THE NUMERICAL PERFORMANCE OF VARIATIONAL METHODS

S. G. MIKHLIN
University of Leningrad, Leningrad, USSR

THE NUMERICAL PERFORMANCE OF VARIATIONAL METHODS

translated from the Russian by

DR. R. S. ANDERSSEN
Computer Centre, The Australian National University, Canberra

WOLTERS-NOORDHOFF PUBLISHING GRONINGEN
THE NETHERLANDS

Library of Congress Catalogue Card Number 78-119883

ISBN 90 01 58865 4

PRINTED IN THE NETHERLANDS
BY BOEKDRUKKERIJ DIJKSTRA NIEMEYER N.V. - GRONINGEN

CONTENTS

CHAPTER III

On the stability of the Bubnov-Galerkin-Process for non-stationary problems

CHAPTER IV

The residual of an approximate solution

CHAPTER V

On the rational choice of coordinate functions

CHAPTER VI

Infinite regions and other singular problems

CHAPTER VII

The stability of the Ritz-process for eigenvalue problems

CHAPTER VIII

The effect of error in the equation

CHAPTER IX

Variational methods for non-linear problems

CHAPTER X

The numerical solution of non-linear variational problems

FOREWORD TO THE ENGLISH TRANSLATION

This English translation of the original Russian book, "The numerical realisation of variation methods", differs from it in some essential ways. The most important difference is the residual theorem (§ 23) which has been considerably sharpened in the English edition (§ 22). Because of this, it is possible to extend the class of coordinate systems for which the convergence of the residual of the approximate solution to zero can be proved. Simultaneously, the examination of the residual can be greatly simplified.

Of the other changes, it is important to mention the following: proof of a theorem about the transformation of minimal systems into strongly minimal ones (§ 2); an estimate for the rate of convergence of polynomial approximation is given (§ 28); a complete investigation of the method of differentiation with respect to a parameter (§ 72); the notion of stability of numerical processes for non-linear problems is improved (§ 76).

On the whole the overall layout of the book remains the same. The basic problem, examined in the book, is the stability of approximate variational processes, the rational choice of coordinate systems and the use of variational methods for the solution of non-linear problems.

I would like to record my pleasure with the high quality of Dr. R. S. Anderssen's translation.

Leningrad
October 9, 1969.

S. Mikhlin

TRANSLATOR'S PREFACE

The translator would like to take this opportunity to record his thanks to Professor Mikhlin for his willingness to supply material which has led to a considerable revision, and consequent improvement, to major sections of the translation as well as the promptness and care with which he answered all questions communicated to him. Without this help the translation would not have had its present potential for success.

In addition, the translator wishes to thank the Australian National University for the opportunity to use an Australian National University-Moscow State University Exchange Scholarship to visit Russia, and thus Professor Mikhlin in Leningrad, earlier this year. Thanks are also due to Mrs Stephanie Larkham and Mrs Pam Hawke of the Australian National University's Computer Centre for typing the translation.

Computer Centre,
Australian National University,
Canberra,
October, 1970

R. S. Anderssen

FOREWORD

This book is a sequal to the author's earlier book *Variational Methods in Mathematical Physics* (Mikhlin [12]) in which the general theory relating to variational methods is presented, applications of them to the most important problems of mathematical physics are given and methods of *a posteriori* estimation for the error in the approximate solution are developed. For purposes of illustration, numerical examples for which variational methods lead to completely satisfactory results are considered in Mikhlin [12]. More general theoretical results relating to variational methods are also presented in the book *The Problem of The Minimum of a Quadratic Functional*, Mikhlin [5].

It appears that a consideration of the numerical performance of such methods involves: (1) the choice of a system of coordinate functions (*coordinate system*); (2) the formation of the Ritz-system; (3) the solution of the Ritz-system; (4) the effect of errors, arising during the formation and solution of the Ritz-system, on the accuracy of the approximate solution.

In practical cases, the second of the mentioned problems reduces to the evaluation of integrals of known functions. Since this problem has already been dealt with in detail* in many monographs and text books, we shall not consider it here. The third problem poses no difficulty for linear problems as the solution of the Ritz system reduces to the solution of some linear algebraic system. Of the many works available on this subject, we mention the books by Faddeev and Faddeeva [1] and Wilkinson [1]. For non-linear problem, this question has not been studied with such success. Accordingly, we shall not be concerned with methods of solution for linear Ritz-systems, but shall devote some attention to methods for such non-linear systems.

The bases for the present book are the first and fourth problems posed

* This excludes the case of oscillatory functions which are often of interest for variational methods.

above: the choice of coordinate systems and the calculation of the effect of errors. These problems, which we investigate in detail for the linear case, have arisen with the widespread use of computers.

The wide availability of computers, which has had such a big impact on all numerical analysis, forces into consideration those aspects of numerical analysis which are connected with variational methods and brings to light new questions which earlier attracted little attention. Computers make possible the construction of significantly more exact approximations with the help of many tens of, rather than a few, coordinate functions. This at once introduces serious difficulties, since computer implementations of the Ritz-method can exhibit instability with respect to an increase in the number of coordinate functions. We note that similar results were observed earlier for calculations connected with the use of a large number of coordinate functions. In this way, the cancellation of terms in the solution of the Ritz-system was discovered by Kachanov [3] who applied the method of Ritz to an investigation of the stress in a turbine blade. An investigation of the concept of stability (and instability) for the Ritz-process and its exact relation to the question of a rational choice of coordinate functions takes a fundamental place in the present book.

Of equal importance are detailed examinations of problems in mathematical physics defined on infinite regions, and questions arising with respect to the solution of integral equations, in particular, singular integral equations. In Mikhlin [5] and [12], these problems were given comparatively little space.

A special chapter, viz. 5, is devoted to the rational choice of coordinate functions for some of the most important classes of practical problems in mathematical physics. This chapter plays the role of a specialised handbook, although all the statements in it are accompanied by either proofs or sufficient remarks for the proofs to carry through.

One of the chapters, viz. 7, is devoted to the stability of the Ritz-method for the calculation of eigenvalues and -vectors for self-adjoint operators. In another, viz. 8, the behaviour of the solution of an equation containing error arising during its formation is examined. The abstractly formulated results are applied to a series of problems in mathematical physics including the theory of shells.

A basic place is occupied by Chapters IX and X which are devoted to non-linear problems. In Chapter IX, some questions from the general theory of variational methods for non-linear problems are presented: reduction to a variational formulation, the convergence of minimising sequences and their construction with the help of the Ritz-method. In Chapter X, methods for the numerical solution of the non-linear Ritz-system are examined. These methods include the use of non-linear finite difference methods.

Sections of the material in this book appeared in the review article of Mikhlin [20] and the book of Mikhlin and Smolitskiy [1].

In variational methods, the most laborious part is the construction of the Ritz- (or Bubnor-Galerkin-) system, demanding often the execution of a large number of simple manipulations with elementary functions: addition, multiplication, differentiation, indefinite integration, the evaluation of functions etc.

In the appendix "Applications", written by Smirnova*, a series of very interesting ideas on the execution of such kinds of manipulations on computers are presented.

An attempt has been made to put the terminology of variational methods on a firm foundation. In the literature, the term "method" is used to refer to two different things: to the process of replacing a boundary value problem of a given differential equation by a corresponding variational problem (the energy method, the method of least squares, etc.) and to the process of generating an approximate representation of the solution of the variational problem (the method of Ritz, the method of Bubnov-Galerkin). Actually, it is not important to object to the use of the term "method" in these two ways, but it does lead to ambiguity. Therefore, we shall refer to "method" only when the reduction of a given boundary value problem to a corresponding variational formulation is involved. The procedure required to generate an approximate representation of the solution of the variational formulation (and hence, the boundary value problem) will be called the process and we shall accordingly speak of the Ritz-process, the Bubnov-Galerkin-process, the moment-process etc. We retain, however, the name "method of nets" which is in wide scientific use.**

* *Translator's Note.* Since it is not intrinsically connected with the main purpose of the book and has since been published as a book (see Smirnova [3]), this appendix has not been translated. The interested reader is also referred to Smirnova [1] and [2].

** *Translator's Note.* This contingency does not arise in English as the common expression is "finite difference methods".

Throughout the book, the following system of theorem and formula numbering will be adopted. Every theorem (corollary, formula etc.) is designated by two numbers: the first denotes the number of the Section while the second is the number of the Theorem (corollary, formula etc.) within this Section.

It will often be necessary to make reference to Mikhlin [5] and [12]. We use the abbreviations "PM" and "VM", respectively.

In this book, the results not only of Mikhlin but also of a number of other people are considered. People who collaborated on the development of questions, formulated by Mikhlin ,on the stability of numerical processes: G. M. Vaynikko, M. A. Veliev, Yu. S. Verzhbinskaya, L. N. Dovbysh (Gagen-Torn), B. A. Samokish, M. N. Yakovlev and G. N. Yaskova. The results of I. V. Gelman, A. Langenbach and L. M. Kachanov on non-linear problems, as well as the corresponding results of S. G. Mikhlin, Z. A. Vlasovta and L. N. Dovbysh (Gagen-Torn) play a very important role in this book.

The calculations were carried out by N. A. Solov'eva and T. A. Tushkina. The author gladly extends to both his warmest thanks. M. K. Gavurin read the manuscript and made many valuable observations To M. K. Gavurin, the author extends his sincerest appreciation.

May, 1965. S. Mikhlin.

INTRODUCTION

The basic tools for the solution of difficult practical problems – variational and finite difference methods – have undergone distinctive evolutions. The process, discovered by V. Ritz in 1908, for the construction of minimizing sequences has given a capable push to applied analysis. The laborious problems of the theory of partial differential equations (for example, problems in the theory of elasticity) are now easily solved. Many workers in the applied sciences, especially Timoshenko, developed very important applications of variational methods. The works of Bubnov and Galerkin played a fundamental role: the process developed by them simplified, in many cases, the formation of the Ritz-equations. Besides this, this process often appeared suitable when the given problems did not admit a reduction to a variational form. Comparatively quickly, however, serious shortcomings in the variational method approach appeared: the difficulty of construction of coordinate functions, satisfying given boundary conditions, for many complex forms of the region, and of forming the Ritz system in connection with the fact that its coefficients and right hand side values are usually expressed by integrals the evaluation of which, particularly for two or more independent variables, can require a large expenditure of labour. This last fact did not have, it is true, serious significance as long as only comparatively crude approximations, consisting of a linear combination of a small number of coordinate functions, were constructed.

Along with variational method, finite difference methods were developed. At first, the theoretical significance of these methods was, perhaps, greater than the practical: for hand calculations, the solution of systems of sufficiently high order, to which finite difference methods led, were often unrealizable.

The appearance of computers changed the situation. Important advantages of finite difference methods over variational became apparent: for finite difference methods, the form of the region is of little importance and the formation of difference systems is based on simple and similar rules. At present, difference methods are used considerably more often than variational.

At this point, it is important to note the basic limitations of difference methods. The laboriousness of the solution of systems of high dimension continues to manifest itself. In Forsythe and Wasow [1], written in 1959, approximate data on the amount of machine time necessary for the solution of the usual problems in mathematical physics by finite difference methods was given. Assuming that the execution of one arithmetic operation requires 50 microseconds of machine time, Forsythe and Wasow concluded: in order to obtain a solution with high accuracy, one dimensional problems require 1 hour, two dimensional require 6 weeks and three dimensional require 100 years of machine time. Of course, with the appearance of faster machines the situation has improved. Nevertheless, it is probable that, for multidimensional problems (starting with the third), the application of finite difference methods will still lead to an excessive outlay of machine time.

Variational methods require considerably fewer operations and correspondingly considerably less outlay of machine time. Although both variational and finite difference techniques can be applied to an extensive class of problems, each, in their own way, has its "domain of optimum application". For finite difference methods, this is two dimensional problems defined on rather complex regions. For variational methods, this is basic multi-dimensional problems as well as problems with different degrees of degeneracy, where difference approximations of the derivative can lead to large error. It is also possible that variational methods have certain advantages for problems defined on infinite regions. It is clear that the separation of "the spheres of influence" of both methods is not simple. Variational methods can be applied to some comparatively complex regions. Using techniques, given in Forsythe and Wasow [1], the solution of three dimensional problems by finite difference methods can be obtained with average accuracy in one week of machine time. This is technically possible, and when absolutely necessary can always be realised. To this it is necessary to add "the sphere of influence" to which each method will extend with its development.

Now, the use of variational methods for the construction of sufficiently accurate approximations requires certain preliminaries. It is clear from the content of VM that, for the construction of more accurate approximations using the Ritz-process, it is first necessary to increase the number of coordinate functions being used. Hence, it is necessary to increase the order of the Ritz-systems. The elements of its matrix and right hand side are calculated with some, no matter how small, error, and thus, for high order systems the error in its solution can be very considerable. In addition, together with the order of these systems, this error can grow without limit independent of its initial size. Calculations show that this phenomenon does indeed occur. We have already cited the work of Kachanov [2]. We also mention Mitkevich [1]. In this connection, it is possible to talk about the "stability" and "instability" of the Ritz-process (an exact formulation is given below in Chapter II). In Mikhlin [13], [15], [16], it is shown that stability and instability of the Ritz-process depends on properties of the coordinate system. The investigation of Mikhlin was continued by Vaynikko [1], Yaskova and Yakovlev [1], who, in particular, examined questions of the stability of the Bubnov-Galerkin-process for stationary problems, and Veliev [1], [2], who studied the same questions for the non-stationary case. We also mention Dovbysh [2], who investigated the stability of the Ritz-process in spectral analysis.

A general treatment of the stability of numerical processes is given in Mikhlin [21]. The results enumerated above constitute a special case of this. The abovementioned work of Mikhlin, together with Mikhlin [11], constitutes a basis for the rational choice of coordinate systems: Mikhlin [17] is also devoted to this.

Of fundamental importance is the fact that the elements of the matrix and right hand side vector of a Ritz-system are usually defined in terms of integrals. Their evaluation usually requires a considerable effort. Sometimes they can be evaluated analytically. In such cases the expenditure of labour is sharply reduced, though the necessity to work by hand is involved. The automation of these analytical computations is highly desirable. Steps in this direction have already been made. In particular, Smirnova [1] and [2] has presented a method for executing on a computer a series of elementary operations on both algebraic and trigonometric polynomials: Arithmetic operations, differentiation, definite and indefinite integration, substitution of particular values of the argument and others. For algebraic polynomials with two independent variables, a number of these elementary operations reduce to the same calculation of a double integral over a rectangle, ellipse or half-ellipse.

The work of Smirnova is one of a big series in a loft project, under the direction of L. V. Kantorovich, to develop computer implementation of analytical operations in many different forms. A series of papers concerned with this were published in the journal: Trudy Matem. in-ta im. V. A. Steklova, No. 66 (1962).

If we compare the contents of this book (as it relates to linear problems) with VM, then it is possible to make the following observations. In VM, questions relating to the construction and convergence of approximate solutions are examined. Here, the choice of coordinate systems is not significant: for whatever be its choice, the convergence of the approximate to the exact w.r.t. (with respect to) the energy norm is valid. In addition, the approximate solution depends not on its coordinate system but only on the subspace generated by them. If, for example, we solve using a variational method the problem

$$-\frac{d}{dx}\left(p(x)\frac{du}{dx}\right)+q(x)u=f(x),$$

$$u(-1)=u(1)=0,$$

$$p(x)\geqq p_0=\text{const.}>0,\ q(x)\geqq 0,$$

then the two coordinate systems

$$\phi_n(x)=(1-x)(1+x)^n\quad (n=1,2,3,\ldots)$$

and

$$\psi_n(x)=\sqrt{2n+1}\int_{-1}^{x}P_n(t)dt\quad (n=1,2,3,\ldots),$$

where P_n denotes the Legendre polynomial of degree n, lead to identical approximate solutions. From the point of view of the problem studied in VM, both coordinate systems are absolutely equivalent.

In this book, we examine questions relating to the stability of the approximate solution for which conditions on the choice of the coordinate system (and not on the subspaces spanned by them) play a decisive role. Thus, in the abovementioned example, the system $\{\phi_n\}$ yields an unstable approximation while the system $\{\psi_n\}$ yields a stable one. If, for simplicity of calculation, the terms $\sqrt{2n+1}$ are discarded from the functions $\{\psi_n\}$, then the approximate solution loses its stability.

The above relates to linear problems, and thus, to the problem of the minimum of a quadratic functional. In the region of non-linear problems a different situation exists. Almost no work discusses in a general manner finite difference method for non-linear problems. Apparently, this can be explained by the difficulty involved in solving non-linear systems of equations with a large number of unknowns. On the other hand, a number of important works dealing with specific applications of variational methods to non-linear problems exist. It is not the author's intention to give some exhaustive review of the appropriate literature, but rather to limit considerations to only certain basic aspects.

First of all one must mention the aspect, developed by S. N. Bernstein, connected with the proof of existence theorems for problems of the calculus of variations. We shall not dwell on this aspect which is unrelated to the subject matter of this book. There are a number of papers which deal with the construction of variational principles for non-linear problems in elasticity and plasticity. These papers are listed in the books of Vol'mir [1], Kachanov [3], [5], Novozhilov [2] and Hill [1]. In addition, we mention the papers by Reissner [1] and Galimov [1]–[4] who gave new formulations for variational principles for non-linear problems in elasticity, and also the paper by Drucker [1] who made an attempt to systematically unify all the variational principles of plasticity on the bases of a single axiom.

Another aspect is connected with the use of variational methods to develop existence proofs and to study the solutions of non-linear problems in elasticity and plasticity. In this connection, we cite the papers by Vorovich [1]–[6] who deals with the non-linear theory of shells. Making use of the case when the principal terms of this theory are linear, Vorovich reduces this problem to the solution of a system of equations which contain non-linear completely continuous operators and, applying topological methods, proves the compactness of a set of approximate Ritz-solutions. Further, it is proved that every limit point of this set is a solution of the problem. A series of theorems, proved in Vorovich [1]–[6], allows estimates for the error in the approximate solution to be derived. The non-linear theory for a plate is presented in Morozov [1]–[5]. This author observed that the solutions of the equation of von Karman, for the plate either rigidly clamped or freely supported, satisfy an interesting integral identity. The use of this identity greatly simplifies the examination and allows existence theorems to be obtained. In Morozov [5], it is proved that under well-known conditions there exist non-symmetric solutions to the problem of bending a symmetrically loaded circular plate the edges of which are firmly clamped. The proof follows in the usual way. Actually a symmetric solution is constructed and proved to be unique. Further, an assumed displacement, for which the potential energy of the bent plate is smaller than for the symmetric solution is constructed. From here it follows that the absolute minimum is achieved for a non-symmetric solution.

Langenbach [1]–[3] examined some classes of minimization problems which contain many variational problems of the theory of plasticity. The general form of the functionals examined by Langenbach were

$$F(u) = \int_{\Omega} \{ \sum_{j=1}^{k} \int_{0}^{\tau_j(u)} g_j(\xi)\, d\xi \}\, dx - \int_{\Omega} f(x)\, u(x)\, dx, \tag{0.1}$$

where Ω is some connected region of m-dimensional Euclidean space, x is a general point in this space, g_j is a non-negative function of ξ and $\tau_j(u)$ is a non-negative quadratic form of u and its derivatives up to some given order. More details about the conditions which the quantities in $F(u)$ satisfy will be given in Chapter 9. With respect to these conditions, the existence of a generalised solution for the minimisation and the convergence, in some appropriate sense, of the Ritz-process are established.

The last aspect which we would like to mention is connected with the numerical performance of the Ritz-process. This aspect is examined fully in Chapter 10 and therefore we limit ourselves to some very general remarks. As mentioned above, the convergence of the Ritz-process holds for isolated classes of non-linear problems – for example, the ones discussed by Vorovich and Langenbach. Results of a general character can be found in Gel'fand and Fomin [1], where it is proved that the Ritz-process reduces to a minimising sequence for an increasing continuous functional. In Mikhlin [18], it is clarified that the condition of continuity of a functional can be replaced by its semi-continuity above.

The examination of the numerical performance of variational methods for non-linear problems is far from complete. The same is also true for the stability of the Ritz-process for such problems.

We discuss in some detail a simpler question – the approximate solution of the non-linear Ritz-system. They arise as a necessary condition for the minimum of some function of many independent variables. On this last aspect, there have appeared a series of papers concerned with examples of both the solution of systems of non-linear algebraic and transcendental equations and the direct minimization of functions. A survey of many papers of this type was given by Spang [1].

In chapter X, we concentrate on three methods of solution for non-linear Ritz-systems. The first of them (called the Method of Newton) was developed by L. V. Kantorovich. We shall use the terminology "The Newton-Kantorovich Method".

Another method of solution is based on an idea of Kiriya [1] and Davidenko [1]. This idea consists of introducing a subsidiary parameter t and a Cauchy problem for a system of ordinary differential equations with independent variable t. In an actual case, the performance of the Kiriya-Davidenko idea rests on the fact that it is necessary to solve the Cauchy problem on the fixed interval $0 \leqq t \leqq 1$. In Dovbysh and Mikhlin [1], it is proved that the mentioned Cauchy problem is solvable on the interval $0 \leqq t \leqq 1$ if the original system of equations be a Ritz-system for a functional which satisfies some conditions which, generally speaking, reduces to requiring that the functional have a polynomial growth at infinity. The equivalence of the Ritz- and Bubnov-Galerkin-methods for non-linear problems is also established in that paper.

Dovbysh [1] proved that functionals of the form (0.1), under realistic restrictions on the functions g_j and the forms $\tau_j(u)$, satisfy the above-mentioned conditions.

Vlasova [1] has established the applicability of the method of reduction to the Cauchy problem for certain classes of nonlinear difference systems.

The third method was presented by Kachanov [4], [6] for problems in non-linear elasticity and plasticity. This method is a variant of the method of successive approximation. At each step it is necessary to solve a linear system with the same number of independent variables as the given non-linear system.

In conclusion, we mention a particular aspect in the development of variational methods for non-linear problems – the construction of actual approximations to the solution of real non-linear problems using variational methods (Methods which are often quite incorrectly called Galerkin and Bubnov-Galerkin and sometimes Bubnov). Usually, the approximate solutions are constructed in the form of linear collection of two or even one coordinate function. We cite some papers which deal with this aspect*: Kornishin and Mushtari [1] solved a problem in the non-linear theory of curved shells, Gorlov [1] the problem of the elasto-plastic twisting of a bar. Stipps [1], Kalender'yan [1], Berger [1], Weil and Newmark [1], Postnov [1], Vinokurov [1], Klyushmkov [1] and Galimov [5] have considered problems in the non-linear theory of plane elasticity. The work of Weil and Newmark is interesting because use is made of a comparatively large number of coordinate functions – namely 11.

Only separable spaces are examined throughout this book since this is quite sufficient for the applied problems of mathematical physics.

* The listed papers are mentioned in the journal (Russian) "Mekhanika".

Chapter I

A CLASSIFICATION OF SYSTEMS OF ELEMENTS IN A HILBERT SPACE

The present chapter is auxiliary. On the whole, its results can be found in the literature. Nevertheless, we list the ideas and facts which will be used widely throughout the book in order to facilitate its use.

§1. Minimal systems

Definition 1.1. A system of elements of a Hilbert space is called *a minimal system in this space,* if the deletion of any one of the elements from the sytem restricts the span of this new set to a proper subspace of the space spanned by the original system (see Lewin [1], and Kaczmarz and Steinhaus [1]).

Note. This basic definition of minimal systems can be extended immediately to any Banach space (see Kaczmarz and Steinhaus [1]).

We give some examples.

Any finite set of linearly independent elements is minimal: the deletion of any element from such a set reduces by one the dimension of the subspace which is spanned by the original set. Conversely, linearly dependent sets of elements form *non-minimal systems*: the deletion of an element, which is linearly dependent with respect to the remaining elements of a set, does not change the subspace which is spanned by the original set.

Any (finite or infinite) system of elements of a Hilbert space, which are orthogonal and different from zero, is minimal. For example, the system of functions $\sin k\pi x$ $(k = 1, 2, \ldots)$ is minimal in the space $L_2(0, \pi)$. In the same space, the system

$$x, \sin \pi x, \sin 2\pi x, \ldots, \sin n\pi x, \ldots$$

is non-minimal: if the function x is deleted, then the space, which is spanned by the remaining elements, coincides with $L_2(0, \pi)$, and hence does not undergo a change.

We shall also give an important example of a non-minimal system.
On the basis of the well-known theorem of C. Müntz (Kaczmarz and Steinhaus [1]), the sequence $\{x^{p_k}\}$ $(k = 1, 2, \ldots)$, $p_1 < p_2 < p_3, \ldots$, is complete in $L_2(0, 1)$, if the exponents $p_k \geqq 0$ and the series $\sum_{k=2}^{\infty} p_k^{-1}$ diverges. Hence, *the sequence* $\{x^{p_k}\}$ *is non-minimal in* $L_2(0, 1)$: on any of its elements, we do not violate the conditions of Müntz. In this way, the space which is spanned by the sequence is not changed if any of its elements are removed. The non-minimality of this sequence in $L_2(0, 1)$ now follows from Definition 1.1. In particular, the sequence $x^n (n = 0, 1, 2, \ldots)$ is non-minimal in $L_2(0, 1)$.
The following definition of minimal systems, which is equivalent to Definition 1.1, will be useful. For simplicity, we restrict attention to finite or countable systems – only these systems are of interest in the present book.

Definition 1.2. Let

$$\{u_n\} = u_1, u_2, \ldots, u_n, \ldots \tag{1.1}$$

be elements of a Hilbert space $\mathfrak{H}$. We denote by $\mathfrak{H}_k$ the subspace spanned by the elements

$$u_1, u_2, \ldots, u_{k-1}, u_{k+1}, \ldots.$$

System (1.1) is *minimal*, if, for all k, the element u_k does not lie in $\mathfrak{H}_k$; and *non-minimal* otherwise.
The following theorem is an immediate consequence of this definition.

Theorem 1.1 *A necessary and sufficient condition that system* (1.1) *be non-minimal is that there exists an integer j satisfying the following conditions: given* $\varepsilon > 0$, *there exist an integer N and constants* $\alpha_1, \ldots, \alpha_{j-1}, \alpha_{j+1}, \ldots, \alpha_N$ *such that the following inequality holds*

$$\|u_j - \sum_{k=1, k \neq j}^{N} \alpha_k u_k\|_{\mathfrak{H}} < \varepsilon. \tag{1.2}$$

Definition 1.3. The system

$$\{v_n\} = v_1, v_2, \ldots, v_n, \ldots \tag{1.3}$$

of elements in the space $\mathfrak{H}$ is *biorthonormal* to the system (1.1), if

$$(u_j, v_k)_{\mathfrak{H}} = \delta_{jk} = \begin{cases} 0, & j \neq k, \\ 1, & j = k. \end{cases} \tag{1.4}$$

Theorem 1.2. *A necessary and sufficient condition for* $\{u_n\}$ *to be minimal is that there exists a system* (1.3) *biorthonormal to* $\{u_n\}$. *This biorthonormal system is defined in a unique way, if its elements lie in the subspace* $\mathfrak{H}$ *spanned by* $\{u_n\}$.

Proof. Necessity: Let $\{u_n\}$ be minimal and $\mathfrak{H}_j$ denote the subspace spanned by $\{u_n\}$ with the element u_j deleted. Then $u_j = \eta + \xi$, where $\eta \in \mathfrak{H}_j$ and ξ is orthogonal to $\mathfrak{H}_j$. The minimality of (1.1) implies $\xi \neq 0$. In fact, any element $u \in \mathfrak{H}$ can have the representation $u = \lambda\xi + \zeta$, where $\zeta \in \mathfrak{H}_j$. In $\mathfrak{H}$, we define the linear functional l_j such that $l_j(u) = \lambda$. This functional is bounded since

$$|l_j(u)| = |\lambda| \leqq \frac{\|u\|_{\mathfrak{H}}}{\|\xi\|_{\mathfrak{H}}}.$$

Since, by a theorem of F. Riesz, there exists in the space $\mathfrak{H}$ a unique element v_j such that $l_j(u) = (u, v_j)_{\mathfrak{H}}$, $\lambda = 1$ for $u = u_j$ and $\lambda = 0$ for $u = u_k$ $(k \neq j)$. Hence, there exists a unique system (1.3) such that (1.4) holds.

Sufficiency (see Kaczmarz and Steinhaus [1]): Let $\{u_n\}$ be non-minimal and assume the existence of a biorthonormal system (1.3) biorthogonal to $\{u_n\}$. Let ε be a suitable small positive number. We choose the numbers $N, \alpha_1, \ldots, \alpha_{j-1}, \alpha_{j+1}, \ldots, \alpha_N$ for which the inequality (1. 2)is satisfied. This implies that

$$|(u_j - \sum_{k=1, k\neq j}^{N} \alpha_k u_k, v_j)_{\mathfrak{H}}| \leqq \varepsilon \|v_j\|_{\mathfrak{H}}.$$

However, it follows from (1.4) that

$$(u_j - \sum_{k=1, k\neq j}^{N} \alpha_k u_k, v_j)_{\mathfrak{H}} = 1,$$

which gives a contradiction with the previous inequality when ε is sufficiently small.

§2. Strongly minimal and almost orthonormal systems

Here we restrict attention to countable systems of elements.

We shall study the countable system of elements

$$\{u_n\} = u_1, u_2, \ldots, u_n, \ldots, \tag{2.1}$$

lying in the Hilbert space $\mathfrak{H}$, and the corresponding Gramm matrix of the first n-elements of $\{u_n\}$:

$$R_n = \begin{bmatrix} (u_1, u_1)_{\mathfrak{H}} & (u_1, u_2)_{\mathfrak{H}} & \ldots & (u_1, u_n)_{\mathfrak{H}} \\ (u_2, u_1)_{\mathfrak{H}} & (u_2, u_2)_{\mathfrak{H}} & \ldots & (u_2, u_n)_{\mathfrak{H}} \\ \cdots & \cdots & \cdots & \cdots \\ (u_n, u_1)_{\mathfrak{H}} & (u_n, u_2)_{\mathfrak{H}} & \ldots & (u_n, u_n)_{\mathfrak{H}} \end{bmatrix}. \tag{2.2}$$

Since this matrix is Hermitian and positive semi-definite, its eigen-values are non-negative and can be written in increasing order as

$$0 \leqq \lambda_1^{(n)} \leqq \lambda_2^{(n)} \leqq \ldots \leqq \lambda_n^{(n)}. \tag{2.3}$$

The numbers $\lambda_m^{(n)}$ can be found by minimising

$$\frac{\sum\limits_{j,k=1}^{n} (u_j, u_k)_{\mathfrak{H}} t_j \bar{t}_k}{\sum\limits_{k=1}^{n} |t_k|^2} = \frac{\|\sum\limits_{k=1}^{n} t_k u_k\|_{\mathfrak{H}}^2}{\sum\limits_{k=1}^{n} |t_k|^2} \tag{2.4}$$

on the subspace of vectors $t = (t_1, t_2, \ldots, t_n)$ which are orthogonal to the eigen-vectors corresponding to the eigen-values $\lambda_1^{(n)}, \ldots, \lambda_{m-1}^{(n)}$. In particular,

$$\lambda_1^{(n)} = \min_t \frac{\|\sum\limits_{k=1}^{n} t_k u_k\|_{\mathfrak{H}}^2}{\sum\limits_{k=1}^{n} |t_k|^2}. \tag{2.5}$$

Note: It follows immediately from the mini-max principle (VM, §40) that, for fixed m and variable n, the number $\lambda_m^{(n)}$ does not increase.

Definition 2.1. System (2.1) is called *strongly minimal in* $\mathfrak{H}$, if

$$\inf \lambda_1^{(n)} = \lim_{n\to\infty} \lambda_1^{(n)} > 0. \tag{2.6}$$

There exists in this case a positive constant λ_0, independent of n, such that

$$\lambda_1^{(n)} \geqq \lambda_0 . \tag{2.7}$$

Note: Strongly minimal is the name introduced by Taldykin [1]; Kaczmarz and Steinhaus [1] use the term "system of Bessel".

The simplest example of a strongly minimal system is given by an orthonormal system. Here, $\lambda_k^{(n)} = 1$ for all n and k and a suitable value for λ_0 is $\lambda_0 = 1$

Theorem 2.1. *Every strongly minimal system in $\mathfrak{H}$ is minimal in $\mathfrak{H}$.*

Proof. Assume that $\{u_n\}$ is both strongly minimal and non-minimal in $\mathfrak{H}$. On the basis of Theorem 1.1, given $\varepsilon > 0$ there exist integers N and j and constants $\alpha_1, \alpha_2, \ldots, \alpha_{j-1}, \alpha_{j+1}, \ldots, \alpha_N$ such that inequality (1.2) holds. In fact,

$$||u_j - \sum_{k=1,\,k\neq j}^{N} \alpha_k u_k||_{\mathfrak{H}}^2 / (1 + \sum_{k=1,\,k\neq j}^{N} |\alpha_k|^2) < \varepsilon^2 . \tag{2.8}$$

The left hand side of (2.7) is the particular case of (2.5) with $t_j = 1$ and $t_k = -\alpha_k (k = j)$. From (2.5) and (2.7), it follows that $\lambda_1^{(n)} < \varepsilon^2$, and hence, that $\inf \lambda_1^{(n)} = 0$. This contradicts Definition 2.1.

Note: The converse of Theorem 2.1 is not true: there exist systems which are minimal, but not strongly minimal. For example, if the system $\{w_n\}$ is orthonormal in $\mathfrak{H}$, then $\{w_n/n\}$ is obviously minimal but not strongly minimal in $\mathfrak{H}$. It is not difficult to see that in this case $\lambda_1^{(n)} = 1/n$ and $\inf \lambda_1^{(n)} = 0$.

Note: If the system (2.1) is strongly minimal in $\mathfrak{H}$, then

$$\sum_{k=1}^{N} |\sigma_{kj}^{(n)}|^2 \leqq \lambda_0^{-2}, \tag{2.9}$$

where $\sigma_{kj}^{(n)}$ are the elements of R_n^{-1}. In fact, the largest eigenvalue of R_n^{-1} equals $[\lambda_1^{(n)}]^{-1}$. Thus, for any vector $t = (t_1, \ldots, t_n)$, one has the inequality

$$||R_n^{-1} t||^2 \leqq [\lambda_1^{(n)}]^{-2} ||t||^2 \leqq [\lambda_0]^{-2} ||t||^2 .$$

Assuming that $t = (0, 0, \ldots, 0, 1, 0, \ldots, 0)$, where unity occupies the jth place, we obtain inequality (2.8).

Theorem 2.2 (see Dovbysh [3]) *Let the system* (2.1) *be minimal in* $\mathfrak{H}$. *Then there exist scalars* $\alpha_n (n = 1, 2, 3, \ldots)$ *such that*

$$\{\alpha_n u_n\} = \alpha_1 u_1, \alpha_2 u_2, \ldots, \alpha_n u_n, \ldots, \tag{2.10}$$

is strongly minimal in $\mathfrak{H}$.

Proof: We assume that the system (2.1) is complete in $\mathfrak{H}$, since, if this were not the case, we could replace $\mathfrak{H}$ by its subspace spanned by (2.1). Hence, in $\mathfrak{H}$, there exists a unique system

$$\{v_n\} = v_1, v_2, \ldots, v_n, \ldots, \tag{2.11}$$

which is biorthogonal to (2.1). We let r_n denote the Gram matrix of the first n elements of $\{v_n\}$, and $\lambda_1^{(n)} \leqq \lambda_2^{(n)} \leqq \ldots \leqq \lambda_n^{(n)}$ and $\mu_1^{(n)} \leqq \ldots \leqq \mu_n^{(n)}$ the eigenvalues of R_n and r_n, respectively. From Wintner [1], it follows that

$$\inf_n \lambda_1^{(n)} = [\sup_n \mu_n^{(n)}]^{-1}. \tag{2.12}$$

We choose the scalars $\alpha_n > 0$ $(n = 1, 2, \ldots)$ so that

$$C^2 = \sum_{n=1}^{\infty} \alpha_n^{-2} \|v_n\|_{\mathfrak{H}}^2 < \infty. \tag{2.13}$$

Hence, the eigenvalues of the Gram matrix of the first n elements of the system $\{\alpha_n^{-1} v_n\}$, for arbitrary n, do not exceed C^2. It follows from (2.12) that the eigenvalues of the Gram matrix of the first n elements of $\{\alpha_k u_k\}$, for arbitrary n, remains greater than C^{-2}, and hence, that (2.10) is strongly minimal in $\mathfrak{H}$.

Definition 2.2. System (2.1) is called *almost orthonormal in* $\mathfrak{H}$, if there exist positive constants λ_0 and Λ_0 such that for every n and $m \leqq n$ the following inequality holds

$$0 < \lambda_0 \leqq \lambda_m^{(n)} \leqq \Lambda_0. \tag{2.14}$$

Note: Taldykin [1] uses the term "normal system", while Kaczmarz and Steinhaus [1] use "system of Riesz-Fisher" and "basis of Riesz".
Any orthonormal system is almost orthonormal with $\lambda_0 = \Lambda_0 = 1$. Every almost orthonormal system is clearly strongly minimal and hence minimal.

§3. Similar and semi-similar operators

Definition 3.1. Two selfadjoint and positive-definite operators are *similar*, if they have a common domain, and *semi-similar*, if their energy spaces consist of one and the same elements.

Note: Throughout this book, the definitions and notation of PM will be used: $\mathfrak{H}$ will denote the Hilbert space in which an operator A is defined. The scalar product and norm in $\mathfrak{H}$ are denoted by $(,)$ and $\|\ \|$, respectively. The domain and range of an operator A are given by $\mathfrak{D}(A)$ and $\mathfrak{R}(A)$, respectively. The energy space denotes the space $\mathfrak{H}_A$ which is the closure of $\mathfrak{D}(A)$ with respect to the metric $[u, v]_A = (Au, v)$ where A is positive-definite.
Heinz [1] has proved that, if the positive operators A and B have a common domain, that is $\mathfrak{D}(A) = \mathfrak{D}(B)$, then $\mathfrak{D}(A^\alpha) = \mathfrak{D}(B^\alpha)$ for any $\alpha \in (0, 1)$. On the other hand, the set of elements forming the energy space of a positive-definite operator A coincides with $\mathfrak{D}(A^{\frac{1}{2}})$. Hence, similar operators are semi-similar, and positive - definite operators A and B are semi-similar, if the operators $A^{\frac{1}{2}}$ and $B^{\frac{1}{2}}$ are similar.

Theorem 3.1. *If the selfadjoint and positive-definite operators* A *and* B *are similar, then the operators* AB^{-1}, BA^{-1}, $A^{-1}B$ *and* $B^{-1}A$ *are bounded and, consequently, there exist positive constants* c_1 *and* c_2 *such that*

$$c_1\|Bu\| \leqq \|Au\| \leqq c_2\|Bu\|, \qquad u \in \mathfrak{D}(A). \tag{3.1}$$

Proof: We first note that $\mathfrak{D}(AB^{-1}) = \mathfrak{H}$. In fact, $\mathfrak{D}(B^{-1}) = \mathfrak{R}(B) = \mathfrak{H}$ since the operator B is selfadjoint and positive-definite (See PM, §5). On the other hand, $\mathfrak{R}(B^{-1}) = \mathfrak{D}(B) = \mathfrak{D}(A)$. Therefore, if f is any element of $\mathfrak{H}$, the expression $AB^{-1}f = A(B^{-1}f)$ is defined.
We now prove that the operator AB^{-1} is closed. Let $f_n \to f$ and $AB^{-1} f_n \to g$. We put $B^{-1} f_n = h_n$. Since the operator B^{-1} is bounded, $B^{-1} f_n \to B^{-1}f$. Writing $B^{-1}f = h$, we have $h_n \to h$ and $Ah_n \to g$. Since A is selfadjoint, A is closed and it follows that $h \in \mathfrak{D}(A)$ and $Ah = AB^{-1}f = g$.
Since the operator AB^{-1} is defined and closed on $\mathfrak{H}$, it follows that AB^{-1} is bounded on $\mathfrak{H}$. The boundedness of BA^{-1} follows by an analogous argument, while the operators $A^{-1}B$ and $B^{-1}A$ are bounded, as they are the adjoints of the bounded operators BA^{-1} and AB^{-1}, respectively. Let $\|AB^{-1}\| = c_2$, $\|BA^{-1}\| = 1/c_1$. Then

$$||AB^{-1}f|| \leqq c_2||f||, \qquad ||BA^{-1}g|| \leqq \frac{1}{c_1}||g||,$$

where f and g are arbitrary elements of $\mathfrak{H}$. Putting $f = Bu$ and $g = Au$, we obtain the desired inequality (3.1).

Corollary 3.1. *If the positive-definite operators A and B are semi-similar, then the operators*

$$A^{\frac{1}{2}}B^{-\frac{1}{2}}, \quad B^{\frac{1}{2}}A^{-\frac{1}{2}}, \quad A^{-\frac{1}{2}}B^{\frac{1}{2}}, \quad B^{-\frac{1}{2}}A^{\frac{1}{2}} \tag{3.2}$$

are bounded in $\mathfrak{H}$, and there exist positive constants c_1 and c_2 such that

$$c_1|||u|||_B \leqq |||u|||_A \leqq c_2|||u|||_B. \tag{3.3}$$

Proof: From the observation above, it is known that $A^{\frac{1}{2}}$ and $B^{\frac{1}{2}}$ are similar and hence, on the basis of Theorem 3.1, the operators (3.2) are bounded. For these operators, the inequality (3.1) becomes

$$C_1||B^{\frac{1}{2}}u|| \leqq ||A^{\frac{1}{2}}u|| \leqq C_2||B^{\frac{1}{2}}u||. \tag{3.4}$$

Further, the positive-definiteness of A implies $|||u|||_A = ||A^{\frac{1}{2}} u||$. In fact, if $u \in \mathfrak{D}(A)$, then

$$|||u|||_A^2 = (Au, u) = (A^{\frac{1}{2}}u, A^{\frac{1}{2}}u) = ||A^{\frac{1}{2}}u||^2.$$

In general, when $u \in \mathfrak{H}_A$, this relationship is obtained by the application of a simple limit process. Hence, inequality (3.3) follows immediately from (3.4).

Theorem 3.2. *Let the positive-definite operators A and B be such that $\mathfrak{H}_A \subset \mathfrak{H}_B$. Then there exists a constant $c > 0$ such that*

$$|||u|||_A \geqq c|||u|||_B, \qquad u \in \mathfrak{H}_A. \tag{3.5}$$

Proof: It follows immediately that $\mathfrak{D}(A^{\frac{1}{2}}) \subset \mathfrak{D}(B^{\frac{1}{2}})$. Repeating the argument of Theorem 3.1, we find that $B^{\frac{1}{2}}A^{-\frac{1}{2}}$ is bounded. Let $||B^{\frac{1}{2}}A^{-\frac{1}{2}}|| = 1/c$, then $||B^{\frac{1}{2}}A^{-\frac{1}{2}}f|| \leqq 1/c||f||$, $f \in H$. Substituting $A^{-\frac{1}{2}}f = u$, we obtain $u \in \mathfrak{D}(A^{\frac{1}{2}})$ and $||B^{\frac{1}{2}}u|| \leqq 1/c||A^{\frac{1}{2}}u||$ which are equivalent to (3.5).

§4. Comparison theorems

Note: The essential results of this section can be found in Mikhlin [15], [16].

Note: For details on the imbedding of spaces (including not only Hilbert) see Sobolev [1], where the author introduced the idea of imbedding, proved the "Theorem of imbedding" and gave many essential applications. Also see Smirnov [3].

Let $\mathfrak{H}_1$ and $\mathfrak{H}_2$ be two Hilbert spaces. We say that the space $\mathfrak{H}_1$ is *imbedded* in $\mathfrak{H}_2$, if there exists a linear operator V (the *imbedding operator*) such that $\mathfrak{D}(V) = \mathfrak{H}_1$ and $\mathfrak{R}(V) \subset \mathfrak{H}_2$, the operator V is bounded

$$||Vu||_2 \leqq K||u||_1, \tag{4.1}$$

where $|| \; ||_k$ denotes the norm in $\mathfrak{H}_k$ $(k = 1, 2)$, and $Vu = 0$ implies $u = 0$. If $\mathfrak{H}_1$ is imbedded in $\mathfrak{H}_2$ then we write $\mathfrak{H}_1 \subset \mathfrak{H}_2$.

Of special interest is the case when all the elements of $\mathfrak{H}_1$ lie in $\mathfrak{H}_2$ and V is the identity operator. In this case, inequality (4.1), defining the imbedding of spaces, takes the simpler form

$$||u||_2 \leqq K||u||_1 . \tag{4.1'}$$

For simplicity, we shall restrict attention to this case. All the statements of this section are true in the general case when the imbedding operator differs from the identity. In order to show this, it is sufficient to replace ϕ_k by $V\phi_k$ in the arguments below when $\phi_k \in \mathfrak{H}_1$ is examined as an element of $\mathfrak{H}_2$.

Theorem 4.1. *Let $\mathfrak{H}_1$ be imbedded in $\mathfrak{H}_2$ and let the system of elements*

$$\{\phi_n\} = \phi_1, \phi_2, \ldots, \phi_n, \ldots \tag{4.2}$$

lie in $\mathfrak{H}_1$. If (4.2) *is minimal in $\mathfrak{H}_2$ then it is minimal in $\mathfrak{H}_1$.*

Proof: We assume that $\{\phi_n\}$ is non-minimal in $\mathfrak{H}_1$. By Theorem 1.1, there exists an element ϕ_j satisfying the inequality

$$||\phi_j - \sum_{k=1, k \neq j}^{N} \alpha_k \phi_k||_1 < \varepsilon, \tag{4.3}$$

where ε is an arbitrary positive number, and the integer N and the constants $\alpha_1, \ldots, \alpha_{j-1}, \alpha_{j+1}, \ldots, \alpha_N$ can be chosen so that (4.3) holds. On the strength of (4.1′), we have

$$||\phi_j - \sum_{k=1, k \neq j}^{N} \alpha_k \phi_k||_2 < K\varepsilon$$

and hence $\{\phi_n\}$ is non-minimal in $\mathfrak{H}_2$, which contradicts the original assumptions of the theorem.

Theorem 4.2. *If, under the conditions of Theorem* 4.1, *system* (4.2) *is strongly minimal in* $\mathfrak{H}_2$, *then it is strongly minimal in* $\mathfrak{H}_1$.

Proof: Let

$$R_n = \begin{bmatrix} (\phi_1, \phi_1)_1 & (\phi_1, \phi_2)_1 & \dots & (\phi_1, \phi_n)_1 \\ (\phi_2, \phi_1)_1 & (\phi_2, \phi_2)_1 & \dots & (\phi_2, \phi_n)_1 \\ \dots & \dots & \dots & \dots \\ (\phi_n, \phi_1)_1 & (\phi_n, \phi_2)_1 & \dots & (\phi_n, \phi_n)_1 \end{bmatrix} \tag{4.4}$$

and

$$r_n = \begin{bmatrix} (\phi_1, \phi_1)_2 & (\phi_1, \phi_2)_2 & \dots & (\phi_1, \phi_n)_2 \\ (\phi_2, \phi_1)_2 & (\phi_2, \phi_2)_2 & \dots & (\phi_2, \phi_n)_2 \\ \dots & \dots & \dots & \dots \\ (\phi_n, \phi_1)_2 & (\phi_n, \phi_2)_2 & \dots & (\phi_n, \phi_n)_2 \end{bmatrix}, \tag{4.5}$$

where $(,)_k$ denotes the inner product in $\mathfrak{H}_k$ $(k = 1, 2)$. The eigenvalues of the matrices (4.4) and (4.5) are denoted by $\lambda_k^{(n)}$ and $\mu_k^{(n)}$, respectively, and satisfy

$$0 \leqq \lambda_1^{(n)} \leqq \dots \leqq \lambda_n^{(n)} \quad \text{and} \quad 0 \leqq \mu_1^{(n)} \leqq \mu_2^{(n)} \leqq \dots \leqq \mu_n^{(n)}.$$

Since $\{\phi_n\}$ is strongly minimal in $\mathfrak{H}_2$, there exists a positive constant μ_0, independent of n, such that $\mu_1^{(n)} \geqq \mu_0$.
We estimate a lower bound for $\lambda_1^{(n)}$ in terms of μ_0:

$$\lambda_1^{(n)} = \inf_t \frac{\sum\limits_{j,k=1}^{n} (\phi_j, \phi_k)_1 t_j \bar{t}_k}{\sum\limits_{k=1}^{n} |t_k|^2} =$$

$$= \inf_t \frac{\sum\limits_{j,k=1}^{n} (\phi_j, \phi_k)_1 t_j \bar{t}_k}{\sum\limits_{j,k=1}^{n} (\phi_j, \phi_k)_2 t_j \bar{t}_k} \cdot \frac{\sum\limits_{j,k=1}^{n} (\phi_j, \phi_k)_2 t_j \bar{t}_k}{\sum\limits_{k=1}^{n} |t_k|^2} \geqq$$

$$\geqq \inf_t \frac{\sum\limits_{j,k=1}^{n} (\phi_j, \phi_k)_1 t_j \bar{t}_k}{\sum\limits_{j,k=1}^{n} (\phi_j, \phi_k)_2 t_j \bar{t}_k} \cdot \inf_t \frac{\sum\limits_{j,k=1}^{n} (\phi_j, \phi_k)_2 t_j \bar{t}_k}{\sum\limits_{k=1}^{n} |t_k|^2},$$

where the infinum is evaluated over the set of all non-zero vectors $t = (t_1, t_2, \ldots, t_n)$.
In the last inequality, the second term on the right hand side equals $\mu_1^{(n)}$, while the first term can be estimated using (4.1′). In fact, from (4.1′),

$$\frac{\sum_{j,k=1}^{n} (\phi_j, \phi_k)_1 t_j \bar{t}_k}{\sum_{j,k=1}^{n} (\phi_j, \phi_k)_2 t_j \bar{t}_k} = \frac{\|\sum_{k=1}^{n} t_k \phi_k\|_1^2}{\|\sum_{k=1}^{n} t_k \phi_k\|_2^2} \geqq \frac{1}{K^2},$$

and hence, we have

$$\inf_t \frac{\sum_{j,k=1}^{n} (\phi_j, \phi_k)_1 t_j \bar{t}_k}{\sum_{k=1}^{n} (\phi_j, \phi_k)_2 t_j \bar{t}_k} \geqq \frac{1}{K^2}.$$

Thus, $\lambda_1^{(n)} \geqq K^{-2}\mu_1^{(n)}$, which implies that

$$\lambda_1^{(n)} \geqq K^{-2}\mu_0. \tag{4.6}$$

This proves the theorem on the basis of Definition 2.1.

Theorem 4.3. *If each of the spaces $\mathfrak{H}_1$ and $\mathfrak{H}_2$ can be imbedded in the other and system* (4.2) *is almost orthonormal in one of them, then it is almost orthonormal in the other.*

Proof: Firstly, there exist constants K_1 and K_2 such that

$$K_1\|u\|_2 \leqq \|u\|_1 \leqq K_2\|u\|_2. \tag{4.7}$$

If $\{\phi_n\}$ is almost orthonormal in $\mathfrak{H}_2$, then it is strongly minimal in this space. By Theorem 4.2, $\{\phi_n\}$ is strongly minimal in $\mathfrak{H}_1$, that is, there exists a positive constant λ_0, independent of n, such that $\lambda_1^{(n)} \geqq \lambda_0$. It remains to prove that the eigenvalues of (4.4) are bounded above by a constant which is independent of n. Since $\{\phi_n\}$ is almost orthonormal in $\mathfrak{H}_2$, there exists a positive constant M_0 such that $\mu_n^{(n)} \leqq M_0$. Also, we have

$$\lambda_n^{(n)} = \sup_t \frac{\sum_{j,k=1}^{n} (\phi_j, \phi_k)_1 t_j \bar{t}_k}{\sum_{k=1}^{n} |t_k|^2} =$$

$$= \sup_t \frac{\sum_{j,k=1}^{n} (\phi_j, \phi_k)_1 t_j \bar{t}_k}{\sum_{j,k=1}^{n} (\phi_j, \phi_k)_2 t_j \bar{t}_k} \cdot \frac{\sum_{j,k=1}^{n} (\phi_j, \phi_k)_2 t_j \bar{t}_k}{\sum_{k=1}^{n} |t_k|^2} \leqq$$

$$\leqq \sup_t \frac{\sum_{j,k=1}^{n} (\phi_j, \phi_k)_1 t_j \bar{t}_k}{\sum_{j,k=1}^{n} (\phi_j, \phi_k)_2 t_j \bar{t}_k} \cdot \sup_t \frac{\sum_{j,k=1}^{n} (\phi_j, \phi_k)_2 t_j \bar{t}_k}{\sum_{k=1}^{n} |t_k|^2},$$

where the supremum is evaluated over the set of all non-zero vectors $t = (t_1, t_2, \ldots, t_n)$. In the last inequality, the second term on the right hand side equals $\mu_n^{(n)}$, while the first can be estimated using (4.7) to give $\lambda_n^{(n)} \leqq K_2^2 \mu_n^{(n)} \leqq K_2^2 M_0$, which proves the theorem.

Corollary 4.1. *Let* $\boldsymbol{A}$ *and* $\boldsymbol{B}$ *be positive-definite operators defined in a Hilbert space* $\mathfrak{H}$, *and let* $\mathfrak{H}_A$ *be contained in* $\mathfrak{H}_B$. *If the system* (4.2) *is (strongly) minimal in* $\mathfrak{H}_B$, *then it is (strongly) minimal in* $\mathfrak{H}_A$. *In particular, if the elements of* (4.2) *lie in* $\mathfrak{H}_A$ *and are orthonormal in* $\mathfrak{H}_B$, *then* (4.2) *is strongly minimal in* $\mathfrak{H}_A$.

Proof: On the strength of Theorem 3.2, $\mathfrak{H}_A$ is imbedded in $\mathfrak{H}_B$ and the Corollary follows on applying Theorems 4.1 and 4.2.

Corollary 4.2. *Let the conditions of Corollary* 4.1 *hold with* $\boldsymbol{B} = \boldsymbol{I}$, *where* $\boldsymbol{I}$ *is the identity operator. If* $\boldsymbol{A}$ *is positive-definite,* (4.2) *lies in* $\mathfrak{H}_A$ *and is (strongly) minimal in* $\mathfrak{H}$, *then* (4.2) *is (strongly) minimal in* $\mathfrak{H}_A$. *In particular, if* (4.2) *lies in* $\mathfrak{H}_A$ *and is orthonormal in* $\mathfrak{H}$, *then it is strongly minimal in* $\mathfrak{H}_A$.

Corollary 4.3. *If* $\boldsymbol{A}$ *and* $\boldsymbol{B}$ *are semi-similar operators and system* (4.2) *is almost orthonormal (in particular, orthonormal) in either* $\mathfrak{H}_A$ *or* $\mathfrak{H}_B$, *then it is almost orthonormal in the other space.*
This corollary follows immediately from inequality (3.3) and Theorem 4.3.

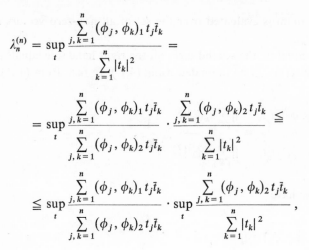

§5. Properties of best approximation

Note. The results of the present section can be found in Lewin [1] and Taldykin [1].

Let

$$\{\phi_n\} = \phi_1, \phi_2, \ldots, \phi_n, \ldots \tag{5.1}$$

be a system of elements in the separable Hilbert space $\mathfrak{H}$, and u any element of $\mathfrak{H}$. The *problem of best approximation* can be formulated as follows: to determine the constants $a_1, a_2, \ldots, a_n$ (where n is fixed) such that

$$\|u - \sum_{k=1}^{n} a_k \phi_k\| = \min.$$

It can be shown (see VM, §83) that the constants a_k are defined by

$$\sum_{k=1}^{n} (\phi_k, \phi_j) a_k = (u, \phi_j) \qquad (j = 1, 2, \ldots, n). \tag{5.2}$$

The constants a_k, which satisfy (5.2), will depend not only on k but also on n. Therefore we denote them by $a_k^{(n)}$. It is clear that

$$u_n = \sum_{k=1}^{n} a_k^{(n)} \phi_k \tag{5.3}$$

is the projection of u on the subspace $\mathfrak{H}_n$ spanned by $\phi_1, \phi_2, \ldots, \phi_n$. We shall assume that for any n the elements $\phi_1, \phi_2, \ldots, \phi_n$ are linearly independent and that $\{\phi_n\}$ is complete in $\mathfrak{H}$. Then (5.2) is solvable for any n and u_n tends to u as $n \to \infty$. In fact, (5.2) is solvable, since its determinant is the Gram determinant of the linearly independent vectors $\phi_1, \phi_2, \ldots, \phi_n$ and therefore differs from zero. Further, u_n is not changed if $\{\phi_n\}$ is subjected to a non-singular linear transformation with triangular matrix, since, for this transformation, the space $\mathfrak{H}_n$ is not changed (See VM, §14). For this reason, we orthonormalise $\{\phi_n\}$ to give the orthonormal system $\{\omega_n\}$ which is clearly complete in $\mathfrak{H}$. If we put

$$u_n = \sum_{k=1}^{n} \alpha_k \omega_k,$$

then (5.2) becomes

$$\alpha_k = (u, \omega_k),$$

and

$$u_n = \sum_{k=1}^{n} (u, \omega_k)\omega_k .$$

Since $\{\omega_n\}$ is orthonormal and complete,

$$u = \sum_{k=1}^{\infty} (u, \omega_k)\omega_k$$

which implies that $\lim_{n\to\infty} u_n = u$.

Theorem 5.1. *If $\{\phi_n\}$ is minimal, then there exist constants a_k such that*

$$a_k = \lim_{n\to\infty} a_k^{(n)} \qquad (k = 1, 2, \ldots). \tag{5.4}$$

If the system, which is biorthonormal to $\{\phi_n\}$ in $\mathfrak{H}$, is bounded, then the limit process in (5.4) *is uniform with respect to k.*

Proof. Let $\{\psi_k\}$ $(k = 1, 2, \ldots)$ be biorthonormal to $\{\varphi_n\}$. Forming the scalar product between u_n and ψ_j, we find that

$$a_j^{(n)} = (u_n, \psi_j).$$

Hence,

$$a_j = \lim_{n\to\infty} a_j^{(n)} = (u, \psi_j). \tag{5.5}$$

If $\{\psi_j\}$ $(j = 1, 2, \ldots)$ is bounded, that is, $||\psi_j|| \leqq C =$ const., then

$$|a_j - a_j^{(n)}| = |(u - u_n, \psi_j)| \leqq C||u - u_n||$$

and the convergence $a_j^{(n)} \to a_j$ is uniform with respect to j.

Theorem 5.2. *If $\{\phi_n\}$ is strongly minimal in $\mathfrak{H}$, then the sequence*

$$a = (a_1, a_2, \ldots, a_n, \ldots),$$

where the a_k are the limits (5.4), *represents an element in the space l_2. In fact, if $a^{(n)} = (a_1^{(n)}, a_2^{(n)}, \ldots, a_n^{(o)}, 0, 0 \ldots)$, then* $\lim_{n\to\infty} ||a^{(n)} - a||_{l_2} = 0$.

Proof. We consider the Gram matrix of elements $\phi_1, \phi_2, \ldots, \phi_n$ and let $\lambda_1^{(n)}$ denote its smallest eigenvalue. The strong minimality of $\{\phi_n\}$ implies the existence of a positive constant λ_0 such that $\lambda_1^{(n)} \geqq \lambda_0$ for all n. By (5.3), we have

$$||u_n||^2 = \sum_{j,k=1}^{n} (\phi_j, \phi_k) a_j^{(n)} \bar{a}_k^{(n)} \geqq \lambda_1^{(n)} \sum_{k=1}^{n} |a_k^{(n)}|^2 \geqq \lambda_0 \sum_{k=1}^{n} |a_k^{(n)}|^2.$$

Hence,

$$\sum_{k=1}^{n} |a_k^{(n)}|^2 \leqq \frac{1}{\lambda_0} ||u_n||^2.$$

Also, $||u_n|| \leqq ||u||$, since u_n is the projection of u on $\mathfrak{H}_n$. This implies that

$$\sum_{k=1}^{n} |a_k^{(n)}|^2 \leqq \frac{1}{\lambda_0} ||u||^2, \tag{5.6}$$

and further

$$\sum_{k=1}^{p} |a_k^{(n)}|^2 \leqq \frac{1}{\lambda_0} ||u||^2, \qquad p \leqq n.$$

Taking the limit as $n \to \infty$ and then as $p \to \infty$, we obtain

$$\sum_{k=1}^{\infty} |a_k|^2 \leqq \frac{1}{\lambda_0} ||u||^2$$

and thus, $a \in l_2$.

Choose $m > n$ and $a_k^{(n)} = 0$, if $k > n$. Then,

$$u_m - u_n = \sum_{k=1}^{m} (a_k^{(m)} - a_k^{(n)})\phi_k.$$

Repeating the above argument, we obtain the inequality

$$\sum_{k=1}^{p} |a_k^{(m)} - a_k^{(n)}|^2 \leqq \frac{1}{\lambda_0} ||u_m - u_n||^2, \qquad p \leqq m.$$

Taking the limit as $m \to \infty$ and then as $p \to \infty$, we find

$$||a - a^{(n)}||_{l_2}^2 \leqq \frac{1}{\lambda_0} ||u - u_n||^2 \underset{n\to\infty}{\to} 0.$$

Chapter II

THE STABILITY OF THE RITZ AND BUBNOV-GALERKIN PROCESSES FOR STATIONARY PROBLEMS

§6. Discussion of the Ritz-process

For the most general variational problems, corresponding to stationary (time independent) linear problems of mathematical physics, we can formulate the *Ritz-process* for their approximate solution in the following way (see PM, §§2–8).

Let $A[u]$ be a homogeneous quadratic functional with domain $\mathfrak{D}(A)$ a linear manifold dense in the Hilbert space $\mathfrak{H}$. Let $A[u]$ correspond to the bilinear form $A[u, v]$ with the same domain such that $A[u] = A[u, u]$. We assume that the functional $A[u]$ is *positive*:

$$A[u] > 0, \qquad u \neq 0.$$

Further, let $l(u)$ be a linear (that is, additive and homogeneous) functional such that its domain $\mathfrak{D}(l) \supset \mathfrak{D}(A)$.

We consider the problem of determining the minimum of the functional

$$F(u) = A[u] - l(u) - \overline{l(u)}. \tag{6.1}$$

As it stands, this problem has, in general, no solution. We introduce the following modification: On $\mathfrak{D}(A)$, we define the new scalar ("energy") product

$$[u, v] = [u, v]_A = A[u, v] \tag{6.2}$$

and the new ("energy") norm

$$|||u||| = |||u|||_A = \sqrt{[u, u]_A} = \sqrt{A[u]} \tag{6.3}$$

and we complete $\mathfrak{D}(A)$ with respect to this norm.

As a result of this completion, we obtain a new Hilbert space $\mathfrak{H}_A$ which is called *the energy space.*

If $l(u)$ is not bounded with respect to (or, more briefly, w.r.t.) the metric $|||u|||_A$, then $F(u)$ is not bounded below, and the problem of the minimum of $F(u)$ lacks sense. Therefore, let $l(u)$ be bounded w.r.t. $|||u|||_A$. Its domain $\mathfrak{D}(l)$ contains $\mathfrak{D}(A)$ which is dense in $\mathfrak{H}_A$. Therefore, $\mathfrak{D}(l)$ is dense in $\mathfrak{H}_A$. The functional $l(u)$, which is defined on a dense set in $\mathfrak{H}_A$ and is bounded in $\mathfrak{H}_A$, can be extended to the whole space $\mathfrak{H}_A$ by continuity. Hence $F(u)$, which can be rewritten in the form

$$F(u) = |||u|||_A^2 - l(u) - \overline{l(u)}, \tag{6.4}$$

can also be extended to the whole space $\mathfrak{H}_A$. Now we can discuss *the problem of the minimum of the functional* $F(u)$ *in the space* $\mathfrak{H}_A$. This problem has a solution which is, moreover, unique: by a theorem of F. Riesz, there exists a unique element $u_0 \in \mathfrak{H}_A$ such that $l(u) = [u, u_0]_A$. Hence,

$$F(u) = |||u - u_0|||_A^2 - |||u_0|||_A^2, \tag{6.5}$$

and u_0 is the solution of this new variational problem. This element u_0 can be regarded as a generalised solution of the problem of the minimum of $F(u)$.

Unless the contrary is stated, we shall assume that $l(u)$ is bounded in $\mathfrak{H}_A$, and thus, that there exists a solution u_0 for the problem of the minimum of $F(u)$ in $\mathfrak{H}_A$.

We suppose that the space $\mathfrak{H}_A$ is separable.

In order to find an approximate representation of u_0, we choose a *coordinate system*: the system of elements $\{\phi_n\} = \phi_1, \phi_2, \ldots, \phi_n, \ldots$, which satisfies the conditions:

1. $\{\phi_n\} \in \mathfrak{H}_A$,
2. for any n, the elements $\phi_1, \phi_2, \ldots, \phi_n$ are linearly independent, and
3. $\{\phi_n\}$ is complete in $\mathfrak{H}_A$.

The elements ϕ_n are usually called *coordinate elements* (see VM, §14). The approximate representation of u_0 is sought in the form (the *Ritz-representation*)

$$u_n = \sum_{k=1}^{n} a_k^{(n)} \phi_k, \tag{6.6}$$

where the constants $a_k^{(n)}$, the *Ritz-coefficients*, are chosen so that $F(u_n) =$ min. From (6.5), it follows that this condition is equivalent to

$$|||u_n - u_0|||_A = |||u_0 - \sum_{k=1}^{n} a_k^{(n)} \phi_k|||_A = \text{min}. \tag{6.7}$$

Note. In VM and PM, the Ritz-coefficients are denoted by a_k. Because we wish to emphasize their dependence on n, they will be written as $a_k^{(n)}$ throughout this book.

Formula (6.7) implies: *the construction of u_n – the nth order Ritz-approximation of u_0 – is equivalent to the construction of the linear combination of the elements $\phi_1, \phi_2, \ldots, \phi_n$, which is the best approximation to u_0 w.r.t. the $\mathfrak{H}_A$-metric.*

The condition $F(u_n) = \min.$ yields easily the *Ritz-system* (for a fixed value of n), or *Ritz-process* (when we are considering a sequence of values of $n = 1, 2, \ldots$) which defines the Ritz-coefficients $a_k^{(n)}$:

$$\sum_{k=1}^{n} [\phi_k, \phi_j] a_k^{(n)} = l\phi_j \qquad (j = 1, 2, \ldots, n). \tag{6.8}$$

We shall examine the significance of (6.8) for standard variational methods. For *the energy method,* $A[u] = (Au, u)$, where A is a positive operator in the Hilbert space $\mathfrak{H}$, and $l(u) = (u, f)$, where f is a given element of $\mathfrak{H}$. If the operator A is positive-definite, then the functional $l(u) = (u, f)$ is bounded in $\mathfrak{H}_A$ and the problem of the minimum of $F(u)$ in $\mathfrak{H}_A$ has sense. If A is only positive, then this problem only holds for those f for which (u, f) is bounded in $\mathfrak{H}_A$. In association with (6.8), the energy method only corresponds to the problems of mathematical physics with homogeneous boundary conditions.

We shall examine some problems with non-homogeneous boundary conditions:

Let Ω be a finite or infinite region in m-dimensional Euclidean space and S its boundary. The Dirichlet problem

$$\Delta v = 0, \quad v|_S = g(x), \qquad x \in S, \tag{6.9}$$

where v is defined on $\Omega + S$, reduces to the variational problem of minimising the integral (See VM, §18)

$$\int_\Omega |\text{grad } v|^2 \, dx \tag{6.10}$$

over the set to functions which have square-summable first derivatives and satisfy the boundary condition in (6.9). Here it is assumed that there exists at least one function $\psi(x)$ such that $\psi|_s = g(x)$ and

$$\int_\Omega |\text{grad } \psi|^2 \, dx < \infty. \tag{6.11}$$

Clearly, the domain of the functional (6.10) is not linear. Therefore, we define $u(x) = v(x) - \psi(x)$ to give

$$u(x)|_S = 0 \tag{6.12}$$

and

$$\int_\Omega |\text{grad } v|^2 dx = \int_\Omega |\text{grad } u|^2 dx - \int_\Omega \text{grad } u \cdot \text{grad } \psi \, dx -$$
$$- \int_\Omega \text{grad } \psi \cdot \text{grad } u \, dx + \int_\Omega |\text{grad } \psi|^2 dx.$$

Since the last integral on the right hand side is constant, the above variational problem reduces to the minimisation of

$$F(u) = \int_\Omega |\text{grad } u|^2 dx -$$
$$- \int_\Omega \text{grad } u \cdot \text{grad } \psi \, dx - \int_\Omega \text{grad } \psi \cdot \text{grad } u \, dx \tag{6.13}$$

on the linear set of functions which have square-summable first derivatives over Ω and satisfy (6.12). In this case,

$$A[u] = |||u|||_A^2 = \int_\Omega |\text{grad } u|^2 dx, \tag{6.14}$$

$$l(u) = \int_\Omega \text{grad } u \cdot \text{grad } \psi \, dx. \tag{6.15}$$

The functional (6.15) is bounded w.r.t. the norm in (6.14), since the inequality of Schwartz (Bunyakovskiy) implies that

$$\left| \int_\Omega \text{grad } u \cdot \text{grad } \psi \, dx \right| \leq \left\{ \int_\Omega |\text{grad } u|^2 dx \right\}^{\frac{1}{2}} \cdot \left\{ \int_\Omega |\text{grad } \psi|^2 dx \right\}^{\frac{1}{2}} =$$
$$= \left\{ \int_\Omega |\text{grad } \psi|^2 dx \right\}^{\frac{1}{2}} |||u|||_A,$$

and the problem of the minimum of (6.13) has sense.

We shall also consider the Neumann problem with non-homogenous boundary conditions. For simplicity, we consider $-\Delta u + u = 0$ instead of the Laplace equation. In fact, we examine the problem

$$-\Delta u + u = 0, \qquad \left. \frac{\partial u}{\partial \nu} \right|_S = h(x), \qquad x \in S. \tag{6.16}$$

The region Ω is assumed to be finite and the boundary S to consist of a finite number of sufficiently smooth surfaces. It is easy to prove (see VM, §18) that the problem (6.16) is equivalent to the minimisation of the functional

$$\int_\Omega \{|\text{grad}\, u|^2 + |u|^2\}\, dx - \int_S u\bar{h}\, dS - \int_S \bar{u} h\, dS \tag{6.17}$$

on a linear set of functions which have square-summable first derivatives. This set is $\mathfrak{H}_A$, where the metric in $\mathfrak{H}_A$ is now defined by

$$|||u|||_A^2 = \int_\Omega \{|\text{grad}\, u|^2 + |u|^2\} dx. \tag{6.18}$$

This variational problem is soluble, if

$$l(u) = \int_S hu\, dS \tag{6.19}$$

is bounded w.r.t. $|||u|||_A$ of (6.18). The boundedness of $l(u)$ follows, $h \in L_2(S)$, that is, if

$$K = \int_S |h|^2 dS < \infty.$$

In fact, by the inequality of Schwartz (Bunyakovskiy),

$$\left| \int_S hu\, dS \right|^2 \leqq K \int_S |u|^2 dS.$$

Further, we have as a result of the imbedding theorem of Sobolev [1; §8] (see also Smirnov [3; §114, Theorem 2]),

$$\int_S |u|^2 dS \leqq K_1 \int_\Omega \{|\text{grad}\, u|^2 + |u|^2\} dx = K_1 |||u|||_A^2, \qquad K_1 = \text{const}.$$

Hence,

$$\left| \int_S hu\, dS \right| \leqq \sqrt{K_1 K}\, |||u|||_A$$

and functional (6.19) is bounded w.r.t. $|||u|||_A$ of (6.18).

Now we consider *the method of least squares*. For this method, the solution of the linear operator (not necessarily symmetric) equation $Au = f$, $f \in H$, is constructed as the function $u \in \mathfrak{D}(A)$ which minimises

$$||Au-f||^2, \tag{6.20}$$

with $A[u] = (Au, Au) = ||Au||^2$. If the operator A is closed and is assumed to have a bounded inverse, then the space $\mathfrak{H}_A$ consists of the elements of $\mathfrak{D}(A)$ with metric

$$|||u|||_A = ||Au||. \tag{6.21}$$

Further, the functional $l(u) = (Au, f)$ is bounded in $\mathfrak{H}_A$ since

$$|l(u)| = |(Au, f)| \leqq ||Au|| \, ||f|| = ||f|| \cdot |||u|||_A.$$

By a theorem of F. Riesz, there exists a function $u_0 \in \mathfrak{D}(A)$ such that

$$(Au, f) = [u, u_0]_A = (Au, Au_0).$$

Hence it is easily seen that

$$||Au-f||^2 = |||u-u_0|||_A^2 + ||f||^2 - ||Au_0||^2,$$

and the minimum of (6.20) is $||f||^2 - ||Au_0||^2$. The application of the Ritz-process (6.8) to this problem is equivalent to the determination of the best approximation ($u_n = \sum_{k=1}^n a_k^{(n)} \phi_k$) to u_0 w.r.t. the metric $|||u|||_A$ of (6.21).

The element u_0 is the minimising element of (6.20). The approximate Ritz-representation (6.6) of u_0 converges to u_0 w.r.t. the metric of (6.21). Since A^{-1} is bounded, the convergence also holds for the metric in $\mathfrak{H}$. If A^{-1} is defined for all elements in $\mathfrak{H}$, then the element u_0 satisfies the original operator equation $Au = f$.

The method of orthogonal projections consists of minimising the quantity

$$||V - \sum_{k=1}^{n} a_k \psi_k||^2,$$

where V is a given element of a Hilbert space $\mathfrak{H}$, and the coordinate elements $\psi_1, \psi_2, \ldots$ lie in some subspace $\mathfrak{H}_2$ of $\mathfrak{H}$. Now, since $V = v_0 + w_0$ where $v_0 \in \mathfrak{H}_1$, which is the subspace orthogonal to $\mathfrak{H}_2$, and $w_0 \in \mathfrak{H}_2$, construction of w_0 yields the required value v_0.

The element

$$w_n = \sum_{k=1}^{n} a_k \psi_k,$$

which reduces

$$||V-w_n||^2 = ||V-\sum_{k=1}^{n} a_k\psi_k||^2,$$

to a minimum, is the best approximation to w_0 in terms of $\psi_1, \psi_2, \ldots, \psi_n$. The method of orthogonal projections leads immediately to the system (6.8). In fact, we can assume that the functional (6.4) has the form $||V-w||^2$, where $w \in \mathfrak{H}_2$. The energy metric coincides with the metric of $\mathfrak{H}$ and the energy space with $\mathfrak{H}_2$. By minimising the above quantity, we construct an approximate Ritz-representation of w_0 with the elements $\psi_1, \psi_2, \ldots$ as coordinate functions.

In conclusion, we discuss *the method of Trefftz*. For simplicity, we restrict attention to problem (6.9). In the method of Trefftz (see VM, §55), we introduce the Hilbert space $\mathfrak{G}_2^1$ of functions which are harmonic and have square-summable first derivatives in Ω. The norm in $\mathfrak{G}_2^1$ is defined by

$$|||u|||^2 = A(u) = \int_\Omega |\text{grad } u|^2 \, dx. \tag{6.22}$$

In introducing this norm, we do not distinguish between functions which differ only by an additive constant. We choose the coordinate functions $\phi_1, \phi_2, \ldots, \phi_n, \ldots$ in $\mathfrak{G}_2^1$, and, for given n, determine the constants $a_1, a_2, \ldots, a_n$ such that

$$A(u_0-u_n) = \min, \qquad u_n = \sum_{k=1}^{n} a_k\phi_k, \tag{6.23}$$

where u_0 is the solution of problem (6.9).

Here $\mathbf{A}[u] = A(u)$, the space $\mathfrak{H}_A$ is the space $\mathfrak{G}_2^1$ of harmonic functions and $|||u|||_A^2 = A(u)$. The method of Trefftz implies that an approximate representation of the minimum of $A(u_0-u)$ can be constructed by the Ritz process (6.8). This approximate representation is the best approximation to u_0 w.r.t. the metric (6.22) and the functions $\phi_1, \phi_2, \ldots, \phi_n$.

§7. Limit properties of the Ritz-coefficients

We shall examine the problem of determining the minimum of the functional (6.1) assuming that this problem has a generalised solution u_0. Let

$$\{\phi_n\} = \phi_1, \phi_2, \ldots, \phi_n, \ldots, \tag{7.1}$$

be a system of coordinate functions satisfying the conditions listed in §6 and let the approximate Ritz-representation of u_0 be

$$u_n = \sum_{k=1}^{n} a_k^{(n)} \phi_k . \tag{7.2}$$

In §6, it was shown that u_n yields the best approximate representation to u_0 w.r.t. the metric in $\mathfrak{H}_A$ and $\phi_1, \phi_2, \ldots, \phi_n$. Hence, from Theorems 5.1 and 5.2, we can list the following limit properties of the Ritz-coefficients:

Theorem 7.1. *If* $\{\phi_n\}$ *is minimal in* $\mathfrak{H}_A$, *then limits for the Ritz-coefficients exist*

$$a_k = \lim_{n\to\infty} a_k^{(n)} \qquad (k = 1, 2, \ldots). \tag{7.3}$$

If the system, which is biorthonormal to $\{\phi_n\}$ *in* $\mathfrak{H}_A$, *is bounded in* $\mathfrak{H}_A$, *then the limit process in* (7.3) *is uniform with respect to* k.

Theorem 7.2. *If* $\{\phi_n\}$ *is strongly minimal in* $\mathfrak{H}_A$, *then the sequence*

$$a = (a_1, a_2, \ldots, a_n, \ldots),$$

where the a_k *are defined in* (7.3), *represents an element of the space* l_2. *In fact, if* $a^{(n)} = (a_1^{(n)}, a_2^{(n)}, \ldots, a_n^{(n)}, 0, 0, \ldots)$, *then*

$$\lim_{n\to\infty} \|a^{(n)} - a\|_{l_2} = 0.$$

If $\{\phi_n\}$ is non-minimal in $\mathfrak{H}_A$, then limits for the coefficients $a_k^{(n)}$ may not exist. Calculations have shown that, for fixed k, the value of $a_k^{(n)}$ can vary greatly for changes in n.

We shall consider two examples.

Example 7.1. We shall solve

$$-\frac{d^2u}{dx^2} = -u''(x) = \frac{1}{1+x}, \qquad u(0) = u'(1) = 0, \tag{7.4}$$

by the method of Ritz. The corresponding variational formulation is

$$F(u) = \int_0^1 \left(u'^2 - 2\frac{1}{1+x}\, u\right) dx, \qquad u(0) = 0, \tag{7.5}$$

where $\mathfrak{H} = L_2\ (0, 1)$. The space $\mathfrak{H}_A$ consists of the functions which are absolutely continuous on the interval $0 \leqq x \leqq 1$, reduce to zero at $x = 0$ and have square-summable first derivatives. The scalar product and norm in $\mathfrak{H}_A$ are defined by

$$[u, v] = \int_0^1 u'(x)v'(x)dx, \qquad |||u|||^2 = \int_0^1 u'^2(x)dx. \tag{7.6}$$

Note. Because the solution of (7.4) will be real, we restrict attention to real functions. This restriction will always be adopted when considering problems with real solutions.

As coordinate functions we choose the system $\{\phi_k\} = \{x^k\}$. It is not difficult to see that the conditions of §6 are satisfied. We calculate the first eight approximate Ritz-representations. The Ritz-system for the eighth approximation is given by:

$$\begin{aligned}
&a_1^{(8)} + a_2^{(8)} + a_3^{(8)} + a_4^{(8)} + a_5^{(8)} + a_6^{(8)} + a_7^{(8)} + a_8^{(8)} = \\
&\qquad = 1 - \ln 2, \\
&a_1^{(8)} + \tfrac{4}{3}a_2^{(8)} + \tfrac{3}{2}a_3^{(8)} + \tfrac{8}{5}a_4^{(8)} + \tfrac{5}{3}a_5^{(8)} + \tfrac{12}{7}a_6^{(8)} + \tfrac{7}{4}a_7^{(8)} + \tfrac{16}{9}a_8^{(8)} = \\
&\qquad = \ln 2 - \tfrac{1}{2}, \\
&a_1^{(8)} + \tfrac{3}{2}a_2^{(8)} + \tfrac{9}{5}a_3^{(8)} + 2a_4^{(8)} + \tfrac{15}{7}a_5^{(8)} + \tfrac{9}{4}a_6^{(8)} + \tfrac{7}{3}a_7^{(8)} + \tfrac{12}{5}a_8^{(8)} = \\
&\qquad = \tfrac{5}{6} - \ln 2, \\
&a_1^{(8)} + \tfrac{8}{5}a_2^{(8)} + 2a_3^{(8)} + \tfrac{16}{7}a_4^{(8)} + \tfrac{5}{2}a_5^{(8)} + \tfrac{8}{3}a_6^{(8)} + \tfrac{14}{5}a_7^{(8)} + \tfrac{32}{11}a_8^{(8)} = \\
&\qquad = \ln 2 - \tfrac{7}{12}, \\
&a_1^{(8)} + \tfrac{5}{3}a_2^{(8)} + \tfrac{15}{7}a_3^{(8)} + \tfrac{5}{2}a_4^{(8)} + \tfrac{25}{9}a_5^{(8)} + 3a_6^{(8)} + \tfrac{35}{11}a_7^{(8)} + \tfrac{10}{3}a_8^{(8)} = \\
&\qquad = \tfrac{47}{60} - \ln 2, \\
&a_1^{(8)} + \tfrac{12}{7}a_2^{(8)} + \tfrac{9}{4}a_3^{(8)} + \tfrac{8}{3}a_4^{(8)} + 3a_5^{(8)} + \tfrac{36}{11}a_6^{(8)} + \tfrac{7}{2}a_7^{(8)} + \tfrac{48}{13}a_8^{(8)} = \\
&\qquad = \ln 2 - \tfrac{37}{60}, \\
&a_1^{(8)} + \tfrac{7}{4}a_2^{(8)} + \tfrac{7}{3}a_3^{(8)} + \tfrac{14}{5}a_4^{(8)} + \tfrac{35}{11}a_5^{(8)} + \tfrac{7}{2}a_6^{(8)} + \tfrac{49}{13}a_7^{(8)} + 4a_8^{(8)} = \\
&\qquad = \tfrac{319}{420} - \ln 2, \\
&a_1^{(8)} + \tfrac{16}{9}a_2^{(8)} + \tfrac{12}{5}a_3^{(8)} + \tfrac{32}{11}a_4^{(8)} + \tfrac{10}{3}a_5^{(8)} + \tfrac{48}{13}a_6^{(8)} + 4a_7^{(8)} + \tfrac{64}{15}a_8^{(8)} = \\
&\qquad = \ln 2 - \tfrac{533}{840}.
\end{aligned} \tag{7.7}$$

The other Ritz-systems for lower order approximations can be obtained from (7.7) by suitable truncation. Solving these numerical systems, including (7.7), we obtain the following table of *exact values* for the Ritz-coefficients (see Table 7.1).

Table 7.1

n	$a_1^{(n)}$	$a_2^{(n)}$	$a_3^{(n)}$	$a_4^{(n)}$	$a_5^{(n)}$	$a_6^{(n)}$	$a_7^{(n)}$	$a_8^{(n)}$
1	$1-\ln 2$							
2	$5\frac{1}{2}-7\ln 2$	$-4\frac{1}{2}+6\ln 2$						
3	$26\frac{1}{3}-37\ln 2$	$-67+96\ln 2$	$41\frac{2}{3}-60\ln 2$					
4	$133\frac{1}{12}-191\ln 2$	$-707\frac{1}{2}+$ $+1\,020\ln 2$	$1\,109\frac{1}{6}-$ $-1\,600\ln 2$	$-533\frac{3}{4}+$ $+770\ln 2$				
5	$694\frac{8}{15}-$ $-1\,001\ln 2$	$9\,120\ln 2-$ $-6\,322$	$17\,952\frac{2}{3}-$ $-25\,900\ln 2$	$29\,120\ln 2-$ $-20\,184\frac{1}{2}$	$7\,860\frac{3}{10}-$ $-11\,340\ln 2$			
6	$3\,698\frac{19}{30}-$ $-5\,335\ln 2$	$74\,130\ln 2-$ $-51\,383\frac{1}{2}$	$228\,239\frac{2}{3}-$ $-329\,280\ln 2$	$636\,880\ln 2-$ $-440\,758\frac{1}{2}$	$386\,376\frac{9}{10}-$ $-557\,424\ln 2$	$182\,028\ln 2-$ $-126\,172\frac{1}{5}$		
7	$19\,972\frac{12}{35}-$ $-28\,813\ln 2$	$567\,168\ln 2-$ $-393\,131\frac{2}{5}$	$2\,506\,559-$ $-3\,616\,200\ln 2$	$10\,496\,640\ln 2-$ $-7\,275\,716\frac{1}{2}$	$10\,638\,813\frac{9}{10}-$ $-15\,348\,564\ln 2$	$11\,028\,864\ln 2-$ $-7\,644\,626$	$2\,148\,129\frac{23}{35}-$ $-3\,099\,096\ln 2$	
8	$108\,951\frac{181}{280}-$ $-157\,183\ln 2$	$4\,161\,528\ln 2-$ $-2\,884\,551\frac{9}{10}$	$24\,929\,343\frac{1}{2}-$ $-35\,965\,440\ln 2$	$145\,285\,140\ln 2-$ $-100\,703\,985\frac{1}{4}$	$216\,181\,005\frac{3}{20}-$ $-311\,883\,264\ln 2$	$366\,870\,504\ln 2-$ $-254\,295\,255\frac{1}{2}$	$154\,836\,614\frac{41}{70}-$ $-223\,382\,016\ln 2$	$55\,070\,730\ln 2-$ $-38\,172\,121\frac{13}{56}$

In Table 7.1, we substitute $\ln 2 = 0.693147180559945$ to obtain the following values for the Ritz-coefficients (accurate to the four decimal places shown):

Table 7.2

n	$a_1^{(n)}$	$a_2^{(n)}$	$a_3^{(n)}$	$a_4^{(n)}$	$a_5^{(n)}$	$a_6^{(n)}$	$a_7^{(n)}$	$a_8^{(n)}$
1	0.3069							
2	0.6480	−0.3411						
3	0.6869	−0.4579	0.0788					
4	0.6922	−0.4899	0.1312	−0.0267				
5	0.6930	−0.4977	0.1547	−0.0541	0.0110			
6	0.6931	−0.4995	0.1631	−0.0708	0.0260	−0.0050		
7	0.6931	−0.4999	0.1657	−0.0786	0.0378	−0.0136	0.0025	
8	0.6931	−0.5000	0.1664	−0.0817	0.0446	−0.0218	0.0075	−0.0013

From Table 7.2, we see that although the approximate Ritz-coefficients exhibit a tendency to stabilise for increasing n, this tendency is non-uniform: the coefficients $a_1^{(n)}$ and $a_2^{(n)}$ stabilise after $n = 5$ and $n = 7$, respectively, while the remaining coefficients exhibit noticeable scattering. Apparently, in this example, the coefficients $a_k^{(n)}$ either diverge as $n \to \infty$ or approach their limits non-uniformly. This irregularity results from the choice of a non-minimal coordinate system in $\mathfrak{H}_A$ with metric (7.6). We prove this last statement: from (7.6), it follows that the minimality of $\{\phi_n\}$ in $\mathfrak{H}_A$ is equivalent to the minimality of $\{\phi'_n\} = \{d\phi_n/dx\}$ in $L_2(0, 1)$; but, $\{n\, x^{n-1}\}$ is non-minimal in L_2 (0, 1) by the Theorem of Müntz. Using Table 7.2, we can construct the approximate solutions. We shall not dwell on this aspect in view of the simplicity of the operation.
In spite of the scattering of the above coefficients, the approximate solutions can be obtained with sufficient accuracy. Thus, for $x = 1$, we have

$$u_1(1) = 0.3069, \quad u_2(1) = 0.3069, \quad u_3(1) = 0.3071,$$
$$u_4(1) = 0.3068.$$

The exact solution is

$$u_0(x) = x(1+\ln 2)-(x+1)\ln(x+1),$$

which yields $u_0(1) = 1-\ln 2 = 0.3069$ and $u_0(1)-u_4(1) = 0.0001$.

The closeness of the approximate solution to the exact becomes clear, if the energy norm of $u_0 - u_k$ is formed. We have (VM, §14 (17)): $|||u_0 - u_n|||_A^2 = |||u_0|||_A^2 - |||u_n|||_A^2$. A value for $|||u_0|||_A^2$ follows immediately from (7.6):

$$|||u_0|||_A^2 = 2(1 - \ln 2) - \ln^2 2 = 0{,}1333.$$

In order to evaluate $|||u_n|||_A^2$, we use, instead of (7.6), the formula (VM, §14(12) and §48(8))

$$|||u_n|||_A^2 = \sum_{k=1}^{n} a_k^{(n)}(f, \phi_k), \tag{7.8}$$

where the (f, ϕ_k) are the right-hand side values for the Ritz-process. This yields, for example,

$$|||u_1|||_A^2 = 0.0942, \qquad |||u_2|||_A^2 = 0.1330, \qquad |||u_3|||_A^2 = 0.1332.$$
$$|||u_4|||_A^2 = 0.1332,$$

and consequently,

$$|||u_0 - u_1|||_A = 0.20, \qquad |||u_0 - u_2|||_A = 0.02,$$
$$|||u_0 - u_3|||_A = 0.01, \qquad |||u_0 - u_4|||_A = 0.01.$$

From (7.6) and the Schwartz inequality, we obtain the uniform error estimate

$$|u_0(x) - u_n(x)| \leqq |||u_0 - u_n|||_A.$$

In particular, $|u_0(1) - u_4(1)| \leqq 0.01$. As we have seen, the real error is considerably smaller.

Example 7.2. Let us consider an example where the scattering of the coefficients is even more marked. This example has been examined in Mikhlin [4; §38].

We shall consider a membrane, which has the shape of a right-angled isosceles triangle and is acted on by a uniform normal force. We shall assume that the membrane is fixed along its perpendicular sides while the hypotenuse remains free. The rectangular x- and y-axes are chosen along the perpendicular sides.

For a suitable choice of units, the problem of determining the displacement $u(x, y)$ in the membrane reduces to the integration of the equation

$$-\frac{\partial^2 u}{\partial x^2} - \frac{\partial^2 u}{\partial y^2} = 1$$

over the triangular region $T = \{(x, y);\ x \geqq 0, y \geqq 0, x+y-1 \leqq 0\}$ under the boundary conditions $u = 0$ on $x = 0$ and $y = 0$, and $\partial u/\partial \nu = 0$ on $x+y-1 = 0$, where ν denotes the normal to the boundary of T in the plane of T. This last problem can be reduced to the problem of minimising the integral

$$F(u) = \int_0^1 \left\{ \int_0^x \left[\left(\frac{\partial u}{\partial x}\right)^2 + \left(\frac{\partial u}{\partial y}\right)^2 - 2u \right] \mathrm{d}y \right\} dx \tag{7.9}$$

under the boundary conditions

$$u(x, 0) = u(0, y) = 0, \tag{7.10}$$

where the space $\mathfrak{H}_A$ consists of the functions which are defined almost everywhere on T with generalised square-summable first derivatives and which satisfy (7.10) – in the sense of Sobolev [1]. The energy inner product and energy norm are defined by

$$\begin{aligned} [u, v]_A &= \int_0^1 \left\{ \int_0^x \left(\frac{\partial u}{\partial x}\frac{\partial v}{\partial x} + \frac{\partial u}{\partial y}\frac{\partial v}{\partial y} \right) dy \right\} dx, \\ |||u|||_A^2 &= \int_0^1 \left\{ \int_0^x \left[\left(\frac{\partial u}{\partial x}\right)^2 + \left(\frac{\partial u}{\partial y}\right)^2 \right] dy \right\} dx. \end{aligned} \tag{7.11}$$

For coordinate functions, we choose the system

$$\{x^k y^m\} \qquad (k, m = 1, 2, \ldots). \tag{7.12}$$

It is not difficult to see that this system satisfies the three conditions listed in §6. This system is non-minimal in $\mathfrak{H}_A$. For the proof, we set $\mathfrak{H}_A = \mathfrak{H}_2$ and examine the space $\mathfrak{H}_1$ of functions which are defined a.e. (almost everywhere) on the square $S = \{(x, y);\ 0 \leqq x \leqq 1, 0 \leqq y \leqq 1\}$, which have generalised square-summable first derivatives and satisfy (in the sense of Sobolev) the condition (7.10). The scalar product and norm in $\mathfrak{H}_1$ are defined by

$$(u, v)_1 = \int_0^1 \int_0^1 \left(\frac{\partial u}{\partial x}\frac{\partial v}{\partial x} + \frac{\partial u}{\partial y}\frac{\partial v}{\partial y} \right) dx\, dy, \tag{7.13}$$

$$||u||_1^2 = \int_0^1 \int_0^1 \left[\left(\frac{\partial u}{\partial x}\right)^2 + \left(\frac{\partial u}{\partial y}\right)^2 \right] dx\, dy. \tag{7.14}$$

Let V be the operator which maps every function $u(x, y)$ defined on S into correspondence with the same function defined only on T. It is clear that V maps $\mathfrak{H}_1$ onto $\mathfrak{H}_A$ and that $|||Vu|||_A \leqq ||u||_1$. Comparing this with inequality (4.1), we see that V defines the imbedding of $\mathfrak{H}_1$ in $\mathfrak{H}_A$. We shall show that system (7.12) is non-minimal in $\mathfrak{H}_1$. The non-minimality of (7.12) in $\mathfrak{H}_A$ then follows from Theorem 4.1.
First, we examine the subspace $\mathfrak{H}_1^{(m)}$ of the space $\mathfrak{H}_1$ spanned by xy^m, $x^2y^m, \ldots$. It is clear that

$$\mathfrak{H}_1 = \bigcup_{m=1}^{\infty} \mathfrak{H}_1^{(m)}.$$

It follows from the Theorem of Müntz (§1) that an arbitrary member can be removed from the sequence nx^{n-1} $(n = 1, 2, \ldots)$ without disturbing its completeness in L_2 (0, 1). Hence it follows that, given k_0 and ε, there exists an integer N and constants $\alpha_1, \alpha_2, \ldots, \alpha_{k_0-1}, \alpha_{k_0+1}, \ldots, \alpha_N$ such that the following inequality

$$||k_0 x^{k_0-1} - \sum_{n=1, n\neq k_0}^{N} \alpha_n n x^{n-1}||_{L_2}^2 = \int_0^1 [k_0 x^{k_0-1} - \sum_{n=1, n\neq k_0}^{N} \alpha_n n x^{n-1}]^2 \, dx < \varepsilon_2$$

holds. On putting

$$f(x) = x^{k_0} - \sum_{n=1, n\neq k_0}^{N} \alpha_n x^n,$$

we obtain

$$||f'(x)||_{L_2}^2 = \int_0^1 [f'(x)]^2 \, dx < \varepsilon^2.$$

We estimate

$$||f(x)||_{L_2}^2 = \int_0^1 [f(x)]^2 \, dx.$$

Since $f(0) = 0$,

$$f(x) = \int_0^x f'(t) dt.$$

Using the Schwartz inequality, we find

$$[f(x)]^2 \leqq x \int_0^x [f'(t)]^2 dt \leqq \|f'(x)\|_{L_2}^2 < \varepsilon^2,$$

which implies

$$\|f(x)\|_{L_2}^2 < \varepsilon^2.$$

Now it is not difficult to arrive at the estimate

$$\|x^{k_0}y^m - \sum_{n=1,\, n\neq k_0}^{N} \alpha_n x^n y^m\|_1 = \|f(x)y^m\|_1.$$

In fact, we have

$$\|f(x)y^m\|_1^2 = \frac{1}{2m+1}\|f'(x)\|_{L_2}^2 + \frac{m^2}{2m-1}\|f(x)\|_{L_2}^2 \leqq C\varepsilon^2,$$

$$C = \text{const.}$$

The last inequality proves the non-minimality of $xy^m, x^2y^m, \ldots,$ in $\mathfrak{H}_1^{(m)}$. Hence, (7.12) is non-minimal in $\mathfrak{H}_1$. The non-minimality of (7.12) in $\mathfrak{H}_A$ follows from the above remark about imbedding

From the symmetric nature of the problem, it is clear that, for the coordinate functions $x^k y^m$ and $x^m y^k$, the approximate solution has identical coefficients. Accordingly, (7.2) can be changed to $(xy)^k(x^m+y^m)$ $(k = 1, 2\ldots;\ m = 0, 1, 2, \ldots)$. If we consider the approximate solution

$$u_4 = a_1^{(4)}xy + a_2^{(4)}xy(x+y) + a_3^{(4)}x^2y^2 + a_4^{(4)}xy(x^2+y^2),$$

we obtain the Ritz-system

$$\begin{aligned}
\tfrac{1}{6}a_1^{(4)} + \tfrac{1}{6}a_2^{(4)} + \tfrac{1}{30}a_3^{(4)} + \tfrac{1}{10}a_4^{(4)} &= \tfrac{1}{24},\\
\tfrac{1}{6}a_1^{(4)} + \tfrac{8}{45}a_2^{(4)} + \tfrac{4}{105}a_3^{(4)} + \tfrac{23}{210}a_4^{(4)} &= \tfrac{1}{30},\\
\tfrac{1}{30}a_1^{(4)} + \tfrac{4}{105}a_2^{(4)} + \tfrac{1}{105}a_3^{(4)} + \tfrac{19}{840}a_4^{(4)} &= \tfrac{1}{180},\\
\tfrac{1}{10}a_1^{(4)} + \tfrac{23}{210}a_2^{(4)} + \tfrac{19}{840}a_3^{(4)} + \tfrac{1}{14}a_4^{(4)} &= \tfrac{1}{60}.
\end{aligned}$$

Solving this system as well as the truncated systems of order 1, 2 and 3, we obtain Table 7.3 for the Ritz-coefficients.

Table 7.3

n	$a_1^{(n)}$	$a_2^{(n)}$	$a_3^{(n)}$	$a_4^{(n)}$	n	$a_1^{(n)}$	$a_2^{(n)}$	$a_3^{(n)}$	$a_4^{(n)}$
1	$\frac{1}{4}$				3	$1\frac{2}{9}$	$-1\frac{1}{6}$	$\frac{35}{36}$	
2	1	$-\frac{3}{4}$			4	$1\frac{6}{19}$	$-1\frac{3}{4}$	$1\frac{8}{13}$	$\frac{14}{39}$

The values of these coefficients, accurate to five decimal places, are given in Table 7.4.

Table 7.4

n	$a_1^{(n)}$	$a_2^{(n)}$	$a_3^{(n)}$	$a_4^{(n)}$
1	0.25000			
2	1.00000	−0.75000		
3	1.22222	−1.16667	0.97222	
4	1.46154	−1.75000	1.61538	0.35897

Table 7.4 shows that for this example, the scattering of the Ritz-coefficients is quite significant: these coefficients change abruptly from one approximation to the next.

In contrast with Example 7.1, we do not know the exact solution for this problem, and therefore it is difficult to give an estimate for the error in the approximate solution. However, we can evaluate the energy norm for the difference $u_n - u_m$ $(n, m = 1, 2, 3, 4)$ and use these norms to examine the closeness between these approximations. Using the formula (VM, §14(16))

$$|||u_m - u_n|||_A^2 = |||u_m|||_A^2 - |||u_n|||_A^2, \qquad m > n,$$

and equation (7.8), we obtain

$$|||u_1|||_A^2 = \tfrac{1}{96} = 0.01042, \qquad |||u_2|||_A^2 = \tfrac{1}{60} = 0.01667,$$

$$|||u_3|||_A^2 = \tfrac{113}{6480} = 0.01744, \qquad |||u_4|||_A^2 = \tfrac{41}{2340} = 0.01752.$$

From here it is clear that the energy norms of the approximate Ritz-solutions only change slightly compared with the sharp changes in the values of the coefficients. From the last results, we obtain

$$|||u_3 - u_2|||_A = \sqrt{|||u_3|||_A^2 - |||u_2|||_A^2} = \sqrt{0.00077} < 0.028,$$

$$|||u_4 - u_3|||_A = \sqrt{|||u_4|||_A^2 - |||u_3|||_A^2} = \sqrt{0.00008} < 0.009.$$

In contrast with Example 7.1, we cannot use these results to ascertain the extent of the uniform closeness of the approximate solutions.

On the basis of the results of the present section we can make the following observation: in itself, the *scattering* of the coefficients is not a defect of the approximate solution. If the approximate solutions u_n ($n = 1, 2, \ldots$) are calculated without serious error, then, for sufficiently large n, u_n will approximate arbitrarily closely to the exact solution independent of the presence, or otherwise, of scattering. Nevertheless, the presence of scattering is not desirable: it hampers the comparison of successive approximations. The presence of scattering serves as an indicator that the coordinate system is not strongly minimal (it may even be non-minimal!) with respect to the energy metric. Also, as will be shown below, this "scattering" may imply instability with respect to the occurrence of small errors at intermediate stages of a calculation.

§8. Examples introducing the concept of numerical stability

We return to the Ritz-system (7.7) and replace its right-hand side values (or, more briefly, r.h.s. values) by values accurate to four decimal places. We obtain the *non-exact* Ritz-system:

$$
\begin{aligned}
&b_1^{(8)}+ b_2^{(8)}+ b_3^{(8)}+ b_4^{(8)}+ b_5^{(8)}+ b_6^{(8)}+ b_7^{(8)} + n_8^{(8)} = 0.3069,\\
&b_1^{(8)}+ \tfrac{4}{3}b_2^{(8)}+ \tfrac{3}{2}b_3^{(8)}+ \tfrac{8}{5}b_4^{(8)}+ \tfrac{5}{3}b_5^{(8)}+\tfrac{12}{7}b_6^{(8)}+\tfrac{7}{4}b_7^{(8)} +\tfrac{16}{9}b_8^{(8)} = 0.1931,\\
&b_1^{(8)}+ \tfrac{3}{2}b_2^{(8)}+ \tfrac{9}{5}b_3^{(8)}+ 2b_4^{(8)}+\tfrac{15}{7}b_5^{(8)}+ \tfrac{9}{4}b_6^{(8)}+\tfrac{7}{3}b_7^{(8)} +\tfrac{12}{5}b_8^{(8)} = 0.1402,\\
&b_1^{(8)}+ \tfrac{8}{5}b_2^{(8)}+ 2b_3^{(8)}+\tfrac{16}{7}b_4^{(8)}+ \tfrac{5}{2}b_5^{(8)}+ \tfrac{8}{3}b_6^{(8)}+\tfrac{14}{5}b_7^{(8)}+\tfrac{32}{11}b_8^{(8)} =0.1098,\\
&b_1^{(8)}+ \tfrac{8}{5}b_2^{(8)}+ 2b_3^{(8)}+\tfrac{16}{7}b_4^{(8)}+ \tfrac{5}{2}b_5^{(8)}+ \tfrac{8}{3}b_6^{(8)} +\tfrac{14}{5}b_7^{(8)} +\tfrac{32}{11}b_8^{(8)} = 0.1098,\\
&b_1^{(8)}+ \tfrac{5}{3}b_2^{(8)}+\tfrac{15}{7}b_3^{(8)}+ \tfrac{5}{2}b_4^{(8)}+\tfrac{25}{9}b_5^{(8)}+ 3b_6^{(8)}+\tfrac{35}{11}b_7^{(8)}+\tfrac{10}{3}b_8^{(8)} = 0.0902,\\
&b_1^{(8)}+\tfrac{12}{7}b_2^{(8)}+ \tfrac{9}{4}b_3^{(8)}+\tfrac{8}{3}b_4^{(8)} +3b_5^{(8)} +\tfrac{36}{11}b_6^{(8)}+ \tfrac{7}{2}b_7^{(8)}+\tfrac{48}{13}b_8^{(8)} = 0.0765,\\
&b_1^{(8)}+ \tfrac{7}{4}b_2^{(8)}+ \tfrac{7}{3}b_3^{(8)}+\tfrac{14}{5}b_4^{(8)}+\tfrac{35}{11}b_5^{(8)}+ \tfrac{7}{2}b_6^{(8)}+\tfrac{49}{13}b_7^{(8)}+ 4b_8^{(8)} = 0.0664,\\
&b_1^{(8)}+\tfrac{16}{9}b_2^{(8)}+\tfrac{12}{5}b_3^{(8)}+\tfrac{32}{11}b_4^{(8)}+\tfrac{10}{3}b_5^{(8)}+\tfrac{48}{13}b_6^{(8)}+ 4b_7^{(8)}+\tfrac{64}{15}b_8^{(8)} = 0.0586.
\end{aligned}
\tag{8.1}
$$

In this *non-exact* system, the matrix does not contain errors, and the errors in the r.h.s.-values are less than 0.00005.

System (8.1) and the corresponding truncated systems have been solved exactly without the introduction of rounding error. The results are given in Table 8.1.

Table 8.1

n	$b_1^{(n)}$	$b_2^{(n)}$	$b_3^{(n)}$	$b_4^{(n)}$	$b_5^{(n)}$	$b_6^{(n)}$	$b_7^{(n)}$	$b_8^{(n)}$
1	0.3069							
2	0.6483	− 0.3414						
3	0.6883	− 0.4614	0.0800					
4	0.6974	− 0.5160	0.1710	− 0.0455				
5	0.7127	− 0.6690	0.6300	− 0.5810	0.2142			
6	0.7633	− 1.4280	4.1720	− 7.6650	6.5898	− 2.1252		
7	0.9141	− 4.5948	25.2840	− 71.0010	101.5938	− 71.7948	19.9056	
8	1.6266	−24.5448	204.8340	−819.1260	1747.4688	−2046.8448	1242.5556	−305.6625

Table 8.2

n	$\eta_1^{(n)}$	$\eta_2^{(n)}$	$\eta_3^{(n)}$	$\eta_4^{(n)}$	$\eta_5^{(n)}$	$\eta_6^{(n)}$	$\eta_7^{(n)}$	$\eta_8^{(n)}$
1	0.0000							
2	0.0003	0.0003						
3	0.0014	0.0035	0.0012					
4	0.0052	0.0261	0.0398	0.0188				
5	0.0197	0.1713	0.4753	0.5269	0.2032			
6	0.0702	0.9285	4.0089	7.5942	6.5638	2.1202		
7	0.2210	4.0949	25.1183	70.9224	101.5560	71.7812	19.9031	
8	0.9335	24.0448	204.6676	819.0443	1747.4242	2046.8230	1242.5481	305.6612

Comparing this table with Table 7.2, which we regard as exact since it is correct to the decimal places shown, we can construct a table of errors (Table 8.2)

$$\eta_k^{(n)} = |b_k^{(n)} - a_k^{(n)}|.$$

We examine the ratio $\eta_k^{(n)}: \delta$, where $\delta = 0.00005$ is an upper bound for the error in the calculation of the r.h.s.-values of (8.1). We see that this ratio grows rapidly for increasing n; it equals 6 when $n = 2$ and reaches the value of 10^7 when $n = 8$.

In making the change from (7.7) to (8.1) and in solving (8.1) and the truncated systems, we have not introduced error into the matrix and have avoided rounding errors. However, if these errors were allowed to occur (for example, if the coefficients in (8.1) were changed to a decimal approximation and if the intermediate calculations in the solution of (8.1) were carried out with less accuracy), then the error in the solution of (8.1) would grow even more.

What is the character of this paradox? In order to extend the accuracy of the approximate Ritz-solution, it is necessary to increase the number n of coordinate functions in its representation – this follows from the fact that the energy norm $|||u_0 - u_n|||_A$, where u_0 is the exact solution of the variational problem and u_n is the nth approximate Ritz-representation of this solution, decreases monotonically as n increases (VM, § 14). But, the process of increasing n can lead to a sharp growth in the numerical error for the corresponding Ritz-systems, and this error can diminish or completely suppress the useful effect of increasing the number of coordinate functions.

However, this unpleasant occurrence does not always occur. A simple and sufficiently important case when this sharp increase in numerical error does not occur is when the coordinate system is orthonormal in the energy space. In fact, if $[\phi_k, \phi_j]_A = \delta_{kj}$ then the Ritz-system assumes the form

$$a_j = (f, \phi_j) \qquad (j = 1, 2, \ldots, n).$$

The error in each of the Ritz-coefficients equals the error in the corresponding r.h.s.-values. For a fixed number j, the error in the coefficient $a_j^{(n)}$ is clearly independent of n since $a_j^{(n)} = a_j = (f, \phi_j)$ is independent of n.

However, it is not necessary that coordinate systems be orthonormal in the energy space, in order to ensure that the numerical error does not grow with increasing n. In order to clarify this point, we shall consider the following example.

The operator $\boldsymbol{A}$, defined by the problem

$$\boldsymbol{A}u = -\frac{d}{dx}\left[(2+x)\frac{du}{dx}\right] + 1, \qquad u(-1) = u(1) = 0, \tag{8.2}$$

is positive-definite in the space $L_2(-1, 1)$. In fact,

$$(\boldsymbol{A}u, u) = -\int_{-1}^{1} \overline{u(x)} \frac{d}{dx}\left[(2+x)\frac{du}{dx}\right] dx = -(2+x)\overline{u(x)}\frac{du}{dx}\bigg|_{-1}^{1} +$$

$$+\int_{-1}^{1}(2+x)\left|\frac{du}{dx}\right|^2 dx = \int_{-1}^{1}(2+x)\left|\frac{du}{dx}\right|^2 dx \geqq \int_{-1}^{1}\left|\frac{du}{dx}\right|^2 dx. \tag{8.3}$$

We introduce the operator $\boldsymbol{B}$ which is defined by the equations

$$\boldsymbol{B}u = -\frac{d^2u}{dx^2}, \qquad u(-1) = u(1) = 0. \tag{8.4}$$

Its energy inner product and norm are

$$[u, v]_{\boldsymbol{B}} = \int_{-1}^{1} \frac{du}{dx}\frac{d\bar{v}}{dx}\, dx, \qquad |||u|||_{\boldsymbol{B}}^2 = \int_{-1}^{1}\left|\frac{du}{dx}\right|^2 dx. \tag{8.5}$$

The operator $\boldsymbol{B}$ has a discrete spectrum. Since the smallest eigenvalue of this operator equals $\pi^2/4$, we have

$$|||u|||_{\boldsymbol{B}}^2 = \int_{-1}^{1}\left|\frac{du}{dx}\right|^2 dx \geqq \frac{\pi^2}{4}||u||^2.$$

Now it follows from inequality (8.3) that

$$(\boldsymbol{A}u, u) \geqq \frac{\pi^2}{4}||u||^2, \tag{8.6}$$

and the positive-definiteness of the operator $\boldsymbol{A}$ is proved.

The energy inner product and norm for the operator $\boldsymbol{A}$ are defined by

$$[u, v]_{\boldsymbol{A}} = \int_{-1}^{1}(2+x)\frac{du}{dx}\frac{d\bar{v}}{dx}\, dx, \qquad |||u|||_{\boldsymbol{A}}^2 = \int_{-1}^{1}(2+x)\left|\frac{du}{dx}\right|^2 dx. \tag{8.7}$$

It follows from (8.7) and (8.5) that

$$|||u|||_B \leqq |||u|||_A \leqq \sqrt{3}|||u|||_B, \tag{8.8}$$

which shows that the operators $\boldsymbol{A}$ and $\boldsymbol{B}$ are semi-similar.
In fact, it is easily seen that $\boldsymbol{A}$ and $\boldsymbol{B}$ are similar.
Since $\boldsymbol{A}$ is positive-definite, problem (8.2) can be solved by the method of Ritz. As coordinate functions we take integrals of the normalised Legendre polynomials:

$$\phi_n(x) = \sqrt{\frac{2n+1}{2}}\int_{-1}^{x} P_n(t)dt \qquad (n = 1, 2, \ldots). \tag{8.9}$$

In fact, these functions satisfy the boundary conditions: clearly, $\phi_n(-1) = 0$, while

$$\phi_n(1) = \sqrt{\frac{2n+1}{2}}\int_{-1}^{1} P_n(t)dt = 0,$$

since the Legendre polynomials $P_n(t)$, with order greater than zero, are orthogonal to $P_0(t) = 1$ in $L_2(-1, 1)$. Also, it is clear that the functions (8.9) lie in $\mathfrak{H}_A$, and that the functions $\phi_1(x), \phi_2(x), \ldots, \phi_n(x)$ are linearly independent for arbitrary n. We shall prove the completeness of system (8.9) w.r.t. the metric (8.7).
Inequality (8.8) implies that the metrics (8.7) and (8.5) are equivalent, and thus, that it is sufficient to prove the completeness of system (8.9) w.r.t. the metric (8.5).
The energy space $\mathfrak{H}_A$ of problem (8.2) consists of the functions which:
(1) are absolutely continuous on the interval $-1 \leqq x \leqq 1$;
(2) equal zero at the ends of this interval;
(3) have square-summable first derivatives on this interval.
If $u(x)$ lies in $\mathfrak{H}_A$, then its derivative $u'(x)$ satisfies

$$\int_{-1}^{1} u'(x)dx = u(1)-u(-1) = 0,$$

and, consequently, the set of first derivatives of $u(x)$ lying in $\mathfrak{H}_A$ can be regarded as a subspace $\tilde{L}_2(-1, 1)$ of functions of $L_2(-1, 1)$ which are orthogonal to unity.
In this subspace, the system of polynomials

$$\phi_n'(x) = \sqrt{\frac{2n+1}{2}}\, P_n(x) \qquad (n = 1, 2, \ldots) \tag{8.10}$$

is complete. Further, it follows from (8.5) that

$$[u, v]_B = (u', v'),$$

and the completeness of (8.9) w.r.t. the metric (8.5) follows at once from the fact that (8.10) is complete in $\tilde{L}_2(-1, 1)$.
With respect to the metric (8.7), the polynomials (8.9) are not orthonormal. However, by inequality (8.8) and Corollary 4.3, the polynomials (8.9) are almost orthonormal with respect to the metric (8.7).
Now, we evaluate the inner products $[\phi_k, \phi_m]$, and r.h.s.-values of the Ritz-process. By (8.7),

$$[\phi_k, \phi_m] = \tfrac{1}{2}\sqrt{(2k+1)(2m+1)}\int_{-1}^{1}(x+2)P_k(x)P_m(x)dx =$$

$$= \tfrac{1}{2}\sqrt{(2k+1)(2m+1)}\left[\int_{-1}^{1} xP_k(x)P_m(x)dx + \frac{4}{2k+1}\delta_{km}\right].$$

Further, the recurrence formula for Legendre polynomials gives

$$xP_k(x) = \frac{k+1}{2k+1}P_{k+1}(x) + \frac{k}{2k+1}P_{k-1}(x),$$

and hence,

$$[\phi_k, \phi_m] = \tfrac{1}{2}\sqrt{(2k+1)(2m+1)}\left[\frac{2(k+1)}{(2k+1)(2k+3)}\delta_{k+1,m} + \right.$$

$$\left. + \frac{2k}{(2k+1)(2k-1)}\delta_{k-1,m} + \frac{4}{2k+1}\delta_{km}\right].$$

Thus, for $k \geqq m$

$$[\phi_k, \phi_m] = \begin{cases} 0, & k-m > 1, \\ 2, & k = m, \\ \dfrac{k}{\sqrt{4k^2-1}}, & k = m+1, \end{cases}$$

while for $k < m$ we use the fact that $[\phi_k, \phi_m] = [\phi_m, \phi_k]$: the Ritz-matrix becomes

$$\begin{pmatrix} 2 & \frac{2}{\sqrt{15}} & 0 & 0 & 0 & \dots \\ \frac{2}{\sqrt{15}} & 2 & \frac{3}{\sqrt{35}} & 0 & 0 & \dots \\ 0 & \frac{3}{\sqrt{35}} & 2 & \frac{4}{3\sqrt{7}} & 0 & \dots \\ 0 & 0 & \frac{4}{3\sqrt{7}} & 2 & \frac{5}{3\sqrt{11}} & \dots \\ \dots & \dots & \dots & \dots & \dots & \dots \end{pmatrix}$$

The r.h.s.-values for the Ritz-process are given by

$$(1, \phi_k) = \int_{-1}^{1} \phi_k(x)dx = x\phi_k(x)\Big|_{-1}^{1} - \int_{-1}^{1} x\phi_k'(x) = \\ = -\sqrt{\frac{2k+1}{2}}\int_{-1}^{1} xP_k(x)dx$$

which simplifies to

$$(1, \phi_k) = \begin{cases} -\sqrt{\frac{2}{3}}, & k = 1, \\ 0, & k > 1. \end{cases}$$

The Ritz-system of order 8 becomes

$$\begin{aligned} 2a_1^{(8)} + \frac{2}{\sqrt{15}}\, a_2^{(8)} &= -\sqrt{\frac{2}{3}}, \\ \frac{2}{\sqrt{15}}\, a_1^{(8)} + 2a_2^{(8)} + \frac{3}{\sqrt{35}}\, a_3^{(8)} &= 0, \\ \frac{3}{\sqrt{35}}\, a_2^{(8)} + 2a_3^{(8)} + \frac{4}{3\sqrt{7}}\, a_4^{(8)} &= 0, \\ \frac{4}{3\sqrt{7}}\, a_3^{(8)} + 2a_4^{(8)} + \frac{5}{3\sqrt{11}}\, a_5^{(8)} &= 0, \\ \frac{5}{3\sqrt{11}}\, a_4^{(8)} + 2a_5^{(8)} + \frac{6}{\sqrt{143}}\, a_6^{(8)} &= 0, \\ \frac{6}{\sqrt{143}}\, a_5^{(8)} + 2a_6^{(8)} + \frac{7}{\sqrt{195}}\, a_7^{(8)} &= 0, \\ \frac{7}{\sqrt{195}}\, a_6^{(8)} + 2a_7^{(8)} + \frac{8}{\sqrt{255}}\, a_8^{(8)} &= 0, \\ \frac{8}{\sqrt{255}}\, a_7^{(8)} + 2a_8^{(8)} &= 0, \end{aligned} \tag{8.11}$$

Table 8.3

n	$\frac{a_1^{(n)}}{\sqrt{6}}$	$\frac{a_2^{(n)}}{\sqrt{10}}$	$\frac{a_3^{(n)}}{\sqrt{14}}$	$\frac{a_4^{(n)}}{\sqrt{2}}$	$\frac{a_5^{(n)}}{\sqrt{22}}$	$\frac{a_6^{(n)}}{\sqrt{26}}$	$\frac{a_7^{(n)}}{\sqrt{30}}$	$\frac{a_8^{(n)}}{\sqrt{34}}$
1	$-\frac{1}{6}$							
2	$-\frac{5}{28}$	$\frac{1}{28}$						
3	$-\frac{131}{730}$	$\frac{14}{365}$	$-\frac{3}{365}$					
4	$-\frac{1\,099}{6\,122}$	$\frac{118}{3\,061}$	$-\frac{27}{3\,061}$	$\frac{18}{3\,061}$				
5	$-\frac{5\,009}{27\,902}$	$\frac{538}{13\,951}$	$-\frac{53}{5\,979}$	$\frac{88}{13\,951}$	$-\frac{20}{41\,853}$			
6	$-\frac{60\,721}{338\,238}$	$\frac{2\,174}{56\,373}$	$-\frac{4\,499}{507\,357}$	$\frac{1\,072}{169\,119}$	$-\frac{260}{507\,357}$	$\frac{20}{169\,119}$		
7	$-\frac{10\,193\,457}{56\,781\,246}$	$\frac{1\,094\,874}{28\,390\,623}$	$-\frac{251\,761}{28\,390\,623}$	$\frac{60\,008}{9\,463\,541}$	$-\frac{14\,620}{28\,390\,623}$	$\frac{1\,200}{9\,463\,541}$	$-\frac{280}{9\,463\,541}$	
8	$-\frac{53\,876\,779}{300\,113\,162}$	$\frac{5\,786\,878}{150\,056\,581}$	$-\frac{1\,330\,667}{150\,056\,581}$	$\frac{951\,528}{150\,056\,581}$	$-\frac{77\,300}{150\,056\,581}$	$\frac{19\,120}{150\,056\,581}$	$-\frac{4\,760}{150\,056\,581}$	$\frac{1\,120}{150\,056\,581}$

while the systems of lower order are obtained by truncation.

In Table 8.3, we give the exact values of the Ritz-coefficients $a_k^{(n)}$ for $1 \leqq n \leqq 8$, while the corresponding values rounded to four decimal places are listed in Table 8.4.

Table 8.4

n	$a_1^{(n)}$	$a_2^{(n)}$	$a_3^{(n)}$	$a_4^{(n)}$	$a_5^{(n)}$	$a_6^{(n)}$	$a_7^{(n)}$	$a_8^{(n)}$
1	−0.4082							
2	−0.4374	0.1129						
3	−0.4395	0.1213	−0.0308					
4	−0.4397	0.1219	−0.0330	0.0083				
5	−0.4397	0.1219	−0.0332	0.0089	−0.0022			
6	−0.4397	0.1220	−0.0332	0.0090	−0.0024	0.0006		
7	−0.4397	0.1220	−0.0332	0.0090	−0.0024	0.0006	−0.0002	
8	−0.4397	0.1220	−0.0332	0.0090	−0.0024	0.0006	−0.0002	0.0001

We note that, in contrast with §7, the phenomenon of *scattering* is not observed: for increasing n, the values in Table 8.4 stabilise quickly and, moreover, uniformly with respect to the subscript k. It is clear that, since the given coordinate system is almost orthonormal in the energy space, it is strongly minimal there.

We turn from the exact Ritz-system (8.11) to the non-exact: we replace the coefficients and r.h.s.-values in (8.11) by their approximate decimal representations, accurate to four decimal places:

$$\begin{aligned} 2b_1^{(8)}+0.5164_2^{(8)} &= -0.8165, \\ 0.5164b_1^{(8)}+2b_2^{(8)}+0.5071b_3^{(8)} &= 0, \\ 0.5071b_2^{(8)}+2b_3^{(8)}+0.5040b_4^{(8)} &= 0, \\ 0.5040b_3^{(8)}+2b_4^{(8)}+0.5025b_5^{(8)} &= 0, \\ 0.5025b_4^{(8)}+2b_5^{(8)}+0.5017b_6^{(8)} &= 0, \\ 0.5017b_5^{(8)}+2b_6^{(8)}+0.5013b_7^{(8)} &= 0, \\ 0.5013b_6^{(8)}+2b_7^{(8)}+0.5010b_8^{(8)} &= 0, \\ 0.5010b_7^{(8)}+2b_8^{(8)} &= 0, \end{aligned} \tag{8.12}$$

In order to avoid the possibility of rounding error effects, the intermediate calculations were carried out with a sufficiently large number of decimal places – with seven places for systems of order $\leqq$ 4 and with 12 places for systems of order 5 to 8. The final results, rounded to four places, are given in Table 8.5.

Table 8.5

n	$b_1^{(n)}$	$b_2^{(n)}$	$b_3^{(n)}$	$b_4^{(n)}$	$b_5^{(n)}$	$b_6^{(n)}$	$b_7^{(n)}$	$b_8^{(n)}$
1	−0.4083							
2	−0.4374	0.1129						
3	−0.4396	0.1213	−0.0308					
4	−0.4397	0.1219	−0.0330	0.0083				
5	−0.4398	0.1220	−0.0332	0.0089	−0.0022			
6	−0.4398	0.1220	−0.0332	0.0089	−0.0024	0.0006		
7	−0.4398	0.1220	−0.0332	0.0089	−0.0024	0.0007	−0.0002	
8	−0.4398	0.1220	−0.0332	0.0089	−0.0024	0.0007	−0.0002	0.0001

Comparing Tables 8.4 and 8.5, we see that the error in the solution of the Ritz-process does not exceed 0.0001, and hence, does not exceed twice the error in the coefficients and r.h.s.-values of the Ritz-process.

§9. On the stability of the Ritz-process

Note. See Mikhlin [15] and [16].

We shall examine the problem of minimising the functional

$$F(u) = A[u] - lu - \overline{lu}, \tag{9.1}$$

where $A[u]$ is a positive quadratic and lu a linear functional. As always, we introduce the energy space $\mathfrak{H}_A$ with energy inner product and norm

$$[u, v] = [u, v]_A = A[u, v], \qquad |||u|||^2 = |||u|||_A^2 = A[u], \tag{9.2}$$

where $A[u, v]$ is a bilinear form with $A[u]$ as its corresponding quadratic form. We assume that the functional lu is bounded w.r.t. the metric (9.2):

$$|||l|||_A \leqq C_0 = \text{const.} \tag{9.3}$$

Then there exists an element $u_0 \in \mathfrak{H}_A$ which minimises $F(u)$ in $\mathfrak{H}_A$. This element is defined by $lu = [u, u_0]$ (see, §6), as a consequence of the theorem of F. Riesz on the general form of a bounded linear functional in a Hilbert space. We note that $|||l|||_A = |||u_0|||_A$, and hence,

$$|||u_0|||_A \leqq C_0. \tag{9.4}$$

We shall construct an approximate representation of the solution of our problem with the help of the method of Ritz: we choose a system of coordinate elements $\{\phi_n\}$ which satisfy the three conditions of §6, and we take for the approximate Ritz-representation (-solution) the element u_n defined by (6.6). The coefficients $a_k^{(n)}$ ($k = 1, 2, \ldots, n$; $n = 1, 2, \ldots$) of u_n are defined by the Ritz-process (6.8).

As we saw in the preceding section, the solutions of Ritz-systems react in different ways for different problems to small errors which arise during the construction of these system, namely, error in the coefficients and r.h.s.-values of these matrix systems: in one case, the error in the solution increased rapidly with increase in the order of the system, while in another the error did not exhibit such a tendency. These results lead to the necessity to formulate some concept of numerical stability for the Ritz-process. We shall now turn attention to this formulation.

Let R_n denote the following Gram-matrix of order n in $\mathfrak{H}_A$ (or, more briefly, the Ritz-matrix),

$$R_n = \begin{pmatrix} [\phi_1, \phi_1]_A & [\phi_2, \phi_1]_A & \cdots & [\phi_n, \phi_1]_A \\ [\phi_1, \phi_2]_A & [\phi_2, \phi_2]_A & \cdots & [\phi_n, \phi_2]_A \\ \cdot & \cdot & \cdot & \cdot \\ [\phi_1, \phi_n]_A & [\phi_2, \phi_n]_A & \cdots & [\phi_n, \phi_n]_A \end{pmatrix},$$

$f^{(n)}$ the column-vector of the r.h.s.-values

$$f^{(n)} = (l\phi_1, l\phi_2, \ldots, l\phi_n),$$

and $a^{(n)}$ the column-vector of Ritz-coefficients

$$a^{(n)} = (a_1^{(n)}, a_2^{(n)}, \ldots, a_n^{(n)}).$$

Using this notation, the Ritz-process becomes

$$\boldsymbol{R}_n a^{(n)} = f^{(n)} \qquad (n = 1, 2, 3, \ldots). \tag{9.5}$$

We shall assume that the energy inner product $[\phi_k, \phi_m]_A$ is evaluated with small error $\gamma_{km} = \gamma_{mk}$ and the scalar product $f_m = (f, \phi_m)$ with small error δ_m. We shall denote by Γ_n the nth order matrix with elements $\gamma_{jk}(j, k = 1, 2, \ldots, n)$ and by $\delta^{(n)}$ the column-vector with components $[\delta_1, \delta_2, \ldots, \delta_n]$. Instead of the process (9.5), we consider the process

$$(\boldsymbol{R}_n + \boldsymbol{\Gamma}_n) b^{(n)} = f^{(n)} + \delta^{(n)} \qquad (n = 1, 2, 3, \ldots), \tag{9.6}$$

where $b^{(n)}$ denotes the column-vector of *non-exact* Ritz-coefficients.

The matrices R_n, R_n^{-1} and Γ_n define in n-dimensional vector space linear operators which we shall denote by the same symbols $\boldsymbol{R}_n$, $\boldsymbol{R}_n^{-1}$, $\boldsymbol{\Gamma}_n$. The symbols $\|\boldsymbol{R}_n\|$, $\|\boldsymbol{R}_n^{-1}\|$ and $\|\boldsymbol{\Gamma}_n\|$ will denote the respective norms of these operators. We observe that

$$||\boldsymbol{R}_n^{-1}|| = \frac{1}{\lambda_1^{(n)}}, \tag{9.7}$$

where grr is the smallest eigenvalue of the matrix Rt. In addition, we note that

$$||\boldsymbol{\Gamma}_n|| \leqq \{\sum_{j,k=1}^{n} |\gamma_{jk}|^2\}^2 = ||\boldsymbol{\Gamma}_n||_E, \tag{9.8}$$

where $||\boldsymbol{\Gamma}_n||_E$ is called the Euclidean norm.
The errors γ_{jk} and δ_j sometimes arise from the fact that the quantities ϕ_j, ϕ_k and $l\phi_j$ are replaced by decimal approximations which retain only a fixed number of decimal places. Let the number of decimal places retained be k, then (restricting attention to a real Hilbert space) $|\gamma_{jk}| < \frac{1}{2}\, 10^{-k}$ and $|\delta_j| < \frac{1}{2}\, 10^{-k}$, whence it follows that

$$||\boldsymbol{\Gamma}_n|| < \frac{n}{2}\, 10^{-k} \quad \text{and} \quad ||\delta^{(n)}|| = \{\sum_{j=1}^{n} \delta_j^2\}^{\frac{1}{2}} < \frac{\sqrt{n}}{2}\, 10^{-k}.$$

We shall say that the Ritz-process is *stable*, if there exist constants p, q and r independent of n such that for $||\boldsymbol{\Gamma}_n|| \leqq r$ and arbitrary $\delta^{(n)}$ the process (9.6) is soluble and the inequality

$$||b^{(n)} - a^{(n)}|| \leqq p||\boldsymbol{\Gamma}_n|| + q||\delta^{(n)}||. \tag{9.9}$$

holds. In the opposite case, we say that the Ritz-process is *unstable*.
This definition assumes that both the *exact* Ritz-process (9.5) and the *non-exact* process (9.6) are solved exactly without error. In this way, our definition of stability does not allow for the occurence of rounding error during the solution of the process.
Stability and instability of a Ritz-process are completely defined by the properties of its coordinate system:

Theorem 9.1. *In order that a Ritz-process be stable, it is necessary and sufficient that its generating coordinate system be strongly minimal in the corresponding energy space.*

Proof. Necessity: Let the Ritz-process (9.5) be stable. We assume that $\Gamma_n = 0$, so that errors in the Ritz-process only arise in the evaluation of the r.h.s.-values. Then

$$||b^{(n)} - a^{(n)}|| \leqq q||\delta^{(n)}||. \tag{9.10}$$

Let $\lambda_1^{(n)}$ denote the smallest eigenvalue of R_n and $x_1^{(n)}$ its corresponding normalised eigenvector.
In equation (9.6) we put $\delta^{(n)} = x_1^{(n)}$ to obtain:

$$\boldsymbol{R}_n b^{(n)} = f^{(n)} + x_1^{(n)}.$$

It follows that

$$b^{(n)} = a^{(n)} + \frac{1}{\lambda_1^{(n)}} x_1^{(n)} \quad \text{and} \quad ||b^{(n)} - a^{(n)}|| = \frac{1}{\lambda_1^{(n)}} = \frac{1}{\lambda_1^{(n)}} ||\delta^{(n)}||.$$

From inequality (9.10), we have $\lambda_1^{(n)} \geqq 1/q$, which proves that the generating coordinate system is strongly minimal.

Sufficiency: Let the coordinate system be strongly minimal, so that $\lambda_1^{(n)} \geqq \lambda_0 = \text{const.} > 0$. We put $r = \beta\lambda_0$, where β is a constant such that $0 < \beta < 1$. We shall assume that $||\boldsymbol{\Gamma}_n|| \leqq \beta\lambda_0$. Then (9.6) has a unique solution for any n.
From equations (9.5) and (9.6), we obtain

$$a^{(n)} = \boldsymbol{R}_n^{-1} f^{(n)}, \qquad b^{(n)} = (\boldsymbol{R}_n + \boldsymbol{\Gamma}_n)^{-1}(f^{(n)} + \delta^{(n)}).$$

However,

$$(\boldsymbol{R}_n + \boldsymbol{\Gamma}_n)^{-1} = [\boldsymbol{R}_n(\boldsymbol{I}_n + \boldsymbol{R}_n^{-1}\boldsymbol{\Gamma}_n)]^{-1} = (\boldsymbol{I}_n + \boldsymbol{R}_n^{-1}\boldsymbol{\Gamma}_n)^{-1}\boldsymbol{R}_n^{-1},$$

where $\boldsymbol{I}_n$ is the operator defined by the identity matrix of order n.
From here it follows that

$$\begin{aligned} b^{(n)} &= (\boldsymbol{I}_n + \boldsymbol{R}_n^{-1}\boldsymbol{\Gamma}_n)^{-1}\boldsymbol{R}_n^{-1}(f^{(n)} + \delta^{(n)}) = \\ &= (\boldsymbol{I}_n + \boldsymbol{R}_n^{-1}\boldsymbol{\Gamma}_n)^{-1} a^{(n)} + (\boldsymbol{I}_n + \boldsymbol{R}_n^{-1}\boldsymbol{\Gamma}_n)^{-1}\boldsymbol{R}_n^{-1}\delta^{(n)} \end{aligned}$$

and hence, that

$$\begin{aligned} ||b^{(n)} - a^{(n)}|| &\leqq ||(\boldsymbol{I}_n + \boldsymbol{R}_n^{-1}\boldsymbol{\Gamma}_n)^{-1} - \boldsymbol{I}_n||\, ||a^{(n)}|| + \\ &+ ||(\boldsymbol{I}_n + \boldsymbol{R}_n^{-1}\boldsymbol{\Gamma}_n)^{-1}||\, ||\boldsymbol{R}_n^{-1}||\, ||\delta^{(n)}||. \end{aligned}$$

Since we have

$$||\boldsymbol{R}_n^{-1}\boldsymbol{\Gamma}_n|| \leqq ||\boldsymbol{R}_n^{-1}||\, ||\boldsymbol{\Gamma}_n|| = \frac{||\boldsymbol{\Gamma}_n||}{\lambda_1^{(n)}} \leqq \frac{||\boldsymbol{\Gamma}_n||}{\lambda_0} \leqq \beta < 1,$$

the operator $(\boldsymbol{I}_n + \boldsymbol{R}_n^{-1}\boldsymbol{\Gamma}_n)^{-1}$ can be expanded as a power series

$$(\boldsymbol{I}_n + \boldsymbol{R}_n^{-1}\boldsymbol{\Gamma}_n)^{-1} = \boldsymbol{I}_n - \boldsymbol{R}_n^{-1}\boldsymbol{\Gamma}_n + (\boldsymbol{R}_n^{-1}\boldsymbol{\Gamma}_n)^2 - \ldots,$$

which yields the result

$$(\boldsymbol{I}_n+\boldsymbol{R}_n^{-1}\boldsymbol{\Gamma}_n)^{-1}-\boldsymbol{I}_n = -\boldsymbol{R}_n^{-1}\boldsymbol{\Gamma}_n+(\boldsymbol{R}_n^{-1}\boldsymbol{\Gamma}_n)^2-\dots$$

The last two expressions are used to give

$$\|(\boldsymbol{I}_n+\boldsymbol{R}_n^{-1}\boldsymbol{\Gamma}_n)^{-1}\| \leqq 1+\|\boldsymbol{R}_n^{-1}\boldsymbol{\Gamma}_n\|+\|(\boldsymbol{R}_n^{-1}\boldsymbol{\Gamma}_n)^2\|+\dots \leqq$$
$$\leqq 1+\frac{\|\boldsymbol{\Gamma}_n\|}{\lambda_0}+\frac{\|\boldsymbol{\Gamma}_n\|^2}{\lambda_0^2}+\dots = \frac{1}{1-\lambda_0^{-1}\|\boldsymbol{\Gamma}_n\|} \leqq \frac{1}{1-\beta}$$

and

$$\|(\boldsymbol{I}_n+\boldsymbol{R}_n^{-1}\boldsymbol{\Gamma}_n)^{-1}-\boldsymbol{I}_n\| \leqq \|\boldsymbol{R}_n^{-1}\boldsymbol{\Gamma}_n\|+\|(\boldsymbol{R}_n^{-1}\boldsymbol{\Gamma}_n)^2\|+\dots \leqq$$
$$\leqq \frac{\lambda_0^{-1}\|\boldsymbol{\Gamma}_n\|}{1-\lambda_0^{-1}\|\boldsymbol{\Gamma}_n\|} \leqq \frac{\lambda_0^{-1}\|\boldsymbol{\Gamma}_n\|}{1-\beta}.$$

Hence,

$$\|b^{(n)}-a^{(n)}\| \leqq \frac{\lambda_0^{-1}\|\boldsymbol{\Gamma}_n\|\,\|a^{(n)}\|+\lambda_0^{-1}\|\delta^{(n)}\|}{1-\beta}. \tag{9.11}$$

Next, we estimate the quantity $\|a^{(n)}\|$. From

$$|||u_n|||^2 = \sum_{j,k=1}^{n}[\phi_k,\phi_j]a_k^{(n)}a_j^{(n)} \geqq \lambda_1^{(n)}\sum_{k=1}^{n}|a_k^{(n)}|^2 =$$
$$= \lambda_1^{(n)}\|a^{(n)}\|^2 \geqq \lambda_0\|a^{(n)}\|^2,$$

we obtain

$$\|a^{(n)}\| \leqq \lambda_0^{-\frac{1}{2}}|||u_n|||.$$

But, $|||u_n||| \leqq |||u_0|||$ (VM, §14 (15)). Hence

$$\|a^{(n)}\| \leqq \lambda_0^{-\frac{1}{2}}|||u_0|||. \tag{9.12}$$

Substituting this in inequality (9.11), we obtain

$$\|b^{(n)}-a^{(n)}\| \leqq \frac{\lambda_0^{-\frac{3}{2}}|||u_0|||\,\|\boldsymbol{\Gamma}_n\|+\lambda_0^{-1}\|\delta^{(n)}\|}{1-\beta}, \tag{9.13}$$

which coincides with inequality (9.9) when

$$p = \frac{\lambda_0^{-\frac{3}{2}}|||u_0|||}{1-\beta}, \qquad q = \frac{\lambda_0^{-1}}{1-\beta}.$$

Note. Clearly, the quantity $|||u_0|||$ is not, in general, known. For a more suitable estimate of the error, it is possible to make use of the formula

$$||b^{(n)}-a^{(n)}|| \leqq \frac{\lambda_0^{-\frac{3}{2}}C||\Gamma_n||+\lambda_0^{-1}||\delta^{(n)}||}{1-\beta}, \tag{9.13'}$$

which follows from inequalities (9.13) and (9.4).

As seen from the structure of the proof, the estimates (9.13) and (9.13′) are only true when both the Ritz-processes (the *exact* (9.5) and the *non-exact* (9.6)) are solved absolutely exactly without the occurrence of rounding errors. If such errors do occur, then the norm of the error $b^{(n)}-a^{(n)}$ can exceed the right-hand sides in each of the expressions (9.13) and (9.13′).

We shall apply these results to the second problem in §8. As noted above, we make use of the fact that the coordinate system (8.9) is almost orthonormal and, hence, strongly minimal in the corresponding energy space. In order to find a value for λ_0, we use results which were obtained for the proof of Theorem 4.2. The system (8.9) is orthonormal, and hence, strongly minimal in $\mathfrak{H}_{\boldsymbol{B}}$, where $\boldsymbol{B}$ is defined by (8.4). We identify the spaces $\mathfrak{H}_{\boldsymbol{A}}$ and $\mathfrak{H}_{\boldsymbol{B}}$ with the spaces $\mathfrak{H}_1$ and $\mathfrak{H}_2$ of §4, respectively. Since the system (8.9) is orthonormal in $\mathfrak{H}_2$, all the eigenvalues of the matrix r_n (equation (4.5)) equal 1 and $\mu_0 = 1$, where μ_0 is the greatest lower bound for the eigenvalues of r_n. Further, the inequality (4.1) becomes (see equation (8.8))

$$||u||_2 \leqq ||u||_1,$$

so that $K = 1$. The estimate (4.6) now gives $\lambda_1^{(n)} \geqq 1$ and, therefore, it is possible to take $\lambda_0 = 1$. For the transition from the exact Ritz-process (8.11) to the non-exact (8.12), we introduce errors which do not exceed $\frac{1}{2}10^{-4}$. Hence, we have

$$|\gamma_{jk}| \leqq \tfrac{1}{2}10^{-4},\ |\delta_k| \leqq \tfrac{1}{2}10^{-4},\ ||\Gamma_8|| \leqq 4 \times 10^{-4},\ ||\delta^{(8)}|| \leqq \sqrt{2} \times 10^{-4}.$$

We can take $\beta = 5 \times 10^{-4}$.

For an estimate of $C \geqq |||u_0|||$, given in (9.13′), we make use of the inequality $|||u_0||| \leqq ||f||/\gamma$, where f is the r.h.s. of the equation (8.2), and γ is the constant in the inequality $(\boldsymbol{A}u, \mathrm{u}) \geqq \gamma^2||u||^2$, which characterises the positive-definiteness of the operator $\boldsymbol{A}$ defined by (8.2). From (8.7), we see that it is possible to take $\gamma = \pi/2$. Further, since $f(x) = 1$,

$$||f|| = \left\{\int_{-1}^{1} dx\right\}^{\frac{1}{2}} = \sqrt{2},$$

and hence, $C = 2\sqrt{2}/\pi$. For simplicity, we replace $2\sqrt{2}/\pi$ by the larger value $C = 1$. Finally, using (9.13′), we obtain the following estimate for the norm of the error vector:

$$||b^{(8)} - a^{(8)}|| \leqq \frac{1 \times 1 \times 4 \times 10^{-4} + \sqrt{2} \times 10^{-4}}{1 - 5 \times 10^{-4}} \approx 5.4 \times 10^{-4}.$$

A comparison of Tables 8.4 and 8.5 yields the following value for this norm:

$$||b^{(8)} - a^{(8)}|| = \sqrt{3} \times 10^{-4} < 1.8 \times 10^{-4}.$$

This bound is less than the theoretically obtained upper bound above, but has the same order of magnitude as the above bound.

§10. The stability of approximate solutions

The solution $b^{(n)}$ of the *non-exact* Ritz-process (9.6) leads to the *non-exact* approximate Ritz-solution

$$v_n = \sum_{k=1}^{n} b_k^{(n)} \phi_k. \tag{10.1}$$

The approximate Ritz-solution

$$u_n = \sum_{k=1}^{n} a_k^{(n)} \phi_k, \tag{10.2}$$

where $a^{(n)} = [a_1^{(n)}, a_2^{(n)}, \ldots, a_n^{(n)}]$ is the solution of the exact Ritz-process (9.5), will be called *stable*, if there exist constants p_1, q_1 and r_1, independent of n, such that for $||\boldsymbol{\Gamma}_n|| \leqq r_1$ and arbitrary $\delta^{(n)}$ the inequality

$$|||u_n - v_n||| \leqq p_1||\boldsymbol{\Gamma}_n|| + q_1||\delta^{(n)}|| \tag{10.3}$$

holds.

Theorem 10.1. *A necessary and sufficient condition for the stability of the approximate Ritz-solution is that the corresponding coordinate system be strongly minimal in the appropriate energy space.*

Proof. Necessity: Let the approximate Ritz-solution be stable. Putting $\boldsymbol{\Gamma}_n = 0$, we obtain

$$|||v_n - u_n||| \leqq q_1 ||\delta^{(n)}||, \tag{10.4}$$

which holds for any vector $\delta^{(n)}$. We put $\delta^{(n)} = x_1^{(n)}$, where $x_1^{(n)}$ was defined in Theorem 9.1, and obtain, as in §9, $b^{(n)} = a^{(n)} + (1/\lambda_1^{(n)})x_1^{(n)}$.
Using this result, we obtain

$$v_n = u_n + \frac{1}{\lambda_1^{(n)}} \sum_{k=1}^{n} x_{1k}^{(n)} \phi_k ,$$

where $x_{1k}^{(n)} (k = 1, 2, \ldots, n)$ are the components of $x_1^{(n)}$. It follows from here that

$$|||v_n - u_n||| = \frac{1}{\lambda_1^{(n)}} |||\sum_{k=1}^{n} x_{1k}^{(n)} \phi_k||| = \frac{||\delta^{(n)}||}{\lambda_1^{(n)}} |||\sum_{k=1}^{n} x_{1k}^{(n)} \phi_k|||.$$

Further, since

$$|||\sum_{k=1}^{n} x_{1k}^{(n)} \phi_k|||^2 = [\sum_{k=1}^{n} x_{1k}^{(n)} \phi_k, \quad \sum_{j=1}^{n} x_{1j}^{(n)} \phi_j] = \sum_{j,k=1}^{n} [\phi_k, \phi_j] x_{1k}^{(n)} \overline{x_{1j}^{(n)}} =$$
$$= (R_n x_1^{(n)}, x_1^{(n)}) = (\lambda_1^{(n)} x_1^{(n)}, x_1^{(n)}) = \lambda_1^{(n)},$$

we obtain

$$|||v_n - u_n||| = \frac{||\delta^{(n)}||}{\sqrt{\lambda_1^{(n)}}} .$$

From inequality (10.4), we obtain $\lambda_1^{(n)} \geqq q_1^{-2}$, which proves that the coordinate system is strongly minimal in the appropriate energy space.

Sufficiency: (see Yaskova and Yakovlev [1]). Let the coordinate system be strongly minimal in the energy space.
Since we know that

$$v_n - u_n = \sum_{k=1}^{n} (b_k^{(n)} - a_k^{(n)}) \phi_k ,$$

it follows that

$$|||v_n - u_n|||^2 = [\sum_{k=1}^{n} (b_k^{(n)} - a_k^{(n)}) \phi_k , \quad \sum_{j=1}^{n} (b_j^{(n)} - a_j^{(n)}) \phi_j] =$$
$$= \sum_{j,k=1}^{n} [\phi_k , \phi_j] (b_k^{(n)} - a_k^{(n)}) (\bar{b}_j^{(n)} - \bar{a}_j^{(n)}) =$$
$$= (\boldsymbol{R}_n (b^{(n)} - a^{(n)}), b^{(n)} - a^{(n)}) \leqq ||\boldsymbol{R}_n b^{(n)} - \boldsymbol{R}_n a^{(n)}|| \; ||b^{(n)} - a^{(n)}||. \tag{10.5}$$

An estimate for the second term on the r.h.s. is given by (9.13). Therefore, we develop an estimate for the first term.
From equations (9.5) and (9.6), it follows that

$$\boldsymbol{R}_n a^{(n)} = f^{(n)}, \qquad \boldsymbol{R}_n b^{(n)} = f^{(n)} + \delta^{(n)} - \boldsymbol{\Gamma}_n b^{(n)},$$

which leads to the results

$$\boldsymbol{R}_n b^{(n)} - \boldsymbol{R}_n a^{(n)} = \delta^{(n)} - \boldsymbol{\Gamma}_n b^{(n)} = \delta^{(n)} + \boldsymbol{\Gamma}_n a^{(n)} - \boldsymbol{\Gamma}_n (b^{(n)} - a^{(n)}), \tag{10.6}$$

and hence,

$$(\boldsymbol{R}_n + \boldsymbol{\Gamma}_n)(b^{(n)} - a^{(n)}) = \boldsymbol{\Gamma}_n a^{(n)} + \delta^{(n)}.$$

The last equation can be rewritten in the form

$$(\boldsymbol{I}_n + \boldsymbol{\Gamma}_n \boldsymbol{R}_n^{-1}) \boldsymbol{R}_n (b^{(n)} - a^{(n)}) = \boldsymbol{\Gamma}_n a^{(n)} + \delta^{(n)},$$

from which it follows that

$$\boldsymbol{R}_n b^{(n)} - \boldsymbol{R}_n a^{(n)} = (\boldsymbol{I}_n + \boldsymbol{\Gamma}_n \boldsymbol{R}_n^{-1})^{-1} (\boldsymbol{\Gamma}_n a^{(n)} + \delta^{(n)}).$$

We assume that $||\boldsymbol{\Gamma}_n|| \leqq \beta \lambda_0$, $0 < \beta < 1$, which implies that

$$||\boldsymbol{\Gamma}_n \boldsymbol{R}_n^{-1}|| \leqq \beta, \qquad ||(\boldsymbol{I}_n + \boldsymbol{\Gamma}_n \boldsymbol{R}_n^{-1})^{-1}|| \leqq \frac{1}{1-\beta},$$

$$||\boldsymbol{R}_n (b^{(n)} - a^{(n)})|| \leqq \frac{1}{1-\beta} [||\boldsymbol{\Gamma}_n|| \; ||a^{(n)}|| + ||\delta^{(n)}||].$$

Using inequality (9.12), the last inequality becomes

$$||\boldsymbol{R}_n (b^{(n)} - a^{(n)})|| \leqq \frac{1}{1-\beta} [\lambda_0^{-\frac{1}{2}} |||u_0||| \; ||\boldsymbol{\Gamma}_n|| + ||\delta^{(n)}||].$$

Inequalities (9.5) and (9.7) yield

$$|||v_n - u_n|||^2 \leqq \frac{1}{1-\beta} [\lambda_0^{-\frac{1}{2}} |||u_0||| \; ||\boldsymbol{\Gamma}_n|| + ||\delta^{(n)}||](p||\boldsymbol{\Gamma}_n|| + q||\delta^{(n)}||),$$

and if we put

$$p_1 = \max\left(p, \frac{\lambda_0^{-\frac{1}{2}}}{1-\beta} |||u_0|||\right), \qquad q_1 = \max\left(q, \frac{1}{1-\beta}\right), \tag{10.7}$$

then we obtain

$$|||v_n - u_n||| \leqq p_1 ||\boldsymbol{\Gamma}_n|| + q_1 ||\delta^{(n)}||,$$

which is the required result.

A practical estimate for the error $|||v_n - u_n|||$ can be obtained from equations (10.5) and (10.6). Namely,

$$|||v_n - u_n|||^2 \leqq ||b^{(n)} - a^{(n)}||\,||\delta^{(n)} - \boldsymbol{\Gamma}_n b^{(n)}||$$

or

$$|||v_n - u_n||| \leqq \sqrt{||b^{(n)} - a^{(n)}||[||\delta^{(n)}|| + ||\boldsymbol{\Gamma}_n||\,||b^{(n)}||]} =$$
$$= \sqrt{||\eta^{(n)}||[||\delta^{(n)}|| + ||\boldsymbol{\Gamma}_n||\,||b^{(n)}||]}. \tag{10.8}$$

We shall apply this formula to the examples in §8.

In both problems in §8, four decimal places have been retained in forming the *non-exact* Ritz-systems from the *exact*. Therefore, $|\gamma_{jk}| < \frac{1}{2}10^{-4}$ and $|\delta_k| < \frac{1}{2}10^{-4}$. Restricting attention to the Ritz-systems of order 4, we obtain in both cases

$$||\boldsymbol{\Gamma}_4|| \leqq 2 \times 10^{-4},\ ||\delta^{(4)}|| \leqq 10^{-4}.$$

Using Tables 8.1 and 8.2, we evaluate $||b^{(4)}||$ and $||\eta^{(4)}|| = ||b^{(4)} - a^{(4)}||$ for the first example to give:

$$||b^{(4)}|| = 0.8854, \qquad ||\eta^{(4)}|| = 0.0514.$$

From (10.8), we obtain

$$|||v_4 - u_4||| \leqq [0.0514(10^{-4} + 2 \times 0.8854 \times 10^{-4})]^{\frac{1}{2}} = 3.77 \times 10^{-3}.$$

Using Table 8.5 we obtain for the second example

$$||b^{(4)}|| = 0.4576.$$

Tables 8.4 and 8.5, in which only four decimal places have been retained, yield $||\eta^{(4)}|| = 0$. Using more exact values for $a_k^{(n)}$ and $b_k^{(n)}$, we obtain $||\eta^{(4)}|| = 2.9 \times 10^{-5}$.

Hence,

$$|||v_4 - u_4||| \leqq [2.9 \times 10^{-5}(10^{-4} + 2 \times 0.4576 \times 10^{-4})]^{\frac{1}{2}} < 7.4 \times 10^{-5}.$$

If we ignore the value for $||\eta^{(4)}||$ and use the theoretical estimate, given by (9.13′) instead, we would obtain

$$|||v_4 - u_4||| \leqq [3 \times 10^{-4}(10^{-4} + 2 \times 0.4576 \times 10^{-4})]^{\frac{1}{2}} \approx 2.4 \times 10^{-4}.$$

We see that the use of the strongly minimal coordinate system in the second example gave an error which is significantly less than that in the first example, where the coordinate system was non-minimal.

The following property is worthy of note: in the second example, that is, in the case with a strongly minimal coordinate system, the estimates for the quantities $||b^{(n)}-a^{(n)}||$ and $|||v_n-u_n|||$ have one and the same order of smallness.

In the same way, the order of smallness for the error in the approximate Ritz-solution in the first example is higher than that for the coefficient-vector. (A phenomenon, analagous to that mentioned above, was discovered also by Mitkevic [1] in an interesting numerical experiment.) The reason for this phenomenon becomes clear on analysing equation (10.8). The order of smallness of the second factor on the r.h.s. of (10.8) is determined by the quantities $||\delta^{(n)}||$ and $||\boldsymbol{\Gamma}_n||$. If the coordinate system is strongly minimal in the energy space then the first factor on the r.h.s. has the same order of smallness as $||\boldsymbol{\Gamma}_n||$ and $||\delta^{(n)}||$ (equation (9.13)), and hence it is clear from equation (10.8) that $|||v_n-u_n|||$ and $||b^{(n)}-a^{(n)}||$ have one and the same order of smallness. If the coordinate system is not strongly minimal, then the order of smallness of $||\eta^{(n)}||$ is lower than that of $||\boldsymbol{\Gamma}_n||$ and $||\delta^{(n)}||$ and it is clear from (10.8) that the order of smallness of $|||v_n-u_n|||$ is higher than that of $||\eta^{(n)}||$.

Also, it is clear that, if the coordinate system is not strongly minimal, then the order of smallness of $|||v_n-u_n|||$ is less than that for $||\boldsymbol{\Gamma}_n||$ and $\delta^{(n)}$ and, in fact, less than $|||v_n-u_n|||$ for a strongly minimal coordinate system.

§11. The condition number of the Ritz-matrix

The concept of stability and the error estimates developed from it for the evaluation of Ritz-coefficients and approximate Ritz-solutions are based on the assumption that the Ritz-process is solved absolutely exactly so that errors arise only from the errors introduced during the construction of this system. However, it is well known that, in practice, the solutions of algebraic systems are intimately connected with rounding error which can have a highly significant effect. It is also known that the influence of rounding error is more noticeable the higher the condition number of the matrix of the system (see Faddeev and Faddeeva [1; §15], and Wilkinson [1]). Since the Ritz-matrix R_n is positive definite, its conditioning can be conveniently characterised by the so-called P-number

$$\rho(R_n) = \frac{\lambda_n^{(n)}}{\lambda_1^{(n)}}, \tag{11.1}$$

where $\lambda_1^{(n)}$ is the smallest and $\lambda_n^{(n)}$ is the largest eigenvalue of the matrix R_n. It is important to require that as n increases the number $\rho(R_n)$ remains bounded. Then it is likely that the effect of rounding error will also remain bounded. It is not difficult to develop conditions for the boundedness of the P-number for a Ritz-matrix. Since, for increasing n, the number $\lambda_1^{(n)}$ does not increase and $\lambda_n^{(n)}$ does not decrease, $\rho(R_n)$ does not decrease (see Note below). Hence, if $\lambda_1^{(n)} \to 0$ or $\lambda_n^{(n)} \to \infty$, then $\rho(R_n) \to \infty$. Therefore, a necessary and sufficient condition for the P-number of R_n to be bounded is that the eigenvalues of R_n be contained between two positive numbers which are independent of n. In other words, the P-number of a Ritz-matrix is bounded (independent of n), if and only if the generating coordinate system is almost orthonormal in the corresponding energy space: if $\lambda_0 \leqq \lambda_k^{(n)} \leqq \Lambda_0$, where λ_0 and Λ_0 are positive numbers independent of n, then

$$\rho(R_n) \leqq \frac{\Lambda_0}{\lambda_0}. \tag{11.2}$$

Note. We prove the above statement that $\lambda_1^{(n)}$ only decreases and $\lambda_n^{(n)}$ only increases for Ritz-matrices: the eigenvalues of the symmetric matrix R_{n+1} are given by

$$\lambda_1^{(n+1)} = \min_t \{ \sum_{j,k=1}^{n+1} [\phi_j, \phi_k] t_j \bar{t}_k / \sum_{k=1}^{n+1} |t_k|^2 \} \tag{*}$$

and

$$\lambda_{n+1}^{(n+1)} = \max_t \{ \sum_{j,k=1}^{n+1} [\phi_j, \phi_k] t_j \bar{t}_k / \sum_{k=1}^{n+1} |t_k|^2 \}; \tag{**}$$

where the maximum and minimum are evaluated over the set of all non-zero vectors $t = (t_1, t_2, \ldots, t_n, t_{n+1})$. It is clear that $\lambda_1^{(n)}$ can be obtained as the minimum of (*) and $\lambda_n^{(n)}$ as the maximum of (**) under the supplementary condition $t_{n+1} = 0$. Hence, it follows that $\lambda_1^{(n)} \geqq \lambda_1^{(n+1)}$ and $\lambda_n^{(n)} \leqq \lambda_{n+1}^{(n+1)}$.

For example, let the operator $\boldsymbol{B}$ be semi-similar to the operator $\boldsymbol{A}$ of a given problem, so that

$$K_1 |||u|||_{\boldsymbol{B}} \leqq |||u|||_{\boldsymbol{A}} \leqq K_2 |||u|||_{\boldsymbol{B}}, \tag{11.3}$$

where K_1 and K_2 are positive constants, and let the coordinate system be orthonormal in $\mathfrak{H}_B$. Since it follows from Theorems 4.2 and 4.3 that $\mu_0 = M_0 = 1$, $K = K_1^{-1}$ and

$$K_1^2 \leqq \lambda_k^{(n)} \leqq K_2^2,$$

we obtain

$$\rho(R_n) \leqq \frac{K_2^2}{K_1^2}. \tag{11.4}$$

Thus, for the second example in §8, it is clear from the inequality (8.7) that $K_1 = 1$, $K_2 = \sqrt{2}$ and, for all n,

$$\rho(R_n) \leqq 3.$$

§12. The solution of the Ritz-process by iteration

The question, examined in this section, is not directly connected with the idea of stability. However, as we shall see below, it is closely connected with the condition imposed on the coordinate system to ensure stability. The Ritz-process

$$\boldsymbol{R}_n a^{(n)} = f^{(n)} \tag{12.1}$$

is equivalent, for arbitrary $\alpha(\neq 0)$, to the system

$$a^{(n)} = (\boldsymbol{I}_n - \alpha \boldsymbol{R}_n) a^{(n)} + \alpha f^{(n)}, \tag{12.2}$$

where $\boldsymbol{I}_n$ is the unit matrix of order n.
If $\lambda_k^{(n)} (k = 1, 2, \ldots, n)$ are the eigenvalues of R_n, then $1-\alpha\lambda_k^{(n)}$ are the eigenvalues of $\boldsymbol{I}_n - \alpha\, \boldsymbol{R}_n$. We choose α so that

$$-1 < 1-\alpha\lambda_k^{(n)} < 1 \qquad (k = 1, 2, \ldots, n). \tag{12.3}$$

Then the iteration, defined by

$$[a^{(n)}]_{m+1} = (\boldsymbol{I}_n - \alpha \boldsymbol{R}_n)[a^{(n)}]_m + \alpha f^{(n)}, \tag{12.4}$$

converges to the solution of (12.1) for any arbitrary initial approximation $[a^{(n)}]_0$.
The number α must be positive, otherwise $1-\alpha\lambda_k^{(n)} > 1$ and the iteration diverges. If $\alpha > 0$, then $1-\alpha\lambda_k^{(n)}$ decreases for increasing k, and it is sufficient to require that

$$1-\alpha\lambda_1^{(n)} < 1, \qquad 1-\alpha\lambda_n^{(n)} > -1, \tag{12.5}$$

which implies that

$$0 < \alpha < \frac{2}{\lambda_n^{(n)}} . \tag{12.6}$$

The most suitable α is one for which both the numbers in (12.5) lie close together in the center of the interval $(-1, 1)$, that is, the value of α is such that

$$\max_{\alpha} \{|1-\alpha\lambda_1^{(n)}|, |1-\alpha\lambda_n^{(n)}|\} = \min. \tag{12.7}$$

For the sake of brevity, we write $\lambda_1^{(n)} = m$ and $\lambda_n^{(n)} = M$ so that $0 < m \leqq M < \infty$. In the plane of $(\alpha, y(\alpha))$ (see Figure 1), we examine the lines

$$y(\alpha) = |1-\alpha m|, \qquad y(\alpha) = |1-\alpha M|. \tag{12.8}$$

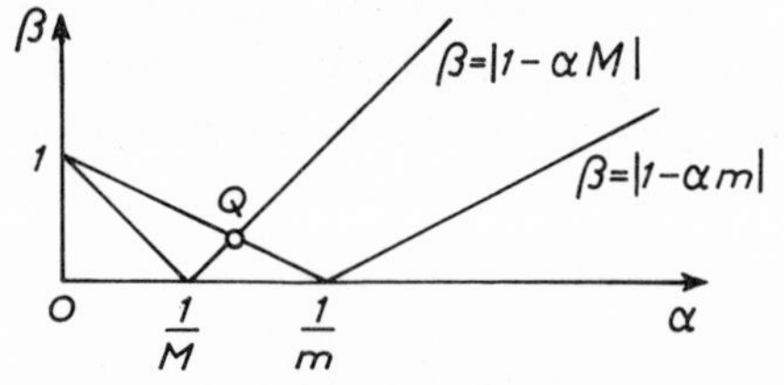

Figure 1.

Condition (12.7) implies that it is necessary to choose the value of α for which the difference between the ordinates of the lines (12.8) has a minimum. From Figure 1, it is clear that this value of α is the abscissa of the point Q, the point of intersection of the lines $y = 1-\alpha m$ and $y = \alpha M-1$. This result yields

$$\alpha = \frac{2}{m+M}, \quad \text{i.e.} \quad \alpha = \frac{2}{\lambda_1^{(n)}+\lambda_n^{(n)}} . \tag{12.9}$$

Hence, α lies in the interval (12.6). For this α, the absolute values of the numbers in (12.5) coincide and are equal to

$$\frac{\lambda_n^{(n)}-\lambda_1^{(n)}}{\lambda_n^{(n)}+\lambda_1^{(n)}} = \frac{\rho(R_n)-1}{\rho(R_n)+1} = r. \tag{12.10}$$

The iteration (12.4) converges no slower than the geometric progression $\{r^n\}$, $(n = 1, 2, \ldots)$.

Note. Equations (12.3) and (12.9) are particular cases of results obtained by Natanson [1] for operator equations of a more general type.

For increasing n, the quantity (12.10) increases. If the coordinate system is not almost orthonormal in the energy space, then this number tends to 1 as $n \to \infty$ and for large n the iteration converges slowly. If the coordinate system is almost orthonormal in the energy space, so that $\lambda_0 \leqq \lambda_k^{(n)} \leqq \Lambda_0$, then $\rho(R_n) \leqq (\Lambda_0/\lambda_0)$ (inequality (11.2)), and

$$\frac{\rho(R_n)-1}{\rho(R_n)+1} \leqq \frac{\Lambda_0-\lambda_0}{\Lambda_0+\lambda_0}.$$

We note that (12.9) requires a knowledge of the eigenvalues of the Ritz-matrix, and therefore, it is not convenient in practice. However, if the coordinate system is almost orthonormal in the energy space and the numbers λ_0 and Λ_0 are known, then it is possible to take

$$\alpha = \frac{2}{\lambda_0+\Lambda_0}. \tag{12.11}$$

In this way,

$$0 < 1-\alpha\lambda_1^{(n)} = \frac{\Lambda_0+\lambda_0-2\lambda_1^{(n)}}{\Lambda_0+\lambda_0} < \frac{\Lambda_0-\lambda_0}{\Lambda_0+\lambda_0},$$

$$0 > 1-\alpha\lambda_n^{(n)} = \frac{\Lambda_0+\lambda_0-2\lambda_n^{(n)}}{\Lambda_0+\lambda_0} > -\frac{\Lambda_0-\lambda_0}{\Lambda_0+\lambda_0}.$$

The spectrum of the matrix $I_n-\alpha R_n$ is contained in the interval

$$\left[-\frac{\Lambda_0-\lambda_0}{\Lambda_0+\lambda_0}, \frac{\Lambda_0-\lambda_0}{\Lambda_0+\lambda_0}\right]$$

and, for arbitrary n, the iteration converges no slower than the geometric progression

$$\left\{\left(\frac{\Lambda_0-\lambda_0}{\Lambda_0+\lambda_0}\right)^n\right\} \qquad (n = 1, 2, \ldots). \tag{12.12}$$

In particular, let the coordinate system be orthonormal in the energy space of an operator $\boldsymbol{B}$, which is semi-similar to a given operator $\boldsymbol{A}$ so that inequality (11.3) holds. Then, as we saw above, $\lambda_0 = K_1^2$ and $\Lambda_0 = K_2^2$.

Using (12.11), we obtain

$$\alpha = \frac{2}{K_1^2 + K_2^2}, \tag{12.13}$$

and the iteration converges like the geometric progression

$$\left\{ \left(\frac{K_2^2 - K_1^2}{K_2^2 + K_1^2} \right)^n \right\} \qquad (n = 1, 2, \ldots). \tag{12.14}$$

Thus, for system (8.9) and system (8.10), which is similar to (8.9), equation (12.13) yields (see §11)

$$\alpha = \frac{2}{1+3} = 0.5.$$

For this problem, (12.2) (obtained from (8.11)) becomes (we restrict attention to the truncated system of order four)

$$\begin{aligned} b_1 &= 0.2b_1 - 0.20656b_2 - 0.32660, \\ b_2 &= -0.20656b_1 + 0.2b_2 - 0.20284b_3, \\ b_3 &= -0.20284b_2 + 0.2b_3 - 0.20160b_4, \\ b_4 &= -0.20160b_3 + 0.2b_4. \end{aligned} \tag{12.15}$$

where the iteration converges like $\{(0.5)^n\}$, $(n = 1, 2, \ldots)$.
Below, we give the solution of (12.15) attained by iteration. The r.h.s.-values were taken as the initial approximation. The first four decimal places stabilised after the 12th iteration:

$$b_1 = -0.4397, \quad b_2 = 0.1219, \quad b_3 = -0.0330, \quad b_4 = 0.0083.$$

We see that the iteration process yields the same values as given in Table 8.5.
In conclusion, we make the following observation: it can happen that, although the system is almost orthonormal, one (or even both) of the numbers λ_0 and Λ_0 are unknown. Then it is not possible to use (12.11). However, if the number Λ_0 is known, the iteration can be used, since any value of α in the interval $0 < \alpha \leqq 2/\Lambda_0$ satisfies the inequality (12.6) and, hence, guarantees the convergence of the iteration process.

§13. Extension of the concept of stability

Note. See Mikhlin [21].

The definition of stability, introduced in §9, has a simple and natural extension.

Let some numerical process be defined by the sequence of equations

$$A_n x^{(n)} = y^{(n)} \qquad (n = 1, 2, \ldots), \tag{13.1}$$

where A_n is an operator which maps from a Banach space $\mathfrak{X}_n$ into another Banach space $\mathfrak{Y}_n$. We assume that the inverse A_n^{-1} is defined for all n and that $\mathfrak{D}(A_n^{-1})$, the domain of A_n^{-1}, equals $\mathfrak{Y}_n$.

Along with equations (13.1), we examine the sequence of equations

$$(A_n + \Gamma_n) z^{(n)} = y^{(n)} + \delta^{(n)} \qquad (n = 1, 2, \ldots). \tag{13.2}$$

We shall say that the given numerical process is *stable*, if there exist constants p, q and r, independent of n, such that, for $\|\Gamma_n\| \leqq r$ and arbitrary $\delta^{(n)}$, equations (13.2) are solvable and inequality

$$\|\eta^{(n)}\| \leqq p\|\Gamma_n\| + q\|\delta^{(n)}\| \tag{13.3}$$

holds with $\eta^{(n)} = z^{(n)} - x^{(n)}$.

Theorem 3.1. *A necessary and sufficient condition for the stability of the numerical process* (13.1) *is that there exist constants* C_1 *and* C_2, *independent of n, such that*

(1) $\|A_n^{-1}\| \leqq C_1$,

(2) *The inequality* $\|A_n^{-1} B_n A_n^{-1} y^{(n)}\| = \|A_n^{-1} B_n x^{(n)}\| \leqq C_2$ *holds for any sequence of operators* $\{B_n\}$ *with unit norm which map from* $\mathfrak{X}_n$ *into* $\mathfrak{Y}_n$.

Proof. Necessity: (1). Let $_n = \Gamma 0$. From inequality (13.3), it follows that $\|\eta^{(n)}\| \leqq \|\delta^{(n)}\|$. However, in the given case, $A_n \eta^{(n)} = A_n z^{(n)} - A_n x^{(n)} = \delta^{(n)}$, and hence, $\|A_n \eta^{(n)}\| \geqq (1/q)\|\eta^{(n)}\|$. The last inequality shows that $\|A_n^{-1}\| \leqq q$. Therefore, we put $C_1 = q$.

(2). Let $\delta^{(n)} = 0$ and $\Gamma_n = \varepsilon B_n$, where $\|B_n\| = 1$ and $\varepsilon = \|\Gamma_n\| \leqq r$. In this case,

$$(A_n + \Gamma_n) z^{(n)} = y^{(n)};$$

from which it follows that

$$z^{(n)} + A_n^{-1} \Gamma_n z^{(n)} = x^{(n)},$$

and

$$z^{(n)}-x^{(n)}+\boldsymbol{A}_n^{-1}\boldsymbol{\Gamma}_n(z^{(n)}-x^{(n)}) = -\boldsymbol{A}_n^{-1}\boldsymbol{\Gamma}_n x^{(n)}. \tag{13.4}$$

Further,

$$||\boldsymbol{A}_n^{-1}\boldsymbol{\Gamma}_n x^{(n)}|| = \varepsilon||\boldsymbol{A}_n^{-1}\boldsymbol{B}_n x^{(n)}|| = ||\boldsymbol{\Gamma}_n||\,||\boldsymbol{A}_n^{-1}\boldsymbol{B}_n x^{(n)}||$$

and

$$||\boldsymbol{A}_n^{-1}\boldsymbol{\Gamma}_n(z^{(n)}-x^{(n)})|| =$$
$$= \varepsilon||\boldsymbol{A}_n^{-1}\boldsymbol{B}_n(z^{(n)}-x^{(n)})|| \leqq \varepsilon||\boldsymbol{A}_n^{-1}||\,||z^{(n)}-x^{(n)}|| \leqq \varepsilon q||z^{(n)}-x^{(n)}||.$$

Using (13.4), one arrives at

$$||\eta^{(n)}|| = ||z^{(n)}-x^{(n)}|| \geqq \frac{||\boldsymbol{\Gamma}_n||\,||\boldsymbol{A}_n^{-1}\boldsymbol{B}_n x^{(n)}||}{1+\varepsilon q}.$$

Comparing this result with inequality (13.3), which has the form $||\eta^{(n)}|| \leqq p||\boldsymbol{\Gamma}_n||$, we find

$$||\boldsymbol{A}_n^{-1}\boldsymbol{B}_n x^{(n)}\,|| \leqq p(1+\varepsilon q).$$

Since ε is arbitrary small,

$$||\boldsymbol{A}_n^{-1}\boldsymbol{B}_n x^{(n)}|| \leqq p,$$

and we can write $C_2 = p$.

Sufficiency: We assume that the conditions of Theorem 13.1 are fulfilled. We put $r = \beta/C_1$, where β is a constant such that $0 < \beta < 1$, and assume that $||\boldsymbol{\Gamma}_n|| \leqq r$.

We examine the equations

$$(\boldsymbol{A}_n+\boldsymbol{\Gamma}_n)z_1^{(n)} = y^{(n)}, \qquad (\boldsymbol{A}_n+\boldsymbol{\Gamma}_n)z_2^{(n)} = \delta^{(n)}. \tag{13.5}$$

It follows that
$z^{(n)} = z_1^{(n)}+z_2^{(n)}$ and $\eta^{(n)} = (z_1^{(n)}-x^{(n)})+z_2^{(n)}$. If $\Gamma_n = 0$, then $z_1^{(n)} = x^{(n)}$ and $z_2^{(n)} = \eta^{(n)} = \boldsymbol{A}_n^{-1}\delta^{(n)}$, and

$$||\eta^{(n)}|| \leqq ||\boldsymbol{A}_n^{-1}||\,||\delta^{(n)}|| \leqq C_1||\delta^{(n)}||,$$

which proves the theorem. If $\Gamma_n \neq 0$, we put $\boldsymbol{\Gamma}_n = ||\boldsymbol{\Gamma}_n||\boldsymbol{B}_n$, where $||\boldsymbol{B}_n|| = 1$. It is quite simple to estimate $||z_2^{(n)}||$:

$$z_2^{(n)} = (\boldsymbol{I}_n+\boldsymbol{A}_n^{-1}\boldsymbol{\Gamma}_n)^{-1}\boldsymbol{A}_n^{-1}\delta^{(n)},$$

where I_n is the identity operator in the space $\mathfrak{X}_n$. Hence,

$$\|z_2^{(n)}\| \leqq C_1 \|(I_n + A_n^{-1}\Gamma_n)^{-1}\| \, \|\delta^{(n)}\|.$$

It is not difficult to show that (see §9)

$$\|(I_n + A_n^{-1}\Gamma_n)^{-1}\| \leqq \frac{1}{1-\beta},$$

which leads to the result

$$\|z_2^{(n)}\| \leqq \frac{C_1}{1-\beta} \|\delta^{(n)}\|. \tag{13.6}$$

If we rewrite (13.5) in the form

$$(I_n + A_n^{-1}\Gamma_n) z_1^n = x^{(n)},$$

we obtain

$$(I_n + A_n^{-1}\Gamma_n)(z_1^{(n)} - x^{(n)}) = -A_n^{-1}\Gamma_n x^{(n)}.$$

Whence, it follows that

$$z_1^{(n)} - x^{(n)} = -(I_n + A_n^{-1}\Gamma_n)^{-1} A_n^{-1}\Gamma_n x^{(n)}$$

and

$$\|z_1^{(n)} - x^{(n)}\| \leqq \frac{\|A_n^{-1}\Gamma_n x^{(n)}\|}{1-\beta} = \frac{\|A_n^{-1}B_n x^{(n)}\|}{1-\beta} \|\Gamma_n\| \leqq \frac{C_2}{1-\beta} \|\Gamma_n\|. \tag{13.7}$$

The combination of (13.6) and (13.7) yields inequality (13.3) with

$$p = \frac{C_2}{1-\beta}, \qquad q = \frac{C_1}{1-\beta}.$$

Note 1. Assume that condition (1) of Theorem 13.1: $\|A_n^{-1}\| \leqq C_1$, is fulfilled. If $\|x^{(n)}\| \leqq C_3 = \text{const.}$, then condition (2) of this theorem is also satisfied:

$$\|A_n^{-1}B_n x^{(n)}\| \leqq \|A_n^{-1}\| \, \|x^{(n)}\| \leqq C_1 C_2.$$

In this way, a sufficient condition for the stability of the process (13.1) is that $\|A_n^{-1}\|$ and $\|A_n^{-1}y^{(n)}\| = \|x^{(n)}\|$ be bounded for all n.

Note 2. If the norms $||A_n^{-1}||$ are positive-bounded-below (bounded below by a positive number), then it follows from condition (2), Theorem 13.1, that the $||x^{(n)}||$ are bounded for all n. For the proof, we assume the opposite: $||x^{(n_k)}|| \to \infty$. We choose $t^{(n_k)}$ so that $||t^{(n_k)}|| = 1$ and $||A_{n_k}^{-1}t^{(n_k)}|| \geqq \frac{1}{2}||A_{n_k}^{-1}||$ and construct the linear functional $f_{n_k}(x)$ so that $f_{n_k}(x^{(n_k)}) = ||x^{(n_k)}||$ and $||f_{n_k}|| = 1$. If we put $B_{n_k}x = f_{n_k}(x)t^{(n_k)}$, then

$$||B_{n_k}x|| = |f_{n_k}(x)| \leqq ||x||;$$

where the equality sign occurs when $x = x^{(n_k)}$. Hence, $||B_{n_k}|| = 1$,

$$A_{n_k}^{-1}B_{n_k}x^{(n_k)} = ||x^{(n_k)}||A_{n_k}^{-1}t^{(n^k)},$$

and

$$||A_{n_k}^{-1}B_{n_k}x^{(n_k)}|| > \tfrac{1}{2}||A_{n_k}^{-1}||\,||x^{(n_k)}|| \to \infty,$$

which contradicts condition (2).

The results of Notes 1 and 2 lead to

Theorem 13.2. *If the norms* $||A_n^{-1}||$ *are positive-bounded-below for all* n, *then a necessary and sufficient condition for the stability of the numerical process* (13.1) *is that* $||A_n^{-1}||$ *and* $||x^{(n)}|| = ||A_n^{-1}y^{(n)}||$ *be bounded above for all* n.

For the Ritz-process, $A_n = R_n$ and the norms $||R_n^{-1}||$ are positive-bounded below: In this case, $||R_n^{-1}|| = [\lambda_1^{(n)}]^{-1}$. Since, for increasing n, the eigenvalues $\lambda_1^{(n)}$ do not increase,

$$[\lambda_1^{(n)}]^{-1} \geqq [\lambda_1^{(1)}]^{-1} = |||\phi_1|||^{-2}.$$

Therefore, Theorem 13.2 can be applied to the Ritz-process.

If the norms $||R_n^{-1}||$ are bounded, then the generating coordinate system is strongly minimal in $\mathfrak{H}_A$. It follows as a corollary that the norms $||x^{(n)}|| = ||a^{(n)}||$ (see equation (9.12)) are bounded. Hence, Theorem 9.1 can be proved as a corollary of Theorem 13.2.

Note 3. Now let $\mathfrak{X}_n$ be a subspace of a Banach space $\mathfrak{X}$.

We say that *the numerical process* (13.1) *is convergent*, if there exists a limit $x_0 = \lim_{n\to\infty} x^{(n)}$. In this way, the $||x^{(n)}||$ are bounded for all n and Theorem 13.1 implies

Theorem 13.3. *If the process* (13.1) *is convergent, then a necessary and sufficient condition for its stability is that the norms* $||A_n^{-1}||$ *be bounded for all* n.

Theorem 13.3 yields a new form for the stability of the approximate Ritz-solution. Here $\mathfrak{X} = \mathfrak{H}_A$, $\mathfrak{X}_n$ is the subspace of $\mathfrak{H}_A$ spanned by $\phi_1, \phi_2, \ldots, \phi_n$ and $\mathfrak{Y}_n$ is the n-dimensional unitary space.

Let S_n denote the operator which brings every element u_n, $\in \mathfrak{X}_n$, into correspondence with the vector $a^{(n)}$ of its coefficients: If

$$u_n = \sum_{k=1}^{n} a_l^{(n)} \phi_k$$

and $a^{(n)} = (a_1^{(n)}, \ldots, a_n^{(n)})$, then $S_n u_n = a^{(n)}$. If u_n is constructed using the Ritz-process, then $a^{(n)}$ is defined in terms of $f^{(n)}$ by (9.5), viz.,

$$R_n a^{(n)} = f^{(n)}.$$

It follows that

$$R_n S_n u_n = f^{(n)}, \tag{13.8}$$

which implies that

$$A_n = R_n S_n. \tag{13.9}$$

Further,

$$A_n^{-1} f^{(n)} = u_n = \sum_{k=1}^{n} a_k^{(n)} \phi_k. \tag{13.10}$$

We now use

$$|||u_n|||_A^2 = (R_n a^{(n)}, a^{(n)}),$$

which coincides with (10.5). Substitution of $a^{(n)} = R_n^{-1} f^{(n)}$ into this formula yields

$$|||A_n^{-1} f^{(n)}|||_A^2 = |||u_n|||_A^2 = (f^{(n)}, R_n^{-1} f^{(n)}). \tag{13.11}$$

From (13.8), it follows that $u_n = S_n^{-1} R_n^{-1} f^{(n)}$ and

$$|||u_n|||_A^2 = [S_n^{-1} R_n^{-1} f^{(n)}, S_n^{-1} R_n^{-1} f^{(n)}]_A =$$
$$= ((S_n^{-1})^* S_n^{-1} R_n^{-1} f^{(n)}, R_n^{-1} f^{(n)})_{\mathfrak{E}_n}.$$

Since $R_n^{-1} f^{(n)}$ is an arbitrary vector, a comparison with (13.11) leads to

$$R_n = (S_n^{-1})^* S_n^{-1}. \tag{13.12}$$

Finally, we obtain

$$A_n = (S_n^{-1})^* \tag{13.13}$$

and

$$||A_n^{-1}|| = ||S_n^*|| = ||S_n|| = \sqrt{||R_n^{-1}||} = \frac{1}{\sqrt{\lambda_1^{(n)}}}. \tag{13.14}$$

Since the approximate solution u_n converges to the exact solution u_0 w.r.t. the $\mathfrak{H}_A$-metric, the process of constructing the approximate solution is convergent. However, by Theorem 13.3: A necessary and sufficient condition for stability is that the norms $||A_n^{-1}||$ be bounded for all n. In turn, it follows from (13.14) that: A necessary and sufficient condition for stability is that the coordinate system be strongly minimal in $\mathfrak{H}_A$. Thus, we have proved: If the coordinate system is strongly minimal in $\mathfrak{H}_A$, then the approximate Ritz-solution is stable in the following sense: there exist three positive constants p', q' and r' such that if the operator A_n (formula (13.9)) is determined with small error $\tilde{\Gamma}_n$, $||\tilde{\Gamma}_n|| \leqq r'$ and the vector $f^{(n)}$ with error $\delta^{(n)}$, then the energy norm of the error in the approximate solution u_n does not exceed the quantity $p'||\tilde{\Gamma}_n||+q'||\delta^{(n)}||$. We shall now prove that the assertion of Theorem 10.1 holds. If R_n is determined with small error Γ_n, let $A_n = (S_n^{-1})^*$ be determined with error $\tilde{\Gamma}_n$. We note that the operator S_n^{-1} is determined without error since

$$S_n^{-1}a^{(n)} = u_n = \sum_{k=1}^{n} a_k^{(n)}\phi_k$$

and the coordinate elements are assumed to be known exactly. We neglect the error generated by the arithmetic operations in the last formula. On the strength of (13.12), we have

$$R_n+\Gamma_n = [(S_n^{-1})^*+\tilde{\Gamma}_n]S_n^{-1}, \qquad \tilde{\Gamma}_n = \Gamma_n S_n,$$

whence, we obtain

$$||\tilde{\Gamma}_n|| \leqq ||\Gamma_n||\,||S_n|| = \frac{1}{\sqrt{\lambda_1^{(n)}}}||\Gamma_n|| < \lambda_0^{-\frac{1}{2}}||\Gamma_n||, \tag{13.15}$$

where $\lambda_0 = \inf \lambda_1^{(n)}$. If the coordinate system is strongly minimal in $\mathfrak{H}_A$, we have $|||v_n-u_n||| \leqq p'||\tilde{\Gamma}_n||+q'||\delta^{(n)}||$. The use of inequality (13.15) now yields the required result

$$|||v_n-u_n||| \leqq p_1||\Gamma_n||+q_1||\delta^{(n)}||, \quad p_1 = p'\lambda_0^{-\frac{1}{2}}, \quad q_1 = q'.$$

§14. The stability of the Bubnov-Galerkin-process for stationary problems

We recall the general character of the Bubnov-Galerkin-process (see VM, §§73, 78 and 82): In the equation

$$Au - f = 0 \tag{14.1}$$

let the operator A have the form

$$A = A_0 + K, \tag{14.2}$$

where A_0 is positive definite in the given separable Hilbert space $\mathfrak{H}$, $\mathfrak{D}(K) \supset \mathfrak{D}(A_0)$ and the product $T = A_0^{-1}K$ can be extended to a completely continuous operator in the energy space $\mathfrak{H}_0 = \mathfrak{H}_{A_0}$. Equation (14.1) is equivalent to the equation

$$u + Tu - A_0^{-1}f = 0. \tag{14.3}$$

Clearly, every solution of (14.1) is a solution of (14.3) and every solution of (14.3), which lies in $\mathfrak{D}(A_0)$, is a solution of (14.1). If (14.3) has a solution (of necessity, it lies in $\mathfrak{H}_0$) which does not lie in $\mathfrak{D}(A_0)$, then we regard it as a generalised solution of (14.1).

For the Bubnov-Galerkin method, we choose a coordinate system

$$\{\phi_n\} = \phi_1, \phi_2, \ldots, \phi_n, \ldots, \tag{14.4}$$

which satisfies conditions analagous to those of §6:

1) $\{\phi_n\} \in \mathfrak{H}_0$;
2) for arbitrary n, the elements $\phi_1, \phi_2, \ldots, \phi_n$ are linearly independent;
3) $\{\phi_n\}$ is complete in $\mathfrak{H}_0$.

An approximate solution of (14.1) or, equivalently, (14.3) is sought in the form

$$u_n = \sum_{k=1}^{n} a_k^{(n)} \phi_k. \tag{14.5}$$

where the coefficients $a_k^{(n)}$ are defined by the condition that, after the substitution of u_n for u, the left-hand side of (14.3) is orthogonal to $\phi_1, \phi_2, \ldots, \phi_n$ w.r.t. the metric of $\mathfrak{H}_0$. Hence, a Bubnov-Galerkin-system takes the form

$$\sum_{k=1}^{n} \{[\phi_k, \phi_j] + [T\phi_k, \phi_j]\} a_k^{(n)} = [A_0^{-1}f, \phi_j] \qquad (j = 1, 2, \ldots, n)$$

or, equivalently,

$$\sum_{k=1}^{n} \{[\phi_k, \phi_j]+[T\phi_k, \phi_j]\}a_k^{(n)} = (f, \phi_j) \qquad (j = 1, 2, \ldots, n), \tag{14.6}$$

where the square brackets denote the energy inner product in $\mathfrak{H}_0$. If $\mathfrak{D}(K) \supset \mathfrak{H}_0$ then $[T\phi_{k'}, \phi_j] = [A_0^{-1}K\phi_{k'}, \phi_j] = (K\phi_{k'}, \phi_j)$, and system (14.6) becomes

$$\sum_{k=1}^{n} \{[\phi_k, \phi_j]+(K\phi_k, \phi_j)\}a_k^{(n)} = (f, \phi_j) \qquad (j = 1, 2, \ldots, n). \tag{14.6'}$$

This representation has an important advantage in that the explicit form of A_0^{-1} is not required. Finally, if $\{\phi_n\} \in \mathfrak{D}(A_0)$, then $[\phi_k, \phi_j] = (A_0\phi_k, \phi_j)$, and we obtain the usual form for the Bubnov-Galerkin-system (14.6)

$$\sum_{k=1}^{n} \{(A_0\phi_k, \phi_j)+(K\phi_k, \phi_j)\}a_k^{(n)} = (f, \phi_k) \qquad (j = 1, 2, \ldots, n). \tag{14.6''}$$

System (14.6″) is obtained independently if, after the substitution of u_n for u, the left-hand side of (4.1) is required to be orthogonal to $\phi_1, \phi_2, \ldots, \phi_n$ w.r.t. the metric in $\mathfrak{H}_0$. It is also known (VM, §78) that, if (14.1) has only one solution, then the approximate solution (14.5) converges to the exact solution w.r.t. the metric in $\mathfrak{H}_0$.

Theorem 14.1 *If the coordinate system* (14.4) *is strongly minimal in* $\mathfrak{H}_0$ *and equation* (14.1) *has only one solution, then the Bubnov-Galerkin-process, based on* (14.6), *is stable.*

Note. In the paper by Yaskova and Yakovlev [1], a discussion of a more general numerical process, the so-called Petrov-Galerkin-process, is given.

Proof. Let R_n and B_n denote the n-th order matrices with elements $[\phi_k, \phi_j]$ and $[T\phi_k, \phi_j]$ $(j, k = 1, 2, \ldots, n)$, respectively, $a^{(n)}$ the vector $[a_1^{(n)}, \ldots, a_n^{(n)}]$ and $f^{(n)}$ the vector $[(f, \phi_1), (f, \phi_2), \ldots, (f, \phi_n)]$. System (14.6) can be rewritten in vector form:

$$(R_n+B_n)a^{(n)} = f^{(n)}. \tag{14.7}$$

According to Note 1, §13, it is sufficient for stability to prove that the quantities $||(R_n+B_n)^{-1}||$ and $||a^{(n)}||$ are bounded for all n. We start by proving the boundedness of $||a^{(n)}||$. As in §9, we find that $||a^{(n)}|| \leq \lambda_0^{-\frac{1}{2}}|||u_n|||$, where $\lambda_0 = \inf \lambda_1^{(n)}$ (the smallest eigenvalue of R_n) – the choice of a strongly minimal coordinate system in $\mathfrak{H}_0$ ensures that $\lambda_0 > 0$. Further, if u_0 is the solution of (14.1), then $|||u_n - u_0||| \to 0$. Hence, $|||u_n||| \to |||u_0|||$. It follows that there exists a constant C_0 such that $|||u_n||| \leqq C_0$. This yields $||a^{(n)}|| \leqq \lambda_0^{-\frac{1}{2}} C_0 = \text{const.}$, which is the required result.

We develop a proof for the boundedness of $||(\boldsymbol{R}_n + \boldsymbol{B}_n)^{-1}||$. Initially, we examine the case when the coordinate system is orthonormal in $\mathfrak{H}_0$. We adopt the following notation: the orthonormal system is $\{\omega_n\}$, where

$$[\omega_k, \omega_j] = \delta_{kj} \quad \text{and} \quad R_n = I_n;$$

the matrix B_n is replaced by the matrix Δ_n with elements $[T\omega_k, \omega_j]$ $(k, j = 1, 2, \ldots, n)$; and $g^{(n)} = [(f, \omega_1), (f, \omega_2), \ldots, (f, \omega_n)]$. Using this notation, equation (14.7) takes the form

$$(\boldsymbol{I}_n + \boldsymbol{\Delta}_n) a^{(n)} = g^{(n)}. \tag{14.7'}$$

Equation (14.3) is identically equivalent to the infinite system (see Mikhlin [4; §52])

$$a_j + \sum_{k=1}^{\infty} [\boldsymbol{T}\omega_k, \omega_j] a_k = (f, \omega_j) \qquad (j = 1, 2, \ldots). \tag{14.8}$$

If Δ denotes the infinite matrix with elements $[T\omega_k, \omega_j]$, $a = [a_1, a_2, \ldots]$ and $g = [(f, \omega_1), (f, \omega_2), \ldots]$, then (14.8) can be rewritten as

$$(\boldsymbol{I} + \boldsymbol{\Delta}) a = g, \tag{14.8'}$$

where $\boldsymbol{I}$ is the infinite unit matrix.

We note that a and g are elements of the l_2-space since $a_j = [u_0, \omega_j]$ are the Fourier coefficients of the solution u_0 w.r.t. the orthonormal (in $\mathfrak{H}_0$) system (14.4) and $g_j = (f, \omega_j) = [\boldsymbol{A}_0^{-1} f, \omega_j]$ the Fourier coefficients of $\boldsymbol{A}_0^{-1} f$ w.r.t. the same system.

The matrix Δ defines a completely continuous opertator in l_2. Being equivalent to (14.3), the infinite system (14.8′) has a unique solution in l_2. In the same way, system (14.7′) also has a unique solution for sufficiently large n. This implies the existence of the matrix $(I + \Delta)^{-1}$ and, for sufficiently large n, the matrices $(I_n + \Delta_n)^{-1}$.

It is also known that the matrix $G = (I + \Delta)^{-1} - I$ defines a completely continuous operator in l_2. We let $G_n = (I_n + \Delta_n)^{-1} - I_n$, while $\widetilde{G}_n$ denotes the infinite matrix with zeros everywhere except for its n-th order truncation which coincides with G_n. Then (see, Kantorovich and Akilov

[1; Chapter X, §1])

$$||\tilde{G}_n - G|| \underset{n\to\infty}{\longrightarrow} 0. \tag{14.9}$$

We prove that

$$||\tilde{G}_n||_{l_2} = ||G_n||_{\mathfrak{E}_n}; \tag{14.10}$$

where the l.h.s. denotes the norm of the operator in l_2 and r.h.s. the norm in the unitary space $\mathfrak{E}_n$. We have,

$$||\tilde{G}_n|| = \sup_{\tilde{x}\in l_2} \frac{||\tilde{G}_n \tilde{x}||}{||\tilde{x}||}. \tag{14.11}$$

Let g_{jk} denote the elements of the matrix G_n. If

$$\tilde{x} = (x_1, x_2, \ldots, x_n, x_{n+1}, \ldots),$$

then the j-th component of the vector $\tilde{G}_n \tilde{x}$ is defined by the formula

$$[\tilde{G}_n \tilde{x}]_j = \begin{cases} \sum_{k=1}^{n} g_{jk} x_k, & j \leqq n, \\ 0, & j > n. \end{cases}$$

Whence, it is clear that

$$[\tilde{G}_n \tilde{x}]_{l_2} = ||\tilde{G}_n \tilde{x}^{(n)}||_{l_2} = ||G_n x^{(n)}||_{\mathfrak{E}_n}, \tag{14.12}$$

where $x^{(n)} \in \mathfrak{E}_n$ is the vector $[x_1, x_2, \ldots, x_n]$, and

$$\tilde{x}^{(n)} = (x_1, x_2, \ldots, x_n, 0, 0, \ldots). \tag{14.13}$$

Further, it is clear that

$$\frac{||\tilde{G}_n \tilde{x}||_{l_2}}{||\tilde{x}||_{l_2}} \leqq \frac{||\tilde{G}_n \tilde{x}^{(n)}||_{l_2}}{||\tilde{x}^{(n)}||_{l_2}} = \frac{||G_n x^{(n)}||_{\mathfrak{E}_n}}{||x^{(n)}||_{\mathfrak{E}_n}}.$$

If $\tilde{\mathfrak{E}}_n \subset l_2$, denotes the set of vectors of the form (14.13), then it follows from the last inequality that

$$\sup_{\tilde{x}\in l_2} \frac{||\tilde{G}_n \tilde{x}||_{l_2}}{||\tilde{x}||_{l_2}} \leqq \sup_{\tilde{x}^{(n)}\in \tilde{\mathfrak{E}}_n} \frac{||\tilde{G}_n \tilde{x}^{(n)}||_{l_2}}{||\tilde{x}^{(n)}||_{l_2}} = \sup_{x^{(n)}\in \mathfrak{E}_n} \frac{||G_n x^{(n)}||_{\mathfrak{E}^n}}{||x^{(n)}||_{\mathfrak{E}_n}}.$$

Since l_2 is larger than $\tilde{\mathfrak{E}}_n$, the first term in the last expression cannot be smaller than the second and we obtain

$$\sup_{x\in l_2} \frac{||\tilde{G}_n\tilde{x}||_{l_2}}{||\tilde{x}||_{l_2}} = \sup_{x^{(n)}\in\mathfrak{E}_n} \frac{||G_n x^{(n)}||_{\mathfrak{E}^n}}{||x^{(n)}||_{\mathfrak{E}_n}},$$

which coincides with (14.10).

From (14.9), it follows that $||\tilde{G}_n||_{l_2} \to ||G||_{l_2}$, or, on the strength of (14.10), $||G_n||_{\mathfrak{E}_n} \to ||G||_{l_2}$. Hence, $||G_n||_{\mathfrak{E}_n}$ and $||(I_n+\Delta_n)^{-1}|| = ||G_n+I_n|| \leqq ||G_n||+1$ are bounded for all n.

We now turn to the general case. Let the coordinate system (14.4) be only strongly minimal in $\mathfrak{H}_0$. We orthonormalise (14.4) w.r.t. the metric in $\mathfrak{H}_0$ to yield the orthonormal system

$$\omega_1, \omega_2, \ldots, \omega_n, \ldots, \quad [\omega_j, \omega_k] = \delta_{jk}.$$

Since ϕ_k is a linear combination of $\omega_1, \omega_2, \ldots, \omega_k$, we have

$$\phi_k = \sum_{s=1}^{k} [\phi_k, \omega_s]\omega_s.$$

Let C_n denote the lower triangular matrix with elements $[\phi_k, \omega_s]$ $(k = 1, 2, \ldots, n, s = 1, 2, \ldots, k)$. It is not difficult to see that

$$R_n = C_n C_n^*, \qquad B_n = C_n \Delta_n C_n^*, \tag{14.14}$$

where C_n^* denotes the conjugate of C_n and Δ_n is defined above. Hence, we have

$$R_n+B_n = C_n(I_n+\Delta_n)C_n^*$$

and

$$(R_n+B_n)^{-1} = (C_n^*)^{-1}(I_n+\Delta_n)^{-1}C_n^{-1}. \tag{14.15}$$

From the first expression in (14.14), it follows that

$$||C_n^{-1}|| = ||(C_n^*)^{-1}|| = \sqrt{||R_n^{-1}||} = \frac{1}{\sqrt{\lambda_1^{(n)}}} \leqq \frac{1}{\sqrt{\lambda_0}},$$

while the expression (14.15) yields

$$||(R_n+B_n)^{-1}|| \leqq \frac{1}{\lambda_0} ||(I_n+\Delta_n)^{-1}||,$$

which is bounded on the strength of the results obtained above.

Just as for the approximate Ritz-solution in §10, we can introduce the concept of stability for the approximate Bubnov-Galerkin-solution. We do not give a definition since it is obvious from the earlier definition in §10.

Theorem 14.2. *A necessary and sufficient condition for the stability of the approximate Bubnov-Galerkin-solution is that the coordinate system be strongly minimal in* $\mathfrak{H}_0$.

Note. The sufficiency condition was proved by Yaskova and Yakovlev [1] and the necessity by Vaynikko [1].

Proof. If Γ_n denotes the error matrix, $\delta^{(n)}$ the error for the r.h.s.-terms and $b^{(n)}$ the vector with the *non-exact* values of the Bubnov-Galerkin-coefficients as components, then

$$(\boldsymbol{R}_n+\boldsymbol{B}_n+\boldsymbol{\Gamma}_n)b^{(n)} = f^{(n)}+\delta^{(n)}. \tag{14.16}$$

Let v_n be the *non-exact* approximate Bubnov-Galerkin-solution:

$$v_n = \sum_{k=1}^{n} b_k \phi_k .$$

Then (see, §10)

$$|||v_n-u_n|||^2 = (R_n(b^{(n)}-a^{(n)}),\, b^{(n)}-a^{(n)}). \tag{14.17}$$

We introduce the notation

$$\boldsymbol{C}_n^* a^{(n)} = \alpha^{(n)}, \qquad \boldsymbol{C}_n^* b^{(n)} = \beta^{(n)}. \tag{14.18}$$

As we saw above (see (14.4)), $\boldsymbol{R}_n = \boldsymbol{C}_n \boldsymbol{C}_n^*$. Hence, (14.17) gives

$$|||v_n-u_n||| = ||\beta^{(n)}-\alpha^{(n)}||. \tag{14.19}$$

On the strength of (14.14), equations (14.7) and (14.16) yield

$$\boldsymbol{C}_n(\boldsymbol{I}_n+\boldsymbol{\Delta}_n)\alpha^{(n)} = f^{(n)},$$
$$[\boldsymbol{C}_n(\boldsymbol{I}_n+\boldsymbol{\Delta}_n)+\boldsymbol{\Gamma}_n(\boldsymbol{C}_n^*)^{-1}]\beta^{(n)} = f^{(n)}+\delta^{(n)},$$

whence, we easily deduce that

$$\begin{aligned}\beta^{(n)}-\alpha^{(n)}+(\boldsymbol{I}_n+\boldsymbol{\Delta}_n)^{-1}\boldsymbol{C}_n^{-1}\boldsymbol{\Gamma}_n(\boldsymbol{C}_n^*)^{-1}(\beta^{(n)}-\alpha^{(n)}) &= \\ = (\boldsymbol{I}_n+\boldsymbol{\Delta}_n)^{-1}\boldsymbol{C}_n^{-1}\boldsymbol{\Gamma}_n a^{(n)}+(\boldsymbol{I}_n+\boldsymbol{\Delta}_n)^{-1}\boldsymbol{C}_n^{-1}\delta^{(n)}.\end{aligned} \tag{14.20}$$

If the coordinate system is strongly minimal in $\mathfrak{H}_0$, then $||(\boldsymbol{I}_n+\boldsymbol{\Delta}_n)^{-1}||$

and $||a^{(n)}||$ are bounded for all n: $||(\boldsymbol{I}_n+\boldsymbol{\Delta}_n)^{-1}|| \leqq c = \text{const.}$ and $||a^{(n)}|| \leqq c' = \text{const.}$ Further, $||\boldsymbol{C}_n^{-1}|| = ||(\boldsymbol{C}_n^*)^{-1}|| \leqq \lambda_0^{-\frac{1}{2}}$. If we assume that

$$||\boldsymbol{\Gamma}_n|| < \frac{1}{2}\frac{\lambda_0}{c},$$

then it follows from (14.19) and (14.20) that

$$|||v_n - u_n||| = ||\beta^{(n)} - \alpha^{(n)}|| < 2(cc'\lambda_0^{-\frac{1}{2}}||\boldsymbol{\Gamma}_n|| + c\lambda_0^{-\frac{1}{2}}||\delta^{(n)}||),$$

which establishes the sufficiency condition of Theorem 14.2.

We turn to the proof of the necessity condition. Assuming that $\Gamma_n = 0$, we obtain from (14.19) and (14.20)

$$|||v_n - u_n||| = ||\beta^{(n)} - \alpha^{(n)}|| = ||(\boldsymbol{I}_n + \boldsymbol{\Delta}_n)^{-1}\boldsymbol{C}_n^{-1}\delta^{(n)}||. \tag{14.21}$$

If we let

$$(\boldsymbol{I}_n + \boldsymbol{\Delta}_n)^{-1}\boldsymbol{C}_n^{-1}\delta^{(n)} = \sigma^{(n)},$$

then

$$||\boldsymbol{C}_n^{-1}\delta^{(n)}|| \leqq ||\boldsymbol{I}_n + \boldsymbol{\Delta}_n||\ ||\sigma^{(n)}||.$$

Above, we saw that $||\boldsymbol{\Delta}_n|| \to ||\boldsymbol{\Delta}||$. Hence, there exists a positive constant μ such that $||\boldsymbol{I}_n + \boldsymbol{\Delta}|| \leqq \mu$. Thus

$$||\sigma^{(n)}|| \geqq \frac{1}{\mu}||\boldsymbol{C}_n^{-1}\delta^{(n)}||.$$

If we now choose $\delta^{(n)}$ so that

$$||\boldsymbol{C}_n^{-1}\delta^{(n)}|| = ||\boldsymbol{C}_n^{-1}||\ ||\delta^{(n)}||,$$

then, on the strength of (14.21),

$$|||v_n - u_n||| \geqq \frac{1}{\mu}||\boldsymbol{C}_n^{-1}||\ ||\delta^{(n)}||.$$

If the coordinate system is not strongly minimal in the space $\mathfrak{H}_0$, then

$$||\boldsymbol{C}_n^{-1}|| = \frac{1}{\sqrt{\lambda_1^{(n)}}} \xrightarrow[n\to\infty]{} \infty,$$

which leads to the contradiction that the approximate Bubnov-Galerkin-solution is not stable.

Vainikko [1] has examined the more general question of necessary conditions for the stability of approximate Petrov-Galerkin-solutions.

§15. Remarks about the use of non-strongly minimal systems

Below, in Chapter 5, methods for the construction of almost orthonormal or, at least, strongly minimal coordinate systems for a comparitatively wide class of problems will be examined. Since this class is far from being comprehensive, it will be necessary to make use of coordinate systems which are not strongly minimal. In the present section, some concepts relating to the use of non-strongly minimal coordinate systems will be introduced. We restrict attention to the most simple and important case: the Ritz-process.

Let the coordinate system $\{\phi_n\}$ be non-strongly minimal in the energy space $\mathfrak{H}_A$. We shall examine the *exact* and the *non-exact* Ritz-systems

$$\boldsymbol{R}_n a^{(n)} = f^{(n)}, \tag{15.1}$$

$$(\boldsymbol{R}_n + \boldsymbol{\Gamma}_n) b^{(n)} = f^{(n)} + \delta^{(n)}. \tag{15.2}$$

As before, $\lambda_1^{(n)}$ and $\lambda_n^{(n)}$ denote the smallest and largest eigenvalues of the matrix R_n. For sufficiently large n, $\lambda_1^{(n)}$ will be small. We assume initially that

$$||\boldsymbol{\Gamma}_n|| \leqq \beta \lambda_1^{(n)}, \tag{15.3}$$

where $0 < \beta = \text{const.} < 1$.

An error matrix is generated because the energy inner products $[\phi_k, \phi_j]$, which represent elements of R_n, are calculated approximately. Inequality (15.3) will be satisfied once the order of the approximation is chosen sufficiently high.

Repeating the argument of §9, we obtain the following expressions, which are equivalent to (9.13) and (9.13′):

$$||\eta^{(n)}|| = ||b^{(n)} - a^{(n)}|| \leqq \frac{[\lambda_1^{(n)}]^{-\frac{1}{2}} ||\boldsymbol{\Gamma}_n|| \, |||u_0||| + [\lambda_1^{(n)}]^{-1} ||\delta^{(n)}||}{1-\beta}, \tag{15.4}$$

$$||\eta^{(n)}|| = ||b^{(n)} - a^{(n)}|| \leqq \frac{C[\lambda_1^{(n)}]^{-\frac{1}{2}} ||\boldsymbol{\Gamma}_n|| + [\lambda_1^{(n)}]^{-1} ||\delta^{(n)}||}{1-\beta}, \tag{15.4′}$$

where, as for (19.13′), C is a known upper bound for $|||u_0|||$.

Expressions (15.4) and (15.4′) hold under the assumption that the vectors $a^{(n)}$ and $b^{(n)}$ satisfy exactly (15.1) and (15.2), respectively: in practice, this implies that a sufficiently large number of additional decimal places must be carried during all intermediate calculations for the solution of system (15.2).

The error of the *non-exact* approximate Ritz-solution

$$v_n = \sum_{k=1}^{n} b_k^{(n)} \phi_k$$

can be estimated by the use of (10.8):

$$|||v_n - u_n|||^2 \leqslant ||\eta^{(n)}||(||\delta^{(n)}|| + ||\boldsymbol{\Gamma}_n||\ ||b^{(n)}||).$$

Since $||b^{(n)}||$ is not known in advance, we rewrite

$$||\eta^{(n)}|| = ||b^{(n)} - a^{(n)}||$$

in the form

$$||b^{(n)}|| \leqq ||a^{(n)}|| + ||\eta^{(n)}||.$$

It is not difficult to obtain a formula analagous to (9.12):

$$||a^{(n)}|| \leqq [\lambda_1^{(n)}]^{-\frac{1}{2}}|||u_0||| \leqq C[\lambda_1^{(n)}]^{-\frac{1}{2}}.$$

Hence,

$$|||v_n - u_n|||^2 \leqq ||\eta^{(n)}||\{||\delta^{(n)}|| + ||\boldsymbol{\Gamma}_n||([\lambda_1^{(n)}]^{-\frac{1}{2}} + ||\eta^{(n)}||)\}. \tag{15.5}$$

From (15.4) and (15.5), we can calculate the error permissible in the evaluation of R_n and $f^{(n)}$.

From (15.4′) and (15.5), it is easy to ascertain values for Γ_n and $f^{(n)}$ which necessarily insure that $v_n - u_n$ is sufficiently small. In fact, if we assume that

$$||\boldsymbol{\Gamma}_n|| = O([\lambda_1^{(n)}]^{1+\kappa}), \qquad ||\delta^{(n)}|| = O([\lambda_1^{(n)}]^{\frac{1}{2}+\kappa}), \tag{15.6}$$

where κ is a positive constant, then

$$||\eta^{(n)}|| = O([\lambda_1^{(n)}]^{\kappa-\frac{1}{2}}), \tag{15.7}$$

and

$$|||v_n - u_n||| = O([\lambda_1^{(n)}]^{\kappa}). \tag{15.8}$$

It is interesting to note that for $0 < \kappa < \frac{1}{2}$ the value $||\eta^{(n)}||$ can increase without bound as $n \to \infty$, while the error in the approximate solution tends to zero.

On the basis of these results, we have

Observation 1. *For the use of non-strongly minimal coordinate systems, the components of the r.h.s.-term $f^{(n)}$ can be calculated with less accuracy than the components in the Ritz-matrix R_n.*

As an example, we consider the problem

$$Au = -\frac{d}{dx}\left(p(x)\frac{du}{dx}\right) + q(x)u = f(x), \qquad u(0) = u(1) = 0, \quad (15.9)$$

where $p(x)$, $p'(x)$ and $q(x)$ are continuous,

$$p_0 \leqq p(x) \leqq p_1, \qquad 0 \leqq q(x) \leqq q_1$$

and p_0, p_1 and q_1 are positive constants. The operator $\boldsymbol{A}$ is positive definite and

$$|||u|||_A^2 = \int_0^1 (pu'^2 + qu^2)dx. \quad (15.10)$$

We note that the operator $\boldsymbol{A}$ is similar to the operator $\boldsymbol{B}$, where

$$Bu = -\frac{d^2u}{dx^2}, \qquad u(0) = u(1) = 0.$$

We compare $|||u|||_A$ and $|||u|||_B$. Now,

$$|||u|||_B^2 = \int_0^1 u'^2 dx,$$

which implies that $|||u|||_A^2 \geqq p_0|||u|||_B^2$. Further,

$$|||u|||_A^2 \leqq p_1 \int_0^1 u'^2 dx + q_1 \int_0^1 u^2 dx = p_1|||u|||_B^2 + q_1||u||^2.$$

Since the smallest eigenvalue of $\boldsymbol{B}$ equals π^2 and $u(0) = u(1) = 0$, we have $||u||^2 \leqq 1/\pi^2|||u|||_B^2$ which leads to the required inequality

$$p_0|||u|||_B^2 \leqq |||u|||_A^2 \leqq (p_1 + \pi^{-2}q_1)|||u|||_B^2. \quad (15.11)$$

Using (15.11) and the inequality

$$||u||^2 \leqq \frac{1}{\pi^2}|||u|||_B^2,$$

we obtain

$$|||u|||_A^2 \geqq p_0 \pi^2 ||u||^2.$$

Hence γ, which characterises the positive definiteness of the operator A, can be taken equal to $\pi\sqrt{p_0}$.
As coordinate functions, we choose the system

$$\{\phi_k(x)\} = \{x^k(1-x)\}.$$

We prove that this system is not strongly minimal in $\mathfrak{H}_B$. On the basis of (2.9), it is sufficient to prove that at least one of the sums

$$\sum_{k=1}^{n} [\sigma_{kj}^{(n)}]^2,$$

where $\sigma_{kj}^{(n)}$ is an element of the inverse Ritz-matrix, is unbounded. We have

$$[\phi_k, \phi_j]_B = \int_0^1 [kx^{k-1}-(k+1)x^k][jx^{j-1}-(j+1)x^j]dx =$$

$$= \frac{2jk}{(j+k)[(j+k)^2-1]}.$$

Since the $\sigma_{kj}^{(n)}$ satisfy the relationship

$$\sum_{k=1}^{n} \frac{2jk\sigma_{kj}^{(n)}}{(j+k)[(j+k)^2-1]} = 1,$$

we obtain, using the inequality of Cauchy,

$$\sum_{k=1}^{n} [\sigma_{kj}^{(n)}]^2 \sum_{k=1}^{n} \frac{4j^2k^2}{(j+k)^2[(j+k)^2-1]^2} \geqq 1.$$

For $j = n$, we have

$$\sum_{k=1}^{n} \frac{4k^2n^2}{(n+k)^2[(n+k)^2-1]} < \sum_{k=1}^{n} \frac{1}{(n+k)^2}.$$

However, since

$$\frac{1}{(n+k)^2} < \int_0^1 \frac{dx}{(n+k-x)^2} = \int_{n+k-1}^{n+k} \frac{dy}{y^2},$$

we obtain

$$\sum_{k=1}^{n} \frac{1}{(n+k)^2} < \int_n^{2n} \frac{dy}{y^2} = \frac{1}{2n},$$

which, with inequality (15.11), yields

$$\sum_{k=1}^{n} [\sigma_{kn}^{(n)}]^2 > 2n.$$

Thus, system (15.12) is not strongly minimal in $\mathfrak{H}_B$. From (15.11) and Corollary 4.1, it follows that this system is not strongly minimal in $\mathfrak{H}_A$. We estimate the eigenvalues of the Ritz-matrix $R_n = ||[\phi_k, \phi_j]_A||_{j,k=1}^{j,k=n}$. Let $\mu_k^{(n)}$ denote an eigenvalue of the matrix $r_n = ||[\phi_k, \phi_j]_B||_{j,k=1}^{j,k=n}$. Using the Minimax Principal and inequality (15.11), we obtain

$$p_0 \mu_k^{(n)} \leqq \lambda_k^{(n)} \leqq (p_1 + \pi^{-2} q_1)\mu_k^{(n)}.$$

Values of $\mu_1^{(n)}$ and $\mu_n^{(n)}$ for various values of n can be found in Mikhlin [16]. We reproduce some of them here:

n	$\mu_n^{(n)}$	$\mu_1^{(n)}$	$\rho(r_n)$
2	0.42769839	0.03896921	10.978
3	0.47572671	0.00270726	175.72
5	0.52695	0.00015	3430
7	0.5552	0.00007	7700

Let an approximate solution of (15.9) be constructed in the form

$$u_7(x) = \sum_{k=1}^{7} a_k^{(7)} \phi_k(x) = x(1-x)(a_1^{(7)} + a_2^{(7)} x + a_3^{(7)} x^2 + \ldots + a_7^{(7)} x^6).$$

For the determination of numerical values, we assume that $p_0 = 1$, $p_1 + \pi^{-2} q_1 = 10$. Then $\lambda_1^{(7)} \geqq 7 \times 10^{-5}$. Further, if u_0 is the exact solution of (15.9), then (see PM, p. 20–21) $|||u_0|||_A \leqq ||f||/\gamma = ||f||/\pi\sqrt{p_0}$ and, in formula (15.4′), $C = ||f||/\pi\sqrt{p_0} = ||f||/\pi$. We also assume that $||f|| = \pi$ and $C = 1$. Finally, let $[\phi_k, \phi_j]_A$ and (f, ϕ_j) be determined to an accuracy of k decimal places. Then

$$|\gamma_{kj}| < \tfrac{1}{2}10^{-k}, \qquad |\delta_k| < \tfrac{1}{2}10^{-k}$$

and

$$\|\Gamma_7\| \leqq 3.5\times 10^{-k}, \qquad \|\delta^{(7)}\| \leqq \frac{\sqrt{7}}{2}\,10^{-k} < 1.5\times 10^{-k}.$$

Since inequality (15.3) implies that $3.5\times 10^{-k} \leqq 7\beta\times 10^{-5}$, we take $\beta = 0.5$ and $k \geqq 5$. Now, by formula (15.4′),

$$\|\eta^{(7)}\| \leqq 2\left[7^{-1.5}\times 3.5\times 10^{7.5-k} + \frac{1.5}{7}\,10^{5-k}\right].$$

Since the second term on the r.h.s. is significantly less than the first, we can discard it without noticeable detriment to the accuracy of the estimate. We assume therefore that

$$\|\eta^{(7)}\| < 2\times 3.5\times 7^{-1.5}\times 10^{7.5-k} = \left(\frac{10}{7}\right)^{\frac{1}{2}} 10^{7-k} < 1.2\times 10^{7-k}.$$

Note. That the second term on the r.h.s. is significantly less than the first is related to Observation 1, above.

We turn to formula (15.5). For this discussion, $[\lambda_1^{(7)}]^{-\frac{1}{2}}$ has order 10^2. For the smallest possible value of $k(=5)$, $\|\eta^{(7)}\| < 1.2\times 10^2$, while for $k > 5$ the order of $\|\eta^{(7)}\|$ is lower. Assuming $k > 5$, we have $\|\eta^{(7)}\| < [\lambda_1^{(7)}]^{-\frac{1}{2}}$ and we substitute $\|\eta^{(7)}\|$ for $[\lambda_1^{(7)}]^{-\frac{1}{2}}$ in (15.5). Further, we neglect $\|\delta^{(7)}\|$ on the basis of a comparison with the essentially larger $\|\Gamma_7\|[\lambda_1^{(7)}]^{-\frac{1}{2}}$. We obtain

$$|||v_7 - u_7|||_A \leqq \sqrt{2\|\eta^{(7)}\|\,\|\Gamma_7\|[\lambda_1^{(7)}]^{-\frac{1}{2}}} < 10^{5-k}.$$

If, however, we require that the error (w.r.t. the energy norm) of the *non-exact* solution v_7 has order 10^{-4}, then the energy inner products must be calculated with an accuracy of 9 decimal places.

We note that this result agrees with equations (15.6)–(15.8) and can be obtained from them with $\kappa = 0.8$.

We also note that it is inappropriate to solve the Ritz systems, considered here, by iteration: for the above choice of numerical values for the given parameters, $\lambda_1^{(n)} \leqq 10\mu^{(n)}$ and $\lambda_n^{(n)} \geqq \mu_n^{(n)}$, and $\rho(R_n) \geqq 0.1\times\rho(r_n)$. In particular, $\rho(R_7) \geqq 770$, and for the optimal choice of α (see, §12) the iteration will converge like the geometric progression $\{(\frac{769}{771})^n\}$.

§16. Another concept of stability

Another concept of stability for numerical processes is presented in Samokish [1]. The numerical process examined by this author will be referred to as *the abstract Bubnov-Galerkin-process* (the author used the name: *the abstract Galerkin-process*).

Let A be a linear operator mapping from $\mathfrak{X}$ into $\mathfrak{Y}$, where $\mathfrak{X}$ and $\mathfrak{Y}$ are Banach spaces. In order to construct an approximate solution for the equation

$$Ax = y, \qquad x \in \mathfrak{X}, \qquad y \in \mathfrak{Y}, \tag{16.1}$$

we choose a system of coordinate elements $\{\phi_n\} \in \mathfrak{X}$ and a system of linear functionals $\{l_n\}$ defined on $\mathfrak{Y}$. An approximate solution is sought in the form

$$x_n = \sum_{k=1}^{n} a_k^{(n)} \phi_k, \tag{16.2}$$

where the coefficients $a_k^{(n)}$ are defined by the system of equations

$$\sum_{k=1}^{n} \alpha_{jk} a_k^{(n)} = l_j y, \qquad \alpha_{jk} = l_l A\phi_k \qquad (j = 1, 2, \ldots, n). \tag{16.3}$$

We note that, if the spaces $\mathfrak{X}$ and $\mathfrak{Y}$ are Hilbert spaces, then *the abstract Bubnov-Galerkin-process* coincides with *the Petrov-Galerkin-process.*

Samokish introduced two numerical tests for the stability of the process (16.3). One of them is the condition number for the matrix $A_n = ||\alpha_{jk}||_{j,k=1}^{j,k=n}$ of system (16.3). When the matrix A_n is non-positive and also non-symmetric, its condition number is defined by (see, Faddeev and Faddeeva [1])

$$H(A_n) = ||A_n||\,||A_n^{-1}||. \tag{16.4}$$

The second test, which we denote by μ_n, consists of the following: in system (16.3), we replace the numbers $l_j y$ by the arbitrary numbers β_j, where

$$\sum_{j=1}^{n} |\beta_j|^2 = 1. \tag{16.5}$$

Further, we determine the coefficients $a_k^{(n)}$ for this system and calculate x_n from (16.2). The number μ_n is defined by

$$\mu_n = \frac{\max ||x_n||}{\min ||x_n||}, \tag{16.6}$$

where the maximum and minimum are evaluated over all possible choices of the numbers $\beta_1, \beta_2, \ldots, \beta_n$ which satisfy (16.5).

Samokish regarded $H(A_n)$ as a test for the stability of the process (16.3), or in other words, the stability of the coefficients $a_k^{(n)}$; and μ_n as a test for the stability of the approximate solution (16.2).

In his paper, Samokish did not give an exact definition of stability: He assumed in every case that a process (16.3) is stable, if $H(A_n)$ is bounded for all n, and computationally-stable, if $H(A_n)$ does not increase too rapidly for increasing n.

Analogously, if μ_n is bounded for all n, then the process of evaluating the approximate solution (16.2) is assumed to be stable. If μ_n does not increase too rapidly for increasing n, then the mentioned process is computationally-stable.

We shall examine in more detail the case when $\mathfrak{X} = \mathfrak{Y}$ and $\boldsymbol{A} = \boldsymbol{I}+\boldsymbol{T}$, where $\boldsymbol{I}$ is the identity operator and $\boldsymbol{T}$ is a completely continuous operator. For this problem, we obtain estimates for $H(A_n)$ and μ_n in the following way.

Let $\mathfrak{X}_n$ denote the n-dimensional subspace of $\mathfrak{X}$ which is spanned by $\phi_1, \phi_2, \ldots, \phi_n$, and $\mathfrak{E}_n$ the n-dimensional unitary space. We introduce into the investigation the operators $\boldsymbol{\Phi}_n$ and $\boldsymbol{\Psi}_n$: $\boldsymbol{\Phi}_n$ maps from $\mathfrak{E}_n$ into $\mathfrak{X}_n$ such that

$$\boldsymbol{\Phi}_n a = \sum_{k=1}^{n} a_k \phi_k, \qquad a = [a_1, a_2, \ldots, a_n] \in \mathfrak{E}_n; \tag{16.7}$$

and $\boldsymbol{\Psi}_n$ maps from $\mathfrak{X}_n$ into $\mathfrak{E}_n$ such that

$$\boldsymbol{\Psi}_n x = [l_1 x, l_2 x, \ldots, l_n x], \qquad x \in \mathfrak{X}_n. \tag{16.8}$$

It is not difficult to see that the inverse operators $\boldsymbol{\Phi}_n^{-1}$ and $\boldsymbol{\Psi}_n^{-1}$ exist, if $\phi_1, \phi_2, \ldots, \phi_n$ are linearly independent and if the functionals l_j are such that

$$l_j x = 0, \qquad x \in \mathfrak{X}_n \qquad (j = 1, 2, \ldots n)$$

only if $x = 0$. We assume below that these conditions are satisfied.

The operator $\boldsymbol{\Psi}_n$ can be extended in an obvious manner to the whole space $\mathfrak{X}$ with the character of (16.8) preserved: Let $\widetilde{\boldsymbol{\Psi}}_n$ denote the operator obtained by such an extension.

We construct the projection operator $\boldsymbol{\Pi}_n$, which maps from $\mathfrak{X}$ into $\mathfrak{X}_n$, such that $l_j \boldsymbol{\Pi}_n x = l_j x$ $(j = 1, 2, \ldots, n)$. This operator is defined in a unique way: it is not difficult to give an explicit formulation, but this will not concern us here. Finally, we put $\tilde{A}_n = \Pi_n \tilde{A}$, where $\tilde{A}$ is the contraction of A to the subspace $\mathfrak{X}_n$.

The estimates mentioned above have the form

$$H(A_n) \leqq \|A\| \, \|\tilde{A}_n^{-1}\| \, \|\tilde{\Psi}_n\| \, \|\Psi_n^{-1}\| \, \|\Phi_n\| \, \|\Phi_n^{-1}\|, \tag{16.9}$$

$$\mu_n \leqq \|A\| \, \|A_n^{-1}\| \, \|\tilde{\Psi}_n\| \, \|\Psi_n^{-1}\|. \tag{16.10}$$

For the Ritz-process, $\mathfrak{X}$ is the energy space corresponding to the problem: $A = I$, $l_j x = [x, \phi_j]$, $A_n = R_n$, and

$$H(A_n) = \rho(R_n) = \frac{\lambda_n^{(n)}}{\lambda_1^{(n)}} .$$

Also, it is a simple matter to estimate μ_n. Namely, system (16.3), in which $l_j y$ is replaced by β_j, takes the form

$$\sum_{k=1}^{n} [\phi_k, \phi_j] a_k^{(n)} = \beta_j$$

or, more briefly, $R_n a^{(n)} = \beta$, where $\beta = [\beta_1, \beta_2, \ldots, \beta_n]$.

Further, since the norms are the energy norms,

$$\max_{\Sigma|\beta_j|^2=1} \|x_n\| = \max_{\|\beta\|=1} |||x_n||| = \max \frac{|||x_n|||}{\|R_n a^{(n)}\|} .$$

Since we know that

$$|||x_n|||^2 = |||\sum_{k=1}^{n} a_k \phi_k|||^2 = (R_n a^{(n)}, a^{(n)}),$$

we obtain

$$\max_{\Sigma|\beta_j|^2=1} \|x_n\|^2 = \max_{a^{(n)} \neq 0} \frac{(R_n a^{(n)}, a^{(n)})}{\|R_n a^{(n)}\|^2} ,$$

or, if we put $R_n a^{(n)} = c^{(n)}$,

$$\max_{\Sigma|\beta_j|^2=1} \|x_n\|^2 = \max_{c^{(n)} \neq 0} \frac{(R_n^{-1} c^{(n)}, c^{(n)})}{\|c^{(n)}\|^2} = \frac{1}{\lambda_1^{(n)}} .$$

Analogously,

$$\min_{\Sigma|\beta_j|^2=1} \|x_n\|^2 = \min_{c^{(n)} \neq 0} \frac{(R_n^{-1} c^{(n)}, c^{(n)})}{\|c^{(n)}\|^2} = \frac{1}{\lambda_n^{(n)}} .$$

Hence,

$$\mu_n = \frac{\max \|x_n\|}{\min \|x_n\|} = \sqrt{\frac{\lambda_n^{(n)}}{\lambda_1^{(n)}}} = \sqrt{\rho(R_n)}. \tag{16.11}$$

In this way, we see that the stability condition of Samokish for the Ritz-process is equivalent to the condition that the coordinate system be almost orthonormal in the energy space for this problem.

A formula like (16.11) does not hold for the abstract Bubnov-Galerkin-process, and μ_n can be bounded when $H(A_n)$ is unbounded.

In connection with the results developed by Samokish for computational stability of the abstract Bubnov-Galerkin-processes, great value is attached to estimates of $H(A_n)$ and μ_n for a concrete class of coordinate functions $\{\phi_n\}$ and functionals l_n. In Samokish [1], a series of examples relating to such estimates is given: we give one of them below after making some introductory remarks.

Let us assume that we deal with either the Ritz- or Bubnov-Galerkin-processes so that the functionals l_n can be identified with the elements ϕ_n which lie in the Hilbert space $\mathfrak{X}$; then $\|\tilde{\boldsymbol{\Psi}}_n\| = \|\boldsymbol{\Psi}_n\|$. We shall prove this result. On the one hand, since $\tilde{\boldsymbol{\Psi}}_n$ is an extension of the operator $\boldsymbol{\Psi}_n$, $\|\tilde{\boldsymbol{\Psi}}_n\| \geqq \boldsymbol{\Psi}_n\|$. On the other hand, if x is an arbitrary element of the space $\mathfrak{X}$ and x' its projection in the space $\mathfrak{X}_n$, which is spanned by $\phi_1, \phi_2, \ldots, \phi_n$, then $\tilde{\boldsymbol{\Psi}}_n x = \tilde{\boldsymbol{\Psi}}_n x' = \boldsymbol{\Psi}_n x'$. Hence,

$$\|\tilde{\boldsymbol{\Psi}}_n x\| = \|\boldsymbol{\Psi}_n x'\| \leqq \|\boldsymbol{\Psi}_n\| \, \|x'\| \leqq \|\boldsymbol{\Psi}_n\| \, \|x\|$$

and, in fact, $\|\tilde{\boldsymbol{\Psi}}_n\| \leqq \|\boldsymbol{\Psi}_n\|$. Further, it is easy to see that, for the Ritz- and Bubnov-Galerkin processes, $\boldsymbol{\Phi}_n$ and $\boldsymbol{\Psi}_n$ are adjoint and, therefore, that $\|\boldsymbol{\Psi}_n\| = \|\boldsymbol{\Phi}_n\|$, $\|\boldsymbol{\Psi}_n^{-1}\| = \|\boldsymbol{\Phi}_n^{-1}\|$.

Now, $\boldsymbol{\Phi}_n = \boldsymbol{S}_n^{-1}$, where $\boldsymbol{S}_n$ is the operator introduced in §13. From (13.12), it follows that

$$\|\boldsymbol{\Phi}_n\| = \|\boldsymbol{\Psi}_n\| = \sqrt{\lambda_n^{(n)}},$$

$$\|\boldsymbol{\Phi}_n^{-1}\| = \|\boldsymbol{\Psi}_n^{-1}\| = \frac{1}{\sqrt{\lambda_1^{(n)}}}.$$

Therefore, estimates (16.9) and (16.10) take the form

$$H(A_n) \leqq \|A\| \, \|\tilde{A}_n^{-1}\| \, \frac{\lambda_n^{(n)}}{\lambda_1^{(n)}}, \qquad \mu_n \leqq \|A\| \, \|\tilde{A}_n^{-1}\| \sqrt{\frac{\lambda_n^{(n)}}{\lambda_1^{(n)}}}.$$

It can be proved that, for the Bubnov-Galerkin-process, $||\tilde{A}_n^{-1}||$ is bounded (for the Ritz-process, $||\tilde{A}_n^{-1}|| = 1$), and the following simpler estimates result

$$H(A_n) \leqq C\frac{\lambda_n^{(n)}}{\lambda_1^{(n)}}, \qquad \mu_n \leqq C\sqrt{\frac{\lambda_n^{(n)}}{\lambda_1^{(n)}}}, \qquad C = \text{const.} \tag{16.12}$$

For the Ritz-process, we saw that $A = I$, $\tilde{A}_n^{-1} = I_n$, $\mu_n = \sqrt{\lambda_n^{(n)}/\lambda_1^{(n)}}$, and, clearly, $H(R_n) = \delta(R_n) = \lambda_n^{(n)}/\lambda_1^{(n)}$.
In this way, the problem reduces to the estimation of the ratio $\lambda_n^{(n)}/\lambda_1^{(n)}$. We shall examine in the real space $\mathfrak{X} = L_2\,(-1, 1)$ the system of functions $\phi_n(t) = t^n$ $(n = 0, 1, 2, \ldots)$. We prove that for this system $\lambda_n^{(n)}/\lambda_1^{(n)} = 0((\sqrt{2}+1)^{2n})$, where

$$\Phi_n a = \sum_{k=0}^{n-1} a_k t^k = p_{n-1}(t)$$

is a polynomial of degree $n-1$ and it is necessary to find upper and lower bounds for

$$\frac{\int_{-1}^{1} p_{n-1}^2(t)dt}{\sum_{k=0}^{n-1} a_k^2}. \tag{16.13}$$

Clearly,

$$\int_{-1}^{1} p_{n-1}^2(t)dt = \int_\gamma p_{n-1}^2(z)dz.$$

where γ is the upper or lower half circle $|z| = 1$ with ends at $z = \pm 1$. Hence, we obtain

$$\int_{-1}^{1} p_{n-1}^2(t)dt = \frac{1}{2}\int_{|z|=1} p_{n-1}^2(z)\,\text{sign Im}\,z\,dz \leqq$$
$$\leqq \frac{1}{2}\int_0^{2\pi} |p_{n-1}(e^{i\theta})|^2\,d\theta = \pi\sum_{k=0}^{n-1} a_k^2.$$

In this way, we see that (16.13) is bounded above by π and $\lambda_n^{(n)} \leqq \pi$.
The ratio (16.13) does not change if the vector a is multiplied by a constant. We choose this constant so that

$$\int_{-1}^{1} p_{n-1}^2(t)dt = 1.$$

In the last integral, we make the substitution $t = \frac{1}{2}(z+z^{-1})$, $z = e^{i\theta}$ and introduce the notation

$$g(z) = \frac{z^{n-1}}{2}\, p_{n-1}(\tfrac{1}{2}(z+z^{-1}))\sqrt{1-z^2}.$$

Then

$$\int_{|z|=1} |g(z)|^2\, d\theta = \int_0^{2\pi} p_{n-1}^2(\cos\theta)|\sin\theta|\, d\theta = 2\int_{-1}^{1} p_{n-1}^2(t)dt = 2.$$

The function $g(z)$ has an analytic continuation within the circle $|z| < 1$ and is regular there. For $|z| < 1$, let

$$g(z) = \sum_{k=0}^{\infty} \alpha_k z^k.$$

Then,

$$|g(z)|^2 \leqq \sum_{k=0}^{\infty} |\alpha_k|^2 \sum_{k=0}^{\infty} |z_k|^{2k} =$$

$$= \frac{1}{2\pi(1-|z|^2)} \int_{|z|=1} |g(z)|^2\, d\theta = \frac{1}{\pi(1-|z|^2)}.$$

Now let t be an arbitrary positive number which is related to z by the formula $t = \frac{1}{2}(z+z^{-1})$, $|z| < |$. Then

$$|p_{n-1}(t)| \leqq |z|^{-n+1}(1-|z|^2)^{-\frac{1}{4}}|g(z)| \leqq \frac{1}{\pi}|z|^{-n+1}(1-|z|^2)^{-5/4}.$$

In the t-plane, we examine the ellipse with focii at ± 1 and passing through the point $t = i$. On this ellipse, $|z| = \sqrt{2}-1$, and hence,

$$|p_{n-1}(t)| \leqq C_1(\sqrt{2}+1)^n, \qquad C_1 = \text{const.}$$

The last estimate is also true on the circle $|t| = 1$. But then

$$\sum_{k=0}^{n-1} a_k^2 = \frac{1}{2\pi}\int_{|t|=1} |p_n(t)|^2\, d\theta \leqq C_2(\sqrt{2}+1)^{2n}, \qquad C_2 = \text{const.}$$

Now, it is clear that the ratio (16.13) is not less than $C_3(\sqrt{2}+1)^{-2n}$, $C_3 = \text{const.}$, and, therefore, $1/\lambda_1^{(n)} \leqq C_4(2+1)^{2n}$, $C_4 = \text{const.}$ Recalling that $\lambda_n^{(n)} \leqq \pi$, we find

$$\frac{\lambda_n^{(n)}}{\lambda_1^{(n)}} \leqq C(\sqrt{2}+1)^{2n}, \qquad C = \text{const.}$$

Chapter III

ON THE STABILITY OF THE BUBNOV-GALERKIN-PROCESS FOR NON-STATIONARY PROBLEMS

§17. The Bubnov-Galerkin-process for non-stationary problems

In this chapter, we shall examine the Cauchy problem for the non-stationary operator equation

$$\frac{d^2}{dt^2} Au + \frac{d}{dt} Bu + Cu = f(t), \tag{17.1}$$

that is, the problem of integrating (17.1) w.r.t. the initial conditions

$$u|_{t=0} = \phi, \qquad \left.\frac{du}{dt}\right|_{t=0} = \psi. \tag{17.2}$$

Problems of this type were studied by S. L. Sobolev [2] when $\boldsymbol{A}$, $\boldsymbol{B}$ and $\boldsymbol{C}$ are differential operators. For this reason, we shall call equations of the form (17.1) Sobolev-equations.

Here, we shall assume that $\boldsymbol{A}$, $\boldsymbol{B}$ and $\boldsymbol{C}$ are operators which act in a separable Hilbert space $\mathfrak{H}$, and $u(t)$ and $f(t)$ are functions of t the values of which lie in this space $\mathfrak{H}$. Accordingly, the elements ϕ and ψ, which arise in the initial conditions (17.2), also lie in $\mathfrak{H}$. If $\boldsymbol{A} = 0$, then the second of the conditions (17.2) does not hold.

The Bubnov-Galerkin-method has been applied by many authors to different forms of the problem (17.1) and (17.2). The most complete examination can be found in Vishik [1], where the case when the operators $\boldsymbol{A}$, $\boldsymbol{B}$ and $\boldsymbol{C}$ are functions of time is examined. Here, we consider the problem when the operators $\boldsymbol{A}$, $\boldsymbol{B}$ and $\boldsymbol{C}$ are independent of time.

Under known assumptions, which we shall not consider here, the Cauchy-problem (17.1) and (17.2) has a unique solution.

We investigate a process, analogous to that of Bubnov-Galerkin, for the construction of a sequence of approximate solutions for this problem. A more detailed account of this process can be found in Vishik [1].

We start by assuming that the operators $\boldsymbol{A}$, $\boldsymbol{B}$ and $\boldsymbol{C}$ are positive definite–

we examine the case where some of the operators $\boldsymbol{A}, \boldsymbol{B}$ and $\boldsymbol{C}$ are only non-negative in subsequent sections of the present chapter. Further, we assume that the domains $\mathfrak{D}(\boldsymbol{A})$, $\mathfrak{D}(\boldsymbol{B})$ and $\mathfrak{D}(\boldsymbol{C})$ intersect in some set $\mathfrak{D}$ which is dense in $\mathfrak{H}$ as well as in each of the energy spaces $\mathfrak{H}_{\boldsymbol{A}}$, $\mathfrak{H}_{\boldsymbol{B}}$ and $\mathfrak{H}_{\boldsymbol{C}}$. Then these energy spaces intersect in some set $\mathfrak{D}_0 \supset \mathfrak{D}$ which is dense in each of them. It is not difficult to see that $\mathfrak{D}_0$ becomes a complete Hilbert space w.r.t. the scalar product

$$[u, v]_0 = [u, v]_{\boldsymbol{A}} + [u, v]_{\boldsymbol{B}} + [u, v]_{\boldsymbol{C}}, \qquad u, v\ \mathfrak{D}_0. \tag{17.3}$$

The norm in $\mathfrak{D}_0$ is denoted by $|||u|||_0$.
We introduce the coordinate system

$$\{\phi_n\} = \phi_1, \phi_2, \ldots, \phi_n \ldots, \tag{17.4}$$

which satisfies the following conditions:
(1) $\{\phi_n\} \in \mathfrak{D}_0$;
(2) the elements $\phi_1, \phi_2, \ldots, \phi_n$ are linearly independent for arbitrary n;
(3) $\{\phi_n\}$ is complete in $\mathfrak{D}_0$. We note that condition (3) implies the completeness of $\{\phi_n\}$ in each of the spaces $\mathfrak{H}_{\boldsymbol{A}}$, $\mathfrak{H}_{\boldsymbol{B}}$ and $\mathfrak{H}_{\boldsymbol{C}}$.
We assume that the elements ϕ and ψ, arising in the initial conditions (17.2), lie in the space $\mathfrak{D}_0$. We seek an approximate solution of (17.1), (17.2) in the form

$$u_n(t) = \sum_{k=1}^{n} a_k^{(n)}(t)\phi_k, \tag{17.5}$$

where the unknown functions $a_k^{(n)}(t)$ are defined by the system of differential equations

$$\sum_{k=1}^{n} \{[\phi_k, \phi_j]_{\boldsymbol{A}} \ddot{a}_k^{(n)} + [\phi_k, \phi_j]_{\boldsymbol{B}} \dot{a}_k^{(n)} + [\phi_k, \phi_j]_{\boldsymbol{C}} a_k^{(n)}\} = (f(t), \phi_j)$$
$$(j = 1, 2, \ldots, n), \tag{17.6}$$

where the dot denotes differentiation w.r.t. t, and the initial conditions become

$$a_k^{(n)}(0) = \alpha_k^{(n)}, \qquad \dot{a}_k^{(n)}(0) = \beta_k^{(n)} \qquad (k = 1, 2, \ldots, n). \tag{17.7}$$

The choice of the constants $\alpha_k^{(n)}$ and $\beta_k^{(n)}$ is to a certain extent arbitrary and only subject to the requirement:

$$|||\phi - \sum_{k=1}^{n} \alpha_k^{(n)}\phi_k||| \underset{n\to\infty}{\to} 0, \qquad |||\psi - \sum_{k=1}^{n} \beta_k^{(n)}\phi_k||| \underset{n\to\infty}{\to} 0. \tag{17.8}$$

One could stipulate, for example, that the sums be, respectively, the projections of the elements ϕ and ψ on the subspaces of $\mathfrak{D}_0$ spanned by $\phi_1, \phi_2, \ldots, \phi_n$. In this way, the constants $\alpha_k^{(n)}$ and $\beta_k^{(n)}$ are defined by the Ritz-systems

$$\sum_{k=1}^{n} [\phi_k, \phi_j]_0 \alpha_k^{(n)} = [\phi, \phi_j]_0 \qquad (j = 1, 2, \ldots, n), \tag{17.9'}$$

$$\sum_{k=1}^{n} [\phi_k, \phi_j]_0 \beta_k^{(n)} = [\psi, \phi_j]_0 \qquad (j = 1, 2, \ldots, n). \tag{17.9''}$$

Below, we consider the case when one of the spaces $\mathfrak{H}_A$, $\mathfrak{H}_B$ and $\mathfrak{H}_C$ lies in the others: if, for example, $\mathfrak{H}_A \subset \mathfrak{H}_B$ and $\mathfrak{H}_A \subset \mathfrak{H}_C$, then the metrics of $\mathfrak{H}_A$ and $\mathfrak{D}_0$ are equivalent and the metric (17.3) can be replaced by the metric of $\mathfrak{H}_A$. Then, $\mathfrak{D}_0 \equiv \mathfrak{H}_A$ and systems (17.9′) and (17.9″) are replaced by the simpler systems

$$\sum_{k=1}^{n} [\phi_k, \phi_j]_A \alpha_k^{(n)} = [\phi, \phi_j]_A \qquad (j = 1, 2, \ldots, n), \tag{17.10'}$$

$$\sum_{k=1}^{n} [\phi_k, \phi_j]_A \beta_k^{(n)} = [\psi, \phi_j]_A \qquad (j = 1, 2, \ldots, n). \tag{17.10''}$$

We clarify to a certain extent the structure of the system of differential equations (17.6). Formally, one can construct this system as follows: we assume that the coordinate elements lie in $\mathfrak{D}$, in other words, that they lie in the common domain of the operators $\boldsymbol{A}$, $\boldsymbol{B}$ and $\boldsymbol{C}$. Then (17.5) can be substituted into the l.h.s. of (17.1). We require (as is usual for the Bubnov-Galerkin-process) that the difference between the result of this substitution and $f(t)$ be orthogonal, w.r.t. the metric of $\mathfrak{H}$, to the elements $\phi_1, \phi_2, \ldots, \phi_n$. As a result, we obtain the system of differential equations

$$\sum_{k=1}^{n} \{(\boldsymbol{A}\phi_k, \phi_j)\ddot{a}_k^{(n)} + (\boldsymbol{B}\phi_k, \phi_j)\dot{a}_k^{(n)} + (\boldsymbol{C}\phi_k, \phi_j)a_k^{(n)}\} = (f, \phi_j)$$
$$(j = 1, 2, \ldots, n).$$

System (17.6) follows immediately, since $(\boldsymbol{A}\phi_k, \phi_j) = [\phi_k, \phi_j]_A$, etc.
The Cauchy-problem (17.6) and (17.7) has a unique solution. The substitution of this solution into (17.5) yields an approximate solution of problem (17.1) and (17.2).
Under certain sufficiently complicated conditions (see Vishik [1]), the approximate solution $u_n(t)$ converges in some approriate sense to the

exact solution $u(t)$. We do not stop to formulate these results, since they are not required for the present investigation of the stability of the Bubnov-Galerkin-process.

We turn to the concept of stability of the Bubnov-Galerkin-process for a non-stationary problem. We introduce the matrix notation

$$R_{A_n} = ||[\phi_k, \phi_j]_A||_{j,k=1}^{j,k=n}, \qquad R_{B_n} = ||[\phi_k, \phi_j]_B||_{j,k=1}^{j,k=n},$$
$$R_{C_n} = ||[\phi_k, \phi_j]_C||_{j,k=1}^{j,k=n}$$

and the vector notation

$$a^{(n)}(t) = \{a_1^{(n)}(t), a_2^{(n)}(t), \ldots, a_n^{(n)}(t)\},$$
$$f^{(n)}(t) = \{(f(t), \phi_1), (f(t), \phi_2), \ldots, (f(t), \phi_n)\},$$
$$\alpha^{(n)} = \{\alpha_1^{(n)}, \alpha_2^{(n)}, \ldots, \alpha_n^{(n)}\}, \quad \beta = \{\beta_1^{(n)}, \beta_2^{(n)}, \ldots, \beta_n^{(n)}\}.$$

Equations (17.6) and (17.7) can be rewritten in the form

$$\boldsymbol{R}_{A_n}\ddot{a}^{(n)}(t)+\boldsymbol{R}_{B_n}\dot{a}^{(n)}(t)+\boldsymbol{R}_{C_n}a^{(n)}(t) = f^{(n)}(t), \tag{17.6'}$$

$$a^{(n)}(0) = \alpha^{(n)}, \qquad \dot{a}^{(n)}(0) = \beta^{(n)} \tag{17.7'}$$

We assume that the matrices R_{A_n}, R_{B_n} and R_{C_n} are calculated with error Γ_{A_n}, Γ_{B_n} and Γ_{C_n} and the vectors $f^{(n)}(t)$, $\alpha^{(n)}$ and $\beta^{(n)}$ with error $\delta^{(n)}(t)$, $\delta_0^{(n)}$ and $\delta_1^{(n)}$, where Γ_{A_n}, Γ_{B_n} and Γ_{C_n} are symmetric matrices of order n and $\delta^{(n)}(t)$, $\delta_0^{(n)}$ and $\delta_1^{(n)}$ are n-component vectors. Instead of (17.6′) and (17.7′), we actually solve

$$(\boldsymbol{R}_{A_n}+\boldsymbol{\Gamma}_{A_n})\ddot{b}^{(n)}(t)+(\boldsymbol{R}_{B_n}+\Gamma_{B_n})\dot{b}^{(n)}(t)+(\boldsymbol{R}_{C_n}+\Gamma_{C_n})b^{(n)}(t) =$$
$$= f^{(n)}(t)+\delta^{(n)}(t), \tag{17.11}$$

$$b^{(n)}(0) = \alpha^{(n)}+\delta_0^{(n)}, \qquad \dot{b}^{(n)}(0) = \beta^{(n)}+\delta_1^{(n)}. \tag{17.12}$$

The concept of stability, introduced in §13, is not satisfactory for the present problem, since it is based on the assumption of the boundedness of $\boldsymbol{\Gamma}_n$. Here it will be necessary to assume that $\boldsymbol{\Gamma}_n$ is unbounded. Accordingly, we change the concept of stability in the following way.

As in §13, we study two sequences of Banach spaces $\mathfrak{X}_n$ and $\mathfrak{Y}_n$ and two sequences of equations

$$\boldsymbol{A}_n x^{(n)} = y^{(n)} \tag{17.13}$$

and

$$(\boldsymbol{A}_n+\boldsymbol{\Gamma}_n)z^{(n)} = y^{(n)}+\Delta^{(n)}. \tag{17.14}$$

As before, we assume that the operator A_n maps from $\mathfrak{X}_n$ into $\mathfrak{Y}_n$ and that A_n^{-1} exists for all n and is defined on the whole space $\mathfrak{Y}_n$. We say that the process (17.13) is *stable*, if there exist three positive constants p, q and r such that, for $||A_n^{-1}\Gamma_n|| \leqq r$, (17.14) is solvable and the following inequality holds:

$$||z^{(n)}-x^{(n)}|| \leqq p||A_n^{-1}\Gamma_n||+q||\Delta^{(n)}||. \tag{17.15}$$

Theorem 17.1. $||A_n^{-1}|| \leqq C_1$ *is a necessary condition and* $||A_n^{-1}|| \leqq C^1$, $||A_n^{-1}y^{(n)}|| = ||x^{(n)}|| \leqq C_2$ *is a sufficient condition for the stability of the process* (17.13), *when* C_1 *and* C_2 *are independent of* n.

Proof. The necessity condition can be proved as in Theorem 9.1. In order to prove the sufficiency conditions, we choose some number r, such that $0 < r < 1$, and put $||A_n^{-1}\Gamma_n|| \leqq r$. We start by considering the equations

$$(A_n+\Gamma_n)z_1^{(n)} = y^{(n)}, \qquad (A_n+\Gamma_n)z_2^{(n)} = \Delta^{(n)},$$

where $z^{(n)}-x^{(n)} = \eta^{(n)} = (z_1^{(n)}-x^{(n)})+z_2^{(n)}$. Since

$$z_2^{(n)} = (I_n+A_n^{-1}\Gamma_n)^{-1}A_n^{-1}\Delta^{(n)},$$

we have

$$||z_2^{(n)}|| \leqq \frac{C_1}{1-r}\,||\Delta^{(n)}||.$$

Further, it is easy to see that

$$z_1^{(n)}-x^{(n)} = -(I_n+A_n^{-1}\Gamma_n)^{-1}A_n^{-1}\Gamma_n x^{(n)},$$

and hence,

$$||z_1^{(n)}-x^{(n)}||\leqq \frac{1}{1-r}\,||A_n^{-1}\Gamma_n||\,||x^{(n)}|| \leqq \frac{C_2}{1-r}\,||A_n^{-1}\Gamma_n||.$$

Finally, we obtain

$$||z^{(n)}-x^{(n)}|| \leqq ||z_1^{(n)}-x^{(n)}||+||z_2^{(n)}|| \leqq$$
$$\leqq \frac{C_2}{1-r}\,||A_n^{-1}\Gamma_n||+\frac{C_1}{1-r}\,||\Delta^{(n)}||,$$

which is equivalent to (17.15) with $p = (C_2/1-r)$, $q = (C_1/1-r)$.

We now develop a concept of stability for the process (17.6′), (17.7′) in connection with the general concept just introduced.

Let $\mathfrak{X}_n$ denote the space of n-vector functions (n-component vector functions) which are continuous on the interval $0 \leqq t \leqq l$, where l is some fixed number which can be infinite. The norm in $\mathfrak{X}_n$ is defined in the following way: if $a^{(n)} = a^{(n)}(t)$ and $a^{(n)} \in \mathfrak{X}_n$, then

$$||a^{(n)}||_{\mathfrak{X}_n} = \max_{0 \leqslant t \leqslant l} ||a^{(n)}(t)||_{\mathfrak{E}_n}. \tag{17.16}$$

We assume that $\mathfrak{Y}_n$ is the space of triple-n-vectors of the form

$$g^{(n)} = (h^{(n)}(t), \rho^{(n)}, \pi^{(n)}),$$

where the $h^{(n)}(t)$ are continuous functions of t for $0 \leqq t \leqq l$, and $\delta^{(n)}$ and $\pi^{(n)}$ are constants. The norm in $\mathfrak{Y}_n$ is defined by

$$||g^{(n)}||_{\mathfrak{Y}_n} = \max_{0 \leqslant t \leqslant l} ||h^{(n)}(t)||_{\mathfrak{E}_n} + ||\rho^{(n)}||_{\mathfrak{E}_n} + ||\pi^{(n)}||_{\mathfrak{E}_n}. \tag{17.17}$$

When $l = \infty$, the symbol "max" in (17.6) and (17.7) is replaced by "sup". Equations (17.6′) and (17.7′) define an operator A_n which maps from $\mathfrak{X}_n$ into $\mathfrak{Y}_n$ and transforms $a^{(n)} = a^{(n)}(t)$ into $g^{(n)} = (f^{(n)}(t), \alpha^{(n)}, \beta^{(n)})$. Equations (17.6′) and (17.7′) can be rewritten in the form (17.13), where $x^{(n)}$ and $y^{(n)}$ are replaced by $a^{(n)}$ and $g^{(n)}$.
We introduce the operator Γ_n which also maps from $\mathfrak{X}_n$ into $\mathfrak{Y}_n$ and which transforms every $a^{(n)} = a^{(n)}(t) \in \mathfrak{X}_n$ into $\zeta^{(n)} \in \mathfrak{Y}_n$ of the form

$$\zeta^{(n)} = (\zeta^{(n)}(t), 0, 0),$$

where

$$\zeta^{(n)}(t) = \boldsymbol{\Gamma}_{A_n} \ddot{a}^{(n)}(t) + \boldsymbol{\Gamma}_{B_n} \dot{a}^{(n)}(t) + \boldsymbol{\Gamma}_{C_n} a^{(n)}(t).$$

Now, equations (17.11) and (17.12) can be rewritten in the form (17.14), where

$$z^{(n)} = b^{(n)}, \qquad \Delta^{(n)} = (\delta^{(n)}(t), \delta_0^{(n)}, \delta_1^{(n)}).$$

In connection with the general definition given above, we call the Bubnov-Galerkin-process (equations (17.6′) and (17.7′)) stable w.r.t. the interval $0 \leqq t \leqq l$, if there exist constants p, q and r, independent of n, such that, for $||A_n^{-1}\boldsymbol{\Gamma}_n|| \leqq r$, an inequality similar to (17.15) holds:

$$||\eta^{(n)}|| = ||b^{(n)} - a^{(n)}||_{\mathfrak{X}_n} \leqq p||A_n^{-1}\boldsymbol{\Gamma}_n||_{\mathfrak{X}_n \to \mathfrak{Y}_n} + q||\Delta^{(n)}||_{\mathfrak{Y}_n}. \tag{17.15′}$$

The stability of the Bubnov-Galerkin-process for non-stationary problems was investigated by Veliev [1], [2]. A somewhat strengthened and generalised version of Veliev's results will be presented below. For this purpose, we shall start with Theorem 17.1 which implies that it is sufficient to establish the boundedness of A_n^{-1} and $x^{(n)} = A_n^{-1} y^{(n)}$ for the proof of stability for the process (17.6) and (17.7).

§18. Equations of parabolic type

We examine the problem of integrating the equation

$$\frac{du}{dt} + Cu = f(t) \tag{18.1}$$

w.r.t. the initial condition

$$u|_{t=0} = \phi, \tag{18.2}$$

where, as in §17, $u(t)$ and $f(t)$ are functions of t which lie in the Hilbert space $\mathfrak{H}$, and C is a selfadjoint and positive definite operator in $\mathfrak{H}$. Using the notation of §17, we have $A = 0$, $B = I$. Hence, it is easy to see that the space $\mathfrak{D}_0$ coincides with $\mathfrak{H}_C$ and $|||u|||^2 = ||u||^2 + |||u|||_C^2$. We assume that $\phi \in \mathfrak{H}_C$ and that the functions $f(t)$ are continuous in the interval $0 \leqq t \leqq l$, where l is a positive number which can be infinite. If $l = \infty$, then we require

$$\sup_{0 \leqslant t < \infty} ||f(t)|| < \infty. \tag{18.3}$$

In addition we demand that $\{\phi_n\} \in \mathfrak{H}_C$. We assume that the remaining conditions, developed for $\{\phi_n\}$ in §17, are satisfied. Let ρ_n denote the matrix $||(\phi_k, \phi_j)||_{j,k=1}^{j,k=n}$, where (,) denotes the scalar product in $\mathfrak{H}$. The Bubnov-Galerkin-system (equations (17.6′) and (17.7′)) for problem (18.1) and (18.2) has the form

$$\rho_n \dot{a}^{(n)}(t) + R_n a^{(n)}(t) = f^{(n)}(t), \qquad R_n = R_{C_n}, \tag{18.4}$$

$$a^{(n)}(0) = \alpha^{(n)}. \tag{18.5}$$

We define the vector $\alpha^{(n)}$ by the condition that the element

$$\sum_{k=1}^{n} \alpha_k^{(n)} \phi_k \tag{18.6}$$

be the projection of ϕ not in $\mathfrak{D}_0$, as in §17, but in $\mathfrak{H}_C$. In this way, condition (17.8) is satisfied and, for the determination of $\alpha^{(n)}$, it is necessary to solve not system (17.9), but the simpler system

$$\sum_{k=1}^{n} [\phi_k, \phi_j]_C \alpha_k^{(n)} = [\phi, \phi_j]_C . \tag{18.7}$$

The definition of $\mathfrak{Y}_n$ can be simplified for the process (18.4) and (18.5). We consider some interval $0 \leqq t \leqq l$, where $l \leqq \infty$: if $l = \infty$, we assume that $0 \leqq t < \infty$. $\mathfrak{Y}_n$ is the space of vector pairs of the form $g^{(n)} = (h^{(n)}(t), \beta^{(n)})$, where $\beta^{(n)}$ is a constant vector and $h^{(n)}(t)$ is a continuous function of t on the interval $0 \leqq t \leqq l$. The norm in $\mathfrak{Y}_n$ is defined by

$$\|g^{(n)}\|_{\mathfrak{Y}_n} = \max_{0 \leqq t \leqq l} \|h^{(n)}(t)\|_{\mathfrak{E}_n} + \|\beta^{(n)}\|_{\mathfrak{E}_n} . \tag{18.8}$$

The operator A_n maps from $\mathfrak{X}_n$ into $\mathfrak{Y}_n$ and transforms the vector $a^{(n)}(t)$ into the vector pair $(\rho_n a^{(n)}(t) + R_n a^{(n)}(t), a^{(n)}(0))$.

Theorem 18.1. *If the coordinate system is almost orthonormal in* $\mathfrak{H}$, *then the process* (18.4) and (18.5) *is stable w.r.t. the interval* $0 \leqq t \leqq l$, *when*

$$\sup_{0 \leqq t \leqq l} \|f(t)\|_{\mathfrak{H}} < \infty.$$

Proof. Since the coordinate system is almost orthonormal in $\mathfrak{H}$, it is strongly minimal there. It follows, on the strength of Corollary 4.2, that this system is strongly minimal in $\mathfrak{H}_C$.

Since the matrices ρ_n and R_n are positive definite, they can be reduced simultaneously to diagonal form: there exists a non-singular matrix Z_n such that (see Gantmakher [1; Chapter X, §6])

$$Z_n^* \rho_n Z_n = I_n , \qquad Z_n^* R_n Z_n = D_n , \tag{18.9}$$

where D_n is the diagonal matrix

$$D_n = \operatorname{diag}[\nu_1^{(n)}, \nu_2^{(n)}, \ldots, \nu_n^{(n)}] \tag{18.10}$$

with the numbers $\nu_k^{(n)}$ the roots of the equation

$$\operatorname{Det}(R_n - \nu \rho_n) = 0. \tag{18.11}$$

It is important to note that the numbers $\nu_k^{(n)}$ are positive-bounded below. In fact, the smallest of them is defined by the formula (see Gantmakher [1, Chapter X, §7])

$$\nu_1^{(n)} = \min \frac{(R_n x^{(n)}, x^{(n)})}{(\rho_n x^{(n)}, x^{(n)})} ,$$

where the minimum is evaluated over all non-zero n-vectors $x^{(n)} = \{x_1^{(n)}, \ldots, x_n^{(n)}\}$. We put

$$u = \sum_{k=1}^{n} x_k^{(n)} \phi_k,$$

where the ϕ_k are the coordinate elements. Then

$$(R_n x^{(n)}, x^{(n)}) = |||u|||_C^2, \qquad (\rho_n x^{(n)}, x^{(n)}) = ||u||^2,$$
$$\nu_1^{(n)} = \min_{x^{(n)} \neq 0} \frac{|||u|||_C^2}{||u||^2}.$$

Since the operator C is positive definite, there exists a constant $\nu_0 > 0$ such that, for every element $u \in \mathfrak{H}_C$, the inequality $|||u|||_C{}^2 \geqq \nu_0 ||u||^2$ holds. Hence, it is clear that

$$\nu_1^{(n)} \geqq \nu_0. \tag{18.12}$$

If we put $Z_n^{-1} = G_n$, we obtain from (18.9) that

$$\rho_n = G_n^* G_n, \qquad R_n = G_n^* D_n G_n. \tag{18.13}$$

The norms of the matrices G_n and G_n^{-1} are bounded. In fact, let the eigenvalues of ρ_n be $\mu_1^{(n)} \leqq \mu_2^{(n)} \leqq \ldots \leqq \mu_n^{(n)}$. Since the coordinate system is almost orthonormal in $\mathfrak{H}$, there exist positive constants μ_0 and M_0 such that $\mu_0 \leqq \mu_k^{(n)} \leqq M_0$. Further, it is easy to see that

$$||G_n||^2 = ||\rho_n|| = \mu_n^{(n)}, \qquad ||G_n^{-1}||^2 = ||\rho_n^{-1}|| = \frac{1}{\mu_1^{(n)}},$$

and hence, that

$$||G_n|| = ||G_n^*|| \leqq \sqrt{M_0}, \qquad ||G_n^{-1}|| = ||(G_n^*)^{-1}|| \leqq \frac{1}{\sqrt{\mu_0}}. \tag{18.14}$$

Putting

$$G_n a^{(n)}(t) = c^{(n)}(t), \qquad G_n \alpha^{(n)} = \gamma^{(n)}, \qquad (G_n^*)^{-1} f^{(n)}(t) = F^{(n)}(t), \tag{18.15}$$

equations (18.4) and (18.5) take thé form

$$\begin{aligned} \dot{c}^{(n)}(t) + D_n c^{(n)}(t) &= F^{(n)}(t), \\ c^{(n)}(0) &= \gamma^{(n)}. \end{aligned} \tag{18.16}$$

System (18.16) decomposes into n independent equations

$$\begin{aligned} \dot{c}_k^{(n)}(t)+\nu_k^{(n)}c_k^{(n)}(t) &= F_k^{(n)}(t), \\ c_k^{(n)}(0) &= \gamma_k^{(n)}. \end{aligned} \tag{18.16'}$$

The solutions of these equations are given by

$$c_k^{(n)}(t) = \gamma_k^{(n)}e^{-\nu_k{}^{(n)}t}+\int_0^t F_k^{(n)}(\tau)\exp(-\nu_k^{(n)}(t-\tau))d\tau, \tag{18.17}$$

$(k = 1, 2, \ldots, n)$.

The next problem is to find an upper-bound for $||A_n^{-1}||$. We assume that, in the system (18.4), $f^{(n)}(t)$ is an arbitrary vector of $\mathfrak{Y}_n$ and, on the basis of this assumption, estimate the value of $||a^{(n)}||_{\mathfrak{N}_n}$.
Using matrix notation, formula (18.17) takes the form

$$c^{(n)}(t) = e^{-D_nt}\gamma^{(n)}+\int_0^t e^{-D_n(t-\tau)}F^{(n)}(\tau)d\tau. \tag{18.17'}$$

We left-multiply both sides of (18.17′) by G_n^{-1} and replace $F^{(n)}(t)$ and $\gamma^{(n)}$ using (18.15). We obtain

$$a^{(n)}(t) = G_n^{-1}e^{-D_nt}G_n\alpha^{(n)}+\int_0^t G_n^{-1}e^{-D_n(t-\tau)}G_n^{*-1}f^{(n)}(\tau)d\tau. \tag{18.18}$$

We note that

$$||e^{-D_nt}|| = e^{-\mu_1{}^{(n)}t} \leqq 1.$$

If we assume that $0 \leqq t \leqq l$, where $l \leqq \infty$, we obtain

$$\begin{aligned} ||a^{(n}(t)||_{\mathfrak{E}_n} &\leqq \sqrt{\frac{M_0}{\mu_0}}\,||\alpha^{(n)}||_{\mathfrak{E}_n}+\frac{1}{\mu_0}\max_{0\leqq t\leqq l}||f^{(n)}(t)||_{\mathfrak{E}_n}\int_0^t e^{-\nu_0 t}dt < \\ &< \sqrt{\frac{M_0}{\mu_0}}\,||\alpha^{(n)}||_{\mathfrak{E}_n}+\frac{1}{\mu_0\nu_0}\max_{0\leqq t\leqq l}||f^{(n)}(t)||_{\mathfrak{E}_n}. \end{aligned} \tag{18.19}$$

Let $g^{(n)}$ denote the vector pair $(f^{(n)}(t), \alpha^{(n)})$ and $q_0 = \max([M_0/\mu_0]^{\frac{1}{2}}, (1/\mu_0\nu_0))$. Then

$$||a^{(n)}||_{\mathfrak{X}_n} = \max_{0\leqq t\leqq l}||a^{(n)}(t)||_{\mathfrak{E}_n} \leqq q_0\,||g^{(n)}||_{\mathfrak{Y}_n}.$$

The last inequality implies that

$$||A_n^{-1}|| \leqq q_0, \tag{18.20}$$

and hence, the norm $||A_n^{-1}||$ is bounded independently of n.
We turn to the original form for $f^{(n)}(t)$:

$$f^{(n)}(t) = ((f(t), \phi_1), (f(t), \phi_2), \ldots, (f(t), \phi_n)),$$

and prove that

$$||f^{(n)}(t)||_{\mathfrak{E}_n} \leqq L, \tag{18.21}$$

where L is a constant independent of t and n. We consider the problem of finding, w.r.t. the metric of $\mathfrak{H}$, the best approximation to $f(t)$ by a linear combination of the form

$$\sum_{k=1}^{n} \alpha_k^{(n)}(t)\phi_k.$$

Then the $\alpha_k^{(n)}(t)$ satisfy the system $\rho_n \alpha^{(n)}(t) = f^{(n)}(t)$ where $\alpha^{(n)}(t) = \{\alpha_1^{(n)}(t), \alpha_2^{(n)}(t), \ldots, \alpha_n^{(n)}(t)\}$ (see §5). On the basis of (5.6), we have

$$||\alpha^{(n)}(t)||_{\mathfrak{E}_n} \leqq \frac{1}{\sqrt{\mu_0}} ||f(t)||_{\mathfrak{H}} \leqq \frac{1}{\sqrt{\mu_0}} \max_{0 \leqq t \leqq l} ||f(t)||_{\mathfrak{H}}.$$

Since

$$||f^{(n)}(t)||_{\mathfrak{E}_n} \leqq ||\rho_n|| \, ||\alpha^{(n)}(t)|| =$$

$$= \mu_n^{(n)} ||\alpha^{(n)}(t)|| \leqq \frac{M_0}{\sqrt{\mu_0}} \max_{0 \leqq t \leqq l} ||f(t)||_{\mathfrak{H}}, \tag{18.22}$$

inequality (18.21) follows.
The vector $\alpha^{(n)}$ solves the problem, w.r.t. the metric of $\mathfrak{H}_C$, of the best approximation to an element ϕ by a linear combination of the coordinate functions $\phi_1, \phi_2, \ldots, \phi_n$. Again, on the basis of (5.6),

$$||\alpha^{(n)}||_{\mathfrak{E}_n} \leqq \frac{1}{\sqrt{\lambda_0}} |||\phi|||_C, \tag{18.23}$$

where λ_0 is a positive lower bound for the eigenvalues of the matrix R_n.
We shall make use of the notation introduced above: $g^{(n)} = (f^{(n)}(t), \alpha^{(n)})$.
Since inequalities (18.21) and (18.23) show that

$$||g^{(n)}||_{\mathfrak{Y}_n} \leqq L_1 = \text{const.},$$

it follows that

$$||a^{(n)}||_{\mathfrak{X}_n} = ||A_n^{-1} g^{(n)}||_{\mathfrak{X}_n} \leqq ||A_n^{-1}|| \, ||g^{(n)}||_{\mathfrak{Y}_n} \leqq q_0 L_1. \tag{18.24}$$

Using inequalities (18.20) and (18.24) and Theorem 17.1, we find that the process (18.4) and (18.5) is stable in the sense of (17.15′).
It is easy to obtain for the error in the approximate solution, constructed by the Bubnov-Galerkin-process, an inequality analogous to (17.15′). In fact, let the *exact* and *non-exact* approximations be, respectively,

$$u_n(t) = \sum_{k=1}^{n} a_k^{(n)}(t)\phi_k,$$

$$v_n(t) = \sum_{k=1}^{n} b_k^{(n)}(t)\phi_k.$$

Then

$$\begin{aligned}||v_n(t)-u_n(t)||_{\mathfrak{H}}^2 &= ||\sum_{k=1}^{n} [b_k^{(n)}(t)-a_k^{(n)}(t)]\phi_k||_{\mathfrak{H}}^2 = \\ &= ||\sum_{k=1}^{n} \eta_k^{(n)}(t)\phi_k||_{\mathfrak{H}}^2 = (\rho_n\eta^{(n)}(t), \eta^{(n)}(t))_{\mathfrak{E}_n} \leqq \\ &\leqq \mu_n^{(n)}||\eta^{(n)}(t)||_{\mathfrak{E}_n}^2 \leqq M_0||\eta^{(n)}(t)||_{\mathfrak{E}_n}^2,\end{aligned}$$

and, on the basis of (17.15′),

$$\begin{aligned}\max_{0\leqq t\leqq l} ||v_n(t)-u_n(t)||_{\mathfrak{H}} &\leqq \\ &\leqq \sqrt{M_0}\{p||A_n^{-1}\boldsymbol{\Gamma}_n||_{\mathfrak{X}_n\to\mathfrak{Y}_n}+q||\Delta^{(n)}||_{\mathfrak{Y}_n}\}. \qquad (18.25)\end{aligned}$$

We estimate $||A_n^{-1}\boldsymbol{\Gamma}_n||_{\mathfrak{X}_n\to\mathfrak{Y}_n}$. Let $\boldsymbol{\Gamma}_{B_n}$ and $\boldsymbol{\Gamma}_{C_n}$ denote the errors arising in the matrices ρ_n and R_n, respectively.
Following the definition given in §17, we define $x^{(n)} = x^n(t)$ by

$$\boldsymbol{\Gamma}_n x^{(n)} = (\zeta^{(n)}(t), 0),$$

where

$$\zeta^{(n)}(t) = \boldsymbol{\Gamma}_{B_n}\dot{x}^{(n)}(t)+\boldsymbol{\Gamma}_{C_n}x^{(n)}(t).$$

If we write $A_n^{-1}\boldsymbol{\Gamma}_n x^{(n)} = \xi^{(n)}(t)$, then $\xi^{(n)}(t)$ is the solution of the Cauchy-problem

$$\begin{aligned}&\boldsymbol{\rho}_n\dot{\xi}^{(n)}(t)+\boldsymbol{R}_n\xi^{(n)}(t) = \boldsymbol{\Gamma}_{B_n}\dot{x}^{(n)}(t)+\boldsymbol{\Gamma}_{C_n}x^{(n)}(t),\\ &\xi^{(n)}(0) = 0.\end{aligned}$$

Using (18.18), we have

$$\xi^{(n)}(t) = \int_0^t \boldsymbol{G}_n^{-1}e^{-D_n(t-\tau)}\boldsymbol{G}_n^{*-1}[\boldsymbol{\Gamma}_{B_n}\dot{x}^{(n)}(\tau)+\boldsymbol{\Gamma}_{C_n}x^{(n)}(\tau)]d\tau.$$

Integrating the first of the integrals on the right hand side of the last expression by parts, we obtain

$$\xi^{(n)}(t) = \rho_n^{-1}\Gamma_{B_n}x^{(n)}(t) - \int_0^t G_n^{-1}D_n e^{-D_n(t-\tau)}G_n^{*-1}\Gamma_{B_n}x^{(n)}(\tau)d\tau + \\ + \int_0^t G_n^{-1}e^{-D_n(t-\tau)}G_n^{*-1}\Gamma_{C_n}x^{(n)}(\tau)d\tau - G_n^{-1}e^{-D_n t}G_n^{*-1}\Gamma_{B_n}x_n(0).$$

As a result, it follows that

$$\begin{aligned} \|\xi^{(n)}(t)\|_{\mathfrak{E}_n} \leqq \frac{1}{\mu_0}\|\Gamma_{B_n}\|\,\|x^{(n)}(t)\|_{\mathfrak{E}_n} + \\ + \frac{1}{\mu_0}\|\Gamma_{B_n}\| \max_{0\leqq t\leqq l}\|x^{(n)}(t)\|_{\mathfrak{E}_n}\int_0^t \|D_n e^{-D_n\tau}\|d\tau + \\ + \frac{1}{\mu_0}\|\Gamma_{C_n}\| \max_{0\leqq t\leqq l}\|x^{(n)}(t)\|_{\mathfrak{E}_n}\int_0^t \|e^{-D_n\tau}\|d\tau + \\ + \frac{1}{\mu_0}\|\Gamma_{B_n}\| \max_{0\leqq t\leqq l}\|x_n(t)\|_{\mathfrak{E}_n}. \end{aligned} \tag{18.26}$$

Since,

$$\int_0^t \|e^{-D_n\tau}\|d\tau = \int_0^t e^{-\mu_1{}^{(n)}\tau}d\tau \leqq \frac{1}{\mu_0},$$

we obtain for

$$\int_0^t \|D_n e^{-D_n\tau}\|d\tau,$$

the estimate

$$\int_0^t \|D_n e^{-D_n\tau}\|d\tau \leqq \|D_n\|\int_0^t \|e^{-D_n\tau}\|d\tau = \frac{\|D_n\|}{\mu_0} = \frac{\nu_n^{(n)}}{\mu_0}. \tag{18.27}$$

This integral can also be estimated by the following procedure:
The eigenvalues of the matrix $D_n e^{-D_n\tau}$ are $\nu_k^{(n)}e^{-\nu_k{}^{(n)}\tau}$ $(k = 1, 2, \ldots, n)$, and its norm equals the largest of these numbers. Let M_k $(k = 1, 2, \ldots, n)$ denote a set of values τ such that

$$\|D_n e^{-D_n\tau}\| = \nu_k^{(n)}e^{-\nu_k{}^{(n)}\tau}.$$

Then

$$\int_0^t ||D_n e^{-D_n\tau}||d\tau \leqq \int_0^\infty ||D_n e^{-D_n\tau}||d\tau =$$
$$= \sum_{k=1}^n \int_{M_k} \nu_k^{(n)} e^{-\nu_k^{(n)}\tau} d\tau < \sum_{k=1}^n \int_0^\infty \nu_k^{(n)} e^{-\nu_k^{(n)}\tau} d\tau = n. \tag{18.28}$$

Let

$$\sigma(n) = \min\left(\frac{\nu_n^{(n)}}{\mu_0}, n\right). \tag{18.29}$$

It follows from (18.27) and (18.28) that

$$\int_0^t ||D_n e^{-D_n\tau}||d\tau \leqq \sigma(n), \tag{18.30}$$

and from (18.26) that

$$||A_n^{-1}\Gamma_n||_{\mathfrak{X}_n\to\mathfrak{Y}_n} \leqq [p' + p''\sigma(n)]||\Gamma_{B_n}||_{\mathfrak{E}_n} + p'''||\Gamma_{C_n}||_{\mathfrak{E}_n}, \tag{18.31}$$

where p', p'' and p''' are constants. Using (17.15′) and which characterises the stability of the process (18.4), (18.5), we obtain

$$||\eta^{(n)}||_{\mathfrak{X}_n} \leqq [p_1 + p_2\sigma(n)]||\Gamma_{B_n}||_{\mathfrak{E}_n} + p_3||\Gamma_{C_n}||_{\mathfrak{E}_n} +$$
$$+ p_4 \max_{0\leqq t\leqq l} ||\delta^{(n)}(t)||_{\mathfrak{E}_n} + p_5||\delta_0^{(n)}||_{\mathfrak{E}_n}, \tag{18.32}$$

where the p_i $(1 \leqq i \leqq 5)$ are constants.

We obtain in an analogous manner from (18.25) the following inequality for the error in the approximate solution:

$$\max_{0\leqq t\leqq l} ||v_n(t) - u_n(t)||_{\mathfrak{H}} \leqq$$
$$\leqq \sqrt{M_0}\{[p_1 + p_2\sigma(n)]||\Gamma_{B_n}||_{\mathfrak{E}_n} + p_3||\Gamma_{C_n}||_{\mathfrak{E}_n} +$$
$$+ p_4 \max_{0\leqq t\leqq l} ||\delta^{(n)}(t)||_{\mathfrak{E}_n} + p_5||\delta_0^{(n)}||_{\mathfrak{E}_n}\}. \tag{18.33}$$

Finally, the estimates (18.32) and (18.33) are true

$$[p' + p''\sigma(n)]||\Gamma_{B_n}||_{\mathfrak{E}_n} + p'''||\Gamma_{C_n}||_{\mathfrak{E}_n} \leqq r < 1. \tag{18.34}$$

Note. We examine the case when the coordinate system is orthonormal in $\mathfrak{H}$. The matrix $\rho_n = I_n$ can be calculated exactly and $\mathrm{F}_{B_n} = 0$. Hence, the constant coefficients of (18.32) and (18.33) are independent of n. This was the case examined in Veliev [1], [2]. Similar remarks apply to the estimates of §21.

§19. A more general equation of the first order

Here, we examine the problem of integrating the equation

$$\frac{d}{dt}Bu + Cu = f(t) \tag{19.1}$$

for the initial condition

$$u|_{t=0} = \phi. \tag{19.2}$$

We assume that the operators B and C are positive definite in the given Hilbert space $\mathfrak{H}$ and that one of the energy spaces $\mathfrak{H}_B$ or $\mathfrak{H}_C$ is contained in the other.

The case $\mathfrak{H}_C \subset \mathfrak{H}_B$ differs little from the case in §18 and the following statement, analogous to Theorem 18.1, is true: the Bubnov-Galerkin-process is stable (in the sense of the definition of §17) if the coordinate system is almost orthonormal in $\mathfrak{H}_B$. The stability holds in the interval where

$$\sup_{0 \leqq t \leqq l} \|f(t)\|_{\mathfrak{H}} < \infty. \tag{19.3}$$

This Bubnov-Galerkin process is defined by the equations

$$\begin{aligned} \rho_n \dot{a}^{(n)}(t) + R_n a^{(n)}(t) &= f^{(n)}(t), \\ a^{(n)}(0) &= \alpha^{(n)}, \end{aligned} \tag{19.4}$$

where $\rho_n = R_{B_n}$ and $R_n = R_{C_n}$, while $f^{(n)}(t)$ and $\alpha^{(n)}$ are defined as in §18. For the error $\eta^{(n)} = b^{(n)} - a^{(n)}$, formulas (17.15′) and (18.32) hold. Corresponding formulae for the error in an approximate solution are obtained from (18.25) and (18.33) by the substitution of $\max_{0 \leqslant t \leqslant 1} |||v_n(t) - u_n(t)|||_B$ on their l.h.s. We shall not dwell on the proof of our statement, since it is sufficient to repeat the argument of §18.

We single out the case when not only $\mathfrak{H}_C \subset \mathfrak{H}_B$ but also $\mathfrak{H}_B \subset \mathfrak{H}_C$: the energy spaces $\mathfrak{H}_B$ and $\mathfrak{H}_C$ consist of one and the same elements and the norms are equivalent.

Here, the numbers $v_k^{(n)}$ (equation (18.10)) are bounded above. In fact, if the $x_k^{(n)}$ are the eigenvectors of $R_n x - v_k^{(n)} \rho_n x = 0$, then

$$v_k^{(n)} = \frac{(R_n x_k^{(n)}, x_k^{(n)})}{(\rho_n x_k^{(n)}, x_k^{(n)})} = \frac{|||u|||_C^2}{|||u|||_B^2}, \qquad u = \sum_{j=1}^{n} x_{kj}^{(n)} \phi_j, \tag{19.5}$$

where $x_{kj}^{(n)}$ are the components of $x_k^{(n)}$ and the ϕ_j are the coordinate functions. Since the norms in $\mathfrak{H}_B$ and $\mathfrak{H}_C$ are equivalent, there exist constants C_1 and C_2 such that $C_1|||u|||_B \leqq |||u|||_C \leqq C_2|||u|||_B$ and $v_k^{(n)} \leqq C_2^2$.

For sufficiently large n, (18.29) yields $\sigma^{(n)} \leqq (C_2^2/\mu_0) = \text{const.}$, and instead of (18.32) and (18.33) we obtain (the notation for the constants is changed):

$$||\eta^{(n)}||_{\mathfrak{X}_n} \leqq p_1||\boldsymbol{\Gamma}_{B_n}||_{\mathfrak{C}_n}+p_2||\boldsymbol{\Gamma}_{C_n}||_{\mathfrak{C}_n}+ \\ +p_3 \max_{0\leqq t\leqq l} ||\delta^{(n)}(t)||_{\mathfrak{C}_n}+p_4||\delta_0^{(n)}||_{\mathfrak{C}_n}, \tag{19.6}$$

$$|||v_n(t)-u_n(t)|||_B \leqq \sqrt{M_0}\{p_1||\boldsymbol{\Gamma}_{B_n}||_{\mathfrak{C}_n}+p_2||\boldsymbol{\Gamma}_{C_n}||_{\mathfrak{C}_n}+ \\ +p_3 \max_{0\leqq t\leqq l} ||\delta^{(n)}(t)||_{\mathfrak{C}_n}+p_4||\delta_0^{(n)}||_{\mathfrak{C}_n}\}, \tag{19.7}$$

where the coefficients are independent of n. It follows from (18.34) that the estimates (19.6) and (19.7) are true if

$$\left(p'+p''\frac{C_2^2}{\mu_0}\right)||\boldsymbol{\Gamma}_{B_n}||_{\mathfrak{C}_n}+p'''||\boldsymbol{\Gamma}_{C_n}||_{\mathfrak{C}_n} \leqq r < 1. \tag{19.8}$$

We prove for the present case that estimates of the form (19.6) and (19.7), with only a change in the values of the constants p_i, hold for the derivatives of the errors: $\dot{\eta}^{(n)}(t)$ and $\dot{v}^{(n)}(t)-\dot{u}^{(n)}(t)$, if the norms $||\boldsymbol{\Gamma}_{B_n}||_{\mathfrak{C}_n}$ and $||\boldsymbol{\Gamma}_{C_n}||_{\mathfrak{C}_n}$ are sufficiently small. On the bais of Theorem 4.3, the coordinate system is almost orthonormal in $\mathfrak{H}_C$.It follows that the eigenvalues $\lambda_k^{(n)}$ of R_n are bounded above and below by positive numbers: $\lambda_0 \leqq \lambda_k^{(n)} \leqq \Lambda_0$. The *non-exact* Ritz-coefficients $b^{(n)}(t)$ satisfies the equation

$$(\boldsymbol{\rho}_n+\boldsymbol{\Gamma}_{B_n})\dot{b}^{(n)}(t)+(\boldsymbol{R}_n+\boldsymbol{\Gamma}_{C_n})b^{(n)}(t) = f^{(n)}(t)+\delta^{(n)}(t).$$

Subtraction of equation (19.4) from this equation yields

$$\dot{\eta}^{(n)}(t) = (\boldsymbol{\rho}_n+\boldsymbol{\Gamma}_{B_n})^{-1}\{\delta^{(n)}(t)-(\boldsymbol{R}_n+\boldsymbol{\Gamma}_{C_n})\eta^{(n)}(t)- \\ -\boldsymbol{\Gamma}_{B_n}\dot{a}^{(n)}(t)-\boldsymbol{\Gamma}_{C_n}a^{(n)}(t)\}. \tag{19.9}$$

The norms $||\boldsymbol{\Gamma}_{B_n}||_{\mathfrak{C}_n}$ and $||\boldsymbol{\Gamma}_{C_n}||_{\mathfrak{C}_n}$ satisfy the inequality (19.8). In addition, we require that $||\boldsymbol{\Gamma}_{B_n}|| \leqq r\mu_0$, where μ_0 is a positive lower bound for the eigenvalues $\mu_k^{(n)}$ of ρ_n. By (18.21) and (18.24), $||f^{(n)}(t)||_{\mathfrak{C}_n}$ and $||a^{(n)}(t)||_{\mathfrak{C}_n}$ are bounded independently of n and t. Further, $||\boldsymbol{\rho}_n^{-1}|| \leqq (1/\mu_0)$ and $||\boldsymbol{R}_n||_{\mathfrak{C}_n} \leqq \Lambda_0$ and, from (19.4), it follows that $||\dot{a}^{(n)}(t)||_{\mathfrak{C}_n}$ is bounded independently of n and t. Finally,

$$\|(\rho_n+\Gamma_{B_n})^{-1}\| \leqq \|\rho_n^{-1}\| \, \|(I_n+\rho_n^{-1}\Gamma_{B_n})^{-1}\| \leqq \frac{M_0}{1-r}.$$

Using (19.7) and (19.9), we obtain an inequality of the form

$$\begin{aligned}\|\dot{\eta}^{(n)}\|_{\mathfrak{X}_n} \leqq\; & q_1\|\Gamma_{B_n}\|_{\mathfrak{E}_n}+q_2\|\Gamma_{C_n}\|_{\mathfrak{E}_n}+ \\ & +q_3 \max_{0\leqq t\leqq l} \|\delta^{(n)}(t)\|_{\mathfrak{E}_n}+q_4\|\delta_0^{(n)}\|_{\mathfrak{E}_n},\end{aligned} \tag{19.10}$$

where the q_i are constants. Using the fact that

$$|||\dot{v}_n(t)-\dot{u}_n(t)|||_B^2 = (\rho_n\dot{\eta}^{(n)}(t), \dot{\eta}^{(n)}(t))_{\mathfrak{E}_n},$$

we find

$$\begin{aligned}|||\dot{v}_n(t)-\dot{u}_n(t)|||_B \leqq\; & \sqrt{M_0}\{q_1\|\Gamma_{B_n}\|_{\mathfrak{E}_n}+q_2\|\Gamma_{C_n}\|_{\mathfrak{E}_n}+ \\ & +q_3 \max_{0\leqq t\leqq l} \|\delta^{(n)}(t)\|_{\mathfrak{E}_n}+q_4\|\delta_0^{(n)}\|_{\mathfrak{E}_n}\}.\end{aligned} \tag{19.11}$$

We now turn to the case when $\mathfrak{H}_B \subset \mathfrak{H}_C$, but $\mathfrak{H}_C \not\subset \mathfrak{H}_B$, where we make the additional assumption that $\phi = 0$. The Bubnov-Galerkin-system (19.4) takes the form

$$\rho_n\dot{a}^{(n)}(t)+R_n a^{(n)}(t) = f^{(n)}(t), \qquad a^{(n)}(0) = 0. \tag{19.12}$$

We also assume that the spaces $\mathfrak{Y}_n$ and $\mathfrak{X}_n$ coincide. Equations (19.12) define an operator which maps from $\mathfrak{X}_n$ to $\mathfrak{Y}_n$ such that

$$A_n a^{(n)} = \rho_n a^{(n)}(t)+R_n a^{(n)}(t), \qquad a^{(n)} = a^{(n)}(t).$$

The domain of this operator consists of the vectors $a^{(n)} \in \mathfrak{X}_n$ which have continuous first derivatives w.r.t. t and equal zero for $t = 0$.

Theorem 19.1. *Let* $\mathfrak{H}_B \subset \mathfrak{H}_C$. *The process* (19.12) *is stable in the interval* $0 \leqq t \leqq l, l < \infty$, *if the coordinate system is almost orthonormal in* $\mathfrak{H}_C$ *and inequality* (19.3) *holds.*

Proof. Retaining the notation of §18, we find that (19.12) has the form

$$\dot{c}_k^{(n)}(t)+v_k^{(n)}c_k^{(n)}(t) = F_k^{(n)}(t), \qquad c_k^{(n)}(0) = 0.$$

Whence, it follows quickly that

$$a^{(n)}(t) = \int_0^t G_n^{-1}e^{-D_n(t-\tau)}(G_n^*)^{-1}f^{(n)}(\tau)d\tau. \tag{19.13}$$

On the basis of our assumptions, the norms of G_n^{-1} and $(G_n^*)^{-1}$ are bounded independently of n. In fact, since the coordinate system is strongly minimal in $\mathfrak{H}_B$, $\mu_k^{(n)} \geqq \mu_0 = \text{const.} > 0$, where the $\mu_k^{(n)}$ are the eigenvalues of ρ_n. We find, as in §18, that

$$||G_n^{-1}|| = ||G_n^{*-1}|| = \sqrt{||\rho_n^{-1}||} = \frac{1}{\sqrt{\mu_1^{(n)}}} \leqq \frac{1}{\sqrt{\mu_0}},$$

where the norms are formed w.r.t. the metric in $\mathfrak{E}_n$. Since the numbers $\nu_k^{(n)}$ are positive, $||e^{-D_n(t-\tau)}|| \leqq 1$ and

$$||a^{(n)}(t)||_{\mathfrak{E}_n} \leqq \frac{1}{\mu_0}\int_0^t ||f^{(n)}(\tau)||_{\mathfrak{E}_n} d\tau \leqq$$
$$\leqq \frac{l}{\mu_0} \max_{0 \leqq t \leqq l} ||f^{(n)}(t)||_{\mathfrak{E}_n} = \frac{l}{\mu_0} ||f^{(n)}||_{\mathfrak{X}_n}.$$

Taking the maximum of the l.h.s., we obtain

$$||a^{(n)}||_{\mathfrak{X}_n} \leqq \frac{l}{\mu_0} ||f^{(n)}||_{\mathfrak{X}_n}. \tag{19.14}$$

This inequality implies that the norms of the operators $||A_n^{-1}||$ are bounded for all n:

$$||A_n^{-1}||_{\mathfrak{X}_n} \leqq \frac{1}{\mu_0}. \tag{19.15}$$

We now prove that $||f^{(n)}||_{\mathfrak{X}_n}$ is bounded for all n. We have:

$$f^{(n)}(t) = \{(f(t), \phi_1), (f(t), \phi_2), \ldots, (f(t), \phi_n)\}.$$

Further

$$(f(t), \phi_k)_{\mathfrak{H}} = (CC^{-1}f(t), \phi_k)_{\mathfrak{H}} = [C^{-1}f(t), \phi_k]_C.$$

As in §18, we consider, w.r.t. the metric of $\mathfrak{H}_C$, the problem of the best approximation to $h(t) = C^{-1}f(t)$ by a linear combination of the form

$$\sum_{k=1}^{n} \alpha_k^{(n)}(t)\phi_k.$$

The vector $\alpha^{(n)}(t) = \{\alpha_1^{(n)}(t), \ldots, \alpha_n^{(n)}(t)\}$ satisfies $R_n\alpha^{(n)}(t) = h^{(n)}(t)$, where

$$h^{(n)}(t) = \{[h(t), \phi_1]_C, [h(t), \phi_2]_C, \ldots, [h(t), \phi_n]_C\}.$$

Since

$$[h(t), \phi_k]_C = (f(t), \phi_k),$$

$h^{(n)}(t) = f^{(n)}(t)$ and $\alpha^{(n)}(t)$ satisfies the equation $R_n \alpha^{(n)}(t) = f^{(n)}(t)$. On the basis of (5.6),

$$||\alpha^{(n)}(t)||_{\mathfrak{E}_n} \leqq \frac{1}{\sqrt{\lambda_0}} |||h(t)|||_C = \frac{1}{\sqrt{\lambda_0}} ||f(t)||_{\mathfrak{H}} \leqq \frac{1}{\sqrt{\lambda_0}} \max_{0 \leqq t \leqq l} ||f(t)||_{\mathfrak{H}}$$

and, hence,

$$||f^{(n)}(t)||_{\mathfrak{E}_n} = ||R_n^{-1} \alpha^{(n)}(t)||_{\mathfrak{E}_n} \leqq \frac{\Lambda_0}{\sqrt{\lambda_0}} \max_{0 \leqq t \leqq l} ||f(t)||.$$

Taking the maximum of the l.h.s., we obtain the required result

$$||f^{(n)}||_{\mathfrak{X}_n} \leqq \frac{\Lambda_0}{\sqrt{\lambda_0}} \max_{0 \leqq t \leqq l} ||f(t)|| = \text{const}.$$

It follows from (19.14) that $||a^{(n)}||_{\mathfrak{X}_n}$ is bounded for all n, while the stability of the process (19.12) is an immediate consequence of Theorem 17.1.

We prove, for the error $\eta^{(n)}(t)$, that the vector of Ritz-coefficients satisfies an estimate of the form (19.6) with the term $p_4 ||\delta_0^{(n)}||_{\mathfrak{E}_n}$ missing. For this purpose we estimate the norm $||A_n^{-1} \Gamma_n||$, where the operator Γ_n maps from $\mathfrak{X}_n$ into $\mathfrak{X}_n$. If we put $\Gamma_n x^{(n)} = \zeta^{(n)}$, then

$$\zeta^{(n)}(t) = \Gamma_{B_n} \dot{x}^{(n)}(t) + \Gamma_{C_n} x^{(n)}(t).$$

Let $A_n^{-1} \Gamma_n x^{(n)} = \xi^{(n)}$. If we repeat the argument of §18, then we obtain again the estimates (18.26) and (18.27). However, since the numbers $v_k^{(n)}$ are bounded (see (19.5)) for the present case, it follows from the above estimates that

$$||A_n^{-1} \Gamma_n|| \leqq p' ||\Gamma_{B_n}||_{\mathfrak{E}_n} + p'' ||\Gamma_{C_n}||_{\mathfrak{E}_n}, \qquad p', p'' = \text{const}.$$

On the basis of this last inequality, we can easily obtain

$$||\eta^{(n)}||_{\mathfrak{X}_n} \leqq p_1 ||\Gamma_{B_n}||_{\mathfrak{E}_n} + p_2 ||\Gamma_{C_n}||_{\mathfrak{E}_n} + p_3 \max_{0 \leqq t \leqq l} ||\delta^{(n)}(t)||_{\mathfrak{E}_n}. \qquad (19.16)$$

Since

$$|||v_n(t) - u_n(t)|||_C^2 = (R_n \eta^{(n)}(t), \eta^{(n)}(t))_{\mathfrak{E}_n},$$

we obtain finally

$$|||v_n(t)-u_n(t)|||_C \leqq \sqrt{\Lambda_0}\{p_1||\Gamma_{B_n}||_{\mathfrak{E}_n}+p_2||\Gamma_{C_n}||_{\mathfrak{E}_n}+ + p_3 \max_{0\leqq t\leqq l} ||\delta^{(n)}(t)||_{\mathfrak{E}_n}\}, \tag{19.17}$$

where Λ_0 is an upper bound for the eigenvalues of R_n.

§20. The S. L. Sobolev equations

We return to the problem in §17 and develop sufficient conditions for the stability of the process (17.6′) and (17.7′). We limit considerations to the simplest case when the metrics in the spaces $\mathfrak{H}_A$, $\mathfrak{H}_B$ and $\mathfrak{H}_C$ are equivalent, and hence, these spaces consist of one and the same elements. For the sake of conciseness, we assume that the vectors $\alpha^{(n)}$ and $\beta^{(n)}$, which arise in the initial conditions (17.1′), are defined by (17.10′) and (17.10″).

Theorem 20.1. *If the metrics in* $\mathfrak{H}_A$, $\mathfrak{H}_B$ and $\mathfrak{H}_C$ *are equivalent and the coordinate system is almost orthonormal in one of these spaces, then the process* (17.6′) and (17.7′) *is stable for any finite interval of t-values.*

Proof. Let $\kappa_k^{(n)}$, $\mu_k^{(n)}$ and $\lambda_k^{(n)}$ denote the eigenvalues of the matrices R_{A_n}, R_{B_n} and R_{C_n}, respectively. Since the coordinate system is almost orthonormal in $\mathfrak{H}_A$, $\mathfrak{H}_B$ and $\mathfrak{H}_C$, these eigenvalues are bounded above and below by positive numbers:

$$\kappa_0 \leqq \kappa_k^{(n)} \leqq K_0, \qquad \mu_0 \leqq \mu_k^{(n)} \leqq M_0, \qquad \lambda_0 \leqq \lambda_k^{(n)} \leqq \Lambda_0, \tag{20.1}$$

where κ_0, K_0, μ_0, M_0, λ_0 and Λ_0 are const. (>0).
We seek an estimate of $||A_n^{-1}||$, where A_n is the operator introduced in §17. As in §18, we obtain

$$R_{A_n} = G_n^* G_n, \qquad R_{B_n} = G_n^* D_n G_n, \qquad D_n = [\nu_1^{(n)}, \nu_2^{(n)}, \ldots, \nu_n^{(n)}].$$

As before, the norms of G_n and G_n^{-1} are bounded:

$$||G_n|| = ||G_n^*|| \leqq \sqrt{M_0}, \qquad ||G_n^{-1}|| = ||G_n^{*-1}|| \leqq \frac{1}{\sqrt{\mu_0}}.$$

It is easy to prove (see §19) that the numbers $\nu_k^{(n)}$ are bounded above and below by positive numbers. In fact, let

$$0 < \nu_0 \leqq \nu_k^{(n)} \leqq N_0, \qquad \nu_0, N_0 = \text{const.} \tag{20.2}$$

We also write

$$G_n a^{(n)}(t) = c^{(n)}(t), \qquad G_n \alpha^{(n)} = \gamma^{(n)}, \qquad G_n \beta^{(n)} = \tilde{\gamma}^{(n)},$$
$$G_n^{*-1} f^{(n)}(t) = F^{(n)}(t). \tag{20.3}$$

Equations (17.6′) and (17.7′) become

$$\begin{aligned} &\ddot{c}^{(n)}(t) + D_n \dot{c}^{(n)}(t) + P_n c^{(n)}(t) = F^{(n)}(t), \\ &c^{(n)}(0) = \gamma^{(n)}, \qquad \dot{c}^{(n)}(0) = \tilde{\gamma}^{(n)}, \end{aligned} \tag{20.4}$$

where

$$P_n = G_n^{*-1} R_{C_n} G_n^{-1}. \tag{20.5}$$

It is not difficult to see that the matrix P_n is positive definite and that its eigenvalues, which we denote by $\theta_k^{(n)}$, are bounded above and below by positive numbers. In fact, let

$$0 < \theta_0 \leqq \theta_k^{(n)} \leqq \Theta_0, \tag{20.6}$$

where θ_0 and Θ_0 are const.
We integrate both sides of the first equation in (20.4) w.r.t. t over the interval $(0, l)$. Taking the remaining equations in (20.4) into account, we obtain

$$\dot{c}^{(n)}(t) + D_n c^{(n)}(t) = \int_0^t F^{(n)}(\tau) d\tau + \tilde{\gamma}^{(n)} + D_n \tilde{\gamma}^{(n)} - \int_0^t P_n c^{(n)}(\tau) d\tau,$$

whence follows a result analogous to (18.17′):

$$c^{(n)}(t) = e^{-D_n t} \gamma^{(n)} + \int_0^t e^{-D_n(t-\tau)} \left[\tilde{\gamma}^{(n)} + D_n \gamma^{(n)} + \int_0^\tau F^{(n)}(\tau_1) d\tau_1 - \right.$$
$$\left. - \int_0^\tau P_n c^{(n)}(\tau_1) d\tau_1 \right] d\tau.$$

This expression can easily be reduced to the following (vector) integral equation of Volterra type

$$c^{(n)}(t) + \int_0^t K_n(t-\tau) c^{(n)}(\tau) d\tau = \Phi^{(n)}(t), \tag{20.7}$$

where

$$K_n(t) = D_n^{-1}(I_n - e^{-D_n t}) P_n, \tag{20.8}$$

$$\Phi^{(n)}(t) = \gamma^{(n)} + \boldsymbol{D}_n^{-1}(\boldsymbol{I}_n - e^{-D_n t})\tilde{\gamma}^{(n)} + \int_0^t \boldsymbol{D}_n^{-1}(\boldsymbol{I}_n - e^{-D_n(t-\tau)})F^{(n)}(\tau)d\tau. \tag{20.9}$$

Equation (20.7) can be solved by a sequence of approximations, and it is not difficult to give an estimate for its solution. First of all,

$$||\boldsymbol{K}_n(t)|| \leqq ||\boldsymbol{D}_n^{-1}||\,||\boldsymbol{I}_n - \mathrm{e}^{-D_n t}||\,||\boldsymbol{P}_n|| =$$
$$= \frac{1}{\nu_1^{(n)}}(1 - \mathrm{e}^{-\nu_1^{(n)}t})\theta_n^{(n)} \leqq q, \quad q = \frac{\theta_0}{\nu_0}.$$

Further,

$$||\Phi^{(n)}(t)||_{\mathfrak{E}_n} \leqq ||\gamma^{(n)}|| + \frac{1}{\nu_1^{(n)}}(1 - e^{-\nu_n^{(n)}t})||\tilde{\gamma}^{(n)}|| +$$
$$+ \frac{l}{\nu_1^{(n)}} \max_{0 \leqq t \leqq l} ||F^{(n)}(t)|| \leqq ||\gamma^{(n)}|| + \frac{1}{\nu_0}||\tilde{\gamma}^{(n)}|| + \frac{l}{\nu_0} \max_{0 \leqq t \leqq l} ||F^{(n)}(t)||_{\mathfrak{E}_n}.$$

Denoting the quantity on the r.h.s. by σ_n, we have

$$||\Phi^{(n)}(t)|| \leqq \sigma_n.$$

The solution of (20.7) has the form

$$c^{(n)}(t) = \sum_{m=0}^{\infty} (-1)^m c^{(n,m)}(t),$$

where

$$c^{(n,0)}(t) = \Phi^{(n)}(t), \qquad c^{(n,m)}(t) = \int_0^t \boldsymbol{K}_n(t-\tau)c^{(n,m-1)}(\tau)d\tau.$$

Consequently, we obtain the estimates

$$||c^{(n,m)}(t)||_{\mathfrak{E}_n} \leqq \frac{\sigma_n q^m t^m}{m!}$$

and

$$||c^{(n)}(t)||_{\mathfrak{E}_n} \leqq \sigma_n e^{qt} \leqq \sigma_n e^{ql}.$$

Since

$$||a^{(n)}(t)||_{\mathfrak{E}_n} = ||\boldsymbol{G}_n^{-1}c^{(n)}(t)||_{\mathfrak{E}_n} \leqq \sigma_n \frac{e^{ql}}{\sqrt{\mu_0}},$$

if we take the maximum of the l.h.s., we obtain

$$||a^{(n)}||_{\mathfrak{X}_n} = \max_{0\leq t\leq l} ||a^{(n)}(t)||_{\mathfrak{E}_n} \leqq \sigma_n \frac{e^{ql}}{\sqrt{\mu_0}} . \qquad \text{t20.10)}$$

Further, using (20.3),

$$\sigma_n = ||G_n\alpha^{(n)}|| + \frac{1}{\nu_0}||G_n\beta^{(n)}|| + \frac{l}{\nu_0}\max_{0\leq t\leq l}||G_n^{*-1}f^{(n)}(t)||_{\mathfrak{E}_n} \leqq$$

$$\leqq \sqrt{M_0}||\alpha^{(n)}|| + \frac{\sqrt{M_0}}{\nu_0}||\beta^{(n)}|| + \frac{l}{\nu_0\sqrt{\mu_0}}\max_{0\leq t\leq l}||f^{(n)}(t)||_{\mathfrak{E}_n}.$$

Let

$$q_1 = \max\left\{\sqrt{M_0}, \frac{\sqrt{M_0}}{\nu_0}, \frac{l}{\nu\sqrt{\mu_0}}\right\}$$

and $g^{(n)}$ denote the vector triple $(f^{(n)}(t), \alpha^{(n)}, \beta^{(n)})$. Then $g^{(n)}$ lies in the space $\mathfrak{Y}_n$ and

$$\sigma_n \leqq q_1||g^{(n)}||_{\mathfrak{Y}_n}.$$

Using the estimate (20.10), it follows that

$$||a^{(n)}||_{\mathfrak{X}_n} \leqq q_2||g^{(n)}||_{\mathfrak{Y}_n}, \qquad q_2 = \frac{q_1 e^{ql}}{\sqrt{\mu_0}} = \text{const.}$$

The last inequality implies that

$$||A_n^{-1}|| \leqq q_2,$$

where A_n is the operator defined in §17 which maps $a^{(n)} \in \mathfrak{X}_n$ into the vector triple $g^{(n)}$.

Repeating the argument of §18 under the same conditions, we find that the norms $||a^{(n)}||_{\mathfrak{X}_n}$ are bounded for all n. Thus, Theorem 20.1 follows from Theorem 17.1.

For the error $\eta^{(n)}(t) = b^{(n)}(t) - a^{(n)}(t)$, it is not difficult to obtain

$$||\eta^{(n)}||_{\mathfrak{X}_n} \leqq p_1||\Gamma_{A_n}|| + p_2||\Gamma_{B_n}|| + p_3||\Gamma_{C_n}|| + p_4\max_{0\leq t\leq l}||\delta^{(n)}(t)|| +$$
$$+ p_5||\delta_0^{(n)}|| + p_6||\delta_1^{(n)}||, \qquad (20.11)$$

where the p_i are constants and the norms on the r.h.s. are evaluated w.r.t. the metric of $\mathfrak{E}_n$. Analogous inequalities can be established for

$$||\dot{\eta}^{(n)}||_{\mathfrak{X}_n}, \; |||v_n(t)-u_n(t)||| \quad \text{and} \quad |||\dot{v}_n(t)-\dot{u}_n(t)|||,$$

where the symbol $|||\ |||$ denotes the norm in any one of the spaces $\mathfrak{H}_A$, $\mathfrak{H}_B$ or $\mathfrak{H}_C$.

§21. Equations of hyperbolic type

The condition that the metrics in $\mathfrak{H}_A$, $\mathfrak{H}_B$ and $\mathfrak{H}_C$ be equivalent, assumed in §20, is not necessary for the stability of the Bubnov-Galerkin-process of the Sobolev equations. We clarify this for the hyperbolic equation

$$\frac{d^2u}{dt^2}+B\frac{du}{dt}+Cu=f(t), \tag{21.1}$$

with the initial condition

$$u|_{t=0}=\phi, \qquad \dot{u}\,|_{t=0}=\psi. \tag{21.2}$$

We assume that B is a non-negative constant and that C is a positive definite operator.
The Bubnov-Galerkin-system has the vector form

$$\rho_n\ddot{a}^{(n)}(t)+B\rho_n\dot{a}^{(n)}(t)+R_n a^{(n)}(t)=f^{(n)}(t), \tag{21.3}$$

$$a^{(n)}(0)=\alpha^{(n)}, \qquad \dot{a}^{(n)}(0)=\beta^{(n)}, \tag{21.4}$$

where

$$\rho_n=||(\phi_k,\phi_j)||_{j,k=1}^{j,k=n}, \qquad R_n=||[\phi_k,\phi_j]_C||_{j,k=1}^{j,k=n}$$

and $f^n(t)$ has the same value as in the previous sections. The vectors $\alpha^{(n)}$ and $\beta^{(n)}$ are defined by

$$R_n\alpha^{(n)}=\phi^{(n)}, \qquad R_n\beta^{(n)}=\psi^{(n)}, \tag{21.5}$$

where the vectors $\phi^{(n)}$ and $\psi^{(n)}$ are defined by

$$\begin{aligned}\phi^{(n)}&=\{[\phi,\phi_1]_C,[\phi,\phi_2]_C,\dots,[\phi,\phi_n]_C\},\\ \psi^{(n)}&=\{[\psi,\phi_1]_C,[\psi,\phi_2]_C,\dots,[\psi,\phi_n]_C\}.\end{aligned} \tag{21.6}$$

We now prove

Theorem 21.1. *Let the coordinate system be almost orthonormal in the given Hilbert space* $\mathfrak{H}$ *and*

$$\max_{0\leq t\leq l}||f(t)||<\infty, \tag{21.7}$$

where $l < \infty$. Then the process (21.3) *and* (21.4) *is stable* (*in the sense of the definition in* §17) *in the interval* $0 \leqq t \leqq l$. *If* $B > 0$, *then the process* (21.3) *and* (21.4) *is stable in the interval* $0 \leqq t < \infty$.

Proof. For simplicity of presentation, we introduce an additional assumption which is discussed below. Writing

$$a^{(n)}(t) = e^{-(B/2)t}\tilde{a}^{(n)}(t), \tag{21.8}$$

system (21.3) and (21.4) becomes

$$\begin{aligned} &\rho_n \ddot{\tilde{a}}^{(n)}(t) + \left(R_n - \frac{B^2}{4}\rho_n\right)\tilde{a}^{(n)}(t) = e^{(B/2)t}f^{(n)}(t), \\ &\tilde{a}^{(n)}(0) = \alpha^{(n)}, \qquad \dot{\tilde{a}}^{(n)}(0) = \frac{B}{2}\alpha^{(n)} + \beta^{(n)}. \end{aligned} \tag{21.9}$$

As in the previous sections, we put

$$\rho_n = G_n^* G_n, \qquad R_n = G_n^* D_n G_n, \qquad D_n = [\nu_1^{(n)}, \nu_2^{(n)}, \ldots, \nu_n^{(n)}],$$

where $\nu_k^{(n)} \geqq \nu_0 = \text{const.} > 0$. *We assume hereafter that* $\nu_0 > (B^2/4)$. On writing

$$G_n \tilde{a}^{(n)}(t) = c^{(n)}(t), \qquad G_n \alpha^{(n)} = \gamma^{(n)}, \qquad G_n\left(\frac{B}{2}\alpha^{(n)} + \beta^{(n)}\right) = \tilde{\gamma}^{(n)},$$
$$e^{(B/2)t} G_n^{*-1} f^{(n)}(t) = F^{(n)}(t),$$

problem (21.9) takes the form

$$\begin{aligned} &\ddot{c}^{(n)}(t) + \left(D_n - \frac{B^2}{4} I_n\right) c^{(n)}(t) = F^{(n)}(t), \\ &c^{(n)}(0) = \gamma^{(n)}, \qquad \dot{c}^{(n)}(0) = \tilde{\gamma}^{(n)}, \end{aligned}$$

with the solution

$$\begin{aligned} c^{(n)}(t) &= \cos\left(\left(D_n - \frac{B^2}{4} I_n\right)^{\frac{1}{2}} t\right)\gamma^{(n)} + \\ &+ \left(D_n - \frac{B^2}{4} I_n\right)^{-\frac{1}{2}} \sin\left(\left(D_n - \frac{B^2}{4} I_n\right)^{\frac{1}{2}} t\right)\tilde{\gamma}^{(n)} + \\ &+ \left(D_n - \frac{B^2}{4} I_n\right)^{-\frac{1}{2}} \int_0^t \sin\left(D_n - \frac{B^2}{4} I_n\right)^{\frac{1}{2}} (t-\tau) F^{(n)}(\tau)\, d\tau. \end{aligned} \tag{21.10}$$

We shall develop an estimate for $c^{(n)}(t)$.

Since $(B^2/4) < v_0$, the matrix $D_n - (B^2/4)I_n$ is positive definite:

$$\left\| \cos\left(D_n - \frac{B^2}{4} I_n\right)^{\frac{1}{2}} t \right\| \leqq 1,$$

$$\left\| \left(D_n - \frac{B^2}{4} I_n\right)^{-\frac{1}{2}} \sin\left(D_n - \frac{B^2}{4} I_n\right)^{\frac{1}{2}} t \right\| \leqq t,$$

and it follows from (21.10) that

$$\begin{aligned} \|c^{(n)}(t)\|_{\mathfrak{E}_n} &\leqq \|\gamma^{(n)}\| + t\|\tilde{\gamma}^{(n)}\| + \int_0^t (t-\tau)\|F^{(n)}(\tau)\| d\tau \leqq \\ &\leqq \|\gamma^{(n)}\| + t\|\tilde{\gamma}^{(n)}\| + \frac{t^2}{2} \max_{0 \leqq t \leqq l} \|F^{(n)}(t)\|_{\mathfrak{E}_n}. \end{aligned} \tag{21.11}$$

If $l < \infty$, then

$$\|c^{(n)}(t)\|_{\mathfrak{E}_n} \leqq \|\gamma^{(n)}\| + l\|\tilde{\gamma}^{(n)}\| + \frac{l^2}{2} \max_{0 \leqq t \leqq l} \|F^{(n)}(t)\|_{\mathfrak{E}_n}.$$

Since $\|G_n\|$ and $\|G_n^{-1}\|$ are bounded,

$$\|c^{(n)}(t)\|_{\mathfrak{E}_n} \leqq q\|g^{(n)}\|_{\mathfrak{Y}_n}, \tag{21.12}$$

where q is a constant, $g^{(n)}$ is the vector triple $(f^{(n)}(t), \alpha^{(n)}, \beta^{(n)})$ and $\mathfrak{Y}_n$ is the space introduced in §17. Further,

$$\|a^{(n)}(t)\|_{\mathfrak{E}_n} = \|e^{-(B/2)t} G_n c^{(n)}(t)\| \leqq \|G_n\| \, \|c^{(n)}(t)\|_{\mathfrak{E}_n} \leqq q_1\|g^{(n)}\|_{\mathfrak{Y}_n},$$

where q_1 = const., and hence,

$$\|a^{(n)}\|_{\mathfrak{X}_n} = \max_{0 \leqslant t \leqslant l} \|a^{(n)}(t)\|_{\mathfrak{E}_n} \leqq q_1\|g^{(n)}\|_{\mathfrak{Y}_n}. \tag{21.13}$$

In this way, the first condition of Theorem 17.1 is fulfilled. Using the same argument of the previous sections in this chapter, we find that $\|g^{(n)}\|_{\mathfrak{Y}_n}$ is bounded, and, on the basis of (21.13), $\|a^{(n)}\|_{\mathfrak{X}_n}$ is bounded so that the second condition in Theorem 17.1 is fulfilled. Hence, the theorem is proved for $l < \infty$.

Letting $l = \infty$, we assume that $B > 0$. On the strength of (21.11), we obtain

$$\begin{aligned} \|a^{(n)}(t)\|_{\mathfrak{E}_n} &\leqq \|G_n\| e^{-\frac{1}{2}Bt} \|c^{(n)}(t)\| \leqq \\ &\leqq \|G_n\| \left\{ \|\gamma^{(n)}\| + \frac{2}{Be} \|\tilde{\gamma}^{(n)}\| + \frac{8}{B^2 e^2} \max_{0 \leqq t \leqq l} \|F^{(n)}(t)\|_{\mathfrak{E}_n} \right\}, \end{aligned}$$

which implies immediately that $a^{(n)}$ satisfies an inequality of the form (12.13). The subsequent argument follows as above.

Chapter IV

THE RESIDUAL OF AN APPROXIMATE SOLUTION

The question, discussed in this chapter, is connected with the application of the Ritz-process to the functional derived for the energy method. Consider the equation

$$Au = f, \tag{IV.1}$$

where A is a positive definite operator in a Hilbert space $\mathfrak{H}$, and let the approximations

$$u_n = \sum_{k=1}^{n} a_k^{(n)} \phi_k \tag{IV.2}$$

to the exact solution u_0 of (IV.1) be constructed by the Ritz-process. The way in which u_n satisfies (IV.1) is, in the general case, devoid of sense: if the coordinate system, and hence u_n, does not lie in $\mathfrak{D}(A)$, then u_n can not be substituted into (IV.1). However, even if $\phi_n \in \mathfrak{D}(A)$, $Au_n \nrightarrow f$. What is more, if for an arbitrary choice of $\{\phi_n\} \in \mathfrak{D}(A)$, $Au_n \to_{n\to\infty} f$, then A is bounded (see PM, Chapter 1, §8).
However, for a special choice of coordinate system, we can show that the residual of the approximate solution, $Au_n - f$, tends to zero for $n \to \infty$ even when the operator A is unbounded. Such a system has been determined by Mikhlin [11] when A has a discrete spectrum. A number of generalisation can be found in Bogaryan [1]. A far deeper result was obtained by Vainikko [2], who also corrected an error in Mikhlin [11]. When differential operators and polynomial coordinate functions are considered, Mikhlin [23] can be used to obtain a general condition for the residual to converge to zero. It is pertinent to note that the method of Mikhlin [23] is closely related to the earlier method of Daugavet [1], [2], [3] who examined only one-dimensional differential operators and obtained some weaker results.
In the present chapter, a detailed account of the results of Mikhlin [11], [23] is presented – Vainikko's very simple proof of the theorem in Mikhlin [11] is given.

§22. A residual theorem

Theorem 22.1. *Let* $\boldsymbol{A}$ *and* $\boldsymbol{B}$ *be similar positive definite operators with domains in the separable Hilbert space* $\mathfrak{H}$ *and* $\boldsymbol{B}$ *have a discrete spectrum. If the system* $\{\phi_k\}$ *of eigenelements of* $\boldsymbol{B}$ *are taken as coordinate elements for the equation.*

$$Au = f \tag{22.1}$$

and if (for simplicity, we write a_k instead of $a_k^{(n)}$)

$$u_n = \sum_{k=1}^{n} a_k \phi_k$$

is the nth *Ritz-approximation to the exact solution of* (22.1), *then the residual* $(Au_n - f)$ *converges to zero as* $n \to \infty$.

Proof. Let $\{\mu_k\}$ denote the eigenvalues of $\boldsymbol{B}$, corresponding to the eigenfunctions ϕ_k, such that $\boldsymbol{B}\phi_k = \mu_k \phi_k$. As usual, we write μ_k in ascending order of magnitude. Let $\boldsymbol{P}_n$ be the operator of orthogonal projection (w.r.t. the metric of $\mathfrak{H}$) which maps onto the subspace $\mathfrak{H}_n$ spanned by the elements $\phi_1, \phi_2, \ldots, \phi_n$, and $\boldsymbol{P}^{(n)} = \boldsymbol{I} - \boldsymbol{P}_n$. For arbitrary $\alpha > 0$, the operators $\boldsymbol{P}_n$ and $\boldsymbol{B}^\alpha$ commute and

$$||\boldsymbol{B}^\alpha \boldsymbol{P}_n|| = \mu_n^\alpha, \qquad ||\boldsymbol{B}^{-\alpha} \boldsymbol{P}^{(n)}|| = \mu_{n+1}^{-\alpha}. \tag{22.3}$$

Let u_0 be the exact solution of (22.1). Since, as was proved in §6, the approximate Ritz-solution u_n gives in $\mathfrak{H}_n$ the best approximation to u_0 (w.r.t. the metric in $\mathfrak{H}_{\boldsymbol{A}}$):

$$\begin{aligned} |||u_0 - u_n|||_{\boldsymbol{A}} &\leqq |||u_0 - \boldsymbol{P}_n u_0|||_{\boldsymbol{A}} = |||\boldsymbol{P}^{(n)} u_0|||_{\boldsymbol{A}} = \\ &= ||\boldsymbol{A}^{\frac{1}{2}} \boldsymbol{P}^{(n)} u_0|| \leqq ||\boldsymbol{A}^{\frac{1}{2}} \boldsymbol{B}^{-\frac{1}{2}}||\ ||\boldsymbol{B}^{\frac{1}{2}} \boldsymbol{P}^{(n)} u_0||. \end{aligned}$$

Further,

$$||\boldsymbol{B}^{\frac{1}{2}} \boldsymbol{P}^{(n)} u_0|| = ||\boldsymbol{B}^{-\frac{1}{2}} \boldsymbol{P}^{(n)} \boldsymbol{P}^{(n)} \boldsymbol{B} u_0|| \leqq ||\boldsymbol{B}^{-\frac{1}{2}} \boldsymbol{P}^{(n)}||\ ||\rho^{(n)} \boldsymbol{B} u_0||.$$

Hence

$$|||u_0 - u_n|||_{\boldsymbol{A}} \leqq \mu_{n+1}^{-\frac{1}{2}} ||\boldsymbol{A}^{\frac{1}{2}} \boldsymbol{B}^{-\frac{1}{2}}||\ ||\boldsymbol{P}^{(n)} \boldsymbol{B} u_0||.$$

On the other hand,

$$||\boldsymbol{B}^{\frac{1}{2}}(u_0 - u_n)|| \leqq ||\boldsymbol{B}^{\frac{1}{2}} \boldsymbol{A}^{-\frac{1}{2}}||\ ||(u_0 - u_n)|| = ||\boldsymbol{B}^{\frac{1}{2}} \boldsymbol{A}^{-\frac{1}{2}}||\ |||u_0 - u_n|||_{\boldsymbol{A}}.$$

Comparing this with the previous inequality, we obtain

$$||B^{\frac{1}{2}}(u_0-u_n)|| \leqq C\mu_{n+1}^{-\frac{1}{2}}||P^{(n)}Bu_0||, \tag{22.4}$$

where, for the sake of brevity, we write

$$C = ||A^{\frac{1}{2}}B^{-\frac{1}{2}}||\ ||B^{\frac{1}{2}}A^{-\frac{1}{2}}||.$$

If $u \in \mathfrak{H}_n$, then $P^{(n)}u = 0$ and it follows that

$$\begin{aligned} B(u_0-u_n) &= B(P_n+P^{(n)})(u_0-u_n) \\ &= B^{\frac{1}{2}}P_nB^{\frac{1}{2}}(u_0-u_n)+BP^{(n)}u_0. \end{aligned}$$

As a result of (22.3) and (22.4), we obtain

$$||B(u_0-u_n)|| \leqq \left[C\sqrt{\frac{\mu_n}{\mu_{n+1}}}+1\right]||P^{(n)}Bu_0|| \leqq (C+1)||P^{(n)}Bu_0||,$$

and hence,

$$\begin{aligned} ||Au_n-f|| &= ||A(u_n-u_0)|| \leqq ||AB^{-1}||\ ||B(u_n-u_0)|| \\ &\leqq ||AB^{-1}||(C+1)||P^{(n)}Bu_0|| \underset{n\to\infty}{\to} 0, \end{aligned}$$

which proves the theorem.

§23. Non-degenerate ordinary differential operators of the second order

In this and the next section, we shall examine some classes of differential operators for which we can select comparatively simple similar operators. Here we examine the problem

$$-\frac{d}{dx}\left(p(x)\frac{du}{dx}\right)+q(x)u = f(x), \tag{23.1}$$

$$u(0) = u(1) = 0, \tag{23.2}$$

for the simplest assumptions relation to $p(x)$ and $q(x)$. We assume that $p(x)$, $p'(x)$ and $q(x)$ are continuous for $0 \leqq x \leqq 1$, that $p(x) \geqq p_0 =$ const. >0, and

$$q(x) > -\mu_1,$$

where μ_1 is the smallest eigenvalue of

$$-\frac{d}{dx}\left(p\frac{du}{dx}\right)$$

w.r.t. the boundary condition (23.2). The l.h.s. of (23.1) and the boundary condition (23.2) define an operator which we denote by $\tilde{A}$ and which acts in the space $\mathfrak{H} = L_2(0,1)$. This operator is defined by

$$\tilde{A}u = -\frac{d}{dx}\left(p(x)\frac{du}{dx}\right) + q(x)u,$$

with $\mathfrak{D}(\tilde{A})$ the set of functions which are twice continuously differentiable on the interval $0 \leqq x \leqq 1$ and equal to zero at its ends. Since the operator $\tilde{A}$ is positive definite (see VM, §20), it possesses a selfadjoint Friedrichs extension which we denote by A (see Friedrichs [1] and PM, §5). We recall that the generalised solution of (23.1) and (23.2), to which the energy method leads, is indeed the solution of $Au = f$.

We examine the set of functions which are contained in $\mathfrak{D}(A)$. As is known (see Friedrichs [1] and PM, §5), it consists of the different generalised solutions of (23.1) and (23.2) corresponding to the different functions $f \in L_2$ (0,1). Such solutions lie in the energy space $\mathfrak{H}_A$ corresponding to our problem.

Starting with the formula (see VM, §20)

$$|||u|||_A^2 = \int_0^1 (p(x)|u'(x)|^2 + q(x)|u(x)|^2)dx, \tag{23.3}$$

it is easy to prove that the space $\mathfrak{H}_A$ consists of the functions which, on the interval $0 \leqq x \leqq 1$, are absolutely continuous, have square summable first derivatives and satisfy (23.2). Conversely, every function which satisfies the above conditions lies in $\mathfrak{H}_A$.

Since the generalised solution of (23.1) and (23.2), corresponding to a given f, yields in $\mathfrak{H}_A$ the minimum of the functional

$$F(u) = |||u|||_A^2 - 2\,\mathrm{Re}\,(u,f) =$$
$$= \int_0^1 \{p(x)|u'(x)|^2 + q(x)|u(x)|^2 - 2\,\mathrm{Re}\,(f(x)u(x))\}dx,$$

$F(u_0+\eta) \geqq F(u_0)$, where η is an arbitrary function of $\mathfrak{H}_A$.

It follows from this that

$$\mathrm{Re}\,\{[u_0, \eta]_A - (f, \eta)\} + |||\eta|||_A^2 \geqq 0,$$

and hence, that $\operatorname{Re}\{[u_0, \eta]_A - (f, \eta)\} = 0$. Replacing η by $i\eta$, where $i = \sqrt{-1}$, we find that $\operatorname{Im}\{[u_0, \eta]_A - (f, \eta)\} = 0$, and, finally,

$$[u_0, \eta]_A - (f, \eta) = 0, \qquad \eta \in \mathfrak{H}_A. \tag{23.4}$$

It follows from (23.4) that, at the minimum, the variation of the functional F equals zero. For the given problem, (23.4) becomes

$$\int_0^1 \{p(x)u_0'(x)\overline{\eta'(x)} + [q(x)u_0(x) - f(x)]\overline{\eta(x)}\}dx = 0. \tag{23.5}$$

The second term can be transformed in the following way

$$\int_0^1 [q(x)u_0(x) - f(x)]\overline{\eta(x)}dx =$$
$$= \int_0^1 \overline{\eta(x)} \frac{d}{dx}\left(\int_0^x [q(t)u_0(t) - f(t)]dt\right) dx =$$
$$= \int_0^1 \overline{\eta'(x)} \int_0^x [q(t)u_0(t) - f(t)]dt\,dx,$$

where the integrated terms vanish since $\eta \in \mathfrak{H}_A$ implies that $\eta(0) = \eta(1) = 0$. Hence, (23.5) becomes

$$\int_0^1 \overline{\eta'(x)}\left\{p(x)u_0'(x) - \int_0^x [q(t)u_0(t) - f(t)]dt\right\} dx = 0. \tag{23.5'}$$

Since the derivative $\eta'(x)$ satisfies

$$\int_0^1 \eta'(x)dx = \eta(1) - \eta(0) = 0,$$

it lies in the subspace $\tilde{L}_2(0,1)$ of $L_2(0,1)$ which is orthogonal to unity. The converse is also obvious: every function in $\tilde{L}_2(0,1)$ can be represented as the derivative of a function which is an element of $\mathfrak{H}_A$. In fact, if $\zeta \in \tilde{L}_2(0,1)$, then

$$\int_0^1 \zeta(x)dx = 0,$$

and the function

$$\eta(x) = \int_0^x \zeta(t)dt$$

is absolutely continuous on the interval [0,1], has almost everywhere the derivative $\eta'(x) = \zeta(x)$ which is square summable on this interval, and $\eta(0) = \eta(1) = 0$. Since (23.5′) implies that the expression in braces is orthogonal to the functions in L_2 (0,1), it follows that

$$p(x)u_0'(x) - \int_0^x [q(t)u_0(t) - f(t)]dt = \text{const.} \tag{23.6}$$

From (23.6), it is clear that if $u_0 \in \mathfrak{D}(A)$, then the first derivative $u_0'(x)$ is absolutely continuous, the second derivative $u_0''(x)$ is square summable and the differential equation

$$-\frac{d}{dx}\left(p(x)\frac{du_0}{dx}\right) + q(x)u_0 = f(x)$$

is satisfied almost everywhere. Conversely, if there exists a function u_0 which possesses the properties just listed and satisfies (25.2), then $u_0 \in \mathfrak{D}(A)$.

In fact, $f(x) \in L_2$ (0,1), where

$$f(x) = -\frac{d}{dx}(pu_0') + qu_0 \tag{23.7}$$

and the function $u_0(x)$ is the generalised solution of (23.1) and (23.2), where $f(x)$ is defined by (23.7).

In this way, the set $\mathfrak{D}(A)$ coincides with the set of functions which satisfy the following properties: their first derivatives $u'(x)$ are absolutely continuous on the interval $0 \leqq x \leqq 1$, their second derivatives $u''(x)$ are square summable on the same interval, and $u(0) = u(1) = 0$.

In particular, it is clear that $\mathfrak{D}(A)$ does not depend on the concrete choice of $p(x)$ and $q(x)$. Therefore, if $\boldsymbol{B}$ denotes the selfadjoint Friedrichs extension of the operator defined by (23.1) and (23.2) when

$$p(x) \equiv 1, \qquad q(x) \equiv 0,$$

then $\mathfrak{D}(A) = \mathfrak{D}(\boldsymbol{B})$: that is, the operators $\boldsymbol{A}$ and $\boldsymbol{B}$ are similar. The eigenvectors of $\boldsymbol{B}$ are the non-trivial solutions of $u'' + \lambda u = 0$ w.r.t. the boundary condition (23.2):

$$\phi_n(x) = c_n \sin n\pi x \qquad (n = 1, 2, \ldots), \tag{23.8}$$

where the coefficients c_n can be chosen using a suitable normalising-condition.

It follows from Theorem 22.1 that, if the functions (23.8) are chosen as coordinate functions for (23.1) and (23.2) and

$$u_n(x) = \sum_{k=1}^{n} a_k \phi_k(x) = \sum_{k=1}^{n} a_k \sin k\pi x$$

is the approximate Ritz-solution for this problem, then the residual $||Au_n - f|| \to 0$ w.r.t. the metric in L_2 (0,1): that is,

$$||p(u_n'' - u_0'') + p'(u_n' - u_0') - q(u_n - u_0)|| \underset{n\to\infty}{\to} 0.$$

Since $u_n \to u_0$ w.r.t. the metric in $\mathfrak{H}_A$.

$$||u_n' - u_0'||_{L_2} \underset{n\to\infty}{\to} 0, \qquad ||u_n - u_0||_{L_2} \underset{n\to\infty}{\to} 0,$$

and since $p(x)$ is positive bounded below:

$$||u_n'' - u_0''||_{L_2} \underset{n\to\infty}{\to} 0.$$

Hence, if the functions (23.8) are used as coordinate functions in (23.1) and (23.2), then the second derivative of the approximate solution converges (w.r.t. the metric in $L_2(0,1)$) to the second derivative of the exact solution. Hence, it follows that, among other things, the first derivatives converge uniformly.

§24. Degenerate ordinary differential operators of the second order

In this section, we examine the second order differential operator

$$Au = -\frac{d}{dx}\left(p(x)\frac{du}{dx}\right) + q(x)u, \tag{24.1}$$

where the functions $p(x)$ and $q(x)$ satisfy, with one exception, the conditions in §23: here, $p(x) > 0$ for $x > 0$ and $p(0) = 0$. In particular, we assume that

$$p(x) = x^\alpha \tilde{p}(x), \qquad \alpha = \text{const}, \qquad 0 < \alpha < 2, \tag{24.2}$$

where $\tilde{p}(x)$ is continuously differentiable and strictly positive ($\tilde{p}(x) \geqq \geqq p_0, p_0 = \text{const.} > 0$) on the interval $0 \leqq x \leqq 1$.

We list some results for degenerate operators of the form given above. We assume that the domain $\mathfrak{D}(A)$ of A, which maps according to (24.1)

in the space $\mathfrak{H} = L_2(0,1)$, is the set of functions $u(x)$ which satisfy the following conditions:
(a) The function $p(x)\, u'(x)$ is absolutely continuous on $0 \leqq x \leqq 1$.
(b) $Au \in L_2(0,1)$.
(c) $u(1) = 0$.
(d) If $1 \leqq \alpha < 2$, then $p(x)\, u'(x) = o(x^{\frac{1}{2}})$.
From conditions (c) and (d), it follows that for x close to zero

$$u(x) = -\int_x^1 u'(t)dt = \begin{cases} o(x^{\frac{3}{2}-\alpha}), & \frac{3}{2} < \alpha < 2, \\ o\left(\ln \dfrac{1}{x}\right), & \alpha = \frac{3}{2}. \end{cases} \tag{24.3}$$

For $0 < \alpha < \frac{3}{2}$, the functions $u(x)$ are continuous at $x = 0$. It is clear that $\mathfrak{D}(A)$, as defined above, is dense in $L_2\,(0,1)$.
(e) If $0 < \alpha < 1$, then $u(0) = 0$.
On the basis of this definition, the operator A is selfadjoint and positive definite and its spectrum is discrete (this result can be obtained as a corollary of a general theorem developed in Achiezer and Glazman [1] and Naimark [1]). We shall prove this result. We introduce the scalar product

$$(Au, u) = -\int_0^1 \overline{u(x)}(p(x)u'(x))'\,dx + \int_0^1 q(x)|u(x)|^2\,dx,$$

and integrate the first integral by parts

$$-\int_0^1 \overline{u(x)}(p(x)u'(x))'\,dx = -\lim_{\delta\to 0}\int_\delta^1 \overline{u(x)}(p(x)u'(x))'\,dx =$$
$$= \lim_{\delta\to 0}\left\{u(\delta)p(\delta)u'(\delta) + \int_\delta^1 p(x)|u'(x)|^2\,dx\right\}.$$

We now show that the integrated term equals zero: it is clear that, if $0 < \alpha < 1$, then $u(\delta) \to 0$ and $p(\delta)\, u'(\delta)$ has a finite limit. If $1 \leqq \alpha < \frac{3}{2}$, then $u(\delta)$ has a finite limit and $p(\delta)u'(\delta) \to 0$. Finally, if $\frac{3}{2} \leqq \alpha < 2$, then $p(\delta)u'(\delta) = o(\delta^{\frac{1}{2}})$ and $u(\delta)$ tends to infinity slower than $\delta^{-\frac{1}{2}}$. Hence, it follows that

$$-\int_0^1 \overline{u(x)}(p(x)u'(x))'\,dx = \int_0^1 p(x)|u'(x)|^2\,dx.$$

Since we now have

$$(Au, u) = \int_0^1 \{p(x)|u'(x)|^2 + q(x)|u(x)|^2\}dx, \tag{24.4}$$

the expression (Au, u) is real (it is also non-negative) and the operator is symmetric.

We now prove that A is a selfadjoint operator. In particular, we examine the case when $1 \leqq \alpha < 2$. Let A^* denote the adjoint of A. Then

$$(Au, v) = (u, A^*v) = (u, v^*),\ u \in D(A),\ v \in D(A^*),\ v^* \in L_2(0, 1).$$

Writing this result in more detail, we obtain

$$-\int_0^1 (p(x)u'(x))'\overline{v(x)}dx + \int_0^1 q(x)u(x)\overline{v(x)}dx = \int_0^1 u(x)\overline{v^*(x)}dx.$$

Putting

$$v^*(x) - q(x)v(x) = v_1(x), \qquad v_1(x) \in L_2(0, 1),$$

and rearranging the last expression,we obtain

$$-\int_0^1 (p(x)u'(x))'\overline{v(x)}dx = \int_0^1 u(x)\overline{v_1(x)}dx. \tag{24.5}$$

We now set

$$v_2(x) = -\int_0^x v_1(t)dt.$$

The function $v_2(x)$ is absolutely continuous on the interval $0 \leqq x \leqq 1$ and $v_2(0) = 0$. Further, by the Schwartz-Buniakovskii inequality,

$$|v_2(x)| \leqq \sqrt{x}\int_0^x |v_1(t)|^2\, dt,$$

and therefore, $v_2(x) = o(\sqrt{x})$. Integrating the r.h.s. of (24.5) by parts, we find

$$\int_0^1 u(x)\overline{v_1(x)}dx = -u(x)\overline{v_2(x)}|_0^1 + \int_0^1 u'(x)\overline{v_2(x)}dx =$$
$$= \int_0^1 u'(x)\overline{v_2(x)}dx.$$

We also define

$$v_3(x) = -\int_x^1 \frac{v_2(t)}{p(t)}\, dt. \tag{24.5'}$$

The product $p(x)v_3'(x) = v_2(x)$ is absolutely continuous on the interval $0 \leqq x \leqq 1$. Further, $v_3(1) = 0$. In conclusion, we observe that the function

$$-\frac{d}{dx}\left(p\frac{dv_3}{dx}\right)+qv_3 = v_1+qv_3$$

lies in the space $L_2(0,1)$.

From the above, it follows that, among other things, $v_3 \in \mathfrak{D}(A)$. Integrating the r.h.s. of the last expression before (24.5′) by parts, we obtain

$$\int_0^1 u'(x)\overline{v_2(x)}dx = p(x)u'(x)\overline{v_3(x)}|_0^1 - \int_0^1 \overline{v_3(x)}(p(x)u(x))'dx.$$

The integrated term vanishes w.r.t. the upper limit since $v_3(1) = 0$. It also vanishes w.r.t. the lower limit since, by (24.5′), $v_3(x) = o(x^{-\frac{1}{2}})$ at the same time as $p(x)u'(x) = o(x^{\frac{1}{2}})$.

In this way, we obtain

$$\int_0^1 u'(x)\overline{v_2(x)}dx = -\int_0^1 \overline{v_3(x)}(p(x)u'(x))'\,dx.$$

If $u \in \mathfrak{D}(A)$, then formula (24.5) leads to the identity

$$\int_0^1 (p(x)u'(x))'(\overline{v(x)}-\overline{v_3(x)})dx = 0. \tag{24.6}$$

We prove that the range of the operator $(p(x)u'(x))'$, with domain $\mathfrak{D}(A)$, coincides with $L_2(0,1)$. For this purpose, we choose an arbitrary function $f(x) \in L_2(0,1)$ and show that there exists a solution $u \in \mathfrak{D}(A)$ for the equation

$$(p(x)u'(x))' = f(x).$$

In fact, this solution is the function

$$u(x) = -\int_x^1 \frac{f_1(t)}{p(t)}\,dt, \qquad f_1(t) = \int_0^t f(t_1)dt_1.$$

It follows from (24.6) that the difference $v-v_3$ is orthogonal to every element of $L_2(0,1)$. This implies that $v_3(x) = v(x)$, $v(x) \in \mathfrak{D}(A)$, and A is selfadjoint.

It is not difficult to establish that A is positive definite. In fact, using

(24.4), we have

$$(Au, u) \geqslant p_0 \int_0^1 x^\alpha |u'(x)|^2 \, dx. \tag{24.7}$$

Further,

$$u(x) = -\int_x^1 u'(t)dt = -\int_x^1 \frac{1}{t^{\alpha/2}} t^{\alpha/2} u'(t)dt$$

and, by the Schwartz-Buniakovskii inequality (for clarity we take $\alpha > 1$),

$$|u(x)|^2 \leqq \frac{1}{\alpha - 1} \left(\frac{1}{x^{\alpha-1}} - 1 \right) \int_0^1 t^\alpha |u'(t)|^2 \, dt.$$

Integrating this last expression w.r.t. x, we find

$$(Au, u) \geqq \gamma^2 ||u||^2, \qquad \gamma^2 = \frac{p_0}{2 - \alpha}.$$

We shall now prove that A has a discrete spectrum. The case when $0 < \alpha < 1$ follows from the results in VM, §35. Therefore, it only remains to examine the case $1 \leqq \alpha < 2$.

From (24.4), it is clear that, for $1 \leqq \alpha < 2$, the energy space consists of the functions $u = u(x)$ which satisfy the following properties:

(1) u is absolutely continuous on the interval $\delta \leqq x \leqq 1$ for arbitrary δ, $0 < \delta < 1$;

(2) $u(1) = 0$;

(3) u is such that the value of (24.7) is finite.

Let $\mathfrak{M} \subset \mathfrak{H}_A$ be a set of functions which have bounded energy: $|||u|||_A \leqq C$, $u \in \mathfrak{M}$. We shall prove that this set is compact in $\mathfrak{H} = L_2\,(0,1)$. First of all, on the strength of inequality (24.7),

$$\int_0^1 x^\alpha |u'(x)|^2 \, dx \leqq \frac{C^2}{p_0},$$

which implies that the set $\mathfrak{M}_1$ of functions $v(x) = x^{\alpha/2} \, u'(x)$ is bounded in $L_2(0,1)$. Further, if $u \in \mathfrak{M}$,

$$u(x) = -\int_x^1 u'(t)dt = -\int_x^1 t^{-\alpha/2} v(t)dt,$$

or, if we put

$$K(x, t) = \begin{cases} 0, & 0 \leqq t < x, \\ -t^{-\alpha/2}, & x < t \leqq 1, \end{cases}$$

we obtain

$$u(x) = \int_0^1 K(x, t)v(t)dt. \tag{24.8}$$

We shall show that $K(x, t)$ is a Fredholm kernel, that is

$$\int_0^1 \int_0^1 K^2(x, t)dx\,dt < \infty.$$

In fact, if $1 < \alpha < 2$, then

$$\int_0^1 \int_0^1 K^2(x, t)dx\,dt = \int_0^1 \frac{1}{\alpha-1}\left(\frac{1}{x^{\alpha-1}} - 1\right) dx = \frac{1}{2-\alpha}.$$

If $\alpha = 1$, then

$$\int_0^1 \int_0^1 K^2(x, t)dx\,dt = \int_0^1 \ln \frac{1}{x}\, dx = 1.$$

It follows that the integral operator (24.8) is completely continuous in $L_2(0,1)$, and hence, transforms the bounded set $\mathfrak{M}_1$ into the compact set $\mathfrak{M}$. Thus, the operator $\boldsymbol{A}$ has a discrete spectrum (PM, §12).

The conditions introduced above for the operator $\boldsymbol{A}$ (the structure of $\mathfrak{D}(\boldsymbol{A})$) are independent of the concrete form of the functions $\tilde{p}(x)$ and $q(x)$. Therefore, putting $\tilde{p}(x) = 1$, $q(x) = 0$ and keeping the domain $\mathfrak{D}(\boldsymbol{A})$ fixed, we obtain the new operator

$$\boldsymbol{B}u = -\frac{d}{dx}\left(x^\alpha \frac{du}{dx}\right), \tag{24.9}$$

which is positive definite and similar to $\boldsymbol{A}$. The spectrum of this new operator is also discrete.

In this way, the use of the Ritz-process to solve

$$-\frac{d}{dx}\left(\tilde{p}(x)x^\alpha \frac{du}{dx}\right) + q(x)u = f(x) \tag{24.10}$$

for the boundary conditions $u(1) = 0$ (and, if $0 < \alpha < 1$, then $u(0) = 0$, also) with the eigenfunctions of $\boldsymbol{B}$ as coordinate functions ensures the convergence of the residual to zero.

The eigenfunctions of B are the solutions of the differential equation

$$\frac{d}{dx}\left(x^{\alpha}\frac{du}{dx}\right)+\lambda u=0,$$

which easily transforms into Bessel's equation (see, for example, Smirnov [1, §49]). Hence, the eigenfunction are defined by

$$\phi_n(x)=c_n x^{(1-\alpha)/2}J_\nu(\gamma_{\nu,n}x^{(2-\alpha)/2}) \tag{24.11}$$

where $\nu=(\alpha-1)/(2-\alpha)$, $\gamma_{\nu,n}$ is the nth postitive root of the Bessel function $J_\nu(x)$ and the coefficients c_n can be determined by an appropriate normalising condition.

§25. Ordinary differential operators with order higher than the second

We examine the operator

$$Au=\sum_{k=1}^{s}(-1)^k\frac{d^k}{dx^k}\left(p_k(x)\frac{d^ku}{dx^k}\right),\qquad a<x<b, \tag{25.1}$$

for the simplest boundary conditions

$$u^{(k)}(a)=u^{(k)}(b)=0\qquad (k=0,1,\ldots,s-1). \tag{25.2}$$

For the sake of simplicity, we assume that the coefficients $p_k(x)$ are non-negative and sufficiently often differentiable on the interval [a, b] and that $p_0(x)$ is strictly positive. Let $\mathfrak{D}(A)$ be the set of functions which are (2s−1)-times continuously differentiable on the interval [a, b], have generalised derivatives of order 2s which are contained in $L_2(a,b)$ and satisfy (25.2).

It is not difficult to prove that A is selfadjoint and positive definite. Its domain does not depend on the form of the $p_k(x)$, if they satisfy the conditions listed above. Hence, it follows that the operator B, which is defined by

$$Bu=(-1)^s\frac{d^{2s}u}{dx^{2s}}$$

with $\mathfrak{D}(B)=\mathfrak{D}(A)$, is similar to A. The spectrum of B is discrete and its eigenfunctions can be used for the solution of $Au=f$, where A is defined by (25.1) and (25.2). Hence, on the basis of Theorem 22.1, the residual of the approximate solution will converge to zero. In the special case when $s = 2$, the eigenfunctions of $\boldsymbol{B}$ are the "beam-functions" which were examined in detail by Krylov [1] and Zamyatina [1]. Comparatively simple similar operators can be constructed in some other cases. For example, if $s = 2$ and condition (25.2) is replaced by

$$u(a) = u(b) = 0, \qquad u''(a) = u''(b) = 0, \tag{25.3}$$

then the operator $\boldsymbol{A}$, as before, is selfadjoint and positive definite in $L_2(a, b)$. The selfadjointness can be established using the argument of §24. We now prove the positive definiteness.

Let $p_2(x) \geqq c = \text{const.} > 0$. Integrating by parts and taking (25.3) into account, we obtain

$$(\boldsymbol{A}u, u) = \int_a^b \{p_2(x)|u''(x)|^2 + p_1(x)|u'(x)|^2 + p_0(x)|u(x)|^2\}dx \geqq$$

$$\geqq c\int_a^b |u''(x)|^2\,dx. \tag{25.3'}$$

We shall make use of Poincaré's inequality for the function $u'(x)$:

$$\int_a^b |u'(x)|^2\,dx \leqq \frac{b-a}{2}\left[\int_a^b |u''(x)|^2\,dx + \left|\int_a^b u'(x)dx\right|^2\right].$$

Note. Poincaré's inequality for a function of one variable, defined on the interval $a \leqq x \leqq b$,

$$\int_a^b |u(x)|^2\,dx \leqq \frac{b-a}{2}\left[\int_a^b |u'(x)|^2\,dx + \left|\int_a^b u(x)dx\right|^2\right]$$

can be easily established. Since

$$u(x) - u(y) = \int_y^x u'(t)dt,$$

it follows that

$$|u(x)|^2 + |u(y)|^2 - u(x)\overline{u(y)} - \overline{u(x)}u(y) = |u(x) - u(y)|^2 \leqq$$
$$|x-y|\left|\int_y^x |u'(t)|^2\,dt\right| \leqq (b-a)\int_a^b |u'(t)|^2\,dt.$$

Integration of this expression w.r.t. x and y between the limits a and b

yields the required inequality (see Courant and Hilbert [1: Chapter 7]; Sobolev [1]).

Since, on the strength of the boundary conditions (25.3),

$$\int_a^b u'(x)dx = u(b)-u(a) = 0,$$

we obtain

$$\int_a^b |u''(x)|^2 \, dx \geqq \frac{2}{b-a}\int_a^b |u'(x)|^2 \, dx.$$

It also follows, on the basis of (27.2), that (see VM, §20)

$$\int_a^b |u'(x)|^2 \, dx \geqq \frac{1}{b-a}\int_a^b |u(x)|^2 \, dx = \frac{1}{b-a}\,||u||^2.$$

Combining these results, we find

$$(Au, u) \geqq \frac{2c}{(b-a)^2}\,||u||^2,$$

which proves the positive definiteness of $\boldsymbol{A}$.

The operator $\boldsymbol{B}$, which is defined by

$$\boldsymbol{B}u = \frac{d^4 u}{dx^4} \tag{25.4}$$

with $\mathfrak{D}(\boldsymbol{B}) = \mathfrak{D}(\boldsymbol{A})$ is similar to $\boldsymbol{A}$.

The eigenfunctions of $\boldsymbol{B}$ are easily found. They satisfy

$$u^{(4)} - \lambda\mu = 0$$

and the boundary condition (25.2). These functions have the form

$$\phi_n(x) = c_n \sin n\pi x \qquad (n = 1, 2, \ldots), \tag{25.5}$$

where the coefficients c_n can be determined by an appropriate normalising condition.

We now examine the problem of integrating the equation

$$\boldsymbol{A}u = \frac{d^2}{dx^2}\left(p_2(x)\frac{d^2u}{dx^2}\right) - \frac{d}{dx}\left(p_1(x)\frac{du}{dx}\right) + p_0(x)u = f(x), \tag{25.6}$$

$f(x) \in L_2(0, 1)$,

w.r.t. the boundary conditions (25.2). If the functions (25.5) are taken as coordinate functions, $u_n(x)$ is the nth Ritz-approximation and $u_0(x)$ is the exact solution, then $||Au_n - f|| \to_{n\to\infty} 0$ or, equivalently,

$$||A(u_n - u_0)|| \to_{n\to\infty} 0.$$

Since the operators $\boldsymbol{A}$ and $\boldsymbol{B}$ are similar, we obtain, on the basis of (3.1),

$$||\boldsymbol{B}(u_n - u_0)|| \leqq \frac{1}{c_1} ||\boldsymbol{A}(u_n - u_0)|| \to_{n\to\infty} 0.$$

The last inequality implies that

$$\left\| \frac{d^4 u_n}{dx^4} - \frac{d^4 u_0}{dx^4} \right\|_{L_2} \to_{n\to\infty} 0.$$

Hence, it follows that the expressions

$$\frac{d^k u_n}{dx^k} - \frac{d^k u_0}{dx^k} \qquad (k = 0, 1, 2, 3)$$

tend uniformly to zero.

For an arbitrary choice of coordinate functions, we can only assert that $|u_n - u_0|_{\boldsymbol{A}} \to_{n\to\infty} 0$, or, on the basis of (3.3), that $|u_n - u_0|_{\boldsymbol{B}} \to_{n\to\infty} 0$, which is equivalent to

$$\left\| \frac{d^2 u_n}{dx^2} - \frac{d^2 u_0}{dx^2} \right\|_{L_2} \to_{n\to\infty} 0.$$

§26. Elliptic operators of the second order

We shall examine the second order elliptic operator

$$Au = -\sum_{j,k=1}^{m} \frac{\partial}{\partial x_j} \left(A_{jk} \frac{\partial u}{\partial x_k} \right) + Cu \tag{26.1}$$

in a finite region Ω of the m-dimensional space with coordinates x_1, $x_2, \ldots, x_m$. We shall assume that the boundary S of Ω is two times continuously differentiable, that C is continuous and that the A_{jk} are two times continuously differentiable in the closed region $\overline{\Omega} = \Omega \cup S$. We shall also assume that the elliptic operator $\boldsymbol{A}$ is non-degenerate: that is, that

$$\sum_{j,k=1}^{m} A_{jk} t_j \bar{t}_k \geqq \mu \sum_{k=1}^{m} |t_k|^2, \qquad \mu = \text{const} > 0.$$

The domain of A is set of functions $\mathring{W}_2^{(2)}(\Omega)$ which have in Ω square-summable second generalised derivatives and which satisfy the boundary condition

$$u|_S = 0. \tag{26.2}$$

A number of authors (see Miranda [1]) have established the following inequality for functions in $\mathring{W}_2^{(2)}(\Omega)$:

$$||Au||^2 = \int_\Omega |Au|^2 \, dx \geqq c \int_\Omega \sum_{j,k=1}^{m} \left| \frac{\partial^2 u}{\partial x_j \partial x_k} \right|^2 dx, \qquad c = \text{const} > 0. \tag{26.3}$$

Using this inequality and the properties of the solution for the Dirichlet problem for an elliptic equation with smooth r.h.s. (see, Sobolev [1] and PM, §17), we can prove that A is selfadjoint. We sketch the proof.
The operator A is positive definite in the space $\mathfrak{H} = L_2(\Omega)$ (VM, §24), and therefore, possesses a selfadjoint Friedrichs extension. Let $\bar{A}$ be this extension, $f \in L_2(\Omega)$ be chosen artibrarily, and u_0 be the generalised solution of $Au_0 = f$, or, equivalently, the solution of $\bar{A}u_0 = f$. From the definition of A, it follows that u_0 satisfies the boundary condition (26.2). We approximate $f(x)$, w.r.t. the metric in $L_2(\Omega)$, by a sequence of sufficiently smooth functions $f_n(x)$.
The equations $Au_n = f_n$ have solutions $u_n(x)$ which for all n, have continuous second derivatives in $\bar{\Omega}$ (Miranda [1, Theorem 36.1]). From inequality (26.3), we obtain

$$\int_\Omega \left| \frac{\partial^2 u_n}{\partial x_j \partial x_k} - \frac{\partial^2 u_p}{\partial x_j \partial x_k} \right|^2 dx \leqq \frac{1}{c} ||f_n - f_p|| \underset{n, p \to \infty}{\to} 0$$
$$(j, k = 1, 2, \ldots, m).$$

Since the positive definite operator A has a bounded inverse in $L_2(\Omega)$ (PM, §5), $||u_n - u_0|| \to 0$. It follows, since the operator of generalised differentiation is closed (see Sobolev [1], and PM, §17), that $u_0(x)$ has square summable generalised second derivatives in Ω. This implies that $\mathfrak{D}(\bar{A}) \subset \mathring{W}_2^{(2)}(\Omega) = \mathfrak{D}(A)$. However, since $\bar{A}$ is the extension of A, $D(\tilde{A}) = D(A)$, $\tilde{A} = A$ and the operator A is selfadjoint.

Since the domain of the operator defined by (26.1) and (26.2) does not depend on the form of the A_{jk} and C , it follows that this operator is similar to, for example, the Laplace operator (taken with a minus sign) with boundary conditions (26.2).

Now, it follows from Theorem 22.1 that, if for the solution of $Au = f$, where A is defined by (26.1) with $\mathfrak{D}(A) = \mathring{W}_2^{(2)}$, we take as coordinate functions the eigenfunctions of the Laplace operator, then the residual $Au_n - f \to 0$ as $n \to \infty$, where u_n is the approximate Ritz-solution of $Au = f$. In turn, the second derivative of the approximate Ritz-solution, w.r.t. the metric in $L_2(\Omega)$, converges to the second derivative of the exact solution. In fact, if u_0 is the exact solution, then it follows from inequality (26.3) that

$$\int_\Omega \left| \frac{\partial^2 u_n}{\partial x_j \partial x_k} - \frac{\partial^2 u_0}{\partial x_j \partial x_k} \right|^2 dx \leqq \frac{1}{c} \, ||Au_n - Au_0||^2 =$$

$$= \frac{1}{c} \, ||Au_n - f||^2 \underset{n \to \infty}{\to} 0.$$

We recall that, for an arbitrary choice of the coordinate functions, we can only assert

$$|||u_n - u_o|||_A^2 = \int_\Omega \left\{ \sum_{j,k=r}^{m} A_{jk} \left(\frac{\partial u_n}{\partial x_j} - \frac{\partial u_0}{\partial x_j} \right) \left(\frac{\partial u_n}{\partial x_k} - \frac{\partial u_0}{\partial x_k} \right) + C|u_n - u_0|^2 \right\} dx \underset{n \to \infty}{\to} 0,$$

which only implies that the first derivatives of the approximate solution converge, w.r.t. the metric in $L_2(\Omega)$, to the first derivative of the exact solution.

We now examine (26.1) w.r.t. the Neumann boundary condition

$$\left[\sum_{j,k=1}^{m} A_{jk} \frac{\partial u}{\partial x^k} \cos(\nu, x_j) \right]_S = 0. \tag{26.4}$$

If the boundary S is sufficiently smooth, then, as can be proved, the self-adjoint extension of the operator defined by (26.1) and (26.4) has as its domain the functions from $W_2^{(2)}(\Omega)$ which satisfy (26.4) - this follows from the results of Ladyzenskaya [1]. Hence, two operators satisfying the Neumann boundary condition will be similar only when the matrices of coefficients for the second derivatives from both operators coincide. In particular, the selfadjoint extensions of the operators

$$-\Delta u + u, \quad \left. \frac{\partial u}{\partial \nu} \right|_S = 0 \tag{26.5}$$

and

$$-\Delta u + C(x)u, \quad \left.\frac{\partial u}{\partial \nu}\right|_S = 0, \tag{26.6}$$

are similar, Hence, the Ritz-solution of

$$-\Delta u + C(x)u = f(x), \quad \left.\frac{\partial u}{\partial \nu}\right|_S = 0$$

can be constructed using the eigenfunctions of (26.5) as coordinate functions, where the second derivatives of the approximate solution will converge w.r.t. the metric in $L_2(\Omega)$ to the corresponding derivatives of the exact solution.

§27. Another approach for studying the residual

1. In 1948, Kantorovich [1] presented a general approach for the investigation of the convergence of projection methods – methods of the Bubnov-Galerkin type. This approach was the basis of the work of Daugavet [3] mentioned at the beginning of this chapter. We now develop the approach of -Kantorovich in connection with a simple case which leads to the Ritzprocess.

In the equation

$$Au = f, \tag{27.1}$$

let A denote a linear operator which is a one-to-one and continuous mapping from the Banach space $\mathfrak{B}_1$ onto the Banach space $\mathfrak{B}_2$ such that $\mathfrak{D}(A) = \mathfrak{B}_1$ and $\mathfrak{R}(A) = \mathfrak{B}_2$ and A and A^{-1} are bounded. The norms in $\mathfrak{B}_k$ $(k = 1, 2)$ will be denoted by $\| \ \|_k$.

We construct a sequence of finite dimensional subspaces $\mathfrak{B}_1^{(n)}$ in $\mathfrak{B}_1$ which satisfies the condition that for arbitrary $u \in \mathfrak{B}_1$

$$E_n(u) = \inf_{v_n \in \mathfrak{B}_1^{(n)}} \|u - v_n\|_1 \underset{n \to \infty}{\to} 0. \tag{27.2}$$

We set $\mathfrak{B}_2^{(n)} = A\mathfrak{B}_1^{(n)}$. For each n, we define the operator Q_n which is the projection of $\mathfrak{B}_2$ on $\mathfrak{B}_2^{(n)}$. The approximate solution of (27.1) is constructed as the element $u_n \in \mathfrak{B}_1^{(n)}$ which satisfies

$$Au_n = Q_n f.$$

If we write $P_n = A^{-1} Q_n A$, then $u_n = P_n u_0$, where u_0 is the exact solution

of (27.1). We shall prove that P_n defines the projection of $\mathfrak{B}_1$ onto $\mathfrak{B}_1^{(n)}$. In fact, if $u \in \mathfrak{B}_1$, then $P_n u = A^{-1}Q_n Au \in A^{-1}Q_n\mathfrak{B}_2 = A^{-1}\mathfrak{B}_2^{(n)} = \mathfrak{B}_1^{(n)}$ and it remains to verify that $P_n^2 = P_n$. Let $u \in \mathfrak{B}_1$ and $P_n u = v_n \in \mathfrak{B}_1^{(n)}$. We set $P_n^2 u = P_n v_n = w_n$, that is, $w_n = A^{-1}Q_n Av_n$ and hence, $Q_n Av_n = Aw_n$. Further, since $Av_n \in A\mathfrak{B}_1^{(n)} = \mathfrak{B}_2^{(n)}$, $Q_n Av_n = Av_n$. In this way, $Av_n = Aw_n$ and hence, $v_n = w_n$ which completes the proof.
We now show that

$$||u_0-u_n|| \leqq (1+||P_n||)E_n(u_0). \tag{27.4}$$

In fact, if v_n is an arbitrary element of $\mathfrak{B}_1^{(n)}$, then

$$\begin{aligned}||u_0-u_n||_1 &\leqq ||u_0-v_n||_1+||v_n-u_n||_1 = ||u_0-v_n||_1+\\ &+||P_n(v_n-u_0)||_1 \leqq (1+||P_n||)||u_0-v_n||_1.\end{aligned}$$

Since the subspace $\mathfrak{B}_1^{(n)}$ is finite dimensional, there exists $\tilde{v}_n \in \mathfrak{B}_1^{(n)}$ such that $E_n(u_0) = ||u_0-\tilde{v}_n||_1$. Putting $v_n = \tilde{v}_n$ in (27.5), we obtain (27.4). From (27.4), we obtain the following sufficient condition for the convergence of $u_n \to u_0$: *if* $||P_n||E_n(u_0) \to_{n\to\infty} 0$, *then* $||u_n-u_0||_1 \to_{n\to\infty} 0$. We note that, since $||P_n|| \leqq$ const. $||Q_n||$, it is sufficient that

$$||Q_n||E_n(u_0) \underset{n\to\infty}{\to} 0. \tag{27.6}$$

If $||u_n-u_0|| \to_{n\to\infty} 0$, then

$$||Au_n-f||_2 = ||A(u_n-u_0)||_2 \leqq ||A||\,||u_n-u_0||_1 \underset{n\to\infty}{\to} 0.$$

In this way, we obtain the result: (27.6) *is a sufficient condition for the convergence of the residual* Au_n-f *to zero w.r.t. the metric in* $\mathfrak{B}_2$.
2. We now assume that $\mathfrak{B}_1 \subset \mathfrak{B}_2 \subset \mathfrak{H}$, where $\mathfrak{B}_2$ and $\mathfrak{H}$ are Hilbert spaces and "$\subset$" denotes dense imbedding. The scalar products and norms in $\mathfrak{H}$ and $\mathfrak{B}_2$ will be denoted by (,) and || ||, and $(\, , \,)_2$ and $|| \, ||_2$, respectively.
We choose in $\mathfrak{B}_1$ a dense coordinate system $\{\phi_k\}$ and define $\mathfrak{B}_1^{(n)}$ as the subspace which spans $\phi_1, \phi_2, \ldots, \phi_n$ so that $\mathfrak{B}_2^{(n)}$ spans $A\phi_1, A\phi_2, \ldots, A\phi_n$. The projection Q_n is defined by

$$(f-Q_n f, \phi_j) = 0 \qquad (j = 1, 2, \ldots, n). \tag{27.7}$$

System (27.7) is the Bubnov-Galerkin-process for equation (27.1) in $\mathfrak{H}$. In fact, the function $Q_n f$ has the form

$$Q_n f = \sum_{k=1}^{n} a_k A\phi_k, \qquad a_k = \text{const.},$$

and (27.7) reduces to the usual form the Bubnov-Galerkin-process

$$\sum_{k=1}^{n} a_k(A\phi_k, \phi_j) = (f, \phi_j) \qquad (j = 1, 2, \ldots, n).$$

If it is solved, them, on the strength of (27.3),

$$u_n = A^{-1}Q_n f = \sum_{k=1}^{n} a_k \phi_k, \tag{27.8}$$

and hence, u_n is the approximate Bubnov-Galerkin-solution of (27.1) in $\mathfrak{H}$.

We now assume that A is positive definite in $\mathfrak{H}$. It follows that u_n (as defined in (27.8)) is the approximate Ritz-solution and (27.7) is the Ritz-process for (27.1) in $\mathfrak{H}$.

We determine an estimate for $||Q_n||$. We first note that

$$||Q_n f||_2^2 = ||\sum_{k=1}^{n} a_k A\phi_k||_2^2 = \sum_{j,k=1}^{n} a_k a_j (A\phi_k, A\phi_j)_2.$$

If we let $\Lambda_n^{(n)}$ denote the largest eigenvalue of the matrix of scalar products

$$\begin{bmatrix} (A\phi_1, A\phi_1) & \ldots & (A\phi_1, A\phi_n) \\ \cdot \quad \cdot \quad \cdot & \cdot & \cdot \quad \cdot \quad \cdot \\ (A\phi_n, A\phi_1) & \ldots & (A\phi_n, A\phi_n) \end{bmatrix}.$$

then

$$||Q_n f||^2 \leqq \Lambda_n^{(n)} \sum_{k=1}^{n} |a_k|^2. \tag{27.9}$$

Using the usual notation for the energy inner product and norm and letting $\lambda_1^{(n)}$ denote the smallest eigenvalue of the Ritz-matrix (see §9), we obtain

$$|||u_n|||^2 = \sum_{j,k=1}^{n} a_k \bar{a}_j (A\phi_k, \phi_j) \geqq \lambda_1^{(n)} \sum_{k=1}^{n} |a_k|^2.$$

However, since $|||u_n||| \leqq |||u_0|||$ (see VM, §92), it follows that

$$\sum_{k=1}^{n} |a_k|^2 \leqq \frac{1}{\lambda_1^{(n)}} |||u_0|||^2 = \frac{1}{\lambda_1^{(n)}} ||A^{-\frac{1}{2}} f||^2.$$

Since A is postitive definite, $A^{-\frac{1}{2}}$ is bounded in $\mathfrak{H}$. Further, on the strength of the the imbedding $\mathfrak{B}_2 \subset \mathfrak{H}$,

$$||f|| \leqq C||f||_2 \quad , \quad f \in \mathfrak{B}_2 \quad ,$$

and thus,

$$\sum_{k=1}^{n} |a_k|^2 \leqq \frac{1}{\lambda_1^{(n)}} ||A^{-\frac{1}{2}}||^2 \, ||f||^2 \leqq \frac{C^2||A^{-\frac{1}{2}}||^2}{\lambda_1^{(n)}} \, ||f||_2^2 .$$

Substitution of this last result in (27.9) yields

$$||Q_n|| \leqq C_1 \left[\frac{\Lambda_n^{(n)}}{\lambda_1^{(n)}}\right]^{\frac{1}{2}}, \qquad C_1 = \text{const.} \tag{27.10}$$

If the coordinate system is strongly minimal in the energy space $\mathfrak{H}_A$, then $\lambda_1^{(n)}$ is bounded below by a postive constant and the estimate becomes

$$||Q_n|| \leqq C_2[\Lambda_n^{(n)}]^{\frac{1}{2}}, \qquad C_2 = \text{const.} \tag{27.11}$$

On the strength of (27.6), the residual of (27.1) converges to zero w.r.t. the metric in $\mathfrak{B}_2$, if

$$\left[\frac{\Lambda_n^{(n)}}{\lambda_1^{(n)}}\right]^{\frac{1}{2}} E_n(u_0) \underset{n\to\infty}{\to} 0. \tag{27.12}$$

In the case when the coordinate system is strongly minimal in $\mathfrak{H}_A$, it is sufficient that

$$[\Lambda_n^{(n)}]^{\frac{1}{2}} E_n(u_0) \underset{n\to\infty}{\to} 0. \tag{27.13}$$

§28. Polynomial coordinate systems

We examine the Dirichlet problem for a system of the form

$$\sum_{|\alpha|+|\beta|=0}^{2k} D^{\alpha}(A_{\alpha\beta}(x)D^{\beta}u) = f(x), \tag{28.1}$$

$$D^{\alpha}u|_S = 0, \qquad 0 \leqq |\alpha| < k-1, \tag{28.2}$$

in the finite region Ω which lies in m-dimensional Euclidean space and is homeomorphic to a ball, where α and β are multi-indices (i.e., sets of m non-negative integers): $\alpha = (\alpha_1, \alpha_2, \ldots, \alpha_m)$ and $\beta = (\beta_1, \ldots, \beta_m)$

such that, if $\gamma = (\gamma_1, \ldots, \gamma_m)$ is a multi-index, then

$$|\gamma| = \sum_{k=1}^{m} \gamma_k,$$

$$D^\gamma w = \frac{\partial^{|\gamma|} w}{\partial x_1^{\gamma_1} \partial x_2^{\gamma_2} \ldots \partial x_m^{\gamma_m}},$$

u and f are vectors and the $A_{\alpha\beta}$ are matrices.

As usual, S denotes the boundary of Ω. We assume that the equation of S has the form $F(x) = 0$, where $F(x)$ is a polynomial such that $F(x) > 0$ in Ω and grad $F(x) \neq 0$ for $x \in S$. In addition, assume that the $A_{\alpha\beta}$ and f are sufficiently smooth for $x \in \bar{\Omega}$, that (28.1) is a non-degenerate elliptic equation for $x \in \bar{\Omega}$, and that the operator defined by (28.1) and (28.2) is positive definite in $L_2(\Omega)$.

We construct an approximate solution for this problem in the form

$$u_n(x) = F^k(x)\, p_n(x), \tag{28.3}$$

where $p_n(x)$ is a polynomial of degree $\leqq n$ with respect to each of the variables $x_1, x_2, \ldots, x_m$. The coefficients of the $p_n(x)$ will be defined by a Ritz-process.

If the functions $A_{\alpha\beta}$ and $f(x)$ have sufficiently many derivatives then, as is well-known, the exact solution u_0 of (28.1) and (28.2) has arbitrarily many continuous derivatives. We assume that $u_0 \in C^r(\bar{\Omega})$, where r is sufficiently large.

In order to examine how the derivatives of the approximate solution converges to the derivatives of the exact solution, we make use of the results of the previous section. We put

$$\mathfrak{B}_1 = \mathring{W}_2^{(s)}(\Omega), \qquad \mathfrak{B}_2 = W_2^{(l)}(\Omega), \qquad \mathfrak{H} = L_2(\Omega),$$

where $s = 2k + l \leqq r$, and $\mathring{W}_2^{(s)}(\Omega)$ denotes the functions of $W_2^{(s)}(\Omega)$ which satisfy (28.2).

We assume that the coordinate system, which we denote by $\{\phi_n\}$, is orthonormal w.r.t. the metric of $W_2^{(k)}(\Omega)$. Hence, $\{\phi_n\}$ is almost orthonormal, and thus, strongly minimal in the energy space of the operator defined by (28.1) and (28.2). Hence, the estimate (27.11) holds for $||Q_n||$. We derive an estimate for $\Lambda_n^{(n)}$. Let N denote the number of coordinate functions in the approximate solution (28.3) It is clear that $N = 0(n^m)$. We have that

$$\Lambda_n^{(n)} = \max_{||t||=1} \sum_{i,j=1}^{N} (A\phi_j, A\phi_i)_l \, t_i \bar{t}_j$$
$$= \max_{||t||=1} ||\sum_{j=1}^{N} t_j A\phi_j||_l^2 \leqq \sum_{j=1}^{N} ||A\phi_j||_l^2,$$

where, here and below (until the end of this section), $(\ ,\ )_l$ and $||\ ||_l$ denote the inner product and norm, respectively, in the Sobolev space $W_2^{(l)}(\Omega)$. Since for $u \in W_2^{(s)}(\Omega)$

$$||Au||_l \leqq C||u||_s, \; C = \text{const.},$$

it follows that

$$||A\phi_j||_l \leqq C||\phi_j||_s,$$

because $\{\phi_j\} \in \mathring{W}_2^{(s)}(\Omega)$.
The norm in $\mathring{W}_2^{(s)}(\Omega)$ has the form

$$||u||_s^2 = ||D^\sigma D^\tau u||_{L_2(\Omega)}^2,$$

where the summation is taken over all values of the multi-indices σ and τ for which $|\sigma| \leqq k+l$ and $|\tau| \leqq l$. If we use estimates for the norms of derivatives of polynomials (see Kantorovich and Akilov [1; chapter 15, §3] and Harrik [1]), then we obtain

$$||\phi_j||_s^2 \leqq C_1 n^{4(k+l)+2m} \sum ||D^\tau \phi_j||_{L_2(\Omega)}^2 \leqq C_1 n^{4(k+l)+2m} ||\phi_j||_k^2$$
$$= C_1 n^{4(k+l)+2m}$$

and

$$\Lambda_n^{(n)} \leqq C^2 C_1 n^{4(k+l)+2m} N = 0(n^{4k+4l+3m}). \tag{28.4}$$

An estimate for $E_n(u_0)$ has been given in the fundamental theorem of Harrik [1]. On the basis of this theorem, we have

$$E_n(u_0) = 0(n^{-r+s}) w_r \left(u_0, \frac{1}{n}\right), \tag{28.5}$$

where $w_\tau(\phi, 1/n)$ denotes the largest absolute value of the continuous derivatives of order τ of the given function ϕ.
Hence, using (27.4), we obtain

$$||u_0 - u_n||_s = 0(n^{-r+4k+3l+\frac{3}{2}m}) w_r \left(u_0, \frac{1}{n}\right). \tag{28.6}$$

In particular, the residual of (28.1) tend to zero w.r.t. the metric in $L_2(\Omega)$, if $r \geqq 4k+[3m/2]+1$.

Chapter V

ON THE RATIONAL CHOICE OF COORDINATE FUNCTIONS

§29. General remarks

The results of the previous chapters (in particular, Chapters II and IV) lead to conclusions which can be characterised as conditions for the rational choice of coordinate functions for the Ritz-process. In the present chapter, we examine these conditions in detail by first restricting attention to the energy method for positive definite differential operators (results of this kind can be found in Mikihlin [17]). At the end of this chapter, we examine briefly the rational choice of coordinate functions for the method of least squares - in particular, for the approximate solution of integral equations.

In Chapter VI, we shall be partly concerned with the rational choice of coordinate functions for positive (but not positive definite) differential operators.

If the problem is the first boundary value problem for an elliptic equation in a region Ω which is homeomorphic to a ball and has a sufficiently smooth boundary S, then it is convenient to use the polynomial coordinate system discussed in §28. It is necessary to ensure that the coordinate system is almost orthonormal (or, at least, strongly minimal) in the energy space of the given problem. We note that the polynomial system can be transformed into a strongly minimal system. The system of functions $\omega \sum_{k=1}^{n} x_k^{n_k} (n_1, n_2, \ldots, n_m = 0, 1, 2, \ldots)$, where $\omega(x_1, \ldots, x_m) = 0$ is the equation of S and satisfies the conditions listed in §28, is complete in the corresponding energy space (see Kantorovich and Krylov [1]). It follows that the system

$$\omega \sum_{k=1}^{n} P_{n_k}(x_k) \, (n_1, n_2, \ldots, n_m = 0, 1, 2, \ldots), \tag{29.1}$$

where the $P_n(x)$ are the normalised Legendre polynomials, is complete in the same energy space.

Inside Ω, we take a cube Q. We place the origin of the coordinate axes at the centre of the cube, position the coordinate axes parallel to the sides of the cube and choose the unit of length so that the sides of the cube have length 2. Since the operation of multiplication by ω is postive definite and bounded in $L_2(Q)$, its energy space coincides with $L_2(Q)$. Using Corollary 4.2., it follows that (29.1) is strongly minimal in $L_2(Q)$. We associate with every function in $L_2(\Omega)$ the same function defined only in Q. In this way, we define the imbedding of $L_2(\Omega)$ in $L_2(Q)$ such that $||u||_{L_2(\Omega)} \geqq ||u||_{L_2(Q)}$. On the basis of Theorem 4.2, (29.1) is strongly minimal in $L_2(\Omega)$. In the same way, it is strongly minimal in the energy space of the first boundary value problem, since the corresponding operator is assumed to be positive definite.

Let the equation

$$Au = f, \tag{29.2}$$

where A is a positive definite operator, be defined in the separable Hilbert space $\mathfrak{H}$.

Keeping in mind our intention to use the Ritz-process, we choose a system of coordinate functions

$$\{\phi_n\} = \phi_1, \phi_2, \ldots, \phi_n, \ldots, \tag{29.3}$$

which, in the first place, satisfies the three conditions of §6:

(1) $\{\phi_n\} \in \mathfrak{H}_A$;

(2) the functions $\phi_1, \phi_2, \ldots, \phi_n$ are linearly independent for arbitrary n;

(3) $\{\phi_n\}$ is complete in $\mathfrak{H}_A$.

The approximate Ritz-solution is constructed in the form

$$u_n = \sum_{k=1}^{n} a_k^{(n)} \phi_k. \tag{29.4}$$

If n is large, then, as we saw in Chapter II, the Ritz-process can prove to be unstable. However, the phrase "large n" has a relative meaning: in the example of §8, the phenomenon of instability has become sufficiently noticeable for $n = 4$. Therefore, acceptable approximate solutions can be obtained in practice under the three conditions listed above only when n is small. If n is compartively large, then the additional requirement that the coordinate system be strongly minimal in $\mathfrak{H}_A$ is necessary. It is desirable to clarify the essence of this requirement. If the coordinate system is strongly minimal, then the Ritz-process is stable w.r.t. the small errors allowed in the construction of the Ritz-systems. However, during the *solution* of such Ritz-system unavoidable rounding errors can lead to large errors in the Ritz-coefficients. Therefore, as was clarified in §11, it is desirable that the coordinate system be almost orthonormal in $\mathfrak{H}_A$. If the coordinate system is only strongly minimal and n is comparatively large, then it is necessary to solve the Ritz-systems with a high degree of accuracy. This in itself can lead to laborious programming problems. Finally, if, as we saw in Chapter IV, we choose as our coordinate system the eigenfunctions (if they are complete) of the operator $\boldsymbol{B}$ which is similar to A, then the residual $Au_n - f$ tends to zero. Moreover, if A is a differential operator, then the following result may hold: derivatives of the approximate solution of order up to and including that of the differential equation tend (w.r.t. the metric of $\mathfrak{H}$) to the corresponding derivatives of the exact solution. For an arbitrary chosen coordinate system, we only know that $|||u_n - u_0|||_A \to 0$: for differential equations, this implies convergence (w.r.t. the metric of $\mathfrak{H}$) for derivatives the order of which does not exceed half the order of the differential equation.

It is important to stress one property: if the eigenfunctions of $\boldsymbol{B}$ are normalised, then the resulting system is almost orthonormal in $\mathfrak{H}_{\boldsymbol{A}}$. In fact, the mentioned eigenfunctions will be orthogonal in $\mathfrak{H}_{\boldsymbol{B}}$ (VM, §29) and after normalisation will be orthonormal in $\mathfrak{H}_{\boldsymbol{B}}$. Since similar operators $\boldsymbol{A}$ and $\boldsymbol{B}$ are semi-similar, it follows from Corollary 4.3 that the eigenfunctions will be almost orthonormal in $\mathfrak{H}_{\boldsymbol{A}}$.

The eigenfunctions of $\boldsymbol{B}$ can be normalised w.r.t. the metric of $\mathfrak{H}_{\boldsymbol{A}}$. It is not difficult to see that we shall again obtain a system which is almost orthonormal in $\mathfrak{H}_{\boldsymbol{A}}$. Such normalisation has its advantages: the values $|\phi_k|_{\boldsymbol{A}}^2$ are the diagonal elements of the Ritz-matrix. Therefore, if the values $|\phi_k|_{\boldsymbol{B}}^2$ cannot be calculated with sufficient ease, then normalisation in $\mathfrak{H}_{\boldsymbol{A}}$ is apparently more appropriate.

On the basis of the above discussion, we formulate a scheme for the choice of coordinate systems for the application of the energy method to positive definite operators (where we shall restrict attention to problems leading to positive definite operators):

1. Initially, we shall try to construct an operator $\boldsymbol{B}$ such that:

(1) $\boldsymbol{B}$ similar to a given $\boldsymbol{A}$;

(2) the spectrum of $\boldsymbol{B}$ is discrete.

In addition, we require that the eigenfunctions of $\boldsymbol{B}$ be easily determined and have a sufficiently simple form.

If, under such circumstances, we take the eigenfunctions of $\boldsymbol{B}$, which are

normalised in $\mathfrak{H}_B$ (or $\mathfrak{H}_A$), as coordinate functions, then:
(a) the Ritz-process and the approximate Ritz-solution will be stable;
(b) the condition number of the Ritz-matrix will be bounded independently of its order. {Hence, among other things, the Ritz-system can be solved by iteration (see §12)};
(c) the coorresponding residual will tend to zero.

2. If we cannot satisfy the requirement of **1**, then we can try to construct an almost orthonormal coordinate system in $\mathfrak{H}_A$ so that (a) and (b) of **1** will hold. If $\boldsymbol{B}$ is semi-similar to $\boldsymbol{A}$, then any complete orthonormal system in $\mathfrak{H}_B$ will define such a system (see Corollary 4.3). In particular, if $\boldsymbol{B}$ has a point spectrum, then we can use the eigenfunctions of $\boldsymbol{B}$ which have been normalised in $\mathfrak{H}_B$.

3. If the construction of a sufficiently simple almost orthonormal coordinate system in $\mathfrak{H}_A$ proves to be difficult, then we can try to construct a strongly minimal coordinate system in $\mathfrak{H}_A$. In this case, (a) of **1** will hold. Strongly minimal coordinate systems can be constructed, for example, in the following manner: If the space $\mathfrak{H}_A$ is imbedded in some space $\mathfrak{K}$ (§4) and system $\{\phi_n\}$ is complete in $\mathfrak{H}_A$ and strongly minimal in $\mathfrak{K}$, then it will be strongly minimal in $\mathfrak{H}_A$ (Theorem 4.2). For example, if $\{\phi_n\}$ is complete in $\mathfrak{H}_A$ and orthonormal in $\mathfrak{K}$, then it is strongly minimal in $\mathfrak{H}_A$.

Note. It should be remembered that the use of the eigenfunctions of a similar operator as coordinate functions yields an approximation which may converge poorly. We clarify this in the following example.

We consider the equation

$$Au = -\Delta u + C(x)u = f(x), \qquad u|_S = 0, \tag{29.5}$$

where Ω is a finite region with a sufficiently smooth boundary S and $C(x) \geqq 0$. The operator $\boldsymbol{B}$ defined by

$$Bu = -\Delta u, \qquad u|_S = 0 \tag{29.6}$$

is similar to $\boldsymbol{A}$.

The spectrum of $\boldsymbol{B}$ is discrete. Let

$$\{\phi_n\} = \phi_1(x), \phi_2(x), \ldots, \phi_n(x), \ldots$$

be the complete system of orthonormal eigenfunctions in $L_2(\Omega)$, and

$$u_n(x) = \sum_{k=1}^{n} a_k^{(n)} \phi_k(x)$$

denote the approximate Ritz-solution of (29.5). Using Theorem 22.1, $Au_n \to f$ in $L_2(\Omega)$. If $u_0(x)$ denotes the exact solution of (29.5), then

$$-\Delta u_n + C(x)u_n \xrightarrow[L_2(\Omega)]{} -\Delta u + C(x)u,$$

and since $u_n \xrightarrow[L_2(\Omega)]{} u_0$,

$$\Delta u_n \xrightarrow[L_2(\Omega)]{} \Delta u_0 .$$

Nevertheless, it does not follow, in general, that Δu_n tends uniformly to Δu_0 in $\bar{\Omega} = \Omega \cup S$. In fact, if uniform convergence did occur, then

$$\Delta u_n|_S \rightrightarrows \Delta u_0|_S ,$$

where $\rightrightarrows$ denotes uniform convergence. However,

$$\Delta u_n = \sum_{k=1}^{n} a_k^{(n)} \Delta \phi_k = -\sum_{k=1}^{n} a_k^{(n)} \mu_k \phi_k ,$$

where the μ_k are the eigenvalues of the operator (29.6). Hence $\Delta u_n|_S = 0$. From (29.5), it follows that

$$\Delta u_0|_S = -f(x)|_S + C(x)u_0|_S = -f(x)|_S ,$$

where the given function $f(x)$ does not tend to zero everywhere on the boundary S. It follows from the examined problem that second or higher order derivatives of the approximate solution will not, in general, converge uniformly to the corresponding derivative of the exact solution. A more general result is: if a differential operator of order k is solved by a Ritz-process with coordinate functions defined by the eigenfunctions of a similar operator, then, in general derivatives of the approximate solution of order $\geq k$ do not converge uniformly in Ω to the corresponding derivative of the exact solution.

On the basis of Theorem 22.1, we make the following observation: if the eigenfunctions of a similar operator are chosen as coordinate functions, then the corresponding approximate solution will not necessarily converge very rapidly to the exact solution. We examine the problem

$$Au = -\frac{d}{dk}\left(p(x)\frac{du}{dx}\right) + q(x)u = f(x), \qquad u(0) = u(\pi) = 0, \quad (29.7)$$

where $p(x)$, $p'(x)$ and $q(x)$ are continuous functions on the interval

$(0, \pi)$ such that $p(x) > 0$, $q(x) \geqq 0$. The operator $\boldsymbol{B}$ defined by

$$\boldsymbol{B}u = -\frac{d^2u}{dx^2}, \qquad u(0) = u(\pi) = 0,$$

is similar to the operator of problem (29.7). The eigenfunctions of $\boldsymbol{B}$ are $\phi_k(x) = (2/\pi)^{\frac{1}{2}} \sin kx$. If

$$u_n(x) = \sqrt{\frac{2}{\pi}} \sum_{k=1}^{n} a_k^{(n)} \sin k\pi x$$

is the approximate Ritz-solution of (29.7) and $u_0(x)$ its exact solution, then (see PM, §38 and the references mentioned there) $|u_n - u_0| = 0(n^{-\frac{3}{2}})$. This estimate can only be improved when $f(x)$ – the r.h.s. term of (29.7) – satisfies some special condition such as $f(0) = f(\pi) = 0$. If polynonials are taken as coordinate functions, then, as was seen in §28, the estimate of $|u_0 - u_0|$ becomes sharper as the smoothness of the functions p, q and f improves.

§30. Ordinary differential equations of the second order

Throughout this section, $\mathfrak{H} = L_2(0,1)$.

1. Let the operator $\boldsymbol{A}$ be defined by

$$\boldsymbol{A}u = -\frac{d}{dx}\left(p(x)\frac{du}{dx}\right) + q(x)u, \qquad 0 < x < 1, \tag{30.1}$$

$$u(0) = u(1) = 0, \tag{30.2}$$

where, as in §25, $p(x)$, $p'(x)$ and $q(x)$ are continuous on $0 \leqq x \leqq 1$, $p(x) \geqq p_0, p_0 = \text{const.} > 0$, and $q(x) \geqq -\mu_1$, where μ_1 is the smallest eigenvalue of the operator

$$-\frac{d}{dx}\left(p(x)\frac{du}{dx}\right) \tag{30.3}$$

w.r.t. the boundary condition (30.2). The operator $\boldsymbol{B}$, defined by

$$\boldsymbol{B}u = -\frac{d^2u}{dx^2}, \qquad u(0) = u(1) = 0, \tag{30.4}$$

is clearly similar to $\boldsymbol{A}$.

For (30.1) and (30.2), we can choose the eigenfunctions of $\boldsymbol{B}$, normalised in $\mathfrak{H}_{\boldsymbol{B}}$, as coordinate functions.
Since the metric in $\mathfrak{H}_{\boldsymbol{B}}$ is defined by

$$[u, v]_{\boldsymbol{B}} = \int_0^1 u'(x)\overline{v'(x)}dx, \qquad |||u|||_{\boldsymbol{B}}^2 = \int_0^1 |u'(x)|^2\, dx,$$

the eigenfunctions (see (25.8)) have the form $\phi_n(x) = c_n \sin n\pi x$, where the c_n are defined by the condition

$$|\phi_n|_{\boldsymbol{B}}^2 = \int_0^1 [\phi_n'(x)]^2\, dx = c_2^n n^2\pi^2 \int_0^1 \cos \; n\pi x\, dx = 1.$$

Hence,

$$c_n = \frac{\sqrt{2}}{n\pi}$$

and

$$\phi_n(x) = \frac{\sqrt{2}}{n\pi} \sin n\pi x\; (n = 1, 2, \ldots). \tag{30.5}$$

Clearly, the conditions (a)–(c) of **1**, §29, must hold for this choice of coordinate functions.
Another simple and suitable system of coordinate function for (30.1) and (30.2) is the system of polynomials

$$Q_n(x) = c_n \int_0^1 P_n(2t-1)dt \qquad (n = 1, 2, \ldots),$$

where the P_n are the Legendre polynomials of order n and the c_n are defined by the condition $|||Q_n|||_{\boldsymbol{B}} = 1$. Now, $Q_n \in \mathfrak{D}(A)$. In fact, these functions have continuous derivatives of all orders and satisfy the boundary conditions (30.2): the result $Q_n(0) = 0$ is obvious, while

$$0 = Q_n(1) = c_n \int_0^1 P_n(2t-1)dt = \tfrac{1}{2}c_n \int_{-1}^1 P_n(z)dz$$

follows from the fact that the Legendre polynomials $P_n(z)$, $n > 0$, are orthogonal to $P_0(z) \equiv 1$ on the interval $[-1, 1]$. Further, the polynomials $Q_n(x)$ are orthonormal in $\mathfrak{H}_{\boldsymbol{B}}$, if the c_n are chosen so that $|||Q_n|||_{\boldsymbol{B}} = 1$.

Since

$$[Q_n, Q_m]_B = \int_0^1 Q_n'(x)\overline{Q_m'(x)}dx = c_n c_m \int_0^1 P_n(2x-1)P_m(2x-1)dx =$$

$$= \frac{c_n c_m}{2}\int_{-1}^1 P_n(z)P_m(z)dz = \frac{c_n c_m}{2n+1}\,\delta_{nm},$$

we find that

$$c_n = \sqrt{2n+1},$$

and hence,

$$Q_n(x) = \sqrt{2n+1}\int_0^x P_n(2t-1)dt \qquad (n = 1, 2, \ldots). \tag{30.6}$$

Since, from the definition of the norm in $\mathfrak{H}_B$, convergence in $\mathfrak{H}_B$ implies convergence of the derivatives in $L_2(0, 1)$, it follows that (see §8) (30.6) is complete in $\mathfrak{H}_B$. Hence, (30.6) is complete and almost orthonormal in $\mathfrak{H}_A$. If (30.6) is chosen as the coordinate system for (30.1) and (30.2), then conditions (a) and (b) of **1**, §29, must hod. From the results of §28, condition (c) is valid for (30.6), if the solution u_0 of (30.1) and (30.2) is contained in $C^4([0,1])$ and d^4u_0/dx satisfies a Lipschitz condition of exponent greater than $\frac{1}{2}$. We also note that the quantity $\sqrt{2n+1}$ in formula (30.6) can be replaced by $[\sqrt{n}]$, where $[x]$ denotes the integral part of x (see the Observation at the end of this section).

2. We again examine (30.1) and (30.2). This time, however, we weaken the conditions on $p(x)$ and $q(x)$: we assume that $p(x)$ is continuous, positive bounded below, $p(x) \geqq p_0 = \text{const.} > 0$, and its first derivative has a finite number of discontinuities of the first kind, and that $q(x)$ is bounded, measurable and $q(x) \geqq -\mu_1+\delta$, where $\delta = \text{const.} > 0$. In this way, $p(x)$ satisfies a Lipschitz condition of exponent 1, and hence, is absolutely continuous on the interval [0,1].

Tracing the argument of §23, it is easy to see that (23.6) remains valid, and hence, that the product $p(x)u_0'(x)$, where $u_0(x)$ is the generalised solution of (30.1) and (30.2), is absolutely continuous. Since the function $p(x)$ does not equal zero and is absolutely continuous, the derivative $u_0'(x)$ is absolutely continuous (see Natanson [2]). It follows from (23.6) that the second derivative $u_0''(x)$ is square summable on the interval [0,1].

Hence, under the conditions of the present sub-section, $\mathfrak{D}(A)$ coincides with that of **1** and, as before, A and B are similar. As a result, the conclusion of **1** must also hold for the corresponding residual w.r.t. (30.6).

3. The situation changes if the coefficient $p(x)$ is discontinuous. We assume, for example, that, except for the continuity of $p(x)$, the conditions in **2** are valid. For the sake of simplicity, let $p(x)$ have a discontinuity of the first kind at the point a, $0 < a < 1$.

If the functions, which lie in $\mathfrak{D}(A)$, only satisfy (30.2), then A is not symmetric. In fact, if $u(0) = u(1) = v(0) = v(1) = 0$ and the manipulations used below are valid, then

$$\begin{aligned}(Au, v) &= \int_0^1 \overline{v(x)}\{-(p(x)u'(x))' + q(x)u(x)\}dx = \\ &= -\int_0^a \overline{v(x)}(p(x)u'(x))'\,dx - \int_a^1 \overline{v(x)}(p(x)u'(x))'\,dx + \\ &\quad + \int_0^1 q(x)u(x)\overline{v(x)}dx = \\ &= -p(x)u'(x)\overline{v(x)}|_0^a - p(x)u'(x)\overline{v(x)}|_a^1 + \\ &\quad + \int_0^1 \{p(x)u'(x)\overline{v'(x)} + q(x)u(x)\overline{v(x)}\}dx, \end{aligned} \tag{30.7}$$

Taking (30.2) into account, we obtain

$$\begin{aligned}(Au, v) &= u'(a)\overline{v(a)}[p(a+0) - p(a-0)] + \\ &\quad + \int_0^1 \{p(x)u'(x)\overline{v'(x)} + q(x)u(x)\overline{v(x)}\}dx;\end{aligned}$$

which is not symmetric w.r.t. u and v.

The operator A, defined by (30.1), becomes symmetric, if $\mathfrak{D}(A)$ is defined as the set of functions u which satisfy:

1) $u \in C([0,1])$, $u(0) = u(1) = 0$;

2) $u'(x)$ has a discontinuity of the first kind at the point a such that

$$p(a-0)u'(a-0) = p(a+0)u'(a+0); \tag{30.8}$$

3) If $u'(x)$ equals $u'(a-0)$ at a, then $u'(x)$ is absolutely continuous on $[0, a]$, while if $u'(x)$ equals $u'(a+0)$ at a, then $u'(x)$ is absolutely continuous on $[a, 1]$;

4) $u''(x)$ is square summable on $[0,1]$.

In fact, under these conditions, (30.7) becomes

$$(Au, v) = [p(a+0)u'(a+0) - p(a-0)u'(a-0)]\overline{v(a)} + \\ + \int_0^1 \{p(x)u'(x)\overline{v'(x)} + q(x)u(x)\overline{v(x)}\}dx = \\ = \int_0^1 \{p(x)u'(x)\overline{v'(x)} + q(x)u(x)\overline{v(x)}\}dx, \tag{30.9}$$

which is symmetric w.r.t. u and v. Moreover, it follows from (30.9) that

$$(Au, u) = \int_0^1 \{p(x)|u'(x)|^2 + q(x)|u(x)|^2\}dx \geqq \\ \geqq \delta \int_0^1 |u(x)|^2 dx = \delta \|u\|^2,$$

which proves that A is positive definite. Repeating the argument of §25, it is not difficult to establish that A is selfadjoint. It is also casy to construct a comparatively simple operator similar to A: for example, the operator B_1 with domain $\mathfrak{D}(B_1) = \mathfrak{D}(A)$ which maps in accordance with

$$B_1 u = \begin{cases} p(a-0)u'', & 0 < x < a, \\ p(a+0)u'', & a < x < 1. \end{cases}$$

Hence, for the solution of (30.1) w.r.t. the boundary conditions (30.2) and (30.8), we can use the eigenfunctions of B_1 as coordinate functions. However, their use is difficult, since the construction of these eigenfunctions is connected with the solutions of a rather complex transcendental equation. We shall derive this equation. These functions satisfy the boundary conditions (30.2) and (30.8) and the differential equations

$$p(a-0)u'' + \lambda u = 0, \qquad 0 < x < a,$$
$$p(a+0)u'' + \lambda u = 0, \qquad a < x < 1.$$

In addition, they are continuous for $x = a$.
Writing, for convenience, $\lambda = \mu^2$, $p(a-0) = r^{-2}$ and $p(a+0) = s^{-2}$, we find that

$$u = \begin{cases} C_1 \cos r\mu x + C_2 \sin r\mu x, & 0 \leqslant x < a, \\ C_3 \cos s\mu x + C_4 \sin s\mu x, & a < x \leqslant 1. \end{cases}$$

Conditions (30.2) and (30.8), as well as the continuity of $u(x)$ at $x = a$, yield

$$C_1 = 0,$$

$$C_3 \cos s\mu + C_4 \sin s\mu = 0,$$

$$C_2 \sin r\mu a - C_3 \cos s\mu a - C_4 \sin s\mu a = 0,$$

$$C_2 r^{-1}\mu \cos r\mu a + C_3 s^{-1}\mu \sin s\mu a - C_4 s^{-1}\mu \cos s\mu a = 0.$$

Hence, we obtain for μ the equation

$$\begin{vmatrix} 0 & \cos s\mu & \sin s\mu \\ \sin r\mu a & -\cos s\mu a & -\sin s\mu a \\ r^{-1}\mu \cos r\mu a & s^{-1}\mu \sin s\mu a & -s^{-1}\mu \cos s\mu a \end{vmatrix} = 0.$$

Since the calculation of the roots for this equation poses quite a laborious problem, it seems appropriate to reject the use of these eigenfunctions and to take instead functions which are complete and orthonormal w.r.t. the metric of some semi-similar operator. It is clear that $\boldsymbol{B}$ (defined by (30.4)) is semi-similar to $\boldsymbol{A}$ and that either (30.5) or (30.6) can serve as coordinate functions. In this way, assertions (a) and (b) of **1**, §29, will hold.

4. Now let $\boldsymbol{A}$ be defined by (30.1) and the boundary conditions

$$u(0) = 0, \qquad u'(1) = 0. \tag{30.10}$$

We retain the assumptions of **1**, where μ_1 is now the smallest eigenvalue of (30.3) and (30.10). Hence, w.r.t. the boundary conditions (30.10), the operator $\boldsymbol{B}_2 = -(d^2/dx^2)$ is similar to $\boldsymbol{A}$. Since its eigenfunctions, which are normalised in $\mathfrak{H}_{\boldsymbol{B}_2}$, are

$$\phi_n(x) = \frac{2\sqrt{2}}{(2n-1)\pi} \sin \frac{2n-1}{2} \pi x \qquad (n = 1, 2, \ldots). \tag{30.11}$$

the conditions (a)–(c) of **1**, §29, will hold if, for the solution of (30.1) and (30.10), we take (30.11) as the system of coordinate functions.

5. We retain the assumptions of **1** with the additional requirement that $q(x) \geqq q_0 = \text{const.} > 0$ and let $\boldsymbol{A}$ be defined by (30.1) and the boundary conditions

$$u'(0) = u'(1) = 0, \tag{30.12}$$

where the operator $\boldsymbol{B}_3$, defined by the differential expression $-(d^2u/dx^2)+u$ and the boundary conditions (13.12), is similar to $\boldsymbol{A}$. Since its eigenfunctions, normalised in $\mathfrak{H}_{\boldsymbol{B}_3}$, are

$$\phi_0(x) = 1, \quad \phi_n(x) = \sqrt{\frac{2}{n^2\pi^2+1}} \cos n\pi x \qquad (n = 1, 2, \ldots), \tag{30.13}$$

the results of **4** carry over without change.

6. We now examine the case when $\boldsymbol{A}$ is defined by (30.1) and the boundary conditions

$$u'(0)-\alpha u(0) = 0, \qquad u'(1)+\beta u(1) = 0, \qquad \alpha, \beta > 0. \tag{30.14}$$

We assume that $p(x)$ and $q(x)$ satisfy the conditions of **1**, where μ_1 is now the smallest eigenvalue of the operator (30.3) and (30.14). Here, the operator $\boldsymbol{B}_4$, defined by the differential expression $-(d^2/dx^2)$ and the boundary conditions (30.14), will be similar to $\boldsymbol{A}$.

However, the construction of the eigenfunctions for this operator is difficult, since they are the solutions of a transcendental equation. On the other hand, it is not difficult to construct an operator semi-similar to $\boldsymbol{A}$, and then to orthonormalise some complete system w.r.t. the metric of the energy space of this operator. In fact, $\boldsymbol{B}_3$ of **5** is semi-similar to $\boldsymbol{A}$. The corresponding spaces $\mathfrak{H}_{\boldsymbol{A}}$ and $\mathfrak{H}_{\boldsymbol{B}_3}$ consist of the functions which are absolutely continuous on [0, 1] and the first derivatives of which are square summable on [0, 1]. If, for the solution of (30.1) and (30.14), the functions (30.13) are used as coordinate functions, then (a) and (b) of **1**, §29, will hold.

The operator $\tilde{\boldsymbol{B}}$, defined by

$$\tilde{\boldsymbol{B}}u = -\frac{d^2u}{dx^2}, \qquad u'(0)-u(0) = 0, \qquad u'(1) = 0,$$

is also semi-similar to $\boldsymbol{A}$. Its corresponding energy inner product and norm are

$$\begin{aligned} [u, v]_{\tilde{\boldsymbol{B}}} &= u(0)\overline{v(0)}+\int_0^1 u'(x)\overline{v'(x)}dx, \\ |||u|||_{\tilde{\boldsymbol{B}}}^2 &= |u(0)|^2+\int_0^1 |u'(x)|^2\,dx. \end{aligned} \tag{30.15}$$

From (30.15), it is at once clear that the spaces $\mathfrak{H}_{\boldsymbol{A}}$ and $\mathfrak{H}_{\boldsymbol{B}}$ consist of one and the same elements. It is not difficult to construct a system of functions which is complete and orthonormal in $\mathfrak{H}_{\tilde{B}}$. Such a system is

$$1,\, x,\, \frac{\sqrt{2}}{\pi}\sin \pi x,\quad \frac{\sqrt{2}}{2\pi}\sin 2\pi x, \ldots,\quad \frac{\sqrt{2}}{n\pi}\sin n\pi x, \ldots \quad . \tag{30.16}$$

Since this system is orthonormal w.r.t. the metric (30.15), it is only necessary to prove its completeness. In order to do this, we determine the function $\omega(x)$ which is orthogonal to the functions

$$\frac{\sqrt{2}}{n\pi}\sin n\pi x \qquad (n = 1, 2, \ldots).$$

w.r.t. the metric (30.15):

$$\left[\omega(x), \frac{\sqrt{2}}{n\pi}\sin n\pi x\right]_{\tilde{B}} =$$
$$= \sqrt{2}\int_0^1 \omega'(x)\cos n\pi x\, dx = 0 \qquad (n = 1, 2, \ldots).$$

This implies that $\omega'(x) = C$ and, thus, that $\omega(x) = Cx + c_1$, where C and c_1 = const., which proves the completeness of (30.16). The use of (30.16) as coordinate functions implies the stability of the approximate Ritz-solution of (30.1) and (30.14) and the boundedness of the condition number of the Ritz-matrix.

7. In an analogous manner, similar to that of **2** and **3**, the boundary value problems of the previous sub-sections can be examined under the weaker assumption of a discontinuity for one or other of the functions $p(x)$, $p'(x)$ or $q(x)$. We leave this analysis to the reader.

Observation. Let A and B be semi-similar operators. As we know, a system of elements which is almost orthonormal in $\mathfrak{H}_B$ is almost orthonormal in $\mathfrak{H}_A$. In the present section we have acted in the following way: starting with a system $\{\phi_n\}$ orthogonal in $\mathfrak{H}_B$, we normalise it w.r.t. the metric of $\mathfrak{H}_B$ by multiplication with appropriate scalars. This yields an orthonormal system in $\mathfrak{H}_B$ which will be almost orthonormal in $\mathfrak{H}_A$. However, in order to achieve this last result, it is not necessary to satisfy $|||\phi_n|||_B = 1$. It is sufficient if $a \leqq |||\phi_n|||_B \leqq b$, where a and b are positive constants. Then, the system $\{\phi_n\}$, which is orthogonal in $\mathfrak{H}_B$, becomes almost orthonormal in $\mathfrak{H}_B$, and hence, almost orthonormal in $\mathfrak{H}_A$. This simple observation allows us to simplify the normalising condition for the construction of coordinate functions. This, in its turn, diminishes the volume of calculations without damaging the quality of the results. Thus, in system (30.5), we can replace $\sqrt{2}/n\pi$ by $1/n$. This yields the following simpler almost orthonormal system

$$\phi_n(x) = \frac{1}{n} \sin n\pi x \qquad (n = 1, 2, \ldots). \tag{30.5'}$$

In an analagous way, systems (30.6), (30.11), (30.13) and (30.16) can be replaced by the following simpler systems which are also almost orthonormal in the corresponding spaces $\mathfrak{H}_A$:

$$Q_n(x) = \sqrt{n} \int_0^x P_n(2t-1)dt \qquad (n = 1, 2, \ldots), \tag{30.6'}$$

$$\phi_n(x) = \frac{1}{2n-1} \sin \frac{2n-1}{2} \pi x \qquad (n = 1, 2, \ldots), \tag{30.11'}$$

$$\phi_0(x) = 1, \qquad \phi_n(x) = \frac{1}{n} \cos n\pi x \qquad (n = 1, 2, \ldots), \tag{30.13'}$$

$$1, x, \sin \pi x, \tfrac{1}{2} \sin 2\pi x, \ldots, \frac{1}{n} \sin n\pi x, \ldots \tag{30.16'}$$

In (30.6′), $\sqrt{n}$ can also be replaced by $[\sqrt{n}]$.
We also note that: the inequality

$$a \leqq |||\phi_n|||_B \leqq b,$$

is satisfied, if we normalise the ϕ_n w.r.t. the metric of $\mathfrak{H}_A$.

§31. Degenerate equations

We restrict attention to some elementary problems. However, an extension of the present results to similar problems defined w.r.t. other boundary conditions does not pose any great difficulty.

1. In §24, we investigated a simple and important example of a degenerate ordinary differential equation. We shall start with this example. We consider the equation

$$-\frac{d}{dx}\left(p(x)\frac{du}{dx}\right) + q(x)u = f(x), \qquad 0 < x < 1, \tag{31.1}$$

where

$$p(x) = \tilde{p}(x)x^\alpha, \qquad 0 < \alpha < 2, \qquad \tilde{p}(x) \geqq p_0 = \text{const} > 0, \qquad (31.2)$$

and retain the other assumptions of §24 regarding the properties of the functions $\tilde{p}(x)$ and $q(x)$.

We seek the solution of (31.1) w.r.t. the boundary conditions

$$u(1) = 0, \qquad (31.3)$$

and, if $0 < \alpha < 1$,

$$u(0) = 0. \qquad (31.4)$$

From the results of §24, it follows that the eigenfunctions of the operator $\boldsymbol{B}$, defined by

$$-\frac{d}{dx}\left(x^\alpha \frac{du}{dx}\right) \qquad (31.5)$$

and the boundary conditions (31.3) and (31.4), can be chosen as coordinate functions. As we saw (equation (24.11)), these functions are

$$\phi_n(x) = c_n x^{(1-\alpha)/2} J_\nu(\gamma_{\nu,n} x^{(2-\alpha)/2}) \qquad (n = 1, 2, \ldots), \qquad (31.6)$$

where the c_n are chosen so that $a \leqq |||\phi_n|||_{\boldsymbol{B}} \leqq b$ (see the Observation at the end of §30). For this choice of the c_n, conditions (a)–(c) of **1**, §29, will hold.

It is simplest to put

$$c_n = \left\{\int_0^1 x^\alpha \left[\frac{d}{dx}(x^{(1-\alpha)/2} J_\nu(\gamma_{\nu,n} x^{(2-\alpha)/2}))\right]^2 dx\right\}^{-\frac{1}{2}} \qquad (n = 1, 2, \ldots), \qquad (31.7)$$

for then $|||\phi_n|||_{\boldsymbol{B}} = 1$ and (31.6) is orthonormal in $\mathfrak{H}_{\boldsymbol{B}}$. However, one can avoid the evaluation of the integral introduced in (31.7) and replace the coefficient (31.7) by something simpler. As a preliminary, we estimate the asymptotic value of the integral

$$K = \int_0^1 x^\alpha \left[\frac{d}{dx}(x^{(1-\alpha)/2} J_\nu(\gamma_{\nu,n} x^{(2-\alpha)/2}))\right]^2 dx$$

for $n \to \infty$.

Evaluating the derivative under the integral sign in K, we obtain

$$K = K_1 + K_2 + K_3,$$

where

$$K_1 = \frac{(2-\alpha)^2}{4}\gamma_{\nu,n}^2 \int_0^1 x^{1-\alpha}[J_\nu'(\gamma_{\nu,n}x^{(2-\alpha)/2})]^2 dx,$$

$$K_2 = \frac{(2-\alpha)(1-\alpha)}{2}\gamma_{\nu,n}\int_0^1 x^{-\alpha/2}J_\nu'(\gamma_{\nu,n}x^{(2-\alpha)/2})J_\nu(\gamma_{\nu,n}x^{(2-\alpha)/2})dx,$$

$$K_3 = \frac{(1-\alpha)^2}{4}\int_0^1 x^{-1}[J_\nu(\gamma_{\nu,n}x^{(2-\alpha)/2})]^2 dx.$$

We seek an asymptotic expression for the integral K_1 for large n. Below, we write γ instead of $\gamma_{\nu,n}$. Putting $\gamma x^{(2\alpha-2)/2} = z$, we obtain (with ε a positive constant such that $0 < \varepsilon < 1$)

$$K_1 = \frac{2-\alpha}{2}\int_0^\gamma z[J_\nu'(z)]dz = \frac{2-\alpha}{2}\int_0^{\gamma^{(1-\varepsilon)/2}} z[J_\nu'(z)]^2 dz +$$

$$+\frac{2-\alpha}{2}\int_{\gamma^{(1-\varepsilon)/2}}^{\gamma} z[J_\nu'(z)]^2 dz = K_1' + K_1''.$$

We use the following results (see Watson [1; §§3.2, 6.2, 7.1]):

$$2J_\nu'(x) = J_{\nu-1}(x) - J_{\nu+1}(x), \tag{31.8}$$

$$J_\nu(x) = \frac{1}{\pi}\int_0^\pi \cos(\nu\theta - x\sin\theta)d\theta - \frac{\sin\nu\pi}{\pi}\int_0^\infty e^{-\nu t - x\,\mathrm{sh}\,t}dt, \qquad x > 0, \tag{31.9}$$

$$J_\nu(x) = \sqrt{\frac{2}{\pi x}}\cos\left(x - \frac{\nu\pi}{2} - \frac{\pi}{4}\right) + O(x^{-\frac{3}{2}}), \qquad x > 0. \tag{31.10}$$

From (31.8) and (31.9), we obtain

$$|J_\nu(x)| \leqq \sigma, \qquad |J_\nu'(x)| \geqq \sigma, \qquad \sigma = 1 + \frac{1}{\pi\nu}. \tag{31.11}$$

Using (31.8) and (31.10), we find an asymptotic expression for $J_\nu'(x)$ for large positive x:

$$J_\nu'(x) = \sqrt{\frac{2}{\pi x}}\cos\left(x - \frac{(\nu-1)\pi}{2} - \frac{\pi}{4}\right) + O(x^{-\frac{3}{2}}). \tag{31.12}$$

On the basis of (31.11),

$$K_1' \leqq \frac{2-\alpha}{2}\sigma^2 \int_0^{\gamma^{(1-\varepsilon)/2}} z\,dz = o(\gamma).$$

Replacing $J_\nu'(z)$ by (31.12), we obtain

$$K_1'' = \frac{2-\alpha}{2}\,\frac{2}{\pi}\int_{\gamma^{(1-\varepsilon)/2}}^{\gamma}\left[\cos^2\left(x-\frac{(\nu-1)\pi}{2}-\frac{\pi}{4}\right)+O(x^{-1})\right]dx =$$

$$= \frac{2-\alpha}{2\pi}\gamma+o(\gamma),$$

and finally,

$$K_1 = \frac{2-\alpha}{2\pi}\gamma+o(\gamma). \tag{31.13}$$

Since, if $\alpha = 1$, $K_2 = K_3 = 0$, it is sufficient to develop estimates for K_2 and K_3 when $\alpha \neq 1$, and hence, $\nu > 0$.

Making use of the substitution $z = \gamma x^{(2-\alpha)/2}$, we find that

$$K_3 = \frac{(1-\alpha)^2}{2(2-\alpha)}\int_0^{\gamma} z^{-1}[J_\nu(z)]^2\,dz =$$

$$= \frac{(1-\alpha)^2}{2(2-\alpha)}\left\{\int_0^1 z^{-1}[J_\nu(z)]^2\,dz+\int_1^{\gamma} z^{-1}[J_\nu(z)]^2\,dz\right\}.$$

The first integral on the right-hand side is constant, while the second, on the basis of (31.11), satisfies

$$\int_1^{\gamma} z^{-1}[J_\nu(z)]^2\,dz \leqq \sigma^2 \ln \gamma.$$

Hence,

$$K_3 = o(\gamma). \tag{31.14}$$

It is quite a simple matter to show that

$$|K_2| \leqq 2K_1^{\frac{1}{2}}K_3^{\frac{1}{2}} = o(\gamma). \tag{31.15}$$

From (31.13)–(31.15), we obtain the required result

$$K = \frac{2-\alpha}{2\pi}\gamma_{\nu,n}+o(\gamma_{\nu,n}). \tag{31.16}$$

Making use of the asymptotic formula for the roots of the Bessel functions (see Watson [1, §15.54]):

$$\gamma_{\nu,n} = \pi n + o(n),$$

we obtain, finally,

$$K = \frac{2-\alpha}{2} n + o(n).$$

It is now clear that, if we put either $c_n = n^{-\frac{1}{2}}$ or $[n^{\frac{1}{2}}]^{-1}$ in (31.6), then (31.6) will be almost orthonormal in $\mathfrak{H}_A$ and conditions (*a*)–(c) of **1**, §29, will be satisfied.

2. We now examine the case when the differential equation is degenerate at both ends of the interval. In the space $L_2(-1, 1)$, we shall examine the operator

$$Au = -\frac{d}{dx}\left[(1-x)^\alpha(1+x)^\beta\tilde{p}(x)\frac{du}{dx}\right] + q(x)u = f(x). \tag{31.17}$$

For simplicity, we assume that $\tilde{p}(x)$, $\tilde{p}'(x)$ and $\tilde{q}(x)$ are continuous on $[-1,1]$, $\tilde{p}(x) \geqq p_0, p_0 = \text{const.} > 0$, and $q(x) \geqq 0$. We also assume that the exponents α and β satisfy $0 \leqq \alpha < 2$ and $0 \leqq \beta < 2$, but exclude from the investigation the trivial non-degenerate case $\alpha = \beta = 0$. When $\alpha > 0$ and $\beta = 0$, we obtain the case examined in **1** of this section.

We define $\mathfrak{D}(A)$ as the set of functions u which satisfy:

(1) $u(x)$ is continuous and $(1-x)^\alpha(1+x)^\beta\, u'(x)$ is absolutely continuous on the interval $[-1, 1]$;

(2) $u(1) = 0;$ (31.18)

(3) if $\alpha < 1$, then

$$u(0) = 0. \tag{31.19}$$

With respect to these conditions, A is positive definite and

$$|||u|||_A^2 = \int_{-1}^{1} \{(1-x)^\alpha(1+x)^\beta\tilde{p}(x)|u'(x)|^2 + q(x)|u(x)|^2\}dx. \tag{31.20}$$

Along with A, we examine the positive definite operator B, with $\mathfrak{D}(B) = \mathfrak{D}(A)$, which maps in accordance with

$$Bu = -\frac{d}{dx}\left[(1-x)^\alpha(1+x)^\beta\frac{du}{dx}\right], \tag{31.21}$$

such that

$$|||u|||_B^2 = \int_{-1}^{1} (1-x)^\alpha (1+x)^\beta |u'(x)|^2 \, dx. \tag{31.22}$$

Repeating the argument of §24, it can be shown that the operators $\boldsymbol{A}$ and $\boldsymbol{B}$ are selfadjoint, and hence, similar. However, since the construction of the eigenfunctions of $\boldsymbol{B}$ is difficult, we limit ourselves to the determination of a system which is orthonormal w.r.t. the metric (31.22), and hence, almost orthonormal w.r.t. the metric (31.20). Such a system is defined by the polynomials

$$q_n^{(\alpha,\beta)}(x) = -\int_x^1 p_n^{(\alpha,\beta)}(t)dt, \tag{31.23}$$

where the $p_n^{(\alpha,\beta)}(x)$ are the normalised Jacobi polynomials (see, for example, Jackson [1]). The choice of the functions $q_n^{(\alpha,\beta)}(x)$ as coordinate functions ensures the validity of (a) and (b) of **1**, §29.

§32. Ordinary differential equations of the fourth order

Consider the equation

$$\frac{d^2}{dx^2}\left(p_2(x)\frac{d^2u}{dx^2}\right) - \frac{d}{dx}\left(p_1(x)\frac{du}{dx}\right) + p_0 u = f(x), \tag{32.1}$$

where the coefficients p_0, p_1 and p_2 satisfy the conditions of §25.
We examine (32.1) w.r.t. some simple types of boundary conditions.
1. We start with the conditions

$$u(0) = u(1) = u''(0) = u''(1) = 0. \tag{32.2}$$

It follows from the results of §25 that the functions $\phi_n(x) = c_n \sin n\pi x$ $(n = 1, 2, \ldots)$ can be taken as coordinate functions, if the coefficients c_n are defined, for example, by the condition $|||\phi_n|||_B = 1$, where $\boldsymbol{B}$ is the operator (25.4). This yields the value $c_n = (\sqrt{2}/n^2\pi^2)$.
The constant factor $\sqrt{2}/\pi^2$ can be discarded. We then obtain

$$\phi_n(x) = \frac{\sin n\pi x}{n^2} \qquad (n = 1, 2, \ldots). \tag{32.3}$$

Conditions (a)–(c) of **1**, §29, will hold for this choice of coordinate functions.

2. We now examine (32.1) w.r.t. the boundary conditions

$$u(0) = u(1) = u'(0) = u'(1) = 0. \tag{32.4}$$

The operator defined by (32.1) and (32.4) is similar and, what is more, semi-similar to the operator $\boldsymbol{B}_1 = (d^4/dx^4)$ with $\mathfrak{D}(\boldsymbol{B}_1)$ contained in the functions which satisfy (32.4). The energy metric corresponding to $\boldsymbol{B}_1$ is defined by

$$|||u|||^2_{\boldsymbol{B}_1} = \int_0^1 |u''(x)|^2 \, dx, \tag{32.5}$$

where the functions of $\mathfrak{H}_{\boldsymbol{B}_1}$ satisfy (32.4). It is easy to establish that the system

$$\phi_n(x) = \sqrt{2n+1}\int_0^x dt \int_0^t P_n(2\tau-1)d\tau =$$
$$= \sqrt{2n+1}\int_0^x (x-t)P_n(2t-1)dt \qquad (n = 2, 3, \ldots), \tag{32.6}$$

where the P_n are Legendre polynomials, is orthonormal and complete in $\mathfrak{H}_{\boldsymbol{B}_1}$. If we take this system as our coordinate system, then conditions (a) and (b) of **1**, §29, will hold. The quantity $\sqrt{2n+1}$ can be replaced by $\sqrt{n}$ or $[\sqrt{n}]$.

If the required solution is contained in $C^9([0,1])$, then (c) of **1**, §29, will also hold.

3. Next, we examine the boundary conditions

$$u(0) = u'(0) = u(1) = u''(1) = 0. \tag{32.7}$$

The operator $\mathfrak{B}_2 = (d^4/dx^4)$ with domain contained in the functions which satisfy (32.7), is similar, and hence, semi-similar to the operator defined by (32.1) and (32.7). The energy metric corresponding to this operator is also defined by (32.5), whereas the functions of $\mathfrak{H}_{\boldsymbol{B}_2}$ only satisfy the conditions $u(0) = u'(0) = u(1) = 0$, since the condition $u''(0) = 0$ is the natural (or transversality) condition (see VM, §17 and PM, §35). System (32.6) is orthonormal, but not complete in $\mathfrak{H}_{\boldsymbol{B}_2}$. We explain how to obtain its completion. Let the function $g(x) \in \mathfrak{H}_{\boldsymbol{B}_2}$ be orthogonal (w.r.t. the metric of this space) to the system (32.6). This implies that

$$\int_0^1 g''(x)P_n(x)dx = 0 \qquad (n = 2, 3, \ldots). \tag{32.8}$$

It follows from here that $g''(x)$ is a polynomial of degree 1, and hence, that $g(x)$ is a polynomial of degree 3. Since $g \in \mathfrak{H}_{B_2}$, and $g(0) = g'(0) = g(1) = 0$, $g(x)$ only differs by a constant factor from $x^2(1-x)$. In this way, a complete and almost orthonormal system (w.r.t. the energy metric of the operator defined by (32.1) and (32.7) is

$$\phi_1(x) = x^2(1-x), \quad \phi_n(x) = [\sqrt{n}]\int_0^x (x-t)P_n(2t-1)dt, \qquad n > 1. \tag{32.9}$$

4. We now examine the case when both boundary conditions at $x = 1$ are natural conditions. In fact, let the boundary conditions take the form

$$u(0) = u'(0) = 0, \quad u''(1) = 0, \quad (p_2(x)u''(x))'|_{x=1} = 0. \tag{32.10}$$

For the problem of bending a beam (VM, §21), these conditions imply that the left-hand end of the beam is rigidly fixed while the right-hand end is free. The operator $\boldsymbol{B}_3 = (d^4/dx^4)$, with domain contained in the functions which satisfy the first three conditions of (32.10) and the additional condition $u'''(1) = 0$, is semi-similar to the operator defined by (32.1) and (32.10). The functions of $\mathfrak{H}_{B_3}$ satisfy the conditions $u(0) = u'(0) = 0$, and the metric in this space is defined by (32.5). Arguing as in **3**, we again find that the functions, orthogonal in $\mathfrak{H}_{B_3}$ to system (32.6), are third degree polynomials. The polynomials, which satisfy the conditions $u(0) = u'(0) = 0$ and are linearly independent, are: x^2 and x^3. Hence, the following system is complete and almost orthonormal w.r.t. the metric of the energy space of the operator defined by (32.1) and (32.10):

$$\phi_0(x) = x^2, \qquad \phi_1(x) = x^3,$$
$$\phi_n(x) = [\sqrt{n}]\int_0^x (x-t)P_n(2t-1)dt \qquad (n = 2, 3, \ldots). \tag{32.11}$$

5. Using the pattern of **2–4** almost orthonormal coordinate systems can be constructed for other types of boundary conditions and for non-degenerate ordinary differential equations of higher order.

§33. Two-dimensional elliptic equations: the first boundary value problem

In this section, we shall assume that $\mathfrak{H} = L_2(\Omega)$ where Ω is a finite plane

region the boundary of which we denote by S.
We shall examine the non-degenerate elliptic equation

$$-\sum_{j,k=1}^{2} \frac{\partial}{\partial x_j}\left(A_{jk}\frac{\partial u}{\partial x_j}\right) + Cu = f(x_1, x_2), \quad x_1 = x, \quad x_2 = y, \tag{33.1}$$

for the boundary condition

$$u|_S = 0. \tag{33.2}$$

Let μ_1 denote the smallest eigenvalue of the operator defined by

$$-\sum_{j,k=1}^{2} \frac{\partial}{\partial x_j}\left(A_{jk}\frac{\partial u}{\partial x_j}\right) \tag{33.3}$$

and the boundary condition (33.2). We assume that $C > -\mu_1$ and that the A_{jk}, the $\partial A_{ik}/\partial x_i$ and C are continuous in the closed region $\bar{\Omega} = \Omega \cup S$.
We assume that the contour S is sufficiently smooth and that there exists a transformation

$$x' = \phi(x, y), \qquad y' = \psi(x, y), \tag{33.4}$$

which defines a one-to-one mapping of $\bar{\Omega}$ onto the disk $\{(x', y');\ (x')^2 + (y')^2 \leqq 1\}$, such that the functions ϕ and ψ are two times continuously differentiable in $\bar{\Omega}$ and that the Jacobian is positive bounded above and below. Applying transformation (33.4), equations (33.1) and (33.2) become

$$-\sum_{j,k=1}^{2} \frac{\partial}{\partial x'_j}\left(A'_{jk}\frac{\partial u}{\partial x'_k}\right) + CJu = fJ, \qquad x'_1 = x', \qquad x'_2 = y', \tag{33.5}$$

$$u|_\Gamma = 0, \tag{33.6}$$

where Γ is the circumference $x'^2 + y'^2 = 1$ and

$$A'_{jk} = J \sum_{r,s=1}^{2} A_{rs} \frac{\partial x'_j}{\partial x_r}\frac{\partial x'_k}{\partial x_s}.$$

Let A denote the operator defined by the l.h.s. of (33.5) and the boundary condition (33.6). It follows from the results of §26 that the operator, defined by

$$B = -\Delta = -\frac{\partial^2}{\partial x'^2} - \frac{\partial^2}{\partial y'^2}$$

and the boundary conditions (33.6), is similar to $\boldsymbol{A}$. The eigenfunctions of $\boldsymbol{B}$ are

$$\phi_{k,n}(x', y') = c_{k,n} J_k(\gamma_{k,n} r) \begin{matrix}\cos\\ \sin\end{matrix} k\theta \qquad (k, n = 0, 1, 2, \ldots), \tag{33.7}$$

where $x' = r\cos\theta$, $y' = r\sin\theta$ and the coefficients $c_{k,n}$ are such that $|||\phi_{k,n}|||_{\boldsymbol{B}} = 1$. The choice of these functions as coordinate functions for the solution of (33.5) and (33.6) ensures the validity of (a)–(c) of **1**, §29. The assertion of §26 holds for the convergence, w.r.t. the metric of $L_2(\Omega)$, of the second derivatives of the approximate Ritz-solution to the corresponding derivative of the exact solution. On the basis of the Sobolev imbedding theorem, it follows that the first derivatives converge w.r.t. the metric of $L_p(\Omega)$ for arbitrary $p > 1$, while the approximate solution itself converges uniformly in Ω.

Let Ω be enclosed between the lines $y = \pm b$, which touch the contour S, and let any arbitrary line $y =$ const. between them intersect S in only two points, with abscissae $\alpha(y)$ and $\beta(y)$. The transformation (33.4) can be defined by

$$x' = \mu(y)x + \nu(y), \qquad y' = \frac{1}{b}y, \tag{33.8}$$

where

$$\mu(y) = \frac{2\sqrt{b^2-y^2}}{b[\beta(y)-\alpha(y)]}, \qquad \nu(y) = \frac{\beta(y)+\alpha(y)}{\beta(y)-\alpha(y)}\,\frac{\sqrt{b^2-y^2}}{b}. \tag{33.9}$$

This transformation satisfies the required conditions, if the functions $\mu(y)$ and $\nu(y)$ have continuous second derivatives in the interval $|y| \leqq b$.

Example 33.1. Let S be the ellipse

$$\frac{x^2}{a^2} + \frac{y^2}{b^2} = 1$$

and Ω its interior. Here,

$$\alpha(y) = -\frac{a}{b}\sqrt{b^2-y^2}, \qquad \beta(y) = \frac{a}{b}\sqrt{b^2-y^2}$$

and hence,

$$\mu(y) = \frac{1}{a}, \qquad \nu(y) = 0,$$

while the transformation (33.8) takes the form

$$x' = \frac{x}{a}, \qquad y' = \frac{y}{b}.$$

The transformation (33.4) can be used to define a one-to-one and sufficiently smooth mapping of Ω onto either a circular section with angle $\beta \leqq \pi$ or a rectangle. The operator $\boldsymbol{B}$ mentioned above (in (33.6), Γ now denotes the contour of either a circular section of a rectangle) is, for both cases, semi-similar to the operator $\boldsymbol{A}$. For the sector $0 < r < 1, 0 < \theta < \beta$ the eigenfunctions of $\boldsymbol{B}$ are

$$\phi_{k,n}(x', y') = c_{k,n} J_{k\pi/\beta}(\gamma_{k\pi/\beta,n} r) \sin \frac{k\pi\theta}{\beta} \quad (k, n = 1, 2, \ldots), \quad (33.10)$$

If $\beta = \pi$ and Ω is such that there exists a sufficiently smooth mapping onto a semi-circular disc, then

$$\phi_{k,n}(x', y') = c_{k,n} J_k(\gamma_{k,n} r) \sin k\theta \qquad (k, n = 1, 2, \ldots). \qquad (33.10')$$

Further, for the rectangle $0 < x' < a, 0 < y' < b$,

$$\phi_{k,n}(x', y') = \frac{2}{\pi}\left(\frac{k^2}{a^2} + \frac{m^2}{b^2}\right)^{-\frac{1}{2}} \sin \frac{k\pi x'}{a} \sin \frac{m\pi y'}{b} \quad (k, n = 1, 2, \ldots). \qquad (33.11)$$

The coefficients in (33.10) are defined by the condition

$$|||\phi_{k,n}|||_{\boldsymbol{B}}^2 = \int_0^1 r\,dr \int_0^\beta \left[\left(\frac{\partial \phi_{k,n}}{\partial r}\right)^2 + \frac{1}{r^2}\left(\frac{\partial \phi_{k,n}}{\partial \theta}\right)^2\right] d\theta =$$

$$= \frac{\beta}{2}\int_0^1 \left[\gamma_{k\pi/\beta,n}^2 J_{k\pi/\beta}'^2(\gamma_{k\pi/\beta,n} r) + \frac{k^2\pi^2}{\beta^2} J_{k\pi/\beta}^2(\gamma_{k\pi/\beta,n} r)\right] r\,dr = 1.$$

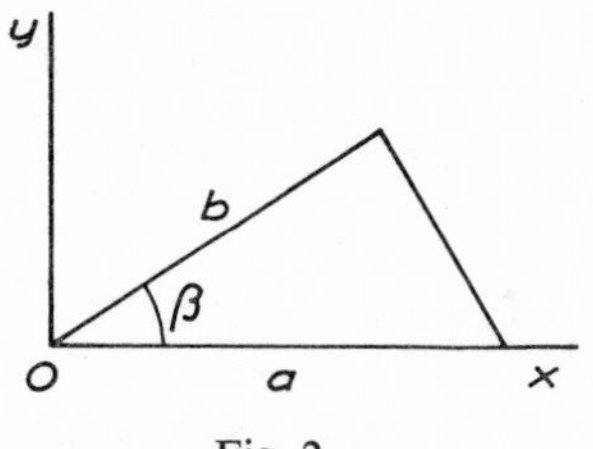

Fig. 2.

If, for the appropriate form of Ω, the functions (33.10), (33.10′) or

(33.11) are used as coordinate functions for the solution of (33.5) and (33.6), then conditions (a) and (b) of **1**, §29, will remain valid.

Example 33.2 As shown in Figure 2, let Ω be a right triangle with acute angle β. The transformation of this triangle onto the circular sector: $0 < r < 1, 0 < \theta < \beta$, is defined by

$$x' = \frac{1}{b}\left\{y \operatorname{ctg} \beta + \frac{b \sin \beta}{a}(x - y \operatorname{ctg} \beta) \frac{\sqrt{b^2 - y^2} - y \operatorname{ctg} \beta}{b \sin \beta - y}\right\}, \tag{33.12}$$

$$y' = \frac{1}{b} y.$$

It is easy to see that this transformation is infinitely often differentiable and that its Jacobian is positive bounded above and below. In fact, we have proved the assertion about the differentiability, if we establish that the quotient

$$\phi(y) = \frac{\sqrt{b^2 - y^2} - y \operatorname{ctg} \beta}{b \sin \beta - y}$$

is infinitely often differentiable w.r.t. y in the interval $0 \leqq y \leqq b \sin \beta$. If we put $y = b \sin \lambda$, $0 \leqq \lambda \leqq \beta$, then

$$\phi(y) = \frac{1}{\sin \beta} \frac{\cos \frac{\beta - \lambda}{2}}{\cos \frac{\beta + \lambda}{2}}$$

and it is obvious that for $0 \leqq \lambda \leqq \beta$ this function is infinitely often differentiable w.r.t. λ and, hence, w.r.t. y. Further, since

$$\frac{D(x', y')}{D(x, y)} = \frac{\sin \beta}{ab} \frac{\sqrt{b^2 - y^2} - y \operatorname{ctg} \beta}{b \sin \beta - \gamma} = \frac{1}{ab} \frac{\cos \frac{\beta - \lambda}{2}}{\cos \frac{\beta + \lambda}{2}},$$

we obtain

$$\frac{1}{ab} \leqq \frac{D(x', y')}{D(x, y)} \leqq \frac{1}{ab \cos \beta}.$$

§34. Two-dimensional elliptic equations with natural boundary conditions

We now examine (33.1) w.r.t. the boundary condition

$$\left[\sum_{j,k=1}^{2} A_{jk} \frac{\partial u}{\partial x_k} \cos(\nu, x_k) + \sigma u\right]_S = 0. \tag{34.1}$$

where ν is the outward normal to the contour S and σ is a bounded, measurable and non-negative function defined on S. We choose the functions σ and C, so that the operator defined by (33.1) and (34.1) is positive definite. This operator (or more exactly, its selfadjoint Friedrichs extension) will be denoted by $\boldsymbol{A}$. Comparatively simple operators, which are similar to $\boldsymbol{A}$, can be constructed for a number of quite different forms of $\boldsymbol{A}$. For example, let (33.1) take the form

$$-\Delta u + C(x, y)u = f(x, y),$$

and (34.1), with $\sigma = 0$,

$$\left.\frac{\partial u}{\partial \nu}\right|_S = 0. \tag{34.1'}$$

The operator $\boldsymbol{B}$, defined by the differential expression $-\Delta u + u$ and the boundary conditions (34.1′), is similar to $\boldsymbol{A}$. The eigenfunctions of $\boldsymbol{B}$ are easily constructed if, for example, S is the unit circle:

$$\phi_{k,n} = c_{k,n} J_k(\tilde{\gamma}_{k,n} r) \begin{matrix}\cos\\ \sin\end{matrix} k\theta \quad (k = 0, 1, 2, \ldots; n = 1, 2, \ldots), \tag{34.2}$$

where $\tilde{\gamma}_{k,n}$ denotes the nth positive root of the derivative $J_k'(x)$. As usual, the coefficients $c_{k,n}$ are defined by either $|||\phi_{k,n}|||_{\boldsymbol{B}} = 1$ or the condition that $|||\phi_{k,n}|||_{\boldsymbol{B}}$ is positive bounded above and below.

If the functions (34.2) are taken as coordinate functions, then (a)–(c) of **1**, §29, will hold.

For the more general case, we assume that there exists a transformation (33.4) which maps Ω onto a disc, a circular sector or a rectangle. We assume that the conditions of §33 hold for this transformation. Using such transformations, (33.1) reduces to (33.5), and (34.1) becomes

$$\left[\sum_{j,k=1}^{2} A'_{jk} \frac{\partial u}{\partial x'_k} \cos(\nu', x_j) + \sigma' u\right]_\Gamma = 0, \tag{34.3}$$

where Γ is the contour of the transformed region, ν' is the outward normal to Γ and

$$\sigma' = \sigma\sqrt{E\cos^2(\nu', y') - 2F\cos(\nu', x')\cos(\nu', y') + G\cos^2(\nu', x')},$$

with

$$E = \left(\frac{\partial x}{\partial x'}\right)^2 + \left(\frac{\partial x}{\partial y'}\right)^2, \qquad F = \frac{\partial x}{\partial x'}\frac{\partial x}{\partial y'} + \frac{\partial y}{\partial x'}\frac{\partial y}{\partial y'},$$

$$G = \left(\frac{\partial y}{\partial x'}\right)^2 + \left(\frac{\partial y}{\partial y'}\right)^2.$$

The operator $\boldsymbol{B}$, defined by

$$\boldsymbol{B}u = -\frac{\partial^2 u}{\partial x'^2} - \frac{\partial^2 u}{\partial y'^2} + u, \qquad \left.\frac{\partial u}{\partial \nu'}\right|_{\Gamma} = 0,$$

is semi-similar to the operator $\boldsymbol{A}'$, defined by (33.5) and (34.3). For the disc, the eigenfunctions of $\boldsymbol{B}$ are defined by (34.2) while, for the sector $0 < r < 1$, $0 < \theta < \beta$, they become

$$\phi_{k,n} = c_{k,n} J_{k\pi/\beta}(\gamma_{k\pi/\beta,n} r) \cos\frac{k\pi\theta}{\beta} \quad (k = 0, 1, 2, \ldots; \quad n = 1, 2, \ldots). \tag{34.4}$$

When the sector corresponds to a semi-circular disc,

$$\phi_{k,n} = c_{k,n} J_k(\tilde{\gamma}_{k,n} r) \cos k\vartheta \quad (k = 0, 1, 2, \ldots; n = 1, 2, \ldots). \tag{34.5}$$

Finally, for the rectangle $0 < x' < a$, $0 < y' < b$,

$$\phi_{k,n} = c_{k,n} \cos\frac{k\pi x'}{a} \cos\frac{n\pi y'}{b} \qquad (k, n = 0, 1, 2, \ldots). \tag{34.6}$$

As usual, the coefficients $c_{k,n}$ are determined by the normalising condition mentioned above: $|||\phi_{k,n}|||_{\boldsymbol{B}}$ is positive bounded above and below. For the functions (34.6), we can have

$$c_{k,n} = \frac{1}{\pi}\left(\frac{k^2}{a^2} + \frac{n^2}{b^2}\right)^{-\frac{1}{2}}$$

or more simply

$$c_{k,n} = \frac{1}{[\sqrt{k^2+n^2}]}.$$

Choosing any one of the systems (34.4)–(34.6), in correspondence with the appropriate region, as a coordinate system, we ensure the validity of (a) and (b) of **1**, §29.
Some additional details can be found in Mikhlin and Smolitskiy [1].
In the case when the coordinate functions are polynomials, the validity of (a) and (b) of **1**, §29, follows from §28.

§35. Three-dimensional problems

We do not attempt a study of equations with an arbitrary number of independent parameters, but limit considerations to the case $m = 3$ as the most interesting from the point of view of applications.
We shall examine the non-degenerate elliptic equation

$$-\sum_{j,k=1}^{3} \frac{\partial}{\partial x_j}\left(A_{jk}(x)\frac{\partial u}{\partial x_j}\right) + C(x)u = f(x), \quad x = (x_1, x_2, x_3) = \\ = (x, y, z), \qquad (35.1)$$

for either one of the boundary conditions

$$u|_S = 0, \qquad (35.2)$$

$$\left[\sum_{j,k=1}^{3} A_{jk}\frac{\partial u}{\partial x_j}\cos(\nu, x_k) + \sigma u\right]_S = 0; \qquad (35.3)$$

where ν is the outward normal to S. We shall assume that the operator A, generated by the l.h.s. of (35.1) and either one of the boundary condition (35.2) or (35.3), is positive definite in $L_2(\Omega)$, where Ω is a finite region with surface S.
We limit the investigation to the cases where there exist sufficiently smooth mappings, with positive Jacobian, which map Ω onto one of the following regions:
(1) a ball,
(2) a right angled parallelepiped,
(3) a right circular cylinder,
(4) a sector of a right circular cylinder formed by two half-planes which intersect on the axis of the cylinder,
(5) a spherical cone – a right circular cone with a spherical cap such that the centre of the spherical cap coincides with the vertix of the cone.
Moreover, we assume that the mapping has been applied, so that Ω already coincides with one of the mentioned regions.

Along with $\boldsymbol{A}$, we examine the operator $\boldsymbol{B}$ defined by

$$\boldsymbol{B}u = -\Delta u + u \tag{35.4}$$

with domain contained in the set of functions which satisfy (35.2), if (35.1) is solved w.r.t. (35.2), and satisfies

$$\left.\frac{\partial u}{\partial \nu}\right|_S = 0, \tag{35.5}$$

if (35.1) is solved w.r.t. (35.3). We assume that $\boldsymbol{A}$ and $\boldsymbol{B}$ coincide with their selfadjoint Friedrichs extensions. If C is a sphere and (35.2) is valid, then $\mathfrak{D}(\boldsymbol{A}) = \mathfrak{D}(\boldsymbol{B})$ consist of the functions $u \in W_2^2(\Omega)$ which equal zero on the boundary of Ω. Hence, $\boldsymbol{A}$ and $\boldsymbol{B}$ are similar.

Note. The term u in (35.4) can be omitted in all cases except the following: the boundary condition is defined by (35.3) with $\sigma(x) = 0$.
Choosing the eigenfunctions of $\boldsymbol{B}$ as coordinate functions, we ensure the validity of (a)–(c) of **1**, §29. In the remaining cases which we study in this section, the operators $\boldsymbol{A}$ and $\boldsymbol{B}$ are at least semi-similar. Hence, the above choice of coordinate functions ensures the validity of (a) and (b) of **1**, §29.
Below, we determine the eigenfunctions of $\boldsymbol{B}$ (which we denote by ϕ_{klm}) – the Laplace operator – for the above mentioned regions w.r.t. the boundary conditions: (35.4) for the Dirichlet problem and (35.5) for the Neuman problem.
1. *The ball with unit radius.* We introduce the spherical coordinates r, θ and ϕ with origin at the centre of the ball. Using separation of variables, it is easy to show that, for the Dirichlet problem,

$$\phi_{klm} = c_{klm} \frac{1}{\sqrt{r}} J_{k+\frac{1}{2}}(\gamma_{k+\frac{1}{2},l}\, r) P_k^{(m)}(\cos\theta) \begin{matrix}\cos m\phi \\ \sin m\phi\end{matrix} \tag{35.6}$$

$$(k = 0, 1, 2, \ldots;\quad l = 1, 2, \ldots;\quad m = 0, 1, 2, \ldots, k),$$

and for the Neuman problem,

$$\phi_{klm} = c_{klm} \frac{1}{\sqrt{r}} J_{k+\frac{1}{2}}(\gamma^*_{k+\frac{1}{2},l}\, r) P_k^{(m)}(\cos\theta) \begin{matrix}\cos m\phi \\ \sin m\phi\end{matrix} \tag{35.7}$$

$$(k = 0, 1, 2, \ldots;\quad l = 1, 2, \ldots;\quad m = 0, 1, 2, \ldots, k).$$

In (35.6) and (35.7), $P_k^{(m)}$ (cos θ) denotes the associated Legendre function,

$\gamma_{k+\frac{1}{2},l}$ is the lth positive root of the Bessel function $J_{k+\frac{1}{2}}(x)$ and $\gamma^*_{k+\frac{1}{2},l}$ is the lth positive root of

$$J'_{k+\frac{1}{2}}(x) - \frac{1}{2x} J_{k+\frac{1}{2}}(x) = 0.$$

2. *The parallelapiped* $0 < x < a, 0 < y < b, 0 < z < c$. Using separation of variables for cartesian coordinates, we obtain, for the Dirichlet problem,

$$\phi_{klm} = c_{klm} \sin \frac{k\pi x}{a} \sin \frac{l\pi y}{b} \sin \frac{m\pi z}{c} \qquad (k, l, m = 1, 2, \ldots). \quad (35.8)$$

The requirement $|||\phi_{klm}|||_{\boldsymbol{B}} = 1$ yields

$$c_{klm} = \frac{1}{\pi} \left(\frac{k^2}{a^2} + \frac{l^2}{b^2} + \frac{m^2}{c^2} + 1 \right)^{-1}. \quad (35.9)$$

The requirement that $|||\phi_{klm}|||_{\boldsymbol{B}}$ be only positive bounded above and below yields

$$c_{klm} = \frac{1}{[\sqrt{k^2 + l^2 + m^2}]}. \quad (35.10)$$

For the Neuman problem,

$$\phi_{klm} = c_{klm} \cos \frac{k\pi x}{a} \cos \frac{l\pi y}{b} \cos \frac{m\pi z}{c} \qquad (k, l, m = 0, 1, 2, \ldots), \quad (35.11)$$

where the c_{klm} can have the values given by (35.9) or (35.10).

3. *The cylinder which is defined, w.r.t. cylindrical coordinates* r, ϕ, z, *by the inequalities* $0 < r < 1, 0 \leqq z \leqq b$. For the Dirichlet problem,

$$\phi_{klm} = c_{klm} J_k(\gamma_{k,l} r) \sin \frac{m\pi z}{b} \begin{matrix} \cos \\ \sin \end{matrix} k\phi \quad (35.12)$$

$$(k = 0, 1, 2, \ldots; \quad l, m = 1, 2, 3, \ldots),$$

while for the Neuman problem,

$$\phi_{klm} = c_{klm} J_k(\tilde{\gamma}_{k,l} r) \cos \frac{m\pi z}{b} \begin{matrix} \cos \\ \sin \end{matrix} k\phi \quad (35.13)$$

$$(k, m = 0, 1, 2, \ldots; \quad l = 1, 2, 3, \ldots),$$

where $\gamma_{k,l}$ and $\tilde{\gamma}_{k,l}$ denote the lth positive roots of the functions $J_k(x)$ and $J_k'(x)$, respectively. The coefficients c_{klm} in (35.12) and (35.13) can be defined by the condition $|||\phi_{klm}|||_A = 1$.

4. *A sector of a circular cylinder defined, w.r.t. cylindrical coordinates, by the inequalities* $0 < r < 1$, $0 < \phi < \beta$, $0 < z < b$.

For the Dirichlet problem,

$$\phi_{klm} = c_{klm} J_{k\pi/\beta}(\gamma_{k\pi/\beta,l}\, r) \sin \frac{k\pi\phi}{\beta} \sin \frac{k\pi z}{b} \qquad (k, l, m = 1, 2, 3, \ldots), \tag{35.14}$$

while for the Neuman problem,

$$\phi_{klm} = c_{klm} J_{k\pi/\beta}(\tilde{\gamma}_{k\pi/\beta,l}\, r) \cos \frac{k\pi\phi}{\beta} \cos \frac{k\pi z}{b} \qquad (k, l, m = 0, 1, 2, \ldots). \tag{35.15}$$

As above, the coefficients c_{klm} can be defined by the condition $|||\phi_{klm}|||_A = 1$.

5. *The spherical cone defined, w.r.t. spherical coordinates by the inequalities* $0 < r < 1$, $0 < \theta < \beta$.

For the Dirichlet problem, separation of variables w.r.t. spherical coordinates again yields the expression (35.6) for the eigenfunctions with, however, this essential difference: the index k takes, in general, non-integral values.

It is important to note that if m is a non-negative integer then (see Erdelyi et al. [1; Vol. 1, p. 148])

$$P_k^{(m)}(\cos\theta) = (-1)^m \sin^m\theta \, \frac{d^m P(\cos\theta)}{(d\cos\theta)^m} \, .$$

where $P_k(x)$ is the generalised Legendre function of the first kind with index k. Since the functions (35.6) equal zero for $r = 1$, it is only necessary that they equal zero for $\theta = \beta$: this defines an equation for k

$$P_k^{(m)}(\cos\beta) = 0. \tag{35.16}$$

We prove that, for arbitrary real m, (35.16) has a countable set of positive roots. If k satisfies (35.16), then the $P_k^{(m)}(x)$ are the eigenfunctions of the operator

$$\boldsymbol{P}u = -\frac{d}{dx}\left[(1-x^2)\frac{du}{dx}\right] + \frac{m^2}{1-x^2}\, u, \qquad u(\cos\beta) = 0. \tag{35.17}$$

For these eigenfunctions, the corresponding eigenvalues are $k(k+1)$. Therefore, it is sufficient to prove that the spectrum of (35.17) is discrete. Since the integral

$$\int_{-1}^{\cos\beta} \frac{1+x}{1-x}\, dx$$

converges, the operator

$$\boldsymbol{P}_0(u) = -\frac{d}{dx}\left[(1-x^2)\frac{du}{dx}\right], \qquad u(\cos\beta) = 0\ , \tag{35.18}$$

has a discrete spectrum (see Mikhlin [9]). Further, since $m^2(1-x^2)^{-1}u$ is non-negative (for $m^2 > 0$, it is positive definite), the operator $\boldsymbol{P}$ is not less than the operator $\boldsymbol{P}_0$:

$$(\boldsymbol{P}u, u) \geqq (\boldsymbol{P}_0 u, u).$$

It is easy to establish that the spectrum of $\boldsymbol{P}$ is discrete. In this way, (35.16) has a countable set of (positive and negative) roots. For each positive root k there corresponds a negative root $-(k+1)$.

Let $k_{n,m}(n = 1, 2, \ldots)$ denote the positive roots of (35.16), then the eigenfunctions of the Dirichlet problem for the given spherical cone can be written as

$$\phi_{nlm} = c_{nlm} J_{k_{n,m}+\frac{1}{2}}(\gamma_{k_{n,m}+\frac{1}{2},l}\, r) P^{(m)}_{k_{n,m}}(\cos\theta) \begin{matrix}\cos m\phi\\ \sin m\phi\end{matrix} \tag{35.19}$$
$$(l, n = 1, 2, 3, \ldots; \quad m = 0, 1, 2, \ldots),$$

where the coefficients c_{nlm} can be defined by the condition $|||\phi_{nlm}|||_A = 1$. For the Neuman problem, an analogous argument gives

$$\phi_{nlm} = c_{nlm} J_{q_{n,m}+\frac{1}{2}}(\tilde{\gamma}_{q_{n,m}+\frac{1}{2},l}\, r) P^{(m)}_{q_{n,m}}(\cos\theta) \begin{matrix}\cos m\phi\\ \sin m\phi\end{matrix} \tag{35.20}$$
$$(l, n = 1, 2, 3, \ldots; \quad m = 0, 1, 2, \ldots),$$

where the $q_{n,m}$ denote the roots of

$$\left[\frac{d}{dx} P^{(m)}_q(x)\right]_{x=\cos\beta} = 0. \tag{35.21}$$

We single out the case $\beta = (\pi/2)$, when the spherical cone becomes a half-ball. In this case, it is easy to see that

$$k_n = k_{n+m} = m+2n-1, \qquad n = 1, 2, 3, \ldots \tag{35.22}$$

This becomes clear, if we note that, on the basis of this definition, k_n runs through all integer values larger than m with different parity than that of m, and the functions $P_{k_n}^{(m)}(x)$ are odd and equal zero at $x = 0$; that is, these functions satisfy (35.16) for $\beta = (\pi/2)$. Other values of k_n do not occur. In fact, if the opposite is assumed, then

$$P_{m+2n-1}^{(m)}(x) \qquad (n = 1, 2, 3, \ldots) \tag{35.23}$$

would not be complete in the interval $0 < x < 1$. Let $w(x) \in L_2(0,1)$ be orthogonal to the functions (35.23), if we now define the odd function extension for $w(x)$ on $-1 < x < 0$, it would follow that (35.23) was not complete in the subspace of odd functions in $L_2(-1,1)$, and this clearly is not true.

For the Neuman problem on the half-ball,

$$q_n = q_{n,m} = m+2n \qquad (n = 1, 2, 3, \ldots). \tag{35.24}$$

§36. Systems of ordinary differential equations

For simplicity, we limit considerations to systems of the second order.

1. *The first boundary value problem.* We examine the system of equations

$$-\frac{d}{dx}\left(p(x)\frac{du}{dx}\right) + q(x)u(x) = f(x), \qquad 0 < x < 1, \tag{36.1}$$

for the boundary conditions

$$u(0) = u(1) = 0, \tag{36.2}$$

where $u(x)$ and $f(x)$ are s-dimensional vector valued functions and $p(x)$ and $q(x)$ are Hermitian matrices of order s. For simplicity, we assume that the matrix $p(x)$ is continuously differentiable and positive definite on the interval $0 \leq x \leq 1$. Hence, there exists a positive constant p_0 such that the smallest eigenvalue of the matrix $p(x)$ is not less than p_0. We also assume that the matrix is measurable, bounded and non-negative. The l.h.s. of (36.1) and the boundary condition (36.2) define an operator, which we shall denote by A, with domain $\mathfrak{D}(A)$ of functions $u = u(x)$ which satisfy the following conditions:

u and u' are absolutely continuous on [0,1];
u satisfies (36.2);
u'' square summable on [0,1].
It is easy to establish that $\boldsymbol{A}$ is positive definite and has a discrete spectrum.

Note. The properties positive definiteness and discreteness of spectrum for $\boldsymbol{A}$ are retained when the matrix $q(x)$ is not non-negative, but satisfies the following more general conditions: its smallest eigenvalue is not less than $\varepsilon - \lambda_1$, where ε is some positive number and λ_1 is the smallest eigenvalue of the operator

$$-\frac{d}{dx}\left(p(x)\frac{du}{dx}\right)$$

defined on $\mathfrak{D}(\boldsymbol{A})$ above.
Since $\mathfrak{D}(\boldsymbol{A})$ is independent of the chosen form for $p(x)$ and $q(x)$, $\mathfrak{D}(\boldsymbol{A}) = \mathfrak{D}(\boldsymbol{B})$ and the operators $\boldsymbol{A}$ and $\boldsymbol{B}$ are similar, if $\boldsymbol{B}$ is defined by

$$\boldsymbol{B}u = -\frac{d}{dx}\left(p_1(x)\frac{du}{dx}\right) + q_1(x)u \tag{36.3}$$

on the set of functions $\mathfrak{D}(\boldsymbol{A})$, where the s-order matrices $p_1(x)$ and $q_1(x)$ satisfy the conditions on $p(x)$ and $q(x)$ listed above.
We put $p_1(x) = I_s$ and $q_1(x) = 0$, where I_s is the unit matrix of order s. Then

$$\boldsymbol{B}u = -\frac{d^2u}{dx^2}, \qquad u(0) = u(1) = 0.$$

The eigenvectors of $\boldsymbol{B}$, normalised w.r.t. the metric of $\mathfrak{H}_{\boldsymbol{B}}$, are

$$\phi_{nl}(x) = \left(0, \ldots, 0, \frac{\sqrt{2}}{\pi n}\sin n\pi x, 0, \ldots, 0\right) \tag{36.4}$$

$$(l = 1, 2, \ldots, s; \quad n = 1, 2, 3, \ldots),$$

where the element differing from zero occurs in the lth place. The factor $\sqrt{2}/\pi$ can be deleted to yield

$$\phi_{nl}(x) = \left(0, \ldots, 0, \frac{1}{n}\sin n\pi x, 0, \ldots, 0\right) \tag{36.4'}$$

$$(l = 1, 2, \ldots, s; \quad n = 1, 2, 3, \ldots).$$

If the vectors (36.4) or (36.4′) are taken as coordinate functions for the solution of (36.1) and (36.2), then conditions (a)–(c) of **1**, §29, are satisfied.

We can also make use of the system

$$\phi_{nl}(x) = (0, \ldots, 0, Q_n(x), 0, \ldots, 0) \qquad (36.5)$$
$$(l = 1, 2, \ldots, s; \quad n = 1, 2, \ldots),$$

where $Q_n(x)$ is defined by (30.6). For this system, only (a) and (b) of **1**, §29, are satisfied.

If the exact solution of (36.1) and (36.2) has five continuous derivatives, then the validity of **1**, §29, is established.

2. *Boundary value problems with natural boundary conditions*. We examine the system of equations (36.1) w.r.t. the boundary conditions

$$u'(0) - M_0 u(0) = 0, \qquad u'(1) + M_1 u(1) = 0. \qquad (36.6)$$

We retain the assumptions of **1** for the matrix $p(x)$. For simplicity, we assume that the matrix $q(x)$ is continuous and non-negative. If $\boldsymbol{A}$ now denotes the operator, defined by the l.h.s. of (36.1) and the boundary conditions (36.6), then

$$(\boldsymbol{A}u, u) = p(0)M_0 u(0) \cdot \overline{u(0)} + p(1)M_1 u(1) \cdot \overline{u(1)} + \\ + \int_0^1 \{p(x)u'(x) \cdot \overline{u'(x)} + q(x)u(x) \cdot \overline{u(x)}\}dx. \qquad (36.7)$$

It is clear that $\boldsymbol{A}$ will be positive definite, if the matrices $p(0)M_0$ and $p(1)M_1$ are non-negative, where at least one of them is positive. Let $\boldsymbol{B}$ denote the operator

$$\boldsymbol{B}u = -\frac{d^2u}{dx^2} + u \qquad (36.8)$$

defined w.r.t. the boundary conditions

$$u'(0) = u'(1) = 0. \qquad (36.9)$$

It is not difficult to see that the operators $\boldsymbol{A}$ and $\boldsymbol{B}$ are semi-similar. The eigenvectors of $\boldsymbol{B}$, normalised in $\mathfrak{H}_{\boldsymbol{B}}$, are

$$\phi_{nl} = \left\{0, \ldots, 0, \sqrt{\frac{2}{n^2\pi^2+1}} \cos n\pi x, 0, \ldots, 0\right\} \qquad (36.10)$$
$$(l = 1, 2, \ldots, s; \quad n = 0, 1, 2, \ldots),$$

where the term differing from zero is in the lth place and the normalisation coefficient equals unity when $n = 0$. The normalisation coefficient $(2/n^2\pi^2+1)^{\frac{1}{2}}$, $n > 0$, can be replaced by the simpler coefficient $1/n$. We then obtain the system

$$\phi_{nl}(x) = \left(0, \ldots, 0, \frac{1}{n}\cos n\pi x, 0, \ldots, 0\right) \tag{36.11}$$

$$(l = 1, 2, \ldots, s; \quad n = 0, 1, 2, \ldots),$$

where $1/n$ is replaced by 1 when $n = 0$. This system is almost orthonormal in $\mathfrak{H}_A$. Taking (36.1) as the coordinate system for the solution of (36.1) and (36.6), conditions (a) and (b) of **1**, §29, are satisfied.

In an analogous manner, as was shown in §30, we can construct a system which is orthonormal in $\mathfrak{H}_B$. We shall not stop to consider this here.

§37. Systems of partial differential equations

As in the preceding section, we limit considerations to second order systems.

We examine the system of s second order equations

$$-\sum_{j,k=1}^{m} \frac{\partial}{\partial x_j}\left(A_{jk}\frac{\partial u}{\partial x_k}\right) + Cu = f(x), \tag{37.1}$$

where $u(x)$ and $f(x)$ are s-dimensional vector valued functions which are defined almost everywhere in a finite region Ω of m-dimensional Euclidean space and the A_{jk} and C are s^{th} order matrices (the elements of which are functions of x) which are defined and, for simplicity, continuous in the closed region $\overline{\Omega} = \Omega \cup S$. With respect to the matrices A_{jk}, we assume also that they are sufficiently often differentiable in Ω and satisfy the following relationships:

$$\text{a)} \quad A_{jk}(x) = A_{kj}^{*}(x), \tag{37.2}$$

where the star denotes the conjugate-transpose of a matrix;

(b) the inequality

$$\sum_{j,k=1}^{m} A_{jk}(x)t_k \cdot t_j \geqq \mu_0 \sum_{k=1}^{m} \|t_k\|^2, \qquad \mu_0 = \text{const} > 0, \tag{37.3}$$

holds for any m s-dimensional vectors $t_1, t_2, \ldots, t_m$, where the dot denotes scalar multiplication of the s-dimensional vectors and $\| \ \|$ denotes the length of a vector.

We shall assume that the boundary S is sufficiently smooth and examine (37.1) w.r.t. one or other of the boundary conditions

$$u|_S = 0 \tag{37.4}$$

or

$$\left[\sum_{j,k=1}^{m} A_{jk} \frac{\partial u}{\partial x_k} \cos(\nu, x_j) + \sigma u\right]_S = 0, \tag{37.5}$$

where σ is a measurable, bounded and non-negative matrix defined on S.

We also consider the operator

$$-\sum_{j,k=1}^{m} \frac{\partial}{\partial x_j}\left(A_{jk} \frac{\partial u}{\partial x_k}\right) \tag{37.6}$$

which is defined w.r.t. one or other of the boundary conditions (37.4) or (37.5). The spectrum of this operator is discrete and positive in all cases except the one when (37.5) holds with $\sigma = 0$. In this case, the smallest eigenvalue of (37.6) equals zero. In the general case, we denote the smallest eigenvalue of (37.6) by $\lambda_1(x)$.

We make the following additional assumptions for the matrix C:

(a) this matrix is Hermitian;

(b) its smallest eigenvalue $\gamma_1(x)$ satisfies the inequality $\gamma_1(x) \geqq -\lambda_1(x) + \varepsilon$, where ε is a positive number.

On the basis of the cited conditions, both operators (37.1), (37.4) and (37.1), (37.5) are positive definite. If we denote the relevant operator by A, we obtain

$$|||u|||_A = \int_\Omega \left\{ \sum_{j,k=1}^{m} A_{jk} \frac{\partial u}{\partial x_k} \cdot \frac{\partial u}{\partial x_j} + Cu \cdot u \right\} dx$$

when the boundary condition is (37.4), and

$$|||u|||_A^2 = \int_\Omega \left\{ \sum_{j,k=1}^{m} A_{jk} \frac{\partial u}{\partial x_k} \cdot \frac{\partial u}{\partial x_j} + Cu \cdot u \right\} dx + \int_S \sigma u \cdot u \, dS$$

when the condition is (37.5). From (37.3) and the continuity of the matrices A_{jk}, it is easy to see that the operator A is semi-similar to the operator $\boldsymbol{B}$ which is defined by

$$\boldsymbol{B}u = -\Delta u + u$$

and the boundary conditions (37.4) or

$$\left.\frac{\partial u}{\partial \nu}\right|_S = 0, \tag{37.4'}$$

depending on whether we consider (37.1) and (37.4) or (37.1) and (37.5). When considering (37.1) and (37.4), it is only necessary to take $\boldsymbol{B}u = -\Delta u$.

Let $\phi_n(x)$ $(n = 1, 2, 3, \ldots)$ denote the eigenfunctions of the scalar Laplace operator for the boundary conditions (37.4) or (37.4′). Then the eigenvectors of the operator $\boldsymbol{B}$ are

$$\phi_{nl}(x) = \{0, \ldots, 0, \phi_n(x), 0, \ldots, 0\} \tag{37.7}$$
$$(l = 1, 2, \ldots, s; \quad n = 1, 2, 3, \ldots),$$

where $\phi_n(x)$ occurs in the lth place. If the functions $\phi_n(x)$ are orthonormalised w.r.t. the metric of the Dirichlet integral, that is

$$\int_\Omega \sum_{k=1}^{m} \frac{\partial \phi_n}{\partial x_k} \frac{\partial \phi_p}{\partial x_k} dx = \delta_{np},$$

then the vectors (37.7) are orthonormalised w.r.t. the metric of $\mathfrak{H}_{\boldsymbol{B}}$, and hence, are almost orthonormal w.r.t. the metric of $\mathfrak{H}_{\boldsymbol{A}}$. The functions $\phi_n(x)$ can be quite easily determined for the cases mentioned in §§33–35. If Ω can be transformed into one of the simple regions, discussed in these sections, then, as a preliminary, one can transform the given problem accordingly.

It is clear that, for the functions ϕ_n, we can take arbitrary functions orthonormalised w.r.t. the metric of the Dirichlet integral instead of the eigenfunctions of the Laplace operator. We also note that (37.3) is not necessary: it is sufficient that

$$|||u|||_{\boldsymbol{A}} \geqq C|||u|||_{\boldsymbol{B}}, \quad C = \text{conts.} > 0.$$

Inequalities of this nature hold, for example, for the basic problems in the static theory of elasticity as a consequence of the well-known *inequality of Korn* (PM, Chapter IV).

§38. Coordinate systems for the method of least squares

We shall assume, as is usual for the method of least squares, that the operator A, defined by the equation

$$Au = f \tag{38.1}$$

is closed (not necessarily symmetric), maps from the separable Hilbert space $\mathfrak{H}$ into the separable Hilbert space $\mathfrak{H}_1$, and is such that the inverse operator A^{-1} is defined on the whole space $\mathfrak{H}_1$, and hence, is bounded. The *method of least squares* is defined in the following manner (see VM, Chapter X): choose a coordinate system $\{\phi_n\}$ which satisfies the conditions:

1) $\{\phi_n\} \in \mathfrak{D}(A)$;
2) the elements $\phi_1, \phi_2, \ldots, \phi_n$ are linearly independent for arbitrary n;
3) the system $\{A\phi_n\}$ is complete in $\mathfrak{H}_1$;

and apply the Ritz-process to the functional $||Au-f||^2$. This leads to the system of equations

$$\sum_{k=1}^{n} (A\phi_k, A\phi_j)a_k^{(n)} = (f, A\phi_j) \qquad (j = 1, 2, \ldots, n), \tag{38.2}$$

where the matrix of the system will be called *the method of least squares-matrix*.

As we saw in §6, the space $\mathfrak{H}_A$ consists of the elements of $\mathfrak{D}(A)$ on which the scalar product and norm are defined by

$$[u, v]_A = (Au, Av), \qquad |||u|||_A = ||Au||. \tag{38.3}$$

From the general results of §§9–11, we obtain:

(1) In order that the last squares-process (the Ritz-process applied to the functional of the method of least squares) and the approximate least squares-solution (obtained by using this process) be stable, it is necessary and sufficient that the coordinate system be strongly minimal w.r.t. the metric (38.3).

(2) In order that the condition number of the least squares-matrix be bounded independent of its order, it is necessary and sufficient that the coordinate system be almost orthonormal w.r.t. the metric of (38.3).

We also note that for an arbitrary choice of coordinate functions, which satisfy conditions 1)–3) listed above, the residual of the approximate least squares-solution tends to zero (see VM, Chapter X).

The space $\mathfrak{H}_A$ can be imbedded in $\mathfrak{H}$. In fact, if $u \in \mathfrak{H}_A$, then $u \in \mathfrak{D}(A)$ and, what is more, $u \in \mathfrak{H}$. Further, from the boundedness of A^{-1} it follows that there exists a constant k such that $||Au|| \geqq k||u||$ or, equivalently, $||u|| \leqq k^{-1}|||u|||_A$ – the imbedding inequality (4.1) holds with $K = k^{-1}$.

From the results of §4, we obtain:

1. If the coordinate system is strongly minimal (for example, orthonormal) in $\mathfrak{H}$, then it is strongly minimal in $\mathfrak{H}_A$ (w.r.t. the metric (38.3)).
2. We extend the concept of similar operators: two *closed operators* $\boldsymbol{A}$ *and* $\boldsymbol{B}$ mapping from $\mathfrak{H}$ into $\mathfrak{H}_1$ are called *similar* if:

(1) $\mathfrak{D}(A) = \mathfrak{D}(B)$;
(2) $\mathfrak{R}(A) = \mathfrak{R}(B) = \mathfrak{H}_1$;
(3) the operators A^{-1} and B^{-1} exist, and hence, are bounded.

It is easy to see that Theorem 3.1 remains valid for such a definition. It is also not difficult to establish that the spaces $\mathfrak{H}_A$ and $\mathfrak{H}_B$ can be imbedded in each other, and hence, a system which is almost orthonormal and complete w.r.t. the metric in $\mathfrak{H}_B$ (that is, the metric defined by

$$[u, v]_B = (Bu, Bv), \qquad |||u|||_B = ||Bu||)$$

will be almost orthonormal and complete w.r.t. the metric (38.3). In particular, if $\mathfrak{H}_1 = \mathfrak{H}$ and the operator $\boldsymbol{B}$ is selfadjoint with a point spectrum, then we can choose the eigenfunctions $\{\phi_n\}$ of this operator (normalised w.r.t. $||B\phi_n|| = 1$) as coordinate functions.

We investigate an important example of a strongly minimal system connected with the method of least squares. Let Γ be a closed curve in the complex plane. We assume that this curve is sufficiently smooth and that it is the boundary of a simply connected region D. As usual, we denote the Cartesian coordinates in the complex plane by x and y, and write $z = x+iy$ and $\bar{z} = x-iy$. We denote the complex coordinates of a variable point on Γ by the points ζ and t. We introduce the Hilbert space $L_2(\Gamma)$ of functions which are defined almost everywhere on Γ and are square summable along Γ. It is easy to prove that $L_2(\Gamma)$ is the direct sum of two spaces, which we shall denote by $\mathfrak{H}_1$ and $\mathfrak{H}_2$. The former is formed by the functions of $L_2(\Gamma)$ which are the limiting values of functions which are holomorphic inside Γ, while the latter is formed by the functions of $L_2(\Gamma)$ which are the limiting values of functions which are the complex conjugates of the functions holomorphic inside Γ and equal to zero at the origin of coordinates. In fact, the above implies that, if

$f(\zeta) \in L_2(\Gamma)$, then, firstly:

$$f(\zeta) = f_1(\zeta) + \overline{f_2(\zeta)}, \tag{38.4}$$

where $f_1(\zeta), f_2(\zeta) \in L_2(\Gamma)$, and there exist analytic continuations $f_1(z)$ and $f_2(z)$ inside Γ, where $f_2(0) = 0$; and, secondly: the representation (38.4) is unique. Assuming that the representation (38.4) exists, we multiply both sides of this expression and $\overline{f(\zeta)} = \overline{f_1(\zeta)} + f_2(\zeta)$ {the conjugate of (38.4)} by the value of the Schwartz kernel $T(z; \zeta)$ on D, which we normalise w.r.t. condition (see Mikhlin [3; §41, (22), (23) and (27)])

$$\operatorname{Im}\{T(0, \zeta)\} = 0.$$

The result of the multiplications we integrate along Γ.
Remembering that $f_2(0) = 0$, we obtain

$$f_1(z) - \tfrac{1}{2} f_1(0) = \frac{1}{4\pi} \int_\Gamma f(\zeta) T(z; \zeta) d\sigma,$$

$$f_2(z) + \tfrac{1}{2} \overline{f_1(0)} = \frac{1}{4\pi} \int_\Gamma \overline{f(\zeta)} T(z; \zeta) d\sigma, \qquad d\sigma = |d\zeta|.$$

Putting $z = 0$ in the first expression, we find,

$$\tfrac{1}{2} f_1(0) = \frac{1}{4\pi} \int_\Gamma f(\zeta) T(0, \zeta) d\sigma,$$

and hence,

$$f_1(z) = \frac{1}{4\pi} \int_\Gamma f(\zeta) [T(z; \zeta) + T(0, \zeta)] d\sigma, \tag{38.5}$$

$$f_2(z) = \frac{1}{4\pi} \int_\Gamma \overline{f(\zeta)} [T(z; \zeta) - T(0, \zeta)] d\sigma. \tag{38.6}$$

Thus, it follows that (38.4) is unique. We shall now prove that (38.4) can be derived from (38.5) and (38.6). From (38.6), it follows immediately that $f_2(0) = 0$.
Further, (38.5) and (38.6) imply

$$f_1(z) + \overline{f_2(z)} = \frac{1}{2\pi} \int_\Gamma f(\zeta) \operatorname{Re}\{T(z; \zeta)\} d\sigma = \frac{1}{2\pi} \int_\Gamma f(\zeta) \frac{\partial G}{\partial v} dv,$$

where G is the Green's function on the region D and v denotes the outward normal to Γ. Letting $z \to t \in \Gamma$, we obtain on the basis of the known

properties of Green functions, that $f_1(t)+f_2(t) = f(t)$.
The expression

$$\frac{1}{4\pi} T(z;\zeta)d\sigma = \frac{1}{2\pi i}\frac{d\zeta}{\zeta-z} + P(z;\zeta)d\sigma,$$

where $P(z;\zeta)$ is continuous as ζ passes through the contour Γ and z is contained in $\bar{D} = D \cup \Gamma$, holds. Making use of the well known limit formula for Cauchy integrals, we obtain

$$f_1(t) = \tfrac{1}{2}f(t) + \frac{1}{2\pi i}\int_\Gamma f(\zeta)\frac{d\zeta}{\zeta-t} + \frac{1}{4\pi}\int_\Gamma [P(t,\zeta)-T(0,\zeta)]d\sigma, \quad t \in \Gamma.$$

The first integral on the r.h.s. is singular – the Cauchy principal value. It is well known (see Zygmund [1; Chapter 7, §2]) that this integral represents a bounded operator in $L_2(\Gamma)$ which acts on f. Hence, it is easily seen that $f_1 \in L_2(\Gamma)$.
By an analogous argument, we find that $f_2 \in L_2(\Gamma)$ which proves our above assertion.
Using well known theorems of the theory of complex variable, it follows that the systems $\{z^n\}$ and $\{\bar{z}^n\}$ are complete in the subspaces $\mathfrak{H}_1$ and $\mathfrak{H}_2$, respectively. Let $\rho_1 = \inf_{\zeta\in\Gamma} |\zeta|$ and choose ρ_0 s.t. $0 < \rho_0 < \rho_1$. We shall prove that: *the systems*

$$\left(\frac{z}{\rho_0}\right)^n \qquad (n = 0, 1, 2, \ldots) \tag{38.7}$$

and

$$\left(\frac{\bar{z}}{\rho_0}\right)^n \qquad (n = 1, 2, 3, \ldots) \tag{38.8}$$

are strongly minimal in the subspaces $\mathfrak{H}_1$ *and* $\mathfrak{H}_2$, *respectively.*
It is sufficient to develop the argument for (38.7). By transforming the variables, we can make $\rho_0 = 1$: then $|\zeta| > 1$ if $\zeta \in \Gamma$. We examine the Gram matrix for $z^k (k = 0, 1, 2, \ldots, n)$ and its smallest eigenvalue $\lambda_1^{(n)}$:

$$\lambda_1^{(n)} = \inf \frac{\|\sum_{k=0}^{n} a_k \zeta^k\|^2}{\sum_{k=0}^{n} |a_k|} = \inf \{\sum_{k=0}^{n} |a_k|^2\}^{-1} \int_\Gamma |\Phi(\zeta)|^2 d\sigma, \tag{38.9}$$

where

$$\Phi(\zeta) = \sum_{k=0}^{n} a_k \zeta^k.$$

The disc $|z| \leqq 1$ is completely contained inside Γ (Figure 3). We prove that

$$\int_{\Gamma} |\Phi(\zeta)|^2 \, d\sigma \geqq c \int_{\Gamma_1} |\Phi(\zeta)|^2 \, d\sigma, \qquad c = \text{const} > 0, \tag{38.10}$$

where Γ_1 is the curve $|\zeta| = 1$. We map the region D conformally onto the unit disc in the τ-plane: Γ is transformed into the unit circle γ and Γ_1 into a curve γ_1 lying inside γ (Figure 4).

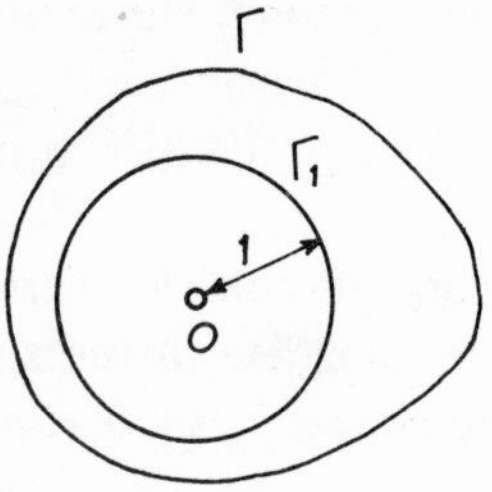

Fig. 3.

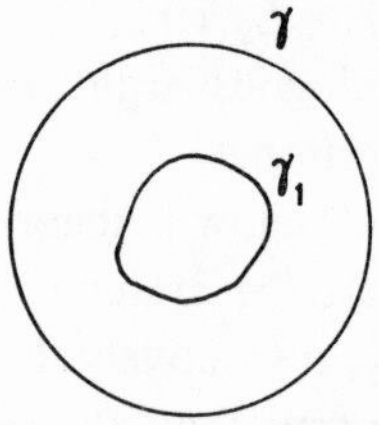

Fig. 4.

We denote the conformal mapping by $w(\tau)$. Since Γ is sufficiently smooth, the derivative $w'(\tau)$ is continuous and different from zero for $|\tau| \leqq 1$. We also write $\Phi(z) = \Phi(w(\tau)) = \phi(\tau)$. Let

$$\phi(\tau) = \sum_{n=0}^{\infty} \alpha_n \tau^n,$$

then

$$\int_{\gamma} |\phi(\tau)|^2 \, |d\tau| = 2\pi \sum_{n=0}^{\infty} |\alpha_n| \, .$$

If $|\tau| < 1$, we obtain using the Cauchy inequality

$$|\phi(\tau)|^2 \leqq \sum_{n=0}^{\infty} |\alpha_n|^2 \sum_{n=0}^{\infty} |\tau|^n = \frac{1}{2\pi(1-|\tau|)} \int_{\gamma} |\phi(\tau)|^2 \, d\tau$$

and hence,

$$\int_{\gamma_1} |\phi(\tau)|^2 |d\tau| \leqq \frac{l}{2\pi(1-\tau_1)} \int_{\gamma} |\phi(\tau)|^2 \, d\tau,$$

where l is the length of the curve γ_1, $\tau_1 = \max |\tau|$, $\tau \in \gamma_1$. Returning to the original variables, we find

$$\int_{\Gamma_1} |\Phi(\zeta)|^2 \frac{d\sigma}{|w'(\tau)|} \leqq \frac{l}{2\pi(1-\tau_1)} \int_{\Gamma} |\Phi(\zeta)|^2 \frac{d\sigma}{|w'(\tau)|}.$$

Since the quantity $|w'(\tau)|$ lies between two positive constants: $0 < \alpha \leqq |\, w'(\tau)| \leqq \beta < \infty$: it follows from the last inequality that (38.10) holds if

$$c = \frac{2\pi\alpha(1-\tau_1)}{\beta l}.$$

It only remains to note that

$$\int_{\Gamma_1} |\Phi(\zeta)|^2 \, d\zeta = 2\pi \sum_{k=0}^{n} |a_k|^2, \tag{38.11}$$

which yields, on the basis of (38.9), that $\lambda_1^{(n)} \geqq 2\pi c$. This proves the above assertion.

Theorem 38.1. *The system, obtained by combining systems* (38.7) *and* (38.8), *is strongly minimal in* $L_2(\Gamma)$.

Proof. As above, we assume that $\rho_0 = 1$.
The smallest eigenvalue $\lambda_{m,n}^{(1)}$ of the Gram matrix of $1, z, \ldots, z^m, \bar{z}, \ldots, \bar{z}^n$ equals

$$\lambda_{m,n}^{(1)} = \inf \frac{\|\Phi(\zeta) + \overline{\Psi(\zeta)}\|^2}{\sum_{k=0}^{m} |a_k|^2 + \sum_{k=1}^{n} |b_k|^2}, \tag{38.12}$$

where

$$\Phi(\zeta) = \sum_{k=0}^{m} a_k \zeta^k, \qquad \Psi(\zeta) = \sum_{k=1}^{n} b_k \zeta^k.$$

We again introduce the conformal mapping $w(\tau)$ of D onto the unit disc. We assume that $w(0) = 0$ and put $\phi(\tau) = \Phi(w(\tau))$ and $\psi(\tau) = \Psi(w(\tau))$.

On the unit circle γ, the functions $\phi(\tau)$ and $\psi(\tau)$ are orthogonal, since $\psi(0) = \Psi(0) = 0$. Therefore,

$$\int_\gamma |\phi(\tau)+\overline{\psi(\tau)}|^2\,|d\tau| = \int_\gamma |\phi(\tau)|^2\,|d\tau| + \int_\gamma |\psi(\tau)|^2\,|d\tau|,$$

or, if we return to our original variable ζ and replace $|w'(\tau)|$ by its smallest value on the right and its largest value on the left,

$$||\Phi(\zeta)+\overline{\Psi(\zeta)}||^2 \geqq \frac{\alpha}{\beta}\{||\Phi(\zeta)||^2+||\Psi(\zeta)||^2\},$$

where the norm is evaluated w.r.t. the metric of $L_2(\Gamma)$.
Above, we saw ((38.10) and (38.11)) that

$$||\Phi(\zeta)||^2 \geqq 2\pi c \sum_{k=0}^{m} |a_k|^2.$$

In an analogous way,

$$||\Psi(\zeta)||^2 \geqq 2\pi c \sum_{k=1}^{n} |b_k|^2.$$

On the strength of (38.12),

$$\lambda_{m,n}^{(1)} \geqq \frac{2\pi c\alpha}{\beta}.$$

Since the r.h.s. of this last expression is positive and independent of m and n, the theorem is proved.

Corollary 38.1 *Let a closed operator A with bounded inverse be defined in* $L_2(\Gamma)$. *If* $\{z^k\} \in \mathfrak{D}(A)$ *and* $\{\bar{z}^k\} \in \mathfrak{D}(A)$, *then the system, obtained by combining* (38.7) *and* (38.8), *is strongly minimal in* $\mathfrak{H}_A$, *where the metric is defined by*

$$[u, v]_A = (Au, Av), \qquad |||u|||_A = ||Au||.$$

It follows from the above that the combined system (38.7) and (38.8) is strongly minimal in the space $\mathfrak{H}_A$ corresponding to the Dirichlet problem, the Neuman problem and the mixed problem for the Laplace equation defined on a finite region of a plane (see VM, §§87 and 90: for the Neuman problem, it is necessary to exclude 1 from the combined system (38.7) and (38.8)).

Choose $\rho^{(0)}$ such that

$$\rho^{(0)} > \max_{\zeta \in \Gamma} |\zeta|.$$

Using an argument analogous to that above, it is easy to prove that the system

$$\left(\frac{\rho^0}{z}\right)^k \quad (k = 0, 1, 2, \ldots), \qquad \left(\frac{\rho}{\bar{z}}\right)^k \quad (k = 1, 2, 3, \ldots) \tag{38.13}$$

is complete and strongly minimal in $L_2(\Gamma)$. Therefore, it is strongly minimal in the space $\mathfrak{H}_A$ corresponding to the Dirichlet problem, the Neuman problem or the mixed problem for the Laplace equation on a finite region of a plane.

We now turn to the case where D is a multi-connected region (see Mikhlin [2]). Let Γ consist of a series of closed and sufficiently smooth curves $\Gamma_0, \Gamma_1, \ldots, \Gamma_s$. We assume that D is a finite region which is bounded on the outside by Γ_0. We place the origin inside D. Inside each of the curves $\Gamma_j (j = 1, 2, \ldots, s)$, we choose a point z_j.

Let

$$\rho_0 < \min_{\zeta \in \Gamma_0} |\zeta|, \quad \rho^{(j)} > \max_{\zeta \in \Gamma_j} |\zeta - z_j| \qquad (j = 1, 2, \ldots, s).$$

Then system (38.7) and (38.8) is strongly minimal in $L_2(\Gamma_0)$ and the system

$$\left(\frac{\rho^{(j)}}{\zeta - z_j}\right)^k \quad (k = 0, 1, 2, \ldots), \qquad \left(\frac{\rho^{(j)}}{\bar{\zeta} - \bar{z}_j}\right)^k \quad (k = 1, 2, \ldots) \tag{38.14}$$

is strongly minimal in $L_2(\Gamma_j)$ $(j = 1, 2, \ldots, s)$.

It is not difficult to see that $L_2(\Gamma)$ is the direct sum of the spaces $L_2(\Gamma_0)$, $L_2(\Gamma_1), \ldots, L_2(\Gamma_s)$. It follows that the combined system (38.7), (38.8) and (38.14) is strongly minimal in $L_2(\Gamma)$. It is now clear that, for the basic problems in the theory of harmonic functions defined on a plane, the above mentioned combination can be used as a coordinate system for the method of least squares. In this way, the coefficients $a_k^{(n)}$ and the approximate solution will be stable.

§39. Integral equations

If in the equation

$$Au = f \tag{39.1}$$

the operator A is bounded, then the choice of a coordinate system is greatly simplified. For example, if (39.1) is solved by the method of least squares, then any orthonormal system in the given Hilbert space will be almost orthonormal w.r.t. the metric $|||u|||_A = ||Au||$. We assume, as is clear, that the inverse A^{-1} exists and is bounded. This is also true if A is a bounded, selfadjoint and positive definite operator and $|||u|||_A^2 = ||A^{\frac{1}{2}}u||^2 = (Au, u)$. Below, we clarify these statements for some simple types of integral equations.

1. *The Fredholm Equation.* If the operator T is completely continuous in the separable space $\mathfrak{H}$ and the equation

$$u + Tu = f, \qquad f \in \mathfrak{H}, \tag{39.2}$$

has a unique solution in $\mathfrak{H}$, then this equation can be solved approximately by the Bubnov-Galerkin-process. As shown in §14, this process is stable, if the coordinate system is strongly minimal in $\mathfrak{H}$. In principle, the construction of such a system is not difficult: it is sufficient to take any complete orthonormal system in $\mathfrak{H}$. It is desirable to choose a system such that the $T\phi_n$, where the ϕ_n are coordinate functions, can be calculated as far as possible with ease. We note that for differential operators an analogous requirement is not of fundamental importance, but that completely continuous operators are usually integral operators and that, if Ω is a region of m-dimensional space and

$$Tu = \int_\Omega K(x, y)u(y)dy,$$

then the expression

$$(T\phi_k, \phi_j) = \int_\Omega \int_\Omega K(x, y)\phi_k(y)\overline{\phi_j(x)}dy$$

represents a $2m$-dimensional integral. If the function

$$T\phi_k = \int_\Omega K(x, y)\phi_k(y)dy$$

is easily determined, then the scalar product $(T\phi_k, \phi_j)$ can be replaced by an m-dimensional integral.

We clarify our remarks with an example: we wish to find the function $u(x, y)$ which is harmonic on the disc $x^2 + y^2 < 1$ and satisfies on the circumference of this disc the condition

$$\left[\frac{\partial u}{\partial \rho} + \sigma(\theta)u\right]_{\rho=1} = f(\theta), \tag{39.3}$$

where ρ and θ are the polar coordinates of the point (x, y) and $\sigma(\theta)$ is a non-negative function, which is not identically equal to zero. We seek the solution in the form of the potential of a simple layer

$$u(x, y) = \int_0^{2\pi} \mu(\theta') \ln \frac{1}{r}\, d\theta', \tag{39.4}$$

where r is the distance between the points (ρ, θ) and $(1, \theta')$. Substitution in (39.3) yields the integral equation

$$\mu(\theta) - \frac{1}{2\pi}\int_0^{2\pi} \mu(\theta')d\theta' + \frac{\sigma(\theta)}{\pi}\int_0^{2\pi} \mu(\theta') \ln \frac{1}{r}\, d\theta' = \frac{1}{\pi} f(\theta). \tag{39.5}$$

The system of functions

$$\begin{matrix}\sin \\ \cos\end{matrix}\, n\theta \qquad (n = 0, 1, 2, \ldots)$$

is orthonormal and complete in $L_2(0, 2\pi)$. We determine the integrals

$$\frac{1}{\pi}\int_0^{2\pi} \cos n\theta' \ln \frac{1}{r}\, d\theta', \qquad \frac{1}{\pi}\int_0^{2\pi} \sin n\theta' \ln \frac{1}{r}\, d\theta'.$$

Since, in (39.5), r is the distance between $(1, \theta')$ and $(1, \theta)$, $r = 2 \times |\sin(\theta - \theta')/2)|$ and

$$\ln \frac{1}{r} = \ln \frac{1}{2\left|\sin \frac{\theta' - \theta}{2}\right|} = \sum_{k=1}^{\infty} \frac{\cos k(\theta' - \theta)}{k}.$$

Hence, we obtain at once

$$\frac{1}{\pi}\int_0^{2\pi} \ln \frac{1}{r}\, d\theta' = 0,$$

$$\frac{1}{\pi}\int_0^{2\pi} \cos n\theta' \ln \frac{1}{r}\, d\theta' = \frac{\cos n\theta}{2n},$$

$$\frac{1}{\pi}\int_0^{2\pi} \sin n\theta' \ln \frac{1}{r}\, d\theta' = \frac{\sin n\theta}{2n}.$$

Thus, the evaluation of the elements of the matrix and the r.h.s.-vector of the Bubnov-Galerkin-process for (39.5) reduces to the evaluation of one-dimensional integrals.

Note. The method of least squares can be applied to (39.2) (see VM, §84). As above, it is sufficient to take a coordinate system which is orthonormal (even only almost orthonormal) in $\mathfrak{H}$. If the operator $(\boldsymbol{I}+\boldsymbol{T})^{-1}$ exists and is bounded, then the coordinate system will be almost orthonormal w.r.t. the metric

$$|||u|||^2 = ||u+\boldsymbol{T}u||^2.$$

In this case, the process for the construction of the coefficients of the approximate solution and the process for the construction of the approximate solution itself will be stable and the condition number of the least squares-matrix will be bounded. This note also applies to singular integral equations, a subject which will be examined below.

2. *One-dimensional singular equations.* We limit considerations to closed paths of integration.

We examine singular equations of the form

$$Au = a(t)u(t)+\frac{b(t)}{\pi i}\int_\Gamma \frac{u(\tau)}{\tau-t}\,d\tau + \\ +\int_\Gamma K(t,\tau)u(\tau)d\tau = f(t), \qquad t\in\Gamma, \tag{39.6}$$

where Γ is a contour which encloses a simply- or multi-connected region in the complex plane. We assume that Γ is a collection of simple closed Lyapunov curves $\Gamma_0, \Gamma_1, \ldots, \Gamma_m$, where Γ_0 is the outside bounding curve (if the region is infinite, then Γ_0 does not exist) and the remainder bound the region internally. We also assume that the coefficients $a(t)$ and $b(t)$ are continuous on Γ and that the kernel $K(t, \tau)$ and the r.h.s.-term $f(t)$ are square summable

$$\int_\Gamma\int_\Gamma |K(t,\tau)|^2\,|dt|\,|d\tau| < \infty, \qquad \int_\Gamma |f(t)|^2\,|dt| < \infty.$$

Finally, we stipulate that

$$a^2(t)-b^2(t) \neq 0, \qquad t\in\Gamma. \tag{39.7}$$

We list some facts on which we shall build (for more details, see Mikhlin [1]):

(1) the operator A defined by l.h.s. of (39.1) is bounded in $L_2(\Gamma)$;
(2) both the equations $Au=0$ and $A^*v=0$ have only a finite number of solutions;
(3) the operator A is normally solvable (or, equivalently, (39.6) has a solution if and only if $f(t)$ is orthogonal to all the solutions of $A^*v = 0$).
We shall assume that $f(t)$ satisfies the above condition of orthogonality and that $Au = 0$ has only the trivial solution. Then the solution of (39.6) exists and is unique, and an approximate representation can be constructed using the least squares-process.
Since the operators A and A^{-1} are bounded, any system which is strongly minimal or almost orthonormal in $L_2(\Gamma)$ will satisfy the same condition w.r.t. the metric

$$|||u|||_A = ||Au||. \tag{39.8}$$

The space $L_2(\Gamma)$ is the orthogonal union of the subspaces of functions which differ from zero on only one of the contours Γ_j. These subspaces can be denoted by $L_2(\Gamma_j)$.
It follows from here that a complete almost orthonormal (or, correspondingly, strongly minimal) system in $L_2(\Gamma)$ can be obtained by collecting the different systems for the individual spaces $L_2(\Gamma_j)$. Thus, one can form the system $\{\omega_{jk}(t)\}$ $(0 \leqq j \leqq m, -\infty < k < \infty)$,

$$\omega_{jk}(t) = \frac{(t-a_j)^k}{\rho_j^k},$$

where ρ_j has the value defined in §38 and the $a_j(j = 1, 2, \ldots, m)$ are fixed points inside the Γ_j. The above collection is used to define the functions

$$\phi_{jk}(t) = \begin{cases} \omega_{jk}(t), & t \in \Gamma_j, \\ 0, & t \in \Gamma_l, \quad l \neq j. \end{cases}$$

The system $\{\phi_{jk}(t)\}$ is almost orthonormal w.r.t. the metric of (39.8).
It is important to note that the singular integral

$$\frac{1}{\pi i}\int_\Gamma \frac{\phi_{jk}(\tau)}{\tau - t}\,d\tau$$

is easily evaluated. In fact,

$$\frac{1}{\pi i}\int_\Gamma \frac{\phi_{jk}(\tau)}{\tau - t}\,d\tau = \frac{1}{\pi i}\int_{\Gamma_j} \frac{\omega_{jk}(\tau)}{\tau - t}\,d\tau.$$

Letting $j = 0$ and denoting an arbitrary point inside Γ_0 by z, we obtain, using the integration formula of Cauchy,

$$\frac{1}{2\pi i}\int_{\Gamma_0} \frac{\omega_{0k}(\tau)}{\tau - z}\,d\tau = \begin{cases} \omega_{0k}(z), & k \geqq 0, \\ 0, & k < 0. \end{cases}$$

Letting $z \to t$, where $t \in \Gamma_0$, and using the known theorem on the limit values of Cauchy integrals, we find

$$\frac{1}{\pi i}\int_{\Gamma_0} \frac{\omega_{0k}(\tau)}{\tau - t}\,d\tau = \begin{cases} \omega_{0k}(t), & t \in \Gamma_0, \quad k > 0, \\ 0, & t \in \Gamma_0, \quad k < 0. \end{cases}$$

In an analogous way, we find

$$\frac{1}{\pi i}\int_{\Gamma_j} \frac{\omega_{jk}(\tau)}{\tau - t}\,d\tau = \begin{cases} -\omega_{jk}(\tau), & t \in \Gamma_j \quad (j = 1, 2, \ldots, m), \quad k < 0, \\ 0, & k \geqq 0. \end{cases}$$

The integration formula of Cauchy gives

$$\frac{1}{\pi i}\int_{\Gamma_0} \frac{\omega_{0k}(\tau)}{\tau - t}\,d\tau = \begin{cases} 2\omega_{0k}(t), & t \in \Gamma_l, \quad l \neq 0, \quad k \geqq 0, \\ 0, & t \in \Gamma_l, \quad l \neq 0, \quad k < 0, \end{cases}$$

$$\frac{1}{\pi i}\int_{\Gamma_j} \frac{\omega_{jk}(\tau)}{\tau - t}\,d\tau = \begin{cases} -2\omega_{jk}(t), & t \in \Gamma_l, \quad l \neq j, \quad k < 0, \\ 0, & t \in \Gamma_l, \quad l \neq j, \quad k \geqq 0. \end{cases}$$

If the equation $Au = 0$ has non-trivial solutions and these solutions are known, then the method of least squares can be applied (see VM, §84). If the solutions of $Au = 0$ are not known, then they can be approximately determined by the Ritz-process as the eigenfunctions of the selfadjoint operator A^*A corresponding to the eigenvalue $\lambda = 0$.

3. *Multi-dimensional singular integral equations.* We shall examine an equation with unknown scalar function $u(x)$ (a more detailed account can be found in Mikhlin [20])

$$Au = a(x)u(x) + \int_{\mathfrak{E}_m} \frac{f(x, \theta)}{r^m}\, u(y)dy + Tu = g(x), \tag{39.9}$$

where $\mathfrak{E}_m$ denotes the m-dimensional Euclidean space, x and y are points of this space, $r = |y - x|$ and $\theta = ((y - x)/r)$. For simplicity, we shall assume that the "characteristic" $f(x, \theta)$ and its derivatives are, to a sufficiently high order, uniformly continuous w.r.t. the Cartesian coordinates of the point θ, when θ passes around the unit sphere, and x is in the space $\mathfrak{E}_m$ with the point at infinity added to it – "the extended Euclidean space $\mathfrak{E}_m$". In this extended Euclidean space, we shall assume that the coefficient $a(x)$ is continuous. Further, let $g(x) \in L_2(\mathfrak{E}_m)$ and the operator $\boldsymbol{T}$ be completely continuous in the same space $\mathfrak{E}_m$. Finally, we stipulate that the symbol in (39.9) is nowhere equal to zero. On the basis of these conditions, the operator defined by the l.h.s. of (39.9) is bounded in $L_2(\mathfrak{E}_m)$ and the basic theorem of the Fredholm theory is true for this equation.

Further, we assume that the homogeneous equation

$$a(x)u(x) + \int_{\mathfrak{E}_m} \frac{f(x.\ \theta)}{r^m} u(y)dy + \boldsymbol{T}u = 0 \tag{39.10}$$

has only the trivial solution. Then (39.9) is always uniquely solvable and the operator $\boldsymbol{A}^{-1}$ is bounded.

Equation (39.9) can be solved approximately by the method of least squares. The corresponding numerical process will be stable, if the coordinate system is strongly minimal in $L_2(\mathfrak{E}_m)$. It is even better if it is orthonormal or, at least, almost orthonormal in $L_2(\mathfrak{E}_m)$.

The choice of the coordinate functions $\phi_n(x)$ is of great importance, so that the singular integral

$$\psi_n(x) = \int_{\mathfrak{E}_m} \frac{f(x, \theta)}{r^m} \phi_n(y)dy \tag{39.11}$$

is easily evaluated. This can be accomplished, if the characteristic (and hence, the symbol) of the singular integral in (39.9) is a spherical polynomial. For ease, we limit considerations to the case $m = 2$. Let the characteristic have the form

$$f(x, \theta) = \sum_{k=-N}^{N}{}' a_k(x)e^{ik\theta}.$$

Then the symbol of the integral (39.11) equals

$$\Phi(x, \theta) = \sum_{k=-N}^{N}{}' b_k(x)e^{ik\theta}, \qquad b_k = \frac{2\pi i^{|k|}}{|k|} a_k. \tag{39.12}$$

When $N = 1$, (39.12) takes the form

$$\Phi(x, \theta) = \beta_1(x) \cos \theta + \beta_2(x) \sin \theta,$$

and the characteristic becomes

$$f(x, \theta) = \alpha_1(x) \cos \theta + \alpha_2(x) \sin \theta, \quad \alpha_j(x) = \frac{\beta_j(x)}{2\pi i} \qquad (j = 1, 2).$$

The singular integral (39.11) can then be written as

$$\psi_n(x) = \alpha_1(x) \frac{\partial}{\partial x_1} \int_{\mathfrak{E}_2} \frac{\phi_n(y)}{r} dy + \alpha_2(x) \frac{\partial}{\partial x_2} \int_{\mathfrak{E}_2} \frac{\phi_n(y)}{r} dy, \tag{39.13}$$

where x_1 and x_2 are the cartesian components of x.

We introduce into the examination the half-space

$$-\infty < x_1 < \infty, \quad -\infty < x_2 < \infty, \quad 0 < x_3 < \infty$$

of $\mathfrak{E}_3$. We denote this half-space by $\mathfrak{E}_3^+$. We choose the system of functions $v_n(x_1, x_2, x_3)$, which are harmonic in $\mathfrak{E}_3^+$, equal to zero at infinity and are continuous together with their first derivatives in the half-space $\mathfrak{E}_3^+$ plus its boundary. We put

$$\phi_n(y) = \left. \frac{\partial v_n(y_1, y_2, y_3)}{\partial y_3} \right|_{y_3 = 0}, \tag{39.14}$$

where y_1 and y_2 are the Cartesian components of y, and then evaluate (39.13).

On the boundary $x_3 = 0$ of $\mathfrak{E}_3^+$, the functions $v_n(x_1, x_2, x_3)$ satisfy the condition of the Neuman problem

$$\frac{\partial v_n}{\partial \nu} = -\phi_n(x),$$

where ν is the outward normal to $x_3 = 0$ (in the $-x_3$ direction). Making use of the known solution for the Neuman problem in $\mathfrak{E}_3^+$, we obtain

$$v_n(x_1, x_2, x_3) = \frac{1}{2\pi} \int_{E_2} \frac{\phi_n(y)}{R} dy,$$

$$R^2 = (x_1 - y_1)^2 + (x_2 - y_2)^2 + x_3^2,$$

whence it follows that

$$\frac{\partial}{\partial x_1} \int_{\mathfrak{E}_2} \frac{\phi_n(y)}{r} dy = 2\pi \frac{\partial v_n(x_1, x_2, 0)}{\partial x_1},$$

$$\frac{\partial}{\partial x_2} \int_{\mathfrak{E}_2} \frac{\phi_n(y)}{r} dy = 2\pi \frac{\partial v_n(x_1, x_2, 0)}{\partial x_2}, \tag{39.15}$$

and the value of (39.13) is determined.

We turn to the general case when the characteristic is a polynomial. We put

$$hu = \frac{1}{2\pi i}\int_{\mathfrak{E}_2} \frac{e^{i\theta}}{r^2}\, u(y)dy.$$

Then, as it follows from (39.12), the integral (39.11) can be expressed in the form

$$\int_{\mathfrak{E}_2} \frac{f(x, \theta)}{r^2}\, u(y)dy = \sum_{k=-N}^{N} b_k(x)h^k u,$$

and the problem reduces to the choice of functions $\phi_n(x)$ so that $h^k\phi_n$ can be easily evaluated. As above, we introduce the system of functions $v_n(x_1, x_2, x_3)$, which are harmonic in $\mathfrak{E}_3^+$ and equal zero at infinity. This time, we only stipulate that the functions be N-times continuously differentiable in the closed half-space $x_3 \geqq 0$. As before, the functions $\phi_n(x)$ are defined by (39.14).

We put

$$w_{n_1}(x_1, x_2, x_3) = 2\pi \left[\frac{\partial v_n}{\partial x_1} + i\,\frac{\partial v_n}{\partial x_2}\right].$$

It is clear that w_{n1} is harmonic in $\mathfrak{E}_3^+$ and $h\phi_n = w_{n1}(x_1, x_2, 0)$. We construct the harmonic functions $\omega_{n1}(x_1, x_2, x_3)$ in $\mathfrak{E}_3^+$, so that $\omega_{n1} = 0$ at infinity and

$$\left.\frac{\partial \omega_{n1}}{\partial x_3}\right|_{x_3=0} = w_{n1}(x_1, x_2, 0).$$

It is easy to see that

$$\omega_{n1} = \int_{+\infty}^{x_3} w_{n1}(x_1, x_2, \xi)d\xi.$$

By an analogous argument,

$$h^2\phi_n = hw_{n1}(x_1, x_2, 0) = 2\pi \left[\frac{\partial \omega_{n1}}{\partial x_1} + i\frac{\partial \omega_{n1}}{\partial x_2}\right]_{x_3=0}.$$

We now put

$$w_{n2}(x_1, x_2, x_3) = 2\pi \left[\frac{\partial \omega_{n1}}{\partial x_1} + i \frac{\partial \omega_{n2}}{\partial x_2}\right]$$

and repeat the process.

For the functions v_n, we could take the Caley transformations for harmonic polynomials.

The extension of the method to multi-dimensional singular integrals is obvious.

Chapter VI

INFINITE REGIONS AND OTHER SINGULAR PROBLEMS

§40. Preliminary remarks

If the region Ω, in which the solution of a boundary-value problem is sought, is infinite, then, for the usual problem of interest (for example, the Dirichlet problem for the Poisson equation), the corresponding operator is often non-positive definite – only positive. Sometimes the operator is positive definite, but its spectrum ceases to be discrete. The spectrum of a positive operator (non-positive definite) is also non-discrete (see below). We recall that, in Chapter V, we made wide use of the discreteness of the spectrum of a given operator for the construction of coordinate systems. In a natural way, the loss of this property makes the choice of coordinate systems more difficult.

Even when the region Ω is finite, the discreteness of the spectrum of an operator and its positive definiteness can be lost, if the differential equation, which is elliptic inside Ω, is degenerate over all or part of its boundary. In the present chapter, we shall study the construction of coordinate systems for operators with non-discrete spectra. At the same time, we shall investigate in more detail the problem

$$Au = f, \qquad f \in \mathfrak{H}, \tag{40.1}$$

where A is a positive, but non-positive definite, operator in the given Hilbert space $\mathfrak{H}$. On $\mathfrak{D}(A)$, the inequality

$$(Au, u) > 0, \qquad u \neq 0, \tag{40.2}$$

holds and

$$\inf_{u \in \mathfrak{D}(A)} \frac{(Au, u)}{(u, u)} = 0. \tag{40.3}$$

Since positive operators are bounded below, they possess selfadjoint Friedrichs extensions. It can happen that the extended operator (denoted by $\tilde{A}$) is no longer positive and satisfies instead of (40.2) the weaker inequality $(\tilde{A}u, u) \geqq 0$, where the equality holds for at least one element $u_0 \neq 0$. We exclude this case from consideration and henceforth stipulate that the Friedrichs extension of a positive operator is a positive operator. Below, we shall assume that in (40.1) the operator A is selfadjoint.

Note $(\tilde{A}u_0, u_0) = 0$ implies $\tilde{A}u_0 = 0$. In fact, let v be an arbitrary element of $\mathfrak{D}(\tilde{A})$. For any real ε,

$$(\tilde{A}(u_0+\varepsilon v), u_0+\varepsilon v) = (\tilde{A}u_0, u_0)+2\varepsilon \operatorname{Re} (\tilde{A}u_0, v)+\varepsilon^2(\tilde{A}v, v) \geqq 0$$

and, since $(\tilde{A}u_0, u_0) = 0$, $\operatorname{Re} (\tilde{A}u_0, v) = 0$. Replacing v by iv, we obtain that $\operatorname{Im} (\tilde{A}u_0, v) = 0$, and hence, $(\tilde{A}u_0, v) = 0$. Being orthogonal to the dense set $\mathfrak{D}(\tilde{A})$, the element $\tilde{A}u_0$ equals zero.

As for positive definite operators, we can introduce an energy inner product and norm (see PM, §6):

$$[u, v] = [u, v]_A = (Au, v), \qquad |||u|||^2 = |||u|||_A^2 = (Au, u) \tag{40.4}$$

and construct the energy space $\mathfrak{H}_A$ as the closure of $\mathfrak{D}(A)$ w.r.t. the metric (40.4). If A is only positive, then $\mathfrak{H}_A$ cannot be imbedded in $\mathfrak{H}$ – among the "minimal" {"ideal"} elements of $\tilde{\mathfrak{H}}_A$ there exist elements for which there are no corresponding elements in $\mathfrak{H}$. Let A be only positive. Then (40.1) has at most one solution in $\mathfrak{H}$. If it is solvable in $\mathfrak{H}$, then its solution will minimise the functional

$$F(u) = |||u|||_A^2-(f, u)-(u,f) \tag{40.5}$$

on the set $\mathfrak{D}(A)$. Conversely, if the functional $F(u)$ attains a minimum on the set $\mathfrak{D}(A)$, then the element $u_0 \in \mathfrak{D}(A)$ which minimises $F(u)$ satisfies (40.1) (see PM, §6).

In general, the element $u_0 \in \mathfrak{H}_A$ which minimises (40.5) on the space $\mathfrak{H}_A$ (if this element exists) does not lie in the original space $\mathfrak{H}$. However, $|||u_0|||_A^2$ is finite. From the physical point of view, this can be interpreted as follows: the state of the required element u_0 has finite energy. On the basis of this interpretation, we say that u_0 *is the solution of* (40.1) *with finite energy*. Fom the results of §6 (for more details of PM, §6), it follows that (40.1) has a solution with finite energy, if and only if the inner product (u,f), $u \in \mathfrak{D}(A)$, is a bounded functional w.r.t. the metric of $\mathfrak{H}_A$.

We can examine the more general variational problem of minimising the functional

$$F(u) = |||u|||_A^2 - lu - \overline{lu}, \qquad \mathfrak{D}(l) \subset \mathfrak{H}_A, \tag{40.5}$$

where lu is a linear functional and the domain $\mathfrak{D}(l)$ is dense in $\mathfrak{H}_A$. It can also be shown that this new problem has a solution (which, as before, we shall call the solution with finite energy), if and only if the functional lu is bounded w.r.t. metric of $\mathfrak{H}_A$.

If the energy space $\mathfrak{H}_A$ is separable and (40.1) has a solution with finite energy, then an approximate representation of the solution can be constructed with the help of the Ritz-process. We prove that, if the original space $\mathfrak{H}$ is separable, then the energy space $\mathfrak{H}_A$ is also separable. The operator $\boldsymbol{B} = \boldsymbol{A}+\boldsymbol{I}$, where $\boldsymbol{I}$ is the identity operator, is selfadjoint and positive definite:

$$|||u|||_B^2 = (\boldsymbol{B}u, u) = |||u|||_A^2 + ||u||^2 \geqq ||u||^2 \qquad u \in \mathfrak{D}(\boldsymbol{B}) = \mathfrak{D}(\boldsymbol{A}).$$

In this way, the space $\mathfrak{H}_B$ is separable (see PM, §8). It follows that the set $\mathfrak{D}(\boldsymbol{B}) = \mathfrak{D}(\boldsymbol{A})$, which is dense in $\mathfrak{H}_B$, is separable w.r.t. the metric in $\mathfrak{H}_B$: there exists a sequence $\{v_k\} \in \mathfrak{D}(\boldsymbol{A})$ such that, whatever may be the element $u \in \mathfrak{D}(\boldsymbol{A})$ and the number $\varepsilon > 0$, we can always find a v_k such that $|||u-v_k|||_B < \varepsilon$. Moreover, $|||u-v_k|||_A \leqq |||u-v_k|||_B < \varepsilon$: the set $\mathfrak{D}(\boldsymbol{A})$ is separable w.r.t. the metric of $\mathfrak{H}_A$, and since this set is dense in $\mathfrak{H}_A$, we can find elements u and $v_k \in \mathfrak{D}(\boldsymbol{A})$, with w an arbitrary element of $\mathfrak{H}_A$, such that $|||w-u|||_A < \varepsilon$ and $|||u-v_k|||_A < \varepsilon$. This implies that $|||w-v_k|||_A < 2\varepsilon$ and that $\mathfrak{H}_A$ is separable.

We consider the well-known and important peculiarity of selfadjoint and *merely positive* operators (we shall call operators *merely positive* if they are positive, but not positive definite): their spectrum is non-discrete. We assume the opposite: there exists a selfadjoint and merely positive operator $\boldsymbol{A}$ with a discrete spectrum. If λ_1 is the smallest eigenvalue of this operator then, on the basis of (40.3),

$$\lambda_1 = \inf_{u \in \mathfrak{D}(\boldsymbol{A})} \frac{(\boldsymbol{A}u, u)}{||u||^2} = 0.$$

We denote by u_1 the normalised eigenfunction corresponding to $\lambda_1 = 0$. Then

$$(\boldsymbol{A}u_1, u_1) = 0, \qquad ||u_1|| = 1,$$

which contradicts inequality (40.2).

If $\boldsymbol{A}$ and $\boldsymbol{K}$ are selfadjoint operators, where $\boldsymbol{A}$ is merely positive and $\boldsymbol{K}$

is bounded, then the sum $A+K$ can be positive definite (for example, when $K = I$), but, in general, its spectrum is non-discrete. This property makes difficult the choice of coordinate functions for problems, related to operators of the above form.

§41. Second order elliptic equations in an infinite region

Let Ω, bounded by a sufficiently smooth surface S, be an infinite region in m-dimensional Euclidean space $\mathfrak{E}_m$ with Cartesian coordinates $x_1, \ldots, x_m$. On the whole, we shall be interested in two types of infinite regions:

(1) regions containing cubes with arbitrarily long sides;

(2) the regions defined by the condition: their surface is enclosed between the two infinite prisms

$$0 \leqq x_k \leqq a, \quad k < m, \quad -\infty < x_m < +\infty,$$
$$0 \leqq x_k \leqq b, \quad k < m, \quad -\infty < x_m < +\infty, \quad a > b,$$

or the two semi-infinite prisms

$$0 \leqq x_k \leqq a, \quad k < m, \quad x_m \geqq \alpha,$$
$$0 \leqq x_k \leqq b, \quad k < m, \quad x_m \geqq \beta, \quad a > b, \quad \beta > \alpha.$$

Regions (1) comprise those outside a finite surface, regions lying inside or outside of a paraboloid, a hyperboloid, a cone, the exterior of a circular cylinder, etc. To regions (2) belong the interior of an infinite or semi-infinite circular cylinder, etc.

In the space $L_2(\Omega)$, we examine the differential operator

$$Au = -\sum_{j,k=1}^{m} \frac{\partial}{\partial x_j}\left(A_{jk}(x)\frac{\partial u}{\partial x_k}\right), \qquad A_{jk} = A_{kj}, \tag{41.1}$$

w.r.t. either of the boundary conditions

$$u|_S = 0 \tag{41.2}$$

or

$$\left[\sum_{j,k=1}^{m} A_{jk}\frac{\partial u}{\partial x_j}\cos(\nu, x_k)+\sigma u\right]_S = 0, \qquad \sigma \geqq 0, \tag{41.3}$$

where the notation used is the same as in the previous chapter. We assume that the eigenvalues of the matrix of the coefficients A_{jk} are positive bounded above and below such that

$$\mu_0 \sum_{k=1}^{m} |t_k|^2 \leqq \sum_{j,k=1}^{m} A_{jk}(x)\bar{t}_j t_k \leqq M_0 \sum_{k=1}^{m} |t_k|^2, \tag{41.4}$$

where μ_0 and M_0 are positive constants. We also assume that the $A_{jk} \in C^{(1)}(\Omega)$.

For $\mathfrak{D}(A)$, we choose the functions of $C^{(2)}(\overline{\Omega})$ with finite support which satisfy either (41.2) or (41.3). In accordance with the general definition, we say that a function *has a finite support*, if it is identically equal to zero outside of some sphere.

It is not difficult to see that this A is positive. In fact, since the functions $u \in \mathfrak{D}(A)$ have finite support, it is only necessary to integrate

$$(Au, u) = -\int_\Omega \bar{u} \sum_{j,k=1}^{m} \frac{\partial}{\partial x_j}\left(A_{jk}\frac{\partial u}{\partial x_k}\right) dx$$

over a finite region. Obviously, integration by parts can be applied. Using the boundary conditions, we obtain

$$(Au, u) = \int_\Omega \sum_{j,k=1}^{m} A_{jk} \frac{\partial \bar{u}}{\partial x_j}\frac{\partial u}{\partial x_k}\, dx \tag{41.5}$$

for (41.2) and

$$(Au, u) = \int_\Omega \sum_{j,k=1}^{m} A_{jk} \frac{\partial \bar{u}}{\partial x_j}\frac{\partial u}{\partial x_k}\, dx + \int_S \sigma |u|^2 dS \tag{41.6}$$

for (41.3). Hence, it is clear that $(Au, u) \geqq 0$. Since $(Au, u) = 0$ implies $u(x) \equiv C \equiv$ const., it follows that $C = 0$, since u equals zero outside of some sphere.

Forming the closure of $\mathfrak{D}(A)$ w.r.t. the metric generated by (41.5) or (41.6), we obtain the space $\mathfrak{H}_A$. It is not difficult to prove that this space consists of the functions which:

1. have generalised first derivatives which are square summable in Ω;
2. can be approximated, w.r.t. the metric of the Dirichlet integral, by continuously differentiable finite functions: In this way, if $u \in \mathfrak{H}_A$, then there exists a sequence of continuously differentiable functions $u_n(x)$ with finite supports in $\overline{\Omega}$ such that

$$\lim_{n\to\infty} \int_{\Omega} |\text{grad}\,(u-u_n)|^2\, dx = 0;$$

3. equal zero on S for (41.2), and are square summable on S with weight σ for the boundary condition (41.3).

From the Sobolev imbedding theorem, it follows that the functions satisfying 1., 2. and 3. are square summable in any finite subregion of C and on any finite and measurable part of the surface S.

The energy inner product and norm will be defined by

$$\begin{aligned} [u, v]_A &= \int_{\Omega} \sum_{j,k=1}^{m} A_{jk} \frac{\partial \bar{v}}{\partial x_j} \frac{\partial u}{\partial x_k}\, dx, \\ |||u|||_A^2 &= \int_{\Omega} \sum_{j,k=1}^{m} A_{jk} \frac{\partial \bar{u}}{\partial x_j} \frac{\partial u}{\partial x_k}\, dx \end{aligned} \tag{41.7}$$

for boundary condition (41.2), and

$$\begin{aligned} [u, v]_A &= \int_{\Omega} \sum_{j,k=1}^{m} A_{jk} \frac{\partial \bar{v}}{\partial x_k} \frac{\partial u}{\partial x_k}\, dx + \int_S \sigma u \bar{v}\, dS, \\ |||u|||_A^2 &= \int_{\Omega} \sum_{j,k=1}^{m} A_{jk} \frac{\partial \bar{u}}{\partial x_j} \frac{\partial u}{\partial x_k}\, dx + \int_S \sigma |u|^2\, dS \end{aligned} \tag{41.8}$$

for boundary condition (41.3).

Theorem 41.1 *The operator A is merely positive, if* Ω *is a region of type* (1), *and positive definite, if* Ω *is a region of type* (2) *and boundary condition* (41.2) *holds.*

Proof. Let Ω be a region of type (1). We construct inside it a cube Q, with sides of length a, and place the coordinate axes along the sides of the cube so that the coordinates of points inside Q will be positive. The functions

$$u_a(x) = \begin{cases} \prod_{k=1}^{m} \sin^3 \dfrac{\pi x_k}{a}, & x \in Q, \\ 0, & x \in Q, \end{cases}$$

lie in $\mathfrak{D}(A)$. On the strength of (41.4), we obtain

$$\frac{(Au_a, u_a)}{||u_a||^2} = \frac{|||u_{aA}^2|||}{||u_a||^2} \leqq \frac{M_0}{||u_a||^2}\int_\Omega \sum_{k=1}^m \left(\frac{\partial u_a}{\partial x_k}\right)^2 dx =$$
$$= \frac{M_0}{||u_a||^2}\int_Q \sum_{k=1}^m \left(\frac{\partial u_a}{\partial x_k}\right)^2 dx = \frac{c}{a^2} \to_{a\to\infty} 0,$$

where c is a constant, whence it follows that

$$\inf_{u\in\mathfrak{D}(A)} \frac{(Au, u)}{||u||^2} = 0.$$

The element $u_0 \neq 0$, for which $(Au_0, u_0) = 0$, does not exist: if such an element exists, then $|||u_0|||_A = 0$. From (41.7), it follows that $u_0 \doteq$ const., and since $u_0 \in \mathfrak{D}(A)$ and therefore $\mathfrak{H}_A$, and since the volume of Ω is infinite, $u_0 \equiv 0$. Hence, it follows that A is a merely positive operator. Now let Ω be a region of type (2) and the boundary condition be (41.2). We assume that it can be placed inside the semi-infinite prism

$$0 \leqq x_k \leqq a, \quad k < m, \qquad 0 \leqq x_m < \infty,$$

where a is fixed. We shall denote this prism by Q. We introduce the operator B acting in the space $L_2(Q)$ in accordance with $Bu = -\Delta u$ and defined on the finite functions of $C^{(2)}(\bar{Q})$ with finite supports, which equal zero on the boundary of Q. Any function $u \in \mathfrak{H}_A$ can be examined as an element of $\mathfrak{H}_B$. For this purpose, it is sufficient to choose the function $u(x)$ and put it equal to zero if $x \in Q\backslash\Omega$. Since, by (41.4),

$$|||u|||_A \geqq \mu_0 \int_\Omega \sum_{k=1}^m \left|\frac{\partial u}{\partial x_k}\right|^2 dx = \mu_0 \int_Q \sum_{k=1}^m \left|\frac{\partial u}{\partial x_k}\right|^2 dx = \mu_0 |||u|||_B^2,$$

it is sufficient to prove that the operator B is positive definite.

Let $u(x)$ be an arbitrary element of $\mathfrak{D}(B)$. Since this function has a finite support, if h is a sufficiently large number, and $x_m > h$, then $u(x) \equiv 0$ and

$$\frac{|||u|||_B^2}{||u||^2} = \frac{\int_0^a \cdots \int_0^a \int_0^h \sum_{k=1}^m \left|\frac{\partial u}{\partial x_k}\right|^2 dx_1 \ldots dx_{m-1}\, dx_m}{\int_0^a \cdots \int_0^a \int_0^h |u|^2 dx_1 \ldots dx_{m-1}\, dx_m} \geqq \lambda_h,$$

where we denote by λ_h the smallest eigenvalue of the Dirichlet problem for the Laplace operator in the parallelepiped: $0 \leqq x_k \leqq a (k < m)$,

$0 \leqq x_m \leqq h$. As is well known,

$$\lambda_h = \pi^2 \left(\frac{m-1}{a^2} + \frac{1}{h^2}\right).$$

Hence,

$$|||u|||_B^2 \geqq \frac{(m-1)\pi^2}{a^2} \, ||u||^2,$$

which proves that $\boldsymbol{B}$ is positive definite. It follows that $\boldsymbol{A}$ is positive definite with

$$|||u|||_A^2 \geqq \frac{(m-1)\mu_0 \pi^2}{a^2} \, ||u||^2.$$

If Ω is a region of type (2) and the boundary condition is (41.3), then $\boldsymbol{A}$ is always positive. This follows immediately from (41.8).

For infinite regions of type (1) and (2), the spectrum of $\boldsymbol{A}$ is non-discrete. For regions of type (1), this follows immediately from the fact that $\boldsymbol{A}$ is merely positive. For regions of type (2), the proof is more complex and we shall not stop to consider it here. (It follows from a very general result found in Glazman [1; §47]).

In conclusion, we shall consider an ordinary differential operator

$$-\frac{d}{dx}\left(p(x)\frac{du}{dx}\right) \tag{41.9}$$

on either one of the infinite intervals $(-\infty, \infty)$ or $(0, \infty)$. We shall assume that, in the given intervals, the function $p(x)$ is continuously differentiable and positive bounded above and below. The operator, defined by (41.9), will be examined in either $L_2(-\infty, \infty)$ or $L_2(0, \infty)$. In the latter case, we assume that $u(x)$ also satisfies either

$$u(0) = 0 \tag{41.10}$$

or

$$u'(0) - \alpha u(0) = 0, \qquad \alpha \geqq 0. \tag{41.11}$$

Here, Ω is an infinite region of type (1): the one-dimensional cube with side of length a is an interval of length a, and the lines $(0, \infty)$ and $(-\infty, \infty)$ both contain intervals of arbitrary length. On the basis of the above results, it follows that the above one-dimensional operators are merely positive, and hence, their spectra are non-discrete.

§42. The divergence condition

Note. The basic results of this section are contained in Mikhlin [8] and [14].

Let Ω be an infinite region of either type (1) or (2) (some of the present results are true for quite general regions) and let it be required to integrate the equation

$$-\sum_{j,k=1}^{m} \frac{\partial}{\partial x_j}\left(A_{jk}\frac{\partial u}{\partial x_k}\right) = f(x) \tag{42.1}$$

in this region for one or other of the boundary conditions (41.2) or (41.3). We assume that the coefficients $A_{jk}(x)$ satisfy the conditions of §41. If $f(x) \in L_2(\Omega)$ and the posed problem has a solution, which also lies in $L_2(\Omega)$, then this solution minimises

$$|||u|||_A^2 - 2\,\mathrm{Re}\int_\Omega u\bar{f}\,dx, \tag{42.2}$$

where $|||u|||_A^2$ is defined by (41.7) or (41.8). In the general problem, we seek the solution of (42.1) with finite energy. From our general considerations (see §40), it is known that such a solution exists, if and only if the integral

$$\int_\Omega u\bar{f}\,dx, \qquad u \in \mathfrak{D}(A), \tag{42.3}$$

is bounded w.r.t. the metric of $\mathfrak{H}_A$. We clarify conditions such that this holds. Let $\mathfrak{M}$ denote the set of functions with finite supports which are continuously differentiable in Ω and equal zero in the boundary region of this region.

Let $G(x)$ be a locally summable (summable in any finite subspace of Ω) vector which is defined almost everywhere in Ω. We also assume that there exists a locally summable scalar function $g(x)$, defined almost everywhere in Ω, which satisfies the condition that the identity

$$\int_\Omega \phi(x)\overline{g(x)}dx = -\int_\Omega \operatorname{grad}\phi \cdot G(x)dx \tag{42.4}$$

is true for any function $\phi(x) \in \mathfrak{M}$. We call the function $g(x)$ the (generalised) *divergence* of the vector $G(x)$ and write $g(x) = \operatorname{div} G(x)$.
It is clear that the concept of generalised divergence can be related to problems with a finite region Ω. For this case, we assume that the functions $g(x)$ and $|G(x)|$ are summable in any internal subregion of Ω and that $\mathfrak{M}$ denotes the set of functions of $C^{(1)}(\Omega)$ which equal zero on some boundary region of Ω. We say that $g(x) = \operatorname{div} G(x)$, if the following identity holds

$$\int_\Omega \phi(x)\bar{g}(x)dx = -\int_\Omega \operatorname{grad} \phi \, . \, G(x)dx.$$

Theorem 42.1. *In order that problem* (42.1) *and* (41.2) *has a solution with finite energy, it is necessary and sufficient that* $f(x) = \operatorname{div} F(x)$, *where* $|F| \in L_2(\Omega)$.

Proof. The condition of Theorem 42.1 is called the *divergence condition.* If (42.1) and (41.2) has a solution $u_0(x)$ with finite energy, then (42.3) can be rewritten in the form (see §41)

$$\int_\Omega \bar{f}(x)u(x)dx = [u, u_0]_A = \int_\Omega \sum_{j,k=1}^m A_{jk}(x) \frac{\partial \bar{u}_0}{\partial x_j} \frac{\partial u}{\partial x_k} dx =$$

$$= -\int_\Omega \operatorname{grad} u \, . \, F(x)dx, \tag{42.5}$$

where $F(x)$ is a vector the kth component of which equals

$$F_k(x) = -\sum_{j=1}^m \bar{A}_{jk} \frac{\partial u_0}{\partial x_j} = -\sum_{j=1}^m A_{kj} \frac{\partial u_0}{\partial x_j}. \tag{42.6}$$

The set $\mathfrak{M}$, defined above, is contained in $\mathfrak{H}_A$. If, in (42.5), u denotes an arbitrary function of $\mathfrak{M}$, then this relationship implies that $f(x) = \operatorname{div} F(x)$. Further, it follows from (41.4) that the coefficients A_{jk} are bounded. Let $|A_{kj}| \leqq N$, then it follows from (42.6), on the strength of Cauchy's inequality, that

$$|F(x)|^2 = \sum_{j=1}^m |F_j(x)|^2 \leqq m^2 N^2 |\operatorname{grad} u_0|^2.$$

Since $u_0 \in \mathfrak{H}_A \subset W_2^{(1)}(\Omega)$, $|F| \in L_2(\Omega)$. Conversely, if $f(x)$ satisfies the divergence condition, then, for arbitrary $u \in \mathfrak{M}$,

$$\int_\Omega \bar{f}(x)u(x)dx = \int_\Omega u \, \overline{\operatorname{div} F} dx = -\int_\Omega \operatorname{grad} u \, . \, F dx.$$

Hence,

$$\left|\int_\Omega \bar{f}(x)u(x)dx\right| \leqq \left\{\int_\Omega |F|^2 dx\right\}^{\frac{1}{2}} \left\{\int_\Omega |\text{grad } u|^2 dx\right\}^{\frac{1}{2}}$$

and, on the basis of (41.4),

$$\left|\int_\Omega \bar{f}(x)u(x)dx\right| \leqq \frac{1}{\mu_0}\left\{\int_\Omega |F|^2 dx\right\}^{\frac{1}{2}} |||u|||_A. \tag{42.7}$$

Since $\mathfrak{M}$ is dense in $\mathfrak{H}_A$, the last inequality shows that the functional (42.3) is bounded in $\mathfrak{H}_A$, and hence, that problem (42.1) and (41.2) has a solution with finite energy.

If $u_0(x)$ is the solution, then

$$\int_\Omega \bar{f}(x)u(x)dx = [u, u_0]_A.$$

In inequality (42.7), which is true not only for the elements of $\mathfrak{M}$ but also for the elements of $\mathfrak{H}_A$, we put $u = u_0$. We then obtain the following estimate for the energy norm of the solution:

$$|||u_0|||_A \leqq \frac{1}{\mu_0}\left\{\int_\Omega |F(x)|^2 dx\right\}^{\frac{1}{2}}. \tag{42.8}$$

Theorem 42.2 *Let Ω be a region of type* (1) *with finite boundary. In order that problem* (42.1) *and* (41.3) *has a solution with finite energy, it is necessary that $f(x) = \text{div } F(x)$, $|F| \in L_2(\Omega)$, and sufficient that, besides this, the formula for integration by parts*

$$\int_\Omega u\bar{f}\, dx = -\int_\Omega (\text{grad } u)\cdot F dx + \int_S u\bar{F}_\nu dS, \tag{42.9}$$

is true for arbitrary functions with finite support $u \in \mathfrak{H}_A$, where F_ν is the projection of the vector F on the outward normal ν to the surface S and $F_\nu \in L_2(S)$.

Proof. We recall that the space $\mathfrak{H}_A$ consists of those functions of $W_2^{(1)}(\Omega)$ which are square summable on the boundary S with weight σ. On noting as a preliminary that $\mathfrak{M} \subset \mathfrak{H}_A$, the necessity is proved as in Theorem 42.1.

We now turn to the proof of sufficiency. Let $u \in \mathfrak{H}_A$ have a finite support.

From (42.9), it follows that

$$\left|\int_\Omega u\bar{f}\,dx\right|^2 \leqq 2\int_\Omega |F|^2\,dx\int_\Omega |\text{grad}\,u|^2\,dx+2\int_S |F_\nu|^2\,dS\int_S |u|^2\,dS. \tag{42.10}$$

We assume initially that $\sigma \not\equiv 0$. It follows from the Sobolev imbedding theorem that

$$\int_S |u|^2\,dS \leqq C_1\left\{\int_\Omega (\text{grad}\,u)^2\,dx+\int_S \sigma|u|^2\,dS\right\}, \qquad C_1 = \text{const},$$

whence it is easily seen that

$$\left|\int_\Omega u\bar{f}dx\right|^2 \leqq C_2\left\{\int_\Omega (\text{grad}\,u)^2\,dx+\int_S \sigma|u|^2\,dS\right\} = C_2|||u|||_A^2, \tag{42.11}$$

$$C_2 = \text{const}.$$

The functional (42.3) is bounded on a dense set of functions with finite supports in $\mathfrak{H}_A$. Hence, problem (42.1) and (41.3) has a solution with finite energy. From (42.10), one easily obtains the estimate $|||u_0|||_A \leqq \sqrt{C_2}$, where u_0 is the solution with finite energy.

The case $\sigma \equiv 0$ requires a special examination. The solution of (42.1) and (41.3), if it exists, will only be determined to within an arbitrary constant. We remove this arbitrariness by replacing $\mathfrak{H}_A$ by the subspace $\tilde{\mathfrak{H}}_A$ of elements of $\mathfrak{H}_A$ which satisfy

$$\int_S u\,dS = 0, \tag{42.12}$$

and stipulate that the required solution with finite energy lies in $\tilde{\mathfrak{H}}_A$. We prove that the inequality

$$\int_S |u|^2\,dS \leqq C_1\int_\Omega |\text{grad}\,u|^2\,dx \leqq \frac{C_1}{\mu_0}\,|||u|||_A^2, \qquad C_1 = \text{const}, \tag{42.13}$$

is true for the elements of $\tilde{\mathfrak{H}}_A$.

We construct the sphere S_R with centre at the origin and fixed radius R, so that S lies inside S_R. We denote by Ω_R that part of Ω which lies inside S_R. If, in the space $W_2^{(1)}(\Omega_R)$, we define the norm by

$$||u||^2_{W_2^{(1)}(\Omega_R)} = \int_{\Omega_R} |\text{grad}\,u|^2\,dx+\left|\int_S u\,dS\right|^2,$$

use of the imbedding theorem yields

$$\int_S |u|^2 dS \leqq C_1 \left\{ \int_{\Omega_R} |\text{grad } u|^2 dx + \left| \int_S u\, dS \right|^2 \right\}, \qquad C_1 = \text{const.}$$

If $u \in \tilde{\mathfrak{H}}_A$, then

$$\int_S |u|^2 dS \leqq C_1 \int_{\Omega_R} |\text{grad } u|^2 dx \leqq C_1 \int_\Omega |\text{grad } u|^2 dx.$$

Combining (42.10) and (42.13), we obtain

$$\left| \int_\Omega u\bar{f}\, dx \right| \leqq 2 \left[\int_\Omega |F(x)|^2 dx + \frac{C_1}{\mu_0} \int_S |F_\nu|^2 dS \right] |||u|||_A^2.$$

Hence, the functional (42.3) is bounded in $\tilde{\mathfrak{H}}_A$ and our problem has a solution with finite energy. Let u_0 be this solution. It minimises

$$|||u|||_A^2 - 2\,\text{Re} \int_\Omega u\bar{f}\, dx$$

on $\tilde{\mathfrak{H}}_A$. Therefore, at u_0, the variation of this functional equals zero

$$[u_0, \zeta]_A - \int_\Omega \zeta \bar{f}\, dx = 0, \qquad \zeta \in \tilde{\mathfrak{H}}_A,$$

and hence,

$$[u_0, \zeta]_A + \int_\Omega \text{grad } \zeta \cdot F\, dx = 0.$$

Putting $\zeta = u_0$ and making use of the Schwartz-Buniakovskii inequality and (41.4), we obtain

$$|||u_0|||_A^2 \leqq \left\{ \int_\Omega |F|^2 dx \right\}^{\frac{1}{2}} \left\{ \int_\Omega |\text{grad } u_0|^2 dx \right\}^{\frac{1}{2}} \leqq$$
$$\leqq \frac{1}{\sqrt{\mu_0}} \left\{ \int_\Omega |F(z)|^2 dx \right\}^{\frac{1}{2}} |||u_0|||_A.$$

This gives us for the solution of the Neuman problem with finite energy the estimate

$$|||u_0|||_A \leqq \frac{1}{\sqrt{\mu_0}} \left\{ \int_\Omega |F|^2 dx \right\}^{\frac{1}{2}}. \tag{42.14}$$

Note 1. Formula (42.9) and the requirement $F_\nu \in L_2(S)$ hold, if, for example, $F_j \in W_p^{(1)}(\omega)$, where the F_j are the components of a vector F, ω is the intersection of Ω with some neighbourhood of S and

$$\frac{(m-1)p}{m-p} > 2 \quad \text{or} \quad p > \frac{2m}{m+1}.$$

Note 2. The relationship $f(x) = \operatorname{div} F(x)$, $F(x) \in L_2(\Omega)$ holds, for example, under the following conditions (see, Mikhlin [14]): let x and y be points of Ω, $\rho = |y|$, $r = |x-y|$ and

$$\alpha(\rho) = \begin{cases} 0, & \rho < 1, \\ 1, & \rho \geqq 1. \end{cases}$$

If there exists a point outside Ω, then we can choose this point as origin and simply put $\alpha(\rho) = 1$. We examine the function

$$\psi(x) = \int_\Omega \left(\frac{1}{r^{m-2}} - \frac{\alpha(\rho)}{\rho^{m-2}} \right) f(y) dy \tag{42.15}$$

and we assume that $m > 2$. If $m = 2$, we put

$$\psi(x) = \int_\Omega \left(\ln \frac{1}{r} - \alpha(\rho) \ln \frac{1}{\rho} \right) f(y) d\gamma. \tag{42.15'}$$

The integral (42.15) exists for almost all $x \in \Omega$, if, for example, $f \in L_p(\Omega)$, $1 < p < m$. If $|\operatorname{grad} \psi| \in L_2(\Omega)$, then we can put $F(x) = C \operatorname{grad} \psi$, where C is a suitably chosen constant.

§43. Other conditions for solvability

Since the existence of a vector $F(x)$ such that $f(x) = \operatorname{div} F(x)$ and $|F| \in L_2(\Omega)$ is not always easy to establish, we determine another easily verifiable sufficiency conditions for the solvability of (42.1) for the boundary conditions (41.2).

For an arbitrary function $u(x)$, which is defined almost everywhere in the m-dimensional Euclidean space $\mathfrak{E}_m$, $m \geqq 3$, has generalised first derivatives and gives finite values to the integrals

$$\int_{\mathfrak{E}_m} |u(x)|^2 \, dx, \qquad \int_{\mathfrak{E}_m} |\operatorname{grad} u|^2 \, dx, \tag{43.1}$$

the following inequality (see Courant and Hilbert [1; chapter 6, §5])

$$\int_{\mathfrak{E}_m} \frac{|u(x)|^2}{|x|^2}\,dx \leqq \frac{4}{(m-2)^2}\int_{\mathfrak{E}_m} |\mathrm{grad}\; u|^2\,dx \tag{43.2}$$

is true.

Starting with this inequality, it is not difficult to prove that problem (42.1) and (41.2) has a solution with finite energy if the dimension of Ω is greater than or equal to 3, the surface S of Ω is finite and

$$\int_\Omega |x|^2 \cdot |f(x)|^2\,dx < \infty. \tag{43.3}$$

In fact,

$$\left|\int_\Omega u(x)\overline{f(x)}dx\right| \leqq \left\{\int_\Omega |x|^2 \cdot |f(x)|^2\,dx\right\}^{\frac{1}{2}}\left\{\int_\Omega \frac{|u(x)|^2}{|x|^2}\,dx\right\}^{\frac{1}{2}}. \tag{43.4}$$

Since $u \in \mathfrak{H}_A$, there exists a sequence $\{u_n(x)\}$ of continuously differentiable finite functions in $\overline{\Omega}$ which equal zero on S such that

$$\int_\Omega |\mathrm{grad}\,(u_n-u)|^2\,dx \underset{n\to\infty}{\to} 0. \tag{43.5}$$

We complete the definition of the functions $u_n(x)$ by setting them equal to zero outside Ω. Functions, defined in this way, have generalised first derivatives and give finite values to the integrals (43.1). On the basis of (43.2),

$$\int_{E_m} \frac{|u_n(x)|^2}{|x|^2}\,dx \leqq \frac{4}{(m-2)^2}\int_{E_m} |\mathrm{grad}\; u_n|^2\,dx,$$

or, if we discard the integrals equal zero on the region added to Ω,

$$\int_\Omega \frac{|u_n(x)|^2}{|x|^2}\,dx \leqq \frac{4}{(m-2)^2}\int_\Omega |\mathrm{grad}\; u_n|^2\,dx. \tag{43.6}$$

We construct a sphere with centre at the origin and radius R, where R is sufficiently large, so that S is contained in the sphere. The intersection of the sphere with Ω is denoted by Ω_R. On the strength of (43.5) and (43.6),

$$\int_{\Omega_R} |\mathrm{grad}\,(u_n-u)|^2\,dx \xrightarrow[n\to\infty]{} 0 \tag{43.7}$$

is true for arbitrary R, and

$$\int_{\Omega_R} \frac{|u_n(x)|^2}{|x|^2} dx \leqq \frac{4}{(m-2)^2} \int_{\Omega} |\text{grad } u|^2 dx. \tag{43.8}$$

Since $u_n(x)$ and $u(x)$ both equal zero on S, it follows from (43.7) (the Sobolev imbedding theorem) that $u_n \to u$ w.r.t. the metric of $L_2(\Omega_R)$. Taking the limit in (43.8), first w.r.t. n then w.r.t. R, we obtain

$$\int_{\Omega} \frac{|u(x)|^2}{|x|^2} dx \leqq \frac{4}{(m-2)^2} \int_{\Omega} |\text{grad } u|^2 dx, \tag{43.9}$$

which is true for arbitrary $u \in \mathfrak{H}_A$. On the basis of (43.4), the functional (42.3) is bounded in $\mathfrak{H}_A$, and hence, problem (42.1) and (41.2) has a solution with finite energy.

§44. Homogeneous differential equations

The present section is devoted to the problem posed by the application of the energy method to boundary value problems for homogeneous differential equations defined on infinite regions.

We limit considerations to the problem of Dirichlet for the Laplace equation. Let Ω be an infinite region with finite boundary S. We seek the harmonic function $v(x)$ in this region which satisfies the boundary condition

$$v|_S = \psi|_S, \tag{44.1}$$

where $\psi \in W_2^{(1)}(\Omega)$ such that

$$\int_{\Omega} |\text{grad } \psi|^2 dx < \infty. \tag{44.2}$$

We consider the problem of minimising

$$\int_{\Omega} |\text{grad } v|^2 dx \tag{44.3}$$

on the set of functions which satisfy (44.1) and give the integral (44.3) a finite value. It is not difficult to see that this problem has a solution. In order to prove this, we introduce the Hilbert space $\mathfrak{H}_0$ which consists of the functions $u(x)$ which satisfy the conditions:

1) $\int_\Omega |\text{grad}\, u|^2 dx < \infty$;

2) $u|_S = 0$; and

3) there exists a sequence $\{u_n(x)\}$ of continuously differentiable finite functions defined on $\bar{\Omega}$ such that

$$\int_\Omega |\text{grad}\,(u_n - u)|^2 dx \underset{n\to\infty}{\to} 0. \tag{44.4}$$

The scalar product in $\mathfrak{H}_0$ is defined by

$$[u_1, u_2]_0 = \int_\Omega \text{grad}\, u_1 \cdot \text{grad}\, u_2\, dx. \tag{44.5}$$

We note that $\mathfrak{H}_0$ coincides with $\mathfrak{H}_A$ of §41, if $Au = -\Delta u$ and (41.2) is satisfied. In integral (44.3), we put $v = \psi - u$. Hence, the problem of minimising (44.3) reduces to the problem of minimising the functional

$$|||u|||_0^2 - 2\,\text{Re} \int_\Omega \text{grad}\, u \cdot \text{grad}\, \psi\, dx \tag{44.6}$$

on $\mathfrak{H}_0$.
Using the Schwartz-Buniakovskii inequality, we find

$$\left| \int_\Omega \text{grad}\, u \cdot \text{grad}\, \psi\, dx \right| \le \left\{ \int_\Omega |\text{grad}\, \psi|^2 dx \right\}^{\frac{1}{2}} |||u|||_0. \tag{44.7}$$

The linear functional in (44.6) is bounded in $\mathfrak{H}_0$ and the problem of minimising (44.6) has a solution $u_0 \in \mathfrak{H}_0$. Hence, $v_0(x) = \psi(x) - u_0(x)$ minimises (44.3).
It is easy to prove (see, PM, §32, Theorem 1) that $v_0(x)$ is harmonic in any finite subregion of Ω. Hence, inside a sufficiently large sphere, this function has a series expansion in terms of spherical harmonics

$$v_0(x) = C + \sum_{n=1}^{\infty} \sum_{k=1}^{k_{n,m}} a_{nk} |x|^n Y_{n,m}^{(k)}(\theta) + \sum_{n=0}^{\infty} \sum_{k=1}^{k_{n,m}} b_{nk} \frac{Y_{n,m}^{(k)}(\theta)}{|x|^{n+m-2}},$$

where $C = \text{const.}$, $\theta = (x/|x|)$, the $Y_{n,m}^{(k)}(\theta)$ are the linearly independent spherical harmonics of order n in $\mathfrak{E}_m$, and $k_{n,m}$ is the number of these linearly independent functions for a given n. Since the integral

$$\int_\Omega |\text{grad}\, v_0|^2 dx$$

must be finite, the $a_{nk} = 0$ and, for sufficiently large x,

$$v_0(x) = C + \sum_{n=1}^{\infty} \sum_{k=1}^{k_n} b_{nk} \frac{Y_{n,m}^{(k)}(\theta)}{|x|^{n+m-2}}. \tag{44.8}$$

If $m = 2$, then $v_0(x)$ is the solution of the problem posed at the beginning of this section. If $m > 2$, then it is usual to include in the definition of the harmonic function $v_0(x)$ the requirement that $C = 0$. Without this requirement, the solution of the Dirichlet problem with finite energy for an infinite region would not be unique.

We put the origin inside S.

Let $C = 0$. Equation (44.8) shows that the integral

$$\int_\Omega \frac{v_0(x)}{|x|^m} dx \tag{44.9}$$

converges. The converse is obvious: if (44.9) converges, then $C = 0$ in (44.8). The function $u_0(x) \in \mathfrak{H}_A$. On the strength of inequality (43.9), the integral

$$\int_\Omega \frac{u_0(x)}{|x|^m} dx$$

converges. In fact, let R be chosen as in §43. Then, if $R_1 > R$,

$$\left| \int_{R<|x|<R_1} \frac{u_0(x)}{|x|^m} dx \right| \leq$$
$$\leq \left\{ \int_{R<|x|<R_1} \frac{|u_0(x)|^2}{|x|^2} dx \right\}^{\frac{1}{2}} \left\{ \int_{S_1} dS_1 \int_R^{R_1} \frac{d|x|}{|x|^{2m-2}} \right\}^{\frac{1}{2}} \leq$$
$$\leq \sqrt{\frac{\omega_m}{2m-3} \left(\frac{1}{R^{2m-3}} - \frac{1}{R_1^{2m-3}} \right)} \left\{ \int_\Omega \frac{|u_0(x)|^2}{|x|^2} dx \right\}^{\frac{1}{2}} \underset{R\to\infty}{\to} 0,$$

where S_1 is the unit sphere in $\mathfrak{E}_m$ and ω_m is the surface area of this sphere. In this way, in order that the function $v_0(x)$, constructed by the energy method, be harmonic in the region Ω of type (1) – with dimension $m \geq 3$ – it is necessary and sufficient that the integral

$$\int_\Omega \frac{\psi(x)}{|x|^m} dx = \int_\Omega \frac{u_0(x)}{|x|^m} dx + \int_\Omega \frac{v_0(x)}{|x|^m} dx \tag{44.10}$$

converges. It is important to note that this can always be achieved: if the integral (44.10) diverges, then the function $\psi(x)$ can be replaced by the product $\psi(x)\zeta(x)$, where $\zeta(x)$ is a continuously differentiable function such that

$$\zeta(x) = \begin{cases} 1, & |x| \leqq R, \\ 0, & |x| \geqq R+1, \end{cases}$$

and R is sufficiently large. Since the conditions (44.1) and (44.2) cannot be violated, the integral

$$\int_\Omega \frac{\psi(x)\zeta(x)}{|x|^m} dx$$

converges.

§45. Degenerate equations in a finite region

We examine the second order elliptic equation

$$-\sum_{j,k=1}^{m} \frac{\partial}{\partial x_j}\left(A_{jk}\frac{\partial u}{\partial x_k}\right) = f(x), \qquad A_{jk} = \bar{A}_{kj}, \tag{45.1}$$

in a given finite region Ω with surface S, where this equation is degenerate on some part S' of S. We assume that there exists a sufficiently smooth transformation (see Mikhlin [9]) which maps the independent variables $x_1, x_2, \ldots, x_m$ into new variables $\xi_1, \xi_2, \ldots, \xi_m$ in such a way that S' is mapped onto a part of the surface $\xi_m = 0$ and the coefficients $A_{jm}(j = 0, 1, \ldots, m-1)$ are removed. We assume that the transformation has been applied to give $A_{jm} \equiv 0$ $(j < m)$ and that S', on which (45.1) is degenerate, lies on the surface $x_m = 0$. We assume that S' is uniquely determined on Ω so that the form

$$\sum_{j,k=1}^{m} A_{jk}\bar{t}_j t_k = \sum_{j,k=1}^{m-1} A_{jk}\bar{t}_j t_k + A_{mm}|t_m|^2$$

is positive definite for all points of $\bar{\Omega}$ for which $x_m > 0$ and is degenerate for $x_m = 0$. We make the following assumption: in the interval $0 \leqq x_m \leqq h$, where h is the maximum value of x_m in Ω, there exists a continuously differentiable function $\phi(x_m)$ such that the quotient $(A_{mm}(x_m))/(\phi(x_m))$ is continuous and bounded above and below by positive numbers.

It is clear that $\phi(0) = 0$ and $\phi(x_m) > 0$ for $x_m > 0$.

We denote the complement of S' w.r.t. S by S''. The differential operator, defined by the l.h.s. of (45.1), will be examined on the set $\mathfrak{N}(\Omega)$ of functions which satisfy the following conditions:
(a) if $u(x) \in \mathfrak{N}(\Omega)$, then the functions

$$u, \quad \frac{\partial u}{\partial x_j}, \quad \frac{\partial^2 u}{\partial x_j \partial x_k}, \qquad (j, k \leqq m-1),$$

$$\phi(x_m)\frac{\partial u}{\partial x_m}, \quad \frac{\partial}{\partial x_m}\left(\phi(x_m)\frac{\partial u}{\partial x_m}\right)$$

are continuous in $\bar{\Omega}$;

(b) $u|_{S''} = 0;$ (45.2)

(c) if the integral

$$\int_0^h \frac{dt}{\phi(t)} \tag{45.3}$$

converges, then we impose the condition

$$u|_{S'} = 0; \tag{45.4}$$

and if the integral (45.3) diverges, then we do not impose a condition on S'.

The operator, which is defined on $\mathfrak{N}(\Omega)$ by the l.h.s. of (45.1), is positive in $L_2(\Omega)$ and therefore possesses a selfadjoint Friedrichs extension. We denote this extension by A. If the integral

$$\int_0^h \frac{t\,dt}{\phi(t)} \tag{45.5}$$

converges, then A is positive definite and its spectrum is discrete. The operator A is positive definite, when $at^2 \leqq \phi(t) \leqq bt^2$, where a and b are positive constants, but the discreteness of the spectrum is lost. Finally, if $C_1 t^\beta \leqq \phi(t) \leqq C_2 t^\beta$, where C_1 and C_2 are positive constants and $\beta > 2$, and if there exists, for $0 \leqq t \leqq h$, a continuous non-negative function $\psi(t)$ such that $\psi(0) = 0$ and

$$\sum_{j,k=1}^{m-1} A_{jk}(x)\bar{t}_j t_k \leqq \psi(x_m) \sum_{k=1}^{m-1} |t_k|^2, \tag{45.6}$$

then A is merely positive – not positive definite.

We can introduce the energy space $\mathfrak{H}_A$ with norm defined by

$$|||u|||_A^2 = \int_\Omega \sum_{j,k=1}^m A_{jk} \frac{\partial \bar{u}}{\partial x_j} \frac{\partial u}{\partial x_k} dx. \tag{45.7}$$

It consists of the functions, defined in Ω, which have generalised first derivatives, give finite values to (45.7) and satisfy the condition (45.2). We pose the *D-problem*: the integration of (45.1) for the conditions (45.2) and (45.4). The last condition does not apply if (45.3) diverges. The D-problem has a solution with finite energy if there exists a function in $\mathfrak{H}_A$ which minimises

$$\int_\Omega \left\{ \sum_{j,k=1}^m A_{jk} \frac{\partial \bar{u}}{\partial x_j} \frac{\partial u}{\partial x_k} - 2 \operatorname{Re} u\bar{f} \right\} dx.$$

Theorem 45.1. *Let* $f(x)$ *in* (45.1) *be summable in any internal subregion of* Ω. *The problem* (45.1) and (45.2) *has a solution with finite energy, if and only if* $f(x) = \operatorname{div} F(x)$, *where the vector* $F(x)$ *is such that*

$$\int_\Omega u \operatorname{div} \bar{F}\, dx = -\int_\Omega \operatorname{grad} u \cdot F\, dx \tag{45.8}$$

is true for any function $u \in N(\Omega)$, *and the integral*

$$\int_\Omega \sum_{k=1}^m F_k \bar{\omega}_k dx, \tag{45.9}$$

converges, where the ω_k *are defined by the system of equations*

$$\sum_{k=1}^m A_{jk} \omega_k = F_j. \tag{45.10}$$

Proof Let $u \in \mathfrak{N}(\Omega)$. We examine the functional

$$lu = \int_\Omega u\bar{f}\, dx = \int_\Omega u \operatorname{div} \bar{F}\, dx, \qquad u \in \mathfrak{H}_A. \tag{45.11}$$

On the basis of (45.8) and (45.10),

$$lu = -\int_\Omega \sum_{j=1}^m \bar{F}_j \frac{\partial u}{\partial x_j} dx + -\int_\Omega \sum_{j,k=1}^m \bar{A}_{jk} \frac{\partial u}{\partial x_j} \bar{\omega}_k dx =$$

$$= -\int_\Omega \sum_{j,k=1}^m A_{jk} \bar{\omega}_j \frac{\partial u}{\partial x_k} dx.$$

The quadratic functional

$$\int_\Omega \sum_{j,k=1}^m A_{jk}(x)\overline{\zeta_j(x)}\zeta_k(x)dx$$

is non-negative and the Cauchy-Buniakovskii inequality can be applied to give

$$|lu| \leqq \left\{\int_\Omega \sum_{j,k=1}^m A_{jk}\overline{\omega}_j\,\omega_k\,dx\right\}^{\frac{1}{2}}\left\{\int_\Omega \sum_{j,k=1}^m A_{jk}\frac{\partial \bar{u}}{\partial x_j}\,\frac{\partial u}{\partial x_k}\,dx\right\}^{\frac{1}{2}} =$$
$$= |||u|||_A\left\{\int_\Omega \sum_{k=1}^m F_j\overline{\omega}_j dx\right\}^{\frac{1}{2}}.$$

The last inequality shows that the functional (45.9) is bounded in $\mathfrak{H}_A$, and hence, that the D-problem has a solution with finite energy.

Conversely, let the D-problem have a solution $u_0(x)$ with finite energy. Then

$$lu = \int_\Omega u\bar{f}\,dx = [u, u_0]_A = \int_\Omega \sum_{j,k=1}^m A_{jk}\frac{\partial u}{\partial x_j}\,\frac{\partial \bar{u}_0}{\partial x_k}\,dx, \qquad (45.12)$$
$$u \in N(\Omega),$$

and it is sufficient to assume that

$$F_j = \sum_{k=1}^m \bar{A}_{jk}\frac{\partial u_0}{\partial x_k} = \sum_{k=1}^m A_{kj}\frac{\partial u_0}{\partial x_k}.$$

We prove this. We take the function $u(x) \in C^{(1)}(\Omega)$, which equals zero on some boundary region of Ω, and construct its average function $u_h(x)$ (see Sobolev [1] and PM, §16). For sufficiently small h, the function $u_h \in \mathfrak{N}(\Omega)$ and satisfies the identity (45.12), which can be rewritten as

$$\int_\Omega u_h\bar{f}\,dx = -\int_\Omega \operatorname{grad} u_h \cdot F\,dx.$$

As $h \to 0$, let u_h and grad u_h tend uniformly to u and grad u, respectively, and the function f and the vector F be summable in any internal subregion of Ω. Then the last inequality becomes, in the limit,

$$\int_\Omega u\bar{f}\,dx = -\int_\Omega \operatorname{grad} u \cdot F\,dx.$$

This implies that $f(x) = \operatorname{div} F(x)$. For the adopted definition of F, it is clear that (45.8) holds. Further, $\omega_k = (\partial u_0/\partial x_k)$ and

$$\int_\Omega \sum_{k=1}^m F_k \bar{\omega}_k dx = \int_\Omega \sum_{j,k=1}^m A_{jk} \frac{\partial u_0}{\partial x_j} \frac{\partial \bar{u}_0}{\partial x_k} dx = |||u|||_A^2,$$

so that integral (45.9) converges.

As an example, we examine the case when $f(x)$ is continuous in $\bar{\Omega}$. For simplicity, we assume that Ω is convex and that its surface S'' is sufficiently smooth. Let the line parallel to the x_1-axis cut the surface S'' in the points $\alpha(x_2, \ldots, x_m)$ and $\beta(x_2, \ldots, x_m)$, $\alpha < \beta$. We put $F = (F_1, F_2, \ldots, F_m)$, where

$$F_1 = \int_\alpha^{x_1} f(\xi, x_2, \ldots, x_m) d\xi, \qquad F_j = 0, \quad j > 1.$$

Then $f(x) = \operatorname{div} F(x)$. If $u \in \mathfrak{N}(\Omega)$, then

$$-\int_\Omega \operatorname{grad} u \cdot F(x) dx = -\int_\Omega \frac{\partial u}{\partial x_1} F_1(x) dx =$$

$$= \int_\Omega u f(x) dx - \int_{S''} u F_1(x) \cos(\nu, x_1) dS,$$

where ν is the outward normal to S''. On the strength of (45.2), the contour integral vanishes and the identiy (45.8) is true. The D-problem has a solution with finite energy, if the integral

$$\int_\Omega F_1 \bar{\omega}_1 dx \tag{45.9'}$$

converges. Taking into account that $A_{jm} = 0$, $j < m$, it follows from (45.10) that $\omega_1 = (F_1/\Delta)\Delta_1$ where

$$\Delta = \begin{vmatrix} A_{11} & A_{12} & \ldots & A_{1,m-1} \\ A_{21} & A_{22} & \ldots & A_{2,m-1} \\ \cdot & \cdot & \cdot & \cdot \\ A_{m-1,1} & A_{m-1,2} & \ldots & A_{m-1,m-1} \end{vmatrix},$$

and Δ_1 is the minor of the element A_{11} in the determinant Δ. We assume that not only the estimate (45.6), but also the double-sided estimate

$$a\psi(x_m) \sum_{k=1}^{m-1} |t_k|^2 \leqq \sum_{j,k=1}^{m-1} A_{jk} \bar{t}_j t_k \leqq \psi(x_m) \sum_{k=1}^{m-1} |t_k|^2, \tag{45.13}$$

is true, where a is a constant such that $0 < a \leqq 1$. Hence, all the eigenvalues of the matrix of coefficients A_{jk} $(j, k \leqq m-1)$ have the estimates $O(\psi(x_m))$. In turn, it follows that, for x_m close to zero, Δ behaves like $0([\psi(x_m)]^{m-1})$.

Putting $t_1 = 0$ in (45.13), we find

$$a\psi(x_m)\sum_{k=2}^{m-1} |t_k|^2 \leqq \sum_{j,k=2}^{m-1} A_{jk}\bar{t}_j t_k \leqq \psi(x_m)\sum_{k=2}^{m-1} |t_k|^2$$

and hence, $\Delta_1 = 0([\psi(x_m)]^{m-2})$. The functions in the integrand of (45.12) have the estimate

$$\frac{|F_1\bar{\omega}_1|}{\Delta} \leqq \frac{|F_1|^2\Delta_1}{\Delta} \leqq C\frac{|F_1|^2}{\psi(x_m)}, \qquad C = \text{const.},$$

and the solution with finite energy exists, if the integral

$$\int_0^h \frac{dt}{\psi(t)}$$

converges. Further,

$$|F_1| \leqq (\beta-\alpha) \max_{\alpha\leqq\xi\leqq\beta} |f(\xi, x_2, \ldots, x_m)| \leqq$$

$$\leqq C_1 \max_{\alpha\leqq x_1\leqq\beta} |f(x_1, x_2, \ldots, x_m)|, \qquad C_1 = \text{const.}$$

Let $f(x) \xrightarrow[x_m\to 0]{} 0$, or more precisely, let $|f(x)| \leqq C_2\chi(x_m)$, where $C_2 = \text{const.}$ and $\chi(0) = 0$. Then the solution with finite energy exists, if the integral

$$\int_0^h \frac{\chi^2(t)}{\psi(t)}\,dt$$

converges.

§46. Coordinate systems for homogeneous problems defined on an infinite interval

Note In this section, we present results based on Verzhbinskaya [1].

1. In the space $L_2(0, \infty)$, we examine the operator defined by

$$Au = -\frac{d^2u}{dx^2} + u \tag{46.1}$$

with $\mathfrak{D}(A)$ the set of finite $C^2(0, \infty)$ functions satisfying the boundary condition

$$u(0) = 0. \tag{46.2}$$

The operator A is positive definite, since

$$(Au, u) = \int_0^\infty (-u''\bar{u}+|u|^2)dx = -u'\bar{u}|_0^\infty + \int_0^\infty (|u'|^2+|u|^2)dx =$$
$$= \int_0^\infty (|u'|^2+|u|^2)dx \geqq \int_0^\infty |u|^2 dx = ||u||^2.$$

The space $\mathfrak{H}_A$ is formed as the closure of $\mathfrak{D}(A)$ w.r.t. the metric

$$[u, v]_A = \int_0^\infty (u'\bar{v}'+u\bar{v})dx.$$

We can prove that $\mathfrak{H}_A$ comprises the functions of $L_2(0, \infty)$ which are absolutely continuous on any finite sub-interval of $(0, \infty)$ and which satisfy $u(0) = 0$ and

$$|||u|||_A^2 = \int_0^\infty (|u'|^2+|u|^2)dx < \infty. \tag{46.3}$$

We examine the system of functions

$$\phi_k = \frac{2}{\sqrt{\pi}} \frac{\sin(2k \operatorname{arctg} x)}{\sqrt{1+x^2}} \qquad (k = 1, 2, \ldots). \tag{46.4}$$

We shall prove that it satisfies the conditions (1), (2) and (3) of §6.
It is obvious that (1) and (2) are satisfied.
We show that $\{\phi_k\}$ is complete in $\mathfrak{H}_A$. For this purpose, it is sufficient to prove that the relationship

$$\int_0^\infty (f\phi_k'+f\phi_k)dx = 0 \qquad (k = 1, 2, \ldots), \tag{46.5}$$

where $f \in \mathfrak{H}_A$, implies $f \equiv 0$.
We have

$$\int_0^\infty \frac{2kf'}{(1+x^2)^{\frac{3}{2}}} \cos(2k \operatorname{arctg} x)dx +$$
$$+\int_0^\infty \left[\frac{-xf'}{(1+x^2)^{\frac{3}{2}}} + \frac{f}{\sqrt{1+x^2}}\right] \sin(2k \operatorname{arctg} x)dx = 0.$$

Integrating the second integral by parts, we obtain

$$\int_0^\infty \frac{2kf'}{(1+x^2)^{\frac{3}{2}}} \cos(2k \operatorname{arctg} x) dx +$$

$$+ \left[\sin(2k \operatorname{arctg} x) \cdot \int_0^x \left[\frac{-tf'}{(1+t^2)^{\frac{3}{2}}} + \frac{f}{(1+t^2)^{\frac{1}{2}}}\right] dt\right]\Bigg|_0^\infty -$$

$$-\int_0^\infty \left[\int_0^x \left[-\frac{tf'}{(1+t^2)^{\frac{3}{2}}} + \frac{f}{(1+t^2)^{\frac{1}{2}}}\right] dt\right] 2k \frac{\cos(2k \operatorname{arctg} x)}{(1+x^2)} dx = 0$$

$$(k = 1, 2, \ldots).$$

It is easy to prove that, since the integrated terms in the last expression vanish, the relationship becomes

$$2k \int_0^\infty \left\{\frac{f'}{(1+x^2)^{\frac{1}{2}}} - \int_0^x \left(-\frac{tf'}{(1+t^2)^{\frac{3}{2}}} + \frac{f}{(1+t^2)^{\frac{1}{2}}}\right) dt\right\} \times$$

$$\times \frac{\cos(2k \operatorname{arctg} x)}{(1+x^2)} dx = 0 \qquad (k = 1, 2, \ldots).$$

We denote the expression in braces by $\Phi(x)$, put $x = \tan(t/2)$ and obtain

$$\int_0^\pi \Phi\left(\operatorname{tg}\frac{t}{2}\right) \cos kt\, dt = 0 \qquad (k = 1, 2, \ldots).$$

Since the system of functions $\{\cos kt\}$ is complete in $L_2(0, \pi)$, $\Phi(x) =$ const. Hence,

$$\frac{f'}{(1+x^2)^{\frac{1}{2}}} = \int_0^x \left[-\frac{tf'}{(1+t^2)^{\frac{3}{2}}} + \frac{f}{(1+t^2)^{\frac{1}{2}}}\right] dt + \text{const}. \tag{46.6}$$

Consequently, the function f which satisfies (46.5) and lies in $\mathfrak{H}_A$ has a second derivative. Differentiating (46.6), we find that $-f''+f = 0$, which solves to give $f = c_1 e^{-x} + c_2 e^x$. However, $c_2 = 0$ since $f \in L_2(0, \infty)$, and $c_1 = 0$ since $f(0) = 0$. Hence $f \equiv 0$, which proves condition (3). The system (46.4) is strongly minimal in $\mathfrak{H}_A$. In fact, $\mathfrak{H}_A$ lies in $L_2(0, \infty)$, since A is positive definite. Further, system (46.4) is orthonormal w.r.t. the metric of $L_2(0, \infty)$. On the basis of Corollary 4.2, it is strongly minimal in $\mathfrak{H}_A$.

We now examine the more general operator

$$A_1 u = -\frac{d}{dx}\left[p(x)\frac{du}{dx}\right] + q(x)u, \tag{46.7}$$

$$u(0) = 0, \qquad x \in [0, \infty).$$

We impose on $p(x)$ and $q(x)$ the following conditions:
(a) $p(x)$ is bounded above and below by positive numbers and has a continuous and bounded first derivative:

$$0 < p_0 \leqq p(x) \leqq p_1; \tag{46.8}$$

(b) $q(x)$ is measurable and is bounded above and below by positive numbers:

$$0 < q_0 \leqq q(x) \leqq q_1. \tag{46.9}$$

In inequalities (46.8) and (46.9), the quantities p_0, q_0, p_1 and q_1 are constants.
The metric in $\mathfrak{H}_{A_1}$ is defined by

$$[u, u]_{A_1} = \int_0^\infty (p(x)u'^2 + q(x)u^2)dx.$$

From inequalities (46.8) and (46.9), it follows that the metric in $\mathfrak{H}_{A_1}$ is equivalent to the metric in $\mathfrak{H}_A$, and hence, that system (46.4) satisfies (1), (2) and (3) of §6 and is strongly minimal in $\mathfrak{H}_{A_1}$.
2. We now examine the operator (46.1) w.r.t. the boundary condition

$$u'(0) = 0, \qquad x \in [0, \infty). \tag{46.10}$$

For the domain of this operator, which we as usual denote by A, we choose the finite $C^2(0, \infty)$ functions which satisfy (46.10). This operator is positive definite. The energy space $\mathfrak{H}_A$ consists of the functions which are absolutely continuous on any finite subinterval of $(0, \infty)$ and satisfy

$$|||u|||_A^2 = \int_0^\infty (u'^2 + u^2)dx < \infty.$$

The boundary condition (46.10) is natural and the functions of $\mathfrak{H}_A$ will not necessarily satisfy it.
We examine the system of functions

$$\psi_k(x) = \frac{2}{\sqrt{\pi}} \frac{\cos(2k \operatorname{arctg} x)}{\sqrt{1+x^2}} \qquad (k = 0, 1, 2, \ldots). \tag{46.11}$$

It is clear that the system $\{\psi_k\}$ satisfies conditions (1) and (2) of §6. We prove that $\{\psi_k\}$ is complete in $\mathfrak{H}_A$. For this purpose, we show that the relationship

$$\int_0^\infty (f'\psi_k'+f\psi_k)dx = 0 \qquad (k = 0, 1, 2, \dots), \tag{46.12}$$

where $f \in \mathfrak{H}_A$, implies that $f \equiv 0$.

We have

$$\int_0^\infty \left[-\frac{f'}{(1+x^2)^{\frac{3}{2}}} 2k \sin(2k \operatorname{arctg} x)\right] dx +$$
$$+\int_0^\infty \left[-\frac{xf'}{(1+x^2)^{\frac{3}{2}}}+\frac{f}{(1+x^2)^{\frac{1}{2}}}\right] \cos(2k \operatorname{arctg} x) dx = 0. \tag{46.13}$$

Integrating the second term by parts, we obtain

$$\int_0^\infty \left[-\frac{f'}{(1+x^2)^{\frac{3}{2}}} 2k \sin(2k \operatorname{arctg} x)\right] dx +$$
$$+\left[\int_0^x \left(-\frac{tf'}{(1+t^2)^{\frac{3}{2}}}+\frac{f}{(1+t^2)^{\frac{1}{2}}}\right) dt \cos(2k \operatorname{arctg} x)\right]_0^\infty +$$
$$+2k\int_0^\infty \left[\int_0^x \left(-\frac{tf'}{(1+t^2)^{\frac{3}{2}}}+\frac{f}{(1+t^2)^{\frac{1}{2}}}\right) dt\right]$$
$$\times \sin(2k \operatorname{arctg} x)\frac{1}{1+x^2}\, dx = 0.$$

We now establish that the integrated terms vanish. In fact, for $x = 0$ it is obvious, while for $x = \infty$ the integrated terms vanish, since for $k = 0$ we have from (46.12)

$$\int_0^\infty \left[-\frac{tf'}{(1+t^2)^{\frac{3}{2}}}+\frac{f}{(1+t^2)^{\frac{1}{2}}}\right] dt = 0.$$

Hence, (46.13) now takes the form

$$2k\int_0^\infty \left\{-\frac{f'}{(1+x^2)^{\frac{1}{2}}}+\int_0^x \left[-\frac{tf'}{(1+t^2)^{\frac{3}{2}}}+\frac{f}{(1+t^2)^{\frac{1}{2}}}\right] dt\right\} \times$$
$$\times \frac{\sin(2k \operatorname{arctg} x)}{1+x^2}\, dx = 0.$$

Let the term in braces be denoted by $\Phi(x)$. We obtain

$$\int_0^\infty \Phi(x)\frac{\sin(2k \operatorname{arctg} x)}{1+x^2}\, dx = 0.$$

Using the same basic argument as in **1**, we obtain from this last expression that $f \equiv 0$.

System (46.11) is strongly minimal in $\mathfrak{H}_A$. In fact, this system is orthonormal in $\mathfrak{H} = L_2(0, \infty)$, since

$$(\psi_k, \psi_m) = \frac{2}{\pi}\int_0^\infty \cos(2k \operatorname{arctg} x)\cos(2m \operatorname{arctg} x)\frac{2}{1+x^2}\,dx = $$
$$= \frac{2}{\pi}\int_0^\pi \cos kt \cos mt\,dt = \delta_{km}.$$

Further, since the operators (46.1) and (46.10) are positive definite in $L_2(0, \infty)$, the strong minimality of (46.11) in $\mathfrak{H}_A$ follows from Corollary 4.2.

We examine the more general operator

$$A_2 u = -\frac{d}{dx}\left[p(x)\frac{du}{dx}\right] + q(x)u, \qquad u'(0) = 0, \qquad x \in [0, \infty),$$

where p and q satisfy the requirements of **1**.

It is obvious that the space $\mathfrak{H}_{A_2}$ with the metric

$$|||u|||^2_{A_2} = \int_0^\infty [p(x)u'^2 + q(x)u^2]\,dx$$

is equivalent to the space $\mathfrak{H}_A$. Hence, the functions (46.11) can be used as coordinate functions for A_2 and the system $\{\psi_k(x)\}$ is strongly minimal in $\mathfrak{H}_{A_2}$.

3. We examine the operator A_3

$$\begin{aligned} &-\frac{d}{dx}\left[p(x)\frac{du}{dx}\right] + q(x)u, \\ &u'(0) - \alpha u(0) = 0, \qquad x \in [0, \infty), \qquad \alpha > 0, \end{aligned} \tag{46.14}$$

where the functions $p(x)$ and $q(x)$ satisfy the conditions of **1**.

The boundary conditions (46.10) and (46.11) are natural boundary conditions for an ordinary differential equation of the second order. It follows that the metrics in $\mathfrak{H}_{A_2}$ and $\mathfrak{H}_{A_3}$ are equivalent. Hence, the system $\{\psi_k\}$ can be chosen as a coordinate system for A_3. It will be strongly minimal in $\mathfrak{H}_{A_3}$.

4. We examine the first and second boundary value problems for the differential operator

$$-\frac{d}{dx}\left[p(x)\frac{du}{dx}\right]+q(x)u$$

in the space $L_2(-\infty, +\infty)$, where $p(x)$ and $q(x)$ satisfy the conditions of **1**. Let A_4 denote the operators defined by these problems.

Using the basic argument developed above, we can show that the system

$$\frac{1}{\sqrt{1+x^2}}, \frac{\sin(2 \operatorname{arctg} x)}{\sqrt{1+x^2}}, \frac{\cos(2 \operatorname{arctg} x)}{\sqrt{1+x^2}}, \ldots$$
$$\ldots, \frac{\sin(2k \operatorname{arctg} x)}{\sqrt{1+x^2}}, \frac{\cos(2k \operatorname{arctg} x)}{\sqrt{1+x^2}}, \ldots$$

serves as a coordinate system for the operators A_4. This coordinate system will be strongly minimal in the related energy spaces $\mathfrak{H}_{A_4}$.

5. We investigate in $L_2(0, \infty)$ the operator A_5, defined by

$$-\frac{d}{dx}\left[p(x)\frac{du}{dx}\right]+q(x)u$$

and the boundary condition (46.2). We denote this operator by A_5.
Here, the functions $p(x)$ and $q(x)$ satisfy:

(a) $p(x)$ is bounded above and below, has a continuous first derivative, and satisfies

$$0 < p_0 \leqq p(x) \leqq p_1, \qquad p_0 = \text{const}, \qquad p_1 = \text{const}.$$

(b) $q(x)$ is measurable, non-negative, bounded above and, for large x, satisfies

$$q(x) = O(x^{-\alpha}), \qquad \alpha \geqq 2.$$

The space $\mathfrak{H}_{A_5}$ consists of those functions of $L_2(0, \infty)$ which are absolutely continuous on any finite subinterval of $(0, \infty)$ and which satisfy $u(0) = 0$ and

$$|||u|||_A^2 = \int_0^\infty [p(x)|u'|^2+q(x)|u|^2]dx < \infty. \tag{46.15}$$

We shall prove that the system

$$\eta_k(x) = \int_0^x \frac{e^{-t/2}L_k(t)}{k!}\,dt \qquad (k = 0, 1, 2, \ldots), \tag{46.16}$$

where $L_k(t)$ is the Laguerre polynomial of order k, satisfies the conditions (1), (2) and (3) of §6. In fact, as is known,

$$L_k(t) = e^t \frac{d^k}{dt^k}(t^k e^{-t}).$$

Integrating by parts, we obtain

$$\eta_k(x) = \int_0^x \frac{e^{t/2}}{k!} \frac{d^k}{dt^k}(t^k e^{-t})dt = (-1)^k 2 + \sum_{m=0}^{k} c_m x^m e^{-x/2}, \tag{46.17}$$

where the c_m are constants.

From (46.17) and $\eta_k(0) = 0$, it follows that $\eta_k \in \mathfrak{H}_{A_5}$. It is also clear that the functions $\eta_0(x), \eta_1(x), \ldots, \eta_n(x)$ are linearly independent for arbitrary n. Finally, we prove that $\{\eta_n\}$ is complete in $\mathfrak{H}_{A_5}$.

We start with Hardy's inequality (Hardy, Littlewood, Polya [1])

$$\int_0^\infty \frac{|u(x)|}{x^2} dx \leqq 4 \int_0^\infty |u'(x)|^2 dx, \tag{46.18}$$

which is true for functions which are absolutely continuous on arbitrary intervals of the form $0 \leqq x \leqq N$ and equal zero at $x = 0$.

From the condition $q(x) = 0(x^\alpha)$, $\alpha \leqq 2$, it follows that

$$q(x) \leqq \frac{C}{x^2}, \qquad C = \text{const.}$$

On this basis, inequality (46.18) yields the estimate

$$\int_0^\infty q(x)|u|^2 dx \leqq 4C \int_0^\infty |u'(x)|^2 dx, \qquad u \in \mathfrak{H}_A, \tag{46.19}$$

from which it follows, in turn, that

$$|||u|||_A^2 \leqq (1+C) \int_0^\infty |u'|^2 dx. \tag{46.20}$$

As is well known, the system

$$\eta_k'(x) = \frac{e^{-x/2} L_k(x)}{k!} \qquad (k = 0, 1, 2, \ldots)$$

is orthonormal and complete in $L_2(0, \infty)$. Consequently, if $u \in \mathfrak{H}_{A_5}$ and ε is an arbitrary positive number, then, for n sufficiently large,

$$\int_0^\infty |u'(x) - \sum_{k=1}^n a_k \eta_k'(x)|^2 dx < \varepsilon^2, \qquad a_k = \int_0^\infty u'(x)\eta_k'(x)dx.$$

Using (46.20),

$$|||u - \sum_{k=1}^n a_k \eta_k|||_{A_5}^2 \leqq (1+C)\varepsilon^2.$$

Since ε is an arbitrary positive number, the last inequality implies that the system $\{\eta_k\}$ is complete in $\mathfrak{H}_{A_5}$.

The system $\{\eta_k\}$ is almost orthonormal in $\mathfrak{H}_{A_5}$. In fact, the system $\{\eta_k'\}$ is orthonormal in $L_2(0, \infty)$, that is, the system $\{\eta_k\}$ is orthonormal in the space $\mathfrak{H}_0$ of functions $u(x)$, which satisfy $u(0) = 0$, with norm

$$||u||_0^2 = \int_0^\infty |u'(x)|^2 dx.$$

Since (46.15) and (46.20) show that the norms $||u||_0$ and $|||u|||_{A_5}$ are equivalent, the almost orthonormality of $\{\eta_k\}$ in $\mathfrak{H}_{A_5}$ follows from Theorem 4.3.

§47. Coordinate systems for multi-dimensional problems defined on infinite regions with finite boundaries

We assume that Ω is the region contained outside a finite number of sufficiently smooth closed surfaces (or lines, if Ω is a region on a surface). As always, we denote the collection of these surfaces – the boundary of Ω – by S. The origin is taken inside S. We investigate the first boundary value problem

$$-\sum_{j,k=1}^m \frac{\partial}{\partial x_j}\left(A_{jk}\frac{\partial u}{\partial x_k}\right) = f(x), \tag{47.1}$$

$$u|_S = 0. \tag{47.2}$$

The coefficients A_{jk} satisfy the requirements of §41 and the function $f(x)$ the divergence condition. Our aim is to construct a system $\{\phi_k\}$ which is strongly minimal or, even better, almost orthonormal w.r.t. the metric

$$|||u|||_A = \int_\Omega \sum_{j,k=1}^m A_{jk}\frac{\partial \bar{u}}{\partial x_j}\frac{\partial u}{\partial x_k}\,dx, \tag{47.3}$$

where

$$u|_S = 0. \tag{47.4}$$

On the basis of inequality (41.4), it is sufficient that the unknown system satisfy the stated condition w.r.t. the metric

$$|||u|||_0^2 = \int_\Omega \sum_{k=1}^{m} \left| \frac{\partial u}{\partial x_k} \right|^2 dx. \tag{47.5}$$

We note that the metric (47.5) is the energy metric for the Laplace operator $-\Delta$ w.r.t. the boundary condition $u|_S = 0$.
We introduce spherical coordinates with origin at $x = 0$. Then

$$|||u|||_0^2 = \int_\Omega \left\{ \left| \frac{\partial u}{\partial \rho} \right|^2 + \frac{1}{\rho^2} \sum_{k=1}^{m-1} \frac{1}{q_k} \left| \frac{\partial u}{\partial \theta_j} \right|^2 \right\} dx, \tag{47.6}$$

where $\rho, \theta_1, \theta_2, \ldots, \theta_{m-1}$ are the spherical coordinates of a general point x. Further,

$$q_1 = 1, \qquad q_k = \prod_{j=1}^{k-1} \sin^2 \theta_j, \qquad k > 1.$$

We put $\rho = (1/\rho')$: the region Ω is transformed into the region Ω'. If x and x' are corresponding points of Ω and Ω', then $dx = |J| dx'$ where J is the Jacobian of the transformation $\rho = (1/\rho')$. Since $|J| = \rho^{2m}$,

$$dx = \rho^{2m}\, dx'.$$

We substitute $u = u'/\rho^{m-2}$ in the integral (47.6) and obtain

$$|||u|||_0^2 = \int_{\Omega'} \left\{ \left| \frac{\partial u'}{\partial \rho'} - \frac{m-2}{\rho'} u' \right|^2 + \frac{1}{\rho'^2} \sum_{k=1}^{m-1} \frac{1}{q_k} \left| \frac{\partial u'}{\partial \theta_k} \right|^2 \right\} dx'. \tag{47.7}$$

Initially, we examine the case when $m = 2$. Denoting the polar angle by θ, we have

$$|||u|||_0^2 = \int_{\Omega'} \left\{ \left| \frac{\partial u'}{\partial \rho'} \right|^2 + \frac{1}{\rho'^2} \left| \frac{\partial u'}{\partial \theta} \right|^2 \right\} dx'. \tag{47.8}$$

The r.h.s. of (47.8) is the square of the energy norm of u' w.r.t. the Laplace operator for the boundary condition $u|_{S'} = 0$, where S' is the surface of Ω'. We denote the energy space of this operator by $\mathfrak{H}_1$ and the energy norm by $|||u|||_1$. Hence, for $m = 2$, the transformation $\rho = (1/\rho')$, $u = u'$ maps $\mathfrak{H}_0$ onto $\mathfrak{H}_1$ isometrically.

We now choose in $\mathfrak{H}_1$ the arbitrary almost orthonormal system $\{\phi_n'(\rho', \theta)\}$, then the system $\{\phi_n\}$, where $\phi_n(\rho, \theta) = \phi_n'(1/\rho' \, \theta)$, is almost orthonormal in $\mathfrak{H}_0$, and hence, in $\mathfrak{H}_A$. If Ω' is one of the regions, listed in §33, then the required almost orthonormal systems in $\mathfrak{H}_A$ are the coordinate systems of §33. In particular, if Ω is the exterior of the circle of unit radius, then we can choose

$$\phi_{kn}(\rho, \theta) = c_n J_n\left(\frac{\gamma_{nk}}{\rho}\right) \begin{matrix}\cos\\ \sin\end{matrix}\, n\theta \qquad (n = 0, 1, 2, \ldots), \tag{47.9}$$

where the c_n are defined by $|||\phi_{kn}|||_A = 1$.
We again turn to (47.7) and assume that $m > 2$. In the standard inequality

$$|a+b|^2 \leqq 2|a|^2+2|b|^2 \tag{47.10}$$

we replace a by $a-b$ and b by $-b$. We then obtain

$$|a+b|^2 \geqq \frac{|a|^2}{2} - |b|^2. \tag{47.11}$$

Whence it follows that

$$\left|\frac{\partial u'}{\partial \rho'} - \frac{m-2}{\rho'}\mu'\right|^2 \geqq \frac{1}{2}\left|\frac{\partial u'}{\partial \rho'}\right|^2 - \frac{(m-2)^2}{\rho'^2}|u'|^2,$$

and hence,

$$|||u|||_0^2 \geqq \frac{1}{2}\int_{\Omega'}\left\{\left|\frac{\partial u'}{\partial \rho'}\right|^2 + \frac{1}{\rho'^2}\sum_{k=1}^{m-1}\frac{1}{q_k}\left|\frac{\partial u'}{\partial \theta_k}\right|^2\right\} dx' -$$
$$-(m-2)^2\int_{\Omega'}\frac{|u'|^2}{\rho'^2}\,dx'. \tag{47.12}$$

As above, we introduce the space $\mathfrak{H}_1$. Then the first integral in (47.12) equals $|||u'|||_1{}^2$. The second integral can be estimated, using (43.9), to give

$$\int_{\Omega'}\frac{|u'|^2}{\rho'^2}\,dx' = \int_{\Omega}\frac{u^2}{\rho^2}\,dx \leqq \frac{4}{(m-2)^2}\int_{\Omega}|\text{grad } u|^2\,dx = \frac{4}{(m-2)^2}|||u|||_0^2.$$

Substituting this result in (47.12), we find

$$|||u|||_0^2 \geqq \tfrac{1}{10}\,|||u'|||_1^2. \tag{47.13}$$

From Theorem 4.2, it follows that every system which is strongly minimal (in particular, orthonormal) in $\mathfrak{H}_1$ is transformed by the mapping $\rho = (1/\rho)'$, $u = (u'/\rho^{m-2})$ into a system which is strongly minimal in $\mathfrak{H}_0$, and hence, in $\mathfrak{H}_A$. If Ω is the exterior of the three-dimensional unit sphere, then

$$\phi_{klm} = \frac{c_{klm}}{\sqrt{\rho'}} J_{k+\frac{1}{2}} \left(\frac{\gamma_{k+\frac{1}{2},l}}{\rho'}\right) P_k^{(m)}(\cos\theta) \begin{matrix}\cos\\ \sin\end{matrix} m\phi \tag{47.14}$$

$$(k = 0, 1, 2, \ldots; \quad l = 1, 2, \ldots; \quad m = 0, 1, \ldots, k),$$

is a strongly minimal system in $\mathfrak{H}_A$, where the coefficients c_{klm} can be determined by the condition $|||\phi_{klm}|||_A = 1$ or some other appropriate condition, such as: the $|||\phi_{klm}|||_A$ are bounded above and below by positive numbers.

We now turn to the second boundary-value problem. We examine (47.1) w.r.t. the boundary conditions

$$\left[\sum_{j,k=1}^{m} A_{jk} \frac{\partial u}{\partial x_j} \cos(\nu, x_k) + \sigma u\right]_S = 0. \tag{47.15}$$

As usual, we assume that σ, defined on S, is measurable, non-negative and bounded. The energy inner product and norm are defined by (41.8). The coordinate system will be strongly minimal or almost orthonormal in $\mathfrak{H}_A$, if it has the same properties in $\mathfrak{H}_0$ (which consists of the same function of $\mathfrak{H}_A$, see §41), where the norm is defined by

$$|||u|||_0^2 = \int_\Omega \sum_{k=1}^{m} \left|\frac{\partial u}{\partial x_k}\right|^2 dx + \int_S \sigma |u|^2 dS =$$

$$= \int_\Omega \left\{\left|\frac{\partial u}{\partial \rho}\right|^2 + \frac{1}{\rho^2} \sum_{k=1}^{m-1} \frac{1}{q_k} \left|\frac{\partial u}{\partial \theta_j}\right|^2\right\} dx + \int_S \sigma |u|^2 dS. \tag{47.16}$$

We apply to (47.16) the transformation $\rho = (1/\rho')$ and $u = \rho^{m-2} u'$ to obtain

$$|||u|||_0^2 = \int_{\Omega'} \left\{\left|\frac{\partial u'}{\partial \rho'} - \frac{m-2}{\rho'} u'\right|^2 + \frac{1}{\rho'^2} \sum_{k=1}^{m-1} \frac{1}{q_k} \left|\frac{\partial u'}{\partial \theta_k}\right|^2\right\} dx' +$$

$$+ \int_{S'} \sigma K |u'|^2 dS', \tag{47.17}$$

where S' is the boundary of Ω' and K is some bounded function.

When $m = 2$, we establish as above that we can take as coordinate functions the eigenfunctions of the Neuman problem for the Laplace operator in Ω' {subjected to the transformation $\rho = (1/\rho')$}. Such a system will be almost orthonormal in $\mathfrak{H}_A$. In particular, if Ω is the exterior of the unit circle, then we can put

$$\phi_{kn}(\rho, \theta) = c_{kn} J_n \left(\frac{\tilde{\gamma}_{n,k}}{\rho}\right) \begin{matrix}\cos\\ \sin\end{matrix}\, n\theta \qquad (n = 0, 1, 2, \ldots; k = 1, 2, \ldots), \tag{47.18}$$

where the c_{kn} are such that $|||\phi_{kn}|||_A = 1$.
If $m > 2$, then, as above, we obtain

$$|||u|||_0^2 \geqq \frac{1}{2}\int_{\Omega'} \left\{\left|\frac{\partial u'}{\partial \rho'}\right|^2 + \frac{1}{\rho'^2} \sum_{k=1}^{m-1} \frac{1}{q_k}\left|\frac{\partial u'}{\partial \theta_k}\right|^2\right\} dx' + \\ + \int_S \sigma K |u'|^2 dS' - (m-2)^2 \int_\Omega \frac{|u|^2}{\rho^2}\, dx. \tag{47.19}$$

The function u can be extended to the whole of E_m in such a manner that the extended function has generalised first derivatives and (see Babich [1])

$$\int_\Omega |\text{grad } u|^2 dx \geqq c \int_{E_m} |\text{grad } u|^2 dx,$$

where c depends only on Ω. In this way, (41.2) leads to the chain of inequalities

$$\int_\Omega \frac{|u|^2}{\rho^2}\, dx \leqq \int_{E_m} \frac{|u|^2}{\rho^2}\, dx \leqq \frac{4}{(m-2)^2} \int_{E_m} |\text{grad } u|^2 dx \leqq \\ \leqq \frac{4}{c(m-2)^2} \int_\Omega |\text{grad } u|^2 dx \leqq \frac{4}{c(m-2)^2}\, |||u|||_0^2 .$$

The estimate

$$|||u|||_0^2 \geqq C_1 \left[\int_\Omega |\text{grad}'\, u'|^2 dx' + \int_{S'} \sigma K |u'|^2 dS'\right] \tag{47.20}$$

follows from (47.19), where $C_1 = \text{const.}$ and grad′ implies differentiation w.r.t. the points x'. The expression in brackets in (47.20) defines a norm in the Sobolev space $W_2^{(1)}(\Omega')$ which is equivalent to the basic norm

$$||u||^2_{W^{(1)}{}_2(\Omega')} = \int_\Omega |[\text{grad}'\, u'|^2 + |u'|^2] dx'. \tag{47.21}$$

Hence, we can now repeat word for word the results obtained above for the first boundary-value problem: any system which is strongly minimal w.r.t. the metric (47.21) is transformed by $\rho = (1/\rho')$ and $u = \rho^{m-2}u'$ into a system which is strongly minimal in the energy space of the second boundary-value problem. In particular, use can be made of the eigenfunctions of the Neuman problem for the Laplace operator in Ω'. If, for example, Ω is the exterior of the three-dimensional unit sphere, we obtain the coordinate system

$$\phi_{klm} = \frac{c_{klm}}{\sqrt{\rho}} J_{k+\frac{1}{2}}\left(\frac{\gamma^*_{k+\frac{1}{2},l}}{\rho}\right) P_k^{(m)}(\cos\theta) \begin{matrix}\cos\\ \cdot \\ \sin\end{matrix}\, m\phi, \tag{47.22}$$

where the coefficients c_{klm} can be defined by the condition $|||\phi_{klm}|||_A = 1$ and γ^* is defined above.

§48. Coordinate systems for regions with infinite boundaries

1. In the present section, we examine the first and second boundary value problems, defined by

$$-\sum_{j,k=1}^{m} \frac{\partial}{\partial x_j}\left(A_{jk}\frac{\partial u}{\partial x_j}\right) = f(x) \tag{48.1}$$

w.r.t. the boundary conditions (41.2) and (41.3), respectively. The self-adjoint extensions of the operators, defined by the first and second boundary-value problems, we denote by A_1 and A_2, respectively. We shall assume that there exists a sufficiently smooth transformation of Ω into a semi-infinite or infinite cylindrical region. If this transformation exists, we assume that it has been applied, so that Ω represents either the cylinder

$$\xi \in \omega, \qquad 0 \leqq x_m < \infty, \tag{48.2'}$$

or

$$\xi \in \omega, \qquad -\infty < x_m < \infty, \tag{48.2''}$$

where ξ denotes a point in the $(m-1)$-dimensional Euclidean space of coordinates $x_1, x_2, \ldots, x_{m-1}$ and ω a region in this space. We limit considerations to the case when the boundary of ω is finite. The region ω can be infinite or finite – the corresponding Ω is a region of type (1) or type (2), respectively (see § 41).

We assume that the coefficients A_{jk} satisfy the conditions of §41. Also, we assume that σ in (41.3) is measurable and that there exists on S a function σ_0 which is non-negative, bounded and measurable such that the relationship

$$c_1\sigma_0 \leqq \sigma \leqq c_2\sigma_0, \qquad c_1, c_2 = \text{const.} > 0 \tag{48.3}$$

holds on the cylindrical part S_0 of S.

The coordinate system will be strongly minimal and complete in $\mathfrak{H}_{A_i}$ $(i = 1, 2)$, if it satisfies the same conditions w.r.t. the metric $|||\,.\,|||_i$ $(i = 1, 2)$, where

$$|||u|||_1^2 = \int_\Omega |\text{grad } u|^2 dx, \qquad u|_S = 0 \tag{48.4}$$

and

$$|||u|||_2^2 = \int_\Omega |\text{grad } u|^2 dx + \int_{S_0} \sigma_0 |u|^2 dS. \tag{48.5}$$

2. Initially, we examine the problem (48.1) and (41.2) and relate it to the operator A_1, where we assume that ω is a finite region and Ω is the cylinder (48.2′). We denote by $\tau_k(\xi)$ the eigenfunctions of

$$-\sum_{j=1}^{m-1} \frac{\partial^2 \tau}{\partial x_j^2}, \qquad \tau|_s = 0. \tag{48.6}$$

These functions are orthogonal and form a complete system both w.r.t. the metric of $L_2(\omega)$ and the metric generated by the inner product

$$[\tau, \chi]_0 = \int_\omega \sum_{j=1}^{m-1} \frac{\partial \tau}{\partial x_j} \frac{\partial \bar{\chi}}{\partial x_j} d\xi. \tag{48.7}$$

We also assume that they are normalised w.r.t. the metric in $L_2(\omega)$, so that

$$\int_\omega \tau_k(\xi)\tau_l(\xi) d\xi = \delta_{kl}. \tag{48.8}$$

For the problem (48.1) and (41.2), we choose the system

$$\phi_{kn}(x) = \frac{\sqrt{2}}{\pi} \tau_k(\xi) \frac{\sin(2n \text{ arctg } x_m)}{\sqrt{1+x_m^2}} \qquad (k, n = 1, 2, \ldots) \tag{48.9}$$

as the coordinate system. It is clear that the $\phi_{kn} \in \mathfrak{H}_{A_1}$. We prove that (48.9) is complete in $\mathfrak{H}_{A_1}$: it is sufficient to prove that this system is complete w.r.t. the metric (48.4). In fact, it is sufficient to prove that, given any $\varepsilon > 0$ and any $v(x)$, which is infinitely often differentiable and has compact support in Ω, there exist constants K, N and α_{nk}, $1 \leqq k \leqq K$, $1 \leqq n \leqq N$, such that

$$|||v - \sum_{k=1}^{K} \sum_{n=1}^{N} \alpha_{nk} \tau_k(\xi) \phi_n(x_m)|||_1 < \varepsilon. \tag{A}$$

For brevity, we write

$$\varphi_n(x_m) = \frac{\sqrt{2}}{\pi} \frac{\sin(2n \operatorname{arctg} x_m)}{\sqrt{1+x_m^2}}.$$

The system $\{\varphi_n(x_m)\}$ is orthonormal and complete in $L_2(0, \infty)$. Let

$$v(x) = \sum_{n=1}^{\infty} v_n(\xi) \varphi_n(x_m).$$

It is easy to see that $v_n(\xi) = O(n^{-q})$, where q is any positive number. Thus,

$$|||v - \sum_{n=1}^{N} v_n(\xi) \varphi_n(x_m)|||_1 < \frac{\varepsilon}{2} \tag{B}$$

is true for sufficiently large N. Let N be fixed and α_{nk} be the Fourier coefficients of $v_n(\xi)$ w.r.t. the orthonormal system $\{\tau_k(\xi)\}$. Then the following relation is true for sufficiently large K

$$|||\sum_{n=1}^{N} \{v_n(\xi) - \sum_{k=1}^{K} \alpha_{nk} \tau_k(\xi)\} \varphi_n(x_m)|||_1 < \frac{\varepsilon}{2}, \tag{C}$$

and (A) follows immediately from (B) and (C).

The metric (48.4) is a particular case of the metric of $\mathfrak{H}_{A_1}$ when $A_{jk} = \sigma_{jk}$. The operator A_1 is positive definite (see, §41) and, by Corrollary 4.2, system (48.9) is orthonormal w.r.t. metric of $L_2(\Omega)$ and strongly minimal in $\mathfrak{H}_{A_1}$.

We note that system (48.9) remains complete and strongly minimal w.r.t. the metric in $\mathfrak{H}_{A_1}$, when (48.1) is replaced by the equation

$$-\sum_{j,k=1}^{m} \frac{\partial}{\partial x_j}\left(A_{jk} \frac{\partial u}{\partial x_k}\right) + Cu = f(x), \tag{48.10}$$

where C is non-negative (this condition can be removed), measurable and bounded in Ω. It quickly follows that the energy metrics of problems (48.1), (41.2) and (48.10), (41.2) are equivalent.
The factor $2/\sqrt{\pi}$ in (48.9) can be omitted.
If Ω is the infinite cylinder (48.2″), then the functions

$$\tau_k(x)\frac{\cos(2n \operatorname{arctg} x_m)}{\sqrt{1+x_m^2}} \qquad (n = 0, 1, 2, \ldots) \tag{48.11}$$

must be added to system (48.9).
3. We now turn to the problem (48.1), (41.3) and the corresponding operator A_2. As in **2**, we assume that the region ω is finite. For the semi-infinite cylinder (48.2′), we choose the coordinate system in the form

$$\phi_{kn}(x) = \frac{\sqrt{2}}{\pi}\chi_k(\xi)\frac{\cos(2n \operatorname{arctg} x_m)}{\sqrt{1+x_m^2}} \tag{48.12}$$

$$(k = 1, 2, \ldots; n = 0, 1, 2, \ldots),$$

where $\chi_k(\xi)$ are the eigenfunctions of

$$-\sum_{j=1}^{m-1}\frac{\partial^2\chi}{\partial x_j^2}, \qquad \left.\frac{\partial\chi}{\partial\nu}\right|_S = 0, \tag{48.13}$$

and ν is the normal to S. For the infinite cylinder (48.2″), we add the functions

$$\chi_k(\xi)\frac{\sin(2n \operatorname{arctg} x_m)}{\sqrt{1+x_m^2}} \qquad (k, n = 1, 2, \ldots), \tag{48.14}$$

to the functions (48.12) to form an appropriate coordinate system.
Repeating word for word the argument of **2**, we establish that system (48.12) {system (48.12) and (48.14) when the cylinder is (48.2″)} is complete and strongly minimal in $\mathfrak{H}_{A_2}$, when the cylinder is (48.2′).
4. If the region ω is infinite, then, for the construction of a strongly minimal coordinate system, it is necessary to replace $\tau_k(\xi)$ and $\chi_k(\xi)$ in (48.9), (48.11), (48.12) and (48.14) by the functions $\tilde{\tau}_k(\xi)$ and $\tilde{\chi}_k(\xi)$ which are constructed in the following way:
We assume that $m \geqq 3$ and $\rho = |\xi|$ and apply the transformation $\rho' = 1/\rho$. We suppose that the origin of the coordinates $x_1, x_2, \ldots, x_{m-1}$

lies inside S, the surface of ω, and that our transformation maps w, S and ξ into a finite region ω', a surface S' and a point ξ'. Let $\tau_k'(\xi')$ and $\chi_k'(\xi')$ be the eigenfunctions of the Dirichlet and Neuman problems for the Laplace operator in the region ω'. We then define

$$\tilde{\tau}_k(\xi) = \frac{1}{\rho^{m-3}}\,\tau_k'(\xi'), \qquad \tilde{\chi}_k(\xi) = \frac{1}{\rho^{m-3}}\,\chi_k'(\xi'). \tag{48.15}$$

Coordinate systems, constructed in this way, will be complete and strongly minimal in the corresponding energy spaces.

§ 49. Examples

All the coordinate systems listed below are strongly minimal in the appropriate energy spaces defined by either the first, second or mixed boundary value problems for non-degenerate second order elliptic equations:

1. For the first boundary-value problem in the region

$$0 < x < 1, \qquad -\infty < y < \infty, \tag{49.1}$$

we can use the coordinate system

$$\frac{1}{\sqrt{1+y^2}}\sin k\pi x \,\begin{matrix}\sin\\ \cos\end{matrix}\,(2n \operatorname{arctg} y) \qquad (k = 1, 2, \ldots;\ n = 0, 1, 2, \ldots).$$

2. For the second boundary-value problem in (49.1), we can use the system

$$\frac{1}{\sqrt{1+y^2}}\cos k\pi x \,\begin{matrix}\sin\\ \cos\end{matrix}\,(2n \operatorname{arctg} y) \qquad (k, n = 0, 1, 2, \ldots).$$

3. For the first boundary-value problem in

$$0 < x < 1, \qquad 0 \leqq y < \infty, \tag{49.2}$$

we can use the coordinate system

$$\frac{1}{\sqrt{1+y^2}}\sin k\pi x \sin (2n \operatorname{arctg} y) \qquad (k, n = 1, 2, \ldots).$$

4. For the second boundary-value problem in (49.2), we can use the system

$$\frac{1}{\sqrt{1+y^2}} \cos k\pi x \cos (2n \operatorname{arctg} y) \qquad (k, n = 0, 1, 2, \ldots).$$

It is also a strongly minimal coordinate system for some problems with mixed boundary conditions.

5. For the mixed boundary-value problem in (49.1), where the first boundary condition acts on the line $x = 0$ and the second boundary condition acts on the line $x = 1$, we can use the coordinate system

$$\frac{1}{\sqrt{1+y^2}} \sin \frac{2k+1}{2} \pi x \begin{matrix} \sin \\ \cos \end{matrix} (2n \operatorname{arctg} y) \qquad (k, n = 0, 1, 2, \ldots).$$

6. For the mixed boundary-value problem in (49.2), where the first boundary condition acts on $x = 0$ and $x = 1$ and the second condition on the interval $y = 0, 0 \leqq x \leqq 1$, we can use the coordinate system

$$\frac{1}{\sqrt{1+y^2}} \sin k\pi x \cos (2n \operatorname{arctg} y) \qquad (k = 1, 2, \ldots; \; n = 0, 1, 2, \ldots).$$

It is not difficult to increase the number of examples of a similar nature.

7. For the first boundary-value problem inside the (3-dimensional) infinite rectangular prism

$$0 < x < a, \qquad 0 < y < b, \qquad -\infty < z < \infty, \tag{49.3}$$

we can use the coordinate system

$$\frac{1}{\sqrt{1+z^2}} \sin \frac{k\pi x}{a} \sin \frac{l\pi y}{b} \begin{matrix} \sin \\ \cos \end{matrix} (2n \operatorname{arctg} z)$$

$$(k, l = 1, 2, \ldots; \; n = 0, 1, 2, \ldots).$$

8. For the second boundary-value problem inside (49.3), we can use the coordinate system

$$\frac{1}{\sqrt{1+z^2}} \cos \frac{k\pi x}{a} \cos \frac{l\pi y}{b} \begin{matrix} \sin \\ \cos \end{matrix} (2n \operatorname{arctg} z) \qquad (k, l, n = 0, 1, 2, \ldots).$$

It is not difficult to determine coordinate systems for some mixed boundary-value problems. We develop one example.

9. For the mixed boundary-value problem in (49.3), where the first boundary condition holds on $x = 0$, $y = 0$ and the second boundary condition holds on $x = a$, $y = b$, we can use the coordinate system

$$\frac{1}{\sqrt{1+z^2}} \sin \frac{2k+1}{2a} \pi x \sin \frac{2l+1}{2b} \pi y \begin{matrix} \sin \\ \cos \end{matrix} (2n \operatorname{arctg} z)$$

$(k, l, n = 0, 1, 2, \ldots)$.

10. For the first boundary-value problem inside the (3-dimensional) semi-infinite rectangular prism

$$0 < x < a, \qquad 0 < y < b, \qquad 0 < z < \infty, \tag{49.4}$$

we can use the coordinate system

$$\frac{1}{\sqrt{1+z^2}} \sin \frac{k\pi x}{a} \sin \frac{l\pi y}{b} \sin (2n \operatorname{arctg} z) \qquad (k, l, n = 1, 2, \ldots).$$

11. A coordinate system for the second boundary-value problem in (49.4) is

$$\frac{1}{\sqrt{1+z^2}} \cos \frac{k\pi x}{a} \cos \frac{k\pi y}{b} \cos (2n \operatorname{arctg} z) \qquad (k, l, n = 0, 1, 2, \ldots).$$

12. A coordinate system for the first boundary value problem in the (3-dimensional) infinite circular cylinder

$$0 < \rho < 1, \qquad 0 \leqq \theta \leqq 2\pi, \qquad -\infty < z < \infty, \tag{49.5}$$

is

$$c_{kln} \frac{1}{\sqrt{1+z^2}} J_k(\gamma_{k,l}\rho) \begin{matrix} \cos \\ \sin \end{matrix} k\theta \begin{matrix} \cos \\ \sin \end{matrix} (2n \operatorname{arctg} z)$$

$(k, n = 0, 1, 2, \ldots; \quad l = 1, 2, \ldots)$,

where $\gamma_{k,l}$ denotes the lth positive root of $J_k(t)$.

13. A coordinate system for the second boundary-value problem in (49.5) is one which has the same form as that in **12**, except that $\gamma_{k,l}$ is replaced by $\tilde{\gamma}_{k,l}$, where $\tilde{\gamma}_{k,l}$ is the lth positive root of $J_k'(t)$.

14. A coordinate system for the first boundary-value problem in the semi-infinite cylinder

$$0 < \rho < 1, \qquad 0 \leqq \theta \leqq 2\pi, \qquad 0 < z < \infty, \tag{49.6}$$

is

$$c_{kln}\,\frac{1}{\sqrt{1+z^2}}\,J_k(\gamma_{k,l}\rho)\,\begin{matrix}\cos\\ \sin\end{matrix}\,k\theta\,\sin(2n\,\mathrm{arctg}\,z)$$

$(k = 0, 1, 2, \ldots;\ l, n = 1, 2, \ldots)$.

15. A coordinate system for the second boundary-value problem in (49.6) is

$$c_{kln}\,\frac{1}{\sqrt{1+z^2}}\,J_k(\tilde{\gamma}_{k,l}\rho)\,\begin{matrix}\cos\\ \sin\end{matrix}\,k\theta\,\cos(2n\,\mathrm{arctg}\,z)$$

$(k, n = 0, 1, 2, \ldots;\quad l = 1, 2, \ldots)$.

16. A coordinate system for the first boundary-value problem in the region exterior to the (3-dimensional) infinite circular cylinder

$$1 < \rho < \infty, \qquad 0 \leqq \theta \leqq 2\pi, \qquad -\infty < z < \infty, \tag{49.7}$$

is

$$c_{kln}\,\frac{1}{\sqrt{1+z^2}}\,J_k\left(\frac{\gamma_{k,l}}{\rho}\right)\begin{matrix}\cos\\ \sin\end{matrix}\,k\theta\,\begin{matrix}\cos\\ \sin\end{matrix}\,(2n\,\mathrm{arctg}\,z)$$

$(k, n = 0, 1, 2, \ldots;\quad l = 1, 2, \ldots)$.

17. A coordinate system for the second boundary-value problem in (49.7) is given by that in **16**, except that $\gamma_{k,l}$ is replaced by $\tilde{\gamma}_{k,l}$.

18. For the first boundary value problem for the semi-infinite region

$$1 < \rho < \infty, \qquad 0 \leqq \theta \leqq 2\pi, \qquad 0 < z < \infty, \tag{49.8}$$

we can use the system

$$c_{kln}\,\frac{1}{\sqrt{1+z^2}}\,J_k\left(\frac{\gamma_{k,l}}{\rho}\right)\begin{matrix}\cos\\ \sin\end{matrix}\,k\theta\,\sin(2n\,\mathrm{arctg}\,z)$$

$(k = 0, 1, 2, \ldots;\quad n, l = 1, 2, \ldots)$.

19. In the same region (49.8), a coordinate system for the second boundary-value problem is

$$c_{kln}\,\frac{1}{\sqrt{1+z^2}}\,J_k\left(\frac{\tilde{\gamma}_{k,l}}{\rho}\right)\begin{matrix}\cos\\ \sin\end{matrix}\,k\theta\,\cos(2n\,\mathrm{arctg}\,z)$$

$(k, n = 0, 1, 2, \ldots;\quad l = 1, 2, \ldots)$.

In examples **13–19**, the coefficients can be normalised w.r.t. the condition that the energy norm of each coordinate function equals 1.
For the regions (49.6) – (49.8), strongly minimal coordinate systems can be constructed for mixed boundary-value problems. Using the results of §33 and §34, it is also easy to construct strongly minimal systems for infinite and semi-infinite cylinders where the cross-sections are circular sectors (in particular, semi-circles). The results of the present section generalise in a straight forward manner to regions in m-dimensional space, $m > 3$.

§50. Coordinate systems for degenerate equations defined in finite regions

We limit considerations to the case when the following conditions apply:
(a) Ω is a cylindrical region of m-dimensional space defined by

$$\xi = (x_1, x_2, \ldots, x_{m-1}) \in \omega, \qquad 0 < x_m < 1, \tag{50.1}$$

where ω is a finite region in $(m-1)$-dimensional space with a sufficiently smooth surface s.
(b) The basic problem is the integration of (45.1) for the boundary condition (45.2) and, if necessary, the additional condition (45.4).
(c) The following two-sided estimate

$$\mu_0[\psi(x_m) \sum_{k=1}^{m-1} |t_k|^2 + \phi(x_m)|t_m|^2] \leqq$$

$$\leqq \sum_{j,k=1}^{m} A_{jk}\bar{t}_j t_k \leqq M_0[\psi(x_m) \sum_{k=1}^{m-1} |t_k|^2 + \phi(x_m)|t_m|^2], \tag{50.2}$$

holds, where μ_0 and M_0 are positive constants, $\phi(t)$ and $\psi(t)$ are functions which are continuous for $0 \leqq t \leqq 1$ and positive for $0 < t \leqq 1$, where only one of the quantities $\phi(0)$ and $\psi(0)$ equals zero.
In order that the coordinate system be complete and strongly minimal w.r.t. the energy metric of our problem it is sufficient that this system be complete and strongly minimal w.r.t. the metric

$$|||u|||_0^2 = \int_\Omega \left\{\psi(x_m) \sum_{k=1}^{m-1} \left| \frac{\partial u}{\partial x_k} \right|^2 + \phi(x_m) \left| \frac{\partial u}{\partial x_m} \right|^2 \right\} dx \tag{50.3}$$

and that the functions, contained in the coordinate system, satisfy the boundary conditions of the problem.

We examine separately the cases when the integral (45.3) diverges and converges. If it diverges, then the above conditions are satisfied by the system of functions

$$\phi_{kn}(x) = \tau_k(\xi) \int_{x_m}^{1} p_n(t)dt, \tag{50.4}$$

where the $\tau_k(\xi)$ are the eigenfunctions of

$$\sum_{j=1}^{m-1} \frac{\partial^2 \tau}{\partial x_j^2} + \mu\tau = 0, \qquad \tau|_s = 0, \tag{50.5}$$

{which are orthonormal w.r.t. the metric of $L_2(\omega)$} and the $p_n(t)$ are polynomials of degree n which are orthonormal with weight $\phi(t)$ on the interval $0 \leqq t \leqq 1$. In (50.4), the indices k and n have the values $k = 1, 2, 3, \ldots$ and $n = 0, 1, 2, 3, \ldots$.

We prove this result. First of all, the functions (50.4) clearly satisfy the boundary conditions of the problem. Further, as we shall now establish, system (50.4) is complete w.r.t. the metric (50.3). As in § 48, it is sufficient to prove that every infinitely often differentiable function $v(x)$ with compact support in Ω can be approximated by a linear combination of the functions (50.4). Let N be any positive integer. It follows from the well known theorems of Jackson (see, for example, Natanson [3]) that there exists a polinomial $t_N(\xi, x_m)$ with argument x_m and degree N such that

$$\left| \frac{\partial^j v}{\partial x_m^j} - \frac{\partial^j t_N}{\partial x_m^j} \right| \leqq \frac{C_{qj}}{N^{q-j}} \qquad (j = 1, 2, \ldots), \tag{50.6}$$

where q is an arbitrary positive number and C_{qj} does not depend on N and ξ. We can represent t_N in the following way:

$$t_N(\xi, x_m) = \sum_{n=0}^{N} v_n(\xi) p_n(x_m).$$

We write for brevity

$$\varphi_n(x_m) = \int_{x_m}^{1} p_n(t)dt.$$

Putting $j = 1$ in (50.6) and integrating, we easily find

$$|v(x) - \sum_{n=1}^{N} v_n(\xi)\varphi_n(x_m)| \leqq \frac{C_{q1}}{N^{q-1}}\,. \tag{50.7}$$

It follows from (50.6) and (50.7) that

$$|||v - \sum_{n=1}^{N} v_n(\xi)\varphi_n(x_m)|||_0 \leqq \frac{C}{N^{q-1}}, \qquad C = \text{const.} \tag{50.8}$$

We choose an arbitrary $\varepsilon > 0$ and fix N so that $C.N^{1-q} > \varepsilon/2$. We expand $v_n(\xi)$ as a series

$$v_n(\xi) = \sum_{k=1}^{\infty} \alpha_{nk}\,\tau_k(\xi),$$

and choose K so that

$$|||\sum_{n=1}^{N} \{v_n(\xi) - \sum_{k=1}^{K} \alpha_{nk}\,\tau_k(\xi)\}\varphi_n(x_m)|||_0 < \frac{\varepsilon}{2} \tag{50.9}$$

Combining (50.8) and (50.9), we obtain the relation

$$|||v - \sum_{K=1}^{K} \sum_{n=1}^{N} \alpha_{nk}\,\tau_k(\xi)\varphi_n(x_m)|||_0 < \varepsilon,$$

which proves our assertion.

System (50.4) is orthonormal and therefore strongly minimal w.r.t. the metric

$$|||u|||_1^2 = \int_\Omega \phi(x_m)\left|\frac{\partial u}{\partial x_m}\right|^2 dx.$$

Since $|||u|||_0 \geqq |||u|||_1$, it follows, on the strength of Theorem 4.2, that system (50.4) is strongly minimal w.r.t. the metric (50.3), which proves the required result.

We now assume that the integral (45.3) converges. System (50.4) will be complete and strongly minimal in $\mathfrak{H}_A$ if we redefine the polynomials $p_n(t)$: as before, the $p_n(t)$ are polynomials of degree n, but they now satisfy the conditions

$$\int_0^1 p_n(t)dt = 0 \qquad (n = 1, 2, 3, \ldots), \tag{50.10}$$

$$\int_0^1 \phi(t)p_r(t)p_s(t)dt = \delta_{rs} \qquad (r, s = 1, 2, 3, \ldots). \tag{50.11}$$

We do not introduce the polynomial $p_0(t)$ into the discussion. It is not difficult to establish that a sequence of polynomials which satisfy (50.10) and (50.11) can be constructed.

We now assume that in (50.4) k and $n = 1, 2, 3, \ldots$.
By (50.10), the functions (50.4) satisfy not only (45.2) but also (45.4) – that is, they satisfy all the boundary conditions of the problem. As above we can show that this system is complete and strongly minimal w.r.t. the metric (50.3).
If $\phi(0) > 0$, then we can take $\phi(x_m) = 1$. In this way,

$$p_n(t) = \sqrt{2n+1}\,P_n(2t-1),$$

where the P_n are Legendre polynomials.

Chapter VII

THE STABILITY OF THE RITZ-PROCESS FOR EIGENVALUE PROBLEMS

In this short chapter, we shall formulate stability conditions for the application of the Ritz-process to the evaluation of approximate eigenvalues and eigenfunctions for a positive definite operator. We present definitions for the corresponding concepts of stability: it is necessary to do this, since eigenvalue problems (even for linear operators) are non-linear problems and the definitions of stability, which were applied to linear problems in earlier chapters, can prove to be inappropriate.

§51. The general theorem

Lemma 51.1 (This is a special case of Weil's Lemma: see Riesz and St Nagy [1]). *Let* $\boldsymbol{S}$ *and* $\boldsymbol{T}$ *be selfadjoint, non-negative and completely continuous operators, acting in a certain Hilbert space* $\mathfrak{H}$, *and let* $\sigma_k^{\boldsymbol{S}}$ *and* $\sigma_k^{\boldsymbol{T}}$ $(k = 1, 2, \ldots)$ *be their eigenvalues presented in descending order, respectively. Then*

$$|\sigma_k^{\boldsymbol{S}} - \sigma_k^{\boldsymbol{T}}| \leqq ||\boldsymbol{S} - \boldsymbol{T}||. \tag{51.1}$$

Proof. We put

$$\begin{aligned} \sigma^{\boldsymbol{S}}(v_1, v_2, \ldots, v_{k-1}) &= \max(\boldsymbol{S}u, u), \\ \sigma^{\boldsymbol{T}}(v_1, v_2, \ldots, v_{k-1}) &= \max(\boldsymbol{T}u, u), \end{aligned} \tag{51.2}$$

where the maxima are evaluated w.r.t. the elements $u \in \mathfrak{H}$ such that $||u|| = 1$ and $(u, v_j) = 0$ $(j = 1, 2, \ldots, k-1)$. On the strength of the mini-max principle,

$$\sigma_k^{\boldsymbol{S}} = \min \sigma^{\boldsymbol{S}}(v_1, v_2, \ldots, v_{k-1}), \tag{51.3}$$

$$\sigma_k^{\boldsymbol{T}} = \min \sigma^{\boldsymbol{T}}(v_1, v_2, \ldots, v_{k-1}), \tag{51.4}$$

where the minima are evaluated w.r.t. all the different sets of elements $v_1, v_2, \ldots, v_{k-1}$ which lie in $\mathfrak{H}$.

For arbitrary real variables x and y, we know that $\sup(x+y) \leqq \sup x + \sup y$. Putting $\boldsymbol{S} = \boldsymbol{T}+\boldsymbol{Q}$, we obtain

$$\sigma^{S}(v_1, v_2, \ldots, v_{k-1}) - \sigma^{T}(v_1, v_2, \ldots, v_{k-1}) \leqq$$
$$\leqq \sup_{\substack{\|u\|=1 \\ (u, v_j)=0}} (\boldsymbol{Q}u, u) \leqq \sup_{\|u\|=1} |(\boldsymbol{Q}u, u)| = \|\boldsymbol{Q}\| = \|\boldsymbol{S}-\boldsymbol{T}\|.$$

Interchanging $\boldsymbol{T}$ and $\boldsymbol{S}$, we also find

$$\sigma^{T}(v_1, v_2, \ldots, v_{k-1}) - \sigma^{S}(v_1, v_2, \ldots, v_{k-1}) \leqq \|\boldsymbol{S}-\boldsymbol{T}\|$$

and hence,

$$|\sigma^{S}(v_1, v_2, \ldots, v_{k-1}) - \sigma^{T}(v_1, v_2, \ldots, v_{k-1})| \leqq \|\boldsymbol{S}-\boldsymbol{T}\|. \tag{51.5}$$

For example, let $\sigma_k^T \leqq \sigma_k^S$. In (51.5), we put $v_j = v_j^0$ $(j = 1, 2, \ldots, k\text{-}1)$, where v_j^0 is the function which minimises (51.4). Hence, (51.5) takes the form

$$\sigma^{S}(v_1^0, v_2^0, \ldots, v_{l-1}^0) - \sigma_k^T \leqq \|\boldsymbol{S}-\boldsymbol{T}\|.$$

However, by (51.3), $\sigma_k^S = \sigma^S(v_1^0, v_2^0, \ldots, v_{k-1}^0)$ and hence, $\sigma_k^S - \sigma_k^T \leqq \|\boldsymbol{S}-\boldsymbol{T}\|$. This result coincides with (51.1), since $\sigma_k^S \geqq \sigma_k^T$.

We now examine a sequence of Hilbert spaces $\{\mathfrak{H}_n\}$, $(n = 1, 2, 3, \ldots)$. In the space $\mathfrak{H}_n$, we define two selfadjoint, positive definite operators $\boldsymbol{A}_n$ and $\boldsymbol{B}_n$, such that the operators $\boldsymbol{A}_n^{-1}$ and $\bar{\boldsymbol{B}}_n = \boldsymbol{A}_n^{-\frac{1}{2}}\boldsymbol{B}_n\boldsymbol{A}_n^{-\frac{1}{2}}$ are completely continuous in $\mathfrak{H}_n$. Since

$$\boldsymbol{A}_n^{-\frac{1}{2}}\boldsymbol{B}_n\boldsymbol{A}_n^{-\frac{1}{2}} = \boldsymbol{A}_n^{-\frac{1}{2}}\boldsymbol{B}_n^{\frac{1}{2}}\boldsymbol{B}_n^{\frac{1}{2}}\boldsymbol{A}_n^{-\frac{1}{2}} = (\boldsymbol{B}_n^{\frac{1}{2}}\boldsymbol{A}_n^{-\frac{1}{2}})^*(\boldsymbol{B}_n^{\frac{1}{2}}\boldsymbol{A}_n^{-\frac{1}{2}}),$$

the operator $\boldsymbol{A}_n^{-\frac{1}{2}}\boldsymbol{B}_n\boldsymbol{A}_n^{-\frac{1}{2}}$ is completely continuous, if $\boldsymbol{B}_n^{\frac{1}{2}}\boldsymbol{A}_n^{-\frac{1}{2}}$ is completely continuous. In turn, it is easy to prove that for this it is necessary and sufficient that every set, which is bounded in the energy space of $\boldsymbol{A}_n$, is compact in the energy space of $\boldsymbol{B}_n$. We denote by $\sigma_k^{(n)}$ the kth eigenvalue (in ascending order) of

$$(\boldsymbol{A}_n - \sigma\boldsymbol{B}_n)u_n = 0. \tag{51.6}$$

Along with (51.6), we examine the equation

$$[(\boldsymbol{A}_n + \boldsymbol{\Gamma}_n) - \mu(\boldsymbol{B}_n + \boldsymbol{\Delta}_n)]v_n = 0, \tag{51.7}$$

where $\boldsymbol{\Gamma}_n$ and $\boldsymbol{\Delta}_n$ are bounded selfadjoint operators acting in the space $\mathfrak{H}_n$.

Definition. The process of determining the kth eigenvalue of (51.6) {or, more briefly, *the process* (51.6)} is *stable*, if there exist constants p, q and

r independent of n (but not necessarily independent of k) such that, for $\|\boldsymbol{\Gamma}_n\| \leqq r$ and for arbitrary $\boldsymbol{\Delta}_n$, the sums $\boldsymbol{B}_n+\boldsymbol{\Delta}_n$ are positive definite and the following conditions are satisfied:

(1) the operators $\boldsymbol{A}_n+\boldsymbol{\Gamma}_n$ are positive definite;

(2) the operators

$$\boldsymbol{T}_n = (\boldsymbol{I}_n+\bar{\boldsymbol{\Gamma}}_n)^{-\frac{1}{2}}(\bar{\boldsymbol{B}}_n+\bar{\boldsymbol{\Delta}}_n)(\boldsymbol{I}_n+\bar{\boldsymbol{\Gamma}}_n)^{-\frac{1}{2}}$$

are completely continuous in $\mathfrak{H}_n$, where $\boldsymbol{I}_n$ is the identity operator in $\mathfrak{H}_n$,

$$\bar{\boldsymbol{\Gamma}}_n = \boldsymbol{A}_n^{-\frac{1}{2}}\boldsymbol{\Gamma}_n\boldsymbol{A}_n^{-\frac{1}{2}}, \qquad \bar{\boldsymbol{\Delta}}_n = \boldsymbol{A}_n^{-\frac{1}{2}}\boldsymbol{\Delta}_n\boldsymbol{A}_n^{-\frac{1}{2}};$$

(3) if $\mu_k^{(h)}$ denotes the kth eigenvalue (in ascending order) of (51.7), then

$$\left| \frac{\sigma_k^{(n)}}{\mu_k^{(n)}} - 1 \right| \leqq p\|\boldsymbol{\Gamma}_n\| + q\|\boldsymbol{\Delta}_n\|. \tag{51.8}$$

Theorem 51.1 *In order that the process* (51.6) *be stable, it is necessary that*

$$\|\boldsymbol{A}_n^{-1}\| \leqq C_1, \tag{51.9}$$

and sufficient that (51.9) *be satisfied and*

$$\sigma_k^{(n)} \leqq C_2, \qquad \frac{(\boldsymbol{B}_n u, u)}{(\boldsymbol{A}_n u, u)} \leqq C_3, \qquad u \in \mathfrak{H}_n, \tag{51.10}$$

where C_1, C_2 and C_3 are constants independent of n (the constant C_2 can depend on k).

Proof of Necessity. If the process (51.6) is stable, then, for $\|\boldsymbol{\Gamma}_n\| \leqq r$, the operator $\boldsymbol{A}_n+\boldsymbol{\Gamma}_n$ is positive definite. If we put $\boldsymbol{\Gamma}_n = -r\boldsymbol{I}_n$, then

$$((\boldsymbol{A}_n - r\boldsymbol{I}_n)u, u) \geqq 0, \qquad u \in \mathfrak{H}_n,$$

whence $(\boldsymbol{A}_n u, u) \geqq r\|u\|^2$, and hence (PM, §5, (5)), $\|\boldsymbol{A}_n^{-1}\| \leqq (1/r)$.

Proof of Sufficiency. Choosing β, $0 < \beta < 1$, we put $r = \beta/C_1$ and write $\|\boldsymbol{\Gamma}_n\| \leqq r$. Using the bound just obtained for $\|\boldsymbol{A}_n^{-1}\|$, we find that the lower bound γ_n^2 for the positive definite operator $\boldsymbol{A}_n$ equals $1/\|\boldsymbol{A}_n^{-1}\|$. Using (51.9), $\gamma_n^2 \geqq (1/C_1)$, and hence,

$$((\boldsymbol{A}_n+\boldsymbol{\Gamma}_n)u, u) = (\boldsymbol{A}_n u, u) + (\boldsymbol{\Gamma}_n u, u) \geqq$$

$$\geqq (\gamma_n^2 - \|\boldsymbol{\Gamma}_n\|)\|u\|^2 \geqq \frac{1-\beta}{C_1}\|u\|^2.$$

Thus the operator $A_n+\Gamma_n$ is positive definite.
It is clear that the operator T_n is non-negative in $\mathfrak{H}_n$. We now prove that it is completely continuous in $\mathfrak{H}_n$. From its spectral decomposition, we obtain

$$||A_n^{-\frac{1}{2}}|| = ||A_n^{-1}||^{\frac{1}{2}} = \frac{1}{\gamma_n},$$

and hence, $||A_n^{-\frac{1}{2}}|| \leqq \sqrt{C_1}$. Further, $||\bar{\Gamma}_n|| \leqq ||\Gamma_n||\, ||A_n^{-\frac{1}{2}}||^2 \leqq \beta < 1$, the operator $I_n+\Gamma_n$ is positive definite and the operator $(I_n+\bar{\Gamma}_n)^{-\frac{1}{2}}$ exists and is bounded. In this way, we obtain

$$||(I_n+\bar{\Gamma}_n)^{-\frac{1}{2}}|| = \left\| \sum_{m=0}^{\infty}(-1)^m \binom{m}{\frac{1}{2}} \bar{\Gamma}_n^m \right\| \leqq$$

$$\leqq \sum_{m=0}^{\infty} \binom{m}{\frac{1}{2}} ||\bar{\Gamma}_n||^m \leqq \sum_{m=0}^{\infty} \binom{m}{\frac{1}{2}} \beta^m = \frac{1}{\sqrt{1-\beta}}. \tag{51.11}$$

The operator $\bar{B}_n$ is completely continuous on the bais of assumptions, and the operator Δ_n is the product of two completely continuous operators and a bounded operator. The complete continuity of T_n is now obvious.
We now turn to a proof of estimate (51.8). Assuming that $A_n^{\frac{1}{2}}u = v$, we have

$$\frac{(B_n u, u)}{(A_n u, u)} = \frac{(B_n A_n^{-\frac{1}{2}}v, A_n^{-\frac{1}{2}}v)}{||v||^2} = \frac{(\bar{B}_n v, v)}{||v||^2}.$$

Since $\bar{B}_n$ is selfadjoint,

$$||\bar{B}_n|| = \sup \frac{(\bar{B}_n v, v)}{||v||^2},$$

and the second inequality (51.10) shows that

$$||\bar{B}_n|| \leqq C_3. \tag{51.12}$$

The substitution

$$A_n^{\frac{1}{2}}u_n = \tilde{u}_n, \qquad (I_n+\bar{\Gamma}_n)^{\frac{1}{2}}A_n^{\frac{1}{2}}v = \tilde{v}_n$$

reduces equations (51.6) and (51.7) to the form

$$(I_n-\lambda\bar{B}_n)\tilde{u}_n = 0, \qquad (I_n-\mu T_n)\tilde{v}_n = 0,$$

whence it is seen that $1/\sigma_k^{(n)}$ and $1/\mu_k^{(n)}$ are the eigenvalues of the selfadjoint and completely continuous operators $\bar{\boldsymbol{B}}_n$ and $\boldsymbol{T}_n$, respectively. On the basis of Lemma 51.1,

$$\left| \frac{1}{\mu_k^{(n)}} - \frac{1}{\sigma_k^{(n)}} \right| \leqq ||\boldsymbol{T}_n - \bar{\boldsymbol{B}}_n||.$$

Further,

$$\begin{aligned} ||\boldsymbol{T}_n - \bar{\boldsymbol{B}}_n|| &= ||(\boldsymbol{I}_n + \bar{\boldsymbol{\Gamma}}_n)^{-\frac{1}{2}} \bar{\boldsymbol{B}}_n (\boldsymbol{I}_n + \bar{\boldsymbol{\Gamma}}_n)^{-\frac{1}{2}} - \bar{\boldsymbol{B}}_n + \\ &\quad + (\boldsymbol{I}_n + \bar{\boldsymbol{\Gamma}}_n)^{-\frac{1}{2}} \bar{\boldsymbol{\Delta}}_n (\boldsymbol{I}_n + \bar{\boldsymbol{\Gamma}}_n)^{-\frac{1}{2}}|| \leqq \\ &\leqq ||[(\boldsymbol{I}_n + \boldsymbol{\Gamma}_n)^{-\frac{1}{2}} - \boldsymbol{I}_n] \bar{\boldsymbol{B}}_n (\boldsymbol{I}_n + \boldsymbol{\Gamma}_n)^{-\frac{1}{2}}|| + \\ &\quad + ||\bar{\boldsymbol{B}}_n [(\boldsymbol{I}_n + \bar{\boldsymbol{\Gamma}}_n)^{-\frac{1}{2}} - \boldsymbol{I}_n]|| + ||(\boldsymbol{I}_n + \bar{\boldsymbol{\Gamma}}_n)^{-\frac{1}{2}} \bar{\boldsymbol{\Delta}}_n (\boldsymbol{I}_n + \bar{\boldsymbol{\Gamma}}_n)^{-\frac{1}{2}}|| \leqq \\ &\leqq \frac{C_3(1+\sqrt{1-\beta})}{\sqrt{1-\beta}} ||(\boldsymbol{I}_n + \bar{\boldsymbol{\Gamma}}_n)^{-\frac{1}{2}} - \boldsymbol{I}_n|| + \frac{C_1 ||\boldsymbol{\Delta}_n||}{1-\beta}. \end{aligned}$$

However, since

$$\begin{aligned} ||(\boldsymbol{I}_n + \bar{\boldsymbol{\Gamma}}_n)^{-\frac{1}{2}} - \boldsymbol{I}_n|| &= \left\| \sum_{m=1}^{\infty} \binom{m}{\frac{1}{2}} \bar{\boldsymbol{\Gamma}}_n^m \right\| \leqq ||\bar{\boldsymbol{\Gamma}}_n|| \left\| \sum_{m=1}^{\infty} \binom{m}{\frac{1}{2}} \bar{\boldsymbol{\Gamma}}_n^{m-1} \right\| \leqq \\ &\leqq C_1 ||\boldsymbol{\Gamma}_n|| \sum_{m=1}^{\infty} \binom{m}{\frac{1}{2}} \beta^{m-1} = \frac{C_1 ||\boldsymbol{\Gamma}_n||}{\sqrt{1-\beta}(1+\sqrt{1-\beta})}, \end{aligned}$$

we obtain

$$\left| \frac{1}{\mu_k^{(n)}} - \frac{1}{\sigma_k^{(n)}} \right| \leqq \frac{C_1 C_3}{1-\beta} ||\boldsymbol{\Gamma}_n|| + \frac{C_1}{1-\beta} ||\boldsymbol{\Delta}_n||.$$

Multiplying this result by $\sigma_k^{(n)}$ and remembering that $\sigma_k^{(n)} \leqq C_2$, we obtain, finally,

$$\left| \frac{\sigma_k^{(n)}}{\mu_k^{(n)}} - 1 \right| \leqq \frac{C_1 C_2}{1-\beta} (C_3 ||\boldsymbol{\Gamma}_n|| + ||\boldsymbol{\Delta}_n||). \tag{51.13}$$

The proof of the theorem is complete on putting in (51.13)

$$p = \frac{C_1 C_2 C_3}{1-\beta}, \qquad q = \frac{C_1 C_2}{1-\beta}.$$

§52. The stability of the Ritz-process for eigenvalue problems

Let A be a positive definite, selfadjoint operator with a discrete spectrum which acts in the separable Hilbert space $\mathfrak{H}$ and let $\lambda_k (k = 1, 2, 3, \ldots)$ be the eigenvalues of A, written in ascending order. For the approximate determination of the numbers λ_k, we can make use of the Ritz-process (see VM, §33): we choose a coordinate system $\{\phi_n\}$ which satisfies conditions (1), (2) and (3) of §6 and form the matrices

$$R_n = \begin{Bmatrix} [\phi_1, \phi_1] & [\phi_2, \phi_1] \ldots [\phi_n, \phi_1] \\ [\phi_1, \phi_2] & [\phi_2, \phi_2] \ldots [\phi_n, \phi_2] \\ \cdot \quad \cdot \quad \cdot & \cdot \quad \cdot \quad \cdot \quad \cdot \quad \cdot \\ [\phi_1, \phi_n] & [\phi_2, \phi_n] \ldots [\phi_n, \phi_n] \end{Bmatrix} \tag{52.1}$$

and

$$r_n = \begin{Bmatrix} (\phi_1, \phi_1) & (\phi_2, \phi_1) \ldots (\phi_n, \phi_1) \\ (\phi_1, \phi_2) & (\phi_2, \phi_2) \ldots (\phi_n, \phi_2) \\ \cdot \quad \cdot \quad \cdot & \cdot \quad \cdot \quad \cdot \quad \cdot \quad \cdot \\ (\phi_1, \phi_n) & (\phi_2, \phi_n) \ldots (\phi_n, \phi_n) \end{Bmatrix}. \tag{52.2}$$

An approximate eigenfunction

$$u_n = \sum_{k=1}^{n} a_k^{(n)} \phi_n$$

and an approximate eigenvalue $\lambda_k^{(n)}$ are defined by

$$(\boldsymbol{R}_n - \sigma \boldsymbol{r}_n) a^{(n)} = 0, \tag{52.3}$$

where

$$a^{(n)} = (a_1^{(n)}, a_2^{(n)}, \ldots, a_n^{(n)}).$$

We recognise within these conditions the general scheme of §51: the space $\mathfrak{H}_n$ is the n-dimensional unitary space $\mathfrak{E}_n$, $\boldsymbol{A}_n = \boldsymbol{R}_n$ and $\boldsymbol{B}_n = \boldsymbol{r}_n$, where on this occasion, the operators $\boldsymbol{R}_n$ an $\boldsymbol{r}_n$ are generated by the matrices (52.1) and (52.2) in $\mathfrak{E}_n$, respectively.
Since they are generated by Gram matrices of linear independent functions, $\boldsymbol{R}_n$ and $\boldsymbol{r}_n$ are positive definite. The question regarding complete continuity does not arise, since linear operators are automatically completely continuous in a finite dimensional space.

Theorem 52.1. *A necessary and sufficient condition for the application of the Ritz-process to the evaluation of the first eigenvalue of a positive definite operator to be stable is that the coordinate system be strongly minimal in the corresponding energy space.*

Proof. (The proof of this theorem is based on Dovbysh [1]). If the process is stable, then, by Theorem 51.1, $||\boldsymbol{R}_n^{-1}|| \leqq C_1$. However, since $||\boldsymbol{R}_n^{-1}|| = (1/\lambda_1^{(n)})$ where $\lambda_1^{(n)}$ is the smallest eigenvalue of the matrix R_n, $\lambda_1^{(n)} \geqq (1/C_1)$ and the coordinate system is strongly minimal in $\mathfrak{H}_A$. The sufficiency proof reduces to the verification of (51.9) and (51.10) for $k = 1$.

If the coordinate system is strongly minimal in $\mathfrak{H}_A$, then there exists a constant $\lambda_0 > 0$ such that $\lambda_1^{(n)} \geqq \lambda_0$. Therefore,

$$||\boldsymbol{R}_n^{-1}|| = \frac{1}{\lambda_1^{(n)}} \leqq \frac{1}{\lambda_0}$$

and we can put $C_1 = (1/\lambda_0)$. Further, $\sigma_1^{(n)}$ is the eigenvalue of (52.3). Since $\sigma_1^{(n)}$ does not increase for increasing n (VM, §32), $\sigma_1^{(n)} \leqq \sigma_1^{(k)} (n > k)$ and we can put $C_2 = \sigma_1^{(k)}$.

Finally, we establish the second condition in (51.10). Since A is positive definite, there exists a constant γ such that $|||u|||_A \geqq \gamma ||u||$, $u \in \mathfrak{H}_A$. Let $a^{(n)} = (a_1^{(n)}, \ldots, a_n^{(n)})$ be an arbitrary vector of $\mathfrak{E}_n$. We put

$$u_n = \sum_{k=1}^{n} a_k^{(n)} \phi_k.$$

It is clear that $u_n \in \mathfrak{H}_A$, and we obtain

$$\frac{(\boldsymbol{r}_n a^{(n)}, a^{(n)})}{(\boldsymbol{R}_n a^{(n)}, a^{(n)})} = \frac{||u_n||^2}{|||u_n|||_A^2} \leqq \frac{1}{\gamma^2}.$$

Since we can put $C_3 = (1/\gamma^2)$, all the conditions of Theorem 51.1 are satisfied, and hence, Theorem 51.2 is proved.

Using (51.13), it is easy to give an estimate for the error of the *non-exact* Ritz-approximation. Namely, if $\boldsymbol{\Gamma}_n$ and $\boldsymbol{\Delta}_n$ are the errors in $\boldsymbol{R}_n$ and $\boldsymbol{r}_n$, respectively, and $||\boldsymbol{\Gamma}_n|| \leqq \beta / C_1 = \beta \lambda_0$, then

$$\left| \frac{\sigma_k^{(n)}}{\mu_k^{(n)}} - 1 \right| \leqq \frac{\sigma_k^{(k)}}{\lambda_0 (1 - \beta)} \left(\frac{||\boldsymbol{\Gamma}_n||}{\gamma^2} + ||\boldsymbol{\Delta}_n|| \right), \tag{52.4}$$

where $\sigma_k^{(n)}$ is the exact and $\mu_k^{(n)}$ is the non-exact n^{th} order Ritz-approximation to the kth eigenvalue of A.

For $k > 1$, Dovbysh [1] has proved

Theorem 52.2 *For the stability of the Ritz-process when used to evaluate the* k^{th} ($k > 1$) *eigenvalue of a positive definite operator, it is sufficient, and for a class of minimal systems necessary, that the coordinate system be strongly minimal in the corresponding energy space.*

The sufficiency can be proved as in Theorem 52.1. We shall not prove the necessity. The stipulation about a class of minimal systems is necessary: examples show that, for $k > 1$, the Ritz-process can be stable for coordinate systems which are non-minimal in the energy space.

§53. The stability of the Ritz-process for the eigenfunction problem

Let $\boldsymbol{A}$ be a positive definite operator with discrete spectrum, let $\sigma_k = \sigma_{k+1} = \ldots = \sigma_{k+l-1}$ be the eigenvalues with multiplicity l and let $\mathfrak{H}^{(k)}$, corresponding to this eigenvalue, be the corresponding eigensubspace of $\boldsymbol{A}$. Let $\sigma_{k+j}^{(n)}(j = 0, \ldots, l-1)$ be the eigenvalues of (52.3) and $\mu_{k+j}^{(n)}$ be the eigenvalues of

$$[(\boldsymbol{R}_n + \boldsymbol{\Gamma}_n) - \mu(\boldsymbol{r}_n + \boldsymbol{\Delta}_n)]b^{(n)} = 0, \tag{53.1}$$

where $\boldsymbol{\Gamma}_n$ and $\boldsymbol{\Delta}_n$ denote the errors in $\boldsymbol{R}_n$ and $\boldsymbol{r}_n$. We denote by $E_{k,l}^{(n)}$ the orthogonal sum of the eigensubspaces of (52.3), corresponding to the eigenvalues $\sigma_k^{(n)}, \sigma_{k+1}^{(n)}, \ldots, \sigma_{k+l-1}^{(n)}$, and by $F_{k,l}^{(n)}$ the orthogonal sum for (53.1) and the eigenvalues $\mu_k^{(n)}, \mu_{k+1}^{(n)}, \ldots, \mu_{k+l-1}^{(n)}$. In the space $\mathfrak{E}^{(n)} = \mathfrak{E}_n$, we introduce the new metric

$$[\alpha^{(n)}, \beta^{(n)}] = (\boldsymbol{R}_n \alpha^{(n)}, \beta^{(n)}), \qquad |||\alpha^{(n)}||| = \sqrt{[\alpha^{(n)}, \alpha^{(n)}]}, \tag{53.2}$$

and, w.r.t. this metric, define the angle θ_n between $E_{k,l}^{(n)}$ and $F_{k.l}^{(n)}$

$$\cos \theta_n = \sup \frac{|[\alpha^{(n)}, \beta^{(n)}]|}{|||\alpha^{(n)}|||\ |||\beta^{(n)}|||}, \tag{53.3}$$

where the upper bound is evaluated w.r.t. all non-zero vectors $\alpha^{(n)} \in \tilde{E}_{k,l}^{(n)}$ and $\beta^{(n)} \in \tilde{F}_{k,l}^{(n)}$, where $\tilde{E}_{k,l}^{(n)}$ and $\tilde{F}_{k,l}^{(n)}$ are the orthogonal complements of $E_{k,l}^{(n)}$ and $F_{k,l}^{(n)}$ w.r.t. their general subspaces. We shall say that the evaluation of $E_{k,l}^{(n)}$ by the Ritz-process is stable, if, for $||\boldsymbol{\Gamma}_n|| \to 0$ and $||\boldsymbol{\Delta}_n|| \to 0$, the angle θ_n tends to zero uniformly w.r.t. the n. That is, given ε, there exist $r > 0$ and $s > 0$ such that, if $||\boldsymbol{\Gamma}_n|| \leqq r$ and $||\boldsymbol{\Delta}_n|| \leqq s$, then $\theta < \varepsilon$.

In Dovbysh [2], the following theorem has been proved: *The process of determining the subspace $E_{k,l}^{(n)}$ is stable, if the coordinate system is strongly minimal in $\mathfrak{H}_A$.*

We present a proof only for the simplest case when $\mathfrak{H}^{(n)} = E_{1,1}^{(n)}$ is the eigensubspace of the operator A which corresponds to its smallest eigenvalue λ_1, where this eigenvalue is simple.

Let $\|\boldsymbol{\Gamma}_n\| \leqq r$ and $\|\boldsymbol{\Delta}_n\| \leqq s$, where r and s are so small that the Ritz-process for the determination of λ_1 is stable. For n sufficiently large, the smallest eigenvalues $\sigma_1^{(n)}$ and $\lambda_1^{(n)}$ of the *exact* and the *non-exact* approximate problems will be simple. Let the corresponding (one-dimensional) eigensubspaces be $\Xi_1^{(n)}$ and $M_1^{(n)}$.

Let the 2-dimensional space P span $\Xi_1^{(n)}$ and $M_1^{(n)}$ and ψ_n denote the angle (w.r.t. the metric generated by the matrix R_n) between the direction $\Xi_1^{(n)}$ and an arbitrary vector $x \in P$:

$$\cos \psi_n = \frac{(\boldsymbol{R}_n x, \xi_n)}{\sqrt{(\boldsymbol{R}_n x, x)(\boldsymbol{R}_n \xi_n, \xi_n)}},$$

where $\xi_n \in \Xi_1^{(n)}$ is the eigenvector of $\boldsymbol{R}_n \xi - \sigma_1^{(n)} \boldsymbol{r}_n \xi = 0$. We can assume that ξ_n is a unit vector: $(\boldsymbol{R}_n \xi_n, \xi_n) = 1$, and then

$$\cos \psi_n = \frac{(\boldsymbol{R}_n x, \xi_n)}{\sqrt{(\boldsymbol{R}_n x, x)}}. \tag{53.4}$$

We prove that, for any vector $x \in P$,

$$\frac{(\boldsymbol{r}_n x, x)}{(\boldsymbol{R}_n x, x)} = a_n \sin^2 \psi_n + b_n \cos^2 \psi_n, \tag{53.5}$$

where the a_n and b_n do not depend on x. In the plane P, we choose η_n such that: $(\boldsymbol{R}_n \eta_n, \eta_n) = 1$ and $(\boldsymbol{R}_n \xi_n, \eta_n) = 0$.

Then $x = (\xi_n \cos \psi_n + \eta_n \sin \psi_n)|x|$, and

$$(\boldsymbol{r}_n x, x) = [(\boldsymbol{r}_n \xi_n, \xi_n) \cos^2 \psi_n + (\boldsymbol{r}_n \eta_n, \eta_n) \sin^2 \psi_n + \\ + 2 \operatorname{Re} (\boldsymbol{r}_n \xi_n, \eta_n) \cos \psi_n \sin \psi_n] |x|^2.$$

However,

$$(\boldsymbol{r}_n \xi_n, \eta_n) = \frac{1}{\sigma_1^{(n)}} (\boldsymbol{R}_n \xi_n, \eta_n) = 0,$$

and we arrive at (53.5) with

$$a_n = (\boldsymbol{r}_n \eta_n, \eta_n), \qquad b_n = (\boldsymbol{r}_n \xi_n, \xi_n). \tag{53.6}$$

From (53.6) and the definition of ξ_n and η_n, it follows at once that

$$b_n = \frac{1}{\sigma_1^{(n)}}, \qquad a_n \leqq \frac{1}{\sigma_2^{(n)}}. \tag{53.7}$$

Further,

$$b_n - a_n \geqq \frac{1}{\sigma_1^{(n)}} - \frac{1}{\sigma_2^{(n)}} \underset{n\to\infty}{\to} \frac{1}{\lambda_1} - \frac{1}{\lambda_2},$$

where λ_2 is the second eigenvalue of A. Since the eigenvalue λ_1 is simple $(1/\lambda_1)$–$(1/\lambda_2) > 0$, and, hence, there exists a constant $\beta > 0$ such that, for n sufficiently large,

$$b_n - a_n \geqq \beta. \tag{53.8}$$

In the plane P, we examine

$$\frac{((\boldsymbol{r}_n + \boldsymbol{\Delta}_n)x, x)}{((\boldsymbol{R}_n + \boldsymbol{\Gamma}_n)x, x)} = \frac{(a_n \sin^2 \psi_n + b_n \cos^2 \psi_n) + \dfrac{(\boldsymbol{\Delta}_n x, x)}{(\boldsymbol{R}_n x, x)}}{1 + \dfrac{(\boldsymbol{\Gamma}_n x, x)}{(\boldsymbol{R}_n x, x)}}. \tag{53.9}$$

where the ratios in the numerator and denominator are independent of $|x|$. We write

$$\frac{(\boldsymbol{\Gamma}_n x, x)}{(\boldsymbol{R}_n x, x)} = \tau_1^{(n)}(\psi_n), \qquad \frac{(\boldsymbol{\Delta}_n x, x)}{(\boldsymbol{R}_n x, x)} = \tau_2^{(n)}(\psi_n),$$

so that

$$\frac{((\boldsymbol{r}_n + \boldsymbol{\Delta}_n)x, x)}{((\boldsymbol{R}_n + \boldsymbol{\Gamma}_n)x, x)} = \frac{a_n + (b_n - a_n)\cos^2 \psi_n + \tau_2^{(n)}(\psi_n)}{1 + \tau_1^{(n)}(\psi_n)}. \tag{53.9'}$$

The absolute maximum of (53.9) is attained for the eigenfunction of the *non-exact* problem corresponding to the eigenvalue $\mu_1^{(n)}$.
We note that $x \in \mathfrak{E}_n$, since the space $\mathfrak{E}_n$ contains both $\Xi_1^{(n)}$ and $M_1^{(n)}$. Hence,

$$|(\boldsymbol{\Gamma}_n x, x)| \leqq \|\boldsymbol{\Gamma}_n\| \, \|x\|^2, \qquad |(\boldsymbol{R}_n x, x)| \geqq \tilde{\lambda}\|x\|^2,$$

where $||x|| = ||x||_{\mathfrak{C}_n}$ and $\tilde{\lambda}$ is the positive lower bound for the eigenvalues of R_n. In this way,

$$|\tau_1^{(n)}(\psi_n)| \leqq \frac{||\boldsymbol{\Gamma}_n||}{\tilde{\gamma}} \leqq \frac{r}{\tilde{\lambda}}. \tag{53.10}$$

and, analogously,

$$|\tau_2^{(n)}(\psi_n)| \leqq \frac{||\boldsymbol{\Delta}_n||}{\tilde{\lambda}} \leqq \frac{s}{\tilde{\lambda}}. \tag{53.11}$$

We denote the r.h.s. of (53.9) by $\Omega(\psi_n)$ so that

$$\Omega(\psi) = \frac{a_n+(b_n-a_n)\cos^2\psi+\tau_2^{(n)}(\psi)}{1+\tau_1^{(n)}(\psi)}.$$

If $\tau_1^{(n)}(\psi) = \tau_2^{(n)}(\psi) = 0$ (the *exact* problem), then, on the basis of (53.8), $\Omega(\psi)$ attains a maximum for $\psi = 0$. We now prove that for small $\tau_1^{(n)}$ and $\tau_2^{(n)}$ the function $\Omega(\psi)$ attains a maximum in the neighbourhood of $\psi = 0$. More specificly, we prove that: given $\varepsilon > 0$, there exist r and s such that, if $||\boldsymbol{\Gamma}_n|| \leqq r$ and $||\boldsymbol{\Delta}_n|| \leqq s$, then $\Omega(\psi)$ attains an absolute maximum in the neighbourhood of $\psi = 0$ defined by $\sin^2\psi < \varepsilon$.
From (53.10) and (53.11), it follows that

$$\Omega(\lambda) \geqq \frac{a_n+(b_n-a_n)\cos^2\psi - \dfrac{s}{\tilde{\lambda}}}{1+\dfrac{r}{\tilde{\lambda}}}.$$

whence letting "max" denote absolute maximum, we obtain

$$\max\Omega(\psi) \geqq \Omega(0) \geqq \frac{b_n - \dfrac{s}{\tilde{\lambda}}}{1+\dfrac{r}{\tilde{\lambda}}}. \tag{53.12}$$

Let $\max\Omega(\psi) = \Omega(\psi_0)$, where $\sin^2\psi_0 \geqq \varepsilon$. Then $\cos^2\psi_0 \leqq 1-\varepsilon$ and

$$\Omega(\psi_0) < \frac{a_n+(b_n-a_n)\cos^2\psi_0+\dfrac{s}{\tilde{\lambda}}}{1-\dfrac{r}{\tilde{\lambda}}} \leqq \frac{a_n+(b_n-a_n)(1-\varepsilon)+\dfrac{s}{\tilde{\lambda}}}{1-\dfrac{r}{\tilde{\lambda}}} =$$

$$= \frac{b_n-(b_n-a_n)\varepsilon+\dfrac{s}{\tilde{\lambda}}}{1-\dfrac{r}{\tilde{\lambda}}} \leqq \frac{b_n-\beta\varepsilon+\dfrac{s}{\tilde{\lambda}}}{1-\dfrac{r}{\tilde{\lambda}}}.$$

For fixed ε and sufficiently small r and s, the last quotient is less than the r.h.s. of inequality (53.12), and we obtain a contradiction.
Thus, the absolute maximum of (53.9) is attained for the vector for which the angle $\psi_n < \arcsin \varepsilon$. However, this function, as is clear, is the eigenfunction corresponding to the eigenvalue $\mu_1^{(n)}$ of the non-exact problem. This proves the theorem.
In a class of minimal systems, the condition of strong minimality is also necessary (see, Dovbysh [2]).

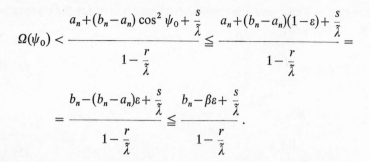

Chapter VIII

THE EFFECT OF ERROR IN THE EQUATION

In the present chapter, we shall conduct the following investigation. With a view to simplifying the operator defined by a given problem, we replace the given operator by a suitably defined approximation (an approximate operator) and ask the question: How bad is the solution of the approximate problem compared with that of the original problem? We conduct similar investigations when, for example, the coefficients of the differential equation or the region of integration are replaced by approximations with a simpler structure. Examples of this kind will be examined here. The question posed above is similar to, but not identical with, the question of stability for a numerical process. In the examination of stability for a numerical process, it was necessary to compare the solutions of two sequences of equations

$$A_n x^{(n)} = y^{(n)} \qquad (n = 1, 2, \ldots)$$

and

$$(A_n + \Gamma_n) z^{(n)} = y^{(n)} + \delta^{(n)} \qquad (n = 1, 2, \ldots).$$

It was also necessary to impose on the error Γ_n of A_n a sufficiently stringent condition – in the cases above, we required that the product $A_n^{-1}\Gamma_n$ be bounded. However, in return, we obtained an estimate uniformly valid w.r.t. n. In the present chapter, instead of two sequences of equations, we shall only investigate two equations which can be written in the form

$$Ax = y, \qquad (A+\Gamma)z = y$$

(below, we shall make use of a different notation). The problem is somewhat simplified, because the parameter n and the necessity for uniform estimates w.r.t. this parameter vanish. Nevertheless, we shall now construct estimates w.r.t. new assumptions on A and Γ. In particular, we shall not assume that the product $A^{-1}\Gamma$ is bounded.

Further, we shall not examine the errors caused by changes in the r.h.s. terms, since they can be determined with ease.

Note. The basic results of this chapter are contained in Mikhlin [6], [7] and [8]. A rather condensed formulation of these results and one illustrative example can be found in VM, §63.

§54. The formulation of the problem and an estimate for the error in the solution

We shall examine the equation

$$Au = f, \tag{54.1}$$

where A is a selfadjoint and positive operator acting in the Hilbert space $\mathfrak{H}$. It is understood that we do not exclude the case when this operator is positive definite. With respect to the r.h.s. value f, we assume that (u, f) is defined on a set $\mathfrak{M}$, which is dense in $\mathfrak{H}_A$, and that this functional (u, f) is linear and bounded in this space. Then equation (54.1) has a solution with finite energy which we shall denote by u_0.
Along with (54.1), we examine

$$Bu = f, \tag{54.2}$$

where B is a selfadjoint and positive operator which is *semi-similar to* A. The energy spaces $\mathfrak{H}_A$ and $\mathfrak{H}_B$ will consist of one and the same elements and their metrics will be equivalent. Hence, there exist constants α and β such that

$$\alpha|||u|||_B^2 \leqq |||u|||_A^2 \leqq \beta|||u|||_B^2, \qquad u \in \mathfrak{H}_A. \tag{54.3}$$

It is not difficult to see that, together with (54.1), equation (54.2) has a solution with finite energy. In fact, it follows from inequality (54.3) that the set $\mathfrak{M}$, which is dense in $\mathfrak{H}_A$, is also dense in $\mathfrak{H}_B$. Further, since the functional (u, f) is bounded in $\mathfrak{H}_A$,

$$|(u, f)| \leqq c|||u|||_A, \qquad c = \text{const.}$$

it follows that

$$|(u, f)| \leqq c\sqrt{\beta}|||u|||_B,$$

which implies that (u, f) is bounded in $\mathfrak{H}_B$, and hence, that (54.2) has a solution with finite energy. We denote this solution by u_1. Our immediate problem is to estimate $|||u_0-u_1|||_{\boldsymbol{B}}$.

For a suitable choice of (u,f), every element $u_1 \in \mathfrak{H}_{\boldsymbol{B}}$ is a solution of (54.2) with finite energy. It is sufficient to put $(u,f) = [u, u_1]_{\boldsymbol{B}}$. The operator which is defined by this relationship (maps u_1 of (54.2) into correspondence with u_0 of (54.1)) is itself defined on the whole space $\mathfrak{H}_{\boldsymbol{A}}$. We shall denote this operator by $\boldsymbol{T}$ such that $u_0 = \boldsymbol{T}u_1$.

We have

$$(u,f) = [u, u_0]_{\boldsymbol{A}}, \qquad (u,f) = [u, u_1]_{\boldsymbol{B}}, \qquad u \in \mathfrak{H}_{\boldsymbol{A}}.$$

Hence,

$$[u, \boldsymbol{T}u_1]_{\boldsymbol{A}} = [u, u_1]_{\boldsymbol{B}}, \qquad u \in \mathfrak{H}_{\boldsymbol{B}}.$$

Putting $u = u_1$, we find

$$[\boldsymbol{T}u_1, u_1]_{\boldsymbol{A}} = |||u_1|||_{\boldsymbol{B}}^2 > 0, \qquad u_1 \neq 0, \tag{54.4}$$

which implies that $\boldsymbol{T}$ is selfadjoint in $\mathfrak{H}_{\boldsymbol{A}}$. From (54.3), we obtain

$$\frac{1}{\beta}\,|||u_1|||_{\boldsymbol{A}}^2 \leqq [\boldsymbol{T}u_1, u_1]_{\boldsymbol{A}} \leqq \frac{1}{\alpha}\,|||u_1|||_{\boldsymbol{A}}^2.$$

This implies that the spectrum of $\boldsymbol{T}$, examined as an operator on $\mathfrak{H}_{\boldsymbol{A}}$, is contained in the interval $[(1/\beta), (1/\alpha)]$. Hence, the spectrum of $\boldsymbol{T}-\boldsymbol{I}$ is contained in $[(1/\beta)-1, (1/\alpha)-1]$ and

$$|||\boldsymbol{T}-\boldsymbol{I}|||_{\boldsymbol{A}} \leqq \max\left(\frac{|\alpha-1|}{\alpha}, \frac{|\beta-1|}{\beta}\right) = \eta. \tag{54.5}$$

Finally, we obtain the required estimate

$$|||u_1-u_0|||_{\boldsymbol{A}} = |||(\boldsymbol{T}-\boldsymbol{I})u_1|||_{\boldsymbol{A}} \leqq \eta|||u_1|||_{\boldsymbol{A}}. \tag{54.6}$$

We determine certain estimates as a consequence of (54.6). Firstly, using (54.3), we obtain

$$|||u_0-u_1|||_{\boldsymbol{A}} \leqq \eta\sqrt{\beta}|||u_1|||_{\boldsymbol{B}}, \tag{54.7}$$

$$|||u_0-u_1|||_{\boldsymbol{B}} \leqq \eta\sqrt{\frac{\beta}{\alpha}}\,|||u_1|||_{\boldsymbol{B}}. \tag{54.8}$$

A useful estimate can be obtained as follows: We replace $\boldsymbol{B}$ by $k\boldsymbol{B}$, where k is a positive constant, and endeavour to select k so that η becomes a minimum. For this purpose, we replace u_1 by $(1/k)u_1$ and α and β by α/k and β/k. The problem reduces to the choice of k for which

$$\max\left(\frac{|\alpha-k|}{\alpha}, \frac{|\beta-k|}{\beta}\right) = \min.$$

Arguing as in §12, we find that the minimum value of η equals $(\beta-\alpha)/(\beta+\alpha)$, where $1/k = \frac{1}{2}(1/\alpha)+(1/\beta)$, and arrive at a formula which was obtained by Slobodyanskiy [1] in the form:

$$\left|\left|\left|\frac{1}{2}\left(\frac{1}{\alpha}+\frac{1}{\beta}\right)u_1-u_0\right|\right|\right|_A \leqq \frac{\beta-\alpha}{2\alpha\beta}|||u_1|||_A. \tag{54.9}$$

Certain other estimates can be obtained, if it is assumed that, in (54.1) and (54.2), $f \in \mathfrak{H}$ and the solutions with finite energy u_0 and u_1 are simultaneously solutions in the usual sense of the word, so that $u_0 \in \mathfrak{D}(A)$ and $u_1 \in \mathfrak{D}(B)$. Hence, $u_0 \in \mathfrak{D}(A^{\frac{1}{2}})$ and $u_1 \in \mathfrak{D}(B^{\frac{1}{2}})$ simultaneously, which can be derived from the corresponding spectral representations. We construct the selfadjoint operator $Y = B^{-\frac{1}{2}}A^{\frac{1}{2}}A^{\frac{1}{2}}B^{-\frac{1}{2}}$ and seek bounds for its spectrum. We put $u = B^{-\frac{1}{2}}v$ in (54.3), where v is an arbitrary element of $\mathfrak{D}(B^{\frac{1}{2}}) = \mathfrak{D}(A^{\frac{1}{2}})$. We recall that

$$|||u|||_B^2 = ||B^{\frac{1}{2}}u||^2 = ||v||^2.$$

Further,

$$|||u|||_A^2 = ||A^{\frac{1}{2}}u||^2 = ||A^{\frac{1}{2}}B^{-\frac{1}{2}}v||^2 = (A^{\frac{1}{2}}B^{-\frac{1}{2}}v, A^{\frac{1}{2}}B^{-\frac{1}{2}}v) = (Yv, v),$$

and inequality (54.3) takes the form

$$\alpha||v||^2 \leqq (Yv, v) \leqq \beta||v||^2. \tag{54.10}$$

Inequality (54.10) holds for $v \in \mathfrak{D}(B^{\frac{1}{2}})$. Since $\mathfrak{D}(B^{\frac{1}{2}})$ is dense in $\mathfrak{H}$ and Y is bounded (A and B are semi-similar), (54.10) can be extended to the whole of $\mathfrak{H}$, and it is clear that the spectrum of Y lies in the interval $[\alpha, \beta]$. We put $v_0 = B^{\frac{1}{2}}u_0$ and $v_1 = B^{\frac{1}{2}}u_1$. Left multiplying $Au_0 = f$ with $B^{-\frac{1}{2}}$ and substituting $B^{-\frac{1}{2}}v_0$ for u_0, we obtain $Yv_0 = B^{-\frac{1}{2}}f = v_1$. It follows that $v_0-v_1 = (Y^{-1}-I)v$, and hence, $||v_0-v_1|| \leqq ||Y^{-1}-I||\,||v_1||$. Since the spectrum of $Y^{-1}-I$ is contained in the interval $[(1/\beta)-1, (1/\alpha)-1]$, $||Y^{-1}-I|| \leqq \eta$, where η is defined by (54.5). This gives

$$||v_0-v_1|| \leqq \eta||v_1||.$$

Since

$$\|v_0 - v_1\| = \|B^{\frac{1}{2}}(u_0 - u_1)\| = |||u_0 - u_1|||_B,$$
$$\|v_1\| = \|B^{\frac{1}{2}}u_1\| = |||u_1|||_B,$$

we obtain, finally,

$$|||u_0 - u_1|||_B \leqq \eta |||u_1|||_B. \tag{54.11}$$

This estimate differs from (54.6) in that it is evaluated w.r.t. the metric in $\mathfrak{H}_B$. A formula, analogous to (54.9), is also true

$$\left|\left|\left| \frac{1}{2}\left(\frac{1}{\alpha} + \frac{1}{\beta}\right) u_1 - u_0 \right|\right|\right|_B \leqq \frac{\beta - \alpha}{2\alpha\beta} |||u_1|||_B. \tag{54.12}$$

§55. Application to second order equations

1. ***The first boundary-value problem.***

Let Ω be a finite region of $\mathfrak{E}_m$ with coordinate $x_1, x_2, \ldots, x_m$ and sufficiently smooth boundary surface S. We pose for this region the problem of integrating the following non-degenerate elliptic equation

$$-\sum_{j,k=1}^{m} \frac{\partial}{\partial x_j}\left(A_{jk}(x)\frac{\partial u}{\partial x_k}\right) + A_0(x)u = f(x), \qquad A_{jk} = \bar{A}_{kj}, \tag{55.1}$$

for the boundary condition

$$u|_S = 0. \tag{55.2}$$

We assume that the coefficients $A_{jk}(x)$ and $A_0(x)$ are bounded and measurable in Ω. For simplicity, we assume also that $A_0(x) \geqq 0$ and $f \in L_2(\Omega)$. We denote the selfadjoint Friedrichs extension of (55.1) and (55.2) by A and the solution of $Au = f$ by $u_0(x)$. Further, u_1 denotes the solution of $Bu = f$, where B is the Friedrichs extension of the operator defined by (55.2) and the non-degenerate elliptic differential expression

$$-\sum_{j,k=1}^{m} \frac{\partial}{\partial x_j}\left(B_{jk}(x)\frac{\partial u}{\partial x_k}\right) + B_0(x)u, \qquad B_{jk} = \bar{B}_{kj}. \tag{55.3}$$

We assume that the coefficients B_{jk} and B_0 satisfy the same conditions as A_{jk} and A_0. We estimate the quotient

$$\frac{|||u_0 - u_1|||_B}{|||u_1|||_B}. \tag{55.4}$$

Since this follows from the results of the previous section, it will be sufficient to determine the constants α and β in (54.3).

We know that

$$|||u|||_A^2 = \int_\Omega \left\{ \sum_{j,k=1}^m A_{jk} \frac{\partial \bar{u}}{\partial x_j} \frac{\partial u}{\partial x_k} + A_0 |u|^2 \right\} dx,$$

$$|||u|||_B^2 = \int_\Omega \left\{ \sum_{j,k=1}^m B_{jk} \frac{\partial \bar{u}}{\partial x_j} \frac{\partial u}{\partial x_k} + B_0 |u|^2 \right\} dx,$$

and consider

$$\text{Det}\, |A_{jk}(x) - \kappa B_{jk}(x)| = 0.$$

We denote by $\kappa_1(x)$ and $\kappa_m(x)$ the smallest and largest roots of this equation. Further, if we put

$$\delta_1 = \inf_{x \in \Omega} \kappa_1(x), \qquad \delta_2 = \sup_{x \in \Omega} \kappa_m(x),$$

then we obtain

$$\begin{aligned}(\delta_1 - 1) \int_\Omega \sum_{j,k=1}^m \frac{\partial \bar{u}}{\partial x_j} \frac{\partial u}{\partial x_k} dx &\leqq \\ \leqq \int_\Omega \sum_{j,k=1}^m (A_{jk} - B_{jk}) \frac{\partial \bar{u}}{\partial x_j} \frac{\partial u}{\partial x_k} dx &\leqq \\ \leqq (\delta_2 - 1) \int_\Omega \sum_{j,k=1}^m B_{jk} \frac{\partial \bar{u}}{\partial x_j} \frac{\partial u}{\partial x_k} dx.&\end{aligned} \tag{55.5}$$

Next, we let λ_0 denote the smallest eigenvalue of

$$-\sum_{j,k=1}^m \frac{\partial}{\partial x_j} \left(B_{jk}(x) \frac{\partial u}{\partial x_k} \right) \tag{55.6}$$

w.r.t. the boundary condition (55.2). On putting

$$\delta_0 = \sup_{x \in \Omega} |A_0(x) - B_0(x)|,$$

we obtain

$$\begin{aligned}-\frac{\delta_0}{\lambda_0} \int_\Omega \sum_{j,k=1}^m B_{jk} \frac{\partial \bar{u}}{\partial x_j} \frac{\partial u}{\partial x_k} dx &\leqq \\ \leqq \int_\Omega (A_0 - B_0) |u|^2 dx \leqq \frac{\delta_0}{\lambda_0} \int_\Omega \sum_{j,k=1}^m B_{jk} \frac{\partial \bar{u}}{\partial x_j} \frac{\partial u}{\partial x_k} dx.&\end{aligned} \tag{55.7}$$

We combine (55.5) and (55.7) and then add $|||u|||_B^2$ to all the terms of the resulting inequality. This yields

$$\left(\delta_1-\frac{\delta_0}{\lambda_0}\right)\int_\Omega \sum_{j,k=1}^m B_{jk}\frac{\partial \bar{u}}{\partial x_j}\frac{\partial u}{\partial x_k}dx+\int_\Omega B_0|u|^2dx \leqq |||u|||_A \leqq$$

$$\leqq \left(\delta_2+\frac{\delta_0}{\lambda_0}\right)\int_\Omega \sum_{j,k=1}^m B_{jk}\frac{\partial \bar{u}}{\partial x_j}\frac{\partial u}{\partial x_k}dx+\int_\Omega B_0|u|^2dx. \tag{55.8}$$

It is now clear that inequality (54.3) is satisfied, if we put

$$\alpha = \min\left(\delta_1-\frac{\delta_0}{\lambda_0},\ 1\right), \qquad \beta = \max\left(\delta_2+\frac{\delta_0}{\lambda_0},\ 1\right). \tag{55.9}$$

We have assumed that $\delta_1-(\delta_0/\lambda_0) > 0$. In the special case when $A_0(x) = B_0(x) \equiv 0$, we can put

$$\alpha = \delta_1, \qquad \beta = \delta_2. \tag{55.10}$$

If $A_{jk}(x) \to B_{jk}(x)$ and $A_0(x) \to B_0(x)$ uniformly in Ω, then $\alpha \to 1$ and $\beta \to 1$. From the estimates of §51 and the positive definiteness of $\boldsymbol{B}$, it follows that

$$||u_0-u_1||_{W_2^{(1)}(\Omega)} \to 0. \tag{55.11}$$

The results of the present section apply, without change, to the case when Ω is an infinite region of type (2) (§41) except that λ_0 is now (not the smallest eigenvalue of (55.6) and (55.2)) the greatest lower bound for its spectrum. For the case of an infinite region of type (1), these results can be extended, if, for example, $A_0(x) = B_0(x)$. If $\inf\{A_0(x)\} = 0$, then (55.11) becomes

$$||\text{grad } u_0-\text{grad } u_1||_{L_2(\Omega)} \to 0. \tag{55.12}$$

2. ***The second boundary-value problem.***

We now assume that (55.1) is solvable w.r.t. the boundary condition

$$\left[\sum_{j,k=1}^m A_{jk}(x)\frac{\partial u}{\partial x_j}\cos(\nu, x_k)+\sigma_0(x)u\right]_S = 0, \tag{55.13}$$

and (55.3) w.r.t. the condition

$$\left[\sum_{j,k=1}^m B_{jk}(x)\frac{\partial u}{\partial x_j}\cos(\nu, x_k)+\sigma_1(x)u\right]_S = 0. \tag{55.14}$$

We subject A_0, B_0, A_{jk} and B_{jk} to the previous assumptions. As before, Ω is finite and S is sufficiently smooth. The functions $\sigma_0(x)$ and $\sigma_1(x)$, defined for $x \in S$, are assumed to be measurable, bounded and, for simplicity, positive, so that

$$\inf \sigma_0 > 0, \qquad \inf \sigma_1 > 0. \tag{55.15}$$

Let $\boldsymbol{A}$ and $\boldsymbol{B}$ denote the Friedrichs extensions of (55.1), (55.13) and (55.3), (55.14), respectively. Since these operators are positive definite and semi-similar, we can obtain an estimate for (55.4) by evaluating the constants α and β contained in (54.3).

Here, we have

$$|||u|||_{\boldsymbol{A}}^2 = \int_\Omega \left\{ \sum_{j,k=1}^m A_{jk} \frac{\partial \bar{u}}{\partial x_j} \frac{\partial u}{\partial x_k} + A_0|u|^2 \right\} dx + \int_S \sigma_0 |u|^2 dS,$$

$$|||u|||_{\boldsymbol{B}}^2 = \int_\Omega \left\{ \sum_{j,k=1}^m B_{jk} \frac{\partial \bar{u}}{\partial x_j} \frac{\partial u}{\partial x_k} + B_0|u|^2 \right\} dx + \int_S \sigma_1 |u|^2 dS.$$

We retain the notation δ_1, δ_2, and δ_0, and let λ_0 denote the smallest eigenvalue of (55.6) w.r.t. the boundary condition (55.14). Then inequalities (55.5) and (55.7) remain valid in this new context.

We put

$$\bar{\delta} = \sup_{x \in S} \frac{|\sigma_0(x) - \sigma_1(x)|}{\sigma_1(x)}. \tag{55.16}$$

It follows from (55.4) that δ is finite and $\delta \to 0$, if $\sigma_0(x) \to \sigma_1(x)$ uniformly on S. We now have

$$-\bar{\delta} \int_S \sigma_1 |u|^2 dS \leqq \int_S (\sigma_0 - \sigma_1)|u|^2 dS \leqq \delta \int_S \sigma_1 |u|^2 dS. \tag{55.17}$$

We first combine (55.5), (55.7) and (55.17), and then add $|||u|||_{\boldsymbol{B}}^2$ to all the terms of the resulting inequality. This yields

$$\left(\delta_1 - \frac{\delta_0}{\lambda_0}\right) \int_\Omega \sum_{j,k=1}^m B_{jk} \frac{\partial \bar{u}}{\partial x_j} \frac{\partial u}{\partial x_k} dx + \int_\Omega B_0 |u|^2 dx +$$

$$+ (1 - \bar{\delta}) \int_S \sigma_1 |u|^2 dS \leqq |||u|||_{\boldsymbol{A}}^2 \leqq$$

$$\leqq \left(\delta_2 + \frac{\delta_0}{\lambda_0}\right) \int_\Omega \sum_{j,k=1}^m B_{jk} \frac{\partial \bar{u}}{\partial x_j} \frac{\partial u}{\partial x_k} dx +$$

$$+ \int_\Omega B_0 |u|^2 dx + (1 + \bar{\delta}) \int_S \sigma_1 |u|^2 dS.$$

Hence, (54.3) is satisfied if we put

$$\alpha = \min\left(\delta_1 - \frac{\delta_0}{\lambda_0},\ 1-\bar{\delta}\right), \qquad \beta = \max\left(\delta_2 + \frac{\delta_0}{\lambda_0},\ 1+\bar{\delta}\right). \quad (55.18)$$

We assume that this last expression yields a positive value for α. A simpler, though somewhat different, case (with $A_0 = B_0 = \sigma_0 \equiv 0$) was explained in VM, §63

§56. Application to the linear theory of shells. Formulation of the problem

In this and the following sections of the present chapter, we shall be concerned with the estimation of the error for the approximation of elastic shells by plane plates. This problem arises in connection with the necessity to investigate the distribution of stresses in the blade of a water turbine. Such an investigation encounters considerable difficulties arising from the rather complex shape of the blade and the external conditions on its supports.

A turbine blade can be represented by a shell of variable thickness, which can be regarded as a weakly curved plate, in other words, as a gently curved shell with part of its edge rigidly fixed while the remainder is free. Thus, the idea of approximating the given shell by a plane plate arises in a natural way (see Kachanov [2]). In connection with this problem, it is useful to estimate the error associated with such an approximation. The general method for obtaining such estimates is given in §51. Below, we only apply it to the special case formulated here.

As is well known, there exist a number of independent forms for the equations of the theory of thin shells. These forms differ from the fundamental form in that certain terms in the latter can be regarded as small and are accordingly neglected. In Mikhlin [10], an independent form of the theory of shells is derived. As usual, the equations are obtained from the principle of minimum potential energy. However, as a preliminary, the energy integral is simplified by rejecting a number of terms which can be shown to be small (see Mikhlin [10]). The difference between the equations of Mikhlin [10] and those presented, for example, in the books of Vlasov [1] and Novozhilov [1], is not very fundamental.

The estimates mentioned above are derived w.r.t. the equations of Mikhlin [10]. The results are presented below. In the general case, the error associated with the replacement of a gently curving shell by a plane plate can be arbitrarily large if the thickness of the shell is sufficiently small. A favourable exception is presented by the purelyrotational stress case. Experimental investigations show (see Shikhobalov, Krasnov, Maksutova, Tseytts and Èdel'shteyn [1]) that, to a rather high degree of accuracy, the state of stress in a turbine blade is purely rotational. Our estimates show that the relative energy error for calculations based on the approximation of the blade by a plane plate, for various conditions on the blade, vary between 12.2% and 96.4%.

In the general case, an analysis of the reasons for the appearance of large errors, arising from the use of the thin plane plate, has resulted in the formulation of simple, more general and, possibly, more exact equations for the equilibrium of gently curving shells.

§57. The potential energy of deformation of a shell

We shall denote by Ω the mean surface of a shell. We assume, for simplicity, that it has a constant thickness of $2h$. We introduce the orthogonal curvilinear co-ordinates α_1, α_2 and α_3, where α_1 = const. and α_2 = const. are the lines of curvature on the mean surface Ω and α_3 is the distance from a given point to the point on Ω along the normal to Ω. With respect to the co-ordinates α_1 and α_2, let the arc length ds' on Ω be defined by

$$(ds')^2 = A_1^2(\alpha_1, \alpha_2)d\alpha_1^2 + A_2^2(\alpha_1, \alpha_2)d\alpha_2^2 .$$

Then, as is known, the arc length ds in space will be defined by

$$ds^2 = (1-2k_1\alpha_3)A_1^2 d\alpha_1^2 + (1-2k_2\alpha_2)A_2^2 s\alpha_2^2 + d\alpha_3^2,$$

where k_1 and k_2 are the principal curvatures of Ω. Hereafter, we assume that the coordinate mesh is such that the coefficients A_1 and A_2 are continuous, continuously differentiable and never equal zero on Ω.

We denote by u_1, u_2 and u_3 the components of the displacement vector $\boldsymbol{u}$ w.r.t. the axes α_1, α_2 and α_3, and by $e_{ik} = e_{ik}(\boldsymbol{u})$ the components of the deformation tensor. With respect to the local coordinates x_1, x_2 and x_3 (formed by the tangents to the coordinate lines), these components satisfy

$$e_{ik} = \frac{1}{2}\left(\frac{\partial u_i}{\partial x_k} + \frac{\partial u_k}{\partial x_i}\right). \tag{57.1}$$

We make the usual assumptions as in the theory of shells. For the evaluation of the potential energy of deformation, we can assume

$$e_{13} = e_{23} = 0, \qquad e_{33} = -\frac{\sigma}{1-\sigma}(e_{11}+e_{22}), \tag{57.2}$$

$$e_{ik} = \varepsilon_{ik}(\alpha_1, \alpha_2) + \alpha_3 \kappa_{ik}(\alpha_1, \alpha_2) \qquad (i, k = 1, 2), \tag{57.3}$$

where σ is Poisson's constant, ε_{ik} denotes the deformation of the mean surface Ω and κ_{ik} its distortion (twist). These quantities can be represented as the components of the two tensor E and K. With respect to the coordinates α_1 and α_2, the deformation and distortion are defined by

$$\begin{aligned}
\varepsilon_{11} &= \frac{1}{A_1}\frac{\partial w_1}{\partial \alpha_1} + \frac{1}{A_1 A_2}\frac{\partial A_1}{\partial \alpha_2} w_2 - k_1 w_3, \\
\varepsilon_{12} &= \frac{1}{2}\left\{\frac{A_1}{A_2}\frac{\partial}{\partial \alpha_2}\left(\frac{w_1}{A_1}\right) + \frac{A_2}{A_1}\frac{\partial}{\partial \alpha_1}\left(\frac{w_2}{A_2}\right)\right\}, \\
\varepsilon_{22} &= \frac{1}{A_1 A_2}\frac{\partial A_2}{\partial \alpha_1} w_1 + \frac{1}{A_2}\frac{\partial w_2}{\partial \alpha_2} - k_2 w_3,
\end{aligned} \tag{57.4}$$

$$\begin{aligned}
\kappa_{11} &= -\frac{1}{A_1}\frac{\partial k_1}{\partial \alpha_1} w_1 - \frac{1}{A_2}\frac{\partial k_1}{\partial \alpha_2} w_2 - k_1^2 w_3 - \\
&\quad - \frac{1}{A_1}\frac{\partial}{\partial \alpha_1}\left(\frac{1}{A_1}\frac{\partial w_3}{\partial \alpha_1}\right) - \frac{1}{A_1 A_2^2}\frac{\partial A_1}{\partial \alpha_2}\frac{\partial w_3}{\partial \alpha_2}, \\
\kappa_{12} &= \frac{1}{2}\left\{(k_2 - k_1)\left[\frac{A_1}{A_2}\frac{\partial}{\partial \alpha_2}\left(\frac{w_1}{A_1}\right) - \frac{A_2}{A_1}\frac{\partial}{\partial \alpha_2}\left(\frac{w_2}{A_2}\right)\right] - \right. \\
&\quad \left. - \frac{A_1}{A_2}\frac{\partial}{\partial \alpha_2}\left(\frac{1}{A_1^2}\frac{\partial w_3}{\partial \alpha_1}\right) - \frac{A_2}{A_1}\frac{\partial}{\partial \alpha_1}\left(\frac{1}{A_2^2}\frac{\partial w_3}{\partial \alpha_2}\right)\right\}, \\
\kappa_{22} &= -\frac{1}{A_1}\frac{\partial k_2}{\partial \alpha_1} w_1 - \frac{1}{A_2}\frac{\partial k_2}{\partial \alpha_2} w_2 - k_2^2 w_3 - \\
&\quad - \frac{1}{A_1^2 A_2}\frac{\partial A_2}{\partial \alpha_1}\frac{\partial w_3}{\partial \alpha_1} - \frac{1}{A_2}\frac{\partial}{\partial \alpha_2}\left(\frac{1}{A_2}\frac{\partial w_3}{\partial \alpha_2}\right),
\end{aligned} \tag{57.5}$$

where $w = (w_1, w_2, w_3)$ is the displacement vector for points on Ω.

If certain small terms are neglected, then the potential energy of deformation of a shell can be developed in the form

$$Э(w) = \frac{E}{2(1-\sigma^2)}\int_\Omega\int\Big\{h[\varepsilon_{11}^2+2\sigma\varepsilon_{11}\varepsilon_{12}+\varepsilon_{22}^2+2(1-\sigma)\varepsilon_{12}^2]+$$
$$+\frac{h^3}{12}[\kappa_{11}^2+2\sigma\kappa_{11}\kappa_{12}+\kappa_{22}^2+2(1-\sigma)\kappa_{12}^2]\Big\}\,dS, \tag{57.6}$$

where E is the modulus of elasticity of the material and $dS = A_1 A_2 d\alpha_1 d\alpha_2$ is an element of surface area of Ω.

A careful examination of the integrand in (57.6) yields the conclusion (for more detail, see Mikhlin [7] and [10]) that, under certain circumstances, terms, depending on the curvature and its derivatives, can be discarded from the expressions (57.5). In particular, this is possible in the following two cases:

(1) the stress condition in the shell is not purely rotational, so that the tensor $\bar{E}$ is not identically zero;

(2) the shell has a sufficiently gently curvature.

We formulate the last condition more exactly. Let the parameters α_1 and α_2 be dimensionless and the coordinate axes a right handed set such that A_1 and A_2 nowhere equal zero on Ω.

Our condition is that the products

$$A_i k_j, \qquad A_i\frac{\partial k_j}{\partial\alpha_m} \qquad (i, j, m = 1, 2), \tag{57.7}$$

must be sufficiently small.

Below we shall assume that one or the other (if not both) of the above conditions is fulfilled. In this way, we can write instead of (57.5) the comparatively simpler system

$$\begin{aligned}
\kappa_{11} &= -\frac{1}{A_1}\frac{\partial}{\partial\alpha_1}\left(\frac{1}{A_1}\frac{\partial w_3}{\partial\alpha_1}\right) - \frac{1}{A_1 A_2^2}\frac{\partial A_1}{\partial\alpha_2}\frac{\partial w_3}{\partial\alpha_2},\\
\kappa_{12} &= -\frac{1}{2}\left\{\frac{A_1}{A_2}\frac{\partial}{\partial\alpha_2}\left(\frac{1}{A_1^2}\frac{\partial w_3}{\partial\alpha_1}\right) + \frac{A_2}{A_1}\frac{\partial}{\partial\alpha_1}\left(\frac{1}{A_2^2}\frac{\partial w_3}{\partial\alpha_2}\right)\right\},\\
\kappa_{22} &= -\frac{1}{A_1^2 A_2}\frac{\partial A_2}{\partial\alpha_1}\frac{\partial w_3}{\partial\alpha_1} - \frac{1}{A_2}\frac{\partial}{\partial\alpha_2}\left(\frac{1}{A_2}\frac{\partial w_3}{\partial\alpha_2}\right).
\end{aligned} \tag{57.8}$$

It is important for the subsequent work that (57.8) remains valid for any orthogonal system of coordinate α_1 and α_2. As for equations (57.4), they are replaced by

$$\begin{aligned} \varepsilon_{11} &= \frac{1}{A_1}\frac{\partial w_1}{\partial \alpha_1} + \frac{1}{A_1 A_2}\frac{\partial A_1}{\partial \alpha_2} w_2 - \frac{L}{A_1^2} w_3, \\ \varepsilon_{12} &= \frac{1}{2}\left\{\frac{A_1}{A_2}\frac{\partial}{\partial \alpha_2}\left(\frac{w_1}{A_1}\right) + \frac{A_2}{A_1}\frac{\partial}{\partial \alpha_1}\left(\frac{w_2}{A_2}\right)\right\} - \frac{M}{A_1 A_2} w_3, \\ \varepsilon_{22} &= \frac{1}{A_1 A_2}\frac{\partial A_2}{\partial \alpha_1} w_1 + \frac{1}{A_2}\frac{\partial w_2}{\partial \alpha_2} - \frac{N}{A_2^2} w_3, \end{aligned} \tag{57.9}$$

where L, M and N are the coefficients of the second fundamental form of the surface Ω, defined w.r.t. some orthogonal coordinate system. We also note that (57.6) is valid for an arbitrary orthogonal coordinate system.

We shall only examine shells which have at least part of their boundary rigidly clamped. We shall prove that, if the deformation and distortion of the shell Ω is identically equal to zero, then the displacement of its points also equals zero.

We make use of an isometric coordinate system for which $A_1 = A_2 = A$. Equating the tensor K to zero, we obtain from (57.8)

$$\begin{aligned} \frac{\partial}{\partial \alpha_1}\left(\frac{1}{A}\frac{\partial w_2}{\partial \alpha_1}\right) + \frac{1}{A^2}\frac{\partial A}{\partial \alpha_2}\frac{\partial w_3}{\partial \alpha_2} &= 0, \\ \frac{\partial}{\partial \alpha_2}\left(\frac{1}{A}\frac{\partial w_3}{\partial \alpha_2}\right) + \frac{1}{A^2}\frac{\partial A}{\partial \alpha_1}\frac{\partial w_3}{\partial \alpha_1} &= 0, \end{aligned} \tag{57.10}$$

$$\frac{\partial}{\partial \alpha_2}\left(\frac{1}{A^2}\frac{\partial w_3}{\partial \alpha_1}\right) + \frac{\partial}{\partial \alpha_1}\left(\frac{1}{A^2}\frac{\partial w_3}{\partial \alpha_2}\right) = 0. \tag{57.11}$$

It follows from (57.11) that there exists a function $\psi(\alpha_1, \alpha_2)$ such that

$$\frac{\partial w_3}{\partial \alpha_1} = A^2 \frac{\partial \psi}{\partial \alpha_1}, \qquad \frac{\partial w_3}{\partial \alpha_2} = -A^2 \frac{\partial \psi}{\partial \alpha_2}. \tag{57.12}$$

Substituting this result in (57.10) and adding the two expressions, we obtain

$$\frac{\partial^2 \psi}{\partial \alpha_1^2} + \frac{\partial^2 \psi}{\partial \alpha_2^2} = 0.$$

In this way, $\psi(\alpha_1, \alpha_2)$ is a harmonic function defined on Ω. On the strength of the condition that some part of Ω is clamped,

$$w_3 = \frac{\partial w_3}{\partial v} = 0,$$

where v is the outward normal to the surface of Ω. It follows from here that

$$\frac{\partial w_1}{\partial \alpha_1} = \frac{\partial w_2}{\partial \alpha_2} = 0$$

on the clamped section of Ω, and, on the strength of (57.12),

$$\frac{\partial \psi}{\partial \alpha_1} = \frac{\partial \psi}{\partial \alpha_2} = 0.$$

Hence, ψ = const. on Ω and (57.12) implies that w_3 = const. Since $w_3 = 0$ on part of the boundary, $w_3 \equiv 0$.
By assumptions, the tensor $\bar{E} \equiv 0$. Taking into account that $w_3 \equiv 0$, we obtain from (57.9)

$$\frac{\partial w_1}{\partial \alpha_1} + \frac{1}{A}\frac{\partial A}{\partial \alpha_2} w_2 = 0, \qquad \frac{1}{A}\frac{\partial A}{\partial \alpha_1} w_1 + \frac{\partial w_2}{\partial \alpha_2} = 0, \tag{57.13}$$

$$\frac{\partial}{\partial \alpha_2}\left(\frac{w_1}{A}\right) + \frac{\partial}{\partial \alpha_1}\left(\frac{w_2}{A}\right) = 0. \tag{57.14}$$

It follows from (57.14) that there exists a function $\phi(\alpha_1, \alpha_2)$ such that

$$w_1 = A\frac{\partial \varphi}{\partial \alpha_1}, \qquad w_2 = -A\frac{\partial \phi}{\partial \alpha_2}.$$

Substituting this in (57.13) and adding the resulting expressions, we find

$$\frac{\partial^2 \phi}{\partial \alpha_1^2} + \frac{\partial^2 \phi}{\partial \alpha_2^2} = 0.$$

In this way, ϕ is harmonic in Ω. Since $w_1 = w_2 = 0$ (or $(\partial\phi/\partial\alpha_2) = (\partial\phi/\partial\alpha_2) = 0$) on the clamped section of the boundary, $\phi \equiv$ const., and hence, $w_1 = w_2 \equiv 0$.

§58. The shell-operator

We shall examine a shell the edge of which is either completely or partially rigidly clamped. In the latter case, we assume that the non-clamped section of the edge is free from the action of external forces.

The differential equations for the equilibrium of the shell and the natural boundary conditions on the non-clamped section of its boundary can be obtained in the usual way from the condition for the minimum of the potential energy of the shell

$$Э(w) - \int_{\Omega}\int qw\,dS, \tag{58.1}$$

where $Э(\omega)$ is defined by (57.6) and q is the external load vector acting on the shell. The operator, generated by the above differential equations and boundary conditions acting on the edge of Ω, will be denoted by $\boldsymbol{P}$, so that the totality of equilibrium equations and boundary conditions can be presented in the form

$$\boldsymbol{P}w = q. \tag{58.2}$$

Since it is not necessary, we shall not describe $\boldsymbol{P}$ in detail.

The operator $\boldsymbol{P}$ will be referred to as *the shell-operator*.

It is important to note that for $L = M = N = 0$, the operator $\boldsymbol{P}$ becomes the operator corresponding to the equilibrium problem for a plane disk, subject to the same loading and boundary conditions.

We introduce into the examination the real Hilbert space $\mathfrak{H}$ of functions defined on Ω. The scalar product and norm in $\mathfrak{H}$ are defined by

$$(W', W'') = \int_{\Omega}\int W'W''\,dS = \int_{\Omega}\int (W_1' W_1'' + W_2' W_2'' + W_3' W_3'')dS,$$

$$||W||^2 = \int_{\Omega}\int |W|^2\,dS = \int_{\Omega}\int (W_1^2 + W_2^2 + W_3^2)dS.$$

It is easily seen that $\boldsymbol{P}$ is symmetric and satisfies the identity

$$(\boldsymbol{P}w, w) = 2Э(w). \tag{58.3}$$

It follows from (58.3) that $\boldsymbol{P}$ is positive. In fact, $(\boldsymbol{P}w, w) \geqq 0$. If $(\boldsymbol{P}w, w) = 0$, then $Э(w) = 0$, and hence $\varepsilon_{ik} = 0$, $\kappa_{ik} = 0$. On the basis of the result in §54, $w \equiv 0$. We now prove that *the operator* $\boldsymbol{P}$ *is positive definite*. Here, we prove this result for the special case when the shell has a unique projection on a certain plane. We assume that the plane is the (x_1, x_2)-plane and define the coordinates x_1, x_2 and x_3 by

$$x_i = x_i(\alpha_1, \alpha_2, \alpha_3) \qquad (i = 1, 2, 3).$$

Then the equations

$$x_i = x_i(\alpha_1, \alpha_2, 0) \qquad (i = 1, 2)$$

define the projection Ω' of the mean surface of the shell on the (x_1, x_2)-plane. Accordingly, α_1 and α_2 can be regarded as orthogonal curvilinear coordinates in Ω' for which

$$ds^2 = dx_1^2 + dx_2^2 = A_1^2\, d\alpha_1^2 + A_2^2\, d\alpha_2^2 .$$

We assume that the operator $\boldsymbol{P}$ is not positive definite. Then there exists a sequence of vectors $\{w_n\} \in \mathfrak{D}(\boldsymbol{P})$ such that

$$Э(w_n) \xrightarrow[n\to\infty]{} 0, \qquad \|w_n\| = 1. \tag{58.4}$$

It follows from (54.6) that all the components of deformation $\varepsilon_{jk}^{(n)}$ and distortion $\kappa_{jk}^{(n)}$, corresponding to the vector w_n, tend to zero in $L_2(\Omega)$. We write

$$w_n = (w_1^{(n)}, w_2^{(n)}, w_3^{(n)}).$$

Equations (57.8) imply that the following limiting relationships are satisfied in $L_2(\Omega)$:

$$\begin{gathered}
\frac{\partial^2 w_3^{(n)}}{\partial \alpha_1^2} - \frac{1}{A_1}\frac{\partial A_1}{\partial \alpha_1}\frac{\partial w_3^{(n)}}{\partial \alpha_1} + \frac{A_1}{A_2^2}\frac{\partial A_1}{\partial \alpha_2}\frac{\partial w_3^{(n)}}{\partial \alpha_2} \to 0,\\
\frac{\partial^2 w_3^{(n)}}{\partial \alpha_1 \partial \alpha_2} - \frac{1}{A_1}\frac{\partial A_1}{\partial \alpha_2}\frac{\partial w_3^{(n)}}{\partial \alpha_1} - \frac{1}{A_2}\frac{\partial A_2}{\partial \alpha_1}\frac{\partial w_3^{(n)}}{\partial \alpha_2} \to 0,\\
\frac{\partial^2 w_3^{(n)}}{\partial \alpha_2^2} + \frac{A_2}{A_1^2}\frac{\partial A_2}{\partial \alpha_1}\frac{\partial w_3^{(n)}}{\partial \alpha_1} - \frac{1}{A_2}\frac{\partial A_2}{\partial \alpha_2}\frac{\partial w_3^{(n)}}{\partial \alpha_2} \to 0.
\end{gathered} \tag{58.5}$$

We prove that the second derivative of $w_3^{(n)}$ is bounded in $L_2(\Omega')$. We assume the opposite: There exists a sequence (as before, we denote it by $w_3^{(n)}$) such that

$$\sum_{j,k=1}^{2} \left\| \frac{\partial^2 w_3^{(n)}}{\partial \alpha_j \partial \alpha_k} \right\| \to \infty.$$

The l.h.s. of this last expression we denote by Q_n. For the functions $\tilde{w}_3^{(n)} = Q_n^{-1} w_3^{(n)}$, the relationships (58.5) remain valid. The norms of the second derivatives of these functions are bounded (they do not exceed unity), and the first derivatives of the same functions equal zero on the rigidly clamped section of the boundary. On the strength of the imbedding theorem, the first derivatives

$$\frac{\partial \tilde{w}_3^{(n)}}{\partial \alpha_1} \quad \text{and} \quad \frac{\partial \tilde{w}_3^{(n)}}{\partial \alpha_2}$$

and the functions $\tilde{w}_3^{(n)}$ are compact in $L_2(\Omega)$. Therefore, we can form a subsequence $\{\tilde{w}_3^{(n_k)}\}$ which converges to $\tilde{w}_3$ in $W_2^{(1)}(\Omega)$ and satisfies the conditions on the clamped section of the boundary.

It is implied by (58.5) that the second derivatives of $\tilde{w}_3^{(n_k)}$ also tend to a limit, and hence, $\tilde{w}_3 \in W_3^{(2)}(\Omega)$, and that the distortions, corresponding to the function $\tilde{w}_3$, are identically equal to zero. It follows, on the basis of §57, that $\tilde{w}_3 = 0$. However, this is not possible, since

$$\sum_{j,k=1}^{2} \left\| \frac{\partial^2 \tilde{w}_3}{\partial \alpha_j \partial \alpha_k} \right\| = \lim_{n\to\infty} \sum_{j,k=1}^{2} \left\| \frac{\partial^2 \tilde{w}_3^{(n)}}{\partial \alpha_j \partial \alpha_k} \right\| = 1.$$

Thus, the norms of the second derivatives of $w_3^{(n)}$ are bounded. Repeating the above argument, we can prove that

$$\|w_3^{(n)}\|_{W^{(2)}{}_2(\Omega)} \to 0,$$

and in particular, that

$$\|w_3^{(n)}\|_{L_2(\Omega)} \to 0.$$

It follows from (58.4) that

$$\|w_1^{(n)}\|^2 + \|w_2^{(n)}\|^2 \to 1, \tag{58.6}$$

and

$$\begin{gathered} \frac{1}{A_1}\frac{\partial w_1^{(n)}}{\partial \alpha_1} + \frac{1}{A_1 A_2}\frac{\partial A_1}{\partial \alpha_2} w_2^{(n)} \to 0, \\ \frac{1}{2}\left\{\frac{A_1}{A_2}\frac{\partial}{\partial \alpha_2}\left(\frac{w_1^{(n)}}{A_1}\right) + \frac{A_2}{A_1}\frac{\partial}{\partial \alpha_1}\left(\frac{w_2^{(n)}}{A_2}\right)\right\} \to 0, \\ \frac{1}{A_1 A_2}\frac{\partial A_2}{\partial \alpha_1} w_1 + \frac{1}{A_2}\frac{\partial w_2}{\partial \alpha_2} \to 0, \end{gathered} \tag{58.7}$$

where the limiting processes hold in $L_2(\Omega)$ and, what is the same thing, in $L_2(\Omega')$.

We shall examine the pair of functions $(w_1^{(n)}, w_2^{(n)})$ as a two-dimensional elastic displacement vector in the plane region Ω', where the l.h.s. of (58.7) become the corresponding deformations. On the basis of the clamped condition, the mentioned vector will equal zero on a section of the boundary of Ω'. In this case (see Eydus [1], [2] and PM, §43), the operator of the problem of the plane theory of elasticity is positive definite, which is inconsistent with the relationships (58.6) and (58.7). Hence, the positive definiteness of $\boldsymbol{P}$ is proved.

§59. Shells similar to plane plates

Consider a shell with a mean surface Ω and a plane plate with mean surface Ω^0. We denote by L and L^0 the boundaries of Ω and Ω^0. We introduce for Ω and Ω^0 the same coordinates α_1 and α_2 and assume, for simplicity, that the coordinates are orthogonal and have the same ranges in both Ω and Ω^0. This allows any function defined on the points of Ω or L to be examined as the same function on the points of Ω^0 or L^0. We assume that the same external load $q(\alpha_1, \alpha_2)$ is applied to the plate and the shell and that the boundary conditions (assumed to be homogeneous) are identical at the points of L and L^0 with the same coordinates. Under these conditions, let the load q determine displacement vectors w for the shell and w^0 for the plate.

Here and below, we shall denote by $\boldsymbol{P}^0$ the operator defined by the conditions on the plate. We recall that $\boldsymbol{P}^0$ is obtained formally from $\boldsymbol{P}$ when $L = M = N = 0$. It is clear that

$$(\boldsymbol{P}^0\boldsymbol{w}^0, \boldsymbol{w}^0) = 2Э^0(\boldsymbol{w}^0), \tag{59.1}$$

where $Э^0(w^0)$ is the potential energy of deformation of the plate corresponding to the displacement w^0.

In general, we shall use the superscript "0" to signify that a term referes to the plate as distinct from the shell. Thus, if ω is the displacement vector, then the deformation of the plate is defined by the following equations, which are marginally simpler for the plate than for the shell:

$$\varepsilon_{11}^0 = \frac{1}{A_1^0}\frac{\partial w_1}{\partial \alpha_1} + \frac{1}{A_1^0 A_2^0}\frac{\partial A_1^0}{\partial \alpha_2} w_2,$$

$$\varepsilon_{12}^0 = \frac{1}{2}\left\{\frac{A_1^0}{A_2^0}\frac{\partial}{\partial \alpha_2}\left(\frac{w_1}{A_1^0}\right) + \frac{A_2^0}{A_1^0}\frac{\partial}{\partial \alpha_1}\left(\frac{w_2}{A_2^0}\right)\right\}, \tag{59.2}$$

$$\varepsilon_{22}^0 = \frac{1}{A_1^0 A_2^0}\frac{\partial A_2^0}{\partial \alpha_1} w_1 + \frac{1}{A_2^0}\frac{\partial w_2}{\partial \alpha_2}.$$

The distortions and potential energy of deformation of the plate are defined by formulas completely analogous to (57.8) and (57.6).

For the usual conditions, one can estimate

$$\frac{\text{Э}^0(\boldsymbol{w}-\boldsymbol{w}^0)}{\text{Э}^0(\boldsymbol{w}^0)} \tag{59.3}$$

or, equivalently, estimate in the mean the error in evaluating the stresses when Ω is replaced by Ω^0.

The shell-operator $\boldsymbol{P}$ is defined on the set of vectors which have the necessary derivatives and satisfy the boundary conditions on L. Analogously, the plate-operator $\boldsymbol{P}^0$ is defined on the set of vectors which have the same derivatives as for $\boldsymbol{P}$ and satisfy the boundary conditions on L^0. Both domains coincide only when L, and hence L_0, are completely clamped. In this case, the boundary conditions on both L and L^0 take the form (58.6). If only sections L' and $L^{0\prime}$ of the contours L and L^0 are clamped, then the boundary conditions on L' and $L^{0\prime}$ coincide and have the form (58.6). On the unclamped sections of the contours, the boundary conditions differ. In this case, the domains of $\boldsymbol{P}$ and $\boldsymbol{P}^0$ differ.

It is not difficult to see that the energy spaces of the operators $\boldsymbol{P}$ and $\boldsymbol{P}^0$ consist of the vectors which have generalised first derivatives w.r.t. α_1 and α_2, are square summable and satisfy (58.6) for the values of α_1 and α_2, defining the sections of the contour L' and $L^{0\prime}$. It follows that $\boldsymbol{P}$ and $\boldsymbol{P}^0$ are semi-similar.

We have estimated (59.3) once we have determined the constants α and β such that

$$\alpha(\boldsymbol{P}^0\boldsymbol{w}, \boldsymbol{w}) \leqq (\boldsymbol{P}\boldsymbol{w}, \boldsymbol{w}) \leqq \beta(\boldsymbol{P}^0\boldsymbol{w}, \boldsymbol{w}),$$

or, equivalently,

$$\alpha\text{Э}^0(\boldsymbol{w}) \leqq \text{Э}(\boldsymbol{w}) \leqq \beta\text{Э}^0(\boldsymbol{w}), \tag{59.4}$$

where $\boldsymbol{w}$ is an arbitrary vector in $\mathfrak{H}_{\boldsymbol{P}}$.

We assume that the shell is similar in shape to the plane plate Ω: namely, we assume that the quantities

$$|A_i - A_i^0|, \qquad \left|\frac{\partial A_i}{\partial \alpha_k} - \frac{\partial A_i^0}{\partial \alpha_k}\right|, \qquad |L|, \qquad |M|, \qquad |N|$$

do not exceed a certain sufficiently small value γ.

We introduce the notation

$$U_\varepsilon = \varepsilon_{11}^2 + 2\sigma\varepsilon_{11}\varepsilon_{22} + \varepsilon_{22}^2 + 2(1-\sigma)\varepsilon_{12}^2,$$
$$U_\kappa = \kappa_{11}^2 + 2\sigma\kappa_{11}\kappa_{22} + \kappa_{22}^2 + 2(1-\sigma)\kappa_{12}^2,$$

while U_ε^0 and U_κ^0 denote the results of replacing ε_{ik} by ε_{ik}^0 and κ_{ik} by κ_{ik}^0 in the expressions for U_ε and U_κ, respectively. We also write

$$2Э_\varepsilon = \frac{Eh}{1-\sigma^2}\int_\Omega\int U_\varepsilon\, dS, \qquad 2Э_\kappa = \frac{Eh^3}{12(1-\sigma^2)}\int_\Omega\int U_\kappa\, dS,$$

$$2Э_\varepsilon^0 = \frac{Eh}{1-\sigma^2}\int_{\Omega^0}\int U_\varepsilon^0\, dS^0, \qquad 2Э_\kappa^0 = \frac{Eh^3}{12(1-\sigma^2)}\int_{\Omega^0}\int U_\kappa^0\, dS,$$

where dS^0 is an element of area in the plane (x_1, x_2). It is clear that

$$Э = Э_\varepsilon + Э_\kappa, \qquad Э^0 = Э_\varepsilon^0 + Э_\kappa^0.$$

Equating the expressions for ε_{ik} and ε_{ik}^0 {equations (57.9) and (59.2)}, corresponding to one and the same displacement vector $\boldsymbol{w}$, we find

$$\varepsilon_{11} = \varepsilon_{11}^0 + \left(\frac{A_1^0}{A_1} - 1\right)\varepsilon_{11}^0 + \frac{1}{A_1}\left(\frac{1}{A_2}\frac{\partial A_1}{\partial \alpha_2} - \frac{1}{A_2^0}\frac{\partial A_1^0}{\partial \alpha_2}\right) w_2 - \frac{L}{A_1^2} w_3,$$

$$\varepsilon_{22} = \varepsilon_{22}^0 + \left(\frac{A_2^2}{A_2} - 1\right)\varepsilon_{22}^0 + \frac{1}{A_2}\left(\frac{1}{A_1}\frac{\partial A_2}{\partial \alpha_1} - \frac{1}{A_1^0}\frac{\partial A_2^0}{\partial \alpha_1}\right) w_2 - \frac{N}{A_2^2} w^3,$$

$$\varepsilon_{12} = \varepsilon_{12}^0 + \frac{1}{2}\left\{\left(\frac{1}{A_2} - \frac{1}{A_2^0}\right)\frac{\partial w_1}{\partial \alpha_2} + \left(\frac{1}{A_1} - \frac{1}{A_1^0}\right)\frac{\partial w_2}{\partial \alpha_2}\right\} - \tag{59.5}$$
$$- \left(\frac{1}{A_1A_2}\frac{\partial A_1}{\partial \alpha_2} - \frac{1}{A_1^0A_2^0}\frac{\partial A_1^0}{\partial \alpha_2}\right) w_1 -$$
$$- \left(\frac{1}{A_1A_2}\frac{\partial A_2}{\partial \alpha_1} - \frac{1}{A_1^0A_1^0}\frac{\partial A_2^0}{\partial \alpha_1}\right) w_2 - \frac{M}{A_1A_2} w_3.$$

Substituting (59.5) in U_ε, we easily obtain the inequality

$$\frac{Eh}{1-\sigma^2}\,|U_\varepsilon - U_\varepsilon^0| \leqq C_1 \gamma h \left\{ \sum_{j,k=1}^{2} \left(\frac{\partial w_j}{\partial \alpha_k}\right)^2 + \sum_{j=1}^{3} w_j^2 \right\},$$

where C_1 is a constant. Here and below, the C_i will denote positive constants which depend only on the form of Ω^0, the clamped condition on the boundary and the constant E and σ. Integrating the last inequality over Ω^0, we obtain

$$\left| \frac{Eh}{1-\sigma^2} \int_{\Omega} \int U_\varepsilon \, dS^0 - 2\mathcal{E}_\varepsilon^0 \right| \leqq C_1 \gamma h \int_{\Omega^0} \int \left\{ \sum_{j,k=1}^{2} \left(\frac{\partial w_j}{\partial \alpha_k}\right)^2 + \sum_{j=1}^{3} w_j^2 \right\} dS^0. \tag{59.6}$$

In an elastic body, for which a section of the boundary is clamped, Korn's inequality is valid (see the introductory remarks at the beginning of this chapter). For a plane plate, it takes the form

$$h \int_{\Omega^0} \int \sum_{j,k=1}^{2} \left(\frac{\partial w_j}{\partial \alpha_k}\right)^2 dS_0 \leqq 2C_2 \mathcal{E}_\varepsilon^0. \tag{59.7}$$

On the basis of the imbedding theorem, an arbitrary function U, which equals zero on the curve $L^{0\prime}$, satisfies

$$\int_{\Omega^0} \int u^2 \, dS^0 \leqq C_3 \int_{\Omega^0} \int \left\{ \left(\frac{\partial u}{\partial \alpha_1}\right)^2 + \left(\frac{\partial u}{\partial \alpha_2}\right)^2 \right\} dS^0.$$

This last inequality, together with Korn's inequality, yields

$$h \int_{\Omega^0} \int (w_1^2 + w_2^2) dS^0 \leqq C_3 h \int_{\Omega^0} \int \sum_{j,k=1}^{2} \left(\frac{\partial w_j}{\partial \alpha_k}\right)^2 dS^0 \leqq 2C_4 \mathcal{E}_\varepsilon^0. \tag{59.8}$$

Using (59.7) and (59.8), (59.6) can be changed to the form

$$\left| \frac{Eh}{1-\sigma^2} \int_{\Omega^0} \int U_\varepsilon \, dS^0 - 2\mathcal{E}_\varepsilon^0 \right| \leqq 2C_5 \gamma h \mathcal{E}_\varepsilon^0 + C_1 \gamma h \int_{\Omega^0} \int w_3^2 \, dS^0. \tag{59.9}$$

We evaluate an estimate for

$$\int_{\Omega^0} \int w_3^2 \, dS^0.$$

The function w_3 and its first derivative equal zero on $L^{0\prime}$. It follows, on using the imbedding theorem, that

$$\int_{\Omega^0}\!\!\int w_3^2\,dS^0 \leqq C_6 \int_{\Omega^0}\!\!\int \left\{\left(\frac{\partial w_3}{\partial x_1}\right)^2 + \left(\frac{\partial w_3}{\partial x_2}\right)^2\right\} dS^0 \leqq$$

$$\leqq C_6^2 \int_{\Omega^0}\!\!\int \sum_{j,k=1}^{2} \left(\frac{\partial^2 w_3}{\partial x_j \partial x_k}\right)^2 dS^0,$$

where x_1 and x_2 are the Cartesian coordinates on Ω^0. With respect to the Cartesian coordinates

$$\kappa_{jk}^0 = -\frac{\partial^2 w_3}{\partial x_j \partial x_k},$$

and since U_κ^0 is a positive definite quadratic form w.r.t. the variables κ_{jk}^0

$$C_1 \int_{\Omega^0}\!\!\int w_3^2\,dS^0 \leqq \frac{2}{h^3} C_7 \ni_\kappa^0.$$

Substituting this result in (59.9), we obtain, finally,

$$\left|\frac{Eh}{1-\sigma^2}\int_{\Omega^0}\!\!\int U_\varepsilon\,dS^0 - 2\ni_\varepsilon^0\right| \leqq 2C_5\gamma\ni_\varepsilon^0 + \frac{2C_7\gamma}{h^2}\ni_\kappa^0. \tag{59.10}$$

It is not difficult to deduce from (54.8) that

$$\kappa_{jk} = \kappa_{jk}^0 + a_{jk}\kappa_{jk}^0 + b_{jk}\frac{\partial w_3}{\partial \alpha_1} + c_{jk}\frac{\partial w_3}{\partial \alpha_2},$$

where a_{jk}, b_{jk} and c_{jk} are of order γ. Substituting this result in U_κ and integrating, we obtain

$$\left|\frac{Eh^3}{12(1-\sigma^2)}\int_{\Omega^0}\!\!\int U_\kappa\,dS^0 - 2\ni_\kappa^0\right| \leqq$$

$$\leqq C_8\gamma\left\{2\ni_\kappa^0 + h^3\int_{\Omega^0}\!\!\int \left[\left(\frac{\partial w_3}{\partial \alpha_1}\right)^2 + \left(\frac{\partial w_3}{\partial \alpha_2}\right)^2\right] dS^0\right\}.$$

Since, as above, the last integral can be estimated in terms of $\ni_\kappa^0$, we obtain

$$\left|\frac{Eh^3}{12(1-\sigma^2)}\int_{\Omega^0}\!\!\int U_\kappa\,dS^0 - 2\ni_\kappa^0\right| \leqq 2C_9\gamma\ni_\kappa^0. \tag{59.11}$$

It follows from (59.10) and (59.11) that

$$\left| \frac{Eh}{1-\sigma^2} \int_{\Omega^0}\!\!\int \left(U_\varepsilon + \frac{h^2}{12} U_\kappa \right) dS^0 - 2\text{Э}^0 \right| \leqq 2\left(C_{10} + \frac{C_7}{h^2} \right) \gamma \text{Э}^0. \tag{59.12}$$

We now examine

$$2\text{Э} = \frac{Eh}{1-\sigma^2} \int_{\Omega^0}\!\!\int \left(U_\varepsilon + \frac{h^2}{12} U_\kappa \right) dS. \tag{59.13}$$

We know that

$$dS = A_1 A_2 \, d\alpha_1 \, d\alpha_2 , \qquad dS^0 = A_1^0 A_2^0 \, d\alpha_1 \, d\alpha_2 ,$$

and hence,

$$dS = \frac{A_1 A_2}{A_1^0 A_2^0} dS^0 = (1+B) dS^0,$$

where $0 \leqq B = 0(\gamma)$. We write $C_{11}\gamma \leqq B \leqq C_{12}\gamma$, where C_{11} can equal zero. Then

$$2\text{Э} = \frac{Eh}{(1-\sigma^2)} \int_{\Omega^0}\!\!\int \left(U_\varepsilon + \frac{h^2}{12} U_\kappa \right) (1+B) dS^0,$$

and hence,

$$\begin{aligned} C_{11}\gamma \frac{Eh}{1-\sigma^2} \int_{\Omega^0}\!\!\int \left(U_\varepsilon + \frac{h^2}{12} U_\kappa \right) dS^0 \leqq \\ \leqq 2\text{Э} - \frac{Eh}{1-\sigma^2} \int_{\Omega^0}\!\!\int \left(U_\varepsilon + \frac{h^2}{12} U_\kappa \right) dS^0 \leqq \\ \leqq C_{12}\gamma \frac{Eh}{1-\sigma^2} \int_{\Omega^0}\!\!\int \left(U_\varepsilon + \frac{h^2}{12} U_\kappa \right) dS^0. \end{aligned}$$

We replace the integrals in the first and third terms of the last inequality by the estimate given by (59.12):

$$2\text{Э}^0(1-\gamma\Gamma) \leqq \frac{Eh}{1-\sigma^2} \int_{\Omega^0}\!\!\int \left(U_\varepsilon + \frac{h^2}{12} U_\kappa \right) dS^0 \leqq 2\text{Э}^0(1+\gamma\Gamma),$$

where, for brevity, we have written

$$\Gamma = C_{10} + \frac{C_7}{h^2}. \tag{59.14}$$

This leads to the inequality

$$2\text{Э}^0 C_{11}\gamma(1-\gamma\Gamma) \leqq 2\text{Э} - \frac{Eh}{1-\sigma^2}\int_{\Omega^0}\!\!\int \left(U_\varepsilon + \frac{h^2}{12}U_\kappa\right) dS^0 \leqq$$

$$\leqq 2\text{Э}^0 C_{12}\gamma(1+\gamma\Gamma),$$

whence we obtain from (59.12)

$$-\gamma[\Gamma - C_{11}(1-\gamma\Gamma)]\text{Э}^0 \leqq \text{Э} - \text{Э}^0 \leqq \gamma[\Gamma + C_{12}(1+\gamma\Gamma)]\text{Э}^0,$$

and, from (59.4)

$$\alpha = 1-\gamma[\Gamma - C_{11}(1-\gamma\Gamma)], \qquad \beta = 1+\gamma[\Gamma + C_{12}(1+\gamma\Gamma)]. \quad (59.15)$$

If (59.15) yields a positive value for α, then the following estimate holds for (59.3):

$$\frac{\text{Э}^0(w-w^0)}{\text{Э}^0(w^0)} \leqq \max\left(\frac{|\alpha-1|}{\alpha}, \frac{|\beta-1|}{\beta}\right) =$$

$$= \max\left\{\frac{\gamma[\Gamma - C_{11}(1-\gamma\Gamma)]}{1-\gamma[\Gamma - C_{11}(1-\gamma\Gamma)]}, \frac{\gamma[\Gamma + C_{12}(1+\gamma\Gamma)]}{1+\gamma[\Gamma + C_{12}(1+\gamma\Gamma)]}\right\}. \quad (59.16)$$

§60. The purely rotational state of stress

We assume that γ is small. If the stress in a shell Ω is determined approximately by replacing Ω by a suitable plane plate Ω^0, then it follows from (59.14) and (59.16) that the error in such a calculation has order $\gamma(a+(b/h^2))$, where a and b are positive constants. It follows that, even for arbitrarily small γ, this error can be arbitrary large, if the shell is sufficiently thin. Hence, in the general case, the replacement of a shell by a suitable plane plate for the calculation of approximate stresses is impossible. The term b/h^2 can be removed from the error estimate if, in the process of obtaining the deformation (59.2) from (57.9), the terms

$$-\frac{L}{A_1^2}w_3, \; -\frac{M}{A_1 A_2}w_3 \quad \text{and} \quad -\frac{N}{A_2^2}w_3$$

are retained. This reduces in the final calculation to the equilibrium equations for a shell with a sufficiently gentle curvature. We shall not stop to do this here (see Mikhlin [7] and [10]), but turn to the case when the term b/h^2 does not occur at all in the estimate. This is the socalled *purely rotational* stress condition where $\varepsilon_{jk} \equiv 0$. We shall examine this case in more detail. We have $Э = Э_\kappa$, $Э^0 = Э_\kappa^0$. Formula (59.11) becomes

$$\left| \frac{Eh^3}{12(1-\sigma^2)} \int_{\Omega^0} \int U_\kappa \, dS^0 - 2Э^0 \right| \leqq 2C_9 \gamma Э^0. \tag{60.1}$$

As in § 59, we set $dS = (1+\mathrm{B})\, dS^0$ and $C_{11}\gamma \leqq B \leqq C_{12}\gamma$. Then

$$C_{11}\gamma \frac{Eh^3}{12(1-\sigma^2)} \int_{\Omega^0} \int U_\kappa \, dS^0 \leqq 2Э - \frac{Eh^3}{12(1-\sigma^2)} \int_{\Omega^0} \int U_\kappa \, dS^0 \leqq$$
$$\leqq C_{12}\gamma \frac{Eh^3}{12(1-\sigma^2)} \int_{\Omega^0} \int U_\kappa \, dS^0. \tag{60.2}$$

It follows from (60.1) that

$$2(1-C_8\gamma)Э^0 \leqq \frac{Eh^3}{12(1-\sigma^2)} \int_{\Omega^0} \int U_\kappa \, dS^0 \leqq 2(1+C_8\gamma)Э^0. \tag{60.3}$$

Substituting this result in the first and last terms of (60.2), we obtain

$$2(1-C_8\gamma)C_{11}\gamma Э^0 \leqq 2Э - \frac{Eh^3}{12(1-\sigma^2)} \int_{\Omega^0} \int U_\kappa \, dS^0 \leqq$$
$$\leqq 2(1+C_8\gamma)C_{12}\gamma Э^0.$$

Combining this with (60.3), we deduce the required estimate

$$(1-C_8\gamma)(1+C_{11}\gamma)Э^0 \leqq Э \leqq (1+C_8\gamma)(1+C_{12}\gamma)Э^0. \tag{60.4}$$

If $\gamma < (1/C_8)$, inequality (60.4) yields an estimate for (59.3):

$$\frac{Э^0(w-w^0)}{Э^0(w^0)} \leqq \max \left\{ \frac{|C_{11}-C_8-C_8 C_{11}\gamma|\gamma}{(1-C_8\gamma)(1+C_{11}\gamma)}, \frac{(C_8+C_{12}+C_8 C_{12}\gamma)\gamma}{(1+C_8\gamma)(1+C_{11}\gamma)} \right\}. \tag{60.5}$$

In general, the r.h.s. of (60.5) can be reduced, if use is made of (54.12).

§61. Helical shells

In connection with the stress in a turbine blade, it proves to be of interest to apply (57.6) to a shell for which the mean surface Ω is part of the right helicoid

$$x = \rho \cos\theta, \qquad y = \rho \sin\theta, \qquad z = \zeta\theta, \tag{61.1}$$

defined by

$$\rho_0 \leqq \rho \leqq \rho_1, \qquad -\theta_0 \leqq \theta \leqq \theta_0, \tag{61.2}$$

where ρ_0, ρ_1 and θ_0 are positive constants. Let the following section of the inner boundary

$$\rho = \rho_0, \qquad \vartheta_1 < \theta < \vartheta_2, \tag{61.3}$$

be rigidly fixed and the remainder of the boundary of the shell be free from external forces. The lines ρ = const. and θ = const. are orthogonal on the helicoid and we take them as coordinates: We put $\alpha_1 = \rho$ and $\alpha_2 = \theta$. With respect to the coordinates ρ and θ, the element of length on the helicoid is defined by

$$ds^2 = d\rho^2 + (\rho^2 + \zeta^2)d\theta^2,$$

so that

$$A_1 = 1, \qquad A_2 = \sqrt{\rho^2 + \zeta^2}.$$

Since the components of displacement w_1 and w_2 will not arise in the following examination, we shall write w instead of w_3. On the basis of (57.8), we have

$$\begin{aligned} \kappa_{11} &= -\frac{\partial^2 w}{\partial \rho^2}, \qquad \kappa_{22} = -\frac{1}{\rho^2+\zeta^2}\frac{\partial^2 w}{\partial \theta^2} - \frac{\rho}{\rho^2+\zeta^2}\frac{\partial w}{\partial \rho}, \\ \kappa_{12} &= -\frac{1}{2}\left\{\frac{1}{\sqrt{\rho^2+\zeta^2}}\frac{\partial^2 w}{\partial \rho\, \partial \theta} + \sqrt{\rho^2+\zeta^2}\,\frac{\partial}{\partial \rho}\left(\frac{1}{\rho^2+\zeta^2}\frac{\partial w}{\partial \theta}\right)\right\}. \end{aligned} \tag{61.4}$$

We replace the shell by a plane plate Ω^0 of the same thickness. We shall assume that Ω^0 is a section of the circular ring defined by (61.2). Hence, we have

$$\begin{aligned} &A_1^0 = 1, \qquad A_2^0 = \rho, \\ &\kappa_{11}^0 = -\frac{\partial^2 w}{\partial \rho^2}, \qquad \kappa_{22}^0 = -\frac{1}{\rho^2}\frac{\partial^2 w}{\partial \theta^2} - \frac{1}{\rho}\frac{\partial w}{\partial \rho}, \\ &\kappa_{12}^0 = -\frac{1}{\rho}\frac{\partial^2 w}{\partial \theta^2} + \frac{1}{2\rho^2}\frac{\partial w}{\partial \theta}. \end{aligned} \tag{61.5}$$

In accordance with the general conditions of §59, we assume that the external load has equal values at the points of the shell and the plate with the same ρ and θ, and that the edge of the plate is free except for the rigidly clamped section (61.3). We estimate the error in the solution arising from this replacement. We have

$$2Э = D\int_{\Omega}\int [\kappa_{11}^2+2\sigma\kappa_{11}\kappa_{22}+\kappa_{22}^2+2(1-\sigma)\kappa_{12}^2]dS, \tag{61.6}$$

$$2Э^0 = D\int_{\Omega^0}\int [\kappa_1^{02}+2\sigma\kappa_{11}^0\kappa_{22}^0+\kappa_{22}^{02}+2(1-\sigma)\kappa_{12}^{02}]dS^0, \tag{61.7}$$

where

$$D = \frac{Eh^3}{12(1-\sigma^2)}.$$

Since D will cancel itself in (59.3), we assume that $D = 1$.
It follows from (61.4) and (61.5) that

$$\begin{aligned} \kappa_{11} &= \kappa_{11}^0, \qquad \kappa_{22} = (1-r)\kappa_{22}^0, \\ \kappa_{12} &= (1-s)\kappa_{12}^0 - t\,\frac{1}{\rho\rho_0}\,\frac{\partial w}{\partial\theta}, \end{aligned} \tag{61.8}$$

where

$$\begin{aligned} r &= \frac{\zeta^2}{\rho^2+\zeta^2}, \qquad s = \frac{\zeta^2}{\sqrt{\rho^2+\zeta^2}(\sqrt{\rho^2+\zeta^2}+\rho)}, \\ t &= \frac{\rho_0\zeta^4}{\rho(\rho^2+\zeta^2)(\sqrt{\rho^2+\zeta^2}+\rho)^2} = \frac{\rho_0}{\rho}\,s^2. \end{aligned} \tag{61.9}$$

We let U and U^0 denote the integrands of (61.6) and (61.7). Using (61.8), we find

$$\begin{aligned} U = U^0 &- [(2r-r^2)\kappa_{22}^{02}+2\sigma r\kappa_{11}^0\kappa_{22}^0] - \\ &-2(1-\sigma)\left[(2s-s^2)\kappa_{12}^{02}+2(1-s)t\kappa_{22}^{02}\left(\frac{1}{\rho\rho_0}\,\frac{\partial w}{\partial\theta}\right) - \right. \\ &\left. -t^2\left(\frac{1}{\rho\rho_0}\,\frac{\partial w}{\partial\theta}\right)^2\right] = U^0-F_1-2(1-\sigma)F_2. \end{aligned} \tag{61.10}$$

Forming elementary estimates and then integrating, we obtain inequalities of the form

$$-\delta'\ni^0(w)-\frac{\delta''}{\rho_0^2}\int_{\Omega^0}\!\!\int\left(\frac{1}{\rho}\frac{\partial w}{\partial\theta}\right)^2 dS^0 \leqq$$

$$\leqq \ni(w)-\ni^0(w) \leqq \delta_1'\ni^0(w)+\frac{\delta_1''}{\rho_0^2}\int_{\Omega^0}\!\!\int\left(\frac{1}{\rho}\frac{\partial w}{\partial\theta}\right)^2 dS^0. \qquad (61.11)$$

Since the construction of (61.11) for a numerical example will be considered in the following section, we return to the problem: in order to proceed from (61.11) to (59.5) it is necessary for us to obtain relationships of the form

$$\int_{\Omega^0}\!\!\int\left(\frac{1}{\rho}\frac{\partial w}{\partial\theta}\right)^2 dS^0 \leqq k\ni^0(w) \qquad (61.12)$$

and to determine the constant k in this expression. The formula

$$(\text{grad } w)^2 = \left(\frac{\partial w}{\partial\rho}\right)^2+\left(\frac{1}{\rho}\frac{\partial w}{\partial\theta}\right)^2$$

allows us to concentrate on the stronger inequality

$$\int_{\Omega^0}\!\!\int (\text{grad } w)^2\, dS^0 \leqq k\ni^0(w). \qquad (61.13)$$

It must be established for functions which, together with their first derivatives, equal zero on the following sections of the boundary:

$$\rho=\rho_0, \qquad \vartheta_1 \leqq \theta \leqq \vartheta_2. \qquad (61.14)$$

We transform (61.13) to Cartesian coordinates to obtain

$$\int_{\Omega^0}\!\!\int\left\{\left(\frac{\partial w}{\partial x}\right)^2+\left(\frac{\partial w}{\partial y}\right)^2\right\} dS^0 \leqq$$

$$\leqq \frac{k}{2}\int_{\Omega^0}\!\!\int\left\{\left(\frac{\partial^2 w}{\partial x^2}\right)^2+2\sigma\frac{\partial^2 w}{\partial x^2}\frac{\partial^2 w}{\partial y^2}+\left(\frac{\partial^2 w}{\partial y^2}\right)^2+\right.$$

$$\left.+2(1-\sigma)\left(\frac{\partial^2 w}{\partial x\,\partial y}\right)^2\right\} dS^0. \qquad (61.15)$$

Since the Poisson constant σ varies in the interval $-1<\sigma<\frac{1}{2}$, $|\sigma|<1$. For arbitrary real a and b, the inequality

$$a^2+2\sigma ab+b^2 \geqq (1-|\sigma|)(a^2+b^2),$$

is valid and, instead of (16.15), we can establish the stronger inequality

$$\int_{\Omega^0}\int \left\{\left(\frac{\partial w}{\partial x}\right)^2 + \left(\frac{\partial w}{\partial y}\right)^2\right\} dS^0 \leqq$$

$$\leqq \frac{k(1-|\sigma|)}{2}\int_{\Omega^0}\int \left\{\left(\frac{\partial^2 w}{\partial x^2}\right)^2 + 2\left(\frac{\partial^2 w}{\partial x\,\partial y}\right)^2 + \left(\frac{\partial^2 w}{\partial y^2}\right)^2\right\} dS^0. \quad (61.16)$$

Let $u(x, y)$ be an arbitrary function of $W_2^{(1)}(\Omega^0)$, which equals zero on the line (61.14), and let us try to find the constant λ_0 such that

$$\int_{\Omega^0}\int u^2\, dS^0 \leqq \frac{1}{\lambda_0}\int_{\Omega^0}\int \left\{\left(\frac{\partial u}{\partial x}\right)^2 + \left(\frac{\partial u}{\partial y}\right)^2\right\} dS^0. \quad (61.17)$$

The existence of λ_0 follows from the imbedding theorem. Putting, in turn

$$u = \frac{\partial w}{\partial x} \quad \text{and} \quad u = \frac{\partial w}{\partial y}$$

and adding, we obtain (61.16) with

$$k = \frac{2}{\lambda_0(1-|\sigma|)}.$$

More generally, we can put

$$k \geqq \frac{2}{\lambda_0(1-|\sigma|)}. \quad (61.18)$$

Our problem reduces to the evaluation of λ_0. In a concrete example, the Ritz-process could be used to construct λ_0 as the smallest eigenvalue of

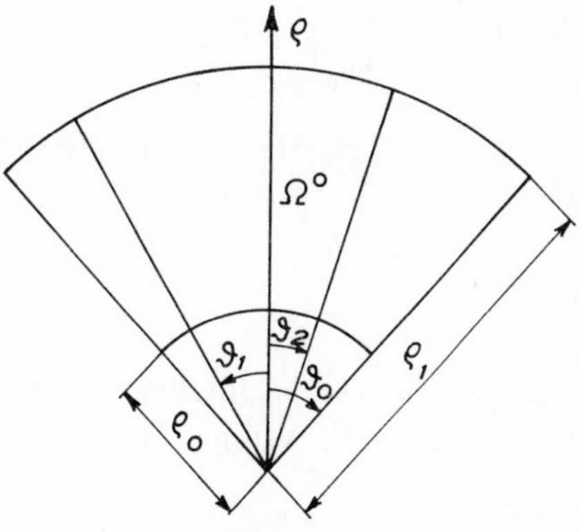

Fig. 5.

the Laplace operator on Ω^0 for the following boundary conditions: $u = 0$ on the line (61.14) and $(\partial u/\partial v) = 0$ on the remainder of the boundary. However, on the one hand, the Ritz-process involves the execution of a sufficiently complex calculation, while, on the other, it yields a value for λ_0 which is consistently too large. In the latter case, this makes the use of (61.17) unreliable. We therefore try to obtain a lower estimate for λ_0, independent of the Ritz-process.

We examine the region in Figure 5 and let $u(\rho, \theta)$ be an arbitrary function, which is continuously differentiable on this region and equal to zero on the line (61.14). If $\vartheta_1 \leqq \theta \leqq \vartheta_2$, then

$$u(\rho, \theta) = \int_{\rho_0}^{\rho} u_\rho(\rho', \theta)d\rho' = \int_{\rho_0}^{\rho} u_\rho(\rho', \theta)\sqrt{\rho'}\frac{d\rho'}{\sqrt{\rho'}}, \qquad u_\rho = \frac{\partial u}{\partial \rho}.$$

Using the Schwartz-Buniakovskiy inequality,

$$u^2(\rho, \theta) \leqq \ln\frac{\rho}{\rho_0}\int_{\rho_0}^{\rho} u_\rho^2(\rho', \theta)\rho' d\rho' \leqq \ln\frac{\rho}{\rho_0}\int_{\rho_0}^{\rho_1} u_\rho^2(\rho', \theta)\rho\, d\rho'.$$

We multiply the last inequality by $dS^0 = \rho\, d\rho\, d\theta$ and integrate over the region $\rho_0 \leqq \rho \leqq \rho_1$, $\vartheta_1 \leqq \theta \leqq \vartheta_2$.

After a simple manipulation, we obtain

$$\int_{\vartheta_1}^{\vartheta_2}\int_{\rho_0}^{\rho_1} u^2(\rho, \theta)dS^0 \leqq \rho_0^2 K \int_{\vartheta_1}^{\vartheta_2}\int_{\rho_0}^{\rho_1} u_\rho^2(\rho, \theta)dS^0, \tag{61.19}$$

where

$$K = \frac{1}{4}\left\{2\left(\frac{\rho_1}{\rho_0}\right)^2 \ln\frac{\rho_1}{\rho_0} - \left(\frac{\rho_1}{\rho_0}\right)^2 + 1\right\}. \tag{61.20}$$

If the whole internal edge is rigidly clamped, so that $\vartheta_1 = -\theta_0$ and $\vartheta_2 = \theta_0$, then $(1/\lambda_0) \leqq K$ and we write

$$k = \frac{2K}{1-|\sigma|}.$$

We now turn to the general case. In (61.19), we extend the integral on the r.h.s. to the whole region Ω^0. Writing, for brevity,

$$A = \int_{\Omega^0}\int u_\rho^2 dS^0,$$

we obtain

$$\int_{\vartheta_1}^{\vartheta_2}\int_{\rho_0}^{\rho_1} u^2\,dS^0 \leqq \rho_0^2 KA. \tag{61.21}$$

The existence of an angle ϕ, $\vartheta_1 < \phi < \vartheta_2$, such that

$$\int_{\rho_0}^{\rho_1} u^2(\rho, \phi)\rho\,d\rho \leqq \frac{\rho_0^2 K}{\vartheta_2-\vartheta_1} A, \tag{61.22}$$

follows from this last inequality. Since, choosing $\theta > \phi$, we obtain

$$u^2(\rho, \theta) = u^2(\rho, \phi)+\int_{\phi}^{\theta} \frac{\partial[u^2(\rho, \theta')]}{\partial\theta'}\,d\theta',$$

it follows that

$$\int_{\rho_0}^{\rho_1} u^2\rho\,d\rho = \int_{\rho_0}^{\rho_1}\int_{\phi}^{\theta} \frac{\partial[u^2(\rho, \theta')]}{\partial\theta'}\,dS^0+\int_{\rho_0}^{\rho_1} u^2(\rho, \phi)\rho\,d\rho. \tag{61.23}$$

We can estimate the second term on the r.h.s. by using (61.22). Further,

$$\left|\frac{\partial u^2(\rho, \theta')}{\partial\theta'}\right| \leqq \varepsilon\rho^2u^2(\rho, \theta')+\frac{1}{\varepsilon}\left[\frac{1}{\rho}\,u_\theta(\rho, \theta')\right]^2,$$

where ε is an arbitrary positive constant. Hence,

$$\begin{aligned}\int_{\rho_0}^{\rho_1} u^2\rho\,d\rho &\leqq \varepsilon\int_{\rho_0}^{\rho_1}\int_{\phi}^{\theta} \rho^2u^2\,dS^0\\ &\quad+\frac{1}{\varepsilon}\int_{\rho^0}^{\rho_1}\int_{\phi}^{\theta}\left(\frac{1}{\rho}\,u_\theta(\rho, \theta')\right)^2 dS^0+\frac{\rho_0^2 K}{\vartheta_2-\vartheta_1}A \leqq\\ &\leqq \varepsilon\rho_1^2\int_{\rho_0}^{\rho_1}\int_{\phi}^{\theta_0} u^2\,dS^0+\frac{1}{\varepsilon}\int_{\rho_0}^{\rho_1}\int_{\phi}^{\theta_0}\left(\frac{1}{\rho}\,u_\theta\right)^2 dS^0+\frac{\rho_0^2K}{\vartheta_2-\vartheta_1}A. \end{aligned}\tag{61.24}$$

We set

$$\varepsilon = \frac{1}{2\rho_1^2(\theta_0-\phi)}.$$

Integrating the last inequality w.r.t. θ and transferring to the left the fi- term on the r.h.s., we derive the inequality

$$\int_{\rho_0}^{\rho_1}\int_{\phi}^{\theta_0} u^2\,dS^0 \leqq 4\rho_1^2(\theta_0-\phi)^2\int_{\rho_0}^{\rho_1}\int_{\phi}^{\theta_0}\left(\frac{1}{\rho}\,u_\theta\right)^2 dS^0+\frac{2\rho_0^2 K(\theta_0-\phi)}{\vartheta_2-\vartheta_1}A. \tag{61.25}$$

Analogously, we derive

$$\int_{\rho_1}^{\rho_0}\int_{-\theta_0}^{\phi} u^2\, dS^0 \leqq 4\rho_1^2(\theta_0-\phi)^2 \int_{\rho_0}^{\rho_1}\int_{-\theta_0}^{\phi}\left(\frac{1}{\rho}\, u_\theta\right)^2 dS^0 + + \frac{2\rho_0^2\, K(\theta_0+\phi)}{\vartheta_2-\vartheta_1}\, A. \tag{61.26}$$

We add (61.25) and (61.26) and note that

$$\theta_0-\phi \leqq \theta_0-\vartheta_1\,, \qquad \theta_0+\phi \leqq \theta_0+\vartheta_2\,.$$

Writing

$$\vartheta = \max\,(\theta_0-\vartheta_1\,, \theta_0+\vartheta_2) \tag{61.27}$$

and using the value of A, we find

$$\int_{\Omega^0}\!\!\int u^2\, dS^0 \leqq 4\rho_1^2\,\vartheta^2 \int_{\Omega^0}\!\!\int \left(\frac{1}{\rho}\, u_\theta\right)^2 dS^0 + \frac{4\rho_0^2\, K\theta_0}{\vartheta_2-\vartheta_1}\int_{\Omega^0}\!\!\int u_\rho^2\, dS^0. \tag{61.28}$$

Finally, putting

$$m = \max\left(4\rho_1^2\,\vartheta^2,\ \frac{4\rho_0^2\, K\theta_0}{\vartheta_2-\vartheta_1}\right), \tag{61.29}$$

we obtain the estimate

$$\int_{\Omega^0}\!\!\int u^2\, dS \leqq m \int_{\Omega^0}\!\!\int (\text{grad}\ u)^2\, dS^0. \tag{61.30}$$

Comparing (61.17) and (61.30), we find that $(1/\lambda_0) \leqq m$. Inequality (61.18) shows that we can put

$$k = \frac{2m}{1-|\sigma|}\,. \tag{61.31}$$

§62. A numerical example

In the present section, we derive a detailed estimate for the helical shell, the projection of which is the region of Figure 5, for the parameter values

$$2\theta_0 = 85°,\ \ \vartheta_1 = -29°30',\ \ \vartheta_2 = 18°30',\ \ \frac{\rho_1}{\rho_0} = 2.50,\ \ \frac{\zeta}{\rho_0} = 0.50.$$

We find from (61.20) that

$$K = 1.55,$$

and we assume that Poisson's constant $\sigma = 0.29$.

The basic aim will be to calculate the constants in (61.11).

We determine the form of F_1 in (61.10) by comparing it with

$$A = \kappa_{11}^{0\,2} + 2\sigma\kappa_{11}^{0}\,\kappa_{22}^{0} + \kappa_{22}^{0\,2}. \tag{62.1}$$

With this aim in view, we form the determinant of $F_1 - \lambda A$

$$\begin{vmatrix} -\lambda & 0.29(r-\lambda) \\ 0.29(r-\lambda) & 2r-r^2-\lambda \end{vmatrix}.$$

Its roots are

$$\lambda' = r - 0.546r^2 - \sqrt{(r-0.546r^2)^2 + 0.092r^2},$$
$$\lambda'' = r - 0.546r^2 + \sqrt{(r-0.546r^2)^2 + 0.092r^2}.$$

For sufficiently small r, the root λ' decreases and the root λ'' increases for increasing r. Therefore, λ' takes the smallest and λ'' the largest value for

$$r = r_{\max} = \frac{\zeta^2}{\zeta^2 + \rho_0^2} = 0.2.$$

Denoting these values by λ_0' and λ_0'', we have $\lambda_0' = -0.010$ and $\lambda_0'' = 0.366$, and hence,

$$-0.010A \leqq F_1 \leqq 0.366A. \tag{62.2}$$

We turn to F_2. For brevity, we write $\kappa_{12}^{0} = u$ and $1/(\rho^0\rho)/(\partial w/\partial\theta) = v$. Then

$$F_2 = (2s - s^2)u^2 + 2(1-s)tuv - t^2v^2. \tag{62.3}$$

Since s is less than unity, $2s - s^2$ takes its maximum value when s is a maximum, which corresponds to the smallest value of $\rho = \rho_0$, and equals

$$\frac{1}{5+2\sqrt{5}} = 0.106.$$

It follows that

$$(2s - s^2)_{\max} = 0.200.$$

The largest value of $t = (\rho_0/\rho)s^2$ equals $s^2_{\max} = 0.011$ and $[2(1-s)t]_{\max} = 0.019$. Finally, $t^2_{\max} = 0.0001$. If, because of its smallness, we neglect this term, we obtain

$$|F_2| \leqq 0.200u^2 + 0.019|uv| \leqq (0.200 + 0.010\varepsilon)u^2 + \frac{0.010}{\varepsilon}v^2,$$

where ε is an arbitrary positive number. We choose ε so that $0.200+0.010\,\varepsilon = 0.366$. Then $\varepsilon = 16.6$ and $(0.010/\varepsilon) = 0.0006$. In this way,

$$0.366\kappa^{0\,2}_{12} - 0.0006\left(\frac{1}{\rho_0\rho}\frac{\partial w}{\partial\theta}\right)^2 \leqq F_2 \leqq$$
$$\leqq 0.366\kappa^{0\,2}_{12} + 0.0006\left(\frac{1}{\rho_0\rho}\frac{\partial w}{\partial\theta}\right)^2. \tag{62.4}$$

From (62.2), (62.4) and (61.10), we obtain

$$-0.366U^0 - 0.0012(1-\sigma)\left(\frac{1}{\rho_0\rho}\frac{\partial w}{\partial\theta}\right)^2 \leqq U - U^0 \leqq$$
$$\leqq 0.010(\kappa^{0\,2}_{11} + 2\sigma\kappa^{0}_{11}\kappa^{0}_{22} + \kappa^{0\,2}_{22}) + 0.366 \times 2(1-\sigma)\kappa^{0\,2}_{12} +$$
$$+0.0012(1-\sigma)\left(\frac{1}{\rho_0\rho}\frac{\partial w}{\partial\theta}\right)^2.$$

Replacing the factor 0.010 by 0.366 on the right, we obtain the simpler inequality

$$|U - U^0| \leqq \left|0.366U^0 + 0.0012(1-\sigma)\left(\frac{1}{\rho_0\rho}\frac{\partial w}{\partial\theta}\right)^2\right|.$$

Integrating over Ω, we obtain

$$\left|\frac{1}{2}\int_{\Omega^0}\!\!\int U\,dS^0 - \mathfrak{I}^0\right| \leqq 0.366\mathfrak{I}^0 + \frac{0.0006(1-\sigma)}{\rho_0^2}\int_{\Omega^0}\!\!\int\left(\frac{1}{\rho}\frac{\partial w}{\partial\theta}\right)^2 dS^0. \tag{62.5}$$

We now make use of (61.12). Using (61.31), we determine the value of k in (61.12). Since the equality (61.29) implies

$$m = \rho_0^2 \max\left(4\left(\frac{\rho_1}{\rho_0}\right)^2 \vartheta^2, \frac{4K\theta_0}{\vartheta_2 - \vartheta_1}\right) = 1.6\pi^2\rho_0^2 = 15.79\rho_0^2,$$

it follows that

$$k = \frac{31.58}{1-\sigma} \rho_0^2$$

and

$$\frac{1-\sigma}{\rho_0^2} \int_{\Omega^0}\int \left(\frac{1}{\rho} \frac{\partial w}{\partial \theta}\right)^2 dS^0 \leqq 31.58Э^0.$$

Substituting this result in (62.5), we obtain

$$\left| \frac{1}{2} \int_{\Omega^0}\int U \, dS^0 - Э^0 \right| \leqq 0.388Э^0. \tag{62.6}$$

We now derive estimates for

$$2Э - \int_{\Omega}\int U \, dS^0 = \int_{\Omega}\int U \, dS - \int_{\Omega^0}\int U \, dS^0 =$$
$$= \int_{\Omega^0}\int U \left[\frac{1}{\rho} \sqrt{\rho^2+\zeta^2} - 1\right] dS^0.$$

The term in square brackets has the form

$$\frac{1}{\rho} \sqrt{\rho^2+\zeta^2} - 1 = \frac{\zeta^2}{\rho(\sqrt{\rho^2+\zeta^2}+\rho)}.$$

Replacing ρ by its largest value $\rho = \rho_1 = 2.5\,\rho_0$ and then by its smallest value $\rho = \rho_0$, we find

$$0.020 \leqq \frac{1}{\rho} \sqrt{\rho^2+\zeta^2} - 1 \leqq 0.118.$$

It follows that

$$0.010 \int_{\Omega^0}\int U \, dS^0 \leqq Э - \frac{1}{2} \int_{\Omega^0}\int U \, dS^0 \leqq 0.059 \int_{\Omega^0}\int U \, dS^0. \tag{62.7}$$

From (62.6), we find

$$1.244Э^0 \leqq \int_{\Omega^0}\int U \, dS^0 = 2.776Э^0. \tag{62.8}$$

We substitute this in the first and third terms of (62.7) to yield

$$0.012Э^0 \leqq Э - \frac{1}{2}\int_{\Omega^0}\int U\, dS^0 \leqq 0.164Э^0. \tag{62.9}$$

Subtracting 2 from (62.8) and adding (62.9), we obtain, finally,

$$0.624Э^0 < Э < 1.552Э^0. \tag{62.10}$$

Hence, the constants in (54.3) take the values

$$\alpha = 0.624, \qquad \beta = 1.552.$$

In this way, we obtain the required estimate

$$\frac{Э^0(w-w^0)}{Э^0(w^0)} \leqq \max\left(\frac{1-0.624}{0.624}\,;\ \frac{1.552-1}{1.552}\right) = 0.60.$$

The use of (54.12) sometimes improves the estimate. If we take for the approximation not w^0 but

$$\tilde{w}^0 = \frac{1}{2}\left(\frac{1}{\alpha} + \frac{1}{\beta}\right) w^0 = 1.123w^0,$$

then we obtain

$$\frac{Э^0(w-\tilde{w}^0)}{Э^0(\tilde{w}^0)} \leqq 0.48.$$

Chapter IX

VARIATIONAL METHODS FOR NON-LINEAR PROBLEMS

§63. Preliminary remarks and auxiliary information

In this and the next chapter, we shall examine non-linear operators which map from one Banach space (in particular, a Hilbert space) into another Banach space. Sometimes (such cases will be mentioned explicitly), we shall examine operators acting in non-normed metric spaces. In this latter case, we shall assume that the elements of the examined space form a linear set.

We shall restrict attention to real spaces.

If u is an element of a Banach space $\mathfrak{B}$ and f is an element of the adjoint space $\mathfrak{B}^*$, then the symbol $(f, u) = (u, f)$ will denote the value of the functional f on the element u.

We make the following assumptions regarding the non-linear operators to be examined here and below:

I. The domain of the operator is a linear manifold and is dense in the examined space.

II. Let $x_0, x_1, x_2, \ldots, x_n$ be linear independent elements of the given space. We shall call a collection of elements of the form

$$x_0 + \sum_{k=1}^{n} a_k x_k,$$

where the a_k are arbitrary (real) constants, *the n-dimensional hyperplane* in the space. We require that, for arbitrary n and arbitrary elements x_0, $x_1, \ldots, x_n$ contained in the domain of the given operator, the values of this operator be strongly differentiable (Fréchet differentiable) functions w.r.t. the numerical variables $a_1, a_2, \ldots, a_n$ for all finite values of these variables. (For more details about abstract functions of numerical variables, see Vainberg[1] and Kantorovich and Akilov [1]). Briefly, we shall formulate this as follows: a given operator is continuously Fréchet differentiabel on any hyperplane of its domain.

We develop the theory, necessary for future concepts and theorems, for non-linear operators in a Banach space. A sufficiently complete presentation of this theory can be found in Kantorovich and Akilov [1] and Vainberg [1].

Let $\boldsymbol{P}(u)$ be a non-linear operator acting in the Banach space $\mathfrak{B}$. Let u, $h \in \mathfrak{B}$. On the basis of II, the following limit exists

$$\lim_{t\to 0} \frac{\boldsymbol{P}(u+th)-\boldsymbol{P}(u)}{t} = \frac{d}{dt}\boldsymbol{P}(u+th)|_{t=0}\,.$$

We denote this limit by

$$\boldsymbol{P}'_u h = \frac{d}{dt}\boldsymbol{P}(u+th)|_{t=0}\,, \tag{63.1}$$

and call it *the Gateaux differential of* $\boldsymbol{P}$. The Gateaux differential can be examined as the value at the point h of a certain operator $\boldsymbol{P}'_u$ which depends on the point u. In general, this operator is homogeneous: $\boldsymbol{P}'_u(ah) = a\boldsymbol{P}'_u h$, and non-additive: $\boldsymbol{P}'_u(a_1 h_1 + a_2 h_2) \neq a_1 P_u h_1 + a_2 P_u h_2$.

Let, at a certain point u, the operator $\boldsymbol{P}'_u$ be additive, when h is contained in a certain set $\mathfrak{M}_u \subset \mathfrak{D}(\boldsymbol{P})$. Then $\boldsymbol{P}'_u$ is a linear (but not necessarily bounded) operator with domain $\mathfrak{D}(\boldsymbol{P}'_u) = \mathfrak{M}_u$. In this case, $\boldsymbol{P}'_u$ is called the *Gateaux derivative* or, more simply, the *derivative of* $\boldsymbol{P}$ *at* u.

III. The derivative $\boldsymbol{P}'_u$ exists for arbitrary $u \in \mathfrak{D}(\boldsymbol{P})$.

The operator and its derivative are connected by the relationship

$$\boldsymbol{P}(u) - \boldsymbol{P}(v) = \int_0^1 \boldsymbol{P}'_{u+t(u-v)}(u-v)dt, \tag{63.2}$$

which is valid if both sides make sense.

The concept of a derivative can be extended in a natural way to a functional.

Let the following assumptions hold for a functional F.

I′. The domain $\mathfrak{D}(F)$ of the functional F is linear and dense in a given Banach space $\mathfrak{B}$.

II′. On any finite-dimensional hyperplane of its domain, the functional F is continuously differentiable.

It follows on the basis of these assumptions that the limit

$$\lim_{t\to 0} \frac{F(u+th)-F(u)}{t} = \frac{d}{dt}F(u+th)|_{t=0} \tag{63.3}$$

exists for arbitrary $u, h \in \mathfrak{D}(F)$. This limit is the Gateaux differential of the functional F. If for some $u \in \mathfrak{D}(F)$ the limit (63.3) is a linear (though, perhaps, unbounded) functional w.r.t. h, then this limit is the Gateaux derivative of the functional F at u. Below, we shall not make use of the concept of the Gateaux differential and Gateaux derivative of a functional. The concept of *the gradient of a functional* proves to be considerably more important.

We investigate the set $\mathfrak{M} \subset \mathfrak{D}(F)$ which satisfies the condition: If $u \in \mathfrak{M}$, then the limit (63.3) is a linear *bounded* functional w.r.t. u. On the set $\mathfrak{M}$, the operator $\boldsymbol{P}$, which maps from a Banach space $\mathfrak{B}$ into its adjoint space $\mathfrak{B}^*$ such that

$$\frac{d}{dt} F(u+th)|_{t=0} = (\boldsymbol{P}u, h), \tag{63.4}$$

is defined. Below, we shall always assume that the set $\mathfrak{M} = \mathfrak{D}(\boldsymbol{P})$ is linear. The operator $\boldsymbol{P}$ is called *the gradient of the functional* F which in its turn is called *the potential of the operator* $\boldsymbol{P}$. Between the potential and its gradient, there exists a simple relationship

$$F(u) = F(u_0) + \int_0^1 (\boldsymbol{P}(u_0 + t(u-u_0)), u-u_0))dt, \tag{63.5}$$

which is valid if u and u_0 are arbitrary elements of the domain of the gradient. In particular, if the zero element lies in this domain, then we can put $u_0 = 0$ and (63.5) becomes

$$F(u) = \int_0^1 (\boldsymbol{P}(tu), u)dt + \text{const.} \tag{63.6}$$

The form of the gradient and its domain depend on the space in which the given functional is examined. In order to clarify this assertion, we examine the functional

$$\Phi(u) = \frac{1}{2}\int_0^1 u'^2(x)dx.$$

As its domain we choose the set of functions of one (real) variable, $x \in [0,1]$, which:

(1) are absolutely continuous on the interval [0, 1];

(2) have first derivatives which are square summable on this interval;

(3) equal zero at the ends of [0, 1], so that $u(0) = u(1) = 0$.
We have

$$\frac{d}{dt}\Phi(u+th)|_{t=0} = \int_0^1 u'(x)h'(x)dx.$$

The domain $\mathfrak{D}(\Phi)$ of the functional Φ is converted into a Hilbert space, if we introduce on $\mathfrak{D}(\Phi)$ the scalar product and norm defined by

$$[u, v] = \int_0^1 u'(x)v'(x)dx, \qquad |||u|||^2 = \int_0^1 u'^2(x)dx.$$

We denote this space by $\mathfrak{H}_0$. If Φ is examined as a functional on $\mathfrak{H}_0$, then

$$\frac{d}{dt}\Phi(u+th)|_{t=0} = [u, h],$$

where the r.h.s. of this relationship represents for arbitrary u a bounded linear functional w.r.t. h. It follows that the gradient of Φ is defined for the whole space $\mathfrak{H}_0$ and, obviously, coincides with the identity operator in this space.

On the other hand, the domain of the functional Φ can be examined, for example, as a linear manifold in $\mathfrak{H} = L_2(0, 1)$. In this space, the functional, defined w.r.t. $h \in \mathfrak{D}(\Phi)$, equals

$$\int_0^1 u'(x)h'(x)dx,$$

where $u(x)$ lies in $\mathfrak{D}(\Phi)$ and is bounded then and only then when $u'(x)$ is absolutely continuous and $u''(x)$ is square summable on [0, 1]. In this way,

$$\int_0^1 u'(x)h'(x)dx = -\int_0^1 u''(x)h(x)dx = (-u'', h),$$

and it is clear that $\boldsymbol{P} = \text{grad}\,\Phi = -(d^2/dx^2)$ where $\mathfrak{D}(\boldsymbol{P})$ does not coincide with $\mathfrak{D}(\Phi)$, but only with the functions which, as just shown, have absolutely continuous first derivatives and square summable second derivatives on [0, 1].

The functional F is called *increasing* if $F(u) \to \infty$ if and only if $||u|| \to \infty$. If the functional is not defined in a normed space, but only in a metric space with distance function $\rho(u, v)$, then the condition $||u|| \to \infty$ is replaced by $\rho(u, u_0) \to \infty$, where u_0 is a fixed element of the space.

The functional F is called *lower-semicontinuous* {and, correspondingly, *upper-semicontinuous*} at the point u_0, if, given $\varepsilon > 0$, there exists a $\delta > 0$ such that, if $\rho(u, u_0) < \delta$, then $F(u) - F(u_0) > -\varepsilon$ $\{F(u_0) - F(u) > -\varepsilon\}$. This can also be formulated as follows: the functional F at the point u is upper-semicontinuous {lower-semicontinuous} if $\underline{\lim}_{u_n \to u_0} F(u_n) \geqq F(u_0)$ $(\overline{\lim}_{u_n \to u_0} F(u_u) \leqq F(u_0))$.

The functional F is called *weakly lower-semicontinuous* {and, correspondingly, *weakly upper-semicontinuous*} at the point u_0, if the relationship $\underline{\lim}\ F(u_n) \geqq F(u_0)$ $\{\overline{\lim}\ F(u_n) \leqq F(u_0)\}$ holds when u_n converges weakly to u_0.

A functional is semicontinuous on a set, if it is semicontinuous at every point of this set.

The functional F is continuous at the point u_0, if, given $\varepsilon > 0$, there exists $\delta > 0$ such that, if $||u - u_0|| < \delta$, then $|F(u) - F(u_0)| < \varepsilon$, and the functional is continuous on a set, if it is continuous at every point of this set. It is clear that a functional is continuous, if and only if it is simultaneously upper- and lower-semicontinuous.

We now state a theorem of Kazimirov [1] which is an important tool for proving the semicontinuity of a suitably wide class of functionals.

Theorem 63.1. *Let*

$$F(U, P) = \int_\Omega G(x, u_1, u_2, \ldots, u_s; p_1, p_2, \ldots, p_k) dx = \int_\Omega G(x, U, P)\, dx, \tag{63.7}$$

where the integrand is defined for $x \in \Omega$ and arbitrary values of the parameters u_i and p_i, and let this integrand satisfy over its domain of definition the conditions:

(1) *G and its derivatives $\partial G/\partial p_j$ are continuous*;

(2) *G is non-negative*;

(3) *the inequality*

$$G(x, U, P) - G(x, U, \bar{P}) - \sum_{j=1}^{k} (p_j - \bar{p}_j) \frac{\partial G(x, U, \bar{P})}{\partial p_j} \geqq 0 \tag{63.8}$$

holds for arbitrary $x \in \Omega$, U, P and $\bar{P}$.

If the functions $u_{in}(x)$ converge strongly to the functions u_{i0} in a space $L_r(\Omega)$, $1 < r < \infty$, and the functions $p_{jn}(x)$ converge weakly to the functions $p_{j0}(x)$, then

$$\varliminf_{n\to\infty} F(U_n, P_n) \geqq F(U_0, P_0).$$

We note that inequality (63.8) is satisfied if the matrix of second derivatives

$$\frac{\partial^2 G}{\partial p_\alpha \partial p_\beta} \qquad (\alpha, \beta = 1, 2, \ldots, k)$$

is non-negative for all value of the arguments $x \in \Omega$, U and P. This is an immediate consequence of the Taylor series representation of the integrand G.

§64. Positive operators in a Banach space

Note. See Birman [1].

This, as the previous section, is auxiliary. Its purpose is to develop the concept of an energy space for the case of a *linear* operator acting in a Banach space.

Let the linear operator A with a dense domain map from the reflexive Banach space $\mathfrak{B}$ into the adjoint space $\mathfrak{B}^*$. Then the adjoint operator A^* also maps from $\mathfrak{B}$ into $\mathfrak{B}^*$. We extend in a natural way to these operator the important concepts of the variational calculus which relate to a Hilbert space; namely, an operator A:

(1) is symmetric if $A \subset A^*$;

(2) is selfadjoint if $A = A^*$;

(3) is positive, if it is symmetric and if $(Au, u) > 0$ if $u \neq 0$;

(4) is positive definite, if it is symmetric and if $(Au, u) \geqq \gamma^2 \|u\|^2$, $\gamma = \text{const.} > 0$.

With a positive operator A, which maps from $\mathfrak{B}$ into $\mathfrak{B}^*$, we can associate a *Hilbert* space $\mathfrak{H}_A$.

In fact, let $u, v \in \mathfrak{D}(A)$. Then the expression (Au, v) satisfies all the axioms for a scalar product in a real Hilbert space:

1. $(Au, v) = (u, Av) = (Av, u)$, since a positive operator A is symmetric.
2. $(A(\alpha u + \beta v), w) = \alpha(Au, w) + \beta(Av, w)$, since A is linear.
3. $(Au, u) \geqq 0$.
4. $(Au, u) = 0$ if and only if $u = 0$.

Axioms 3. and 4. follow directly from the positiveness of $\boldsymbol{A}$.
Introducing the scalar (*energy*) product

$$[u, v]_A = (Au, v), \qquad u, v \in \mathfrak{D}(A), \tag{64.1}$$

we transform $\mathfrak{D}(A)$ into a Hilbert space – if it proves to be non-complete, we complete it. We shall denote the complete Hilbert space, obtained in this way, by $\mathfrak{H}_A$ and call it *the energy space of the operator* $\boldsymbol{A}$.
If $\boldsymbol{A}$ is a positive definite operator, then $\mathfrak{H}_A$ lies in the original space $\mathfrak{B}$. This will not be the case if $\boldsymbol{A}$ is positive, but not positive definite.
The problem of minimising the quadratic functional

$$(Au, u) - 2(f, u), \qquad u \in \mathfrak{B}, \quad f \in \mathfrak{B}^*$$

is solved in exactly the same way as when $\mathfrak{B}$ is a Hilbert space. We shall not stop to consider this problem further.

§65. Some theorems of the calculus of variations

We shall examine the functional $\Phi(u)$ which is defined on a linear set $\mathfrak{D}(\Phi)$ dense in a reflexive Banach space $\mathfrak{B}$. In correspondence with the results of §63, we shall assume that the mentioned functional $\Phi(u)$ is continuously differentiable on any finite-dimensional hyperplane lying in $\mathfrak{D}(\Phi)$. We put $\boldsymbol{P} = \operatorname{grad} \Phi$ and assume that the domain $\mathfrak{D}(\boldsymbol{P})$ is linear and dense in $\mathfrak{B}$. It is clear that $\mathfrak{D}(\boldsymbol{P}) \subset \mathfrak{D}(\Phi)$. We also assume that the operator $\boldsymbol{P}$ is Frechét differentiable on any finite dimensional hyperplane of its domain and that the Gateaux derivative $\boldsymbol{P}'_u$ is defined on the set $\mathfrak{D}(\boldsymbol{P}'_u)$ dense in $\mathfrak{B}$.
We put

$$F(u) = \Phi(u) - (f, u), \tag{65.1}$$

where f is a fixed element of the adjoint space $\mathfrak{B}^*$.

Theorem 65.1 (Gel'man [1]) *If the element* u_0 *is a relative minimum of the functional* $F(u)$, *then* $u_0 \in \mathfrak{D}(\boldsymbol{P})$ *and*

$$\boldsymbol{P}u_0 = f. \tag{65.2}$$

Proof. In fact, for arbitrary $h \in \mathfrak{D}(\Phi)$,

$$\frac{d}{dt} F(u_0 + th)|_{t=0} = \frac{d}{dt} \Phi(u_0 + th)|_{t=0} - (f, h) = 0.$$

It follows that

$$\frac{d}{dt}\,\Phi(u_0+th)|_{t=0} = (f, h),$$

and the expression on the left is a bounded functional w.r.t. h. Hence, $u_0 \in \mathfrak{D}(\boldsymbol{P})$ and $\boldsymbol{P}u_0 = f$, which proves the theorem.

In a certain sense, the following theorem is a converse of Theorem 65.1.

Theorem 65.2 (This theorem is very nearly that proved by Langenbach [1], [2], [3] and earlier, but under stricter conditions, by Vainberg [1]). *Let the functional* Φ *and its gradient* $\boldsymbol{P}$ *be defined on the linear sets* $\mathfrak{D}(\Phi)$ *and* $\mathfrak{D}(\boldsymbol{P}) \subset \mathfrak{D}(\Phi)$, *respectively, where* $\mathfrak{D}(\Phi)$ *and* $\mathfrak{D}(\boldsymbol{P})$ *are dense in the Banach space* $\mathfrak{B}$. *Let the derivative* $\boldsymbol{P}'_u$ *exist and be positive for arbitrary* $u \in \mathfrak{D}(\boldsymbol{P})$ *and, for fixed* h, *let the element* $\boldsymbol{P}'_u h$ *change continuously as* u *changes continuously along any straight line, and let* $\mathfrak{D}(\boldsymbol{P}'_u) \supset \mathfrak{D}(\boldsymbol{P})$ *for arbitrary* u.

If there exists a solution u_0 *of* (65.2), *then this solution is unique and*

$$F(u_0) = \min_{u\in\mathfrak{D}(\boldsymbol{P})} F(u), \tag{65.3}$$

where the functional F *is defined by* (65.1). *If, further, the functional* Φ *is upper-semicontinuous then*

$$F(u_0) = \min_{u\in\mathfrak{D}(\Phi)} F(u). \tag{65.4}$$

Proof. Let u_0 satisfy (65.1) and let this equation also have the solution u_1. Then

$$(\boldsymbol{P}u_1-\boldsymbol{P}u_0,\, u_1-u_0) = 0.$$

We put $\xi = u_0+t(u_1-u_0)$, where t is a real number, and obtain

$$\frac{d}{dt}\,\boldsymbol{P}(\xi) = \frac{d}{d\tau}\,\boldsymbol{P}(u_0+(t+\tau)(u_1-u_0))|_{\tau=0} = \boldsymbol{P}'_\xi(u_1-u_0).$$

It follows that

$$\int_0^1 \boldsymbol{P}'_\xi(u_1-u_0)dt = \int_0^1 \frac{d}{dt}\,\boldsymbol{P}(\xi)dt =$$
$$= \boldsymbol{P}(t(u_1-u_0)+u_0)|_{t=0}^{t=1} = \boldsymbol{P}u_1-\boldsymbol{P}u_0.$$

Hence,

$$0 = (Pu_1 - Pu_0, u_1 - u_0) = \int_0^1 (P'_\xi(u_1 - u_0), u_1 - u_0)dt,$$

and, since the derivative P'_ξ is positive, $u_1 = u_0$ – the solution of (65.1) is unique.

We now prove that u_0 minimises (65.2) on $\mathfrak{D}(P)$. In order to do this, we establish the identity

$$F(u+h) - F(u) = \int_0^1 (P(u+\tau h), h)d\tau - (f, h), \qquad u, h \in \mathfrak{D}(P). \quad (65.5)$$

On the basis of (63.6),

$$\begin{aligned} F(u+h) - F(u) &= \\ &= \int_0^1 [(Pt(u+h), u+h) - (Ptu, u)]dt - (f, h) = \\ &= \int_0^1 (Pt(u+h), h)dt + \int_0^1 (Pt(u+h) - Ptu, u)dt - (f, h). \quad (65.6) \end{aligned}$$

We manipulate the second integral in the following manner:

$$\begin{aligned} \int_0^1 (Pt(u+h) - Ptu, u)dt &= \int_0^1 dt \int_0^t \frac{d}{d\tau}(P(tu+\tau h), u)d\tau = \\ &= \int_0^1 d\tau \int_\tau^1 (P'_{tu+\tau h} h, u)dt = \int_0^1 d\tau \int_\tau^1 (P'_{tu+\tau h} u, h)dt = \\ &= \int_0^1 (P(u+\tau h) - P\tau(u+h), h)d\tau. \end{aligned}$$

Substituting this in (65.6), we obtain (65.5).

Let u denote an arbitrary element of $\mathfrak{D}(P)$. Putting $u = u_0 + h$, we obtain from (65.5)

$$\begin{aligned} F(u_0+h) - F(u_0) &= \int_0^1 (P(u_0+\tau h), h)d\tau - (f, h) = \\ &= \int_0^1 (P(u_0+\tau h) - Pu_0, h)d\tau = \\ &= \int_0^1 \frac{d\tau}{\tau} \int_0^1 (P'_{u_0+t\tau h} \tau h, \tau h)dt \geqq 0, \end{aligned}$$

which proves the required result.

We now assume that the functional Φ is upper-semicontinuous and prove (65.4). If it is not true, then there exists an element $u_1 \in \mathfrak{D}(\Phi)$ such that $F(u_1) < F(u_0)$. Since $\mathfrak{D}(\boldsymbol{P})$ is dense in $\mathfrak{B}$, there exists, for arbitrary $\delta > 0$, an element $v \in \mathfrak{D}(\boldsymbol{P})$ which satisfies $||v - u_1|| < \delta$.
Together with Φ, F is upper-semicontinuous: given $\varepsilon > 0$, there exists $\delta > 0$ such that, if $||u_1 - w|| < \delta$, then $F(u_1) - F(w) > -\varepsilon$.
We choose

$$\varepsilon = \tfrac{1}{2}[F(u_0) - F(u_1)]$$

and $w = v$, where v is the above-mentioned element of $\mathfrak{D}(\boldsymbol{P})$. Then

$$F(v) < \tfrac{1}{2}[F(u_0) + F(u_1)] < F(u_0),$$

which contradicts the relationship (65.3).

§66. The existence of a solution of a variational problem

The functional Φ is called *convex on the linear set* $\mathfrak{M} \subset \mathfrak{D}(\Phi)$, if

$$\Phi(u) + \Phi(v) - 2\Phi\left(\frac{u+v}{2}\right) \geqq 0, \qquad u, v \in M. \tag{66.1}$$

This functional is called *essentially convex* on the same set if the equality sign only holds for $u = v$.

Theorem 66.1. *If the operator* $\boldsymbol{P} = \operatorname{grad} \Phi$ *has a derivative, which is positive for arbitrary* $u \in \mathfrak{D}(\boldsymbol{P})$, *where* $\mathfrak{D}(\boldsymbol{P}'_u) \supset \mathfrak{D}(\boldsymbol{P})$ *whatever be the value of* $u \in \mathfrak{D}(\boldsymbol{P})$, *the functional* Φ *is essentially convex on* $\mathfrak{D}(\boldsymbol{P})$. *If, in addition,* Φ *is continuous, then it is convex on the set* $\mathfrak{D}(\Phi)$. *Finally, if* Φ *is continuous and the derivative of its gradient is uniformly positive bounded below, that is, if*

$$(\boldsymbol{P}'_u h, h) \geqq \gamma^2 ||h||^2, \qquad \gamma = \text{const.} > 0, \tag{66.2}$$

and, as before, $\mathfrak{D}(\boldsymbol{P}'_u) \supset \mathfrak{D}(\boldsymbol{P})$, *then* Φ *is essentially convex on* $\mathfrak{D}(\Phi)$.

Proof. (1) We write $v = u + h$. If $u, v \in \mathfrak{D}(\boldsymbol{P})$ then we obtain, on the basis of (65.5),

$$\begin{aligned}\Phi(u+h)+\Phi(u)-2\Phi\left(u+\frac{h}{2}\right) &= \\ &= \left[\Phi(u+h)-\Phi\left(u+\frac{h}{2}\right)\right]-\left[\Phi\left(u+\frac{h}{2}\right)-\Phi(u)\right] = \\ &= \int_0^1 \left(P\left(u+\frac{h}{2}+t\frac{h}{2}\right)-P\left(u+t\frac{h}{2}\right),\ \frac{h}{2}\right) dt = \\ &= \int_0^1\int_0^1 \left(P'_\xi\frac{h}{2},\frac{h}{2}\right) dt\, d\tau \geqq 0, \qquad \xi = u+(t+\tau)\frac{h}{2}. \end{aligned} \tag{66.3}$$

It is clear that the equality sign holds only when $h = 0$ or $u = v$. This result was proved by Langenbach [1], [2], [3] who examined operators acting in a Hilbert space.

(2) We assume, further, that Φ is continuous. It is necessary to prove that (66.1) holds for arbitrary $u \neq v \in \mathfrak{D}(\Phi)$. If this is not true, there exist elements $u_0 \neq v_0 \in \mathfrak{D}(\Phi)$ such that

$$\Phi(u_0)+\Phi(v_0)-2\Phi\left(\frac{u_0+v_0}{2}\right) = -k < 0. \tag{66.4}$$

We put

$$\varepsilon = \frac{k}{6}.$$

Since Φ is continuous, there exists $\delta > 0$ such that, if $||u_0-u|| < \delta$ and $||v_0-v|| < \delta$, then

$$\begin{gathered}\Phi(u_0) > \Phi(u)-\varepsilon, \qquad \Phi(v_0) > \Phi(v)-\varepsilon, \\ \Phi\left(\frac{u_0+v_0}{2}\right) < \Phi\left(\frac{u+v}{2}\right)+\varepsilon.\end{gathered} \tag{66.5}$$

Since $\mathfrak{D}(P)$ is dense in $\mathfrak{B}$, the elements u and v can be chosen from this set. It follows from (66.4) and (66.5) that

$$\Phi(u)+\Phi(v)-2\Phi\left(\frac{u+v}{2}\right) < -k+4\varepsilon = -\frac{k}{3} < 0,$$

which contradicts the results in (1).

(3) We now assume that Φ is continuous and satisfies (66.2). We suppose that Φ is not essentially convex in $\mathfrak{D}(\Phi)$. Then there exist $u_0, v_0 \in \mathfrak{D}(\Phi)$,

$u_0 \neq v_0$, such that

$$\Phi(u_0)+\Phi(v_0)-2\Phi\left(\frac{u_0+v_0}{2}\right) \leqq 0.$$

Given an arbitrary small $\varepsilon > 0$, there exists a $\delta > 0$ such that for u, $v \in \mathfrak{D}(\boldsymbol{P})$, $||u-u_0|| < \delta$, $||v-v_0|| < \delta$ and

$$\Phi(u)+\Phi(v)-2\Phi\left(\frac{u+v}{2}\right) < \varepsilon. \tag{66.6}$$

Since δ can be made arbitrarily small, we choose $\delta \leqq \frac{1}{3}\,||u_0-v_0||$ so that $||u-v|| > \frac{1}{3}||u_0-v_0||$. Further, as in (2), it can be assumed that $u, v \in \mathfrak{D}(\boldsymbol{P})$. It follows from (66.2) and (66.3) that

$$\Phi(u)+\Phi(v)-2\Phi\left(\frac{u+v}{2}\right) \geqq \frac{\gamma^2}{36}\,||u_0-v_0||^2,$$

which contradicts (66.6) if ε is sufficiently small.

Theorem 66.2 (Gel'man [1]) *Let the functional F be defined in a Banach space, in which the sphere is weakly compact, and let it be increasing, essentially convex and weakly lower-semicontinuous. Then it is bounded below, and its lower bound is the value of F at the unique point to which every minimising sequence converges weakly.*

Proof. First of all, the functional F is bounded below. In fact, we assume the opposite: there exists a sequence $\{u_n\}$ such that $F(u_n) \to -\infty$. Since the functional is increasing, the sequence is necessarily bounded and therefore weakly compact. Let $\{u_{n_k}\}$ be a weakly convergent subsequence of $\{u_n\}$ and let u_0 be the weak limit of this subsequence. Since F is weakly lower-semicontinuous, $F(u_0) \leqq \underline{\lim}\, F(u_{n_k}) = -\infty$ which is absurd. We write $d = \inf F$ and let $\{u_n\}$ be a minimising sequence. As above, we can establish that it is bounded, and therefore weakly compact. Let $\{u_{n_k}\}$ be the weakly convergent subsequence of $\{u_n\}$ and let u_0 be a weak limit of this subsequence. Since F is lower-semicontinuous, $d = \lim F(u_{n_k}) \geqq F(u_0)$. But $d = \inf F(u)$, therefore $F(u_0) = d$ and the lower bound of F occurs at u_0. This point is unique: if there exists a $u_1 \neq u_0$ such that $F(u_1) = d$, then the essential convexity of F implies

$$F\left(\frac{u_0+u_1}{2}\right) < \tfrac{1}{2}F(u_0)+\tfrac{1}{2}F(u_1) = d,$$

which is impossible.

It remains to prove that the minimising sequence $\{u_n\}$ converges weakly to u_0. We assume the opposite: there exists a linear bounded functional f such that

$$(f, u_n) \nrightarrow (f, u_0).$$

It follows, in turn, that there exists a subsequence $\{u_{n_k}\}$ and $\varepsilon_0 > 0$ such that

$$|(f, u_{n_k})-(f, u_0)| \geqq \varepsilon_0 . \tag{66.7}$$

The sequence $\{u_{n_k}\}$ is also a minimising sequence. On the basis of the above results, we can select a subsequence $\{u_{n_{kl}}\}$ from $\{u_{n_k}\}$ which converges weakly to u_0. This contradicts inequality (66.7).

Gel'man [1] proved that the problem of minimising the functional

$$\int_\Omega F(x_1, \ldots, x_m, \ldots, u^{i,j}_{j_1,\ldots,j_m}, \ldots)dx,$$

$$u^{i,j}_{j_1,\ldots,j_m}|_S = 0 \qquad (i = 1, 2, \ldots, N, \;\; j = 0, 1, \ldots, l-1), \tag{66.8}$$

has a solution, when Ω is a finite region of m-dimensional Euclidean space, S is its boundary, with

$$u^{i,j}_{j_1,\ldots,j_m} = \frac{\partial^j u^{i,0}_{0,\ldots,0}}{\partial x_1^{j_1} \ldots \partial x_m^{j_m}},$$

where $u^{i,0}_{0,\ldots,0} \in W_b^{(l)}(\Omega)$, $1 < p < \infty$, and the function F satisfies the following restrictions:

(1) This function and its first and second partial derivatives w.r.t. the arguments $u^{i,j}_{j_1,\ldots,j_m}$ are continuous for arbitrary values of $u^{i,j}_{j_1,\ldots,j_m}$ and $x \in \bar{\Omega}$.

(2) The two-sided inequality

$$K_1 \sum_{i=1}^{N} [\sum_{j_1+\ldots+j_m=l} |u^{i,l}_{j_1,\ldots,j_m}|^2]^{\frac{1}{2}p} \leqq F \leqq$$

$$\leqq K_2 \sum_{i=1}^{N} [\sum_{j=0}^{l} \sum_{j_1+\ldots+j_m=j} |u^{i,j}_{j_1,\ldots,j_m}|^2]^{\frac{1}{2}p},$$

$$K_1, K_2 = \text{const.} > 0 \tag{66.9}$$

is valid.

(3) The matrix of elements

$$\frac{\partial^2 F}{\partial u^{i,j}_{j_1,\ldots,j_m} \partial u^{k,s}_{s_1,\ldots,s_m}} \tag{66.10}$$

is positive definite.

The proof of the existence of the solution of this variational problem depends on Theorem 63.1 of Kazimirov as well as on Theorem 66.2.

Other approaches to the solution of variational problems have been developed by Langenbach [1], [2], [3]. This work relates to functional and gradients defined in a Hilbert space.

We examine the functional (65.1) under the assumptions that the derivative $\boldsymbol{P}'_u$, where $\boldsymbol{P} = \operatorname{grad} \Phi$, is an operator which is positive for arbitrary $u \in \mathfrak{D}(\boldsymbol{P})$. We restrict the domain of this Φ to the set $\mathfrak{D}(\boldsymbol{P})$. For simplicity of presentation, we put $\boldsymbol{P}(0) = 0$. This does not reduce the generality: it is sufficient to replace $\boldsymbol{P}u = f$ by $\boldsymbol{P}u - \boldsymbol{P}(0) = f - \boldsymbol{P}(0)$, so that $\boldsymbol{P}u$ is replaced by $\boldsymbol{P}u - \boldsymbol{P}(0)$ and the functional $\Phi(u)$ by $\Phi(u) - (\boldsymbol{P}(0), u)$ {this substitution does not change any of the properties of the functionals examined here}. We neglect the constant in (63.6) which is independent of the minimisation process and obtain:

$$F(u) = \int_0^1 (\boldsymbol{P}(tu), u) - (f, u), \qquad \mathfrak{D}(F) = \mathfrak{D}(\boldsymbol{P}). \tag{66.11}$$

It follows from Theorem 65.2 that the solution of $\boldsymbol{P}u = f$ minimises the functional (66.11) and, from Theorem 65.1, the converse. We assume, in addition, that the derivative $\boldsymbol{P}'_u$ satisfies inequality (66.2), so that it is positive bounded below uniformly w.r.t. u. We prove that under this condition the functional (66.11) is bounded below. In fact, since $\boldsymbol{P}(0) = 0$,

$$F(u) = \int_0^1 (\boldsymbol{P}(tu) - \boldsymbol{P}(0), u)dt - (f, u).$$

Since, on the basis of (63.2),

$$\boldsymbol{P}(tu) - \boldsymbol{P}(0) = \int_0^1 P'_{(t+\tau)u}\, tu\, d\tau,$$

it follows that

$$F(u) = \int_0^1 \int_0^1 t(\boldsymbol{P}'_{(t+\tau)u} u, u)dt\, d\tau - (u, f),$$

and hence, on the basis of (66.2),

$$F(u) \geqq \tfrac{1}{2}\gamma^2 \|u\|^2 - (u, f).$$

Applying Cauchy's inequality, we obtain

$$F(u) \geqq \tfrac{1}{2}\gamma^2\|u\|^2 - \|u\|\,\|f\| = \frac{\gamma^2}{2}\left(\|u\| - \frac{\|f\|}{\gamma^2}\right)^2 - \frac{\|f\|^2}{2\gamma^2} \geqq -\frac{\|f\|^2}{2\gamma^2},$$

which implies that (66.1) is bounded below.

We write

$$d = \inf F(u).$$

Theorem 66.3. *If* (66.2) *is satisfied, then any minimising sequence for the functional* (65.1) *converges in* $\mathfrak{B}$ *to a limit which does not depend on the choice of the minimising sequence.*

Proof. On the basis of Theorem 66.1, the functional Φ is essentially convex. We put

$$\rho(u, v) = \left[\Phi_1(u) + \Phi(v) - 2\Phi\left(\frac{u+v}{2}\right)\right]^{\frac{1}{2}},$$
$$\Phi(u) = \int_0^1 (P(tu), u)dt. \tag{66.12}$$

Using (66.3), we obtain

$$\rho(u, v) = \left[\int_0^1\int_0^1 \left(P'_\xi \frac{h}{2}, \frac{h}{2}\right) dt\, d\tau\right]^{\frac{1}{2}}, \qquad h = u - v, \tag{66.13}$$

and, on the basis of (66.2),

$$\rho(u, v) \geqq \frac{\gamma}{2}\|u - v\|. \tag{66.14}$$

Let $\{u_n\}$ be a minimising sequence for F, so that $F(u_n) \to d$.

We estimate $\rho(u_m, u_n)$. First, we note that

$$\rho(u, v) = \left[F(u) + F(v) - 2F\left(\frac{u+v}{2}\right)\right]^{\frac{1}{2}}$$

is valid. Here, we put $u = u_m$ and $v = u_n$. Remembering that

$$F\left(\frac{u_m + u_n}{2}\right) \geqq \inf F(u) = d,$$

we obtain

$$\rho(u_m, u_n) \leqq [F(u_m) + F(u_n) - 2d]^{\frac{1}{2}}.$$

We choose m and n sufficiently large, so that the inequalities $F(u_m) < d+$ $+\varepsilon$ and $F(u_n) < d+\varepsilon$ are satisfied, where ε is an arbitrary positive number. Then $\rho(u_m, u_n) < \sqrt{2\varepsilon}$ and

$$\lim_{m,n\to\infty} \rho(u_m, u_n) = 0.$$

It follows from (66.14) that $||u_m - u_n|| \underset{m,n\to\infty}{\to} 0$ and the minimising sequence converges in $\mathfrak{B}$ to a limit u_0. This element does not depend on the choice of the minimising sequence: if $\{u_n\}$ and $\{v_n\}$ are two such sequences, then the sequence

$$u_1, v_1, u_2, v_2, \ldots, u_n, v_n, \ldots$$

is also a minimising sequence and has a limit, and its subsequences $\{u_n\}$ and $\{v_n\}$ have one and the same limit.

This common limit u_0 of the minimising sequences will be called the *generalised solution of the problem of minimising the functional* (66.11). We look at the case when $\boldsymbol{P}'_u$ satisfies not only (66.2) but also the stronger inequality

$$(\boldsymbol{P}'_u h, h) \geqq \gamma_1^2(\boldsymbol{P}'_{u_0} h, h), \qquad \gamma_1^2 = \text{const} > 0, \tag{66.15}$$

where u_0 is fixed. We write $\mathfrak{B}_0 = \mathfrak{B}_{Pu_0}$ for the energy space of the linear operator $\boldsymbol{P}u_0$, and $[\ ,\ ]_0$ and $|||\ \ |||_0$ for the energy product and norm in this space. Then $(\boldsymbol{P}'_u h, h) \geqq \gamma_1^2\ |||h|||_0^2$ and, from (66.13), we obtain

$$\rho(u, v) \geqq \frac{\gamma_1^2}{4}\ |||u-v|||_0^2. \tag{66.16}$$

If $\{u_n\}$ is a minimising sequence for the functional (65.1), then $\rho(u_m, u_n) \underset{n,m\to\infty}{\to} 0$. On the basis of (66.16),

$$|||u_m - u_n|||_0 \underset{m,n\to\infty}{\to} 0,$$

and hence, the generalised solution of the variational problem lies not only in the original space $\mathfrak{B}$ but also in the energy space $\mathfrak{B}_0$.

§67. The energy space of a non-linear problem

We retain the assumptions at the end of the previous section: the domain of Φ coincides with the domain of its gradient $\boldsymbol{P}$ and the derivative $\boldsymbol{P}'_u$

satisfies (66.2). In this way, a concept of the energy space of the functional Φ, w.r.t. a metric analogous to that introduced for linear problems, can be developed.

The domain $\mathfrak{D}(\Phi) = \mathfrak{D}(\boldsymbol{P})$ of Φ and its gradient are converted into a topological space by the introduction of the closed sets: $\rho(u, v) \leqq \varepsilon$ and $\rho(u, v) \geqq \varepsilon$, where $\rho(u, v)$ is defined by (66.12), ε is an arbitrary positive number and u is a fixed and v is a variable element of $\mathfrak{D}(\Phi)$. The closed sets also include the union of any finite number and the intersection of arbitrarily many of the mentioned sets.

If $\mathfrak{M}$ is an arbitrary subset of $\mathfrak{D}(\Phi)$, then its closure $\overline{\mathfrak{M}}$ is, as usual, the intersection of all closed sets which contain $\mathfrak{M}$. If $\mathfrak{M}$ is the empty set or $\mathfrak{M} = \mathfrak{D}(\Phi)$, then we put $\overline{\mathfrak{M}} = \mathfrak{M}$. As is known, Hausdorff's separation axion [1; §22] is satisfied in the above topological space.

Let the sequence $\{u_n\} \in \mathfrak{D}(\boldsymbol{P})$ be a Cauchy sequence: $\rho(u_n, u_m) \underset{n, m\to\infty}{\rightarrow} 0$. Inequality (66.2) implies that $\{u_n\}$ converges in $\mathfrak{B}$, and hence, that there exists an element $\tilde{u} \in \mathfrak{B}$ such that $||u_n - \tilde{u}|| \to 0$. We assume that all such *limit* elements u are adjoined to $\mathfrak{D}(\Phi)$, and we call the resulting set the energy space $\mathfrak{B}_{\boldsymbol{P}}$ of the operator $\boldsymbol{P}$. The name *energy space* is highly artificial, since, in the general case, we do not introduce a topology into $\mathfrak{B}_{\boldsymbol{P}}$.

We single out a case when a topology (and even a metric) can be introduced into the energy space.

From (66.12), it is seen that $\rho(u, v)$ satisfies two of the three metric-axioms:

(1) $\rho(u, v) = \rho(v, u)$;

(2) $\rho(u, v) \geqq 0$ such that $\rho(u, v) = 0$ if and only if $v = u$.

Let $\rho(u, v)$ satisfy the *weak triangular inequality*

$$\rho(u, v) \leqq a[\rho(u, w) + \rho(w, v)], \qquad a = \text{const.} \tag{67.1}$$

It is clear that $a \geqq 1$. If $a = 1$, then $\rho(u, v)$ is a metric and the energy space $\mathfrak{B}_{\boldsymbol{P}}$ is simply the completion of $\mathfrak{D}(\boldsymbol{P})$ w.r.t. the metric ρ. If $a > 1$, then there exists a metric $\tilde{\rho}(u, v)$ topologically equivalent to $\rho(u, v)$, and $\mathfrak{B}_{\boldsymbol{P}}$ is the completion of $\mathfrak{D}(\boldsymbol{P})$ w.r.t. $\tilde{\rho}$.

Note. Chittenden [1] proved the following more general assertion: Let $\rho(x, y)$ be defined for pairs of elements in $\mathfrak{M}$ and satisfy the following conditions: $\rho(x, y) = \rho(y, x)$; $\rho(x, y) \geqq 0$ such that $\rho(x, y) = 0$ if and only if $x = y$; there exists a function $f(t)$, defined for $t \geqq 0$, for which $\lim_{t\to 0} f(t) = 0$, such that, if $\rho(x, z) < t$ and $\rho(z, y) < t$, then $\rho(x, y) <$

$f(t)$. Then there exists on $\mathfrak{M}$ a metric $\tilde{\rho}(x, y)$ which is topologically equivalent to $\rho(x, y)$.

Condition (67.1) is fulfilled in the following case: there exist positive constants α and β, such that for arbitrary $u, h \in \mathfrak{D}(\boldsymbol{P})$

$$\alpha^2(\boldsymbol{P}'_0 h, h) \leqq (\boldsymbol{P}'_u h, h) \leqq \beta^2(\boldsymbol{P}'_0 h, h), \tag{67.2}$$

where $\boldsymbol{P}'_0$ denotes the derivative of $\boldsymbol{P}$ w.r.t. $u = 0$. Let $\mathfrak{H}_0 = \mathfrak{H}'_{\boldsymbol{P}_0}$ be the energy space of the linear operator $\boldsymbol{P}'_0$ (see §64). Inequality (67.2) can be rewritten as

$$\alpha^2|||h|||_0^2 \leqq (\boldsymbol{P}'_u h, h) \leqq \beta^2|||h|||_0^2 .$$

It follows from (63.13) that

$$\frac{\alpha}{2}|||u-v|||_0 \leqq \rho(u, v) \leqq \frac{\beta}{2}|||u-v|||_0 ,$$

and inequality (67.1) is satisfied for $a = \beta/\alpha$.

§68. Functionals in the theory of plasticity and their extension

Note. See Langenbach [2].

Some of the problems in the theory of plasticity can be reduced to the problem of minimising the functional

$$F(u) = \int_\Omega \sum_{j=1}^{s} \int_0^{\tau_j(u)} g_j(\xi)d\xi\, dx - \int_\Omega fu\, dx, \tag{68.1}$$

where Ω is a finite region of Euclidean space, $f(x)$ is a function which is defined almost everywhere in Ω and lies in some functional space, u is a scalar or vector function which satisfies a certain homogeneous boundary condition and $\tau_j(u)$ $(j = 1, 2, \ldots, s)$ is a non-negative quadratic form w.r.t. u and its derivatives. The coefficients of $\tau_j(u)$ can be functions of x. Further, the $g_j(\xi)$ $(j = 1, 2, \ldots, s)$ are non-negative functions of ξ which are defined almost everywhere and are locally summable on the interval $0 \leqq \xi < \infty$. There exists at least one integer k, $1 \leqq k \leqq s$, such that

$$g_k(\xi) \geqq a, \qquad a = \text{const} > 0, \tag{68.2}$$

and, if u satisfies the boundary condition of the problem,

$$\int_\Omega \tau_k(u)dx \geqq \gamma_0^2 \int_\Omega u^2\, dx, \qquad \gamma_0 = \text{const} > 0. \tag{68.3}$$

We consider some examples.

1. *The twisting of reinforced bars* (see Kachanov [3]). If Ω is a simply connected region of the x, y-plane, then the equation and boundary conditions defining elasto-plastic twisting can be written in the form

$$P(u) = -\frac{\partial}{\partial x}\left[\bar{g}(T^2)\frac{\partial u}{\partial x}\right] - \frac{\partial}{\partial y}\left[\bar{g}(T^2)\frac{\partial u}{\partial y}\right] = \omega, \tag{68.4}$$

$$u|_S = 0, \tag{68.5}$$

where S is the boundary of Ω,

$$T^2 = (\text{grad } u)^2 = \left(\frac{\partial u}{\partial x}\right)^2 + \left(\frac{\partial u}{\partial y}\right)^2,$$

ω is the angle of twist per unit length of the bar, and $g(T^2)$ is a function which is characterised by the material of the bar in the state of stress and satisfies the constraint equation

$$\Gamma = \bar{g}(T^2)T \tag{68.6}$$

between the maximum tangential stress T and the shear intensity Γ. Since it is well known that Γ is an increasing function of T, $d\Gamma/dT \geqq 0$, or, equivalently,

$$\bar{g}(\xi^2)+2\bar{g}'(\xi^2)\xi^2 \geqq 0.$$

We assume that the function $\bar{g}$ satisfies the stronger inequality

$$\bar{g}(\xi^2)+2\bar{g}'(\xi^2)\xi^2 \geqq C_1, \qquad C_1 = \text{const.} > 0. \tag{68.7}$$

It is also known that

$$\bar{g}(\xi^2) \geqq C_2, \qquad C_2 = \text{const.} > 0, \tag{68.8}$$

where $C_2 = 1/G$ with G the shear modulus of the stressed material. We assume that $\bar{g}$ has two continuous derivatives. We shall examine P as an operator $\boldsymbol{P}$ in $L_2(\Omega)$, and assume that $\mathfrak{D}(\boldsymbol{P})$ is the linear set of functions which are twice continuously differentiable in Ω and satisfy (68.5) where S is sufficiently smooth. It is clear that condition II of §63 is satisfied. We shall prove that $\boldsymbol{P}$ has a derivative which is a linear operator and satisfies inequality (66.2). A direct calculation yields

$$\lim_{t\to 0}\frac{\boldsymbol{P}(u+th)-\boldsymbol{P}(u)}{t} = -\frac{\partial}{\partial x}\left\{\left[\bar{g}(T^2(u))+2\bar{g}'(T^2(u))\left(\frac{\partial u}{\partial x}\right)^2\right]\frac{\partial h}{\partial x}+\right.$$

$$\left.+2\bar{g}'(T^2(u))\frac{\partial u}{\partial x}\frac{\partial u}{\partial y}\frac{\partial h}{\partial y}\right\} - \frac{\partial}{\partial y}\left\{2\bar{g}'(T^2(u))\frac{\partial u}{\partial x}\frac{\partial u}{\partial y}\frac{\partial h}{\partial x}+\right.$$

$$\left.+\left[\bar{g}(T^2(u))+2\bar{g}'(T^2(u))\left(\frac{\partial u}{\partial y}\right)^2\right]\frac{\partial h}{\partial y}\right\}, \qquad h|_S = 0, \tag{68.9}$$

which shows that this operator is linear w.r.t. h. As usual, we denote this operator by $\boldsymbol{P}'_u h$. Now, $\boldsymbol{P}'_u$ is symmetric and

$$(\boldsymbol{P}'_u h, h) = \iint_\Omega \{\bar{g}(T^2(u))(\text{grad } h)^2 +$$

$$+2\bar{g}'(T^2(u))(\text{grad } u \text{ grad } h)^2\}dx\,dy, \tag{68.10}$$

where Ω is the region of cross-section of the bar.

We rewrite $\bar{g}'$ as the difference between its positive and negative parts

$$\bar{g}' = g_1 - g_2, \qquad g_1 = \begin{cases}\bar{g}', & \bar{g}' \geqq 0,\\ 0, & \bar{g}' < 0,\end{cases} \qquad g_2 = \begin{cases}0, & \bar{g}' \geqq 0,\\ -\bar{g}', & \bar{g}' < 0.\end{cases}$$

Since, on the basis of Cauchy's inequality,

$$(\text{grad } u \text{ grad } h)^2 \leqq (\text{grad } u)^2(\text{grad } h)^2 = T^2(u)(\text{grad } h)^2,$$

it follows from inequality (68.10) that

$$(\boldsymbol{P}'_u h, h) \geqq \iint_\Omega \{\bar{g}(T^2(u)) - 2g_2(T^2(u))T^2(u)\}(\text{grad } h)^2\,dx\,dy. \tag{68.11}$$

If $\bar{g}'(T^2(u)) \geqq 0$, then $g_2 = 0$ and

$$\bar{g}(T^2(u)) - 2g_2(T^2(u))T^2(u) = \bar{g}(T^2(u)) \geqq C_2;$$

if $\bar{g}'(T^2(u)) < 0$, then $g_2(T_2(u)) = -\bar{g}'(T^2(u))$ and

$$\bar{g}(T^2(u)) - 2g_2(T^2(u))T^2(u) = \bar{g}(T^2(u)) + 2\bar{g}'(T^2(u))T^2(u) \geqq C_1.$$

Since, in both cases,

$$\bar{g}(T^2(u)) - 2g_2(T^2(u))T^2(u) \geqq \mu = \min(C_1, C_2),$$

(68.11) yields

$$(\boldsymbol{P}'_u h, h) \geqq \mu \iint_\Omega (\text{grad } u)^2\,dx\,dy. \tag{68.12}$$

Using the Friedrichs' inequality (VM, p. 146) with constant κ, one obtains

$$(\boldsymbol{P}'_u h, h) \geqq \gamma^2 \|u\|^2, \qquad \gamma^2 = \mu\kappa. \tag{68.13}$$

We note that the derivative $\boldsymbol{P}'_u$ satisfies not only (66.2) but also (66.15) with $u_0 = 0$. In fact, if $u = u_0 \equiv 0$, then $T^2(u) = (\text{grad } u)^2 \equiv 0$ and (68.10) becomes

$$(\boldsymbol{P}'_0 h, h) = \bar{g}(0) \int_\Omega \int (\text{grad } h)^2 \, dx \, dy.$$

On the strength of (68.12),

$$(\boldsymbol{P}'_u h, h) \geqq \gamma_1^2 (\boldsymbol{P}'_0 h, h), \qquad \gamma_1^2 = \frac{\mu}{\bar{g}(0)}. \tag{68.14}$$

It follows from Theorems 65.1 and 65.2 that problem (68.4) and (68.5) is equivalent to the problem of minimising

$$F(u) = \int_0^1 (\boldsymbol{P}(tu), u) dt - (\omega, u), \qquad u|_S = 0.$$

We have

$$\int_0^1 (\boldsymbol{P}(tu), u) dt =$$
$$= -\int_0^1 t \, dt \int_\Omega \int u \left\{ \frac{\partial}{\partial x} \left[\bar{g}(t^2 T^2(u)) \frac{\partial u}{\partial x} \right] + \right.$$
$$\left. + \frac{\partial}{\partial y} \left[\bar{g}(t^2 T^2(u)) \frac{\partial u}{\partial y} \right] \right\} dx \, dy,$$

which becomes, on integrating the inner integral by parts and using the boundary condition $u|_S = 0$,

$$\int_0^1 (\boldsymbol{P}(tu), u) dt = \int_0^1 t \, dt \int_\Omega \int \bar{g}(t^2 T^2(u)) T^2(u) dx \, dy =$$
$$= \int_\Omega \int dx \, dy \int_0^1 t \bar{g}(t^2 T^2(u)) T^2(u) dt.$$

The substitution $\xi = t^2 T^2(u)$ gives

$$\int_0^1 (\boldsymbol{P}(tu), u) dt = \int_\Omega \int dx \, dy \int_0^{T^2(u)} \tfrac{1}{2} \bar{g}(\xi) d\xi,$$

and hence,

$$F(u) = \int_{\Omega}\int dx\,dy \int_0^{T^2(u)} \tfrac{1}{2}\bar{g}(\xi)d\xi - \omega \int_{\Omega}\int u\,dx\,dy. \tag{68.15}$$

The functional (68.15) is obtained from the general expression (68.1) when $s = 1$, $g_1(\xi) = \frac{1}{2}\bar{g}(\xi)$, $f(x) = \omega$ and $\tau_1(u) = T^2(u)$. All the assumptions at the beginning of this section are fulfilled.

2. *Elasto-plastic bending of a plane plate which is rigidly clamped at its edge.* (This problem was posed by Kachanov [1] and examined by Langenbach [1]–[4]. Langenbach also examined the cases when the edge of the plate is both freely supported and free). The equation defining elasto-plastic bending in a plate is

$$\boldsymbol{P}w = \frac{\partial^2}{\partial x^2}\left[g(H)\left(\frac{\partial^2 w}{\partial x^2} + \frac{1}{2}\frac{\partial^2 w}{\partial y^2}\right)\right] + \frac{\partial^2}{\partial x\,\partial y}\left[g(H)\frac{\partial^2 w}{\partial x\,\partial y}\right] + \\ + \frac{\partial^2}{\partial y^2}\left[g(H)\left(\frac{\partial^2 w}{\partial y^2} + \frac{1}{2}\frac{\partial^2 w}{\partial x^2}\right)\right] = f(x, y), \tag{68.16}$$

where $f(x, y)$ is proportional to the external normal load per unit area, g depends on the given material, and

$$H = H(w) = \left(\frac{\partial^2 w}{\partial x^2}\right)^2 + \left(\frac{\partial^2 w}{\partial y^2}\right)^2 + \left(\frac{\partial^2 w}{\partial x\,\partial y}\right)^2 + \frac{\partial^2 w}{\partial x^2}\frac{\partial^2 w}{\partial y^2}. \tag{68.17}$$

It is clear that $H(w)$ is a positive definite quadratic form w.r.t. the second derivatives of w. The deflection w must satisfy the boundary condition

$$w\Big|_S = \frac{\partial w}{\partial v}\Big|_S = 0, \tag{68.18}$$

where S is the contour of the plate and v is normal to S.

We assume that $g(\xi)$ is three times continuously differentiable and satisfies

$$g(\xi) \geqq c_1, \qquad g(\xi) + 2g'(\xi)\xi \geqq c_2, \tag{68.19}$$

where c_1 and c_2 are positive constants. We shall examine $\boldsymbol{P}$ (formula (68.16)) as an operator in $L_2(\Omega)$, where Ω is the region of the plate. We assume that $\mathfrak{D}(\boldsymbol{P})$ is the set of functions which are four times continuously differentiable in the closed region $\bar{\Omega} = \Omega \cup S$ and satisfy the boundary condition (68.18). The operator $\boldsymbol{P}$ has a derivative $\boldsymbol{P}'_w$ which represents a linear symmetric operator which satisfies inequalities (66.2) and (66.15). The last inequality holds for $w_0 = 0$. We prove these assertions.

Let w and h be arbitrary elements of $\mathfrak{D}(\boldsymbol{P})$ and t a real variable. A simple calculation yields

$$\begin{aligned} \boldsymbol{P}'_w h = \lim_{t\to\infty} \frac{\boldsymbol{P}(w+th)-\boldsymbol{P}(w)}{t} &= \frac{\partial}{\partial x^2}\left\{ g(H(w))\left(\frac{\partial^2 h}{\partial x^2}+\frac{1}{2}\frac{\partial^2 h}{\partial y^2}\right)+\right. \\ &\left. +2g'(H(w))\left(\frac{\partial^2 w}{\partial x^2}+\frac{1}{2}\frac{\partial^2 w}{\partial y^2}\right)H(w,h)\right\}+ \\ &+\frac{\partial^2}{\partial y^2}\left\{ g(H(w))\left(\frac{\partial^2 h}{\partial y^2}+\frac{1}{2}\frac{\partial^2 h}{\partial x^2}\right)+\right. \\ &\left. +2g'(H(w))\left(\frac{\partial^2 w}{\partial y^2}+\frac{1}{2}\frac{\partial^2 w}{\partial x^2}\right)H(w,h)\right\}+ \\ &+\frac{\partial^2}{\partial x\,\partial y}\left\{ g(H(w))\frac{\partial^2 h}{\partial x\,\partial y}+2g'(H(w))\frac{\partial^2 w}{\partial x\,\partial y}H(w,h)\right\}, \end{aligned} \tag{68.20}$$

where

$$\begin{aligned} H(w,h) = &\frac{\partial^2 w}{\partial x^2}\frac{\partial^2 h}{\partial x^2}+\frac{\partial^2 w}{\partial y^2}\frac{\partial^2 h}{\partial y^2}+\frac{\partial^2 w}{\partial x\,\partial y}\frac{\partial^2 h}{\partial x\,\partial y}+ \\ &+\frac{1}{2}\left(\frac{\partial^2 w}{\partial x^2}\frac{\partial^2 h}{\partial y^2}+\frac{\partial^2 w}{\partial y^2}\frac{\partial^2 h}{\partial x^2}\right) \end{aligned} \tag{68.21}$$

is the bilinear form corresponding to the quadratic form $H(w)$. Since $h\in\mathfrak{D}(\boldsymbol{P})$, h satisfies the boundary condition

$$h\Big|_S = \frac{\partial h}{\partial \nu}\Big|_S = 0. \tag{68.22}$$

It is clear that $\boldsymbol{P}'_w$ defined by (68.20)–(68.22) is linear and symmetric. We consider

$$(\boldsymbol{P}'_w h, h) = \int_\Omega\!\!\int h\boldsymbol{P}'_w h\,dx\,dy.$$

Integration by parts twice and the use of (68.22) yields

$$(\boldsymbol{P}'_w h, h) = \int_\Omega\!\!\int \{g(H(w))H(h)+2g'(H(w))H^2(w,h)\}dx\,dy. \tag{68.23}$$

Repeating the argument in **1**, we obtain

$$(\boldsymbol{P}'_w h, h) \geqq c' \int_\Omega\int H(h) dx\, dy, \qquad c' = \text{const} > 0. \tag{68.24}$$

Condition (68.22) leads to the identity (see VM, §27(6))

$$\int_\Omega\int H(h) dx\, dy = \int_\Omega\int \left\{ \left(\frac{\partial^2 w}{\partial x^2}\right)^2 + 2\left(\frac{\partial^2 w}{\partial x\, \partial y}\right)^2 + \left(\frac{\partial^2 w}{\partial y^2}\right)^2 \right\} dx\, dy,$$

and hence (see VM, §27), to

$$(\boldsymbol{P}'_w h, h) \geqq c'\kappa^2 \|w\|^2, \tag{68.25}$$

where κ is the constant in the Friedrichs' inequality. This proves that $\boldsymbol{P}'_w$ satisfies (66.2).

For $w = 0$, we have $H(w) = 0$, $H(w, h) = 0$, and it follows from (68.23) and (68.24) that

$$(\boldsymbol{P}'_w h, h) \geqq \frac{c'}{g(0)} (\boldsymbol{P}'_0 h, h), \tag{68.26}$$

which is equivalent to (66.15) with $w_0 = 0$.

The problem (68.16)–(68.18) is equivalent to the problem of minimising

$$F(w) = \int_0^1 (\boldsymbol{P}(tw), w) dt - (f, w).$$

Proceeding as in **1**, we easily find

$$\int_0^1 (\boldsymbol{P}(tw), w) dt = \int_\Omega\int dx\, dy \int_0^{H(w)} \tfrac{1}{2} g(\xi) d\xi,$$

and hence,

$$F(w) = \int_\Omega\int dx\, dy \int_0^{H(w)} \tfrac{1}{2} g(\xi) d\xi - \int_\Omega f w\, dx\, dy, \tag{68.27}$$

which can be derived from (68.1).

3. Gröger [1], [2] examined the case when the forms $\tau_j(u)$ are degenerate as well as the case when Ω is infinite. Langenbach [5] examined the general problem of the non-linear behaviour of an elastic plate under the assumption that the potential energy of deformation depends in a definite way on the first two invariants of the deformation tensor. This reduces to the functional form (68.1) with $s = 2$.

§ 69. Functionals in the theory of plasticity and their extension (continuation)

In the present section, we turn to the question regarding the existence of generalised solutions for the problem of minimising the functional (68.1).

For ease of presentation, we limit considerations to the case when the sum in (68.1) contains only one term, so that (68.1) becomes

$$F(u) = \int_\Omega dx \int_0^{\tau(u)} g(\xi)d\xi - (f, u). \tag{69.1}$$

Instead of the assumptions of §68, we assume that the ones cited below hold (some are is new, the remainder are similar to those in §68):

(1) $\tau(u)$ is a non-negative quadratic form w.r.t. the (scalar or vector) function u and its derivatives upto and including the order l. In fact, $\tau(u) = \tau^{(1)}(u)+\tau^{(2)}(u)$, where $\tau^{(1)}(u)$ depends only on the lth derivative and $\tau^{(2)}(u)$ only on u and its derivatives of order less than l. The coefficients of $\tau(u)$ can depend on x.

(2) The function $g(\xi)$ satisfies the inequalities

$$g(\xi) \geqq a, \tag{69.2}$$

$$g(\xi)+2\xi g'(\xi) \geqq a_1, \tag{69.3}$$

where a and a_1 are positive constants.

(3) For $\xi \to \infty$, the quotient $g(\xi)/\xi^{\frac{1}{2}p-1}$, where p $(2 \leqq p < \infty)$ is a constant, is bounded above and below by positive constants. We restrict attention to $p \leqq 2$, since $p > 2$ would violate (69.2). Assumption (3) is equivalent to the inequality

$$\alpha_0+\alpha_1 \xi^{\frac{1}{2}p-1} \leqq g(\xi) \leqq A_0+A_1 \xi^{\frac{1}{2}p-1}, \qquad 0 \leqq \xi < \infty, \tag{69.4}$$

where α_0, α_1, A_0 and A_1 are positive constants.

(4) As $\xi \to \infty$,

$$g'(\xi) = O(\xi^{\frac{1}{2}p-2}). \tag{69.5}$$

(5) For arbitrary $\xi \geqq 0$, $g(\xi)$ has a continuous second derivative.

Before formulating the remaining assumptions, we introduce the functional space which will play a fundamental role in the subsequent investigation. As usual, the problem of minimising the functional (69.1) is solved under the assumption that the function u satisfies a certain *linear* and *homogeneous* boundary condition. We introduce the space $\overline{W}_p^{(l)}(\Omega)$, which is a subspace of the Sobolev space $W_p^{(l)}(\Omega)$ and represents the closure w.r.t. the metric of $W_p^{(l)}(\Omega)$ of the set of sufficiently smooth functions, satisfying the boundary condition of the variational problem.

We now assume that:

(6) The norm in $W_p^{(l)}(\Omega)$ for elements of the subspace $\overline{W}_p^{(l)}(\Omega)$ is equivalent to the quantity

$$\left\{\int_\Omega [\tau(u)]^{\frac{1}{2}p}\, dx\right\}^{1/p}.$$

This allows the mentioned quantity to be taken as the norm in $\overline{W}_p^{(l)}(\Omega)$. If, for brevity, we put $\mathfrak{B} = \overline{W}_p^{(l)}(\Omega)$, then we obtain

$$||u||_{\mathfrak{B}} = \left\{\int_\Omega [\tau(u)]^{\frac{1}{2}p}\, dx\right\}^{1/p}. \tag{69.6}$$

In the subsequent work, we shall write $|| \;\; ||$ instead of $|| \;\; ||_B$.

(7) Finally, we assume that f in (69.1) is an element of the adjoint space $\mathfrak{B}^*$ of $\mathfrak{B}$.

On the strength of (1) and (3), the functional

$$\Phi(u) = \int_\Omega dx \int_0^{\tau(u)} g(\xi)d\xi \tag{69.7}$$

is defined on $\mathfrak{B}$. From (7), it follows that the functional

$$F(u) = \Phi(u) - (f, u)$$

is defined on the same space.

Note. In Langenbach [2], the more general case when (68.1) contains an arbitrary number of terms and the functions $g_j(\xi)$ satisfy a more general relationship than (69.3) is examined. It is shown that it is necessary to introduce the Orlicz spaces.

Below, we formulate and prove a series of theorems relating to the functional (69.1). We assume, for ease of formulation, that all the assumptions (1)–(7) hold, although not all of them are necessary for every one of the theorems.

Theorem 69.1. *The functional* (69.1) *is continuous in* $\mathfrak{B}$.

Proof. It is sufficient to prove the theorem for the functional (69.7). Let $||u_n - u|| \to 0$. We have

$$\Phi(u_n) - \Phi(u) = \int_\Omega dx \int_{\tau(u)}^{\tau(u_n)} g(\xi)d\xi.$$

From inequality (69.4), it follows that

$$|\Phi(u_n)-\Phi(u)| \leqq \int_\Omega [A_0|\tau_n-\tau|+A_2|\tau_n^{\frac{1}{2}p}-\tau^{\frac{1}{2}p}|]dx, \tag{69.8}$$

where, for brevity, we have written $\tau = \tau(u)$, $\tau_n = \tau(u_n)$ and $A_2 = (2/p)\,A_1$.

We estimate each term individually. We have

$$\tau_n-\tau = \tau(u_n)-\tau(u) = \tau(u_n-u, u_n+u),$$

where $\tau(u, v)$ is the bilinear form corresponding to the quadratic form $\tau(u)$. This expression is non-negative. Since, by Cauchy's inequality

$$|\tau(u_n-u, u_n+u)| \leqq \sqrt{\tau(u_n-u)}\sqrt{\tau(u_n+u)},$$

we obtain

$$\int_\Omega |\tau_n-\tau|dx \leqq \int_\Omega [\tau(u_n-u)]^{\frac{1}{2}}[\tau(u_n+u)]^{\frac{1}{2}}\cdot 1 \cdot dx.$$

We apply Hölder's inequality to the integral on the r.h.s. and obtain

$$\int_\Omega |\tau_n-\tau|dx \leqq$$

$$\leqq \left\{\int_\Omega [\tau_n(u_n-u)]^{\frac{1}{2}p}\,dx\right\}^{1/p}\left\{\int_\Omega [\tau(u_n+u)]^{\frac{1}{2}p}\,dx\right\}^{1/p}\left\{\int_\Omega dx\right\}^{1/r} =$$

$$= (\mu\Omega)^{1/r}||u_n-u||\;||u_n+u||,$$

where $2/p+1/r = 1$ and $\mu\Omega$ denotes the volume of Ω. Since $||u_n-u|| \to 0$, the norm $||u_n+u||$ is bounded and

$$\lim_{u_n\to u}\int_\Omega |\tau_n-\tau|dx = 0. \tag{69.9}$$

We now turn to the estimation of the second integral on the r.h.s. of (69.8). On the basis of Lagrange's formula, we find

$$\frac{\tau_n^{\frac{1}{2}p}-\tau^{\frac{1}{2}p}}{\tau_n-\tau} = \frac{p}{2}\,\sigma_n^{\frac{1}{2}p-1}, \qquad \sigma_n = (1-\theta_n)\tau+\theta_n\tau_n, \qquad 0 < \theta_n < 1.$$

For arbitrary non-negative numbers a, b and k the following inequality

$$(a+b)^k \leqq 2^k \max(a^k, b^k) \leqq 2^k(a^k+b^k) \tag{69.10}$$

holds. Hence,

$$\sigma_n^{\frac{1}{2}p-1} \leqq 2^{\frac{1}{2}p-1}(\tau_n^{\frac{1}{2}p-1}+\tau^{\frac{1}{2}p-1})$$

and

$$\int_\Omega |\tau_n^{\frac{1}{2}p}-\tau^{\frac{1}{2}p}|dx \leqq 2^{\frac{1}{2}p-2}p\int_\Omega |\tau_n-\tau|(\tau_n^{\frac{1}{2}p-1}+\tau^{\frac{1}{2}p-1})dx \leqq$$
$$\leqq 2^{\frac{1}{2}p-2}p\int_\Omega [\tau(u_n-u)]^{\frac{1}{2}}[\tau(u_n+u)]^{\frac{1}{2}}(\tau_n^{\frac{1}{2}p-1}+\tau^{\frac{1}{2}p-1})dx.$$

Applying Hölder's inequality to the integral on the r.h.s. of this last expression, we obtain

$$\int_\Omega |\tau_n^{\frac{1}{2}p}-\tau^{\frac{1}{2}p}|dx \leqq$$
$$\leqq 2^{\frac{1}{2}p-2}p\|u_n-u\|\,\|u_n+u\|\left\{\int_\Omega (\tau_n^{\frac{1}{2}(p-2)}+\tau^{\frac{1}{2}(p-2)})^r\,dx\right\}^{1/r}.$$

Since $r = p/(p-2)$, we find, on the basis of (69.10), that

$$\int_\Omega (\tau_n^{\frac{1}{2}(p-2)}+\tau^{\frac{1}{2}(p-2)})^r\,dx \leqq 2^r\int_\Omega (\tau_n^{\frac{1}{2}p}+\tau^{\frac{1}{2}p})dx = 2^r(\|u_n\|^p+\|u\|^p).$$

Taking into account that $\|u_n\|$ is bounded, we deduce, finally,

$$\lim_{u_n\to u}\int_\Omega |\tau_n^{\frac{1}{2}p}-\tau^{\frac{1}{2}p}|dx = 0. \tag{69.11}$$

It follows from (69.8), (69.9) and (69.11) that

$$\lim_{u_n\to u}[\Phi(u_n)-\Phi(u)] = 0,$$

which proves the required result.

Theorem 69.2. *The functional* (69.1) *is essentially convex in* $\mathfrak{B}$.

Proof. It is sufficient to prove that the functional (69.7) is essentially convex. We divide the proof of this last assertion into several steps:
1. The functional Φ has a gradient $\boldsymbol{P}$ = grad Φ, defined on $\mathfrak{B}$. In fact,

$$\frac{d}{dt}\Phi(u+th)|_{t=0} = \frac{d}{dt}\int_\Omega dx\int_0^{\tau(u+th)} g(\xi)d\xi|_{t=0} =$$
$$= 2\int_\Omega g(\tau(u))\tau(u,h)dx. \tag{69.12}$$

We prove that the r.h.s. of (69.12) is a functional w.r.t. h which is bounded in $\mathfrak{B}$ for arbitrary $u \in \mathfrak{B}$. We have

$$\left| \int_\Omega g(\tau(u))\tau(u, h)dx \right| \leqq \int_\Omega g(\tau(u))[\tau(u)]^{\frac{1}{2}}[\tau(h)]^{\frac{1}{2}}\, dx.$$

Application of Hölder's inequality with indices $r = p/(p-2)$, p and p to the integral on the r.h.s. yields

$$\left| \int_\Omega g(\tau(u))\tau(u, h)dx \right| \leqq \left\{ \int_\Omega [g(\tau(u))]^r\, dx \right\}^{1/r} ||u|| \cdot ||h||.$$

On the strength of (69.4),

$$\int_\Omega [g(\tau(u))]^r\, dx \leqq \int_\Omega \{A_0 + A_1[\tau(u)]^{\frac{1}{2}(p-2)r}\, dx \leqq$$

$$\leqq 2^r \int_\Omega \{A_0^r + A_1^r[\tau(u)]^{\frac{1}{2}p}\}dx = 2^r\{A_0^r\, \mu\Omega + A_1^r ||u||^p\}, \qquad (69.13)$$

which proves our assertion.

2. The derivative $\boldsymbol{P}'_u$ exists for arbitrary $u \in \mathfrak{B}$ and its domain $\mathfrak{D}(\boldsymbol{P}'_u) = \mathfrak{B}$. For the proof, we use an expression which defines $\boldsymbol{P}$ and follows from the identity (69.12):

$$(\boldsymbol{P}(u), h) = 2 \int_\Omega g(\tau(u))\tau(u, h)dx.$$

In this way, we obtain

$$\frac{d}{dt}(\boldsymbol{P}(u + th_1), h)|_{t=0} =$$

$$= 2 \int_\Omega \{g(\tau(u))\tau(h_1, h) + 2g'(\tau(u))\tau(u, h_1)\tau(u, h)\}dx. \qquad (69.14)$$

We prove that the r.h.s. of (69.14) is a bilinear operator w.r.t. h and h_1, which is defined on $\mathfrak{B}$ and is bounded for arbitrary $u \in \mathfrak{B}$. We find

$$\left| \int_\Omega \{g(\tau(u))\tau(h_1, h) + 2g'(\tau(u))\tau(u, h_1)\tau(u, h)\}dx \right| \leqq$$

$$\leqq \int_\Omega g(\tau(u))[\tau(h_1)]^{\frac{1}{2}}[\tau(h)]^{\frac{1}{2}}\, dx +$$

$$+ 2 \int_\Omega |g'(\tau(u))|\tau(u)[\tau(h_1)]^{\frac{1}{2}}[\tau(h)]^{\frac{1}{2}}\, dx. \qquad (69.15)$$

The application of Hölder's inequality with indices $r = p/(p-2)$, p, p to the first term on the r.h.s. yields

$$\int_\Omega g(\tau(u))[\tau(h_1)]^{\frac{1}{2}}[\tau(h)]^{\frac{1}{2}}\,dx \leqq C_1\|h_1\|\,\|h\|, \tag{69.16}$$

where, on the strength of (69.13),

$$C_1 = 2^r\{A_0^r\,\mu\Omega + A_1^r\|u\|^p\}.$$

Further, it follows from (69.5) that

$$|g'(\tau(u))|\tau(u) \leqq b_0\,\tau(u) + b_1[\tau(u)]^{\frac{1}{2}p-1}, \qquad b_0, b_1 = \text{const} > 0.$$

Again applying Hölder's inequality in the above form to the second integral on the r.h.s. of (69.15), we easily obtain the estimate

$$\int_\Omega |g'(\tau(u))|\tau(u)[\tau(h_1)]^{\frac{1}{2}}[\tau(h)]^{\frac{1}{2}}\,dx \leqq C_2\|h_1\|\,\|h\|, \tag{69.17}$$

where C_2 is a constant. It follows from (69.16) and (69.17) that the bilinear functional (69.14) is bounded. In its turn, it follows that the derivative $\boldsymbol{P}'_u$ exists for arbitrary $u \in \mathfrak{B}$ and its domain coincides with $\mathfrak{B}$ for arbitrary u.

3. The derivative $\boldsymbol{P}'_u$ is positive. For $p = 2$, it is uniformly positive definite. For the proof, we rewrite (69.14) in the form

$$(\boldsymbol{P}'_u h_1, h) = 2\int_\Omega \{g(\tau(u))\tau(h_1, h) + 2g'(\tau(u))\tau(u, h_1)\tau(u, h)\}dx.$$

It is clear from this result that $\boldsymbol{P}'_u$ is symmetric. Putting $h_1 = h$, we obtain

$$(\boldsymbol{P}'_u h, h) = 2\int_\Omega \{g(\tau(u))\tau(h) + 2g'(\tau(u))\tau^2(u, h)\}dx.$$

Repeating the argument in **1** of §68 and applying inequality (69.3), we find

$$g(\tau(u))\tau(h) + g'(\tau(u))\tau^2(u, h) \geqq c\tau(h), \qquad c = \text{const} > 0.$$

Hence, for arbitrary $p \geqq 2$, the operator $\boldsymbol{P}'_u$ is positive. If $p = 2$, then

$$(\boldsymbol{P}'_u h, h) \geqq c\int_\Omega \tau(u)dx = c\|u\|^2,$$

and the operator is uniformly positive definite.

4. The essential convexity of (69.7) in $\mathfrak{B}$ now follows from the first assertion of Theorem 66.1, since $\mathfrak{D}(\boldsymbol{P}) = \mathfrak{B}$.

Theorem 69.3 *The functional* (69.1) *is increasing in* $\mathfrak{B}$.

Proof. On the strength of (69.4),

$$\Phi(u) \geqq \frac{2\alpha_1}{p}\int_\Omega [\tau(u)]^p \, dx = \frac{2\alpha_1}{p} \|u\|^p,$$

and hence,

$$F(u) \geqq \frac{2\alpha_1}{p} \|u\|^p - \|f\| \, \|u\| \underset{\|u\| \to \infty}{\longrightarrow} \infty.$$

On the other hand, it follows from (69.4) that

$$F(u) \leqq A_0 \int_\Omega \tau(u) dx + \frac{2A_1}{p} \|u\|^p + \|f\| \, \|u\|.$$

Using Hölders inequality,

$$\int_\Omega \tau(u) dx \leqq \left\{ \int_\Omega [\tau(u)]^{\frac{1}{2}p} \, dx \right\}^{2/p} (\mu\Omega)^{(p-2)/p} = (\mu\Omega)^{(p-2)/p} \|u\|^2,$$

and it is clear that $F(u)$ is bounded, if the norm of u is bounded.

Theorem 69.4 *The functional* (69.1) *is weakly lower semi-continuous in* $\mathfrak{B}$.

Proof. It is sufficient to prove the assertion for the functional (69.7). We show that this functional has the form of that in Theorem 63.1. We assume that $U = (u_1, u_2, \ldots, u_s)$ is the aggregate consisting of the function u and its derivatives of orders $\leqq l-1$, while $P = (p_1, p_2, \ldots, p_k)$ is the aggregate consisting of the lth order derivatives of u. Then

$$G(x, U, P) = \int_0^{\tau(u)} g(\xi) d\xi.$$

It is clear that conditions (1) and (2) of Theorem 63.1 are satisfied. We verify the validity of (3): As was mentioned in §63, it is sufficient to verify that the matrix of the second order derivatives

$$\frac{\partial^2 G}{\partial p_\alpha \partial p_\beta} \qquad (\alpha, \beta = 1, 2, \ldots, k)$$

or, equivalently, the quadratic form

$$\sum_{\alpha,\beta=1}^{k} \frac{\partial^2 G}{\partial p_\alpha \partial p_\beta} t_\alpha t_\beta \tag{69.18}$$

with variable $t_1, t_2, \ldots, t_k$ is non-negative. We recall that $\tau(u) = \tau^{(1)}(u) + \tau^{(2)}(u)$, where $\tau^{(1)}(u)$ depends only on the variables $p_1, p_2, \ldots, p_k$ and represents a non-negative form w.r.t. these variables.
Since $\tau^{(1)}(u)$ is a non-negative quadratic form w.r.t. the independent variables $p_1, p_2, \ldots, p_k$, we write

$$\tau^{(1)}(u) = \sum_{\alpha,\beta=1}^{k} a_{\alpha\beta}\, p_\alpha p_\beta .$$

We note that the coefficients $a_{\alpha\beta}$ can depend on x. We now have

$$\frac{\partial G}{\partial p_i} = 2g(\tau(u)) \sum_{\beta=1}^{k} a_{i\beta} p_\beta ,$$

$$\frac{\partial^2 G}{\partial p_i \partial p_j} = 2a_{ij}\, g(\tau(u)) + 4g'(\tau(u)) \sum_{\beta=1}^{k} a_{i\beta}\, p_\beta \sum_{\gamma=1}^{k} a_{j\gamma}\, p_\gamma .$$

In this way, we obtain

$$\sum_{i,j=1}^{k} \frac{\partial^2 G}{\partial p_i \partial p_j} t_i t_j = 2\tau^{(1)}(t) g(\tau(u)) + 4g'(\tau(u)) \tau^{(1)2}(u, t), \tag{69.19}$$

where we have written for brevity

$$\tau^{(1)}(t) = \sum_{\alpha,\beta=1}^{k} a_{\alpha\beta}\, t_\alpha t_\beta , \qquad \tau^{(1)}(u, t) = \sum_{\alpha,\beta=1}^{k} a_{\alpha\beta}\, t_\alpha u_\beta .$$

If $g'(\tau(u)) \geqq 0$, then it follows from (69.19) that (69.18) is non-negative.
We now consider the case when $g'(\tau(u)) < 0$.
By Cauchy's inequality

$$\tau^{(1)2}(u, t) \leqq \tau^{(1)}(u) \tau^{(1)}(t).$$

It follows from (69.19) that

$$\sum_{i,j=1}^{k} \frac{\partial^2 G}{\partial p_i \partial p_j} t_i t_j \geqq 2\tau^{(1)}(u)[g(\tau(u)) + 2\tau^{(1)}(u) g'(\tau(u))].$$

Since $\tau^{(2)}(u)$ is non-negative, $\tau^{(1)}(u) \leqq \tau(u)$ and

$$\sum_{i,j=1}^{k} \frac{\partial^2 G}{\partial p_i \partial p_j} t_i t_j \geqq 2\tau^{(1)}(u)[g(\tau(u))+2\tau(u)g'(\tau(u))].$$

Using the argument of **1**, §65, and inequality (69.3), we easily find that the form (69.18) is non-negative for arbitrary values of $p_1, p_2, \ldots, p_n$. Let $\{u_n\}$ converge weakly to u in $\mathfrak{B}$. It follows that the derivatives of order l of the u_n converge weakly in $L_p(\Omega)$ to the corresponding derivatives of u. The Sobolev imbedding theorem implies that the derivatives of order less than l of the u_n converge strongly in $L_p(\Omega)$ to the corresponding derivatives of u. Since all the conditions of Theorem 63.1 are satisfied,

$$\underline{\lim}\, \Phi(u_n) \geqq \Phi(u_0)$$

and the functional $\Phi(u)$ is weakly lower semi-continuous.

Using the Sobolev imbedding theorem, Theorems 69.1–69.4 and 63.1 imply

Theorem 69.5 *Let the conditions* (1)–(7), *above, be satisfied. Then the functional* (69.1) *has an absolute minimum in* $\mathfrak{B}$ *which is attained at a unique point. If* u_0 *is this point and* $\{u_n\}$ *is an arbitrary minimising sequence, then the derivatives of order* l *of the* u_n *converge weakly to the corresponding derivatives of* u_0 *in* $L_p(\Omega)$ *and the derivatives of order less than* l *of the* u_n *converge strongly to the corresponding derivatives of* u_0 *in* $L_p(\Omega)$.

In the case when $p = 2$, Theorem 69.5 can be sharpened in the following way.

Theorem 69.6 *Let the functional* (69.1) *attain its absolute minimum at* u_0, *and* $\{u_n\}$ *be a minimising sequence for this functional. If* $p = 2$, *then the derivatives of order* l *of the* u_n *converge strongly in* $L_2(\Omega)$ *to the corresponding derivatives of* u_0.

In fact, in the proof of Theorem 69.2 (**3**), it was established for $p = 2$ that the derivative $\boldsymbol{P}_u'$ is uniformly positive definite in $\mathfrak{B}$. Hence, it follows from Theorem 66.3 that

$$||u_n - u_0|| = ||u_n - u_0||_{W_2^{(l)}(\Omega)} \underset{n\to\infty}{\to} 0.$$

The assertion of Theorem 69.6 is a direct corollary of this last relationship.

We turn to the examples in §68. In the problem relating to the twisting of reinforced bars,

$$\tau(u) = T^2(u) = \left(\frac{\partial u}{\partial x}\right)^2 + \left(\frac{\partial u}{\partial y}\right)^2, \qquad g(\xi) = \tfrac{1}{2}\bar{g}(\xi).$$

If we assume that, for $\xi \to \infty$, the quotient $\bar{g}(\xi)/\xi^{\frac{1}{2}p-1}$ is bounded above and below by positive numbers, and the quotient $|\bar{g}'(\xi)|/\xi^{\frac{1}{2}p-2}$ is bounded above for a certain $p \geqq 2$, then all the assumptions of the present section will be satisfied for $l = 1$. The problem of minimising (68.15) has a solution in $W_p^{(l)}(\Omega)$. If u_0 is this solution and $\{u_n\}$ is a minimising sequence, then grad $u_n \to$ grad u_0 weakly and $u_n \to u_0$ strongly in $L_p(\Omega)$. If $p = 2$, then grad $u_n \to$ grad u_0 strongly in $L_2(\Omega)$.
In the problem relating to the elasto-plastic bending of a plane plate, rigidly clamped at its edge, $l = 2$ and

$$\tau(w) = H(w) = \left(\frac{\partial^2 w}{\partial x^2}\right)^2 + \left(\frac{\partial^2 w}{\partial y^2}\right)^2 + \left(\frac{\partial^2 w}{\partial x\,\partial y}\right)^2 + \frac{\partial^2 w}{\partial x^2}\,\frac{\partial^2 w}{\partial y^2}.$$

If the function $g(\xi)$ satisfies the conditions which were listed above for $\bar{g}(\xi)$, then our problem has a solution $w_0 \in W_2^{(2)}$. If w_n is a minimising sequence, then

$$\frac{\partial^2 w_n}{\partial x^2} \to \frac{\partial^2 w_0}{\partial x^2}, \qquad \frac{\partial^2 w_n}{\partial x\,\partial y} \to \frac{\partial^2 w_0}{\partial x\,\partial y}, \qquad \frac{\partial^2 w_n}{\partial y^2} \to \frac{\partial^2 w_0}{\partial y^2} \tag{69.20}$$

converge weakly in $L_p(\Omega)$ and

$$\frac{\partial w_n}{\partial x} \to \frac{\partial w_0}{\partial x}, \qquad \frac{\partial w_n}{\partial y} \to \frac{\partial w_0}{\partial y}, \qquad w_n \to w_0,$$

converge strongly in $L_p(\Omega)$. If $p = 2$, then the relationships (69.20) converge strongly in $L_2(\Omega)$.

Chapter X

THE NUMERICAL SOLUTION OF NON-LINEAR VARIATIONAL PROBLEMS

§70. The Ritz-process and Bubnov-Galerkin-process

As results of the previous chapters indicate, the solutions of a wide class of variational problems can be obtained, if minimising sequences for the appropriate functionals are constructed. If the minimising sequence $\{u_n\}$ converges, then for sufficiently large n, u_n can be taken as an approximate solution of the given variational problem. Hence, questions relating to the construction of numerical representations of the solution reduce to questions connected with the construction of minimising sequences. Just as for linear problems, the construction of minimising sequences for non-linear problems can, in many cases, be achieved with the help of the Ritz-process.

We pose the problem of minimising the functional F with a linear domain $\mathfrak{D}(F)$. We assume that the set $\mathfrak{D}(F)$ is dense in a certain separable linear metric space $\mathfrak{M}$ (not necessarily a normed space) with distance function $\rho(u, v)$. We consider a system of elements, *coordinate elements*,

$$\{\phi_n\} = \phi_1, \phi_2, \ldots, \phi_n, \ldots, \tag{70.1}$$

which satisfies the usual conditions:

(1) $\{\phi_n\} \in \mathfrak{D}(F)$;

(2) the elements $\phi_1, \phi_2, \ldots, \phi_n$ are linearly independent for arbitrary n;

(3) the system (70.1) is complete in $\mathfrak{M}$; as always, this implies that the set of all finite linear combinations of elements of (70.1) is dense in $\mathfrak{M}$.

As usual for the Ritz-process, we choose n and reduce the problem of minimising F on $\mathfrak{D}(F)$ to the problem of minimising F on the n-dimensional subspace spanned by $\phi_1, \phi_2, \ldots, \phi_n$. We assume that the solution of this new problem exists. It has the form

$$u_n = \sum_{k=1}^{n} a_k \phi_k. \tag{70.2}$$

Although the coefficients a_k depend on n, we shall not signify this in any special way. The element u_n (defined by (70.2)) is called the approximate Ritz-solution of the variational problem corresponding to the given functional F.

We assume that F is continuously differentiable on any finite-dimensional hyperplane within its domain. Hence, the Ritz-coefficients a_k satisfy the system of equations

$$\frac{\partial F(\sum_{k=1}^{n} a_k \phi_k)}{\partial a_j} = 0 \qquad (j = 1, 2, \ldots, n). \tag{70.3}$$

Theorem 70.1 *Let the conditions relating to the functional F and the coordinate system* (70.1) *which were formulated above, be satisfied. If the functional F w.r.t. the metric* $\rho(x, y)$ *is increasing and upper-semicontinuous then the approximate Ritz-solutions can be constructed for arbitrary n and this sequence of approximate solutions is a minimising sequence of F* (see Mikhlin [18]; the following error occurs in the theorems of this paper: "lower-semicontinuous" is written instead of "upper-semicontinuous").

Proof. The expression $F(\sum_{k=1}^{n} a_k \phi_k)$ is a function of the variables a_1, $a_2, \ldots, a_n$ which is continuously differentiable w.r.t. all these variables and tends to $+\infty$ as $a_1^2 + a_2^2 + \ldots + a_n^2 \to \infty$. This function attains its absolute minimum for at least one point which is at a finite distance from the origin and for which

$$\frac{\partial F(\sum_{k=1}^{n} a_k \phi_k)}{\partial a_j} = 0 \qquad (j = 1, 2, \ldots, n).$$

In this way, the Ritz-system (70.3) has at least one solution for any integer n, and hence, there exists at least one approximate Ritz-solution for the problem of minimising F for a given n.

We now prove that these approximate solutions form a minimising sequence for the functional F. We let $\inf F(u) = d$. We construct the minimising sequence $u^{(n)}$ such that

$$F(u^{(n)}) \leqq d + \frac{1}{n}.$$

On the basis of the completeness of the coordinate system, we can choose for each $u^{(n)}$ a linear combination

$$v^{(N_n)} = \sum_{k=1}^{N_n} \alpha_k^{(n)} \phi_k,$$

so that $\rho(u^{(n)}, v^{(N_n)}) < \delta_n$. We choose δ_n sufficiently small, so that for any v which satisfies $\rho(u^{(n)}, v) < \delta_n$, we have $F(u^{(n)}) - F(v) \geqq -1/n$. This is possible, because F is upper-semicontinuous. Now, we know that

$$F(v^{(N_n)}) \leqq F(u^{(n)}) + \frac{1}{n}$$

and, what is more, that

$$F(v^{(N_n)}) \leqq d + \frac{2}{n}.$$

It follows that $\{v^{(N_n)}\}$ is a minimising sequence.
Let

$$u_p = \sum_{k=1}^{p} a_k \phi_k$$

denote the pth approximate Ritz-solution. Then

$$F(u_{N_n}) \leqq F(v^{(N_n)}) \leqq d + \frac{2}{n}$$

and $\{u_{N_n}\}$ is also a minimising sequence. Finally, since $F(u_n)$ is monotonicly decreasing for increasing n, the sequence $\{F(u_{N_n})\} \to d$, and hence, $\{F(u_n)\} \to d$. – the required result.
In the problems of §68, the functional F is not only upper-semicontinuous, but is also continuous in the corresponding space $\mathfrak{B}$. In both these problems, the functionals are also increasing. Hence, in both these problems, the approximate Ritz-solution can be constructed for arbitrary n. The results at the end of the last section, connected with the convergence of a minimising sequence, also apply to the convergence of the approximate Ritz-solutions.
The element which attains the minimum of the functional F, satisfies the equation

$$\boldsymbol{P}u = 0, \qquad \boldsymbol{P} = \text{grad}\, F. \tag{70.4}$$

We assume that the domain $\mathfrak{D}(F)$ of F lies in a certain separable Banach space $\mathfrak{B}$ and is dense in $\mathfrak{B}$. Further, we assume that grad F has a linear domain, which is also dense in $\mathfrak{B}$. Then (70.4) can be solved by the Bubnov-Galerkin-process. We consider a coordinate system (70.1), which satisfies conditions (2) and (3) above as well as the stronger condition (1′): $\{\phi_n\} \in \mathfrak{D}(\boldsymbol{P})$, which replaces (1). We choose an element of the form (70.2) and define the coefficients a_k by the Bubnov-Galerkin-system

$$(\boldsymbol{P}(\sum_{k=1}^{n} a_k \phi_k), \phi_j) = 0 \qquad (j = 1, 2, \ldots, n). \tag{70.5}$$

If the equations (70.5) have a solution, then substitution of the a_k so determined into (70.2) yields an element which will be called the approximate Bubnov-Galerkin-solution of (70.4).

We note at once that the Bubnov-Galerkin-process can also be applied when $\boldsymbol{P}$ is non-potential: it is sufficient that $\mathfrak{D}(\boldsymbol{P})$ be a linear set which is dense in $\mathfrak{B}$, that the range $\mathfrak{R}(\boldsymbol{P})$ lie in the adjoint space $\mathfrak{B}^*$ and that the co-ordinate system satisfy conditions (1′), (2) and (3). Further, it is not necessary that $\boldsymbol{P}$ acts from $\mathfrak{B}$ into $\mathfrak{B}^*$. It is sufficient, if $\boldsymbol{P}$ maps from $\mathfrak{B}$ into a Banach space $\mathfrak{B}_1$. In this case, the Bubnov-Galerkin-system takes another form: for more details see Krasnosel'skiy [1]. In the case when $\boldsymbol{P} = \boldsymbol{I}+\boldsymbol{T}$, where $\boldsymbol{I}$ is the identity and $\boldsymbol{T}$ is a completely continuous non-linear operator in a certain Banach space, the convergence of the Bubnov-Galerkin-process was analysed by Krasnosel'skiy [1].

Theorem 70.2 (see Dovbysh and Mikhlin [1]). *Let the domain* $\mathfrak{D}(F)$ *of* F *and the domain* $\mathfrak{D}(\boldsymbol{P})$ *of* $\boldsymbol{P} =$ grad F *be linear and dense in a separable Banach space* $\mathfrak{B}$ *and let* F *be continuously differentiable on any finite-dimensional hyperplane of* $\mathfrak{D}(F)$. *If the coordinate system* (70.1) *satisfies conditions* (1′), (2) *and* (3) *above, then the Ritz-system* (70.3) *and the Bubnov-Galerkin-system* (70.5) *are equivalent.*

Proof. The proof is very simple. Equations (70.3) can be rewritten in the form

$$\frac{\partial F(u_n)}{\partial a_j} = 0,$$

where the u_n are defined by (70.2). However, since

$$\frac{\partial F(u_n)}{\partial a_j} = \frac{d}{dt} F(u_n + t\phi_j)|_{t=0} = (\boldsymbol{P}(u_n), \phi_j),$$

it follows that (70.3) and (70.5) are identical.
The most important consideration in the use of variational methods for the solution of non-linear problems is the choice of the procedure for the construction of the approximate Ritz-solution.
In the following sections, we shall examine three such procedures: the Newton-Kantorovich-method, the method of differentiation w.r.t. a parameter and the Kachanov-method.

§71. Application of the Newton-Kantorovich-method

The implementation of the Newton-Kantorovich-method, conditions for convergence and estimates for the rate of convergence are presented in sufficient detail in Kantorovich and Akilov [1]. Here, we only indicate how this method is applied to system (70.3) and present a numerical example.
We write

$$F\Big(\sum_{k=1}^{n} a_k \phi_k\Big) = \tilde{F}(a_1, a_2, \ldots, a_n).$$

For the Newton-Kantorovich-method, we start with a certain initial approximation $a_{10}, a_{20}, \ldots, a_{n0}$ and construct the approximation a_{11}, $a_{21}, \ldots, a_{n1}$, as the solution of the linear system:

$$\sum_{k=1}^{n} \frac{\partial^2 \tilde{F}}{\partial a_j \partial a_k}\bigg|_0 (a_{k1} - a_{k0}) = \frac{\partial \tilde{F}}{\partial a_j}\bigg|_0 \qquad (j = 1, 2, \ldots, n),$$

where the symbol $|_0$ implies that the arguments $a_1, a_2, \ldots, a_n$ are replaced by $a_{10}, a_{20}, \ldots, a_{n0}$. More generally, if the sth approximation a_{1s}, $a_{2s}, \ldots, a_{ns}$ has been constructed, then the $(s+1)$th approximation $a_{1,s+1}$ $a_{2,s+1,\ldots,} a_{n,s+1}$ is constructed as the solution of the linear system

$$\sum_{k=1}^{n} \frac{\partial^2 \tilde{F}}{\partial a_j \partial a_k}\bigg|_s (a_{k,s+1} - a_{ks}) = \frac{\partial \tilde{F}}{\partial a_j}\bigg|_s \qquad (j = 1, 2, \ldots, n),$$

where the symbol $|_s$ implies that the arguments $a_1, a_2, \ldots, a_n$ are replaced by $a_{1s}, a_{2s}, \ldots, a_{ns}$.
The application of the Newton-Kantorovich-method to the Ritz-system encounters certain difficulties: a simple procedure for the choice of a

reliable initial approximation is far from being always satisfactory; in any case, the convergence of the method depends on the choice of this initial approximation. One procedure for making this choice is mentioned below in §72. In the example which we now consider, a randomly chosen initial approximation proves to be successful.

Example. We seek the function which satisfies the boundary conditions

$$y(0) = 1, \qquad y(1) = 0$$

and minimises the integral

$$F(y) = \int_0^1 (\tfrac{1}{48} y'^4 + y'^2 + y^6 - 6y)dx.$$

If we put $y = z+1-x$, then $z\ (0) = z(1) = 0$ and z will run through values in a linear set. As coordinate functions, we choose

$$\sin k\pi x \qquad (k = 1, 2, 3, \ldots).$$

The above problem has the exact solution $y = 1-x^2$. If the Fourier sine series of the function $z = y-(1-x) = x(1-x)$ is formed, then the terms in this series containing $\sin 2k\pi x$ $(k = 1, 2, \ldots)$ will be missing. Since test calculations also show that the terms with even k introduce terms with very small coefficients into the approximate solutions, we have only retained the coordinate functions

$$\sin (2k-1)\pi x \qquad (k = 1, 2, 3, \ldots)$$

in the final calculation.

We choose the coordinate functions corresponding to $k = 1, 2, 3, 4$ and 5, so that the approximate solution takes the form

$$y_5 = 1-x+\sum_{k=1}^{5} a_k \sin (2k-1)\pi x.$$

Substituting this result in the given functional, we obtain

$$\begin{aligned} F(y_5) &= F(a_1, a_2, a_3, a_4, a_5) = \\ &= -1.6458333-3.1830989a_1-1.0610330a_2-0.63661978a_3- \\ &\quad -0.45472841a_4-0.35367765a_5+6.0516525a_1^2+50.464872a_2^2+ \\ &\quad +139.29131a_3^2+272.53097a_4^2+450.18385a_5^2+0.76100853a_1^4+ \\ &\quad +61.641691a_2^4+475.63033a_3^4+1827.1815a_4^4+ \\ &\quad +4992.9770a_5^4+27.396307a_1^2 a_2^2+76.100853a_1^2 a_3^2+ \end{aligned}$$

$$+149.15767a_1^2 a_4^2+246.56676a_1^2 a_5^2+684.90767a_2^2 a_3^2+$$
$$+1342.4190a_2^2 a_4^2+2219.1009a_2^2 a_5^2+3728.9418a_3^2 a_4^2+$$
$$+6164.1691a_3^2 a_5^2+12081.771a_4^2 a_5^2+45.660512a_1^2 a_2 a_3+$$
$$+106.54119a_1^2 a_3 a_4+191.77415a_1^2 a_4 a_5+136.98153a_1 a_2^2 a_3+$$
$$+191.77415a_1 a_2^2 a_4+1598.1179a_2 a_3^2 a_4+684.90767a_1 a_3^2 a_5+$$
$$+6712.0952a_3 a_4^2 a_5+3.0440341a_1^3 a_2+246.56676a_2^3 a_5+$$
$$+319.62358a_1 a_2 a_3 a_4+410.94460a_1 a_2 a_3 a_5 +$$
$$+575.32244a_1 a_2 a_3 a_4+2876.6122a_2 a_3 a_4 a_5 .$$

Differentiating $F(y_5)$ w.r.t. the a_j and equating the results to zero, we obtain the Ritz-system:

$$\frac{\partial F(y_5)}{\partial a_1} = -3.1830989+12.103305a_1+3.0440341a_1^3+$$
$$+54.792614a_1 a_2^2+152.20171a_1 a_3^2-398.31534a_1 a_4^2+$$
$$+493.13352a_1 a_5^2+91.321024a_1 a_2 a_3+213.08238a_1 a_3 a_4+$$
$$+383.54830a_1 a_4 a_5+136.98153a_2^2 a_3+191.77415a_2^2 a_4+$$
$$+684.90767a_3^2 a_5+9.1321023a_1^2 a_2+319.62358a_2 a_3 a_4+$$
$$+410.94460a_2 a_3 a_5+575.32244a_2 a_4 a_5 = 0,$$

$$\frac{\partial F(y_5)}{\partial a_2} = -1.0610330+100.92974a_2+246.56676a_2^3+$$
$$+1369.8153a_2 a_3^2+2684.8380a_2 a_4^2+4438.2018a_2 a_5^2+$$
$$+45.660512a_1^2 a_3+273.96306a_1 a_2 a_3+383.5483a_1 a_2 a_4+$$
$$+1598.1179a_3^2 a_4+739.70028a_2^2 a_5+319.62358a_1 a_3 a_4+$$
$$+410.94460a_1 a_3 a_5+575.32244a_1 a_4 a_5+2876.6122a_3 a_4 a_5+$$
$$+54.792614a_1^2 a_2+3.0440341a_1^3 = 0,$$

$$\frac{\partial F(y_5)}{\partial a_3} = -0.63661978+278.58262a_3+1902.5213a_3^3+$$
$$+7457.8836a_3 a_4^2+12328.338a_3 a_5^2+152.20171a_1^2 a_3+$$
$$+1369.8153a_2^2 a_3+45.660512a_1^2 a_2+106.54119a_1^2 a_4+$$
$$+136.98153a_1 a_2^2+3196.2358a_2 a_3 a_4+1369.8153a_1 a_3 a_5+$$
$$+6712.0952a_4^2 a_5+319.62358a_1 a_2 a_4+410.94460a_1 a_2 a_5+$$
$$+2876.6122a_2 a_4 a_5 = 0,$$

$$\frac{\partial F(y_5)}{\partial a_4} = -0.45472841+545.06194a_4+7308.7260a_4^3+$$
$$+298.31534a_1^2a_4+2684.8380a_2^2a_4+7457.8836a_3^2a_4+$$
$$+24163.542a_4a_5^2+106.54119a_1^2a_3+191.77415a_1^2a_5+$$
$$+191.77415a_1a_2^2+1598.1179a_2a_3^2+13424.190a_3a_4a_5+$$
$$+319.62358a_1a_2a_3+575.32244a_1a_2a_5+2876.6122a_2a_3a_5=0,$$

$$\frac{\partial F(y_5)}{\partial a_5} = -0.35367765+900.36770a_5+19971.908a_5^3+$$
$$+493.13352a_1^2a_5+4438.2018a_2^2a_5+12328.338a_3^2a_5+$$
$$+24163.542a_4^2a_5+181.77415a_1^2a_4+684.90767a_1a_3^2+$$
$$+6712.0952a_3a_4^2+410.94460a_1a_2a_3+575.32244a_1a_2a_4+$$
$$+2876.6122a_2a_3a_4+246.56676a_2^3 = 0.$$

This system is now solved by the Newton-Kantorovich-method with the initial approximation

$$a_{10} = a_{20} = a_{30} = a_{40} = a_{50} = 0.$$

We present below the values obtained at the third iteration. For comparison purposes, the second iteration is also included:

n	the second approximation	the third approximation	n	the second approximation	the third approximation
a_1	0.25801631	0.25801628	a_4	0.00075839	0.00075838
a_2	0.00956008	0.00956007	a_5	0.00036394	0.00036394
a_3	0.00206908	0.00206907			

We compare this with the exact solution $y = 1-x^2$. It is easy to obtain the Fourier sine series representation

$$1-x^2 = 1-x+\sum_{k=1}^{\infty} \frac{8}{(2k-1)^3\pi^3} \sin(2k-1)\pi x.$$

In the Table below, we have evaluated the first five coefficients to an accuracy of eight decimal places:

k	$\frac{8}{(2k-1)^3\pi^3}$	k	$\frac{8}{(2k-1)^3\pi^3}$
1	0.25801227	4	0.00075222
2	0.00955601	5	0.00035393
3	0.00206410		

We see that the approximate values are accurate to five decimal places for the first four coefficients, while the fifth approximation only differs by one in the fifth place.
The value of $F(y_5)$, corresponding to the third iteration, equals

$$F(y_5) = -2.0666036,$$

while the exact solution of our variational problem $y = 1-x^2$ yields the value

$$F_{\min} = -2\tfrac{1}{15} = -2.0666667.$$

§72. Differentiation with respect to a parameter

The method of differentiation w.r.t. a parameter was proposed almost simultaneously by several authors (see Kiriya [1] and Davidenko [1]). Even though this method can be extended to a wide class of equations in a metric space, we limit consideration to its applications to a finite system of non-linear equations with a number of unknowns – in particular, a Ritz-system.
We wish to solve the system of equations

$$f_i(a_1, a_2, \ldots, a_n) = 0 \qquad (i = 1, 2, \ldots, n). \tag{72.1}$$

We construct the functions $F_1(a_1, a_2, \ldots, a_n; \lambda)$ as functions of the variables $a_1, a_2, \ldots, a_n$ and the subsidiary parameter λ, so that:
(a) these functions are continuously differentiable w.r.t. all the variables $a_1, a_2, \ldots, a_n$ and the parameter λ for $0 \leqq \lambda \leqq 1$;
(b)

$$F_i(a_1, a_2, \ldots, a_n; 1) \equiv f_i(a_1, a_2, \ldots, a_n) \; (i = 1, 2, \ldots, n); \tag{72.2}$$

and
(c) the system of equations

$$F_i(a_1, a_2, \ldots, a_n; 0) = 0 \qquad (i = 1, 2, \ldots, n) \tag{72.3}$$

can be solved with sufficient ease.
Let its solution be $a_i^{(0)}$ $(i = 1, 2, \ldots, n)$.
Instead of (72.1), we solve the system

$$F_i(a_1, a_2, \ldots, a_n; \lambda) = 0 \qquad (i = 1, 2, \ldots, n) \tag{72.4}$$

which, generally speaking, defines $a_1, a_2, \ldots, a_n$ as functions of λ. We observe that it is sufficient for us to know the values of these functions for $\lambda = 1$.

It is clear that (72.4) is equivalent to the system of ordinary differential equations

$$\sum_{k=1}^{n} \frac{\partial F_i}{\partial a_k} \frac{da_k}{d\lambda} + \frac{\partial F_i}{\partial \lambda} = 0, \tag{72.5}$$

which are obtained by differentiating (72.4) w.r.t. λ, and the initial condition

$$a_i|_{\lambda=0} = a_i^{(0)}. \tag{72.6}$$

In this way, we obtain the Cauchy problem (72.5) and (72.6) for the determination of the functions $a_i(\lambda)$. As is known, methods for its approximate solution have been developed. If (72.5) and (72.6) have a solution for $0 \leqq \lambda \leqq 1$, then we solve system (72.1) on substituting $\lambda = 1$.

The problem reduces to that of clarifying the conditions for which the Cauchy problem (72.5) and (72.6) has a solution on the *finite* interval $0 \leqq \lambda \leqq 1$. Below, we state sufficient conditions for the solvability of the Cauchy problem defined by the Ritz-process (for more general conditions, see Dovbysh and Mikhlin [1]).

We examine the functional $F(x)$, which is defined on the linear set $\mathfrak{D}(F)$ and is dense in a certain separable Banach space $\mathfrak{B}$. As usual, we assume that this functional is continuously differentiable on any finite-dimensional hyperplane of $\mathfrak{D}(F)$. Let the operator $Q = \operatorname{grad} F$ satisfy similar conditions: its domain $\mathfrak{D}(Q)$ is linear and dense in $\mathfrak{B}$, and it is continuously differentiable on any finite-dimensional hyperplane of $\mathfrak{D}(Q)$. Finally, we assume that for arbitrary $u \in \mathfrak{D}(Q)$ there exists a derivative Q'_u, which is defined on a dense set, which is independent of u and is contained in $\mathfrak{D}(Q)$, and is symmetric and positive:

$$(Q'_u h_1, h_2) = (h_1, Q'_u h_2), \qquad (Q'_u h, h) > 0, \qquad h \neq 0.$$

Let $\{\phi_k\}$ be a coordinate system. We assume that $\{\phi_k\} \in \mathfrak{D}(Q)$. Then the Ritz-system can be written in the form (70.5). Following the method of differentiation w.r.t. a parameter, we construct a new system which depends on a parameter λ, so that for $\lambda = 0$ the system is solvable without difficulty, while for $\lambda = 1$ it coincides with (70.5). We take this new system in the form

$$a_j+\lambda[(Q(u_n),\phi_j)-a_j] = 0 \quad (j = 1, 2, \ldots, n), \quad u_n = \sum_{k=1}^{n} a_k\phi_k, \tag{72.7}$$

where for $\lambda = 0$ we have

$$a_j|_{\lambda=0} = 0 \qquad (j = 1, 2, \ldots, n). \tag{72.8}$$

We differentiate (72.7) w.r.t. λ to give

$$\frac{da_j}{d\lambda}+\lambda\left\{\sum_{k=1}^{n}[(Q'_{u_n}\phi_k,\phi_j)-\delta_{jk}]\frac{da_k}{d\lambda}\right\}+(Q(u_n),\phi_j)-a_j = 0 \tag{72.9}$$

$$(j = 1, 2, \ldots, n).$$

Since the operator Q'_{u_n} is positive, we can introduce the energy inner product

$$[u, v] = (Q'_{u_n}u, v).$$

In this way, the coefficient-matrix for the derivatives $da_k/d\lambda$ can be written in the form

$$(1-\lambda)I+\lambda\begin{pmatrix}[\phi_1,\phi_1] & [\phi_2,\phi_1] \ldots [\phi_n,\phi_1]\\ [\phi_1,\phi_2] & [\phi_2,\phi_2] \ldots [\phi_n,\phi_2]\\ \cdot\ \cdot\ \cdot & \cdot\ \cdot\ \cdot\ \cdot\ \cdot\ \cdot\ \cdot\ \cdot\ \cdot\\ [\phi_1,\phi_n] & [\phi_2,\phi_n] \ldots [\phi_n,\phi_n]\end{pmatrix}, \tag{72.10}$$

where I is the identity matrix. Since the second matrix in (72.10) is the Gram matrix of the linearly independent elements $\phi_1, \phi_2, \ldots, \phi_n$, it is positive definite. Hence, the matrix (72.10) will be positive definite for arbitrary $\lambda \in [0, 1]$. It follows that for $\lambda \in (0, 1]$ the determinant Δ_n of (72.10) differs from zero and equations (72.9) can be solved for $da_j/d\lambda$. Using Cramer's rule, we obtain

$$\frac{da_j}{d\lambda} = \frac{\Delta_n^{(j)}}{\Delta_n} \equiv g_j(a_1, a_2, \ldots, a_n; \lambda) \qquad (j = 1, 2, \ldots, n). \tag{72.11}$$

We make the following assumptions:
(1) The functions $(Q(u_n), \phi_j)$ and $(Q'_{u_n}\phi_k, \phi_j)$ tend to infinity as rapidly as polynomials:

$$|(Q(u_n), \phi_j)| \leqq P_m(|a_1|, |a_2|, \ldots, |a_n|), \tag{72.12}$$

$$|(Q'_{u_n}\phi_k, \phi_j)| \leqq P_{m-1}(|a_1|, |a_2|, \ldots, |a_n|), \tag{72.13}$$

where P_m and P_{m-1} are polynomials of degree m and $m-1$, respectively. The form of these polynomials and m can depend on n.
(2) In every interval $\delta \leqq \lambda \leqq 1$, where $\delta > 0$, the lower bound

$$(Q'_{u_n} h, h) \geqq N(\sum_{j=1}^{n} a_j^2)^{\frac{1}{2}(m-1)} ||h||^2 \tag{72.14}$$

holds, where N can depend on n and δ.
Using (72.13) and (72.14), we obtain for the determinant Δ_n the estimate

$$N_1(\sum_{k=1}^{n} a_k^2)^{\frac{1}{2}n(m-1)} \leqq \Delta_n \leqq P_{n(m-1)}(|a_1|, |a_2|, \ldots, |a_n|), \tag{72.15}$$

where N_1 is a positive constant and $P_{n(m-1)}$ is a polynomial of degree $n(m-1)$. Since the inequality on the r.h.s. of (72.15) is an immediate consequence of (72.13), it only remains to establish the l.h.s. inequality. We have

$$\sum_{j,k=1}^{n} [\phi_k, \phi_j] t_k t_j = |||\sum_{j=1}^{n} \phi_j t_j|||^2 = (Q'_{u_n} v_n, v_n),$$

where

$$v_n = \sum_{j=1}^{n} \phi_j t_j .$$

As a consequence of (72.14),

$$(Q'_{u_n} v_n, v_n) \geqq N(\sum_{k=1}^{n} a_k^2)^{\frac{1}{2}(m-1)} ||\sum_{k=1}^{n} t_k \phi_k||^2.$$

On the unit sphere, the expression

$$||\sum_{k=1}^{n} t_k \phi_k||^2$$

is a continuous, non-negative function of $t_1, t_2, \ldots, t_n$, where not all the t_i are zero simultaneously. In the opposite case, the functions ϕ_1, $\phi_2, \ldots, \phi_n$ would be linearly dependent. This implies that the last expression has a positive lower bound

$$||\sum_{k=1}^{n} t_k \phi_k||^2 \geqq L = \text{const} > 0, \qquad \sum_{k=1}^{n} t_k^2 = 1.$$

Hence,

$$\sum_{j,k=1}^{n} [\phi_k, \phi_j] t_k t_j \geqq LN(\sum_{k=1}^{n} a_k^2)^{\frac{1}{2}(m-1)}, \qquad \sum_{k=1}^{n} t_k^2 = 1.$$

This inequality shows that all the eigenvalues of the matrix

$$\begin{pmatrix} [\phi_1, \phi_1] & [\phi_2, \phi_1] \ldots [\phi_n, \phi_1] \\ [\phi_1, \phi_2] & [\phi_2, \phi_2] \ldots [\phi_n, \phi_2] \\ \cdot \quad \cdot \quad \cdot & \cdot \quad \cdot \quad \cdot \quad \cdot \quad \cdot \\ [\phi_1, \phi_n] & [\phi_2, \phi_n] \ldots [\phi_n, \phi_n] \end{pmatrix}$$

are larger than

$$LN(\sum_{k=1}^{n} a_k^2)^{\frac{1}{2}(m-1)} \qquad (\delta \leqq \lambda \leqq 1).$$

In this way, all the eigenvalues of (72.10) are larger than

$$\delta LN(\sum_{k=1}^{n} a_k^2)^{\frac{1}{2}(m-1)},$$

and the determinant Δ_n is larger than

$$N_1(\sum_{k=1}^{n} a_k^2)^{\frac{1}{2}n(m-1)}, \qquad N_1 = (\delta LN)^n.$$

This proves the l.h.s. inequality in (72.15).

We now prove that the Cauchy problem (72.8) and (72.9) has a solution for $0 \leqq \lambda \leqq 1$. First of all, we note that the l.h.s. of (72.9) is continuous and continuously differentiable w.r.t. all arguments for $0 \leqq \lambda \leqq 1$ and $-\infty < a_j < \infty$ $(j = 1, 2, \ldots, n)$. This follows from the fact that for these values of the arguments the determinant Δ_n is positive bounded below.

We choose the numbers $\lambda^* \in (0, 1)$ and $a^* \in (0, \infty)$ and we examine the region

$$0 \leqq \lambda \leqq \lambda^*, \qquad -a^* \leqq a_j \leqq a^* \qquad (j = 1, 2, \ldots, n). \tag{72.16}$$

In this region, all the conditions of the classical existence theory for the solutions of a Cauchy problem are satisfied, and hence, problem (72.8) and (72.9) has a unique solution for $\lambda \in [0, \sigma]$, where $\sigma = \min(\lambda^*, a/M)$ and M is the largest of the maxima of the g_j on the region (72.16).

We now choose a number δ, $0 < \delta < \sigma$, and assume for $\lambda = \delta$ that $a_j = \tilde{a}_j$ $(j = 1, 2, \ldots, n)$. We examine the region

$$\delta \leqq \lambda \leqq 1, \qquad -\infty < a_j < +\infty \qquad (j = 1, 2, \ldots, n) \tag{72.17}$$

and consider the Cauchy problem for (72.9) with the initial conditions

$$a_j|_{\lambda=\delta} = \tilde{a}_j \qquad (j = 1, 2, \ldots, n). \tag{72.18}$$

From the estimates (72.12)–(72.15), it is clear that the derivatives $\partial g_j/\partial a_k$ are bounded in the region (72.17), and hence, (see Sansone [1]) there exists a unique solution of (72.9) and (72.18) which is defined on the interval $\delta \leqq \lambda \leqq 1$.

Now, it is clear that (72.8) and (72.9) have a solution which is defined for $0 \leqq \lambda \leqq 1$. It follows, in particular, that the Ritz-system (67.5) is solvable. Dovbysh [1] has shown that estimates of the form (72.12)–(72.14) hold for functionals (68.1) under very wide conditions when $m = 1$.

In connection with the method of differentiation w.r.t. a parameter, the following difficulty arises. In the general case, the Ritz-system (70.3) does not have a unique solution. Such is the case, for example, when $\boldsymbol{P}u$, where $\boldsymbol{P} = \text{grad } F$, is a polynomial in u and its derivatives. From the solution of system (70.3), it is necessary to choose the one which minimises F. It is also important to clarify that this solution coincides with the one which is defined by the method of differentiation w.r.t. a parameter. A positive answer to this question (see Mikhlin [22]) is a consequence of the following conjecture:

Let F satisfy conditions I–III, §63, and inequality (66.2), where $\boldsymbol{P} = \text{grad } F$. For arbitrary λ, $0 \leqq \lambda \leqq 1$, the system, defined by the method of differentiation w.r.t. a parameter,

$$(1-\lambda)a_j^{(i)} + \lambda \frac{\partial F(\sum_{k=1}^{n} a_k^{(n)}\phi_k)}{\partial a_j} = 0 \qquad (j = 1, 2, \ldots, n), \tag{72.19}$$

has only one solution with respect to which

$$\Phi_\lambda(a^{(n)}) = \frac{1-\lambda}{2} \sum_{k=1}^{n} (a_k^{(n)})^2 + \lambda F(\sum_{k=1}^{n} a_k^{(n)}\phi_k) \tag{72.20}$$

has a real value. This solution also minimises (72.20).

In order to prove this proposition, let the value of (72.20) be real for the vectors $a^{(n)} = (a_1^{(n)}, a_2^{(n)}, \ldots, a_n^{(n)})$ and $b^{(n)} = (b_1^{(n)}, b_2^{(n)}, \ldots, b_n^{(n)})$, and $a^{(n)}$ satisfy (72.19). Using Taylor's Theorem, we obtain $(0 < \theta < 1)$

$$\Phi_\lambda(b^{(n)}) - \Phi_\lambda(a^{(n)}) = \frac{1-\lambda}{2} \sum_{k=1}^{n} (b_k^{(n)} - a_k^{(n)})^2 +$$

$$+ \frac{\lambda}{2} \sum_{j,k=1}^{n} \frac{\partial^2 \Phi_\lambda}{\partial a_j \partial a_k} (a^{(n)} + \theta(b^n - a^{(n)})(b_j^{(n)} - b_k^{(n)})(a_j^{(n)} - a_k^{(n)}).$$

It is clear that, since the matrix of second derivatives of Φ_λ is positive definite, $\Phi_\lambda(b^{(n)}) > \Phi_\lambda(a^{(n)})$, which proves the conjecture. Hence, for $\lambda = 1$, we find that the solution, defined by the method of differentiation w.r.t. a parameter, minimises

$$F(\sum_{k=1}^{n} a_k^{(n)}\phi_k).$$

Note 1. In our presentation, the system of differential equations, obtained by differentiation w.r.t. a parameter, serves not only as a means for the approximate solution of our given problem, but also as a means for the proof of the existence of its actual solution. One can act in a different way: using the above procedure, conditions can be established w.r.t. which (72.4) has a solution which is defined and continuously differentiable for $0 \leqq \lambda \leqq 1$. The existence of a solution of the Cauchy problem (72.5) and (72.6) is automatically proved, and it only remains to construct this solution using some approximate method. Such a procedure was developed in Vlasova [1] using finite difference methods. The nature of this work will be discussed in the next section. This procedure has also been applied to the Ritz-process by Yakovlev [1] (the results of Yakovlev are based on a result of Lozinskiy [1] the complete proof of which, as far as the Author knows, has not yet been published).

We present the basic results of Yakovlev [1]. For brevity, we let a, f and F denote the vectors with components a_j, f_j and F_j $(j = 1, 2, \ldots, n)$, respectively, and J the Jacobian of the matrix of the vectors f. The system $a+\lambda(f-a) = 0$ has a continuously differentiable solution on the interval $0 \leqq \lambda \leqq 1$, if the following conditions are satisfied:

(a) There exists a number r^*, $0 < r^* \leqq \infty$, such that within the sphere $||a|| \leqq r$, $0 \leqq r < r^*$, the inequality

$$(J(a)h, h) \geqq m(r)||h||^2$$

holds, where h is arbitrary and $m(r)$ is a function which is positive and non-increasing in the interval $0 \leqq r < r^*$.

(b) The following inequality is true

$$||f(0)|| \leqq \int_0^{r^*} m^*(\rho)d\rho, \qquad m^*(\rho) = \min\{1, m(\rho)\}.$$

Under these conditions, the Cauchy problem

$$\frac{da_j}{d\lambda} + \lambda\left[\sum_{k=1}^{n} \frac{\partial f_j}{\partial a_k} - \delta_{jk}\right]\frac{da_k}{d\lambda} + f_j - a_j = 0, \qquad a_j|_{\lambda=0} = 0,$$

has a solution. Yakovlev [1] also examined a method for the introduction of the parameter: he defined the vector function $F(x, \lambda)$ by the formula

$$F(x, \lambda) = f(x) - (1-\lambda) f(0).$$

The existence and continuous differentiability of the solution of $F(x, \lambda) = 0$ and the corresponding Cauchy problem are established, if condition (a) above and conditions (c) and (d) below are satisfied:

(c) For $0 \leqq r \leqq r^*$, $\|J^{-1}(a)\| \leqq D(r)$, where $D(r)$ is a continuous and non-decreasing function

(d) $\|f(0)\| \leqq \rho^*$, where $\rho^* = \int_0^{r^*} \frac{1}{D(\rho)} \, d\rho.$

Note 2. As numerical examples show, the accuracy of the method of differentiation w.r.t. parameter is not good. However, it is appropriate to use the approximation obtained by this method as an initial (starting) solution for the Newton-Kontorovich-method.

§73. The application to finite difference equations

Usually, problems in the calculus of variations reduce to problems connected with the extremum of certain integrals. In such cases, an approximate solution of the problem can be constructed by finite difference methods. For this purpose, we replace the integral by a finite sum w.r.t. a certain quadrature formula, and replace the derivatives under the integral sign by equivalent finite difference representations. In this way, we obtain problems connected with the extrema of the new functionals defined on finite dimensional spaces. The Euler-Lagrange equations for such functionals are defined by systems of finite difference equations. If the original functionals are not quadratic, then the finite difference systems are non-linear and use of the method of differentiation w.r.t. a parameter can be made for their solution. Below, we reproduce in essence the results of Vlasova [1] for the so-called "simplest problem in the calculus of variations".

We consider the problem: find the curve which passes through the points A, (a, a_1), and B, (b, b_1), and minimises the integral

$$\int_a^b \phi(x, y, y') dx. \tag{73.1}$$

We assume that for $x \in [a, b]$ and any finite value of y and y' the function

$\phi(x, y, y')$ is continuous together with its derivatives upto the second order, inclusive.

On the interval $[a, b]$, we choose the $n+2$ points

$$x_0 = a, x_1, \ldots, x_n, x_{n+1} = b.$$

Using for these points a quadrature foımula with coefficients $C_k > 0$ and replacing the derivatives by first differences defined on these points, we obtain the approximation

$$\int_a^b \phi(x, y, y')dx \approx \sum_{k=0}^{n} C_k \phi\left(x_k, y_k, \frac{y_{k+1}-y_k}{\Delta x_k}\right),$$

where

$$\Delta x_k = x_{k+1} - x_k, \qquad y_0 = a_1, \qquad y_{n+1} = b_1.$$

The replacement of $y'(x_k)$ by the equivalent expression $(y_{k+1}-y_k)/\Delta x_k$, though not very exact, is the simplest. In the example below (see §74), we shall make use of a more exact substitution.

We introduce into the considerations a sufficiently smooth function $C(x)$ which has the values C_k at the point x_k.

We write

$$\psi(x, y, y') = C(x)\phi(x, y, y').$$

The exact variational problem, formulated above, is now replaced by the approximate problem: find the vector $Y = (y_1, \ldots, y_n)$ w.r.t. which the sum

$$\sum_{k=0}^{n} \psi\left(x_k, y_k, \frac{y_{k+1}-y_k}{\Delta x_k}\right) = f(Y) \tag{73.2}$$

takes its minimum value.

The necessary condition for the existence of a minimum leads to the following system for the determination of Y:

$$\left.\frac{\partial\psi}{\partial y}\right|_k - \frac{1}{\Delta x_k}\left.\frac{\partial\psi}{\partial y'}\right|_k + \frac{1}{\Delta x_{k-1}}\left.\frac{\partial\psi}{\partial y'}\right|_{k-1} = 0. \tag{73.3}$$

Here and below, $\partial\psi/\partial y|_k$ denotes the partial derivative of $\psi(x, y, y')$ w.r.t. y which is evaluated at the point $(x_k, y_k, (y_{k+1}-y_k)/\Delta x_k)$. A similar notation is used for the other derivatives.

As is well known, in order that Y satisfies (73.3) and attains the required minimum of (73.2), it is sufficient that the derivative of its gradient be positive definite for arbitrary Y and $H = [h_1, h_2, \ldots, h_n]$. We write

$\boldsymbol{P} = \operatorname{grad} f$. On performing the necessary calculations, we obtain

$$(\boldsymbol{P}'_Y H, H) = \sum_{k=0}^{n} [(p_k - q_k + q_{k-1}) h_k^2 + (r_k - q_k)(h_{k+1} - h_k)^2], \tag{73.4}$$

where

$$p_k = \left.\frac{\partial^2 \psi}{\partial y^2}\right|_k, \qquad q_k = \frac{1}{\Delta x_k} \left.\frac{\partial^2 \psi}{\partial y\, \partial y'}\right|_k, \qquad r_k = \frac{1}{(\Delta x_k)^2} \left.\frac{\partial^2 \psi}{\partial y'^2}\right|_k .$$

We assume that the integrand $\phi(x, y, y')$ and the quadrature formula, defined at the points x_k with coefficients C_k, are such that for arbitrary finite y_k the inequalities

$$r_k - q_k > 0, \tag{73.4'}$$

$$p_k - q_k + q_{k-1} \geqq \delta \qquad (k = 1, 2, \ldots, n), \tag{73.4''}$$

are satisfied, where δ is a certain positive constant. Then, for arbitrary Y,

$$(\boldsymbol{P}'_Y H, H) \geqq \delta \sum_{k=1}^{n} h_k^2 > 0.$$

Hence, if conditions (73.4′) and (73.4″) are satisfied, it is sufficient to solve (73.3), in order to determine the approximate minimising vector.

Note 1. For sufficiently small Δx_k, condition (73.4′) follows from the strengthened condition of Legendre (see, Achiezer [1; §15]). For small Δx_k and $C_1 = C_2 = \ldots = C_n$, condition (73.4″) is a consequence of the Bernstein condition (see, Bernstein [1; p. 37] or Achiezer [1; §9]), which applies to the Euler equation of our problem and the strengthened condition of Legendre. For equations of the form $y'' = f(x, y, y')$, the Bernstein condition takes the form $\partial f / \partial y \geqq K$, where K is a positive constant.

For the solution of (73.3), which is in general non-linear, we apply the method of differentiation w.r.t. a parameter.

We form the following system, which contains the parameter λ, $0 \leqq \lambda \leqq 1$,

$$N_k(\lambda, y_{k-1}, y_k, y_{k+1}) = (1-\lambda)(-\delta^2 y_k + T_k y_k) + \\ + \lambda \left(\left.\frac{\partial \psi}{\partial y}\right|_k - \frac{1}{\Delta x_k} \left.\frac{\partial \psi}{\partial y'}\right|_k + \frac{1}{\Delta x_{k-1}} \left.\frac{\partial \psi}{\partial y'}\right|_{k-1} \right) = 0 \tag{73.5}$$

$(k = 1, 2, \ldots, n)$,

where

$$\delta^2 y_k = R_k y_{k+1} - (R_k + R_{k-1}) y_k + R_{k-1} y_{k-1},$$

and the R_k and T_k are arbitrarily chosen positive constants.

For $\lambda = 1$, (73.5) coincides with (73.3), and for $\lambda = 0$ it reduces to the linear system

$$-\delta^2 y_k + T_k y_k = 0 \qquad (k = 1, 2, \ldots, n). \tag{73.6}$$

The quadratic form, corresponding to the coefficient-matrix of (73.6), which has the structure

$$\sum_{k=0}^{n} [R_k(h_{k+1} - h_k)^2 + T_k h_k^2]$$

is positive definite. Hence, the solution of (73.6) exists and is unique. In particular, if $a_1 > b_1 \geqq 0$, then we can take

$$R_k = \frac{1}{2^{k-n}} \frac{1}{\Delta x_k}, \qquad T_k = \frac{a_1 - b_1}{2^{k-n}[a_1(b - x_k) + b_1(x_k - a)]}.$$

In this way, the vector Y with components defined by

$$y_k = \frac{a_1(b - x_k) + b_1(x_k - a)}{b - a} \qquad (k = 1, 2, \ldots, n)$$

satisfies (73.6).

We differentiate system (73.5) w.r.t. the parameter λ. This yields a system of linear equations with unknowns $\partial y_l / \partial \lambda$:

$$\begin{aligned} &\sum_{l=k-1}^{k+1} \frac{\partial N_k}{\partial y_l} \frac{\partial y_l}{dy} = -\frac{\partial N_k}{\partial \lambda} \qquad (k = 1, 2, \ldots, n), \\ &\frac{dy_0}{d\lambda} = \frac{dy_{n+1}}{d\lambda} = 0. \end{aligned} \tag{73.7}$$

We introduce the notation

$$\begin{aligned} \alpha_{k-1} &= -\frac{\partial N_k}{\partial y_{k-1}} = \lambda(r_{k-1} - q_{k-1}) + (1 - \lambda)R_{k-1}, \\ \beta_k &= \frac{\partial N_k}{\partial y_k} = \lambda(p_k - 2q_k + r_k + r_{k-1}) + (1 - \lambda)[T_k + R_k + R_{k-1}], \\ \alpha_k &= -\frac{\partial N_k}{\partial y_{k+1}} = \lambda(r_k - q_k) + (1 - \lambda)R_k, \\ y_k &= \frac{\partial N_k}{\partial \lambda} = \delta^2 y_k - T_k y_k + \left.\frac{\partial \psi}{\partial y}\right|_k - \frac{1}{\Delta x_k} \left.\frac{\partial \psi}{\partial y'}\right|_k + \frac{1}{\Delta x_{k-1}} \left.\frac{\partial \psi}{\partial x'}\right|_{k-1}. \end{aligned} \tag{73.8}$$

It is clear that the coefficient-matrix A of (73.7) is a symmetric, tri-diagonal matrix of the form

$$A_n = \begin{pmatrix} \beta_1 & -\alpha_1 & 0 & \dots & 0 & 0 \\ -\alpha_1 & \beta_2 & -\alpha_2 & \dots & 0 & 0 \\ \cdot & \cdot & \cdot & \cdot & \cdot & \cdot \\ 0 & 0 & 0 & \dots & -\alpha_{n-1} & \beta_n \end{pmatrix}.$$

We show that (73.7) is solvable w.r.t. the unknowns $dy_l/d\lambda$. We consider the quadratic form which corresponds to the matrix A_n and is defined by the expression

$$(A_n H, H) = \sum_{k=1}^{n} \{(1-\lambda)T_k + \lambda(p_k - q_k + q_{k-1})\} h_k^2 + \\ + \sum_{k=0}^{n} \{(1-\lambda)R_k + \lambda(r_k - q_k)\}(h_k - h_{k+1})^2.$$

It follows from (73.4′) and (73.4″) that the inequality

$$(A_n H, H) \geqq \delta_1 \sum_{k=1}^{n} h_k^2, \qquad 0 < \delta_1 \leqq \delta\lambda + (1-\lambda) \min_{1 \leqq k \leqq n} T_k$$

guarantees the positive definiteness of the quadratic form $(A_n H, H)$ as well as a lower bound for the determinant Δ_n of A_n:

$$\Delta_n \geqq \delta_1^n > 0. \tag{73.9}$$

In this way, system (73.7) can be solved for the unknowns $dy_l/d\lambda$ and Cramer's formula yields

$$\frac{dy_l}{d\lambda} = \frac{\Delta_n^l}{\Delta_n}, \qquad \lambda \in [0, 1] \qquad (l = 1, 2, \dots, n). \tag{73.10}$$

We now establish that there exists a unique solution of system (73.10) on the interval [0, 1] w.r.t. the initial condition

$$\lambda = 0, \quad y_0 = a_1, \quad y_k = \bar{y}_k \qquad (k = 1, 2, \dots, n), \qquad y_{n+1} = b_1,$$

where the $\bar{y}_k$ are the solutions of (73.6) for the chosen values of R_k and T_k.

For this purpose, we prove that (73.5) is uniquely solvable for the unknowns $y_1, y_2, \dots, y_k$ with $\lambda \in [0, 1]$ and the functions $y_k(\lambda)$ $(k = 1, 2, \dots, n)$ are continuous and continuously differentiable w.r.t. λ.

As a preliminary, we establish an *a priori* estimate for the solution of (73.5).

Lemma 73.1. *If system* (73.5) *has a solution, then it is uniformly bounded for* $\lambda \in [0, 1]$.

Proof. Let $y_k(\lambda)$ and $\bar{y}_k$ be the solutions of (73.5) and (73.6), respectively, $\delta y_k(\lambda) = y_k(\lambda) - \bar{y}_k$ and $\lambda_0 \neq 0$ be a fixed value of λ.
Using the mean value theorem, we obtain

$$-N_k(\lambda_0, \bar{y}_{k-1}, \bar{y}_k, \bar{y}_{k+1}) = \\ = \frac{\partial \tilde{N}_k}{\partial y_{k-1}} \delta y_{k-1}(\lambda_0) + \frac{\partial \tilde{N}_k}{\partial y_k} \delta y_k(\lambda_0) + \frac{\partial \tilde{N}_k}{\partial y_{k+1}} \delta y_{k+1}(\lambda_0).$$

The mark $\sim$ implies that all the partial derivatives of $\phi(x, y, y')$ in $\partial N_k / \partial y_{k-1}$, $\partial N_k / \partial y_k$ and $\partial N_k / \partial y_{k+1}$ are evaluated at the points

$$\left(x_k, \bar{y}_k + \theta_k \delta y_k(\lambda_0), \frac{\bar{y}_{k+1} - \bar{y}_k}{\Delta x_k} + \theta_k \frac{\delta y_{k+1}(\lambda_0) - \delta y_k(\lambda_0)}{\Delta x_k} \right)$$

and

$$\left(x_{k-1}, \bar{y}_{k-1} + \theta_k \delta y_{k-1}(\lambda_0), \frac{\bar{y}_k - \bar{y}_{k-1}}{\Delta x_{k-1}} + \theta_k \frac{\delta y_k(\lambda_0) - \delta y_{k-1}(\lambda_0)}{\Delta x_k} \right).$$

We rewrite the previous expression, making use of the notation (73.8),

$$-N_k(\lambda_0, \bar{y}_{k-1}, \bar{y}_k, \bar{y}_{k+1}) = \\ = \tilde{\alpha}_{k-1}[\delta y_k(\lambda_0) - \delta y_{k-1}(\lambda_0)] + (\tilde{\beta}_k - \tilde{\alpha}_{k-1} - \tilde{\alpha}_k)\delta y_k(\lambda_0) + \\ + \tilde{\alpha}_k[\delta y_k(\lambda_0) - \delta y_{k+1}(\lambda_0)]. \tag{73.11}$$

It follows from conditions (73.4′) and (73.4″) and the positiveness of the constants T_k and R_k that, for $\lambda \in [0, 1]$,

$$\lambda_k \geqq 0, \\ \beta_k = \alpha_k + \alpha_{k-1} + \lambda(p_k - q_k + q_{k-1}) + (1-\lambda)T_k \geqq \\ \geqq \alpha_k + \alpha_{k+1} + \delta_1. \tag{73.12}$$

Let the function $|\delta y_k(\lambda_0)|$ attain a maximum for $k = t$,

$$\delta y_t(\lambda_0) > 0, \qquad \delta y_t(\lambda_0) \geqq \delta y_{t-1}(\lambda_0), \\ \delta y_t(\lambda_0) \geqq \delta y_{t+1}(\lambda_0).$$

It follows from (73.11) and (73.12) that

$$[y_t(\lambda_0)-\bar{y}_t] \leqq -\frac{1}{\delta_1} N_t(\lambda_0, \bar{y}_{t-1}, \bar{y}_t, \bar{y}_{t+1}).$$

If $\delta y_k(\lambda_0)$ has a negative minimum, an analogous inequality is introduced for $-\delta y_t(\lambda_0)$.

Since λ_0 is an arbitrary point on the interval [0, 1], we can form the following estimate for the solution of (73.5)

$$|y_k(\lambda)-\bar{y}_k| \leqq \frac{1}{\delta_1} \max_{\substack{1\leqq k\leqq n\\ 0\leqq\lambda\leqq 1}} |N_k(\lambda, \bar{y}_{k-1}, \bar{y}_k, \bar{y}_{k+1})| = m.$$

Hence, the Lemma is proved.

For a proof of the existence of a solution of the system (73.5), it will be necessary for us to use an implicit function theorem for equations of the form $F(x, y, z) = 0$.

As is known, such theorems have a local character. They indicate that the solvability of $F(x, y, z) = 0$ w.r.t. z holds in a certain neighbourhood around the initial point.

We shall define more precisely the size of this region in connection with system (73.8).

Lemma 73.2. *Let the function $F(x, y, z)$ be continuous and have continuous partial derivatives in the region D defined by*

$$\begin{aligned} &0 \leqq x-x_0 \leqq \Delta x, && \Delta x > 0,\\ &|y-y_0| \leqq \Delta y, && \Delta y > 0,\\ &|z-z_0| \leqq \Delta z, && \Delta z > 0, \end{aligned}$$

and moreover

$$\begin{aligned} &|F_x| \leqq M, \quad |F_y| \leqq M,\\ &F_z \geqq k > 0,\\ &F(x_0, y_0, z_0) = 0. \end{aligned} \tag{73.13}$$

Then the implicit function theorem is valid in the region

$$\begin{aligned} &0 \leqq x-x_0 \leqq \min\left\{\frac{k}{2M}\Delta z, \Delta x\right\},\\ &|y-y_0| \leqq \min\left\{\frac{k}{2M}\Delta z, \Delta y\right\}. \end{aligned} \tag{73.14}$$

Proof. For the proof, we apply the mean value theorem to the function $F(x_0, y_0, z)$:

$$F(x_0, y_0, z_0+\Delta z) = F_z(x_0, y_0, z_0+\theta_1 \Delta z)\Delta z, \qquad 0 < \theta_1 < 1.$$

It follows, on using the estimate (73.13), that

$$F(x_0, y_0, z_0+\Delta z) \geqq k\Delta z.$$

We determine the segment on the half-line

$$x \geqq x_0, \qquad y = y_0, \qquad z = z_0+\Delta z,$$

for which the following inequality holds

$$F(x, y_0, z_0+\Delta z) \geqq \frac{k}{2}\Delta z. \tag{73.15}$$

Let

$$F(\xi, y_0, z_0+\Delta z) = \frac{k}{2}\Delta z$$

be satisfied at the point $\xi \in [x_0, x_0+\Delta x]$. Using the mean value theorem, we obtain

$$F(\xi, y_0, z_0+\Delta z) = F(x_0, y_0, z_0+\Delta z)+$$
$$+F_x[x_0+\theta_2(\xi-x_0), y_0, z_0+\Delta z](\xi-x_0), \qquad 0 < \theta_2 < 1.$$

If $(\xi-x_0) < \Delta x$, then

$$\xi-x_0 \geqq \frac{k}{2M}\Delta z.$$

Hence, (73.15) is satisfied for

$$0 \leqq x-x_0 \leqq \min\left\{\frac{k}{2M}\Delta z, \Delta x\right\}.$$

In a similar way, we find that in the region d, defined by inequalities (73.14), the function $F(x, y, z_0+\Delta z)$ is non-negative.
Repeating the argument for the plane $z = z_0-\Delta z$, we establish that in the region d the function $F(x, y, z_0-\Delta z)$ is non-positive.
The existence of the required implicit function in d now follows from the results above. Its continuity and continuous differentiability is proved in the usual way.

Theorem 73.1. *If conditions* (73.4') *and* (73.4'') *as well as the smoothness conditions, formulated above for the integrand function* $\phi(x, y, y')$, *are satisfied, then system* (73.5) *is uniquely solvable on the interval* [0, 1] *and defines the functions*

$$y_k = Q_k(\lambda) \qquad (k = 1, 2, \ldots, n),$$

which are continuous together with their first derivatives on the same interval.

Proof. If follows from the continuity of $\phi(x, y, y')$ and its derivatives, which are contained in (73.8), as well as from the estimate (73.9), that there exist constants S and δ_0 such that, for $\lambda \in [0, 1]$ and $|y_k(\lambda) - \bar{y}_k| \leqq 3m$ for all k, the inequalities

$$\begin{gathered} |\gamma_k| \leqq S, \qquad \alpha_k \leqq S, \qquad \beta_k \leqq S, \qquad \Delta_k \leqq S, \\ \frac{\alpha_{k-1}\Delta_{k-2}}{\Delta_{k-1}} \leqq S, \qquad \frac{\Delta_k}{\Delta_{k-1}} \geqq \delta_0, \\ \left| \gamma_k + \frac{\alpha_{k-1}\Delta_{k-2}}{\Delta_{k-1}} \left(\gamma_{k-1} + \ldots + \frac{\alpha_1 \Delta_0}{\Delta_1} \gamma_1 \right) \right| \leqq S, \end{gathered} \tag{73.16}$$

hold.

Choosing S sufficiently large, we can assume that

$$\frac{1}{S} \cdot \frac{\delta_0}{2} \leqq 1.$$

For $\lambda = 0$, (73.5) has the solution $\bar{y}_k$ $(k = 1, 2, \ldots, n)$. We continue this solution w.r.t. the parameter λ.

It follows from Lemma 73.2 and the implicit function theorem that, in the region defined by

$$0 \leqq \lambda \leqq \min \left\{ 2m \left(\frac{\delta_0}{2S} \right)^{n-1}, 1 \right\},$$

$$|y_{j+1} - \bar{y}_{j+1}| \leqq 2m \left(\frac{\delta_0}{2S} \right)^{j} \qquad (j = 0, 1, 2, \ldots, n-1),$$

system (73.5) defines the recursion formula

$$y_j = \phi_j(\lambda, y_{j+1}), \qquad \phi_j(0, \bar{y}_{j+1}) = \bar{y}_j \qquad (j = 1, 2, \ldots, n-1),$$

where the functions $\phi_j(\lambda, y_{j+1})$ are continuous and have continuous partial derivatives

$$\begin{aligned}\frac{\partial \phi_j}{\partial \lambda} &= -\frac{\Delta_{j-1}}{\Delta_j}\left\{\gamma_j + \frac{\alpha_{j-1}\Delta_{j-2}}{\Delta_{j-1}}\left[\gamma_{j-1} + \ldots + \frac{\alpha_1 \Delta_0}{\Delta_1}\gamma_1\right]\right\}, \\ \frac{\partial \phi_j}{\partial y_{j+1}} &= \frac{\alpha_j \Delta_{j-1}}{\Delta_j}.\end{aligned} \tag{73.17}$$

In fact, we assume that the above assertion is true for $n = k$: for $n = 2$, this is obtained by the immediate application of Lemma 73.2 and the implicit function theorem to the first equation of system (73.5).
We apply Lemma 73.2 and the implicit function theorem to the $(k+1)^{\text{th}}$ equation of (73.5).
As $F(x, y, z)$, we choose the function

$$N_k[\lambda, \phi_{k-1}(\lambda, y_k), y_k, y_{k+1}] = \Phi_k(\lambda, y_k, y_{k+1})$$

and put

$$x = \lambda, \qquad y = y_{k+1}, \qquad z = y_k.$$

We define the region D by

$$\begin{aligned}&0 \leqq \lambda \leqq \min\left\{2m\left(\frac{\delta_0}{2S}\right)^{k-1}, 1\right\}, \\ &|y_k - \bar{y}_k| \leqq 2m\left(\frac{\delta_0}{2S}\right)^{k-1}, \\ &|y_{k+1} - \bar{y}_{k+1}| \leqq 2m.\end{aligned}$$

We calculate the partial derivatives of $\Phi_k(\lambda, y_k, y_{k+1})$, used in Lemma 73.2, employing the expressions for $\partial\phi_{k-1}/\partial\lambda$, $\partial\phi_{k-1}/\partial y_k$:

$$\begin{aligned}\frac{\partial \Phi_k}{\partial \lambda} &= \frac{\partial N_k}{\partial \lambda} + \frac{\partial N_k}{\partial y_{k-1}}\frac{\partial \phi_{k-1}}{\partial \lambda} = \\ &= \gamma_k + \frac{\alpha_{k-1}\Delta_{k-2}}{\Delta_{k-1}}\left\{\gamma_{k-1} + \ldots + \frac{\alpha_1\Delta_0}{\Delta_1}\gamma_1\right\}, \\ \frac{\partial \Phi_k}{\partial y_k} &= \frac{\partial N_k}{\partial y_k} + \frac{\partial N_k}{\partial y_{k-1}}\frac{\partial \phi_{k-1}}{\partial y_k} = \frac{\Delta_k}{\Delta_{k-1}}, \\ \frac{\partial \Phi_k}{\partial y_{k+1}} &= -\alpha_k.\end{aligned}$$

On the basis of (73.13) and (73.16), we can put $M = S$ and $k = \delta_0$. Using Lemma 73.2 and the implicit function theorem, we establish in the region

$$0 \leqq \lambda \leqq \min \left\{2m \left(\frac{\delta_0}{2S}\right)^k, 1\right\}, \qquad |y_{k+1} - \bar{y}_{k+1}| \leqq 2m \left(\frac{\delta_0}{2S}\right)^k$$

that the functions $y_k = \phi_k(\lambda, y_{k+1}), \phi_k(0, \bar{y}_{k+1}) = \bar{y}_k$ are continuous and single-valued and their partial derivatives reduce to the form (73.17) with j replaced by k.

Repeating this process, we reach the last equation of (73.5)

$$N_n[\lambda, \phi_n(\lambda, y_n), y_n, b_1] = \Phi_n(\lambda, y_n, b_1) = 0,$$

which determines in the region $d^{(n)}$:

$$0 \leqq \lambda \leqq \min \left\{2m \left(\frac{\delta_0}{2S}\right)^n, 1\right\} = \Delta\lambda, \tag{73.18}$$

the function $y_n = \phi_n(\lambda, b_1) = Q_n(\lambda)$ which satisfies all the conditions mentioned in Lemma 73.2 and the implicit function theorem.

Further, performing the inverse process, we construct successively in the region $d^{(n)}$ continuous single-valued functions

$$y_k = Q_k(\lambda), \qquad Q_k(0) = \bar{y}_k \qquad (k = 1, 2, \ldots, n),$$

which have continuous first derivatives.

In this way, we have proved the validity of Theorem 73.1 for the segment $[0, \Delta\lambda]$, where $\Delta\lambda > 0$ is defined by (73.18). This segment can either contain the interval [0, 1] or be a part of it.

In the latter case, it is necessary to continue the solution throughout the interval [0, 1].

We take as our new initial condition the value of the functions $y_k(\lambda)$ at $\lambda = \Delta\lambda/2$

$$y_k\left(\frac{\Delta\lambda}{2}\right) = \bar{\bar{y}}_k \qquad (k = 1, 2, \ldots, n).$$

It follows from Lemma 73.1 that $|\bar{y}_k - \bar{\bar{y}}_k| \leqq m$, $|\bar{\bar{y}}_k - \bar{y}_k| \leqq 2m$.

Since the estimate (73.16), used in the proof of the theorem, is valid for arbitrary $\lambda \in [0,1]$, we prove by an analogous argument the validity of the theorem in either the interval [0, 1] or the interval $[0, \Delta\lambda/2 + \Delta\lambda]$.

It follows from (73.18) that

$$\Delta\lambda \geqq 2m\left(\frac{\delta_0}{2S}\right)^n.$$

Hence, performing less than $(1/m)\ (2s/\delta_0)^n$ steps, we reach the point $\lambda = 1$.

Note 2. If the point $x_{n+1} = b$ is a point of the quadrature formula, that is, if we perform the following substitution in the sum representing the integral

$$\int_a^b \phi(x, y, y')dx =$$

$$= \sum_{k=0}^{n} C_k \phi\left(x_k, y_k, \frac{y_{k+1}-y_k}{\Delta x_k}\right) +$$

$$+ C_{n+1}\phi\left(x_{n+1}, y_{n+1}, \frac{y_{n+1}-y_n}{\Delta x_n}\right),$$

then a term is added to the last equation in (73.3) and this equation takes the form

$$\psi_y\Big|_n - \frac{1}{\Delta x_n}\psi_{y'}\Big|_n + \frac{1}{\Delta x_{n-1}}\psi_{y'}\Big|_{n-1} -$$

$$- \frac{1}{\Delta x_n}\psi_{y'}\left(x_{n+1}, y_{n+1}, \frac{y_{n+1}-y_n}{\Delta x_n}\right) = 0.$$

Besides this, the values of β_n and λ_n are changed:

$$\beta_n = \lambda(p_n - 2q_n + r_n + r_{n-1}) + (1-\lambda)(R_n + R_{n-1} + T_n) +$$

$$+ \frac{1}{(\Delta x_n)^2}\psi_{y'y'}\left(x_{n+1}, y_{n+1}, \frac{y_{n+1}-y_n}{\Delta x_n}\right),$$

$$\gamma_n = \delta^2 y_n - T_n y_n + \psi_y\Big|_n - \frac{1}{\Delta x_n}\psi_{y'}\Big|_n + \frac{1}{\Delta x_{n-1}}\psi_{y'}\Big|_{n-1} -$$

$$- \frac{1}{\Delta x_n}\psi_{y'}\left(x_{n+1}, y_{n+1}, \frac{y_{n+1}-y_n}{\Delta x_n}\right).$$

All the remaining equations of (73.3) and (73.7) retain their original form. Lemma 73.1 and Theorem 73.1 are also valid.

§74. An example

In this section, we examine a numerical example to which the considerations of the previous section are applied (this is the example considered by Vlasova and Rybakova [1]).

Before considering the example, we explain some general concepts which will be used. We restrict somewhat the generality of the construction of the previous section and waive a subdivision of the basic interval by an arbitrary sequence of step lengths. We assume that the interval $[a, b]$ is subdivided by n equally spaced points $x_k = a+kh\,(k = 0, 1, \ldots, n)$, $h = (b-a)/n$. Simultaneously, we use a more exact approximation than that in §73 for the derivative. In fact, we put

$$\begin{aligned} y'_k &= y'(x_k) \approx \frac{y_{k+1}-y_{k-1}}{2h} \qquad (k = 1, 2, \ldots, n-1), \\ y'_0 &= y'(x_0) \approx \frac{-3y_0+4y_1-y_2}{2h}, \\ y'_n &= y'(x_n) \approx \frac{y_{n-2}-4y_{n-1}+3y_n}{2h}. \end{aligned} \tag{74.1}$$

As in §73, we replace the exact variational problem by an approximate problem: find the vector $Y = (y_1, y_2, \ldots, y_{n-1})$ so that the sum

$$\begin{aligned} f(y_1, y_2, \ldots, y_{n-1}) &= \sum_{k=0}^{n} C_k \phi(x_k, y_k, y'_k) = \\ &= \psi\left(x_0, y_0, \frac{-3y_0+4y_1-y_2}{2h}\right) + \sum_{k=1}^{n-1} \psi\left(x_k, y_k, \frac{y_{k+1}-y_{k-1}}{2h}\right) \\ &+ \psi\left(x_n, y_n, \frac{y_{n-2}-4y_{n-1}+3y_n}{2h}\right) \end{aligned} \tag{74.2}$$

attains its minimum value.

From the necessary condition for a minimum, we obtain a system of $(n-1)$ non-linear equations with unknowns $y_1, y_2, \ldots, y_{n-1}$:

$$
\begin{aligned}
&\frac{\partial f}{\partial y_1} = \left.\frac{\partial \psi}{\partial y}\right|_1 - \frac{1}{2h}\left.\frac{\partial \psi}{\partial y'}\right|_2 + \frac{2}{h}\left.\frac{\partial \psi}{\partial y'}\right|_0 = 0,\\
&\frac{\partial f}{\partial y_2} = \left.\frac{\partial \psi}{\partial y}\right|_2 - \frac{1}{2h}\left.\frac{\partial \psi}{\partial y'}\right|_3 + \frac{1}{2h}\left.\frac{\partial \psi}{\partial y'}\right|_1 - \frac{1}{2h}\left.\frac{\partial \psi}{\partial y'}\right|_0 = 0,\\
&\frac{\partial f}{\partial y_k} = \left.\frac{\partial \psi}{\partial y}\right|_k - \frac{1}{2h}\left.\frac{\partial \psi}{\partial y'}\right|_{k+1} + \frac{1}{2h}\left.\frac{\partial \psi}{\partial y'}\right|_{k-1} = 0,\\
&\qquad (k = 3, 4, \ldots, n-3), \qquad\qquad (74.3)\\
&\frac{\partial f}{\partial y_{n-2}} = \left.\frac{\partial \psi}{\partial y}\right|_{n-2} - \frac{1}{2h}\left.\frac{\partial \psi}{\partial y'}\right|_{n-3} + \frac{1}{2h}\left.\frac{\partial \psi}{\partial y'}\right|_{n-1} + \frac{1}{2h}\left.\frac{\partial \psi}{\partial y'}\right|_n = 0,\\
&\frac{\partial f}{\partial y_{n-1}} = \left.\frac{\partial \psi}{\partial y}\right|_{n-1} - \frac{2}{h}\left.\frac{\partial \psi}{\partial y'}\right|_n + \frac{1}{2h}\left.\frac{\partial \psi}{\partial y'}\right|_{n-2} = 0,
\end{aligned}
$$

where, for example,

$$
\left.\frac{\partial \psi}{\partial y}\right|_1 = \frac{\partial \psi\left(x_1, y_1, \dfrac{y_2 - u_0}{2h}\right)}{\partial y}.
$$

We solve system (74.3) by the method of differentiation w.r.t. a parameter. We introduce the following system which contains the parameter $\lambda, 0 \leqq \lambda \leqq 1$,

$$
N_k(\lambda, y_{k-2}, y_{k-1}, y_k, y_{k+1}, y_{k+2}) = (1-\lambda)\Delta_k + \lambda \frac{\partial f}{\partial y_k} = 0 \qquad (74.4)
$$

$$(k = 1, 2, \ldots, n-1),$$

where the linear function $\Delta_k = \Delta_k(y_{k-1}, y_k, y_{k+1})$ is chosen so that the system

$$
\begin{aligned}
&\Delta_k(y_{k-1}, y_k, y_{k+1}) = 0 \qquad (k = 1, 2, \ldots, n-1),\\
&y_0 = A, \qquad y_n = B, \qquad\qquad (74.5)
\end{aligned}
$$

is symmetric and has a unique solution $y_k = \bar{y}_k$ $(k = 1, 2, \ldots, n-1)$ for $\lambda = 0$. In this way, if the solution of (74.4) is denoted by $y_k(\lambda)$ $(k = 1, 2, \ldots, n-1)$, then

$$y_k(0) = \bar{y}_k.$$

For $\lambda = 1$, (74.4) becomes (74.3) the solution of which we require.

We differentiate (74.4) w.r.t. λ to obtain

$$\sum_{l=-2}^{2} \frac{\partial N_k}{\partial y_{k+l}} \frac{\partial y_{k+l}}{d\lambda} = -\frac{\partial N_k}{\partial \lambda} \qquad (k = 1, 2, \ldots, n-1), \tag{74.6}$$

or, more briefly,

$$A_{n-1} V_{n-1} = \Gamma_{n-1}, \tag{74.7}$$

where V_{n-1} and Γ_{n-1} are the vector defined by

$$V_{n-1} = \left[\frac{dy_1}{d\lambda}, \frac{dy_2}{d\lambda}, \ldots, \frac{dy_{n-1}}{d\lambda}\right],$$

$$\Gamma_{n-1} = [\gamma_1, \gamma_2, \ldots, \gamma_{n-1}], \qquad \gamma_k = -\frac{\partial N_k}{\partial \lambda}$$

$$(k = 1, 2, \ldots, n-1),$$

and A_{n-1} is the matrix of system (74.6). As is easily seen, it is a symmetric band matrix of order 5.

We introduce the notation

$$\begin{aligned}
b_1 &= \frac{\partial N_1}{\partial y_1} = (1-\lambda)\frac{\partial \Delta_1}{\partial y_1} + \lambda(p_1 + r_2 + 16 r_0),\\
b_2 &= \frac{\partial N_2}{\partial y_2} = (1-\lambda)\frac{\partial \Delta_2}{\partial y_2} + \lambda(p_2 + r_3 + r_1 + r_0),\\
b_k &= \frac{\partial N_k}{\partial y_k} = (1-\lambda)\frac{\partial \Delta_k}{\partial y_k} + \lambda(p_k + r_{k+1} + r_{k-1})\\
&\quad (k = 3, 4, \ldots, n-3),\\
b_{n-2} &= \frac{\partial N_{n-2}}{\partial y_{n-2}} = (1-\lambda)\frac{\partial \Delta_{n-2}}{\partial y_{n-2}} + \lambda(p_{n-2} + r_{n-2} + r_{n-3} + r_n),\\
b_{n-1} &= \frac{\partial N_{n-1}}{\partial y_{n-1}} = (1-\lambda)\frac{\partial \Delta_{n-1}}{\partial y_{n-1}} + \lambda(p_{n-1} + 16 r_n + r_{n-2}),
\end{aligned} \tag{74.8}$$

$$\begin{aligned}
a_1 &= \frac{\partial N_1}{\partial y_2} = \frac{\partial N_2}{\partial y_1} = (1-\lambda)\frac{\partial \Delta_2}{\partial y} + \lambda(-q_2 + q_1 - 4 r_0),\\
a_k &= \frac{\partial N_k}{\partial y_{k+1}} = \frac{\partial N_{k+1}}{\partial y_k} = (1-\lambda)\frac{\partial \Delta_k}{\partial y_{k+1}} + \lambda(-q_{k+1} + q_k)\\
&\quad (k = 2, 3, \ldots, n-3),
\end{aligned}$$

$$a_{n-2} = \frac{\partial N_{n-2}}{\partial y_{n-1}} = \frac{\partial N_{n-1}}{\partial y_{n-2}} =$$

$$= (1-\lambda)\frac{\partial \Delta_{n-2}}{\partial y_{n-1}} + \lambda(q_{n-2} - q_{n-1} - 4r_n),$$

$$c_k = \frac{\partial N_{k-1}}{\partial y_{k+1}} = \frac{\partial N_{k+1}}{\partial y_{k-1}} = -\lambda r_k \qquad (k = 2, 3, \ldots, n-2),$$

where

$$r_k = \frac{1}{4h^2} \frac{\partial^2 \psi}{\partial y' \partial y'}\bigg|_k, \qquad q_k = \frac{1}{2h}\frac{\partial^3 \psi}{\partial y' \partial y}\bigg|_k, \qquad p_k = \frac{\partial^2 \psi}{\partial y \, \partial y}\bigg|_k.$$

Then

$$A_{n-1} = \begin{bmatrix} b_1 & a_1 & c_2 & & & & & & & 0 \\ a_1 & b_2 & a_2 & c_3 & & & & & & \\ c_2 & a_2 & b_3 & a_3 & c_4 & & & & & \\ & \ddots & \vdots & \vdots & \vdots & \ddots & & & & \\ & & c_{k-1} & a_{k-1} & b_k & a_k & c_{k+1} & & & \\ & & & \ddots & \vdots & \vdots & \vdots & \ddots & & \\ & & & & c_{n-4} & a_{n-4} & b_{n-3} & a_{n-3} & c_{n-2} \\ & & & & & c_{n-3} & a_{n-3} & b_{n-2} & a_{n-2} \\ 0 & & & & & & c_{n-2} & a_{n-2} & b_{n-1} \end{bmatrix}. \tag{74.9}$$

The required solution of (74.3) is the solution of the Cauchy problem for (74.6) with $\lambda = 1$ which satisfies the condition

$$y_k(0) = \bar{y}_k \qquad (k = 1, 2, \ldots, n-1).$$

We evaluate this solution numerically. Namely, we subdivide the interval [0,1] into m sub-intervals by points λ_i $(i = 1, 2, \ldots, m)$ and apply, for example, the Runge-Kutta method.

For a system of differential equations of the form

$$\frac{dy_l}{d\lambda} = Z_l(\lambda, y_1, y_2, \ldots, y_{n-1}) \qquad (l = 1, 2, \ldots, n-1), \tag{74.10}$$

the Runge-Kutta formula takes the form

$$y_l(\lambda_{i+1}) = y_l(\lambda_i) + \tfrac{1}{6}[k_1^{(li)} + 2k_2^{(li)} + 2k_3^{(li)} + k_4^{(li)}],$$

where

$$
\begin{aligned}
k_1^{(li)} &= \Delta\lambda \cdot Z_l[\lambda_i, y_1(\lambda_i), y_2(\lambda_i), \ldots, y_{n-1}(\lambda_i)],\\
k_2^{(li)} &= \Delta\lambda \cdot Z_l\left[\lambda_i + \frac{\Delta\lambda}{2}, y_1(\lambda_i) + \frac{k_1^{(1i)}}{2}, \ldots\right.\\
&\qquad \left.\ldots, y_{n-1}(\lambda_i) + \frac{k_1^{(n-1,i)}}{2}\right],\\
k_3^{(li)} &= \Delta\lambda \cdot Z_l\left[\lambda_i + \frac{\Delta\lambda}{2}, y_1(\lambda_i) + \frac{k_2^{(1i)}}{2}, \ldots\right.\\
&\qquad \left.\ldots, y_{n-1}(\lambda_i) + \frac{k_2^{(n-1,i)}}{2}\right],\\
k_4^{(li)} &= \Delta\lambda \cdot Z_l[\lambda_i + \Delta\lambda, y_1(\lambda_i) + k_3^{(1i)}, \ldots\\
&\qquad \ldots, y_{n-1}(\lambda_i) + k_3^{(n-1,i)}],\\
&\qquad (i = 1, 2, \ldots, n-1;\ l = 1, 2, \ldots, n-1).
\end{aligned}
\tag{74.11}
$$

We see that for the implementation of the Runge-Kutta formula, it is necessary to present (74.6) in the form (74.10). However, it is very difficult to solve (74.6) in a general form.

Using numerical integration, this difficulty can be by-passed: For each fixed value of λ_i, we solve numerically the system obtained from (74.6) {after substitution of λ_i into the coefficients of the unknowns and the r.h.s.-values $y_k(\lambda_i)$ obtained above}.

For the solution of this numerical system, we use the upper and lower triangular decomposition for A_{n-1} (see Gantmakher [1] or Faddeev and Faddeeva [1]):

$$A_{n-1} = C_{n-1} \cdot B_{n-1}, \tag{74.12}$$

where

$$
C_{n-1} = \begin{bmatrix}
\beta_1 & & & & & & 0\\
\alpha_1 & \beta_2 & & & & & \\
\delta_2 & \alpha_2 & \beta_3 & & & & \\
& \ddots & \ddots & \ddots & & & \\
& & \delta_{k-1} & \alpha_{k-1} & \beta_k & & \\
& & & \ddots & \ddots & \ddots & \\
0 & & & & \delta_{n-2} & \alpha_{n-2} & \beta_{n-1}
\end{bmatrix},
$$

$$B_{n-1} = \begin{bmatrix} 1 & \mu_1 & v_1 & & & & & 0 \\ & \ddots & \ddots & \ddots & & & & \\ & & 1 & \mu_k & v_k & & & \\ & & & \ddots & \ddots & \ddots & & \\ & & & & 1 & \mu_{n-3} & v_{n-3} \\ & & & & & 1 & \mu_{n-2} \\ 0 & & & & & & 1 \end{bmatrix}$$

The elements of C_{n-1} and B_{n-1} are defined recursively by the expressions

$$\beta_1 = b_1, \quad \mu_1 = \frac{a_1}{\beta_1}, \quad \alpha_1 = a_1, \quad \beta_2 = b_2 = \alpha_2 \mu_1,$$

$$v_k = \frac{c_{k+1}}{\beta_k} \quad (k = 1, 2, \ldots, n-3),$$

$$\mu_k = \frac{a_k - \alpha_{k-1} v_{k-1}}{\beta_k} \qquad (k = 2, 3, \ldots, n-2),$$

$$\alpha_{k-1} = a_{k-1} - \delta_{k-1} \mu_{k-2} \qquad (k = 3, 4, \ldots, n-1),$$

$$\beta_k = b_k - \delta_k v_{k-2} - \alpha_{k-1} \mu_{k-1} \qquad (k = 3, 4, \ldots, n-1),$$

$$\delta_k = c_k \qquad (k = 2, 3, \ldots, n-2).$$

On the basis of (74.7) and (74.12),

$$C_{n-1} B_{n-1} V_{n-1} = \Gamma_{n-1}.$$

If we write

$$B_{n-1} V_{n-1} = D_{n-1}, \tag{74.13}$$

then (74.7) becomes

$$C_{n-1} D_{n-1} = \Gamma_{n-1}.$$

The components of the vector $D = (d_1, d_2, \ldots, d_{n-1})$ can be determined immediately by

$$d_1 = \frac{\gamma_1}{\beta_1}, \qquad d_2 = \frac{\gamma_2 - \alpha_1 d_1}{\beta_2},$$

$$d_k = \frac{\gamma_k - \delta_{k-1} d_{k-2} - \alpha_{k-1} d_{k-1}}{\beta_k} \qquad (k = 3, 4, \ldots, n-1).$$

Hence, from (74.13), we can define the components of the vector V_n:

$$\frac{dy_{n-1}}{d\lambda} = d_{n-1},$$

$$\frac{dy_{n-2}}{d\lambda} = d_{n-2} - \mu_{n-2}\frac{dy_{n-1}}{d\lambda},$$

$$\cdots\cdots\cdots\cdots\cdots$$

$$\frac{dy_k}{d\lambda} = d_k - \mu_k \frac{dy_{k+1}}{d\lambda} - \nu_k \frac{dy_{k+2}}{d\lambda} \qquad (k = n-3, n-4, \ldots, 1),$$

which correspond to the functions $Z_l(\lambda, y_1, t_2, \ldots, y_{n-1})$ when $\lambda = \lambda_i$. We consider the same example as in §71: we wish to determine the function which minimises

$$\int_0^1 [\tfrac{1}{48}y'^4 + y'^2 + y^2 - 6y]dx$$

and satisfies the boundary conditions

$$y(0) = 1, \qquad y(1) = 0.$$

For the quadrature formula, we use a trapezoidal rule, that is, we put

$$C_k = \frac{1}{n}h \qquad (k = 0, 1, \ldots, n-1), \qquad C_n = 0,$$

and then calculate p_k, q_k and r_k:

$$p_k = \frac{2}{n}, \quad q_k = 0, \quad r_k = \frac{n}{4}[2 + \tfrac{1}{4}(\bar{y}_k)] \qquad (k = 0, 1, \ldots, n-1).$$

The functions Δ_k in (74.4) are chosen in the form

$$\Delta_k = -R_k y_{k+1} + (R_k + R_{k-1} + T_k)y_k - R_{k-1}y_{k-1},$$

where

$$R_k = \frac{n-k}{4h^3}, \qquad T_k = \frac{1}{4h^2(1-kh)}.$$

The solution of the corresponding system (74.5) is

$$y_k(0) = \bar{y}_k = 1 - kh \qquad (k = 1, 2, \ldots, n-1).$$

Implementing the procedure outlined above, we obtained the results listed in Tables 74.1, 74.2 and 74.3, and Figure 6.

Table 74.1

The approximate solutions $y_n(x_k)$, obtained by the method of differentiation w.r.t. a parameter for different values of n (with $\Delta\lambda = \frac{1}{16}$)

No of steps	x_k	Exact solution	Approximate solutions for								
			$n = 10$	$n = 20$	$n = 30$	$n = 40$	$n = 50$	$n = 60$	$n = 70$	$n = 80$	$n = 90$
1	0.1	0.99	0.9925	0.9925	0.9865	0.9898	0.9864	0.9882	0.9859	0.9879	0.9865
2	0.2	0.96	0.9738	0.9664	0.9632	0.9614	0.9606	0.9587	0.9596	0.9575	0.9529
3	0.3	0.91	0.8977	0.9218	0.9034	0.9148	0.9049	0.9113	0.9103	0.9095	0.9065
4	0.4	0.84	0.8723	0.8584	0.8529	0.8497	0.8480	0.8453	0.8469	0.8430	0.8369
5	0.5	0.75	0.7240	0.7756	0.7451	0.7654	0.7489	0.7604	0.7483	0.7579	0.7527
6	0.6	0.65	0.6914	0.6730	0.6656	0.6612	0.6586	0.6558	0.6557	0.6531	0.6471
7	0.7	0.51	0.4700	0.5497	0.5063	0.5363	0.5126	0.5303	0.5138	0.5275	0.5173
8	0.8	0.36	0.4297	0.4051	0.3953	0.3895	0.3895	0.3829	0.3818	0.3797	0.3758
9	0.9	0.19	0.1374	0.2384	0.1795	0.2197	0.1877	0.2123	0.1905	0.2086	0.1928
10		−2.0667	−2.3318	−2.2034	−2.1576	−2.1345	−2.1207	−2.1115	−2.1048	−2.0998	−2.0959

In Table 74.1, the approximate values for $y_n(x_k)$, obtained by integrating (74.6) for various value of n and a fixed $\Delta\lambda = \frac{1}{16}$, are shown.

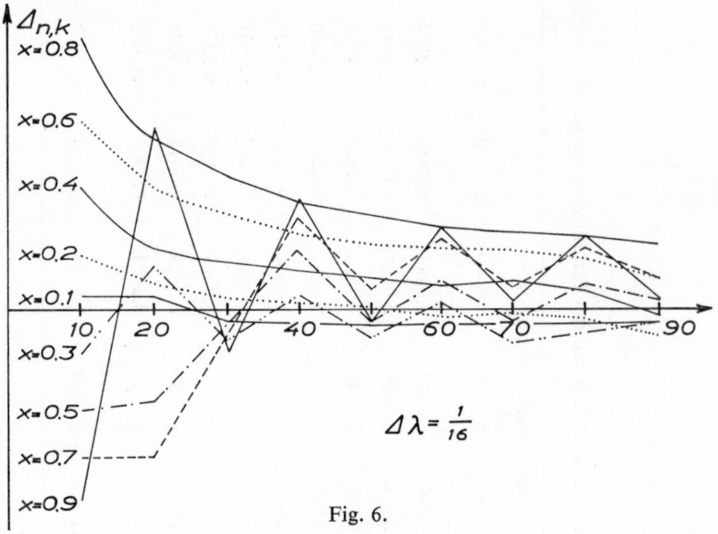

Fig. 6.

Figure 6 can be used to observe the error between the approximate solutions $y_k(x_k)$ and the exact-solutions $y(x_k)$ (with $\Delta\lambda = \frac{1}{16}$). The abscissa define values of n, while the ordinates define values of $\Delta_{n,k} = y_n(x_k) - y(x_k)$. For each x_k ($x_k = kh$, $k = 1, 2, \ldots, 9$, $h = \frac{1}{10}$), the curve $y = \Delta_{n,k}$ is shown.

Table 74.2

Table of maximum error between approximate solution and exact solution for different values of $\Delta\lambda$

$\Delta\lambda$	$n = 10$	$n = 20$	$n = 30$	$n = 40$	$n = 50$	$n = 60$	$n = 70$	$n = 80$
$\frac{1}{16}$	0.0697	0.0484	0.0353	0.0297	0.0259	0.0223	0.0218	0.0197
$\frac{1}{32}$	0.0665	0.0444	0.0337	0.0288	0.0255	0.0232	0.0204	0.0191
$\frac{1}{64}$	0.0657	0.0336	0.0310	0.0275	0.0248	0.0225	0.0226	0.0182
$\frac{1}{128}$	0.0657	0.0331	0.0272	0.0250	0.0232	0.0216	0.0222	0.0175

From the Tables and the Figure, it is clear that only an insignificant decrease in $\Delta_{n,k}$ is observed for increasing n.

Table 74.3

Application of Newton's method

No of steps	x_k	Exact solution	Approximate values $y_n(x_k)$, obtained by Newton-Kantorovich-method					
			$n = 10$		$n = 20$		$n = 30$	
			I	II	I	II	I	II
1	0.1	0.99	0.9970	0.9901	0.99802	0.99011	0.9908	0.98996
2	0.2	0.96	0.9741	0.9601	0.97594	0.96021	0.9616	0.95994
3	0.3	0.91	0.9303	0.9102	0.93339	0.91031	0.9124	0.90993
4	0.4	0.84	0.8666	0.8402	0.86974	0.84040	0.8430	0.83992
5	0.5	0.75	0.7781	0.7503	0.78418	0.75050	0.7535	0.74992
6	0.6	0.64	0.6713	0.6404	0.67573	0.64062	0.6435	0.63993
7	0.7	0.51	0.5327	0.5105	0.54335	0.51072	0.5131	0.50994
8	0.8	0.36	0.3790	0.3606	0.38547	0.36072	0.3620	0.35996
9	0.9	0.19	0.1869	0.1899	0.20105	0.19047	0.1893	0.18997
10		−2.0667	−2.3001	−2.3105		−2.2034	−2.3104	−2.3105
11			−2.0813	−2.0813		−2.0799		

No of steps	x_k	Approximate values $y_n(x_k)$, obtained by Newton-Kantorovich-method					
		$n = 40$		$n = 60$		$n = 80$	
		I	II	I	II	I	II
1	0.1	0.99857	0.99014	0.99854	0.99014	0.99756	0.99013
2	0.2	0.97698	0.96027	0.97690	0.96027	0.97501	0.96025
3	0.3	0.93488	0.91038	0.93477	0.91038	0.93223	0.91036
4	0.4	0.87168	0.84049	0.87155	0.84049	0.86881	0.84046
5	0.5	0.78664	0.75061	0.78660	0.75061	0.78421	0.75057
6	0.6	0.67880	0.64074	0.67896	0.64073	0.67732	0.64069
7	0.7	0.54703	0.51087	0.54746	0.51085	0.54683	0.51081
8	0.8	0.39002	0.36088	0.39087	0.36089	0.39117	0.36086
9	0.9	0.20636	0.19065	0.20773	0.19067	0.20865	0.19068
10			−2.1346		−2.1115		−2.0999
11			−2.0745		−2.07213		−2.0708

It follows from Table 74.2 that a decrease in the integration step length $\Delta\lambda$ does produce a qualitative improvement in results.

In order to obtain a better result for the solution of (74.3), the Newton-Kantorovich-method was applied, where the initial approximation was taken as the solution of (74.3), obtained by using the method of differentiation w.r.t. a parameter.

The numerical results, obtained using the Newton-Kantorovich-method, are listed in Table 74.3, where the initial approximations were chosen from the results listed in Table 74.1.

It is clear from Table 74.3 that the second approximations, obtained using the Newton-Kantorovich-method, differ only slightly from the exact solution – the largest error does not exceed 0.3 %.

We can calculate approximate values for the minimum of the integral by substituting the numerical values for y_k in (74.2).

In the 10th rows of Tables 74.1 and 74.3, the numerical values for the sum (74.2) are presented for the cases when the solution was found by the method of differentiation w.r.t. a parameter and refined by the Newton-Kantorovich-method.

A comparison between the numerical values for the sum (74.2) and the exact value of the minimum of the integral shows that the relative error lies in the range 12.5 %–1.3 %. We see that this error is not diminished, when we use the more accurate values of y_k from Table 74.3.

This situation arises because approximate values for the derivatives are used in (74.2) and the accuracy estimate for the evaluation of the function is not suitable for the evaluation of the derivatives.

A more precise estimate for the approximate value of the minimum can be obtained by using, for example, a Lagrange interpolation formula in order to generate approximate values for the derivatives in the quadrature formula at a larger number of points than are used in (74.1).

In the example, we made use of fourth order approximations which yielded essential improvements. For example, with $n = 10$, the relative error was reduced from 12.5 % to 0.75 % (see Table 74.3, row 11).

§75. The Kachanov-method

The method of solution for a non-linear Ritz-system, which is considered in this section, was developed by Kachanov [4] for the solution of certain problems in the theory of plasticity and applied by Kachanov [6] to the problem of elasto-plastic twisting of a bar with square cross-section. Rose [1] improved the formulation of Kachanov [6] and showed that his method can be applied to general functionals of the form (68.1) {results of Rose [1] can be found in Mikhlin and Smoliškiĭ [1]}. A rigorous proof of this result does not exist (unfortunately, the convergence proof of Rose [1] contains an error.) However, it deserves attention because of its simplicity and its corroboration with numerical results.

For the functional (68.1), we construct the Ritz-system. It has the form

$$\frac{\partial F(u_n)}{\partial a_j} = 0 \qquad (j = 1, 2, \ldots, n), \tag{75.1}$$

where F is the functional (68.1),

$$u_n = \sum_{k=1}^{n} a_k \phi_k, \tag{75.2}$$

and the ϕ_n are coordinate functions. The Kachanov-method is: In the functional (68.1), we replace the functions $g_j(\xi)$ by the constants $g_j(0)$ and consider the problem of minimising the resulting quadratic functional

$$F_1(u) = \int_\Omega \sum_{j=1}^{s} g_j(0)\tau_j(u)dx - (f, u). \tag{75.3}$$

Seeking an approximate solution of this problem by the Ritz-process and putting

$$u_{n1} = \sum_{k=1}^{n} a_{k1} \phi_k, \tag{75.4}$$

we can determine the coefficients a_{k1} by solving a certain linear algebraic system. The coefficients $(a_{11}, a_{21}, \ldots, a_{n1})$ are regarded as defining a first approximation to the solution of the Ritz-system (75.1). In general, if the r-th approximation to the solution of (75.1) is

$$(a_{1r}, a_{2r}, \ldots, a_{nr}), \tag{75.5}$$

then the $(r+1)$-th approximation

$$(a_{1,r+1}, a_{2,r+1}, \ldots, a_{n,r+1})$$

is constructed as follows: in the functional (68.1), we replace $g_j(\xi)$ by the expression

$$g_j(\tau_j(u_{nr})) = g_j(\tau_j(\sum_{k=1}^{n} a_{kr} \phi_k)),$$

and seek the minimum of the resulting quadratic fuhctional

$$F_k(u) = \int_\Omega \sum_{j=1}^{s} g_j(\tau_j(u_{nr}))\tau_j(u)dx-(f, u)$$

by solving the corresponding Ritz-system with

$$u_{n,r+1} = \sum_{k=1}^{n} a_{k,r+1}\phi_k,$$

where the coefficients $a_{k,r+1}$ are defined by a linear algebraic system. If the Gateaux derivative of grad F is uniformly positive definite, then the set of approximate solutions (75.5), corresponding to the values $r = 1, 2, 3, \ldots$, is bounded, and hence, compact. If this set converges, then its limit is the solution of (75.1).

In practice, the above numerical procedure should be performed until its stabilisation or until the onset of instability.

§76. The stability of the Ritz-process for non-linear problems

Let the functional F, the minimum of which is required, satisfy the conditions of Theorem 70.1. We also assume that the derivative $\boldsymbol{P}'_u$, where $\boldsymbol{P}$ = grad F, satisfies inequalities (66.2) and (66.15), so that

$$(\boldsymbol{P}'_u h, h) \geqq \gamma_1^2(\boldsymbol{P}'_{u_0} h, h) \geqq \gamma^2\|h\|^2, \tag{76.1}$$

where γ and γ_1 are positive constants, u_0, u and h are elements of $\mathfrak{D}(\boldsymbol{P})$, where u_0 is fixed and u and h are arbitrary. As elsewhere in this chapter, we assume that F is defined on a linear set dense in a Banach space $\mathfrak{B}$. Then the operators $\boldsymbol{P}$ and $\boldsymbol{P}'_u$ map from $\mathfrak{B}$ into $\mathfrak{B}^*$. Let $\mathfrak{D}$ $(\boldsymbol{P})$ and $\mathfrak{D}(\boldsymbol{P}'_u)$ be dense in $\mathfrak{B}$.

We assume that the coordinate system $\{\phi_n\}$ satisfies conditions (2) and (3) of §70 and that condition (1) of §70 is replaced by the stronger condition: (1′) $\{\phi_n\} \in \mathfrak{D}(\boldsymbol{P})$. Then the Ritz-system can be rewritten in the Bubnov-Galerkin-form (70.5):

$$(\boldsymbol{P}(\sum_{k=1}^{n} a_k^{(n)}\phi_k), \phi_j) = 0 \qquad (j = 1, 2, \ldots, n).$$

We denote by $a^{(n)}$ the vector with components $(a_1^{(n)}, a_2^{(n)}, \ldots, a_n^{(n)})$, set

$$(\boldsymbol{P}(\sum_{k=1}^{n} a_k^{(n)}\phi_k), \phi_j) = P_j^{(n)}(a^{(n)})$$

and denote by $P^{(n)}(a^{(n)})$ the vector with components

$$P_1^{(n)}(a^{(n)}), P_2^{(n)}(a^{(n)}), \ldots, P_n^{(n)}(a^{(n)}).$$

The Ritz-system now becomes

$$P^{(n)}(a^{(n)}) = 0. \tag{76.2}$$

The composition of the vector $P^{(n)}$ is associated with numerical error. In fact, we obtain as a result of a calculation the vector

$$Q^{(n)} = P^{(n)} + T^{(n)} \tag{76.3}$$

instead of the vector $P^{(n)}$. We assume that, for the approximate determination of $P^{(n)}$, we are able to satisfy the following condition: there exist two functions C_t and C'_t with non negative argument t for which

$$||T^{(n)}(a^{(n)})|| \leqq \delta C_t, \qquad ||T_{b^{(n)}}^{(n)\prime}(a^{(n)})|| \leqq \delta C'_t, \tag{76.4}$$

if

$$||a^{(n)}|| \leqq t, \, ||b^{(n)}|| \leqq t,$$

where δ is a quantity which characterises the accuracy of the calculation of $P^{(n)}$. We assume that δ can be made arbitrarily small. For the norms in (76.4), we use the Euclidean vector norms.

Applying the Ritz-process, we solve instead of equation (76.2) the equation

$$Q^{(n)}(b^{(n)}) = P^{(n)}(b^{(n)}) + T^{(n)}(b^{(n)}) = 0. \tag{76.5}$$

We say that the Ritz-process is *stable*, if, given $\varepsilon > 0$, there exists $\delta > 0$ such that, if (76.4) holds, then equation (76.5) has a solution $b^{(n)}$ for which $||b^{(n)} - a^{(n)}|| < \varepsilon$ where $a^{(n)}$ is the solution of (76.2).

We mention a result, in the form suggested by Langenbach [6], about the existence of abstract implicit functions: an implicit function theorem. Let the operator $\boldsymbol{P}$, which is the gradient of the functional F, satisfy the conditions cited in the present section. As is known, the problem of minimising $F(u) - (f, u), f \in H$, has a generalised solution $\tilde{u}$. We set $\tilde{u} = \tilde{\boldsymbol{P}}^{-1} f$. It is not difficult to prove that different $\tilde{u}$ correspond to different f. This implies that $\tilde{\boldsymbol{P}}$, the inverse of $\tilde{\boldsymbol{P}}^{-1}$, exists such that $\tilde{\boldsymbol{P}}\tilde{u} = f$. If $\tilde{u} \in \mathfrak{D}(\boldsymbol{P})$, then $\boldsymbol{P}\tilde{u} = f$. Hence, it follows that $\tilde{\boldsymbol{P}}$ is an extension of $\boldsymbol{P}$.

Consider the operator $\boldsymbol{K}$, the domain of which is at least as large as the domain of $\boldsymbol{P}$ and such that $\boldsymbol{K}$ satisfies a Lipschitz condition of the form

$$||\boldsymbol{K}u_1 - \boldsymbol{K}u_2|| \leqq \alpha|||u_1 - u_2|||_{\boldsymbol{P}'u}.$$

The implicit function theorem, mentioned above, can be stated as: If $\gamma_1/\alpha > 1$, then

$$\tilde{\boldsymbol{P}}u - \boldsymbol{K}u = f$$

has one and only one solution $\bar{u}$, which approximates to $\tilde{u}$ in the sense

$$\lim_{\alpha \to 0} |||\bar{u} - \tilde{u}|||_{\boldsymbol{P}'u} = 0.$$

Theorem 76.1 (see Mikhlin [23]). *If the functional F and its gradient satisfy the conditions listed above and the co-ordinate system is strongly minimal in the energy space of* $\boldsymbol{P}'_{u_0}$, *then the Ritz-process is stable.*

Proof. Firstly, we prove that, for the conditions of the theorem, the quantities $||a^{(n)}||$ are bounded for all n. We write $\boldsymbol{P}(0) = f$. Equation (70.5) becomes

$$(\boldsymbol{P}(u^{(n)}) - \boldsymbol{P}(0), \phi_j) = (f, \phi_j)\ (j = 1, 2, \ldots, n),\ u^{(n)} = \sum_{k=1}^{n} a_n^{(k)} \phi_k$$

However, since

$$\boldsymbol{P}(u^{(n)}) - \boldsymbol{P}(0) = \int_0^1 \boldsymbol{P}'_{tu^{(n)}} u^{(n)}\, dt,$$

we obtain

$$\int_0^1 (\boldsymbol{P}'_{tu^{(n)}} u^{(n)}, \phi_j) dt = (f, \phi_j) \qquad (j = 1, 2, \ldots, n).$$

Multiplying by $a_j^{(n)}$ and adding, we obtain

$$\int_0^1 (\boldsymbol{P}'_{tu^{(n)}} u^{(n)}, u^{(n)}) dt = (f, u^{(n)}).$$

We replace the integrand on the l.h.s. by the smaller quantity $\gamma_1^2(\boldsymbol{P}'_{u_0} u^{(n)}, u^{(n)})$, while the r.h.s. is replaced by the larger estimate $||f||\ ||u^{(n)}||$. We make use of the notation [,] and ||| ||| for the energy inner product and energy norm of $\boldsymbol{P}'_{u_0}$. In this way, we obtain

$$\gamma_1^2 |||u^{(n)}|||^2 \leqq ||f||\ ||u^{(n)}||.$$

On the basis of inequality (76.1),

$$||u^{(n)}|| \leqq \frac{\gamma_1}{\gamma} |||u^{(n)}|||,$$

and we obtain

$$|||u^{(n)}||| \leqq \frac{||f||}{\gamma\gamma_1}. \tag{76.6}$$

Further,

$$|||u^{(n)}|||^2 = (R_n a^{(n)}, a^{(n)}) \geqq \lambda_1^{(n)}||a^{(n)}||^2,$$

where R_n is the matrix with elements $[\phi_k, \phi_j]$, and $\lambda_1^{(n)}$ is its smallest eigenvalue. On the strength of the conditions of the theorem, there exists a constant $\lambda_0 > 0$ such that $\lambda_1^{(n)} \geqq \lambda_0$. Hence,

$$||a^{(n)}|| \leqq \frac{1}{\sqrt{\lambda_0}} |||u^{(n)}||| \leqq \frac{||f||}{\gamma\gamma_1\sqrt{\lambda_0}} = \sigma = \text{const.}, \tag{76.7}$$

which is the required result. It follows from (76.4) and (76.7) that

$$||T^{(n)}(a^{(n)})|| \leqq \delta C_\sigma, \qquad ||T_{b^{(n)}}^{\prime(n)}(a^{(n)})|| < \delta C'_\sigma, \tag{76.8}$$

if $||b^{(n)}|| \leqq 2$.

It follows from (76.8) that, in the ball of radius 2σ, the operator $T^{(n)}$ satisfies a Lipschitz condition with arbitrary small constant, if δ is sufficiently small. As a consequence of the implicit function theorem cited above, it follows that (76.5) has for sufficiently small δ a solution $b^{(n)}$ such that $||b^{(n)} - a^{(n)}|| < \varepsilon$, for arbitrarily small positive ε. Hence, on the strength of our definition, the Ritz-process is stable.

As a consequence of the results of this section, we find that the Ritz-process is stable for the functionals discussed in §§68 and 69, if the co-ordinate system is strongly minimal w.r.t. the corresponding energy metric.

We also consider the following example. In the square $0 \leqq x, s \leqq 1$, we consider the kernel $K(x, s)$ defined by

$$K(x, s) = \int_0^1 L(x, t)L(t, s)dt,$$

where the kernel $L(x, s)$ is real, symmetric, continuous, non-negative and positive definite (the last condition implies that all its eigenvalues are positive). It is clear that $K(x, s)$ will also satisfy these conditions. It is obvious that $L(x, s)$ is bounded, $L(x, s) \leqq M$, and hence, $K(x, s) \leqq M^2$. The domain of the functional

$$F(u) = \frac{1}{2}\int_0^1 u^2(x)dx + \frac{1}{4}\int_0^1\int_0^1 K(x, s)u^2(x)u^2(s)dx\,ds - \\ - \int_0^1 f(x)u(x)dx, \qquad f \in L_2(0, 1), \tag{76.9}$$

defined in the real space L_2 (0, 1), is properly contained in this space. In fact, if $u \in L_2$ (0, 1), then the first and third integrals in (76.9) are defined. Since the second integral also makes sense, it follows that

$$\int_0^1\int_0^1 K(x, s)u^2(x)u^2(s)dx\,ds \leqq M\|u\|^4.$$

We examine the operator $\boldsymbol{P} = \text{grad } F$. We have,

$$\left.\frac{dF(u+\alpha h)}{d\alpha}\right|_{\alpha=0} = \int_0^1 u(x)h(x)dx + \\ + \int_0^1 h(x)dx \int_0^1 K(x, s)u(x)u^2(s)ds - \int_0^1 f(x)h(x)dx. \tag{76.10}$$

The r.h.s. of (76.10) is a linear functional w.r.t. h and is bounded in L_2 (0, 1). In order to establish this result, it is sufficient to verify that the integral

$$\int_0^1 K(x, s)u^2(s)ds$$

is bounded for $u \in L_2(0, 1)$. However, this is obvious, since this integral does not exceed $M^2\|u\|^2$. Now, it is clear that

$$\boldsymbol{P}u = u(x) + u(x)\int_0^1 K(x, s)u^2(s)ds - f(x). \tag{76.11}$$

Further,

$$\boldsymbol{P}'_u h = \left.\frac{d\boldsymbol{P}(u+\alpha h)}{d\alpha}\right|_{\alpha=0} = h(x) + h(x)\int_0^1 K(x, s)u^2(s)ds + \\ + 2u(x)\int_0^1 K(x, s)u(s)h(s)ds. \tag{76.12}$$

Hence,

$$(P'_u h, h) = ||h||^2 + \int_0^1 \int_0^1 K(x, s)u^2(s)h^2(x)dx\,ds +$$
$$+2\int_0^1 \int_0^1 K(x, s)u(x)u(s)h(x)h(s)dx\,ds. \qquad (76.13)$$

Both the integrals on the r.h.s. make sense if $u, h \in L_2(0, 1)$. In fact,

$$\int_0^1 \int_0^1 K(x, s)u^2(x)u^2(s)dx\,ds \leqq M^2||u||^4$$

and

$$\int_0^1 \int_0^1 K(x, s)u(x)u(s)h(x)h(s)dx\,ds =$$
$$= \int_0^1 \int_0^1 \int_0^1 L(x, t)L(s, t)u(x)u(s)h(x)h(s)dx\,ds\,dt =$$
$$= \int_0^1 dt \left\{ \int_0^1 L(x, t)u(x)h(x)dx \right\}^2,$$

where the inner integral has sense and is bounded, since

$$\left| \int_0^1 L(x, t)u(x)h(x)dx \right| \leqq M \int_0^1 |u(x)|\,|h(x)|dx \leqq M||u||\,||h||.$$

Since the integrals in (76.13) are also non-negative,

$$(P'_u h, h) \geqq ||h||^2 \qquad (76.14)$$

and P'_u satisfies inequality (66.2). Formula (76.14) implies that P'_u satisfies (66.15) with $u_0 = 0$. Since $P'_o = I$, the energy space of P_0 coincides with $L_2(0, 1)$.

In this way, all the conditions of Theorem 76.1 are satisfied. Hence, it follows that: for the problem of minimising the functional (76.9) or, equivalently, the non-linear integral equation

$$u(x)\left[1 + \int_0^1 K(x, s)u^2(s)ds\right] = f(x), \qquad (76.15)$$

the Ritz-process is stable if the kernel $K(x, s)$ satisfies the conditions listed above and the coordinate system is almost orthonormal in $L_2(0, 1)$.

BIBLIOGRAPHY

AKHIEZER, N. I., [1] *Lectures on the calculus of variations* (Moscow, 1955), English translation by Blaisdell, New York, 1962.

————, and I. M. GLAZMAN, [1] *Theory of linear operators in Hilberts pace* (Moscow, 1950), English translation by Ungar, New York, 1962.

BABICH, V. M., [1] On questions connected with extention of functions, *Uspehi. Mat. Nauk* 8 (1953), 111–113.

BERGER, H. M., [1] A new approach to the analysis of large deflections of plates, *J. Appl. Mech.* 22 (1955), 465–472.

BERNSTEIN, S. N., [1] Sur les équations du calcul des variations, *Ann. Sci. Ecole Norm. Sup.* 29 (1912), 431–485.

BIRMAN, M. SH., [1] On the method of Friedrichs for the extension of positive definite operators up to the self-adjoint, *Zap. Len. gorn. in-ta* 33 (1956), 132–136.

BOGARYAN, O. K., [1] On the convergence of the residual of the Bubnov-Galerkin and Ritz methods, *Dokl. Akad. Nauk* SSSR 141 (1961), 267–269. English translation: *Soviet Math. Dokl.* 2 (1961), 1413–1415.

CHITTENDEN, E. W., [1] On the equivalence of ecart and voisinage, *Trans. Amer. Math. Soc.* 18 (1917), 161–166.

COURANT, R. and D. HILBERT, [1] *Methods of mathematical physics*, Vol. 1., J. Wiley, New York, 1962.

DAVIDENKO, D. F., [1] On a new method for the numerical solution of systems of non-linear equations, *Dokl. Akad. Nauk SSSR* 88 (1953), 601–603.

DAUGAVET, I. K., [1] On the rate of convergence of the Galerkin method for ordinary differential equations, *Izv. Vys. Uch. Zav., Matem* 5 (1958), 158–165.

————, [2] On the method of moments for ordinary differential equations, *Sib. Matem. Zhurn.* 6 (1) (1965), 70–85.

————, [3] *An examination of the problem of convergence of the method of Galerkin for ordinary differential equations*, Candidate's Thesis, Leningrad, 1959.

DOVBYSH (GAGEN-TORN), L. N., [1] On the solvability of the Ritz system for functions from the theory of plasticity, *Trudy Matem. in-ta im. V. A. Steklov* 66 (1962), 190–195.

————, [2] On the stability of the method of Ritz for problems from the spectral theory of operators, *Trudy Matem. in-ta im. V. A. Steklov* 84 (1965), 78–92.

————, [3] A note on minimal systems, *Trudy Matem. in-ta. im. V. A. Steklov* 96 (1968), 188–189.

————, and S. G. MIKHLIN, [1] On the solvability of the non-linear Ritz system, *Dokl. Akad. Nauk SSSR* 138 (1961), 258–260.

DRUCHER, D. C., [1] Variational principles in the mathematical theory of plasticity, *Proc. Sympos. Appl. Math.* 8 (1958), 7–22.

ERDELYI, A., W. MAGNUS, F. OBERHETTINGER and F. G. TRICOMI, [1] *Higher transcendental functions*, Vols. 1–3, McGraw-Hill, New York, 1953.

EYDUS, D. M., [1] On mixed problems of the theory of elasticity, *Dokl. Akad. Nauk SSSR* 76 (1951), 181–184.

——————, [2] Contact problems of the theory of elasticity, *Matem. Sb.* 54 (96): 3 (1954), 429–440.

FADDEEV, D. K., and FADDEEVA, V. N. [1] *Numerical methods of linear algebra* (Moscow, 1963), English translation by Freeman, San Francisco, 1963.

FADDEEVA (ZAMYATINA), V. N., [1] On the fundamental functions of the operator $X^{(iv)}$, *Trudy Matem. in-ta im. Steklova* 28 (1949), 157–159.

FORSYTH, G. E. and W. R. WASOW, [1] *Finite difference methods for partial differential equations*, John Wiley, New York, 1960.

FRIEDRICKS, K. O., [1] Spektraltheorie Halbbeschränkter Operatoren und Anwendung auf der Spektralzerlegung von Differentialoperatoren, *Math. Ann.* 109 (1934), 465–487.

GALIMOV, K. E., [1] On variational principles of the non-linear theory of elasticity, *Uch. zap. Kazansk. un-ta.* 113 (10) (1953), 115–160.

——————, [2] On some variational formulations of the non-linear theory of elasticity, *Uch. zap. Kazansk. un-ta* 115 (12) (1955), 111–118.

——————, [3] On variational methods of solution of problems in the non-linear theory of plates and shells, *Uch. zap. Kazansk. un-ta* 116 (1) (1956), 36–40.

——————, [4] On one method of solution of boundary problems of non-linear equations of the theory of gently curved shells, *Uch. zap. Kanansk. un-ta* 116 (5) (1956), 19–26.

——————, [5] On large deflections of cylindrical rectangular panels, *Inzh. Sb.* 25 (1959), 20–36.

GANTMAKHER, F. R., [1] *The theory of matrices* (Moscow, 1953), English translation by Interscience, J. Wiley, New York, 1959.

GEL'MAN, I. V., [1] On the problem of the minimum of non-linear functionals, *Uch. zap. Leningr. ped. in-ta* 116 (1958), 255–263.

GEL'FAND, I. M., and S. V. FOMIN, [1] *The calculus of variations* (Moscow, 1961), English translation by Prentice Hall, Englewood Cliffs, N.I., 1963.

GIRAUD, G., [1] Sur différentes questions relatives aux équations du type elliptique, *Ann. Sci. Ecole Norm. Sup.* 47 (1930).

GLAZMAN, I. M., [1] *Direct method of qualitative spectral analysis of singular differential operators*, Fizmatgiz, Moscow, 1963.

GORLOV, A. M., [1] The application of variational methods to the solution of problems of the elasto-plastic twisting of bars, *Trudy Mosk. in-ta ini. i.-d. transp* 122 (1959), 407–419.

GRÖGER, K., [1] Einführung und Anwendung Sobolewscher Räume für beliebige Gebiete, *Math. Nachr.* 28 (1965), 123–144.

——————, [2] Nichtlineare ausgeartete elliptische Differentialgleichungen, *Math. Nachr.* 28 (1965), 181–205.

GUSEVA, O. V., [1] On boundary value problems for strongly elliptic systems, *Dokl. Akad. Nauk SSSR* 102 (1955), 1069–1072.

HARDY, G. G., J. E. LITTLEWOOD and G. POLYA, [1] *Inequalities*, Cambridge University Press, 1934.

HAUSDORF, F., [1] *The theory of sets*, Chelsea, New York, 1957.

HEINZ, E., [1] Beiträge zur Störungstheorie der Spektralzerlegung, *Math. Ann.* 123 (1951), 415–438.

HILL, R., [1] *The mathematical theory of plasticity*, Clarendon Press, Oxford, 1950.

JACKSON, D., [1] *Fourier series and orthogonal polynomials*, Amer. Assoc. Math., 1948.

KACHANOV, L. M., [1] *Some questions regarding the theory of creep*, Moscow, Gostekhizdat, 1949.

————, [2] Calculation of the strength of blades of water turbines, in '*Questions regarding the strength of blades of water turbines*', Leningr. Gos. Univ., 1954, p. 93–173.

————, [3] *The basic theory of plasticity*, Gostekhizdat, Moscow, 1956.

————, [4] On variational methods of solution of problems in the theory of plasticity, *Prikl. Matem. i mekh.* 23 (1959).

————, [5] *The theory of creep*, Fizmatgiz, Moscow, 1960.

————, [6] An example of the solution by variational methods of problems in elasto-plastic twisting, *Issled. po uprugosti i plastichnosti* 1 (1961).

KACZMARZ, S., and H. STEINHAUS, [1] *Theorie der Orthogonalreihen*, Chelsea Publ. Co., New York, 1951.

KALENDER'YAN, L. I., [1] The application of variational methods in the non-linear theory of the bending of plates, *Nauchn. Trudy Odessk. in-ta ini. morsk. flota* 11 (1954–1955), 69–95.

KANTOROVICH, L. V., [1] Functional analysis and applied mathematics, *Usp. Matem. Nauk* III, 6 (28), 1948, 89–185. English translation: Nat. Bureau Standards Project 1101–10–5100, Report 1509.

————, [2] On a mathematical symbolism suitable for numerical computations on a computer, *Dokl. Akad. Nauk SSSR* 113 (1957), 738–741.

————, and G. P. AKILOV, [1] *Functional analysis in normed spaces* (Moscow, 1959), English translation by Pergamon Press, Oxford, 1964.

————, and V. I. KRYLOV, [1] *Approximate methods in higher analysis* (Moscow, 1949), English translation by Noordhoff, Groningen, 1958.

KAZIMIROV, V. I., [1] On the semicontinuity of the integrals of the calculus of variations, *Usp. Matem. Nauk* 11 (69) (1956), 125–130.

KHARRIK, I. YU., [1] On the approximation of functions, which vanish with their partial derivatives on the boundary of a region, with functions of a particular form, *Sibir. Matem. Zhurn.* 4 (2) (1963), 408–425.

KIRIYA, V. S., [1] Motion of a solid in a resisting medium, *Trudy Tbil. un-ta* 44(1951), 1–20.

KLYUSHNIKOV, V. D., [1] The bending of a rectangular plate with regard to large deflections, *Inzh. Sb.* 24 (1956), 62–72.

KORNISHIN, M. S., and KH. M. MUSHTARI, [1] On an algorithm for the solution of non-linear problems in the theory of gently curving shells, *Prikl. Matem. i Mekh.* 23 (1959), 62–72.

KOSHELEV, A. I., [1] A priori estimate in Lp and generalised solutions of elliptic equations and systems, *Usp. Matem. Nauk* 13 (82) (1958), 29–88.

KRAVCHUK, M., [1] Resolution of linear differential equations and integrals by the method of moments, *Vidavnitstvo Ukr. Akad. Nauk*, Kiev, 1936, 1–212.

KRASNOSEL'SKIY, M. A., [1] *Topological methods in the theory of non-linear integral equations* (Moscow, Gostekhizdat, 1956), English translation by Pergamon Press, Oxford, 1964.

KRYLOV, A. N., [1] *On calculations for beams resting on elastic supports*, Leningrad, 1931.

LADYZHENSKAYA, O. A., [1] *Mixed problems for hyperbolic equations* (Moscow, Gostekhizdat, 1953).

LANGENBACH, A., [1] On the application of variational principles to some non-linear variational equations, *Dokl. Akad. Nauk SSSR* 121 (1958), 214–217.

——————, [2] Variationsmethoden in der nichtlinearen Elastizität- und Plastizitätstheorie, *Wiss. Z. Humbolt-Univ., Berlin, Math.-Nat. R.* IX (1959/1960).

——————, [3] On some non-linear operators of the theory of elasticity in Hilbert space, *Vestn. Leningr. Gos. Univ.*, 1, *ser. matem. mekh i astr.* 1 (1961), 38–50.

——————, [4] Elastisch-plastische Deformationen von Platten, *ZAMM* 41 (1961), 126–134.

——————, [5] Zur Losung eines Minimum-Problems der nichtlinearen Plattentheorie, *Math. Nachr.* 26 (1965) 339–351.

——————, [6] Die Linearisierung nichtlinearen Gleichungen, *Math. Nachr.* 24 (1962), 33–51.

LEWIN, S., [1] Über einige mit der Konvergenz im Mittel verbundenen Eigenschaften von Funktionalfolgen, *Math. Zeitschr.* 32 (1930).

LOZINSKIY, S. M., [1] Inverse functions, implicit functions and the solution of equations. *Vestn. Leningr. Gos. Univ.*, 7, *ser. matem mekh. i astr.* 2 (1957), 131–142.

MIKHLIN, S. G., [1] Singular integral equations, *Uspehi. Matem Nauk* 3 (1948), 29–112. English translation: *Amer. Math. Soc. Trans., Series* 1, Vol. 10, 84–198.

——————, [2] The method of least squares in problems of mathematical physics, *Uch. zap. Len. gos. un-ta*, 111, *ser. matem. nauk*, 16 (1949), 167–206.

——————, [3] *Integral equations and their application* (2nd ed. Moscow, 1949), English translation by Pergamon Press, New York, 2nd edition, 1964.

——————, [4] *Direct methods in mathematical physics*, Gostekhizdat, Moscow, 1950.

——————, [5] *The problem of the minimum of a quadratic functional* (Moscow, 1952), English translation by Holden-Day, San Francisco, 1965.

——————, [6] Some theorems in the theory of operators and their application to the theory of gently curved shells, *Dokl. Akad. Nauk SSSR* 84 (3) (1952), 909–917.

——————, [7] An estimate of the error of approximating elastic shells as plane plates, *Prikl. Matem i Mekh* 16 (4) (1952), 399–418.

——————, [8] The integration of Poisson's equation in infinite regions, *Dokl. Akad. Nauk SSSR* 91 (5) (1953), 1015–1017.

——————, [9] Degenerate elliptic equations, *Vest. Leningr. Gos. Univ.* 9 (8) (1954), 19–48.

——————, [10] Elastic shells similar to plane plates, in '*Questions regarding the strength of blades of water turbines*', Leningr. Gos. Univ., 1954, p. 5–92.

——————, [11] On the Ritz method, *Dokl. Akad. Nauk SSSR* 106 (3) (1956), 391–394.

——————, [12] *Variational methods in mathematical physics* (Moscow, 1957), English translation by Pergamon Press, New York, 1964.

——————, [13] A note on coordinate functions, *Izv. Vys. Uch. Zav., Matem* 5 (6) (1958), 91–94.

——————, [14] On solutions with finite energy of elliptic differential equations, *Leningr. Gos. Ped. Inst. Uch. Zap.* 183 (1958), 5–21.

——————, [15] On the stability of the method of Ritz, *Dokl. Akad. Nauk SSSR* 135 (1960), 16–19. English translation: *Soviet Math. Dokl.* 1 (1961), 1230–1233.

——————, [16] Some conditions for the stability of the Ritz method, Vest. Leningr. Univ. 16 (13) (1961), 40–51.

——————, [17] On the rational choice of coordinate functions for the method of Ritz, *Zhurn. Vychisl. Matem. i Matem. Fiz.* 2 (3) (1962), 437–444.

——————, [18] On the method of Ritz in non-linear problems, *Dokl. Akad. Nauk SSSR* 142 (4) (1962), 792–793. English translation: *Soviet Math. Dokl.* 3 (1962), 170–171.

——————, [19] Multidimensional singular integrals and integral equations (Moscow, 1962), English translation by Pergamon, 1965.

——————, [20] Variational methods of solving linear and non-linear boundary value problems, in '*Differential equations and their applications*', Proceedings of Conference, Prague, 1962; Publishing House of the Czechoslovak Acad. Science, Prague, 1963.

——————, [21] On the stability of some numerical processes, *Dokl. Akad. Nauk SSSR* 157 (2) (1964). 271–273. English translation: *Soviet Math. Dokl.* 5 (1964), 931–933.

——————, [22] *Numerische Methoden zur Lösung von Differential- und Integralgleichungen der Mathematischen Physik*, Vorträge d. 3 Tagung über Probleme und Methoden d. Mathematischen Physik, 2 (1966), 1–46, Karl-Marx-Stadt.

——————, [23] Some properties of polynomial approximation in the sense of Ritz, *Dokl. Akad. Nauk SSSR* 180 (2) (1968), 276–278. English translation: *Soviet Math Dokl* 9 (1968), 614–616.

——————, and Kh. M. Smolitskiy, [1] *Approximate methods of solution for differential and integral equations* (Moscow, Nauka, 1965), English translation by American Elsevier, New York, 1967.

Miranda, K., [1] Equazione alle derivate parziali di tipo ellitico, Springer, Berlin, 1955.

Mitkevich, V. M., [1] The application of the method of Ritz to a problem on the bending of cantilevered section of a slab, *Sb. trudov Labor. gidravl. mashin Akad. Nauk. Ukr. SSSR* 9 (1961), 48–57.

Morozov, N. F., [1] On the non-linear theory of thin plates, *Dokl. Akad. Nauk SSSR* 114 (5) (1957), 968–971.

——————, [2] The uniqueness of symmetric solutions of problems relating to large deflections of symmetrically loaded circula plates, *Dokl. Akad. Nauk SSSR* 123 (3) (1958), 417–419.

——————, [3] Non-linear problems of the theory of thin plates, *Vestn. Leningr. Gos. Univ.*, 19, *ser. matem. mekh. i astr.* 4 (1958), 100–124.

——————, [4] Non-linear problems of the theory of thin anisotropic plates, *izv. Vys. Uch. Zav., Matem* 6 (19) (1960), 170–173.

——————, [5] On questions regarding the existence of non-symmetric solutions in problems related to big deflections in circular plates which are loaded symmetrically, *Izv. Vys. Uch. Zav., Matem* 2 (1961), 126–129.

NATANSON, I. P., [1] On the theory of approximate solutions of equations, *Uch. Zap. Leningr. ped. in-ta* 64 (1948), 3–8.

——————, [2] *Theory of functions of a real variable* (Moscow, 1957), English translation by Ungar, New York, 1960.

——————, [3] *The constructive theory of functions*, Moscow, 1949.

NAYMARK, M. A., [1] *Linear differential operators* (Moscow, 1954), English translation by Ungar, New York, 1967.

NOVOZHILOV, V. V., [1] *The theory of thin shells* (Moscow, Sudpromgiz, 1951), English translation by Noordhoff, Groningen, 1964.

——————, [2] *The theory of elasticity* (Moscow, Sudpromgiz, 1958).

POSTNOV, V. A., [1] Large deflections for one particular case when the fastening of the edge of a supporting contour is not symmetric with respect to the center, *Trudy Leningr. Korablestroit. in-ta* 16 (1955), 21–33.

REISSNER, E. L., [1] On a variational theorem for finite elastic deformations, *J. Math. Phys.* 32 (1953), 129–135.

RIESZ, F., and B. ST. NAGY, [1] *Functional analysis*, Blackie, London, 1956.

ROSE, S. N., [1] On the convergence of the method of L. M. Kachanov, *Vest. Leningr. Gos. Univ.* 19 (1961), 170–174.

SAMOKISH, B. A., [1] On the stability of the abstract method of Galerkin, *Vestn. Leningr. Gos. Univ., ser matem mekh i astr.* 1 (1964), 160–162.

SANSONE, J., [1] *Ordinary differential equations* (Italian), Vol. 1, Zanichelli, Bologna, 1963.

SHIKHOBALOV, S. P., V. M. KRASNOV, T. D. MAKSUTOVA, V. V. TSEYTTS, and E. I. EDEL'SHTEYN, [1] An experimental investigation of the stress conditions of the blades of water turbines, in '*Questions regarding the strength of blades of water turbines*', Leningr. Gos. Univ., 1954, 174–215.

SLOBODYANSKIY, M. G., [1] An estimate of the error of approximate solutions of linear problems, *Prikl. Matem. i Mekh.* 17 (2) (1953), 229–244.

SMIRNOV, V. I., [1] *A course in higher mathematics*, Vol. 2 (Moscow, 1952), English translation by Pergamon Press, Oxford, 1964.

——————, [2] *A course in higher mathematics*, Vol. 3 (Moscow, 1949), English translation by Pergamon Press, Oxford, 1964.

——————, [3] *A course in higher mathematics*, Vol. 5 (Moscow, 1959), English translation by Pergamon Press, Oxford, 1964.

SMIRNOVA, T. N., [1] Polynomial calculations on the computer 'Strela', *Zhurn. Vychisl. Matem. i Matem. Fiz.* 1 (5) (1961), 903–916.

——————, [2] Polynomial calculations and the execution of analytic calculations on the computer EVM, *Trudy Matem. in-ta im. Steklov* 66 (1962), 77–112.

——————. [3] *The execution, on computers of type M–20, of polynomial cal-*

culations with the help of prorabs, Nauka Publishers, Leningrad, 1967.

SOBOLEV, S. L., [1] *Some applications of functional analysis to mathematical physics*, Leningr. Gos. Univ., 1950, English translation by Amer. Math. Soc., Transl. Math. Monograph 7, 1963.

——————, [2] On a new problem of mathematical physics, *Izv. Akad. Nauk SSSR, ser. matem* 18 (1) (1954), 3–50.

SPANG, H. A., [1] A review of minimisation techniques for non-linear functions, *SIAM Review* 4 (1962), 343–365.

STIPPES, M., [1] Large deflections of rectangular plates, *Proc. first U.S. Nat. Congr. Appl. Mech.*, Publ. Amer. Soc. Mech. Eng., New York, 1952, p. 339–345.

TALDYKIN, A. T., [1] Systems of elements of a Hilbert space and series constructed with them, *Matem. Sb.* 29 (71): 1 (1951), 79–120.

VAINBERG, M. M., [1] *Variational methods for the study of non-linear operators* (Moscow, 1956), English translation by Holden Day, San Francisco, 1964.

——————, [2] On the stability of the Bubnov-Galerkin method for non-stationary problems, in *Voprosy Vychisl. Matem. i Vychisl. Tekhn.* 3 (Akad. Nauk Azerb. SSR, 1964).

VAYNIKKO, G. M., [1] Necessary and sufficient conditions for the stability of the Bubnov-Galerkin method, *Uch. Zap. Tartusk. un-ta* (1965).

——————, [2] On similar operators, *Dokl. Akad. Nauk SSSR* 179 (1968), 1029–1031. English translation: *Soviet Math. Dokl.* 9 (1968), 477–480.

VELIEV, M. A., [1] An examination of the stability of the Bubnov-Galerkin method for non-stationary problems, *Dokl. Akad. Nauk SSSR* 157 (1964), 16–19; correction: *Dokl. Akad. Nauk SSSR* 161 (1965).

VERZHBINSKAYA, YU. S., [1] On the choice of coordinate functions for the Ritz method for ordinary differential equation defined on an infinite interval, in *Metody Vychisleniy* No. 4 (Len. Gos. Univ., 1967), 3–12.

VINOKUROV, S. G., [1] The application of the method of Galerkin to the solution of the problem on large deflections of a hinge supported circular plate, *Izv. Kazansk. Fil. Akad. Nauk SSSR, Ser. fiz-matem i tekhn nauk*, No. 10 (1956), 57–61.

VISHIK, M. I., [1] The Cauchy problem for equations with operator coefficients, mixed boundary value problems for systems of differential equations and approximate methods for their solution, *Matem. Sb.* 39 (81) (1956), 51–148.

VLASOV, V. Z., [1] *The general theory of shells* (Moscow, 1941).

VLASOVA, Z. A., [1] A finite difference method for a non-linear one-dimensional variational problem, *Trudy Matem. in-ta im. V.A. Steklov* 66 (1962).

——————, and YU. V. RYBAKOVA, [1] On the question of the numerical performance of finite difference methods for non-linear one-dimensional variational problems, *Trudy Matem. in-ta V. A. Steklov* 84 (1956).

VOL'MIR, A. S., [1] *The bending of plates and shells* (Moscow, 1956).

VOROVICH, I. I., [1] On some direct methods in the non-linear theory of gently curving shells, *Dokl. Akad. Nauk SSSR* 105 (1955), 42–45.

——————, [2] On the existence of solutions in the non-linear theory of shells, *Izv. Akad. Nauk SSSR, ser. matem.* 19 (1955), 173–186.

——————, [3] On the method of Bubnov-Galerkin in the non-linear theory of vibrations of gently curving shells, *Dokl. Akad. Nauk SSSR* 110 (1956), 723–726.

————, [4] On some direct methods in the non-linear theory of shells, *Prikl. matem. i mekh.* 20 (1956), 449–474.

————, [5] On the existence of solutions in the non-linear theory of shells, *Dokl. Akad. Nauk SSSR* 117 (1957), 203–206.

————, [6] The error in direct methods in the non-linear theory of shells, *Dokl. Akad. Nauk SSSR* 122 (1958), 196–199.

WATSON, G. N., [1] *The theory of Bessel functions*, Cambridge University Press, 1962.

WEIL, N. A. and N. M. NEWMARK, [1] Large deflections of elliptical plates, *Amer. Soc. Engrs.* A–2 (1955).

WILKINSON, J. H., [1] Rounding error in algebraic processes, *Nat. Phys. Lab., Notes on appl. sci.* 32, London, 1963.

WINTNER, A., [1] *Spektraltheorie der unendlichen Matrizen*, Leipzig, 1929.

YAKOVLEV, M. N., [1] On the solution of systems of non-linear differential equations by the method of differentiation with respect to a parameter, *Zhurn. Vychisl. Matem i Matem. Fiz.* 4 (1) (1964), 146–149.

YASKOVA, G. N., and M. N. YAKOVLEV, [1] Some condition for the stability of the method of Petrov-Galerkin, *Trudy Matem. in-ta im. Steklova* 66 (1962), 182–189.

ZYGMUND, A., [1] *Trigonometric Series*, Vol. 1, Cambridge University Press, 1959.

INDEX